MOMSTROLOGY

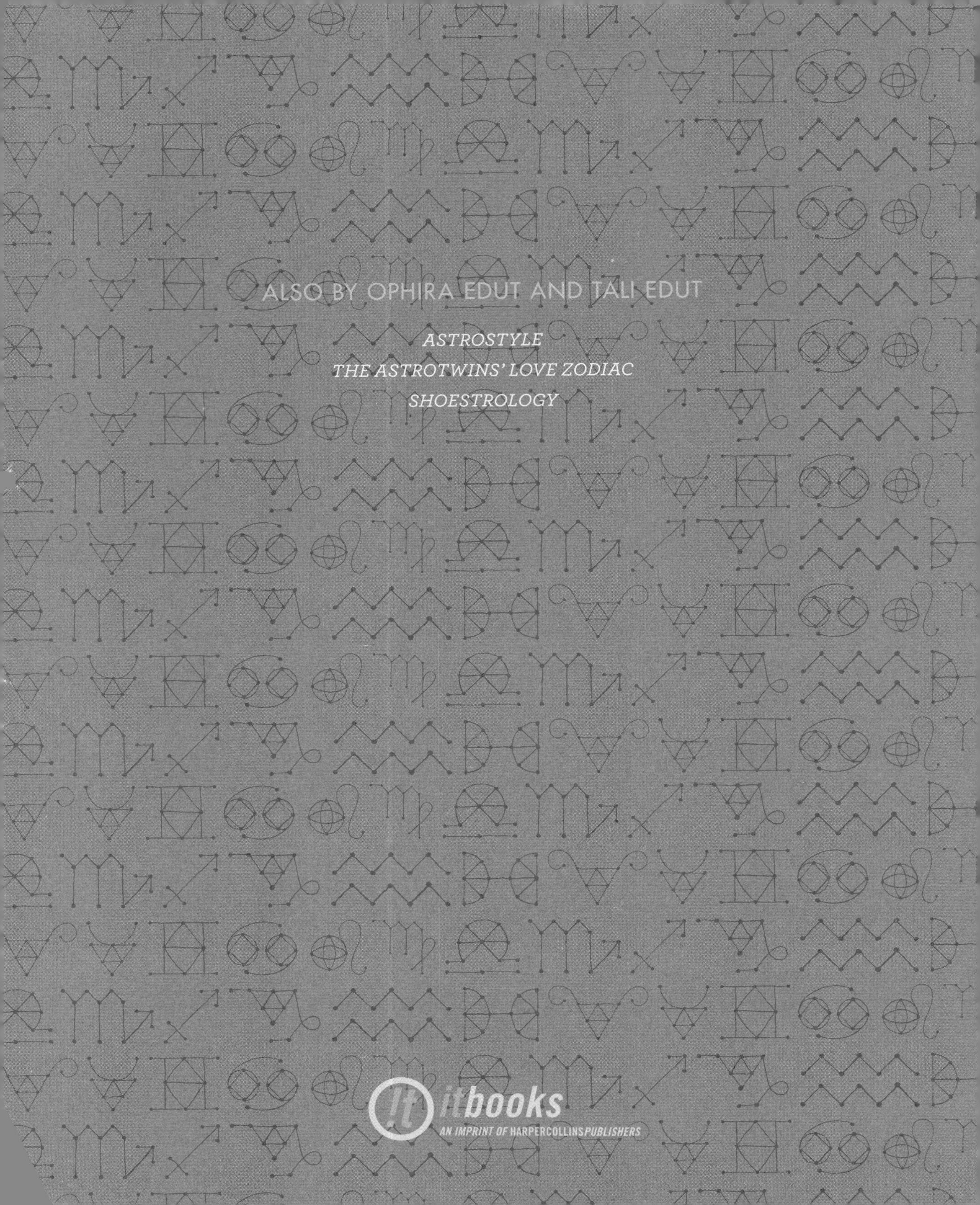

ALSO BY OPHIRA EDUT AND TALI EDUT

ASTROSTYLE

THE ASTROTWINS' LOVE ZODIAC

SHOESTROLOGY

itbooks
AN IMPRINT OF HARPERCOLLINS*PUBLISHERS*

MOMSTROLOGY

The AstroTwins' Guide to Parenting Your Little One by the Stars

OPHIRA EDUT

AND

TALI EDUT

Illustrations on pages iii, xxxii, 196, and 412 are by Yoko Furusho. All other line art illustrations are by Gabriel Stromburg.

HarperCollins books may be purchased for educational, business, or sales promotional use. For information please e-mail the Special Markets Department at SPsales@harpercollins.com

FIRST EDITION

Designed by Shannon Plunkett

Library of Congress Cataloging-in-Publication Data

Edut, Ophira.
Momstrology : the AstroTwins' guide to parenting your little one by the stars / Ophira Edut and Tali Edut. — First edition.
pages cm
ISBN 978-0-06-225046-9 (pbk.)
1. Astrology and child rearing. 2. Astrology and child development. 3. Parenting. 4. Mother and child. I. Edut, Tali. II. Title.
BF1729.C45E38 2014
649'.1—dc23

2013045768

14 15 16 17 18 OV/RRD 10 9 8 7 6 5 4 3 2 1

Momstrology is dedicated to the beloved memory of our dear friend Denyse Thomasos (1964–2012), who passed unexpectedly just as we started writing this book. A brilliant painter, devoted professor, and mother to sweet Syann, Denyse's parenthood was an adventure of the heart and spirit. As an adoptive mama, Denyse proved that love, not biology, is what matters. She was more afraid of *not living* than she was of dying—and she had few regrets. However, if Denyse ever were to allow a sorrow, it would be missing the life she planned to share with her daughter. To Denyse, we raise a cup of black coffee (hazelnut, from the Open Pantry on Second Avenue) and feel the ache of your absence. For a mother—and a true friend—can never be replaced.

A special dedication goes to our own mothers, too. Our textbook Leo mom, Doris Edut, taught us to have a wide-eyed wonder about the world. An ever-present support and endlessly optimistic playmate, she taught us to never stop growing, learning, or celebrating life. Our aunt Carolyn Mickelson is our second mother, a creative Aquarius who taught us to march to the beat of our own drum. She inspired us to be fearless in our self-expression, to honor our emotions, and to take a time-out and laugh at the absurdity of life. Our beloved Cancer grandmother, Sophie Seligson, was the heartbeat of the family, and her unconditional warmth and love was our shelter as children.

Much love and gratitude goes to our girls (Ophira's daughters/Tali's nieces), Leo Clementine and Libra Cybele. They leave us in awe with their beauty, talent, and wisdom every day. As the saying goes, "The mother is born with the child." We thank these two special souls for "birthing" new dimensions and discoveries in us.

CONTENTS

INTRODUCTION

*

They say your kids don't come with instructions. We beg to differ.

It's been said that kids don't come with an owner's manual. Actually, they do . . . in a way. Some real clues to understanding your children are written in their astrological signs. Each zodiac sign is encoded with amazing information to help you understand your child's "automatic settings."

Yes, we have free will. Sure, nature *and* nurture both play a role in shaping our lives and the lives of our children. But the seasons and the stars carry energies, too. We stumbled into astrology over twenty years ago, purely for entertainment, while studying at the University of Michigan. Our hobby later became an obsession and then a career. Now, after studying thousands of people's birth charts, we firmly believe that astrology has a huge hand in shaping people's destinies.

The other hand that guides who your child becomes? Well, it's the one that rocks the cradle—yours!

Looking to astrology can help you tailor your parenting in ways that play to the strengths, and sometimes weaknesses, that are unique to you and your child. It explains why despite your best intentions to teach restraint and responsibility your Aries child rides a tricycle through the house and knocks over your favorite vase. Or why a Taurus baby can be known to sleep fifteen hours, whereas a Leo infant is up demanding attention at dawn.

As a mom and stepmom (Ophira) and an aunt/mama by association (Tali), we've read every motherhood book on the market. While the theories have been helpful (Attachment parenting! Ferberizing! Breast, no, bottle!), the overall MO seems to be a one-size-fits-all parenting. As it turns out, there's no "right" way to raise a child. But we *do* feel that certain techniques fit some zodiac signs better than others.

In *Momstrology*, we help you make sense of parenting, from an astrological point of view. We start by offering a crib sheet (if you will) to the in-and-outs of your child's sign. From choosing a school (private or public?) to picking hobbies and activities, to understanding what it means when they talk back, get clingy, or won't eat the broccoli, the kid chapters will guide you through the practicalities of day-to-day parenthood with cosmic insight. Then we shed light on the moms of every sign, offering advice on how you handle each age and stage. At the end, you'll find an insightful "mom matcher" that explains how your sign meshes with your child's.

While a few books have been written about baby zodiac signs, we haven't seen much written about moms, much less the mother–child dynamic in astrology. Yet it's a bond so deep and unique, it begs to be explored! A December 4, 2012, *Scientific American* article by Robert Martone even found that mothers' bodies may carry the cells of their children (passed through the placenta or even during nursing). If this is a fact, then we all are indeed our mothers—literally!

More than any group, mothers are constantly judged—and often unkindly. As a mom, every day is a minefield of worries about whether you're screwing up your kids' lives, making the right choices, balancing your own needs with theirs, and well, doing it "right." The crush of mommy blogs and mom-targeted marketing in the last decade, especially, has spawned both catharsis and confusion, upping the whole competitive mothering game. In 2012, moms comprised $2 *trillion* of purchasing power (a figure that's only going up), making everyone hungry for our dollars. We also deal with an onslaught of articles questioning whether women can be successful in both our careers and our families—such as the *Atlantic*'s incendiary cover story "Why Women Still Can't Have It All" in July 2012. Who needs the "mommy wars" when you're already fighting so many battles on native soil with your little one—and yourself for that matter!

That's why we created *Momstrology*—to give you tons of support, a bundle of time-tested secrets, and a unique resource for your journey. Motherhood's not for sissies, as you've well discovered by now—or will once your little one arrives. But your child picked *you* as his or her mother for a special, spiritual reason. You've got karmic ties to each other and lots to learn and share. The better you understand each other, the easier it will be.

Does astrology make motherhood a perfect process or provide a magic pill? Alas, no. That's simply not the nature of parenting. It's a constant balancing act among your needs, their needs, family dynamics, and well, *life*.

But what if some of the answers just happen to be written in the stars? Then reach up to the cosmos and grab yourself some extra help. Mama, you deserve it.

 **ARIES** March 21—April 19 

 **TAURUS** April 20—May 20 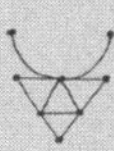

 **GEMINI** May 21—June 20 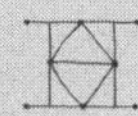

 **CANCER** June 21—July 22 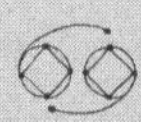

 **LEO** July 23—August 22 

 **VIRGO** August 23—September 22 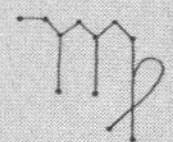

 **LIBRA** September 23—October 22 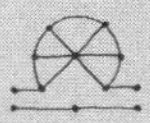

 **SCORPIO** October 23—November 21

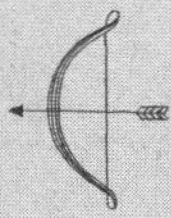 **SAGITTARIUS** November 22—December 21 

 **CAPRICORN** December 22—January 19 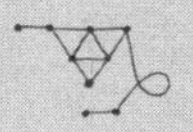

 **AQUARIUS** January 20—February 18 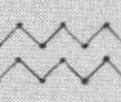

 **PISCES** February 19—March 20 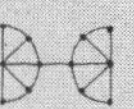

ASTROLOGY 101

*

Welcome, Astromama! We're so happy you've picked up this book. We wrote it with love and a genuine desire to help you build a happy, harmonious family. Before we dive into the mom and children's chapters, we wanted to cover a few astrology basics that will broaden your understanding of your little one's planet-powered personality—and your own. Whether you're a total newbie to astrology or you won't leave the house without checking your daily horoscope, there's always more to learn on this topic. So here's a little refresher for the pros and some new know-how for the neophytes. Enjoy!

SUN SIGNS AND THE ZODIAC WHEEL

Hey, baby, what's your sign? When people ask you that, what they're actually referring to is your sun sign—in other words, the zodiac sign that the sun was visiting when you were born. The sun travels around the earth once a year, slowly passing through each of the zodiac signs over the course of a month. Whichever sign the sun was visiting when we were born is our sun sign, or zodiac sign. In astrology, this reveals someone's essential character and personality.

Knowing your own or your child's sun sign can provide huge insight into what makes you both tick—and the dynamic between your two personalities. If you want an even deeper look, you can cast a complete chart (free on our website and many other astrology sites) by plugging in anyone's time, date, and location of birth. The astrology chart, a wheel divided into twelve segments (called houses), reveals where every planet was positioned when you were born. Each planet represents a different aspect of your nature. For instance, Venus is the planet of love, beauty, and harmony. It influences your personal style, your aesthetic tastes, and how smoothly you get along with others. So a child born with Venus in peacekeeper Libra might be more prone to sharing with friends and siblings, whereas a kid with Venus in me-first Aries can be competitive.

The moon sign is also especially helpful

for parents to know, since it reveals a person's deepest emotional needs, what makes him feel secure, and the mother–child relationship. The moon changes signs every two to three days, which also accounts for the variations between people of the same sun sign.

All of the planets cruise around the sun at varying speeds, which can add a lot of complexity to the birth chart. Based on their proximity to the sun, each planet takes a different amount of time to change zodiac signs (Mercury takes two to three weeks, whereas Jupiter takes twelve to thirteen months, and faraway Neptune takes about twelve years). So one Leo's chart, for instance, can look vastly unlike another Leo's. We ourselves are Sagittarians, but most of the other planets in our chart are in Scorpio or Capricorn, adding an intense, businesslike dimension to our happy-go-lucky sun sign nature. This is why your generic newspaper horoscope or a quickie sun sign description might not totally feel accurate at times. There's a lot more that goes into the whole birth chart business!

We like to say that the chart is a road map to the soul and personality—sort of like learning a person's factory settings. Just like you'd customize a computer or a device with your own screensavers and programs, human beings have free will, consciousness, and the ability to make choices. However, we believe that your "internal processor" is determined—or at least strongly influenced by—your zodiac sign and birth chart.

RULING PLANETS

Each of the twelve zodiac signs has been assigned a planetary/celestial ruler. At times in this book, you may read that a certain planet is the "ruler" of a zodiac sign. The ruling planet exerts its influence over that sign, shaping its traits and qualities.

ZODIAC SIGN	RULING PLANET
Aries	**Mars,** the planet of drive and aggression
Taurus	**Venus,** the planet of love, beauty, and harmony
Gemini	**Mercury,** the planet of communication and ideas
Cancer	**Moon,** the ruler of emotions and nurturing
Leo	**Sun,** the ruler of courage and the self
Virgo	**Mercury,** the planet of communication and ideas

ZODIAC SIGN	RULING PLANET
Libra	**Venus,** the planet of love, beauty and harmony
Scorpio	**Pluto,** the ruler of power and control (minor rule by Mars)
Sagittarius	**Jupiter,** the planet of luck and optimism
Capricorn	**Saturn,** the planet of discipline and perseverance
Aquarius	**Uranus,** the planet of liberation and radical change (minor rule by Saturn)
Pisces	**Neptune,** the planet of compassion and imagination (minor rule by Jupiter)

ZODIAC SIGNS AND THE BODY

But wait . . . there's more! Each of the twelve zodiac signs is also associated with a specific area of the body. The sequence begins with Aries, the zodiac's first sign, ruling the head. Next comes Taurus, which rules the neck and throat . . . and so on, ending with Pisces, the last sign, ruling the feet. The region that your sign rules could be a focal point, one you emphasize when dressing, or that people notice, or even that can be problematic. For example, Capricorn rules the teeth, and many kiddie Caps have toothpaste-commercial smiles (or they're clear-cut candidates for braces). Little Pisces can be serious shoe addicts—or may be prone to having foot problems. And Virgo, ruler of the digestive system, could be on feeding and diapering or potty schedules that go like clockwork.

ZODIAC SIGN	BODY AREA
Aries	Head, face, hair
Taurus	Neck, throat
Gemini	Arms, hands, shoulders
Cancer	Chest, stomach

ZODIAC SIGN	BODY AREA
Leo	Heart, spine, upper back
Virgo	Waist, digestive system
Libra	Lower back, backside
Scorpio	Crotch, reproductive organs
Sagittarius	Hips, thighs, midsection
Capricorn	Knees, teeth, skin, bone structure
Aquarius	Calves, ankles
Pisces	Feet

THE FOUR ELEMENTS

Each zodiac sign is one of four natural elements: fire, earth, air, or water.

FIRE SIGNS:

Aries, Leo, Sagittarius

Fire signs are known for being creative initiators. They are dynamic and active, sometimes "hot"-tempered and impulsive. They crave variety and new experiences and might be constantly on the go. While adventure is their calling card, parents of fire signs may need to teach these kids to finish what they start rather than moving on the second they lose interest. Pursuing passions may be their main goal, but fire signs also need to learn survival skills in the material world.

Fire sign parents are active, impatient, and spontaneous. They're lifelong learners who evolve along with their kids. They may need to work on consistency, though, since their own full agendas may leave them scrambling to juggle their own lives with child-rearing duties.

EARTH SIGNS:

Taurus, Virgo, Capricorn

Earth signs are the builders who create lasting structures. They are often loyal and stable, craving deep roots and security. Change needs to be introduced slowly, as these steady signs are rather traditional. However, they can get stuck in their ways, so parents of earth signs may need to push them out of their comfort zones from time to time. Earth signs can also focus too heavily on material concerns, neglecting their dreams or judging people at face value.

Earth sign parents can be traditional, structured, and consistent, providing a wonderful safety net for children. However, they can also become creatures of habit at their own expense. They need to be adaptable as their kids grow, learning to evolve in their own lives, too.

AIR SIGNS:

Gemini, Libra, Aquarius

Air signs are the communicators who spread ideas. Like the wind, they can be scattered in many directions or have "breezy" personalities that make them witty and popular. They are versatile, with lots of hobbies and interests. While they're good at being objective, they can also get lost in their heads. Parents of air signs need to teach these kids decision-making skills, helping them out of "analysis paralysis." Encourage them to tune into their emotions and intuition, not just their intellect. Push them to pursue a passion, and make it okay for them to express their feelings openly.

Air sign parents are fun, youthful, and intelligent and are able to step back and look at most situations objectively. This can make them easy to talk to, a friend and a parent in one. However, they might be a little too cool at times, having a conversation when the kid just needs a hug.

WATER SIGNS:

Cancer, Scorpio, Pisces

Water signs are emotional and family-oriented. They need comfort, security, and lots of understanding. These deep feelers and empaths are often the nurturers in their families from an early age, and they are slow to trust anyone outside of their immediate families. Parents of water signs need to build these kids' confidence in the wider world. While their intuition is amazing, water signs need to learn how to use their heads, not just their hearts. Thin-skinned, they tend to take things personally. Make it safe for them to step back from their strong emotions and analyze situations objectively.

Water sign parents are sentimental, protective, and nurturing. They tune in on exactly what their kid is feeling and make sure their family wants for nothing. Separation can be hard for water signs, who get deeply attached. Learning to let kids struggle or figure things out on their own is an important lesson.

QUALITIES: CARDINAL, MUTABLE, AND FIXED SIGNS

Each zodiac sign is also assigned a quality: cardinal, fixed, or mutable. Every season contains three zodiac signs. The cardinal signs start each season. Fixed signs are in the middle. Mutables finish it off. Knowing your sign's quality helps you discover whether you're a starter, a doer, or a finisher. Each quality plays an important role in the world, and it's good to have a balance of each on every team (or family, if you should be so lucky). If you were putting together a record deal, for example, it would work like this: Cardinal signs would be the stars, promoters, or trendsetters who create the act. Fixed signs would be the patient workhorses who produce the album. Mutable signs would be the editors who take the near-finished product and do the final mastering and remixing.

CARDINAL SIGNS

Aries, Cancer, Libra, Capricorn

Cardinal signs are the initiator and leaders. They take charge and get a mission off the ground. Born alphas, they like to be large and in charge.

FIXED SIGNS

Taurus, Leo, Scorpio, Aquarius

Fixed signs are the builders and worker bees. They tough out the hard parts and take the job to the finish line. They are resilient but can be resistant to change.

MUTABLE SIGNS

Gemini, Virgo, Sagittarius, Pisces

Mutable signs are the travelers and ambassadors. Flexible and changeable, they like variety and can adapt to new circumstances quickly. Mutable signs are the bridge between new ideas and time-tested traditions.

TWELVE HOUSES OF THE ZODIAC

The zodiac wheel is divided into twelve houses, each one representing a different part of our identities and lives.

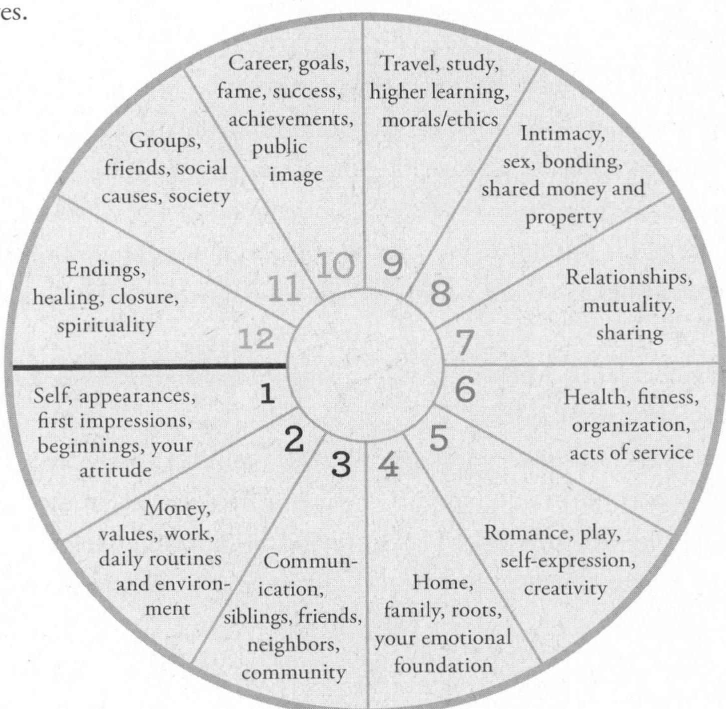

When examining charts for parenting clues, we look at three of the houses in particular.

FOURTH HOUSE —THE MOMMY HOUSE

The zodiac's fourth house is associated with home, family, children, mothers, and femininity. This house shows what kind of mother you'll be and how you'll nurture. It predicts your natural parenting strengths and reveals the ways you'll approach child rearing. In a child's chart, the fourth house can show what kind of mothering or nurturing she needs.

SIXTH HOUSE —THE CAREGIVER HOUSE

Whether you send your child to day care or hire someone for the occasional date night, the sixth house gives clues as to what kind of babysitter or caregiver is best for your child. Permissive playmate or no-nonsense nanny? The sixth house will say.

TENTH HOUSE —THE DADDY HOUSE

Who's your daddy? The zodiac's tenth house is associated with men, rules, structure, authority, fathers, and masculinity. It reveals a man's fathering style. In a child's chart, it can reveal what kind of fathering and discipline he needs.

WHO'S IN THE HOUSE? HOUSE RULERS AND THEIR INFLUENCE

Depending on your sun sign, each house on your zodiac wheel will be ruled, or governed, by a particular sign. The ruler, or zodiac sign on the cusp (borderline), of each zodiac house plays a strong role, too. When a sign rules a house, that means it exerts a strong influence over whatever that house symbolizes. So the ruler of the fourth (motherhood) house will color your approach to mothering. The ruler of the sixth (caregiver) house will reveal what kind of babysitter works best for your babe. A house ruler can shape your behavior, beliefs, responses, and needs.

This is especially fascinating when it comes to the parent houses, because it adds a whole new dimension to your self-understanding. Why? The ruler of your motherhood house is a zodiac sign that's quite different from your sun/birth sign. For example, a fiercely independent Sagittarius mom has superdependent Pisces ruling her motherhood house. As a result, becoming a mom will bring out an entirely different facet of her personality, one that could feel uncomfortable or unfamiliar at first. No wonder so many mamas have an identity crisis after the baby arrives. Beyond the diapers and sleepless nights, it's astrologically a whole new world, too.

Don't worry—you don't have to become an astrologer to learn this. We've provided handy charts for each of the parenting houses. But first we explain the process of finding your house rulers.

FINDING YOUR MOTHERHOOD (FOURTH) HOUSE RULER

To find the ruler of your fourth (motherhood) house, just count through the zodiac signs in order, beginning with your sign, until you get to the fourth one:

Aries > Taurus > Gemini > Cancer

Cancer rules the fourth house for the Aries mom.

Thus, an Aries mom will be Cancerian in her mothering style.

Cancer > Leo > Virgo > Libra

Libra rules the fourth house for the Cancer mom.

Thus, a Cancer mom will be Libran in her mothering style.

FINDING DAD'S FATHERHOOD (TENTH) HOUSE RULER

To find a dad's fatherhood style—or the ruler of his tenth house—begin with his sign and count through the zodiac signs in order from there until you get to the tenth one:

Taurus > Gemini > Cancer > Leo > Virgo > Libra > Scorpio > Sagittarius > Capricorn > Aquarius

Aquarius rules the tenth house for the Taurus dad.

Thus, a Taurus dad will be Aquarian in his fathering style.

FINDING YOUR CHILD'S CAREGIVER HOUSE RULER

To pinpoint the ruler of the sixth (caregiver) house, begin with your child's zodiac sign and count through the zodiac from there until you get to the sixth one:

Scorpio > Sagittarius > Capricorn > Aquarius > Pisces > Aries

Aries rules the sixth house for the Scorpio kid.

Thus, a Scorpio child will benefit from a caregiver with Aries-like traits.

YOUR MOTHERING STYLE: WHAT SIGN RULES YOUR MOTHERHOOD (FOURTH) HOUSE?

Mom's Sun Sign	Fourth House Ruler	Your Mothering Style
Aries	Cancer	Like a crab tightly clutching all that it cherishes, you're a tad possessive of your wee ones. Children bring out the mother hen in independent Aries, much to your surprise. Since Cancer is driven by emotions, kids can also evoke strong feelings (and at times reactions, which isn't always a great mix with your hot Aries temper). Mushball alert: if you've always been the tough chick, prepare to meet your sentimental side.
Taurus	Leo	Proud and regal, you're the queen of your clan. With showy Leo in the fourth house, you like to spoil your kids and brag about their achievements, putting every trophy and stellar report card on display. You might be the best-dressed mama at drop off or the PTA meetings—and if you're not, your child will certainly have serious kiddie style. Lavish birthday parties and elaborate holiday decorations are a given in your family.
Gemini	Virgo	With fastidious Virgo in the fourth house, freewheeling Gemini becomes surprisingly type A. Virgo is the sign of health, so you might be a natural mom, into gluten-free alternatives, home birth, and eco-chic baby products. Watch a tendency to micromanage your kids, since analytical Virgo can make you a wee bit critical.
Cancer	Libra	Mommy and me! Libra is the sign of togetherness, and you can't get enough time with your kids. (Can you say "joined at the hip"?) Being with your child can have a soothing effect for you both, and with patient Libra here, you love to experience every wonder through their eyes. Libra is an aesthetic sign, so you love shopping for your kid, decorating the nursery, and exposing them to the arts. Your kids will be well groomed and well mannered.

Mom's Sun Sign	Fourth House Ruler	Your Mothering Style
Leo	Scorpio	Leos already like to be in charge, and with powerful Scorpio here you're as hands-on as they get. The difference? While Leo is known for courage and openheartedness, Scorpio energy is cautious, even suspicious. Your trademark "trust first, ask questions later" policy does not extend to childrearing. Scorpio is the sign of intimate and permanent bonding, making it hard to cut the cord. While your active involvement in every facet of your kids' lives is admirable, it can be too much. Learn when to step back and allow them to become their own people.
Virgo	Sagittarius	Micromanager no more! With worldly and adventurous Sagittarius in the driver's seat, you become a free thinker instead of a rigid rule follower. Sure, you may still fret over your kids' dairy intake or growth chart percentiles (you *are* a Virgo), but you also expose your children to the wider world, introducing them to cultural diversity, enriching activities, and travel. As a mom, you don't sweat the small stuff the way you normally do. No wonder motherhood is so enjoyable for many Virgos—you actually let yourself lighten up and have fun.
Libra	Capricorn	Order to chaos? While airy Libras are known as scattered, you benefit from structured Capricorn governing your motherhood house. As a mom, you're suddenly able to set rules, follow a routine, and be an authority figure without worrying that your kids won't like you. Even the most conflict-avoiding Libra will deal with misbehavior in a firm and commanding way. With your sign's tendency to run late, parenting can even make you more punctual. Goal-oriented Capricorn can make you worry about status and your children's future. You'll be the first in line for preschool applications, or to butter up the admissions counselor at an elite private high school.

Mom's Sun Sign	Fourth House Ruler	Your Mothering Style
Scorpio	Aquarius	You're the zodiac's most intense sign, yet motherhood brings out a laid-back, bohemian part of your nature. With quirky Aquarius shaping your parenting style, you could be the hippest mama in town, dressing youthfully and being a friend *and* a mom to your kids. Dichotomy alert: while Scorpio gets intensely attached to people, Aquarius is the sign of emotional detachment. This contrast can make you run hot and cold with your kids at times. One minute, you're possessive, the next, you're all "live and let live."
Sagittarius	Pisces	Freedom doesn't look quite as sweet anymore when your independent sign feels the bonding vibes of nurturing Pisces. While Sagittarians tend to be blunt, compassionate Pisces helps soften your edges, giving you a gentler touch. Under Pisces' influence watch out for maternal guilt and a tendency to get overwhelmed by the day-to-day details of motherhood. Your normally firm sign can also be a bit of a pushover with the kids, and setting firm boundaries could be a challenge. Your already generous sign might give a little too much; beware any "martyr mom" tendencies from this house ruler.
Capricorn	Aries	Who's the boss? Your Capricorn sun sign makes you a natural leader, but take-charge Aries adds an assertive punch. While Capricorn can be reserved, fiery Aries is impulsive and direct, making you a lot bolder in your mama life than elsewhere. You're also a strong and capable role model, trying things your cautious sign normally wouldn't. If you know you'll inspire your kids by taking a risk, you'll do it. Both Aries and Capricorn are "masculine" signs, so you may end up being the family provider or disciplinarian, acting as stereotypical mom *and* dad in one.

Mom's Sun Sign	Fourth House Ruler	Your Mothering Style
Aquarius	Taurus	Who, you? Grounded and structured? Maybe not in your pre-mama lifetime, but when it comes to motherhood, yes! Freewheeling Aquarian mums become master planners under the spell of capable Taurus. Once impossible to pin down, you become a reliable go-to as a mother. Your latent type A inclinations can even come out full force with your kiddos. Elsewhere, your life status might be "It's complicated." Here, however, keep-it-simple Taurus helps you prioritize and streamline. It can also make you great with family budgeting, scheduling, party planning, nursery decorating, and keeping the day-to-day routines running smoothly.
Pisces	Gemini	Mommy or BFF? While Pisces is an old soul, youthful Gemini puts a spring in your step, adding a playful twist to your parenting style. Your kids pull you out of your emotional depths, making you laugh and lighten up. Since Gemini rules communication, open dialogue with your children is essential to you. You might talk for hours, share books and music, and even dress alike, as Gemini is the sign of the twins. A natural nurturer, Pisces tend to overgive and even make excuses for bad behavior. Fortunately, Gemini is not pulled by its heartstrings the way Pisces is, so you're able to take a step back and recognize when your kid is taking you for a ride.

COSMIC CAREGIVERS: THE ULTIMATE BABYSITTER FINDER!

It's a reality: the majority of US nuclear families now have two working parents. That means you'll need to find an ideal person to help with daily duties—and astrology can help. But before you try to clone yourself . . . wait. What your child needs from a caregiver is different from what you provide. Ever notice how your kid will listen to the nanny, day-care owner, or babysitter—but not to you? Or how your clingy little kiddo becomes surprising independent with a caregiver? That's because the sign that rules the sixth house of helpers is unique. Here's how to find the right caretaker personality to match your child's temperament.

Sun Sign	Sixth House Ruler	The best caregiver style for this sign
Aries	Virgo	Attention, attention! One-on-one Aries crave someone who really focuses on them and gives them honest feedback. They thrive with a sitter who's health conscious, rule-oriented (without being suffocating), and assigns tasks that build a sense of responsibility. It's all too easy to spoil an Aries, so find a caregiver who's not afraid to say no.
Taurus	Libra	Your bossy Bull needs boundaries, yes. But above all, Taurus kids needs a loving and fair caregiver to bring out their peaceful natures. Look for a balanced babysitter who can teach this rough-and-tumble sign how to be a kinder, gentler human with a sense of right and wrong. Bonus if your sitter has artistic or musical inclinations (or, say, happens to be a Parisian-bred au pair) and can expose Taurus to some culture.
Gemini	Scorpio	Tricky Geminis know how to pull a fast one on adults, so place them with an astute nanny who doesn't miss a beat. Hire someone sharp and witty but *just* intimidating enough to avoid being outsmarted by fast-talking Gemini. With a clever caretaker, this can be a real meeting of the minds!
Cancer	Sagittarius	Who better to draw little Crabs out of their shells than a worldly and adventurous sitter? Forget coddling or catering to Cancer's shyness. A caregiver who gets Cancer excited to leave the house will build this sign's confidence in the world beyond his comfort zone. A sense of humor and lots of compassion are a must. Find a good-natured babysitter who lightens up this moody kid and provides levity when he loses perspective.

Sun Sign	Sixth House Ruler	The best caregiver style for this sign
Leo	Capricorn	Aim for a structured sitter who understands child development and gives restless Leo a few healthy boundaries. An accomplishment-driven person can help teach fiery Leo how to channel confidence into competence, building skills, and earning their keep. It's okay to hire someone a little stern to teach your Leo to be a good sport and a gracious winner and loser.
Virgo	Aquarius	Virgos can develop tunnel vision, so they benefit from an easygoing sitter who teaches them not to sweat the small stuff. These self-critical kids need a kind and tolerant role model who teaches them that it's okay to make mistakes—and to experiment!
Libra	Pisces	Daydream believer? Creative Libras thrive with intuitive nannies who nurture their imaginations. Forget about tough love. Libras need a gentle and compassionate caretaker—more of a fairy godmother than a firm disciplinarian. In some cases, Libras may even develop an intuitive or psychic bond with their babysitters.
Scorpio	Aries	Action! Intense Scorpios need a strong-willed and physically active babysitter who's not afraid to say no. Although they may wrap their mama around their fingers, a little tough love does this powerful sign good. Otherwise, savvy Scorpios can end up running the show.
Sagittarius	Taurus	Earth to Sag! These impulsive tykes can barely sit still—they've got a million dreams, projects, games, and adventures going at once. A steady and consistent sitter can be the earth beneath their fast-moving feet. Find someone patient who supplies Sagittarius with a sense of routine but doesn't fence them in.
Capricorn	Gemini	Who's the adult here, anyway? Cautious Capricorns need a lighthearted and versatile sitter who encourages them to have fun—and plays right along with them. Aim for a creative person who helps linear Cap color outside the lines, teaching them that it's okay to make mistakes—and to experiment.

Sun Sign	Sixth House Ruler	The best caregiver style for this sign
Aquarius	Cancer	Quirky Aquarians savor their freedom, but they need hugs and doting, too. Believe it or not, these independent kids love a nurturing and affectionate sitter with a strong maternal instinct. It doesn't hurt if this person is a tad overprotective—if only to keep fearless Aquarius from running into danger.
Pisces	Leo	Little Pisces may act shy, but these sensitive souls contain multitudes. A warm, protective and expressive caregiver can cultivate the artist in these kids, encouraging them to lighten up and share their talents with the world. A confident go-getter will model the self-assuredness that Pisces need to learn.

WHO'S YOUR DADDY: WHAT SIGN RULES DAD'S FATHERHOOD (TENTH) HOUSE?

Dad's Sun Sign	Tenth House Ruler	His fathering style
Aries	Capricorn	Taming the wild man? With structured Capricorn ruling Aries' fatherhood house, this carpe diem dude becomes a capable dad. Kids can bring out the responsible and reliable side of Aries, inspiring him to be a role model. He'll also help them set goals and earn lofty achievements. The only potential drawback is that Aries can already be a little intimidating, and with authoritarian Capricorn's influence, he might be a bit of an iron-fisted ruler. Or he'll put way too much pressure on himself and the kids instead of enjoying the moment.
Taurus	Aquarius	He's a man with a plan—except when it comes to the kids. While Taurus is normally a structured creature of habit, fatherhood brings out his quirky and spontaneous side. He loves to laugh and explore the world with his children, and he can be quite the entertainer. (Who knew that this buttoned-up dude could mimic the voices of every cartoon character, for example?) If you're a busy working parent, delegate playtime duties to the Taurus dad. He'll happily reconnect with his youth—or finally experience it—through his kids. You might even see his progressive side emerge (hello, Mr. Mom?), since he becomes far less conventional about gender roles as a parent.

Dad's Sun Sign	Tenth House Ruler	His fathering style
Gemini	Pisces	Man of mystery? Verbal Gemini becomes a lot more reflective as a dad, perhaps getting lost in his thoughts and emotions. The influence of perceptive Pisces can bring out the Gemini dad's sensitive side. This can overwhelm his cerebral sign at first, as the flood of emotions is unfamiliar to him. He may need periods of solitude to recharge. Still, if he surrenders to the love, the Gemini man can get out of his head and into his heart, which does this overthinking sign a world of good.
Cancer	Aries	Big papa in the house! While Cancer can be sentimental and even insecure at times, he becomes assertive and confident as a dad. Being a great role model becomes his primary concern, and he loves having adventures with his kids. The Aries-ruled jock within can emerge, and he could be a big sports or outdoor adventure dad. He needs his children to respect and admire him and might even be competitive with other dads. Temper alert: Cancer's normal patience can wear thin under the short-fused Aries influence.
Leo	Taurus	Hello, proud patriarch. Under the spell of stable Taurus, confident Leo becomes even more rooted in his trademark pride and dignity. As a dad, he's all about passing on traditions, leaving a legacy, and honoring the ancestral lineage. (Don't be surprised if he names a son after himself.) While he may be stubborn and hard to budge in his values, the kids know where their Leo daddy stands. The only possible pitfall is that he can become *too* stern or set in his ways. Or indulgent Taurus can turn the Lion lazy: you'll catch him gorging on sweet treats with the kiddos and spoiling them with material gifts.
Virgo	Gemini	Cerebral Mercury rules both Virgo and Gemini, making this dad especially intellectual and observant. Mercury is the communication planet, so the Virgo dad is always learning, talking, teaching (and yes, preaching). Conversation with the kids will be a cherished pastime. He may be the father whose children can talk to him about anything, with no topic being taboo. He'll enjoy learning, reading, and exploring new ideas with his children, making sure they're critical thinkers with solid opinions.

Dad's Sun Sign	Tenth House Ruler	His fathering style
Libra	Cancer	The Libra man is already in touch with his feminine side, and with maternal Cancer ruling his fatherhood house his nurturing nature comes out full force. He loves to be home with his family, bonding, entertaining, and building memories. Say cheese! This sentimental daddy wants to capture every sweet moment on camera. You'll find him creating a comfortable and well-appointed home, cooking, cleaning, changing diapers, and overturning gender role stereotypes at every chance. While he'll provide affection in spades, doling out discipline isn't always his strong suit. When he does, he may get way too emotional, his temper going from zero to sixty in a very un-Libra way. Deep breath, daddy-o!
Scorpio	Leo	Come out, come out! While Scorpios are known for being mysterious, expressive, Leo draws them out from behind their stoic masks. When it comes to his kids, the Scorpio dad is playful, affectionate, and fiercely protective. And finally, he lets himself have a little fun, too. Leo is one of the most creative zodiac signs, and fatherhood might be his favorite outlet. He'll bake cookies, roll around on the floor, and stage elaborate art projects with the kids. So much for looking like he's got it all under control. The normally restrained Scorpio dad will spoil his kids and expose them to the good life, sparing no expense.
Sagittarius	Virgo	Class is in session! Brainy Virgo rules the fatherhood house for Sagittarius the seeker. This didactic daddy loves to teach what he knows, imparting skills and wisdom to the kids. A love of books, media, and learning can be a shared passion with his kids, and he'll cultivate their curiosity. Sagittarius may have been a wild man in his pre-papa days, but as a dad he can be a little uptight or moralistic. He may have a short attention span elsewhere, but as a father he becomes ultraobservant. At times, he can be preachy and even a little critical.

Dad's Sun Sign	Tenth House Ruler	His fathering style
Capricorn	Libra	A softer side of stern Capricorn emerges under the vibes of loving Libra. While Capricorn can be all about his career and ten-year plans, the live-for-now Libra influence gets this future-focused father out of his head. He lets himself enjoy the little things and savor the moment instead of fretting over where everything is going. Exposing his children to arts, culture, and the finer things becomes a priority for Capricorn, who may connect with his own creativity more through the kids. The only possible drawback is that he can become conflict averse, shying away from setting firm boundaries or disciplining the children when needed. Since Libra rules the scales, balancing between work and family life can also be a constant juggling act.
Aquarius	Scorpio	Airy Aquarius gains a steely sense of direction under Scorpio's ruling influence. While he may once have been a nomadic jack-of-all-trades, Aquarius finds a focal point in fatherhood. He doesn't miss a detail, either, tuning into every little nuance of his child's personality. Observing the intricacies of each phase and spending meaningful quality time could become his new passion—can you say "joined at the hip"? While this sign is normally a bit detached, as a father, Aquarius becomes emotionally (and even psychically) bonded with his kids, even if he doesn't always show it openly. Since Scorpio has a suspicious nature, he may be especially protective and even a tiny bit paranoid about safety. In some cases, his children may find him mysterious, complex, or hard to understand, all of which are Scorpionic traits.
Pisces	Sagittarius	Sensitive Pisces finds his worldly, adventurous side as a dad. While he might be thin-skinned or take everything personally, as a father he develops a wider perspective and the ability to laugh at himself. Life, after all, is a divine comedy—and he'll enjoy watching the show with his little ones by his side. Sagittarius is the zodiac's advice giver and ethicist, known for pondering every situation from all angles. Philosophical and open-minded as a dad, he could be the parent that the children confide in or solicit for wisdom about life and love.

COSMIC CONCEPTION CALENDAR

Personally, we like to leave this one up to Mother Nature, but sometimes you've got your heart set on having a child of a certain zodiac sign. Shoot for the moon (or sun sign), we guess! Here are your approximate baby-making dates to increase the odds of getting an astrologically compatible child.

So you want your kid's sign to be . . .	Target Conception Dates
Aries	June 25–July 15
Taurus	July 25–August 15
Gemini	August 25–September 15
Cancer	September 25–October 15
Leo	October 25–November 15
Virgo	November 25–December 15
Libra	December 25–January 15
Scorpio	January 25–February 15
Sagittarius	February 25–March 15
Capricorn	March 25–April 15
Aquarius	April 25–May 15
Pisces	May 25–June 15

MOMSTROLOGY

PART I

Child Signs

THE ARIES CHILD

(March 21–April 19)

SYMBOL: The Ram

COSMIC RULER: Mars

ELEMENT: Fire

BODY PART: Head, face, brain

GEMSTONE: Diamond

COLOR: Red

GOOD DAY: Dynamic
Competitive
Independent
Self-confident

BAD DAY: Bossy
Bratty
Aggressive
Selfish or demanding

LIKES: Autonomy and being in charge
Having things his way
Winning and being "the best"
Affection and reassurance
Attention and genuine praise
Freedom
Living on the edge and taking risks
Bright colors and things that are shiny and new

DISLIKES: Restrictions and rules
Repetitiveness
Forced participation
Sensory overload
Being talked down to or patronized
Being left alone too long
Dishonesty and indirectness
Being ignored

* SO, YOU WANT TO HAVE AN ARIES? *

Target Conception Dates for an Aries Child: **June 25–July 15**

FAMOUS ARIES KIDS, PAST AND PRESENT

*

Abigail Breslin, Haley Joel Osment, Jamie Lynn Spears, Harper Beckham, America Ferrera, Moses Martin, Elle Fanning, Keshia Knight-Pulliam, Emma Watson, Keri Russell, Kristen Stewart, Claire Danes, Hayden Christensen, Melissa Joan Hart, Shannen Doherty, Jennie Garth, Paris Jackson, Jesse McCartney, Lukas Haas, Ricky Schroder, Moises Arias

PARENTING YOUR ARIES CHILD: THE ESSENTIALS

*

Lace up your running shoes, Mama! Aries is a fire sign ruled by Mars, the red-hot warrior planet of aggression and ambition. Impatient and eager for excitement, this energetic kid is in perpetual motion. As the zodiac's first sign, Aries likes to stand out in a crowd and do everything first. Although your little Ram's competitiveness might be off-putting to peers at times (cue the overachieving, would-be class president Tracy Flick in *Election*, played by Aries Reese Witherspoon), you may also have a child star on your hands. Ready or not, you could soon be adding "stage parent" to your résumé, thanks to your precocious wunderkind.

Aries children tend to be utterly adorable when they're young, so lucky you! As praise for your Aries pours in from all directions, try to keep a level head—you may need to stop yourself from letting him or her run the show, because your Aries is just so darn cute! It will be hard to say no to this determined fireball, but keep reminding yourself that you'll end up with an entitled mini-monster down the line if you allow yourself to be strong-armed time and again.

As the zodiac's "baby," Aries also has a lesser-known shy side. This kid is both breathtakingly fearless and utterly terrified of abandonment. As an infant and young child, Aries can be a major squaller and apron stringer, which can make his parents feel helpless—or like hostages! A little Aries can morph from rough-and-tumble to clingy faster than you can say "ma-ma." Parents of Aries must be sensitive to this child's dueling needs for both safety and independence.

It's particularly important to give your little Ram a strong sense of security in the formative years. He has equal doses of old-soul wisdom *and* naïveté, so teach him to trust his intuition but also to look before he leaps. You might have to adopt a "hindsight is 20/20" approach, letting your Ram hit a (gentle) rock bottom, then helping her learn better foresight by talking through her mistakes. Encouragement works wonders for this sign, as a competitive Aries has never met a shiny gold star he didn't like. Above all else, this child wants—*needs*—your undivided attention. Parenting an Aries can feel exhausting, since there will be no sneaking glances at your email or throwing in a load of laundry as your kid recounts every detail of his day. (One friend's Aries toddler marched up to mama and plainly stated, "I need attention.")

Frustrating as this can be for accomplishment-driven mommy types (kiss your productivity good-bye), there *is* a silver lining: multitasking actually isn't healthy or even that fruitful. An Aries child will inadvertently force you to prioritize and be more present, kind of like a baby Buddha. Of course, this can sometimes require an entire reconfiguration of your identity and lifestyle—perhaps one parent stays home with the Aries while she is young, or you appoint a go-to grandparent as primary caregiver while you're at work. Although the Aries child can be wide-eyed and openhearted, this kid doesn't trust just anyone!

You also must learn to set limits—with yourself, your friends and family, and your little one, who will gladly devour every ounce of attention that you've got, and then some. Aries is a one-on-one sign, and can lean too heavily on a single person to meet all of his needs. Steering your Aries into activities where he can build a sense of confidence and accomplish goals can be the antidote. (Having a sibling or pet to look after can do the trick, but you might not want to add that responsibility to *your* roster!) Once this kid gets consumed with a hobby or interest, all that intense neediness gets absorbed into the task at hand. Whew! Soon enough, you could be hearing, "I want to do it all by myself!"

Impatience is a habit you'll want to nip in the bud with this sign, since Aries like to start things but not always finish them. Train your restless Aries in the art of follow-through whenever you can. It's a fine line: don't force your Aries to stick with things that she genuinely dislikes, as that is a recipe for mutiny. However, the mantra "Winners never quit and quitters never win" might need to be invoked now and again in your household. Allowing this child to learn from mistakes is a must! While your Aries can get frustrated easily by demanding tasks, don't rush in for the save every time. Let your kid struggle for a bit and figure it out without assistance. This will hone a sense of pride and accomplishment, the building blocks for a successful Aries adult. Imagine you're shaping a future CEO or world leader, because you very well could be. Finding strength in adversity is a key skill that this kid needs to develop.

ARIES: HOW THEY DEAL WITH . . .

*

RULES AND AUTHORITY

For Aries, respect is earned, not given. Little Rams don't trust readily, and they need to feel safe before handing *anyone* the reins. If this highly sensitive sign suspects that you're fibbing, strong-arming, or talking down to him, expect to be blatantly disregarded. Aries respond best to direct and simple instructions, and they want to be treated like they're competent enough to handle the truth.

LIMITS

What are those? But seriously, independent Aries are born trailblazers, so they regard limits as something to test or even defy. It helps if you explain the theory or reason behind the rule once Aries is old enough to understand. That way, Aries feels like you're dealing with him as more of an equal and not patronizing him. For younger or preverbal Aries, set up the most exciting space possible within safe confines (e.g., a colorful and well-padded playroom that's so fun she'll never want to leave).

SEPARATION AND INDEPENDENCE

The Aries child will want to play independently, but not necessarily alone. When this attention-loving sign performs stunning feats of stardom, he wants an admiring audience! As confident as this child seems, Aries can also have abandonment issues (they're the babies of the zodiac, after all). Gentle, gradual separation works best. For example, you might choose a preschool that allows parents to be in the classroom for the first few weeks, phasing out your presence as your Aries gets used to the environment. Or prepare to hover at the monkey bars perimeter or at the bottom of the big-kid slide when your daredevil Aries comes whizzing down at warp speed.

YOUNGER SIBLINGS

Someone to admire, follow, and worship them? Yes, please. Thank you, Mom, may I have another?

OLDER SIBLINGS

This can go either way. If the older sib is attentive, the little Aries will idolize her, soaking up the spotlight. A resentful older sister or brother can be a challenge. However, the little Aries' charm will quickly melt most defenses. Even an indifferent sibling will get wrapped around the younger Aries' finger sooner or later. This sign will not be ignored! Since Aries can be wise beyond their years (and fiercely loyal), the older sib may eventually lean on Aries for advice and protection.

BYE-BYE, BABY: WEANING AND POTTY TRAINING

He'll do it on his time, thank you very much. Aries kids love a fun challenge, so make growing up into a game. While the Aries kid takes pride in being a big boy or big girl, he still wants to be your baby. So if he thinks he'll lose cuddling status by growing up, he'll resist the transitions. Turn the nighttime nursing session into a cuddling session instead.

SEXUALITY

Aries is ruled by potent Mars and this child may express her sexuality from an early age. If you were taught modesty by your parents, prepare yourself for an education. This kid might prefer to run around naked, expressing comfort and pride in her body. Get used to it.

LEARNING: SCHOOL, HOMEWORK, AND TEACHERS

"I'll do it my way!" The Aries child has his own intuitive process and needs plenty of autonomy in his schooling. While this kid can't go structure-free, too many rules and restrictions are a spiritual buzzkill for young Aries. The opinionated Ram thrives in schools with a more interactive philosophy, where he can raise his hand, ask incisive questions, and work at his own pace (bonus points for a school that assigns independent study projects). Since Aries have a lot of physical energy, they also need to run or roam around. Sitting still and being quiet are a challenge for this sign—so avoid the strict conventional settings if you can.

HOUSEHOLD CONFLICT

Aries are born with a hero complex and will jump in to save the day, standing up for the underdog. Beware though, many times, Aries *are* the source of conflict. When this kid is angry, all hell can break loose. Temper, temper! Aries kids may also intuitively stir up trouble when the rest of the family is in denial about a problem, forcing everyone to deal.

THE ARIES BOY

Make way for the zodiac's sensitive stud. The Aries boy is both macho and mushy in equal parts. Ruled by potent, passionate Mars—the planet of masculinity—Aries is certainly a guy's guy. It was Aries philosopher Joseph Campbell who coined the idea of the monomyth, or hero's journey from boy to man, and it was Aries Russell Crowe who epitomized it in the film *Gladiator.* A natural alpha male, this is the guy that other boys want to be like. Yet Aries can also be a total sweetheart, charming the ladies at hello. The Aries boy typically has a posse of little girls swarming around him on the playground. Famous ladies' men Hugh Hefner and Warren Beatty are both Aries!

Impatient Aries boys can be in perpetual motion, and they have concentrated energy that needs to be channeled. Your Aries might be a brawny lad who can hold his own, but even wiry Aries boys can be surprisingly strong and physically daring. You might need to teach him a few important lessons in nonviolence—or pad the floors and walls—when his roughhousing gets a little too aggressive. Prepare to see any pacifist parenting ideals disintegrate as your Aries demands toy swords, guns, and weapons, or shows a propensity for martial arts. You can try to curb this instinct, but handing him the dreaded Jedi light saber or plastic Super Soaker might be easier in the long run—as long as he knows the difference between what's real and pretend.

What can you do if swordplay makes you squirm? Not much. There's an action hero in every Aries boy. Movie stuntman Jackie Chan is an Aries, as is actor Steven Seagal, who boasts an Aikido black belt. Illusionists Harry Houdini and David Blaine, both Aries, shocked and awed the public with their death-defying stunts. Get this kid a *sensei* or a soccer coach, stat. With a strong guiding hand, your restless little Aries will develop discipline and persistence, skills that he might not otherwise acquire on his own. He'll also learn to answer to authority figures, which is probably a good thing to cultivate early for this know-it-all sign.

While some Aries boys aren't sports-inclined, they're still competitive—perhaps your guy is more of a "mathlete" than an athlete or is the star of the chess club, debate team, and honor society. He might be verbally gifted, a great public speaker who always has an answer at the ready. Hello, future trial lawyer—this kid doesn't shy away from an argument! Aries boys also excel at strategy games, a great outlet for his considerable mental energy. These competitive guys can be steely in their focus when they're in it to win it.

In fact, your Aries son may get a little too cocky for his own good at times, fancying himself smarter than his teachers and authority figures. He wants to be recognized for his cleverness—and if you don't acknowledge it, watch out. Aries Matthew Broderick nailed the Ferris Bueller character, becoming an icon for lovable bad boys who could outfox any adult. Physical comedy and impressions can be this entertaining sign's forte, too. Aries Eddie Murphy and Martin Lawrence have both filmed movies where they famously played more than one character to hilarious result. Get ready to laugh.

While the Aries boy's confidence is unparalleled, he can be hard on himself when the chips are down. Each zodiac sign is associated with a different part of the body, and Aries happens to rule the head and brain. As a result, this sign has some real overthinkers in its ranks. Your son can swing from total self-assurance to "analysis paralysis," lapsing into doom and gloom when things don't fall into his lap. Your Aries needs large doses of praise, which can be challenging, since you don't want to give him false kudos—especially if he's underperforming. Make sure you're bolstering his confidence, not his ego.

Instead of pumping your Aries up by acting like he walks on water, give him what the experts call a "praise sandwich." Try to bookend your (extremely) constructive criticism with mentions of his talents and strengths. Be very specific about what he *can* improve upon, as this sign does not do well with generalization. Keep it simple, clear, and direct. Criticize the behavior, not the child. And yes, there will be times you have to put this kid in his place, as old school as that sounds. The Aries boy's energy knows no bounds, especially once he's comfortable around a person. It's okay to let your son know that the sky's the limit in terms of his dreams but that real-life limits are a part of the deal, too.

THE ARIES GIRL

*

All hail the diva! Whether she's an all-star athlete or a pint-sized pageant queen, this girl knows what she wants and goes for it without apology. You could call her stubborn, but why not just praise her self-awareness and determination? Confidence is her calling card, so don't try to force her to sit down and be a "nice girl." Feminist pioneer Gloria Steinem is an Aries, as are chart toppers Aretha Franklin and Celine Dion, and mega-actresses Reese Witherspoon and Sarah Jessica Parker. Superstardom suits the Aries female like Manolos fit Sarah Jessica Parker (or those controversial kiddie heels and red lipstick fit Aries Suri Cruise).

Each zodiac sign has a ruling planet, which shapes the personality. Aries is ruled by Mars, the planet of aggression and drive. No surprise, then, that your little warrior princess needs big dreams to pursue. Don't worry—she'll come up with them herself. Your only job is to cheer her on, even if her follow through is sometimes lacking. One day, she'll talk at length about building an animal rescue that throws going-away parties whenever a cat or dog is adopted. The next week, she'll want to be the first female president and she'll spend an entire Saturday designing ballot boxes and campaign posters. When she fixes her mind on the right project, however, Aries is unstoppable. At age ten, Aries Jackie Evancho scored second place on *America's Got Talent*. By thirteen, she'd released five albums (including one that reached platinum status), and several Billboard Top 10 releases.

Let your Aries daughter imagine without interference. Words like *realistic* and *reasonable* don't register with her. So even if you think you're protecting her from getting her hopes dashed, don't bother. Mistakes don't deter Aries and well-intended parental advice falls on deaf ears. This girl lives by her instincts and learns by her own experience, even if that means stepping in the same quicksand twice. She'd rather beg for forgiveness later than ask for permission first.

Aries is a highly "masculine" sign, so playing

well with her female peers isn't always easy. An everything-is-equal power structure, common among girls, just doesn't appeal to Aries. She likes to compete and, yes, to win, and that kind of open ambition can be frowned upon in girl culture. Yet her presence isn't always welcomed in the boys' club either—not that it will deter her. (Champion race-car driver Danica Patrick is an Aries.) In some cases, if she can't be the alpha female, she'd rather not participate at all. Some might brand the Aries girl as bossy, but parents should encourage her leadership—a skill that, frankly, our society could stand to cultivate in more girls. Sure, you'll probably need to teach her how to take turns, share, and let others lead, too—just don't put her down in the process. A good litmus test for parents of Aries girls is to ask yourself, if she were a boy, would I be praising her instead of chastising her for this?

The Aries girl is known for setting lofty standards for herself. While her confidence can help her achieve these sky-high goals, the Aries who is taught to be fearful of her impulses and raw energy (perhaps by a more conservative family) may begin to second-guess herself. Or she can get into the nasty habit of bargaining: proving that she's "good" (read: cooperative and willing to conform to the family/culture) in order to buy herself permission to be "bad" (e.g., individualistic). As much as she may seem to disregard your advice, she is still sensitive to criticism and approval, especially from her parents. Be mindful to let your Aries daughter blaze her own trail, even if it's a different one than you hoped she'd follow.

Aries girls can be precocious (like Aries child star Abigail Breslin in her early movies) and even racy. One mom of a little Aries wondered aloud, "Is she going to be the kind of teenager that I have to keep locked up?" And yes, her bids for attention *can* get exhausting. Yet there's a refreshing innocence to Aries girls, who can be honest to a fault. Why should she pretend that someone did a good job when he didn't? False praise is repellent to her—both giving and receiving it. She wants to strive to be her best, and she'll encourage her female friends to do the same. When the troops need motivating, there's no better class president, team captain, or BFF than an Aries girl.

BEHAVIOR DECODER: THE ARIES KID

WHEN ARIES . . .	IT MEANS . . .	SO YOU SHOULD . . .
Cries	Fear: his abandonment issues have been stoked. Frustration: he's trying to make a point and you're not getting it.	Hold him and deliver the reassurance of physical touch. Set aside your ego and give your Aries the space to talk, uninterrupted.
Withdraws socially or gets quiet or moody	He feels ignored or doesn't see an opportunity to engage with the group.	Help Aries find an "entry point" by suggesting ways he can break the ice.
Acts out (hitting, kicking, talking back)	Aries has too much energy pent up and needs a release. Or your Aries is angry and doesn't feel heard.	Get moving and transfer all that energy into a positive physical outlet. Slow down and really *listen*—Aries needs your full attention, stat!
Gets clingy	Attention deficit: she needs some all-to-myself mommy/daddy time.	Stop, drop, and roll with your mini-me. Leave the siblings and smartphone at home and do something special together.
Won't eat what you serve	He's not being difficult; he just doesn't like what you made.	Give your Aries something else or adapt the dish to her preferences; this highly sensory sign is a notorious picky eater. Try planning meals in advance that are healthy, balanced, and to Aries' liking, but keep in mind you may end up repeating the same few dishes again and again.
Can't sit still	Too much energy and emotion has built up and needs to be released.	Open the doors and send Aries out to play. Physical activity is a cure-all for Aries!

THE SOCIAL ARIES

*

ROLE IN THE FAMILY

Attention, attention! If you're easily driven to distraction by everyday stresses, the Aries child will snap you back to reality. Avoidance and denial won't fly with a Ram under your roof. This is not the child who goes along and gets along. Got an issue? Here's a tissue. There's no sweeping problems under the rug in this household. The karmic role of the Aries child may involve conflict and confrontation, especially if he is born or adopted into a family that has allowed unhealthy dynamics to fester for generations. This kid is a fighter (and a fierce lover, too). If you've been avoiding confronting core issues when it comes to tough problems, Aries will force you to face the facts and deal head-on.

This observant sign doesn't miss a thing—even from early on you'll feel your little one tracking your every move like a panther. Later, your Aries will plainly point out what he thinks is unjust. While it may be uncomfortable or even infuriating to be called out on your inconsistencies by a pint-sized police officer (who's the parent here, anyway?), take a deep breath. Rather than silence your Aries, extract the nugget of gold from his harsh words. The kid might just have a point. However, you might need to teach this über-direct sign to be more tactful in delivery, since at times this brand of honesty can be a little too brutal!

FRIENDS AND PEERS

Bossypants alert! Solo star Aries isn't much of a team player. This kid loves to win and makes no bones about boasting when she does. Even shy-seeming Aries kids have a competitive streak that comes out during board games, relay races, and anything interactive. Teaching your Aries how to be a good sport is essential, since this sign can be domineering and not always the most gracious loser—or winner!

The Aries child knows how to work power dynamics among his peers to get his way. "I'm taking my ball and going home" is an ultimatum perfected by many an Aries to establish alpha status. There might even be a few Oscar-worthy temper tantrums staged for effect (heck, if you know any adult Aries, this trait never really disappears). Other Aries have perfected the art of the "poker face" (popularized as a song title by Aries Lady Gaga), innately knowing that the person who talks first loses the negotiation.

The Aries child is a trendsetter who prefers to be the leader of the pack. In group settings, she might hang back and avoid joining the crowd—at least until she's observed a way to establish dominance. Parents and caregivers should be sure to teach Aries how to be not only a star but a "best supporting actor" sometimes, pointing out how powerful the second-in-command role is, too. Show your Aries relatable examples, like how the backup singer enriches vocals on a favorite song or the drummer keeps time for their favorite band—this might help improve your Aries' ability to roll with the punches when she can't be in charge of the group.

At the same time, look for leadership opportunities for your Aries, and cultivate this trait, too. The Aries whose initiative is discouraged can become lazy or self-doubting later in life, a real tragedy. Save your kid years of therapy by providing safe, appropriate outlets to take charge and blaze a trail.

BROTHERS AND SISTERS: ARIES AS A SIBLING

A new sibling can be a mixed bag for Aries. Both birth order and gender influence brother and sister dynamics. Aries tend to do best with a sibling of the opposite sex, since there's less competition. If your Aries has been the baby up until now, there may be some resentment about sharing Mommy and Daddy's attention with a newcomer. This is definitely a child who will need some solo excursions and special bonding once the interloper arrives. Don't let the new sib invade that sacred turf, and you'll lessen the chance of Aries feeling threatened. Soon enough, your child's proud and protective side will emerge, and you'll have a built-in babysitter and watchdog. Praise your Aries for doing a great job and remind him what a special place he has as a mentor and role model.

When the Aries is the middle or younger sibling, he will want someone to look up to, so encourage your older child to take little Aries under his wing. Since Aries is a performer, he might demand tons of attention from his older siblings. However, he's probably so cute and playful, he'll quickly win them over. And when your older kids need backup or moral support, little Aries will stick by his much-adored sibling.

DISCIPLINING AN ARIES

*

Best of luck to you, Mama. A willful and stubborn Aries can be tough to keep in line. Daredevils and risk takers, they're the kids you could be calling "stop!" to all the time. They can also be aggressive, acting out physically. Aries children aren't always aware of their own strength. You may have a few dents in the walls from your Aries kicking during a time-out or from hurling objects in a fit of rage.

With this child, your best defense is prevention. Keep your little Aries active and in motion to channel his intense and fast-building energy stores. Impatient Aries get restless (and soon, aggressive) from sitting around too much. Limiting computer and TV time is also a good idea, since passive activities cause frustration to build up. At the very least, get a video game console that combines jumping, dancing, or simulated martial arts, so your Aries isn't just sitting on his rear in front of a screen for hours. Group sports programs or trampolines (even indoor ones) are helpful, and after-dinner wrestling or dance parties can ease bedtime battles.

Positive reinforcement is another great motivator for this proud sign. Applaud Aries when he does something well, and he just might keep doing it. But know that Aries children are sensitive to manipulation, so if you've got an agenda they'll sniff it out pretty quickly. If your Aries hates putting his toys away, no amount of lavish praise will work. Just look for genuine opportunities to point out when your Aries does something right instead of wrong, and commend his efforts.

When verbally disciplining Aries, you need to be direct and to the point. Name the offending behavior and supply a consequence that's appropriate to the crime. (No TV for a week because Aries won't eat her vegetables? Guaranteed hell for *you*. Can you say "mutiny"?) Sugarcoating the situation or giving lengthy explanations about how your Aries' behavior makes *you* feel will be tuned out. Think business, not personal—like a supervisor directing a valued employee. When Aries feel seen and respected, that increases the odds that they will actually listen.

HANDLING TRANSITIONS: MOVING, DIVORCE, DEATH, AND OTHER TOUGH STUFF

*

Gentle honesty is the best policy when explaining the facts of life or a change of circumstances to your Aries. Aries is an innocent sign that tends to romanticize life, so the first realization that life is unfair can be tough to swallow. Aries may have extremely emotional reactions to upsets, like sobbing loudly or making a scene. However, an Aries child still dislikes being lied to, so do your best with a just-the-facts approach. He might also need a lot of room to talk about his feelings, so plan to make time to listen to your Aries process the emotions that come up. This sign prides itself on bravery, so Aries will often take on the hero role, especially for a younger sibling.

SCHOOL'S IN SESSION

*

BEST EDUCATION STYLE

The Aries child needs autonomy and independence, so a school that encourages individuality is best for this headstrong sign. Rigid rules, starched uniforms, and too much predictability will practically guarantee that your Aries rebels or zones out. This kid is a leader, not a follower, and needs a classroom where opinions are heard and respected. Look for a flexible curriculum that lets Aries follow her own intuitive process and learn at her own speed.

Micromanaging is a no-no for Aries, who hates people looking over his shoulder or meddling in his process. The Aries child wants to be praised for figuring things out on his own—even if he arrives at the solution in a unique way. He's not interested in a set of rote instructions or mind-numbing drills. Creative problem solving thrills little Aries. A critical teacher, an authoritarian approach, or a faculty that insists on things being done a certain way is not a great fit for this kid.

That said, you don't want a school that's *too* touchy-feely (e.g., one that discourages hierarchy and competitive sports or has a no-grades policy). Aries like to compete—they've never met a shiny gold star they didn't like (or feel they deserved)—and will thrive when there are opportunities to shine. Aim for a healthy mix of alternative and traditional methods, so that your child still gets the benefit of structure without feeling suppressed.

BEST HOBBIES AND ACTIVITIES

Competitive Aries has brains and brawn. Contact sports like football, hockey, soccer, or even roller derby could appeal to Aries kids with a rough-and-tumble side. If you're the protective or nonviolent type, you'll need to toughen up, because your Aries *will* come home with a few cuts and bruises (badges of honor in Aries' book).

Chess club, anyone? Strategy games are popular with Aries, who like to use their wits and make bold, calculated decisions. Ruled by warrior Mars, there's a hint of military leader in every Aries (retired four-star general Colin Powell is born under this sign). Your Aries may be involved in elaborate, multiplayer video or fantasy games. Prepare to host a few Dungeons & Dragons marathons at your home later on.

Lights, camera, action! Your Aries child's star power could emerge on stage. Kids of this sign can be fearless in the spotlight, with stunning singing voices, acting abilities, or other talents. One friend recently posted a picture of her four-year-old Aries son with spiked hair and a real guitar, looking every inch the rock star. As the zodiac's first (and therefore "youngest") sign, these precocious kiddos are ready for their close-ups.

GIFT GUIDE:
BEST PRESENTS FOR ARIES

* Action-oriented toys, including sports equipment, climbing structures, and tumbling mats
* A video game console that includes movement elements (Wii Sports, for example)
* Martial arts lessons
* Mental strategy games like Risk, chess, and puzzles
* Jewelry and hair accessories that accent the face (the Aries-ruled area)
* Starter kits that help them create their own cottage industry, such as an ice-cream maker, a tool kit, or a calligraphy set

THE TAURUS CHILD

(April 20–May 20)

SYMBOL: The Bull

COSMIC RULER: Venus

ELEMENT: Earth

BODY PART: Neck, shoulders, throat

GEMSTONE: Emerald

COLOR: Green, brown

GOOD DAY: Determined
Artistic and aesthetic
Self-assured
Reliable

BAD DAY: Stubborn or willful
Blunt
Lazy
Destructive

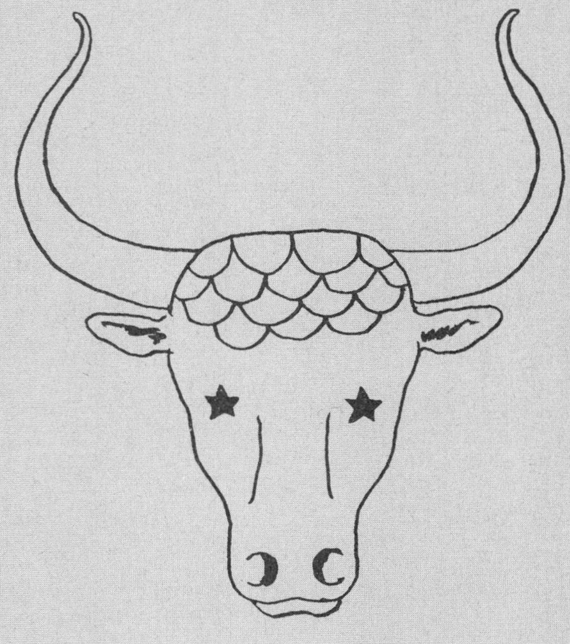

LIKES: Beauty and pleasure
Fresh air and the outdoors
Structure and predictability
Pretty, well-made clothes
Thrills: fast cars, roller coasters, motorcycles, and action movies
Music, concerts, and shows
The finer things (this kid has expensive taste!)
Feeling a little bit superior to all their friends

DISLIKES: Ugliness, bad smells, cheap fabrics, and loud noises
Inconsistency
Change, especially without advance notice
Being forced to do anything they don't want to do
Being physically uncomfortable or confined
Losing or being the low person on the totem pole

* SO, YOU WANT TO HAVE A TAURUS? *

Target Conception Dates for a Taurus Child: **July 25–August 15**

FAMOUS TAURUS KIDS, PAST AND PRESENT

*

Kirsten Dunst, Robert Pattinson, Stevie Wonder, Shirley Temple, Apple Martin, Jason Biggs, Miranda Cosgrove, Melissa Gilbert, Janet Jackson, Lance Bass, Tori Spelling

PARENTING YOUR TAURUS CHILD: THE ESSENTIALS

*

A Bull is born! Prepare for some blissful moments—and a few battles of will. Your little Taurus runs on two speeds: either totally relaxed (think Ferdinand the bull munching clover in his field) or downright unstoppable (the Tasmanian devil comes to mind). There's not much middle ground, so you'll need a parenting persona to match your little one's on and off settings.

Despite the Bull's rep for destruction, Taurus is actually one of the most peaceful signs in the zodiac. Ruled by Venus, the planet of love and beauty, your Taurus is a miniature aesthete who may have strikingly refined taste in food, clothes, and ambience from an early age. Even rough-and-tumble Taureans know what they like and can be uncompromising in their standards. This sign definitely has an appetite for pleasure. Prepare to serve second and third helpings of your Bull's favorite dishes, or to splurge on name-brand clothing pricier than anything *you* ever wore as a kid.

There's a competitive side to Taurus, which is a status-oriented and sometimes even materialistic sign. Ruled by flashy Venus, your Bull is a bit of a show pony who wants to outdress or outdo the other children. If (or likely when) you overhear little Taurus bragging about his name-brand shoes or even what kind of car *you* drive, a little lecture on humility might be in order. Encourage your Taurus to take pride in having good taste, but steer her away from snobbery. Tempted as you are to indulge this sign's exacting whims, don't let Taurus get competitive or, worse, exclusionary. Birthday parties are not a "who's who" of the local elementary school, kiddo! You might even start a tradition of letting your Taurus donate to a charity of his choice each year so he learns the joy of giving, not just receiving.

Your Bull can become a bully without much prompting. You can nip a judgmental streak in the bud through regular family charity or volunteer work. Spare yourself from raising a future elitist by cultivating compassion in your Taurus at an early age. This is a kid who learns and evolves through experience. While little

Taurus may show disdain for people different from him, when he witnesses human suffering or struggle firsthand, he will soften his judgment and often champion the issue. The key is to let this visual sign see things with her own eyes, so don't shelter your Taurus from difficult situations, even if they can seem harsh and unfair.

Taurus is an earth sign, so stability and routine are vital to this kid's happiness. Dinnertimes, bedtimes, knowing what to expect every day—structure is important with a Taurus, so try and minimize chaos, both in your life and your child's. Bulls are the ultimate creatures of habit, and these meat-and-potatoes kids thrive in a predictable environment with calm and consistency. True, this could be said of any child, but Taurus is the zodiac's most sensory sign and is particularly attuned to when things are off at home.

Don't expect to have any deep psychological conversations about family problems or household turmoil. While your child may seem as sensitive as asphalt (and equally as tough), Taurus is actually incredibly perceptive—but his "knowing" comes from what he picks up bodily. For example, your little Taurus might call attention to a strange scent, disturbing noises outside his window, or a piece of furniture he finds ugly when he really feels that something larger is going on. Or she'll throw an epic tantrum when you try to make her wear something she dislikes or feels uncomfortable in. Don't invalidate your Taurus's bodily reactions. These are your clues that little Taurus detects a deeper discontent but is experiencing it through touch, smell, taste, hearing, or sight. Follow the smoke signals with your Taurus and you'll soon uncover the underlying issue.

Because Taurus is so body-oriented, physical touch and affection are important to these kids. Brush their hair, hold and cuddle them, even learn infant massage for your newborn. As Taurus gets older and more independent, he will enjoy just having you physically present, even when going out for grown-up indulgences like mani-pedis and stadium sports games or when eating out at restaurants. As mature and capable as this sign may seem, Taurus likes to know his mom and dad are close by.

Watch out: during stubborn moments, your Bull can and will charge! An angry little Taurus can be fierce and fearsome, stamping her feet, ramming into furniture, or even breaking things. Since Taurus rules the throat, yours might have a powerful voice—and he won't hesitate to bellow so loud that the neighbors peek out of their doors. Many times, your Taurus child doesn't know her own strength, and you'll need to gently but firmly physically restrain this kid to keep her from hurting herself. You might need to hand little Taurus a pillow or sofa cushion to punch, just so the intense emotions can be channeled out of her body. When this Bull sees red, duck! Your Taurus can be a force of nature.

Speaking of nature, fresh air can be the cure-all for this earth sign. Although Taurus kids do enjoy the culture and action of a big city, the sights, sounds, and smells can overwhelm their senses. There's only so much stimulation this sign can process before shutting down. If you live in an urban area, make an effort to take your Taurus to the park or for day trips away from the concrete jungle. Wide-open spaces and a little greenery can really help a Taurus reset and energize. And fair warning: once a Taurus hits the couch, it's potato time all the way. So rather than pry Taurus off the cushions, be proactive in getting this kid outside to play. Try arranging playdates in advance, or sign Taurus up for sports and activities that will keep him (and you!) from the temptation of staying indoors all day. Music also soothes the savage beast, so lull your Taurus back to serenity by playing his favorite tunes.

As willful as your Taurus can be, there's a flip side to that stubbornness. Taurus is one of the most loyal and tenacious signs in the zodiac. Remember that today's defiant child could be tomorrow's forward-thinking CEO. Don't break this kid's spirit—as if anyone even could! Your kid knows what he wants, and when the Bull sets his sights on a target it's often best to just move out of his way.

Of course, you'll want to set limits for the sake of safety and respect. But if you want to bring out the best in your Bull, play to her strengths. Give this kid some real responsibilities, something (or someone) to be in charge of, and he'll step up to the plate. Don't micromanage your Taurus. This sensible sign intuitively knows how to simplify tasks into a step-by-step process. Give your Taurus some sovereignty and let the kid reign over his turf. This "builder" sign loves to see the results of his efforts, so offer your Taurus the wooden blocks and let him construct a small empire. Sure, he might be more of a dictator than a democrat at times, but give him the freedom to develop confidence and determination. Once a Taurus kid cultivates those traits, the sky is the limit—even if his feet remain on terra firma.

TAURUS: HOW THEY DEAL WITH . . .

*

RULES AND AUTHORITY

Rules make children feel safe and secure, and that's really all a Taurus wants. However, many parents' rules can seem arbitrary or subject to change without notice, which are major no-nos with this sign. Headstrong Taurus will constantly test the boundaries if he senses that you don't mean what you say. Follow-through is a must. Taurus needs someone strong enough to handle him—and that will take a lot of self-discipline for parents. As much of a drag as it can be, you'll have to set rules and reinforce them until Taurus sees that you mean business. The good news? Kids of this sign will gladly defer to a consistent, confident authority figure who doesn't back down from challenges. For example, the caregiver who remains unfazed by a young Bull's foot-stomping "no!" or who puts her back into time-out each time she scurries out will eventually win the battle of wills. And if you start strong with Taurus, you can stay strong. Your own consistency from day one could spell the difference between a golden child and a problem child.

LIMITS

A Taurus will happily set limits for everyone else (younger siblings, friends, pets), but only the strong survive when trying to place restrictions on the Bull. Authority figures must be unwavering and firm when Taurus tries to charge through boundaries.

SEPARATION AND INDEPENDENCE

Confident Taurus isn't really a clinger as long as she has someone she knows and trusts around. Luckily, it doesn't matter if this person is an aunt, uncle, grandparent, sibling, or sitter—a familiar face will ease a Taurus into any difficult situation.

YOUNGER SIBLINGS

Taurus kids take a shine to their little brothers and sisters. Rather than feel replaced as the family baby, this managerial sign enjoys being regarded as the older, responsible sibling—and he will milk this position of power for all he can. In fact, you might need to make sure your Taurus is not bossing around the littler ones *too* much.

OLDER SIBLINGS

Your Bull may be the baby of the family, but make no mistake about who's in charge. Affectionate Taurus will love being protected by an adoring older sib. But if rivalry occurs, this cute little brute can hold his own—and will push right back if someone tries to steamroll him.

BYE-BYE, BABY: WEANING AND POTTY TRAINING

Pass the Pull-Ups! Little Taurus is eager to grow up and be the one telling everyone else what to do. While this sign dislikes being dependent, Taurus can be equally averse to change. You'll need to handle transitions with sensitivity. Try warming up your Taurus to a new idea gradually, letting her know what to expect each step of the way. Putting the potty in plain view before suggesting she try to use it will help her get accustomed to the new piece of furniture in the house. Praising her big-girl behavior and pointing out the perks that come along with it can also work well with this results-driven sign. Cold turkey tactics will backfire, as Taurus will resist with all her might.

SEXUALITY

Is that a full moon? As prim or metrosexual as your Taurus might be, this kid will shuck that elegant party outfit and go naked in a heartbeat. Taurus is a sensual sign, and those born under it love to feel the sun or grass or fresh air on their skin. This earth sign is just fine going au naturel, so the key is for you not to freak out or get embarrassed by it. Parents might need to steer Taurus toward "designated naked zones" so he can maintain a sense of body confidence without alarming the mailman. Teaching your Taurus about healthy sexuality and the facts of life is important, as this pleasure-centric sign sometimes begins exploration early. Do your best to impart responsibility and avoid passing on a burden of shame. Teach Taurus that having sexual feelings is normal but that he or she doesn't necessarily need to act on every one.

LEARNING: SCHOOL, HOMEWORK, AND TEACHERS

Taurus kids often fall into one of two camps: either the prim, grade-grubbing teacher's pets (it's all about status) or lazy students who only apply themselves to subjects that truly interest them. The nonacademic Taurus types, however, tend to have street smarts in spades, which will serve them well in sales or "schmoozer"-type jobs later in life. If your Taurus is underachieving in school, consider steering him into a different curriculum than the standard "reading, writing, and 'rithmetic"—possibly even a technical or trade school. You might even give your Bull some real-world work experience, even starting with simple tasks helping out at a relative's shop or business.

HOUSEHOLD CONFLICT

Taurus kids are like dormant volcanoes: serene until too much heat and pressure build up under the surface. To prevent epic explosions, don't expose your Taurus kid to chaos. Or, if you sense that tension is building in the atmosphere, remove Taurus from the environment. Taurus will soak up stress like a sponge, so the less you expose her to, the better.

THE TAURUS BOY

*

Dress him up, dress him down. The Taurus boy is a prince one minute and a hooligan the next. Sometimes he'll come home grass-stained and sweaty from the park; other days he'll spend more time fixing his hair in the mirror than you do. This kid can get dirty with the best of 'em, but he cleans up well. You won't get an argument from this boy when you outfit him in Armani Junior and other formal finery. But don't mistake his wingtips for weakness: this sartorialist has swagger.

There's a delicate beauty to the Taurus boy that can make him look almost angelic, especially when looks are coupled with charm. He's kiddie-model material—provided he's willing to sit still and pose. The Taurus boy has limitless patience when he's interested in something and zero tolerance when he's not. He might be the hardest-working lazy person you've ever met—showing total dedication to, say, building his own soapbox derby race car, but totally blowing off his social studies homework. He can also be a real prankster, playing practical jokes on his unsuspecting friends and family.

As a baby, Taurus can be one of the calmest signs, content to sleep, eat, and cuddle non-stop. In fact, you might need to wake your boy up from his marathon naps now and then! But once he's on his feet, *you'll* be the one who needs a snooze. There's no stopping this little speed demon once he gets going. Get him a kiddie bike, a little scooter . . . or a padded room! You definitely want to keep your Taurus boy in an enclosed area, although don't be surprised if this crafty kid finds a way to break out of his confines.

The Taurus boy is a straightforward kid who calls it like he sees it. This guy only wants the facts, Mom, so you'll want to get to the point, and fast. Not that he won't argue with you if he thinks his way is more sensible (and he usually does). Taurus is also a sign that likes to be right, and he'll dig his heels in during an argument until he gets his point across. Prepare for some fierce battles of will with this guy. Some of the fieriest, most controversial political figures—from Saddam Hussein to Malcolm X—were Tauruses. This sign can bullishly defend his convictions and, yes, even be a dictator.

Headstrong as Taurus can be, home is where his heart lives. A volatile household is especially tough for a Taurus boy, who loves his thrills but hates not knowing what to expect. He's a family guy who craves secure roots, time-honored traditions, and happy memories with his clan. He may not be mushy, but he's nostalgic, and will relish favorite vacation spots and holiday traditions. "Every Christmas, my son makes me take him to see our town's model train display," recalls the mom of a Taurus.

The Taurus boy may idolize his father (or father figure), especially if dad is exceptionally dependable. This is the boy who will take over the family business or dutifully ensure that his parents retire comfortably someday. Taurus is the sign of the provider, and your son will want to express this side. Beware the urge to coddle or spoil him, or you could end up with a lazy "sitting bull" or an entitled little prince. If you're a single parent or a two-mom family, you'll need to find this kid a strong male role model to guide him. Aim for a "gentle giant" type: someone who can do manly man things with him but also build his character and reinforce values such as loyalty, integrity, and earning his keep.

Pass the power drill! Taurus boys can be extremely technical, gifted at taking things apart and putting them back together. No appliance, DVD player, or gadget is safe from your Taurus's tool kit and prying fingers. Bonus: he might just rig up great-sounding speakers throughout your home or miraculously repair your favorite watch when it stops ticking. Even if he's not a Mr. Fix-It, he'll still have great taste in electronics, bikes, even cars. Only the best for Taurus! You'll be glad to have your little handyman around when he changes your car's oil or even advises intelligently on the purchase of a new family sedan. Of course, when he requests a motorcycle as a teenager, you won't be so thrilled with his mechanical inclinations.

With pleasure planet Venus as his ruler, your

little Taurus has an appetite for the finer things, especially when it comes to cuisine. If you're a foodie or a gourmet cook, he may peer over your shoulder at the stove or help with chopping, learning the finer points of your culinary prowess. Or, like one Taurus boy we know, he might be banned from your kitchen and delicate plates. (Can you say "bull in a china shop"?) Either way, he'll happily eat any hearty dish you want to serve. While some Bulls go vegetarian later in life if they suddenly become über-principled (a kick that doesn't always last), this kid is usually a solid meat-and-potatoes guy.

Taurus boys are often physical and/or musical. Some tend toward the stocky side, and these "strong like bull" Taurus dudes excel in contact sports like ice hockey. Other Taurus boys are more lithe and have an extraordinary ear for tune and tone (we know several Taurus guys who work as sound engineers). If music seems his forte, steer him into singing lessons, playing an instrument, even competitive dance. Legendary dancer Fred Astaire was a Taurus (as was "Godfather of Soul" James Brown), and your son may be graceful on his feet, too.

If anyone is self-assured enough to get away with wearing a leotard or ballroom dance shoes, the Taurus boy is. You got a problem with that? Any parent struggling to understand the Taurus boy's nature should just rent the movie *Scent of a Woman*. Watch Taurus Al Pacino's famous scenes as a blind lieutenant colonel dancing the tango, renting a Waldorf-Astoria suite, and even driving a Ferrari in Manhattan (yes, sightless). The Taurus boy plays it safe while also living on the edge. He's a little bit timeless and a little bit rock 'n' roll. And while he may be a daredevil, there's nothing he craves more than returning from his adventures to a safe and happy home.

THE TAURUS GIRL

*

The Taurus girl is a curious mix of sweetness and strength. She's a mild-mannered girl one minute, in your face the next—a princess and a powerhouse in one. Your little steel magnolia may flounce around in a tutu but she means business, and you'll learn that early on. Taurus rules the throat, and when your daughter wants to be heard her voice can carry. Many of the toughest female world leaders—Eva Perón, Golda Meir, Madeleine Albright—were born under the Taurus sign. Prepare for the occasional power struggle when she digs in her fancy heels.

Because Taurus is an earth sign ruled by beauty-loving Venus, your girl will have a taste for pretty things, even from an early age. It's important for moms of Taurus girls to steer them away from materialism. Taurus girls are status conscious and can come off as boastful. One woman we know still shudders at second-grade memories of a Taurus classmate who made fun of her imitation Nikes. Since Taurus is a possessive sign, she can easily accumulate toys and play clothes that she doesn't want to share. ("Mine!" may be a common refrain from your bossy Bull.)

Teaching Taurus girls moderation and practical limits will take time. They might want to have the most stylish and put-together outfit for the first day of school, for example, and no pricey label is beyond their discriminating tastes. Beware creating a monster—or a "mean girl," to use a term coined by Taurus Tina Fey.

A good form of prevention is to encourage your daughter's creativity. Many among this sign love a good DIY project, so set her up with paper, paints, glitter, and glue, and watch her make a masterpiece (and yeah, a huge mess). Rather than criticize her for having extravagant desires, just train her to be resourceful. Before you know it, she could be hosting jewelry-making parties, or rallying friends for an elaborate picnic on the grass, organizing everyone into roles and tasks. Onward, little sandwich makers!

In fact, there's a miniature manager in training in your Taurus daughter. This girl is not afraid to give anyone orders. Straight to the point, the Taurus girl tells it like it is—which might not make her a fan favorite among her female peers. However, the loyal friends who can handle her no-nonsense style will be in Taurus's tribe for life. Organized Taurus girls can later end up as the de facto event planner, movie ticket procurer, and parent persuader for all of her friends. She also has a nurturing side and might even be a bit of a mother hen with some of her pals.

Though Taurus girls can seem lazy when they're relaxing, a worthy goal will get these she-Bulls charging. Idle hands are the devil's playground, as the saying goes, so keep your Taurus busy. She may at first be resistant to new ideas, people, and activities, but once Taurus finds her groove she sticks with it loyally. With artsy Venus as their ruler, Taurus girls can be talented singers, dancers, and instrumentalists. Since this sign can also be a champion couch potato, consider organized sports for your daughter like softball or volleyball. Taurus girls enjoy the camaraderie of reliable teammates—and they also love to win.

Taurus rules the zodiac's second house of work and money, so this girl likes to feel productive. Since Taurus can be driven by the dollar early on, you might consider giving her an allowance for doing chores. Or supply her with the tools for a creative project that she can turn into a profitable little enterprise. Taurus Lena Dunham created a sensation with her HBO series *Girls*, winning two Golden Globes at age twenty-six. Taurus wunderkind Tavi Gevinson was barely a teen when she became a fashion-world darling. As an eleven-year-old, her fashion blog drew thirty thousand readers a day and acclaim from the *New York Times*. She went on to launch the online magazine *Rookie*, publish a spin-off book, and is now off to Hollywood. Don't underestimate your Taurus daughter's homegrown creations; they could be a business in the making!

BEHAVIOR DECODER: THE TAURUS KID

WHEN TAURUS . . .	IT MEANS . . .	SO YOU SHOULD . . .
Cries	Something is genuinely wrong, since this kid isn't usually a big crier.	Stop, soothe, and investigate.
Withdraws socially or gets quiet or moody	Taurus is focused and lost in her thoughts, possibly plotting or pondering how to handle a situation. This sign can fixate and obsess, so it's possible your little Taurus is feeling stuck on something.	Ask a neutral question, like "So, what's on your mind?" Don't make a big deal out of it. Taurus might just need a sounding board to talk things through.
	Taurus is tired.	Sometimes, a cigar is just a cigar (as Taurus Sigmund Freud said, according to urban legend). A cuddle and a nap will chase the moody blues away.
Acts out (hitting, kicking, talking back)	Miniature Mussolini didn't get his way—and man, is he pissed!	Charge! Physically restrain the angry Bull before anyone gets hurt. Give him a pillow to punch or a send him outside to get the pent-up energy out of his system.
Gets clingy	Taurus is a possessive sign, so if you've been spreading your attention around too much, Taurus will mark his territory.	Give your baby Bull some focused one-on-one time and special attention he doesn't have to share. Gifts and material expressions of your love are welcome, too.
Won't eat what you serve	Your junior gourmand may have a refined palate at an early age, so it could be a fussiness issue. However, the Bull can be a major grazer, so she may have filled up on snacks between meals.	If pickiness is the culprit, you may (sigh) need to serve a separate menu for little Taurus, stocking up on her favorite staples. If snacking is the problem, keep healthy ones on hand so that Taurus doesn't gorge on empty calories and ruin her appetite.
Can't sit still	This might be a good problem for Taurus, a sign that can lounge like a champion. Nervous energy is usually the culprit here.	Send Taurus outside to run around, or if it's too cold outdoors, a little wrestling or dance party will do. Taurus needs to release that pent-up mental and physical energy through activity.

THE SOCIAL TAURUS

*

ROLE IN THE FAMILY

Wake-up call! Taurus rules the five senses and is one of the zodiac's most grounded—and therefore present—signs. A Taurus child can teach distracted parents how to live in the now—something we could all use in our multitasking world. Taurus knows how to soak up the beauty of the moment: a great song, a delicious meal, or a breathtaking view. As John Lennon said, "Life is what happens to you while you're busy making other plans." Well, not once a Taurus is born into your family. It's a lovely chance to slow down and savor each day.

At the same time, a Taurus child can make you a better planner, helping you prioritize. Unexpected change can really throw off this sign, as Taurus doesn't adapt easily. You need to be prepared with the Bull's favorite foods, toys, clothes, and accoutrements, keeping a steady schedule and consistent environment. Taurus will force parents to simplify, to say what you mean and mean what you say. While some signs (especially fire and air sign parents) might feel a little trapped or bored by all the sameness, a Taurus child can help you find a pleasant daily rhythm, teaching you that predictability doesn't have to equal boredom.

FRIENDS AND PEERS

Loyal and nostalgic, Taurus is a friend for life. Unless you do wrong by them (Tauruses also make formidable foes), Bulls will stick by their cronies forever. Taurus girls can be the nurturers of their flock, giving advice and supporting their friends. Taurus boys like to have a steady "band of brothers" as their gang. Although they can have a real macho side, Taurus boys are also sweet and sensitive. Taurus boys and girls will usually have a mix of friends from both sexes.

Steady Tauruses are often the rock among their peers. They like to keep entertaining people around them, if only for the colorful stories. Yet this self-assured sign is not afraid to disagree with his friends or voice an unpopular opinion when standing up for his beliefs. Often, Taurus is the voice of reason among her wild-child friends, a goody-goody in values, though not in tastes. One Taurus we knew in high school openly identified as "straight edge" (in other words, she didn't drink, smoke, or do drugs) but attended concerts for her favorite bands and had a few edgy piercings. Taurus kids can be prim and punk rock all at once, and their friends will respect and rely on them as a result. "My daughter made some bold choices in her teens, but I always trusted her to do the right thing," recalls the mom of a Taurus.

BROTHERS AND SISTERS: TAURUS AS A SIBLING

Loyal Tauruses can be protective siblings, especially to younger sisters and brothers. They love to manage and direct others and will enjoy holding this influential position. Taurus takes pride when a little sib starts to copycat or do his bidding and might even spend hours patiently teaching a skill to his young protégé. Imitation, after all, is the highest form of flattery. However, you'll need to keep an eye out that Taurus doesn't get *too* bossy. This sign can definitely veer into domineering terrain, acting more like a parent than a sister or brother. A more submissive sibling can easily get overshadowed or cowed into doing Taurus's bidding.

Older siblings can be a badge of honor (and status) for Taurus, who will brag about a big sister or brother's accomplishments as if they were her own. You might hear little Taurus boast, "*My* sister's the star of the high school play" or "*My* brother won a talent search for the whole state." Clan-centric Taurus has a strong sense that her family reflects on her. For this reason, a scheming, selfish, or manipulative sibling can receive Taurus's wrath. Your little Bull doesn't want to be associated with anyone whose unsavory reputation could rub off on her.

Sibling rivalry can arise with another child born under an equally strong-willed sign. Can you say "bullfight"? A battle for supremacy can go down under your roof unless boundaries are distinctly drawn. You'll need to keep things fair, too, as Taurus is sensitive to favoritism. "If *I* can't have ice cream/a toy/a later bedtime, nobody can!" is this sign's attitude. Territorial Taurus doesn't always like to share his things (or friends), either. This possessive sign could go through a phase where his favorite word seems to be *mine*. You may need to referee a few turf wars and land grabs with a Taurus (or two!) in your house.

DISCIPLINING A TAURUS

*

Have you ever been in the path of a charging bull? Unless you're a matador, you might not have the natural skills to stop El Toro in his tracks. Getting through to a determined Taurus who has set his sights on something is *not* easy! In fact, you might just take a cue from professional bullfighters. Their secret is to work *with* the natural energy of the beast, not against it. They don't calmly try to rationalize with an angry bull; they piss him off more so he stomps around blowing hot air . . . and eventually loses steam.

Often, it makes the most sense just to let your Taurus "get it out of her system." Send her to her room or outside to release that aggression, so she doesn't destroy your delicate furniture or hurt anyone. If your Taurus is very young, invest in a cushiony baby gym or membership to one of those kiddie climbing places where children can run around for hours, crashing into padded enclosures if they are feeling frustrated or upset.

Once your Taurus is calm and able to hear you (or old enough to understand), explain things clearly and simply. As long as Taurus understands the reason behind the rules—and buys into it—you're golden. Believe it or not, this sign also has a "good boy/good girl" complex, which you can cultivate with a few techniques. Giving your Taurus a post of responsibility—a designated pet, plant, or even a sibling to mind—will encourage the desire to be her best, since she's now a role model.

Just as grown-ups love "rewards cards" and loyalty programs, Taurus kids also respond very well to these time-tested marketing moves. Cooperation can be (cautiously) encouraged with material perks. One mom of a Taurus put gold stars on a chart when she caught her son doing something good. Once he earned enough stars, they could be redeemed for rewards. However, she realized that she'd created a monster once she heard his demands for pricey sneakers and toys. Don't deliver this sign into temptation—set clear limits and expectations, because when Taurus doesn't get what he wants, you could have an upset and angry kid on your hands.

Taurus kids are creatures of habit, so entrenched behaviors require a little time to undo. Be compassionate: it takes hard work to break a behavior pattern at *any* age. A gentle and consistent introduction of change works best for Taurus. Of course, you'll have to make some changes, too, since "Do as I say, not as I do" will never fly with this sign. If you want your Taurus to cut back on sugar, for example, you can't keep Popsicles in the freezer for a sibling or munch on sweets in front of him. Get ready to make that change yourself.

HANDLING TRANSITIONS: MOVING, DIVORCE, DEATH, AND OTHER TOUGH STUFF

*

Taurus is one of the zodiac's most steadfast signs, and these kids dislike change—especially when they haven't initiated it. Comforting objects such as a blanket, a bear, or a soothing sound machine that travels with Taurus can help. Introduce change slowly, and find a continuous thread to help smooth the road. For example, if you move to a new home, either reset the child's room to be a replica of the old one or get her excited about what will be an upgraded version 2.0 of her former life.

If dealing with divorce, keep your Taurus's routine as steady and unchanged as possible. Don't rip off the bandage and make her change homes, neighborhoods, and schools all at once if you can help it. Minimize the impact of what is changing. A sense of belonging is important to Taurus, so if you have religious affiliations, your child may find solace in your church or temple's congregation. Taurus gains strength as part of a secure, ongoing community—a youth group, an after-school program, or a safe space that feels like a second home.

Taurus is also a realist and can be shockingly matter-of-fact about death and other tough issues. You might be surprised by your child's maturity, and you can even talk to Taurus like a little adult. Your Taurus may even take on the role of explaining the tough stuff to younger siblings. He's also traditional, so if a pet or family member dies, Taurus will need to do a formal ceremony or commemoration to keep the lost loved one's presence around.

SCHOOL'S IN SESSION

*

BEST EDUCATION STYLE

Taurus kids learn best in a simple, structured educational system. The open-classroom model in which Taurus self-directs his education or an egalitarian school that doesn't give grades might be too loosey-goosey for most Taurus kids. Taurus needs rules and routines, enforced by strong, caring faculty. This sign usually learns best in a classical education system in which her talents and achievements are acknowledged and rewarded. Public school is fine, and even private school (with uniforms) can work for this traditional sign—provided the teachers aren't *too* strict and autocratic.

When a Taurus is engaged in her education, she can be a precocious teacher's pet. But if school isn't stimulating enough for Taurus, this sign gets bored and restless. It's not that Taurus is lazy, but when this kid isn't interested in a subject no amount of coercion can force her to be. Your Taurus may start acting out when asked to sit still during a "boring" lesson. If this happens, you might need to switch to a more interactive teacher or school. When Taurus is invited to express an opinion on a subject, or to apply what she learns to her own life, this practical sign becomes much more engaged.

Business-minded Taurus also likes to make money and may from an early age have a few enterprising schemes in mind. Give your Bull the tools to build his kiddie empire. One Taurus we know began fixing cars at age fifteen, and another started her own advertising-funded website during high school, way back before blogs became the rage. Some Taurus kids may also do well in a technical school where they can learn a craft or trade. Or they may be more street smart than book smart. Begin cultivating your Taurus child's talents early by bringing his hobbies and passions to life. Expose Taurus to the inner workings of his interests—for example, if your Bull loves to dabble in the kitchen, take him on an inside tour of a bakery or a real-life chocolate factory (paging Mr. Wonka!), and let him experiment with simple recipes. Take family cooking classes. Remember that for Taurus the best education often happens outside of the classroom, out in the school of life.

BEST HOBBIES AND ACTIVITIES

Taurus is ruled by Venus, the planet of art, culture, and beauty. Many kids of this sign have real talent for music, fine art, dance, and working with their hands. You could be shuttling this child to lessons and even auditions, since performing competitively is a strong possibility. Patient Taurus is a craftsperson and may have the tolerance to learn technique—perhaps she is first in the ballet class to go *en pointe*, or even to star in *The Nutcracker*. Taurus loves to eat and can be a little foodie, so your Taurus might love to cook. While a pretend kitchen is fun, a Taurus kid will probably want to get his hands on a real stove and ingredients soon. He'll want the gratification of enjoying his creations and might also love to feed friends and family as he gets older.

Other Taurus children seem to be mechanically inclined, with a real passion for understanding how things work. Cars, motorcycles, and all kinds of machinery fascinate them, and you may need to give this Taurus a set of toy wrenches, screwdrivers, and hammers before the kid can walk! Banging on drums—or pots and pans—helps this kid vent frustration *and* express her rhythmic side. Remember, though—soon enough, your little Taurus might be taking apart everything in the house to see how it works. If you have a garage, it could be converted into a wood shop, music studio, or creation station for your little Bull.

GIFT GUIDE: BEST PRESENTS FOR TAURUS

* Tickets to a fun show or concert
* Anything music-related: iPods, instruments, a karaoke machine
* Dinner at a special restaurant or a basket of treats
* Plush, comfy accessories for their rooms—or a chance to redecorate
* Nice-smelling body products like bubble bath, cologne, or lotion

THE GEMINI CHILD

(May 21–June 20)

SYMBOL: The Twins

COSMIC RULER: Mercury

ELEMENT: Air

BODY PART: Arms, hands

GEMSTONE: Pearl

COLOR: Yellow, orange

GOOD DAY: Clever
Original
Charming
Curious

BAD DAY: Restless
Distracted or overwhelmed
Two-faced or gossipy
Sarcastic or back talking

LIKES: Gadgets of any kind
Books and educational toys
Music, movies, and media
Lots of stimulation
Sweets and "impulse foods"
Variety
Being up on the latest trends

DISLIKES: Sitting still
Rules and authority
Silence
Old-fashioned anything; Gemini wants "new and now"
The word *no*
Boredom, routines, sameness

* SO, YOU WANT TO HAVE A GEMINI? *

Target Conception Dates for a Gemini Child: **August 25–September 15**

FAMOUS GEMINI KIDS, PAST AND PRESENT

*

Natalie Portman, Mary-Kate and Ashley Olsen, Michael J. Fox, Judy Garland, Kingston Rossdale, Shiloh Jolie-Pitt, Venus Williams, Anna Kournikova, Shia LaBeouf, Joshua Jackson, Sasha Obama

PARENTING YOUR GEMINI CHILD: THE ESSENTIALS

*

Gemini is the sign of the Twins, a cast of characters rolled into one little person. Who needs to have actual "multiples," when you get a variety pack of personalities in a single child? With Gemini, the only thing constant is change, so expect lots of action and variety. Born with a twinkle in his eye, "mischief" is Gemini's middle name. This kid loves to see what he can get away with and is forever pulling pranks and sly jokes. Gemini has an angel on one shoulder and a devil on the other—and they're usually talking to him at once.

Curious about everything under the sun, this is not a child you can leave unsupervised for long. Gemini rules the hands, so your little Gem's fingers are always going to be exploring, touching, and grabbing. Childproofing is essential when Geminis are young, since they'll seize anything within reach. You'll need to keep your Gemini's busy hands occupied with crafts, LEGOs, musical instruments, and tasks. Enroll in sign language classes together—or teach him baby signing yourself when he's an infant. Visual and audio stimulation that annoys the rest of us can soothe little Gemini. One mom told us that she drives her two-year-old Gemini daughter through Times Square . . . to calm the little girl down!

Fortunately, you can also explain the whys and why-nots to Geminis early. But just because they understand doesn't mean they'll obey. Ruled by Mercury, the planet of communication, your Gemini may talk, read, gesture, and express herself from an early age. This child is a real chatterbox once she gets going, never seeming to run out of steam. Even when Gemini is quiet, there's always something going on in that little head. There's never a dull moment when you're a Gemini—or the parent of one.

If you're a creature of habit or a big "rules" person, prepare for a lesson in flexibility if you have a Gemini child. Too much structure doesn't work for curious Gemini, who needs you to mix it up. Bedtimes, meals, and other routines might need to be flexible. Or, if you're adamant about lights-out time, spice up the agenda: give your Gemini washable bath crayons and fun new shampoos, and create an à la carte menu of bedtime stories.

These children have active imaginations, which can be both a blessing and a curse. To ever-shifting Geminis, reality is often subject to change without notice. Just because they felt one way an hour ago doesn't mean they feel the same way *now*. Their grasp on the "truth" can be slippery, and as a result this sign gets a rep for being fickle or two-faced. Gemini president George Bush Sr. became notorious for pledging "Read my lips . . . no new taxes" and then raising existing taxes. Wordsmith Geminis certainly know how to get by on a technicality. But there's more going on. The multifaceted Gemini can truly see a situation from numerous, even contradictory, points of view. Each version of the "truth" seems valid to this sign, which has a knack for getting swept up in captivating stories and even tall tales. What this whimsical sign loves to do is "mirror" the person she's engaged with—lapsing into a pleasant synergy makes Gemini happiest. After hanging with a hip-hop-loving pal, your Gem will throw you a peace sign and walk out the door with a swagger. An hour later, after video chatting with her bubbly bestie, she's full-on Valley Girl. Which one is the *real* Gemini? Well, maybe all of them are!

Still, Gemini can fall into fibbing, which you'll want to watch. Your little Gemini can spin tales so rich that even *he* believes them. Some Gemini kids can look you in the eye and tell a bald-faced lie. They figure if they can convince you (and themselves), then their fictionalized account is as good as real. One mom of a Gemini recalls her son telling an elaborate tale about robbers breaking in and polishing off the cupcakes she'd prepared for the school bake sale, not realizing the damning evidence (in this case, fudge frosting) was smeared on the corners of his mouth. "I finally marched him over to the mirror—but even then, he still denied that he was guilty!" she said, laughing and shaking her head. "I was actually a little worried by that, and we're still working on the whole honesty thing." Geminis' ability to argue a point until your head spins (talking at warp speed all the while) can make you wave the white flag out of sheer exhaustion. Once you recover, you may find yourself scratching your head, wondering, *What the heck did I just agree to exactly?*

Playful Gemini is an imp but usually means no harm in his or her antics. So what's a parent to do? Cultivate Gemini's imagination while teaching her the importance of honesty. Keep paper, crayons, costumes, and recorder at the ready when Gemini's inner storyteller makes a showing. And pay attention: Geminis' colorful anecdotes are often studded with clues to what they might really be thinking or feeling. Learn how to decode their double-speak and elaborate whoppers. If you read their lips (à la George Bush), make sure you also read between the lines.

To understand Geminis, look to their ruling planet Mercury, the planet closest to the sun. Mercury the messenger speeds around in its orbit, gathering data that it spreads to the rest of the planets. That's why this sign is always up on the latest gossip or the first to discover a new toy, book, gadget, or idea. So take note and don't start Christmas shopping for this kid in July. (Heck, even Black Friday might be too soon.) As quickly as Geminis get enamored with a new friend, plaything, or movie premiere (declaring it the "Best. Thing. Ever."), their interest cools just as fast. Prepare for sudden temperature drops to follow each Gemini heat wave. Yep, that's tornado weather. And like a twister, little Gemini blows into your life, turning a few things upside down but also transporting you to her own magical Oz. Click those heels, Mama, and follow Gemini down a golden road to adventure.

GEMINI: HOW THEY DEAL WITH . . .

*

RULES AND AUTHORITY

Gemini's favorite word is *why* and as soon as he's old enough to ask it, he will. This sign could make a career out of bending the rules and will cleverly find the loophole in any policy you try to create. The Gemini kid enjoys playing the devil's advocate and might rebel just for the sake of rebellion—or for his own entertainment. An iron fist will only make Gemini rail against you even more. As the sign of the Twins, Gemini needs to feel like everything is a dialogue. Throw out the rule book, or at least be willing to make edits to your edicts. A conversational tone, even treating Gemini like (gulp) a peer, will actually get the best response out of these kids.

LIMITS

. . . are only limits until Gemini finds a way to get around them. And since Gemini *will* find that loophole, you'll have to be especially firm about your absolute no-nos. Avoid being overly restrictive and pick the truly important behaviors (talking to strangers, touching hot stoves, violence) to prohibit. At times, explaining *why* something is forbidden can help inquisitive Gemini understand your motives. However, don't let Gemini manipulate you into changing the rules to suit him. Make it clear that no means no, and not everything is up for discussion.

SEPARATION AND INDEPENDENCE

Many Geminis are joined at the hip with their moms (it's that Twin thing), and they're reluctant to venture off . . . at first. The first separation will be the hardest. Once they get the hang of interacting with other kids, though, Geminis' social natures kick in. (Mommy *who*?) Soon your main concern will be making sure Gemini doesn't talk to every stranger—or wander off chasing butterflies and other whims.

YOUNGER SIBLINGS

Interactive Geminis love to teach and will patiently take a little brother or sister under their wing. They love to lead, mentor, and mold an adoring younger sibling. If your Gemini is the family baby, she might adopt a neighbor or younger cousin. Of course, Gemini may not take to the idea right away. One mom recalls her Gemini daughter begging for a little sibling. Shockingly, when she announced that she was pregnant, her little girl got mad and didn't speak to her for a day! With this ever-changing sign, you just never know.

OLDER SIBLINGS

Copycat Gemini can irk his older siblings, helping himself to their toys, clothes, and even friends. Gemini kids are communal by nature and may clash with possessive older sisters or brothers who "want their space."

BYE-BYE, BABY: WEANING AND POTTY TRAINING

Eager for independence, Geminis can be fabulous students when learning the ropes of becoming a big boy or girl. This smart sign can handle change and likes to learn new things. Lucky you: you might not have too much trouble sleep training your Gemini or getting her out of diapers.

SEXUALITY

Precocious Geminis are full of questions, but they also know how to find the answers for themselves. Ruled by speedy Mercury, the messenger planet, your little Gemini might give *you* an earful about the birds and bees, which she's no doubt been buzzing about on the school yard. Touchy-feely Gemini also rules the hands and might do a little, er, exploring with theirs. Rather than get embarrassed, advise your child to do this in private. Little ringleaders, Geminis might be the kids telling their schoolmates how babies are made as soon as they find out.

LEARNING: SCHOOL, HOMEWORK, AND TEACHERS

Brainy, verbal, and keen to learn, Geminis can be enthusiastic students. Their award-winning poems, drawings, and reports on obscure topics can crowd your bulletin board. Geminis are less interested in grades than they are in satisfying their curiosity, though. Easily distracted, your Gemini may not score perfectly on tests or bring home straight A's, even if she has Mensa-level smarts. Working one-on-one with a fun but firm tutor can help, since Gemini learns best in an interactive setting where questions and dialogue are encouraged.

HOUSEHOLD CONFLICT

Diplomat or double-crosser? Dualistic Geminis can switch loyalties faster than you can change a television channel. One minute, they're on Team Mom; the next, they're pleading the other person's case. Their gift for seeing both sides of the situation can make them fabulous mediators, or it can give you whiplash. Be mindful what you let Geminis overhear, because they don't miss a thing. Also, you need to be aware that some Geminis choose denial as a response to stress, inventing their own imaginary worlds and playmates as an alternative escape route.

THE GEMINI BOY

✳

The Gemini boy is curious, in every sense of the word. He's an open book and a mystery all at once. Although he may chatter nonstop—then suddenly go radio silent and get absorbed by a toy, project, or gadget—you might still have no idea *who* this kid really is. And that's the way your Gemini son likes it. *Predictable* is the last adjective this sign ever wants as his descriptor.

Gemini's verbal skills can be exceptional compared to that of other boys, and these kids can make gifted writers and speakers. Rappers Tupac Shakur and Biggie Smalls, known for their intricate wordplays, were both Geminis. Words and trivia can be favorite hobbies of the Gemini guy, and he can be a brilliant mimic, like Gemini comic Mike Myers, who played both Austin Powers *and* Dr. Evil. He might also love doing research, digging for data on topics that fascinate him. Your son may have several collections of obscure things that only a Gemini could find. Or he might request an unusual pet, like a ferret, an iguana, or a hermit crab. Since you'll soon learn that Gemini's attention span is shorter than the hemlines on a spring couture runway, you should probably avoid anything that requires elaborate care and feeding. Even if he's raptly attentive for months, once Gemini loses interest, he's just done and you'll be doing the feeding and the cage cleaning.

When the Gemini boy actually talks about his feelings (which may or may not happen), he can be surprisingly literate. Getting him to open up is the challenge. Because Gemini is the sign of the Twins, this boy has both a strong masculine and feminine side. He may weep openly after losing an intense football game, for example. Or he'll explain his feelings in painstaking detail, then put the sentimental genie right back into the bottle when he's done sharing. He can flip from sensitive to callous in a nanosecond. In fact, his sarcastic remarks can make him a regular seat warmer in the time-out chair.

Some Geminis express their duality through style. Famous gender benders Prince, Lenny Kravitz, Johnny Depp, and André 3000 are all Gemini guys. (Guyliner, anyone?) Even conservative politician Rudolph Giuliani, a Gemini, has an ongoing tradition of dressing as a woman every Halloween. So if your Gemini son wants to walk around in your heels or rummage through your makeup bag, it doesn't necessarily mean he's headed for the drag queen circuit. He might just be creating his own signature look, which is important for this expressive sign as he develops his individuality—a long and winding process. Let him march to his own beat, even if it happens in your snazzy spectator pumps.

Of course, Gemini boys might weather a few identity crises for a host of other reasons. They analyze and question everything, and their brains never shut off—ever! The best way to keep Gemini out of trouble is to keep him busy. Many Gemini boys can be technical and love to tinker with whatever they can. Similar to Taurus, this sign is curious about the inner workings of everything (although unlike patient Taurus, your Gemini might take something apart, then lose interest before he puts it back together!). Easily bored, dexterous Gemini needs to fiddle around with something that can absorb his attention, such as a musical instrument, an art project, or a gadget. In fact, a playroom set up with multiple activity stations suits this boy best, since this variety-loving sign enjoys having a few projects going at once. Idle (Gemini) hands are the devil's playground indeed. Physical activity also helps, since restless Geminis need to be on the move, seeing new sights that stoke his vivid imagination. Drag him away from the computer or TV for a bike ride or a pickup game with the neighbor kids. If he's not playing sports, he may be a superfan of a specific team (or MVP of his fantasy football league). Bonus points if this trivia hound can keep stats on his favorite players.

While your Gemini son might worry you by seeming all over the place, restless and a jack-of-all-trades, he'll eventually find his way—or a couple of niches that hold his attention for longer than a week. With Gemini boys, it's a snowball effect: they gather knowledge and experience from a million different outlets. Then, somehow, it all comes together in a fascinating fusion that's completely unique. Your Gemini son might drive you crazy, but one day he'll also make you proud. Reserve your tickets early—it's gonna be a great show.

THE GEMINI GIRL

*

The Gemini girl will keep everyone around her on their toes. Whip-smart and verbal, these twinkly little fairies talk a mile a minute and can be wise beyond their years. Then they break into a roguish smile, reminding you that they're eternally young spirits who also love to play. That's the duality of the Gemini girl. She's a hard worker and a free spirit in equal measure, a true original!

The Gemini girl is a quick study who loves to learn, talk, and interact. As the sign of the Twins, she's a mimic, too. You might be shocked—and totally tickled—when you hear your own phrases repeated in her little voice. Geminis may read, count, and recite their ABCs early. She can also be a graceful dancer and, as an air sign, a fearless daredevil on the playground climbing gym. (Gravity? Pssshht.) With her precocious personality and adorable smile, your daughter might make a talented child model or actor. Geminis Mary-Kate and Ashley Olsen began filming *Full House* at nine months old. Bright little Gemini Natalie Portman turned down a Revlon modeling agent at ten to act, debuting at thirteen in *Léon: The Professional*. And what girl born after 1940 hasn't tried to channel sixteen-year-old Gemini Judy Garland as Dorothy in *The Wizard of Oz*?

These are no flighty screen starlets, though. After high school, Portman decamped to Harvard, the Olsen twins to NYU. Gemini girls have strong opinions, distinctive goals, and ambitions far beyond the white picket fence. Gemini Angelina Jolie proved she was more than just a sexy action figure when she became a UN goodwill ambassador, inspiring the world's interest in becoming international do-gooders. Born without a filter, these blunt girls don't hold back, either. Gemini's provocative comments can land her in hot water (or offend her peers), but the words are usually out of her mouth before she's had a chance to consider their impact.

The Gemini girl needs a lot of hobbies and intellectual stimulation, too—she's a true Renaissance woman in training. Creative and trendy, she keeps a catalog of pop culture and trivia in her head and can rattle off songs, book passages, birthdays, and other fun facts on a dime. Nurture Gemini's love of learning and expose her to a wide variety of experiences. This is not a kid you want to shelter. And even if you try, good luck. When the Gemini girl wants something, nothing can stop her from figuring out how to get it.

While your Gemini daughter will cherish one-on-one time with her mom—you're her first and original BFF—she also thrives in the company of other children. Playgroups, dance troupes, art and music classes—try them all. This kid needs to mingle. Even if your wee Gemini clings to you or gets upset when you leave, with a little nudging, she'll branch out. Besides, you need to spread the attention around for your own sake, since Gemini girls don't come with an off switch. They love to wrangle partners in crime into all of their schemes and adventures. If only the other kids were clever enough to keep up with her! Early on, Gemini girls can be flirts and might be aggressors who pursue their male playmates. Angelina Jolie has said in interviews that, as a kid, she was part of a club called the Kissy Girls, whose primary purpose was to chase the boys and smooch them until they cried uncle. Dualistic Gemini manages to be both masculine and feminine at the same time—a feat the rest of the zodiac signs only wish they could pull off.

Geminis are said to have multiple personas, and indeed, you may wonder which daughter you're talking to today. She might sprout a new identity or accent every so often or suddenly become raptly interested in new hobbies, each one requiring elaborate supplies or equipment. Costume change! Still, you never know where one of your daughter's alter egos might take her. A shy Gemini named Norma Jean Rae left her broken home and reinvented herself as the iconic Marilyn Monroe. Remember that when you're compelled to dismiss her imaginary identity as fictional. If anyone can weave a dream into reality, it's the Gemini girl.

BEHAVIOR DECODER: THE GEMINI KID

WHEN GEMINI . . .	IT MEANS . . .	SO YOU SHOULD . . .
Cries	Gemini is hurt or something is actually wrong.	Grab the first-aid kit and investigate.
	Gemini is having an emotional moment and may have been teased or gotten his feelings hurt.	Let him talk it out. Or just give a reassuring hug.
Withdraws socially or gets quiet or moody	Gemini's "other side" (the quiet, introverted one) is making an appearance. Like an Energizer bunny that keeps going, she may have finally conked out!	Hand Gemini a book or a quiet activity. Or tuck her in with a story and let her drift off for a rejuvenating nap.
Acts out (hitting, kicking, talking back)	Hyperactive Gemini has too much energy to burn. She may be bored, restless, or feeling suppressed. She needs to fly free!	Make sure Gemini has adequate intellectual and physical outlets. Cut down on sugar and other stimulants in Gemini's diet if they are present.
Gets clingy	The separation process is not complete, and Gemini still sees you as his main "wingman." He's hesitant to engage with anyone else yet.	Wonder Twin powers, activate! Help Gemini find a compatible playmate, and before you know it, he'll forget you even exist. Parallel play also helps, so set up a playdate and a "mom date" in one, during which you bond over coffee or tea while the kiddies frolic nearby.

WHEN GEMINI . . .	IT MEANS . . .	SO YOU SHOULD . . .
Won't eat what you serve	Gemini rules the hands, so these kids tend to "graze," picking up any quick fix they can find to munch on. Did someone fill up on animal crackers again?	Keep healthy snacks on hand (and don't bother hiding the sugary ones; Gemini will find them). These antsy kids love the quick energy spike that sweets give them, but this will lead to an inevitable crash. When Gemini gets older, let him in the kitchen, as this sign can be a talented foodie with a flair for mixing interesting ingredients
Can't sit still	So what's new? Life with Gemini is short-attention-span theater. They bore and grow restless easily.	Short of getting a kiddie leash, there's not much you can do but roll with it. Keep a stash of toys, books, gadgets, and other options on hand at all times, so Gemini can stay engaged.

THE SOCIAL GEMINI

ROLE IN THE FAMILY

How deep are your roots? If you're set in your ways or averse to change, buckle up. Or don't . . . since you're about to be launched into a whole new kind of ride. Experimental Gemini arrives on the scene to mix things up and challenge your assumptions. If this kid came with a road sign, it would be CAUTION: CURVES AHEAD. While this unplanned interruption to your family traditions can be trying, Gemini opens you to creating new customs and helps you view the world through a fascinating kaleidoscope rather than a microscope.

INTERACTIONS WITH FRIENDS AND PEERS

Social butterfly Gemini is a "people person," and this sign has never met a stranger. In fact, Gemini may not get much more acquainted than that before losing interest and flitting off to the next exciting new contact. Gemini will have pals in every port and a lot more acquaintances than actual friends. This sign excels at breadth more than depth. Although Geminis will form a handful of cherished lifelong bonds, the holder of "best friend" status may rotate frequently and without notice. Partly it's because this sign needs to be free. Spontaneous Gemini can't stand being tied down by someone else's agenda. Friends who attempt to saddle Gemini with guilt trips or too many obligations will get the heave-ho. But an adventurous, no-strings pal who can explore a million curiosities in a single day? That person will quickly become Gemini's favorite wingman or wingwoman. While Geminis don't appreciate being snapped out of their dream worlds, when they want to talk, game on. Friends of Gemini need to be able to hold a conversation and keep up with Gemini's mile-a-minute chitchat. Thick skin is also a requirement, since Gemini can dish out blunt observations or teasing that cuts a little close to the bone.

Gemini kids can also be gossipy, so make sure your little Twin isn't throwing grist into the rumor mill. While they don't mean to be cruel, they can't keep a juicy tidbit to themselves. They're ruled by Mercury the messenger, after all. Geminis can end up in divided allegiances just because they spread an unconfirmed story to the wrong person. (Should you become famous one day, the "source" that the paparazzi always seems to hit up for dirt will probably be a Gemini.)

At times, Gemini kids can be out of sync with their peers, especially since their minds are always buzzing. Like little data storage devices, Geminis are full of facts and ideas. They might be light-years ahead of their peers intellectually, whereas emotionally, they're a few paces behind. While their enthusiasm is contagious, Geminis might talk too much or get a little *too* exuberant, which can annoy other kids. They go from zero to sixty so fast that it's overwhelming. Geminis need clusters of friends who will "geek out" with them over their latest obsessions, as well as a couple of easygoing besties who can roll with the many faces, moods, and personalities of a Gemini. Inside jokes and shared (obscure) interests can form the Gemini ties that bind. Just don't get too attached to the kids they bring home or want to invite over for playdates. You never know when Gemini will have a change of heart, rotating the cast of characters once again.

BROTHERS AND SISTERS: GEMINI AS A SIBLING

Gemini rules the zodiac's third house of siblings, and these interactive kids love having brothers and sisters—in theory, anyway. A sibling gives Gemini someone to play with *and* to fight with around the clock. They will do both in spades. Devoted allies and fierce sibling rivals (depending on the hour), Geminis are not always the easiest relatives with whom to share DNA, much less a bedroom or a toy. Don't bother trying to debate with them, either. A battle of wits with clever, fast-talking Gemini can end in tears, torment, and timeouts. Natural mediators, Geminis can step in to settle a family dispute or to argue a sibling's case—sounding much like seasoned trial lawyers. The caveat? They could end up switching sides before the issue is even resolved!

On a good day, Geminis provide their sibs

with endless entertainment and practical jokes. Or they'll dream up elaborate projects that can occupy the family for days, if not months. There won't be any long, boring winters with Gemini in the house! With their boundless imaginations, these Pied Pipers will lead an impressionable sibling on adventures—often the kind that ends with both kids being grounded! Still, Gemini will be planning the next naughty excursion from her prison cell, er, bedroom. As mad as Geminis can make their siblings, those born under this sign have enough charm to be forgiven (although *they* can hold a mean grudge). Flashing a twinkly-eyed glance is all it takes for Gemini to score a second, third, or fiftieth chance from a ticked-off brother or sister.

DISCIPLINING A GEMINI

Smack-talker alert! This forked-tongued child can flip from saccharine to sarcastic, zinging you right where it hurts. Nine times out of ten, it's Gemini's mouth that gets him in trouble. You might catch him in a lie—or shall we say a half-truth. This kid has an answer for everything, even when you didn't ask for one! He also knows just how to rope you into a no-win conversation, whereupon he will talk circles around you. Your Gemini child can be argumentative, and indeed this sign enjoys playing devil's advocate. Some days, you might suspect that Gemini actually *wants* to get in trouble, just for his own entertainment. (Watching you huff and puff and get red in the face is pure comic relief to him.) One of our Gemini playmates growing up convinced a few kids (ahem, including us) to toss pebbles at his next-door neighbor's car. He spun an elaborate tale of conspiracy, assuring us that revenge was the only way to stop these evil, plotting people. After a few days of our top-secret mission, the neighbors noticed dents in the body of their car and called our parents, leaving us busted and in the biggest trouble of our lives.

Mischievous Gemini can be a wild child, forever testing the rules. Yet making stricter and more prohibitive policies only eggs Gemini on. She figures if she could break this many barriers, she might as well keep going. In fact, it's a badge of pride to Gemini when she manages to get away with murder.

What actually *does* work is to talk to your Gemini like a combination of a life coach and a peer. If you condescend, he'll shut down. Make him think changing the behavior is *his* idea, though, and he might go along with it. Geminis are natural marketers, so sometimes you've got to sell them the idea of straightening out. You might even adapt a few cognitive behavioral therapy techniques, which focus on changing the behavior more than the mind-set. You can even slip these into Gemini's daily routines (much like author Jessica Seinfeld suggested sneaking spinach into your kid's smoothie in her cookbook *Deceptively Delicious*). Rather than lecture, which Gemini will only tune out, make a game out of a new behavior pattern. Is it crafty and a little bit manipulative? Sure. Are Geminis those things, too? Yup. So beat them at their own game. Think like a party planner instead of a parent, and you'll proactively change your Gemini into the world's most well-behaved scamp.

HANDLING TRANSITIONS: MOVING, DIVORCE, DEATH, AND OTHER TOUGH STUFF

*

Change and loss affect every child, but for adaptable Gemini certain transitions are actually welcomed. This is not a kid who will stay in a miserable school setting because he prefers "the devil he already knows." Gemini kids reinvent themselves on a daily basis, so what's the big deal about doing that with a new school or group of friends? Besides, they know that they can always use their cleverness to win friends and influence people wherever they go.

Objective Geminis can be emotional but also coolly observant. Death is a part of life, and they might be able to grasp that notion from an early age. Or perhaps they'll just mask their feelings behind an unexpressive face. Don't believe the hype if Gemini acts like everything is fine after a loss or traumatic event. In adulthood, many Geminis are prone to depression as a result of not processing their early emotions. Start 'em young with the "talking cure," even if that means using art or music therapy to draw them out first. Intellectual Gemini would rather make a painting or write a story than sit on a child psychologist's couch and discuss his feelings. But eventually, most Geminis can become quite responsive, especially to a life-coaching style of communication. It just takes practice and a little prodding. Like a windup toy, once little Geminis get flowing, it's all you can do to get them to stop talking. They don't like feeling on the spot or criticized, though, so be sparing with your feedback when your Gemini opens up or she will stop confiding in you.

SCHOOL'S IN SESSION

*

BEST EDUCATION STYLE

Just the facts! Speedy Geminis want to get to the point as fast as possible. Long, drawn-out lessons will cause their eyes to glaze over. These are dilettantes who enjoy a wide range of subjects, and prefer to learn at their own pace. Often that's at a much faster clip than their classmates, so a school that allows independent study and self-directed projects can be a good fit for this creative sign. For Geminis, extracurricular activities are equally as important as their reading, writing, and 'rithmetic and can pave the way for a future career much more than a yawn-inducing geography or Spanish class (no offense to the teachers of those subjects, of course!). One successful Gemini media maven we know cut her teeth as editor of her high school yearbook, for example.

If your Gemini acts out in school, chances are she feels bored and stifled. Desk position is an important factor, too. Geminis are social creatures and can be distracted by a noisy or note-passing kid sitting nearby. Curious Geminis also like to ask a lot of questions, so an interactive classroom setting draws out the best parts of their inquisitive natures. They need to grasp the "why" of a lesson and can improve their grades with a study buddy or an attentive, one-on-one tutor.

A teacher who values Gemini's insights and unique way of looking at things will bring out this sign's academic best. Old-school or authoritarian instructors, on the other hand, will misinterpret Gemini's questions as defiance, and there could be a two-way lane between the classroom and the principal's office reserved for Gemini. If your child starts to act up, then act fast. Switch her to a teacher or school that appreciates the learning style of forward-thinking Gemini—the kid who fancies herself smarter than the teacher. In some cases, Gemini might just be right. Just don't tell her so until after graduation.

BEST HOBBIES AND ACTIVITIES

Gemini kids love culture, arts, and entertainment. Ruled by messenger Mercury, they're often little media moguls in the making, practically shouting "Extra! Extra!" wherever they go. Geminis can be gifted writers and speakers, so get them a post on the school paper or the debate team. When they're little, story hour at the bookstore or a public library card can be a passport to new worlds. Geminis might also have technical inclinations, and (sigh) they can spend hours engrossed in a video game, especially the multiplayer kind. (World of Warcraft, anyone?) Your outspoken little Gemini might even want to create his own multimedia projects once he can tinker with the tools. As Geminis get older, keep them busy with photography workshops, video cameras, and acting or dance class. Err on the side of too many involvements rather than letting them get bored. Variety is the spice of Gemini's life, and these kids were born multitaskers.

Limber Geminis can be daredevils, and they may have strong arms or above-average flexibility. Classes in gymnastic or trapeze can thrill this air sign with the sensation of taking flight. They can also be gifted dancers, especially hip-hop, break dancing, or a style that allows them to break form and invent their own moves. Clear your schedule, because you could be attending a lot of performances, auditions, and even casting calls if you birth a little Gemini. When ambitious Gemini sets her sights on going big, nothing short of the top spot will do. Of course, this kid's interest can fizzle as quickly as it flamed. So before you shuttle Gemini to Hollywood to break into show business, make sure your little one's big dream has actual staying power.

GIFT GUIDE: BEST PRESENTS FOR GEMINI

* Credits to download music from their favorite bands
* Books that stoke their imaginations and have fun wordplays (Dr. Seuss, Shel Silverstein, a choose-your-own adventure when they're older) and a journal to record the creative musings the reading material inspires
* Sketchpads, art supplies, and mixed-media materials
* Tech toys or any of the latest gadgets
* A karaoke machine or semiprofessional equipment for recording audio and/or video
* Tickets to a play or concert or backstage passes to a favorite TV show
* Day trips and short excursions to fun places like a zoo, the circus, or an amusement park with great roller coasters and rides

THE CANCER CHILD

(June 21–July 22)

SYMBOL: The Crab

COSMIC RULER: The moon

ELEMENT: Water

BODY PART: Chest and stomach

GEMSTONE: Ruby

COLOR: Silver, aqua

GOOD DAY: Affectionate and caring
Creative
Helpful
Intuitive

BAD DAY: Moody or hypersensitive
Pessimistic
Clingy or possessive
Insecure

LIKES: Rich foods (especially dessert)
Team sports (playing and/or watching)
Dolls, tea parties, old-fashioned or pretty things
Being at home and around family
Water—beaches, pools, bathtubs
Hugs, cuddling, comfort, and affection
Arts and culture: plays, concerts, and ballets

DISLIKES: Uncomfortable clothes and fabrics
Being forced out of his shell before he's ready
Flavorless, uninspired meals
Insensitive or unsentimental people
Too much time away from home and family
Being put on the spot
Crowds

* SO, YOU WANT TO HAVE A CANCER? *

Target Conception Dates for a Cancer Child: **September 25–October 15**

FAMOUS CANCER KIDS, PAST AND PRESENT

*

Selena Gomez, Jaden Smith, Lindsay Lohan, Knox and Vivienne Jolie-Pitt, Ashley Tisdale, Akiane Kramarik, Fred Savage, Tia and Tamera Mowry, Malia Obama, Prince William

PARENTING YOUR CANCER CHILD: THE ESSENTIALS

*

Did someone say "ma-ma"? Domestic Cancer is one of the zodiac's most family-oriented signs, with an intense need to nurture and be nurtured. Cancer is the sign associated with mother–child relationships, so these kids are strongly affected by "maternal energy." These little empaths need to be around people who take the time to listen to their feelings and respect their often-lengthy emotional processes (easy on the tough love with this kiddo, please). No matter who their primary caretakers are, Cancers will be attached to them at the hip. They're also protective of younger siblings, pets, dolls, and anyone they love. Prepare to have lots of tea parties, imaginary games of house, and even dolls that simulate wetting their diapers or drinking from a bottle around the house.

Cancer is one of the most emotional signs, with moods that fluctuate without warning. These sensitive children may cry easily or express their intense feelings with tiny, tumultuous tantrums. When their emotions reach critical mass, watch out! Other times, Cancers can get quiet or withdrawn. Perhaps they're feeling shy or hesitant, and need you to draw them out. However, your little Crab may just need to retreat into his shell for some alone time with a book, a favorite stuffed animal, or his thoughts. When Cancers are old enough to read and write, a diary (with lock) is an ideal gift to help them process their feelings. Writing is often Cancers' favorite outlet, though they can be talented in music, dance, singing, and other arts, too.

Like the Crab that symbolizes this sign, Cancers like to carry their homes on their backs. This kid needs "transitional objects" more than any other—for example, a toy, sweater, or object that makes them feel like they're still safe at home in your arms when sent out into the wider world. You might need to let your Cancer wear pajama bottoms to preschool—or comfy shoes that feel like slippers. If that's what it takes to prod Cancer out of the house, so be it!

Prone to feelings of abandonment, Cancers may cling to your side. Long after other kids have clipped the apron strings, Cancers need the reassuring comfort of your presence. Like it or not, Cancer will make an attachment parent out of you—crawling into your bed even after you've put them back in their cribs, for example. One Cancer's parents woke up every morning with their toddler Crab asleep at the foot of their bed. "It happened so often, we just gave up trying to make her sleep in her own bed," her mother said, laughing. You might as well study up on attachment parenting principles, since you're likely to adopt them by default with this kid. Cancer is the sign associated with the chest, so these babies may be reluctant to wean if you breast-feed them. These children idealize their mothers, which can be both flattering and overwhelming. Living up to this pedestal comes with a lot of pressure. It may be hard to establish healthy boundaries without feeling guilty or worried about your Cancer. However, if you find yourself sacrificing date nights or your rejuvenating solo time, some gentle separation is in order. Create a few transition rituals—such as reading a book or cuddling before you leave. Be careful about using food as a bribe, though. Cancers can be emotional eaters, so too much chicken soup (and chocolate . . . and ice cream . . .) for their souls can accidentally teach them to self-soothe by bingeing on treats.

Shoring up Cancer's self-confidence will be an ongoing job for their parents. When an inevitable mood swing strikes, Cancers can sink into a state of despair. They can be Debbie Downers or "crabs in a barrel," pulling others into their misery. If you relocate while your Cancer is young, make sure you plan to stay where you are going for the long haul. Nothing makes or breaks the Crab's security quite like having to start over with new friends, babysitters, schools, and people—because they do not like leaving the comfort of the familiar.

Intuitive Cancers are tuned into everyone's feelings, the first to notice when a friend or loved one is upset. They always know who needs a hug and can sense when a fight is brewing between their parents. This perceptive sign can be downright psychic, having hunches that come true. It's critical that you respect your Crab's responses and insights, even if you think he's being paranoid. By waving away Cancer's feelings or telling him "You're imagining things," your child gets the message that he can't trust his own emotions. You don't want to break these kids' connection with their own instincts, which will guide them safely through their lives.

When Cancer speaks with passion and certainty, listen. Even if her interpretation is off, her intuition isn't. Just like animals will sense a storm hours before it happens and start acting strange, Cancer's emotional weather system operates via satellite. While you don't want them to become sheltered and fearful, Cancer kids need to be reassured that they're not crazy for feeling the way they do. Whether it's you or a caring, emotionally literate role model, validating Cancer's feelings (while teaching them not to overreact) is one of the best gifts you can give them.

∗

RULES AND AUTHORITY

Dutiful Cancers seek powerful authority figures and can be quite the obedient little soldiers. They prefer to have someone telling them what to do and where to be than to navigate the wider world themselves. Not that they're sheep by any stretch—they just like knowing what to expect. In fact, this sign can be quite bossy and enjoys taking on the role of den mother/wrangler, telling the other kids what they can and can't do!

LIMITS

Cancer wants to know the rules and boundaries at all times. Security-minded Cancers actually *like* some limits, because it makes them feel safe. In fact, you might have to remember to push these kids beyond their limits, teaching them how to take more risks and build confidence.

SEPARATION AND INDEPENDENCE

The apron strings are never truly clipped for Cancer, the ultimate mama's boys and girls. These kids want Mommy or Daddy by their sides at all times, and it could take real effort to get them to venture away from your protective presence. If you return to work after maternity leave, taking them to a small, family-like day care (or a loving relative's house) is better than leaving them at a larger facility that lacks a personal touch. These children will need lots of familiar objects to ease their transition, and you might need to start with a "gentle separation" process.

YOUNGER SIBLINGS

This could go one of two ways: either your Cancer becomes your mini-me and mother's helper, nurturing his little sibs, or he'll get possessive and not want to share your attention. Sensitive Cancer kids need to know they haven't been replaced as the apple of your eye once the younger ones come along.

OLDER SIBLINGS

The loyal Crab is a devoted little sibling who craves strong bonds and might cling to an older brother or sister for protection. Even though Cancer is the younger one, this sign's maternal instincts are strong, and Cancer might even try to mother older siblings—or boss them around, too.

BYE-BYE, BABY: WEANING AND POTTY TRAINING

"Don't leave, Mommy!" Separation is tough for these mama's boys and girls, who would probably breast-feed until kindergarten if you let them. One tactic to try is to put Cancer in the teacher role. For example, give your young Crab a bear or doll that learns how to use the potty along with them. Reassuring books, songs, rituals, and treats also work as incentives. Find the right balance between coddling and pushing Cancers out of their comfort zones too soon. "My son did a lot better at independence when I was hovering nearby," says one mom of a Cancer. "It took him awhile to be okay with me leaving him alone physically—so I hung out on the sidelines to cheer him on as we separated step-by-step."

SEXUALITY

Modest Cancers get embarrassed easily, so talking too openly about the birds and bees can make them uncomfortable. At the same time, they can be a little aggressive once they feel comfortable with other kids, coming on strong. If anything, you'll need to teach sensitive Cancer the rules of courtship and perhaps even that sex and love are best when they go hand in hand.

LEARNING: SCHOOL, HOMEWORK, AND TEACHERS

Cancers aim to please and are often obedient students, even teacher's pets.

HOUSEHOLD CONFLICT

Home is where the little Crab's heart is, and sensitive Cancer can't bear to have conflict in his sanctuary. Like an emotional sponge, your little Cancer will absorb any intense emotions, either withdrawing into his metaphorical crab shell (becoming silent and moody, hiding in his room), or will externalize it with extreme and aggressive behavior, such a hitting, breaking things or bellowing at the top of his lungs.

THE CANCER BOY

*

Calling all mama's boys! You're the center of your sensitive son's world when he's little—and even as he grows up. If your Crab doesn't tattoo MOM on his chest someday, this kid will remain your devoted fanboy, bringing flowers on Mother's Day, confiding in you, and striving for your approval. Even Cancers with "difficult" moms are still dutiful sons, putting them first (much to the chagrin of their future partners).

Empathic as they are, *sensitive* doesn't necessarily equal *gentle* when it comes to Cancer boys. Their emotions can be intense, overloading their little bodies with energy that turns into aggression if it's not released. Without a physical outlet, your well-mannered little angel can develop quite the violent streak. Anyone who's seen Cancerian Tom Cruise jump on Oprah's couch—or perform his own movie stunts—knows how crazy a *verklempt* Cancer guy can be. But in tender moments, when the Cancer boy feels safe enough to be vulnerable, he can touch your heart like no other sign (to wit: Tom Cruise nailing the tear-jerking line "You complete me").

In a way, the Cancer boy can seem as dualistic as a Gemini, morphing from shy to hyperactive. But unlike whimsical Gemini, the Crab doesn't necessarily flip from one personality to another for no reason. The male Cancer's expressiveness depends on his feeling "safe" enough to reveal his complete emotional spectrum. Will he be made fun of, rejected, or teased for showing his true colors? Has he been immersed in a "boys don't cry" environment? If so, he's not likely to reveal himself—at least, not unless he has a posse of unconditionally supportive friends who have his back. Sometimes his periods of withdrawal mean he's been around too many people, absorbing too much of their energy, and he needs to decompress. Cancer's ruling planet (the celestial body that his sign most resembles) is the ever-shifting moon. Just as the moon comes in and out of "hiding"—or a crab peeks out of its shell—the Cancer boy can retreat into his own private world, emerging after a restorative break with full-bodied self-expression. (Just don't force him out during moody moments or, like a crab, he'll deliver a vengeful pinch to anyone who pokes his soft, sentimental underbelly.) If you follow astrology, you might even track the phases of the moon. You may notice your boy is quieter near new moons (when there's barely a sliver of light) but totally "out there," like *la luna*, when the shining moon is full.

Acting can actually be a fantastic outlet for the Cancer boy's extreme emotions, a safe space where he can channel them into a character. As he simulates strong emotions through a role, he can test the waters, seeing that it's okay to publicly play out his inner monologues and feelings. Hyperactive Cancer comedian Robin Williams was reportedly a quiet kid until joining his high-school drama club. His warp-speed improv monologues are now as memorable as his tear-jerking roles in *Good Will Hunting* and *Dead Poets Society*. Interestingly, Williams's earliest stab at comedy was imitating his grandmother to make his mother laugh. A round of his mama's applause can be all the motivation the Cancer boy needs! Before you know it, this once-shy kid could be seeking an encore on a public stage.

Cancer rules the chest, and this boy may walk with his puffed out. While his body language may read as cocky, the swagger only masks his sensitivity. There's a tender heart beating beneath any tough outer expression, so "manning up" is actually a self-protective measure for Cancer. Early on, he may adopt an aloof or alpha male persona, brooding, bragging, or making obnoxious ploys for attention. Make sure your guy isn't getting bullied for his sensitive nature or overcompensating with aggression to avoid being teased by other boys. (One round of being called a sissy for crying in class can do it.) Unless you want to breed an angry ultraconservative, or shut down a guy who's masking insecurity and frustration, make sure he knows that in your home, it is okay for boys to cry.

Steering your Cancer son into the arts or sending him to a nurturing private school can bolster his self-acceptance. Cancer boys need to know that their compassionate natures are an asset, not a detriment. These guys are also graceful and can be amazing athletes, like baseball's Derek Jeter or Olympic swimmer Michael Phelps, both Cancers. If they're not playing sports, Cancers can often be found watching them, cheering loyally for their favorite players.

Being part of a sports team can anchor Cancer, lending him a sense of family and belonging. As much as Cancer guys adore the company of women—and often have a posse of female friends (picture a male Queen Bee manning the hive)—this sign practically invented the "bromance." A loyal band of brothers plays to Cancer's sentimental ways and also supplies a couple built-in wingmen that have his back. Save up your money for dues and pledge pins, because this kid *will* want to join a fraternity in college. In the meantime, he'll start his own version of a clubby secret society as soon as he can, forming lifelong friendships with a couple fellas who can keep his secrets and let him be sappy without making him feel like "less of a guy" for it.

THE CANCER GIRL

*

Who's the mom here, anyway? Cancer girls are natural nurturers, the zodiac's mini-mamas who mother their friends, toys, pets, even you! These intuitive girls are also sensitive to a fault, easily wounded and in need of frequent reassurance. If you're a sentimentalist who's dreamed of her little girl's precious moments (first steps, first dates, the wedding day), Cancer will provide you with enough frame-worthy mother–daughter montages to fill a foyer. Adorable and angelic, she'll happily pose for the camera, too. Shy in public, the Cancer girl is quite a ham once she feels comfortable. To help her come out of her shell, try to minimize change for Cancer. Help her find hobbies, social groups, and clubs (such as Girl Scouts) that she can stick with through the years.

Although her heart is tender, the female Crab's shell can be tough. There are quite a few bruisers among the Cancer ranks. We know a Cancer girl who, in high school, fought to be on the varsity football team. Title IX (the law mandating gender equality in sports) was practically invented for this sign. Another Cancer woman lived in a Victorian fraternity house during college, the honorary female mascot of sorts. We're not sure if she did it for the instant surrogate family, the historic accommodations, or the unlimited male attention (which Cancer girls soak up like gravy on a biscuit). Many Cancers enjoy being "one of the guys"—the alpha female among the fellas—and might prefer this to the jealousy, betrayal and mean-girl politics that taint so many female friendships.

That said, Cancer is a girls' girl at heart. Although she might have just one or two close girlfriends, she bonds for life—and takes what she perceives as rejection from a friend like a stab to the heart. "I didn't have many hobbies growing up," says one Cancer. "I guess my friends were my hobby!" Cancer prefers a tight-knit clique of loyal female friends, who act as emotional anchors when she feels shy or insecure. She loves planning outings, sleepovers, craft sessions, and other elaborately detailed events she can share with her besties. Nobody can throw a birthday or slumber party quite like Cancer. For this sign, it's all about making memories and sharing special moments with her nearest and dearest. Say cheese!

Since Cancers are so attuned to their environments—and their mothers—you might need to force them to cut the cord. Your Cancer daughter can become your main confidante, which is both heartwarming and thorny. Although she might offer tea and sympathy from an early age, Cancer will absorb your moods, even becoming codependent. Be careful what you expose her to, especially during chaotic times. Although she might seem mature enough to grasp adult problems, even offering shockingly sage advice, turning your Cancer into a little sounding board is unfair. Talented child actor Lindsay Lohan, a Cancer, became deeply troubled around the time her "momager" Dina and troubled dad got divorced. These family-oriented girls do not recover from domestic discord easily. So unless you want to spend years footing *her* therapy bill, get yourself a good shrink in times of turmoil and let your kid be a kid!

The adolescent years can be turbulent for Cancer girls, so handle their passage into womanhood delicately. As the sign of femininity, they often have curvy or rounder bodies (busty Cancerian Jessica Simpson, for example, became better known for her double-D chest than her music). Since Cancer girls often develop physically long before they do emotionally, your daughter might feel self-conscious, in need of resources for positive body image (with you, Mom, leading by example). Celebrate your shared femininity with rituals and special mother–daughter dates, such as mani-pedis and tickets to a play. Give her empowering books like *The Red Tent*, which retells a major biblical story from a female viewpoint, or anything by Jane Austen.

One way or another, your Cancer daughter will want to follow in your footsteps—especially if they're well-shod ones. Keep a trunk of your old clothes (and Grandma's, too), because the Cancer girl loves to play dress-up. Hats, gowns, gloves, faux furs, strands of costume jewelry—she'll dive right in and stay entertained for hours. Help her feel connected to a long line of female ancestors by handing down heirlooms such as your old dollhouse, a treasured ring or something else symbolic of her deep roots—the very ones that make the Cancer girl feel grounded and secure.

BEHAVIOR DECODER: THE CANCER KID

WHEN CANCER . . .	IT MEANS . . .	SO YOU SHOULD . . .
Cries	So what's new? This sensitive sign is often on the verge of tears, for any of a million reasons.	Do a quick check and see what's up. Is Cancer genuinely hurt or upset, or is he perhaps just having a sentimental (or moody) moment? It could be crocodile tears, too.
Withdraws socially or gets quiet or moody	Shy Crabs can be socially anxious and might feel uncomfortable entering an already established group. The energy might be overwhelming and Cancer needs to retreat into his shell.	If Cancer's having a moody moment, let him be—or give a reassuring hug. Never abandon a Cancer during these times, though. Don't pressure Cancer to be "on" or to join the other kids when the Crab is feeling vulnerable.
Acts out (hitting, kicking, talking back)	Emotion overload! Cancer's little body can't hold all the feelings and needs to release them through a physical outlet.	Move the energy physically; e-motion = energy in motion. Try an impromptu dance break, bike ride, pillow fight, or anything to snap Cancer out of it.
	Revenge! The tender Crab feels hurt and is pinching back.	Time out!
Gets clingy	Business as usual. Cancer is feeling shy, vulnerable, or fearful and is clinging on for reassurance.	Start with a hug or a pep talk, and then gently disengage from Cancer's grip. If possible, help Cancer break the ice with the new people, or give her a transitional object like a blanket, teddy bear, or even a picture of you.

WHEN CANCER . . .	IT MEANS . . .	SO YOU SHOULD . . .
Won't eat what you serve	Cancer is an emotional eater and might be craving comfort food. You may have introduced an unfamiliar flavor that doesn't register with the Crab as her favorite home cooking.	Serve up an old standby when introducing new dishes (e.g., Cancer's favorite mashed potatoes with the new turkey meat loaf). Unveil dietary change slowly, and even let this domestic sign help with meal preparation. You might try recipes from Jessica Seinfeld's cookbook *Deceptively Delicious*, to sneak in healthy ingredients (such as spinach in a fruit smoothie). If all else fails, threaten to cancel dessert!
Can't sit still	Pent-up emotion has reached critical mass and Cancer needs a physical release.	See "Acts out" section above.

THE SOCIAL CANCER

ROLE IN THE FAMILY

Cancers are the heartbeat of their homes and the guardians of family ties. This domestic sign craves a secure home base and reminds us that family is the foundation for, well, everything. At least, that's how this traditional sign sees it. There's nothing little Cancer loves more than to have his nearest and dearest gathered round for the holidays or a special occasion. From an early age, Cancer may be interested in family history, wanting to look through photo albums and hear stories about how his grandparents met. Do you have relatives you don't speak to? Issues with your own parents? Even in families more divided than the Montagues and Capulets, sentimental Cancer will still try to mediate or bring the warring factions together. When you welcome a Cancer to your clan, family comes first.

FRIENDS AND PEERS

BFFs forever! Loyal Cancers roll with a tight-knit crew, forming lifelong friendships. Once you pinky-swear your way onto Team Cancer, don't bother trying to defect. Sensitive Cancers might just have a handful of people whom they trust, and they'll stick doggedly by them through thick and thin. This sign can even be cliquey. Partly this is because Cancers can take awhile to truly open up. Once they've finally gotten comfortable enough to let their guards down, they'd rather not repeat that painful process, preferring instead to stick close to the ones they love.

Chicken soup for the school yard soul? Little Crabs are intuitive, caring confidantes who are always ready to comfort a friend in need. Sentimental souls, they never miss a Hallmark moment and will plan elaborate birthday celebrations or holiday presents for their besties. They enjoy nurturing their pals and might even worry about a friend who's upset or struggling. Both male and female Cancers can "mother" their friends, at times verging on overbearing or possessive.

When their feelings are hurt, Cancers can also lash out at their friends, causing a rift. This usually happens when Cancers feel "abandoned," as when, for example, the joined-at-the-hip BFF forms loyalties with someone else. You may need to comfort your brooding little Crab when her buddy makes a playdate elsewhere—reminding her that it's okay for people to have more than one best friend. Push Cancer out of her comfort zone and into new social situations so she doesn't rely too heavily on just one person. Shy Cancers might also try to hide behind their friends. Steer them into sports, arts, drama, or other activities where they can learn that the spotlight can be enjoyable, not threatening.

BROTHERS AND SISTERS: CANCER AS A SIBLING

The possessive Crab can cling tight, which is either good or bad news, depending on who's in their grip. If caring Cancer takes ownership of a sibling, lucky you—you've got a built-in mother's helper around the clock. Score! A sibling close in age can double as Cancer's best friend, and Cancer will happily share a bedroom, look out for her sibling, and create picture-perfect moments together.

But if Cancer's marked *you* as his turf, beware. (Can you say "mine"?) This sign isn't fond of sharing your attention and affection and is prone to jealousy. Sibling rivalry can flare, and Cancer can turn into a tattletale or attention hog. He doesn't take kindly to being overshadowed, especially if you start fawning over a new baby or focusing on another sibling. Ever fearful of abandonment, Cancer needs enough of your quality time to know he's not lost in the shuffle. Otherwise, a poor sibling will get the brunt of his frustration.

DISCIPLINING A CANCER

*

Deep. Breath. Out. Yelling at Cancers is futile, even when they're misbehaving in the worst way imaginable. As the zodiac's most emotional sign, these kids can be volcanic, exploding in crying, kicking, object-hurling rages. While you might need to restrain them to avoid damaged property, know that Cancers' aggression stems from their sensitivity. Picture a scared animal that bites in self-defense (the pinching crab). They've been hurt—and they want to hurt back.

A volatile Cancer can provoke your anger, so you might need to go scream in the car or punch a pillow for a mommy time-out. If you want to get to the root of any problematic issue, however, you must acknowledge Cancers' feelings. Soothe first; ask questions later. Validate their right to be upset, even if you forbid them to express it destructively. Sometimes a strong hug provides a sense of physical safety and comfort while Cancer sobs it out of her system. Little Cancers might also cling to comforting toys, blankets, or objects in order to calm down and feel safe.

Other times, you need to let them rage alone in a time-out—but do remain nearby. Losing control of their emotions is scarier to Cancers than you realize, and if they feel "abandoned" in this overwhelmed state it only makes things worse. When the storm has passed, your Cancer will probably just rush into your arms, sheepish and apologetic. "So many of the parenting books I read suggested a 'calm-down corner' or letting your kid cry it out," says the mama of one young Cancer. "But that never worked with my daughter. One time, in the midst of her sobbing, she insisted, 'You don't love me, Mommy!' Turns out she was scared that her misbehavior had cost her my love. When I was able to assure her that I loved her no matter what she did—even if I didn't love her *behavior*—disciplining her became a lot easier."

Remember, too, that Cancers are hypersensitive to chaos and emotional turbulence around them. If your angelic Cancer morphs from halo-wearer to hell-raiser, investigate the environment at home, school, day care, or anywhere she spends a significant amount of time. Sensitive Cancers absorb everyone's moods and may be reacting to chaos or change. Rather than lecture or punish Cancer, use this sign's misbehavior as a smoke signal that something is off—then get to the bottom of it.

HANDLING TRANSITIONS: MOVING, DIVORCE, DEATH, AND OTHER TOUGH STUFF

*

Break the news to them gently! Sentimental Cancers hate change, especially within their cherished homes and families. Moving away from a childhood house or beloved school can be traumatic, as shy Crabs loathe having to break the ice all over again. It took them long enough to form a comfort zone and they don't want to do it again if they don't have to! Try not to take them in and out of schools, clubs, and activities. These kids can have mega abandonment issues, so if there's a divorce, make sure they have on-demand access to both parents, even if it's just by phone or video chat. Something is better than nothing. Make every effort to get them together with their bestie, even if that friend now lives a few towns or school districts away.

Death can be especially tough for this easily attached sign. Losing a relative or pet will hit Cancers hard, and they will want to keep objects, framed pictures, and other memorabilia close at hand. Do something to honor this loved one's memory: walk through a favorite park where a departed pet used to play, make a grandparent's favorite dish for a special meal, even set a place at the table in this person's honor. It may seem like Cancers cling to the past, and maybe they do. These kids may move on, but they never really let go. *C'est la vie.* Don't tell Cancers to "get over it" or rush their grieving process. Honor their need for transitional objects and rituals, which help Cancers feel the security of a loved one's presence.

SCHOOL'S IN SESSION

*

BEST EDUCATION STYLE

School is Cancer's "home away from home," and as such, this sign needs to feel comfortable in its hallowed halls and classrooms. A large public school can make shy Cancer feel swallowed up and intimidated. The cold, institutional vibe—fluorescent lights, flimsy metal desks, and other 1970s relics—equals pure misery for this homey sign.

Private and parochial school can be a good fit for Cancer, and if uniforms are required all the better. While a dress code may feel confining to some kids, it gives Cancer an automatic sense of belonging. It also alleviates some of the social anxiety Cancer can feel among his peers. The ideal environment is one where Cancer's classmates feel like family members and the teachers are loving authority figures, personally invested in your Cancer's success. In turn, Cancer will respond with bottomless school spirit and pride. (Hello, future alumni board member.)

Cancer is a highly creative sign, so a strong arts program can help these imaginative kids find a niche. While some Crabs thrive in a nurturing, noncompetitive curriculum (such as the Rudolf Steiner schools), they also need to be pushed. Otherwise, comfort-seeking Cancers can get lazy and begin underperforming in subjects that intimidate them. While a barrage of standardized tests and performance-based academics can stress this kid out, you also don't want Cancer graduating with low math scores or a heavy dependency on spell-checkers. Arm your Crab with the tools for self-sufficiency, even if that means (gently) cracking the whip.

BEST HOBBIES AND ACTIVITIES

Express yourself! Imaginative Cancers need an outlet for their cultural and artistic leanings. A drawing workshop, the school newspaper, acting and singing lessons—these kids may be shy, but when it comes to talent they contain multitudes. A picture really *can* say a thousand words for Cancer, who may not be able to verbalize his true feelings but can share them articulately in a poem, a photograph, or a song.

Smells like team spirit? Cancers excel when they participate in a safe, close-knit group, where there are inside jokes and the opportunity to form lifelong bonds. Don't drag them from activity to activity or enroll them in short-term extracurriculars where they have to meet a whole new group of people every time. Empaths to a fault, Cancers get intertwined with people, and they want to invest in lasting friendships, not fleeting ones. Although they may socialize with kids of the opposite gender, Cancers also do well in same-sex crews, like a scout troop, sports team, or youth group. When Cancers get older, send them off to summer camp, first as participants, then counselors. They love a good slumber party and also nurturing younger kids. One Cancer we know even married a guy she'd had a crush on at her annual sleepaway camp. He'd been a counselor whom she'd idolized as a child, and the enchantment never quite wore off. That's how sentimental—and devoted—the Crab can be!

GIFT GUIDE: BEST PRESENTS FOR CANCER

* Anything historical, such as an old-fashioned tea set or vintage model train set (bonus points if it's a family heirloom)
* Art supplies; sewing, knitting, or other craft kits
* A dollhouse or a tree house (or something that lets this nesting-inclined sign simulate her own miniature home)
* Musical instruments
* Sports equipment—or jerseys (patriotic Cancer is a true-blue fan)
* Tickets to a play, ballet, concert, circus, or sports game
* A special day on the town reenacting one of her favorite things (e.g., an *Eloise at the Plaza* high tea or backstage tour of a beloved show

THE LEO CHILD

(July 23–August 22)

SYMBOL: The Lion

COSMIC RULER: The sun

ELEMENT: Fire

BODY PART: Heart, upper back

GEMSTONE: Peridot

COLOR: Gold

GOOD DAY: Brave
Generous
Protective
Entertaining

BAD DAY: Self-centered or vain
Greedy
Aggressive
Demanding

LIKES: Praise and attention
Movies, plays, and concerts
Arts and crafts, DIY projects
Bright colors, shiny surfaces, and furry textures
Unlimited playtime
Big parties and events
Giving and receiving presents

DISLIKES: Being ignored
Second place, losing
Good-byes
Too much quiet or alone time
Criticism
Unsentimental or uptight people
Bland foods, neutral colors, dressing down, lack of pizzazz, or modesty

* SO, YOU WANT TO HAVE A LEO? *

Target Conception Dates for a Leo Child: **October 25–November 15**

FAMOUS LEO KIDS, PAST AND PRESENT

*

Anna Paquin, Daniel Radcliffe, Demi Lovato, Soleil Moon-Frye, Maddox Jolie-Pitt, Dylan and Cole Sprouse, Hallie Kate Eisenberg, JC Chasez, Joe Jonas, Kylie Jenner, L'il Romeo, Rico Rodriguez, Maureen McCormick, Tempestt Bledsoe, Zuma Rossdale, Dorothy Hamill

PARENTING YOUR LEO CHILD: THE ESSENTIALS

*

Your attention, please! Roll out the red carpet *and* the receiving blankets: a future Lion king or queen is born. Affectionate and proud, your Leo child needs to adore and be adored. Lucky you! These can be some of the easiest kids to parent. Leos are well-behaved but not passive, independent but still loyal to their clans. Many Leo kids wake up at the first sign of daylight—smiling, happy, and eager to greet the new day. Even as babies, they might not cry much. Are they for real?

Most Leos readily show their feelings, even to the point of wearing their hearts on their sleeves. Others are more of the quiet powerhouses, saying little but still emanating a strong presence. Either way, these kids command attention, sometimes without uttering a word. While they may have no problem sharing their emotions, Leo kids are not wimps. One minute, their arms are wrapped tightly around your neck; the next second, Leos stun you with their bravery, running off to swing from the highest jungle gym or turn perfect cartwheels in the grass. This sign's boundless enthusiasm and childlike wonder never subside. There's always an impromptu tea party, picnic, outdoor adventure, fashion show, or interactive game waiting to be staged. Tickets, please! Leo rules the theater, and this kid might even be an adorable junior playwright, staging shows that she directs and stars in, with the neighborhood kids cast in supporting roles.

While Leo's demands for your attention can get exhausting at times, few kids are more devoted to their parents, siblings, and loved ones. Like playful cubs, they'll tag along at your heels, wanting to spend as much time with you as they can. Little Leos take great pride and interest in their family history, much like a monarch tracing her dynasty's origins. Prepare to drag out the photo albums, if not to become an amateur genealogist. Leos want to hear every nostalgic story about how their grandparents met or your favorite vacation spot as a child. They might even want to relive your history or retrace their roots by visiting ancestral towns and countries.

Expressive, exuberant, and ruled by the sun, these solar-powered babies are a dynamic force to behold. Since the sun *is* the center of our solar system, Leo often needs to be the focus of all attention, lavished with praise and appreciation. Even a seemingly modest Leo child warms to the sound of applause and loves to impress you with a stellar performance or achievement. Make room on the mantel for Leo's blue ribbons, trophies, newspaper features, and plaques. And don't even *think* about tossing out their award-winning stories and A+ report cards. Every accomplishment counts to Leo.

And why shouldn't they? Leos put their hearts into everything they do. Their early activities could become lifelong passions and even careers. Our Leo friend Jiba, an artist and comic-book geek since childhood, created a line of black superheroes called the Horsemen. Long after anyone else would have given up, Jiba kept developing and exhibiting his work. One day, we opened the *New York Times* and there were Jiba's characters included in a feature story. The top-tier talent agency William Morris Endeavor called and signed him soon after.

The lesson: encourage your Leo to stick with those lofty and "impossible" dreams, even if you think he's being cocky or unrealistic. The Leo imagination is a powerful manifesting machine. Phrases that sound like platitudes to most of us actually work for Leo: "Ask, believe, receive" or "If you can dream it, you can do it." Creative visualization is a Leo sweet spot, so no surprise, this kid can attract whatever he wants. This stunning self-belief took a Leo named Madonna Louise Ciccone from Michigan to New York with $35 in her pocket. Baby, look at her now.

Leo rules the zodiac's fifth house of creativity and self-expression. If these kids aren't singing, dancing, and performing, they'll make their mark with colors, artwork, or personal style. Leos love to appoint their royal quarters in vivid hues and might frequently redecorate their bedrooms. They love crafts, interactive play, and even sports—anything that inspires camaraderie and fun for all.

Friends are important to Leos, and with their natural leadership traits they become the obvious alphas of their social circles. *Someone* has to take charge—and since so few people step up willingly, Leos often become the directors, planners, and organizers. Secretly, they don't mind one bit, since it gives them a chance to show off their fabulous taste *and* get their way. While your little Leo might need gentle reminders to "let someone else have a turn," her star power can't be dimmed. And while your wrists might ache from constant applause, proud Leo will return the ovation, either with fierce loyalty or gushing, effusive praise.

It's impossible to stay mad at Leos, even when their excessive demands take you to the brink of frustration. That's because the road to hell—and Leo missteps—is paved with (mostly) good intentions. It just takes one dazzling smile, sincere compliment, or heartfelt apology from Leo and all is forgiven. Leo Bill Clinton charmed his way out of the world's most, uh, creative use of a cigar. And Leo Martha Stewart became a billionaire *after* doing prison time for securities fraud at Club Fed. No scandal or sin ever sticks to the Lion's fur. Your little Leo is the prince or princess of reinvention—bold, resilient, and like Leo's ruler the sun, always certain that he will rise again.

LEO: HOW THEY DEAL WITH . . .

*

RULES AND AUTHORITY

Leo is not often the "problem child." In fact, these kids can be a dream, skipping the whole teenage rebellion and back-talk phases. As future kings and queens of the jungle, the zodiac's Lion understands hierarchy and respects it. After all, the crown will be on Leo's head one day! Meantime, Leo will cut his chops by bossing other kids around or taking charge wherever he can. You'll find a high number of Leo "Pollyannas," teacher's pets, and even tattletales in the ranks. Dignified Leos dislike people who use brute force and will only "roar" if they feel controlled or dominated. Don't suppress these kids or overtake their turf. Lead by being a fair role model with high integrity who commands (rather than demands) respect.

LIMITS

. . . are nearly invisible to Leos unless you point them out. The world is their playground, after all! In fact, they're often blissfully unaware of boundaries in their exuberant, arms-wide-open approach to life. (Yes, your kid *will* talk to strangers, so keep an eye out.) In general, Leos are obedient if the limits are fair and don't constrict their creativity or freedom. But when these kids set their sights on something, they won't give up that dream easily—if ever.

SEPARATION AND INDEPENDENCE

This is no biggie for little Lions. Leos make friends wherever they go, so you can feel good about dropping and driving. They just want you there as their admiring audience at every school play, concert, game, awards ceremony, and so on. Some Leos can be shy at first, but they're not often scared. They just like to observe the environment before diving in . . . and inevitably taking over.

YOUNGER SIBLINGS

Protective Leos are loving mentors and proud older sibs who always have their little brother or sister's back. They'll want to diaper, bathe, and help raise the little ones and will keep them entertained. What a blessing!

OLDER SIBLINGS

Can you say "number-one fan"? Devoted Leos will want to do everything with (and for) their older siblings. However, if that brother or sister is dismissive, mean, or competitive, the haughty lion will fight back and then take her affections elsewhere. Nobody pushes a fearless Leo around!

BYE-BYE, BABY: WEANING AND POTTY TRAINING

Little Leos are cooperative and flexible, often among the easiest babies to raise. Praise motivates this little achiever, so hearty applause will inspire Leo to show you just how fast she can ditch her diapers. Treats and rewards also do the trick, so set up an incentive program. Just go easy on the bribes or Leo could become demanding. Every successful round on the potty does *not* have to be rewarded with an ice-cream sundae or a new Spider-Man toy.

SEXUALITY

Leo is a romantic sign, ruler of the heart. When the time comes, sex should be presented to young Leos as an expression of genuine love between two adults. Leos can be matter-of-fact about the facts of life and, since they're full of eager questions, will want to know the proper names of body parts and how babies are made. However, they are a romantic sign that prefers a rose-colored tint on their views. So as much as Leos want to know where babies come from, they don't want their innocence tainted, either, and may voluntarily avoid anything with mature subject matter until they're ready.

LEARNING: SCHOOL, HOMEWORK, AND TEACHERS

"Pick me, pick me!" You know the kid waving his hand around, vying to be called on in class? There's a good chance she's a Leo. This expressive sign doesn't bother masking the intense desire to be called on or to share first at show-and-tell. In many cases, Leos don't even have to jump out of their seats for the spotlight. Talented and adorable, they may simply shine above other students. Classmates come to expect that Leo will win the spelling bee, get the lead in the school play, or win a seat on student council. Fortunately, Leos' warm personalities ensure that if not popular, they will have a loyal crew of friends. In the rare cases that Leos can't get positive attention at school—either through academic or extracurricular achievements—they might swing to the other extreme, becoming the children who act out and end up in the principal's office. If your Leo starts having behavior issues, find an activity in which she can shine: sports, piano lessons, earning scout badges, an after-school chess club. Praise and encouragement keep this kid motivated like nothing else.

HOUSEHOLD CONFLICT

Leos only get involved in family fights to protect a younger or weaker relative who is being bullied—or to roar fiercely at anyone who dares to encroach upon their rights. While Leo is known for drama, this sign wants no part of other people's craziness. They'll block out the commotion around them by escaping into their creative projects. Imaginative Leos will repair to their rooms and sing, read, play games—or dream of their inevitable stardom, when the only shouting they'll hear is the fans chanting their names . . .

THE LEO BOY

*

Ta-daaaa! The Leo boy arrives with fiery fanfare and boundless enthusiasm, ready to take a huge bite out of life. Sunny and charming from day one, the Leo boy will capture your heart and never let it go. Not that he's all angelic: like a playful cub, the Leo boy loves rough-and-tumble play, and he can be quite a wild child when he lets loose. This kid may need frequent reminders to use his "inside voice"—which can still be loud enough to shatter the sound barrier (or rock a glee club solo). Forever in motion, the intrepid Leo explorer is always hunting for the next kiddie conquest. Invest in a top-of-the-line camera with zoom lens and a swift shutter speed, as you'll want to capture his adorable moments without blurring!

Later, you'll also need a camera with low-light settings (and video), since you may spend lots of time in auditoriums watching Leo accept awards, steal scenes in the school play, or give tear-jerking commencement speeches. Leo is the zodiac's most dramatic sign, so he could be a talented actor or even a graceful dancer, like Leos Patrick Swayze and Gene Kelly. Oh, how your little boy makes you proud! Leo boys love their mamas, too, so you could quickly form a mutual admiration society. Presidents Bill Clinton and Barack Obama, both Leos, credit their mothers as driving influences.

Speaking of presidents, these extroverts can be politicians in the making. Leo boys are natural leaders—or at least, ringleaders—among their band of brothers. As a tribal sign, the male Lion needs to bond, and he can get downright sentimental about his cronies. Leo Ben Affleck inspired the term *bromance* because of his effusive relationship with BFF and *Good Will Hunting* cowriter Matt Damon. This huggy sign rules the heart, and Leo wears his on his sleeve. He's unabashed in showing affection for his bros—and confident enough in his masculinity not to care. He's equally chummy with the girls and will often be surrounded by an adoring posse of female friends (many of whom will harbor a fierce crush on him).

Of course, that confidence can veer into cockiness, so keep tabs on your little Leo's self-promotion. French military leader Napoleon Bonaparte was a Leo. (Hello, Napoleon complex.) Leos Arnold Schwarzenegger, Fred Durst, and Robert De Niro are as famous for their work as for their big personalities. And yes, there's the occasional outsized ego among

Leo males: upon winning an Oscar for *Titanic*, Leo director James Cameron crowed, "I'm the king of the world!" The Leo boy can have his own unique form of attention deficit disorder, which manifests whenever the attention isn't directed at him. His need to be noticed can turn into an irksome trait that turns people off.

Is it nature or nurture? In the animal kingdom, male lions sleep up to twenty hours a day, and the females do the majority of the hunting. The males only jump in for a big, spectacular kill. In the same way, your Leo boy might rest on his laurels, only springing into action when he can put on a huge, dazzling show.

Little Simba knows he's a future Lion king, so you can hardly blame him for having such a sense of entitlement. However, he may need to be reminded that he's not an automatic heir to the throne. Leo boys can be entitled, expecting everything to land in their laps. They can be sore losers and ungracious winners. And nobody throws a pity party quite like a Leo boy who didn't get his way. You may need to teach him some stern lessons about sportsmanship. One mom made her Leo son skip an entire season on his baseball team because he would pout and even start fights when he didn't get to bat. After missing out on postgame ice-cream outings, camaraderie, and sliding into home base, he stopped being "self-centered and oversensitive," as she put it. "It broke my heart to see him moping around," she recalls. "But he needed to learn a bigger lesson: that it's not always going to be about him."

You can also help Leo gain a sense of importance by giving back. Channel Leo's dynamic energy into acts of service, so that he discovers the joy of life even when it's not all about him. Great outlets can be Boy Scouts or volunteer work when he's young. Later, Leo makes a devoted camp counselor, tutor, or mentor. After all, Leo is an eternal child. Working with younger kids is a special talent—we even know a Leo guy who started a successful practice as a life coach for kids. Put Leo in situations where he can be the star but also play the role of best supporting actor. He loves to leave his mark, and taking someone under his wing gives Leo pride and a noble purpose—bringing out his dignified best.

THE LEO GIRL

✳

Her future's so bright, you've gotta wear shades! The Leo girl is a star in the making, an empire builder who shines at whatever she tries. Similar to Aries, fiery Leo attracts the spotlight, but this girl's got a people-pleasing streak that Aries doesn't. While autonomous Aries can be her own number-one fan, the Leo girl wants to be adored, admired, and applauded by the masses. She also genuinely loves to connect with people and could play social director among friends from a young age. Like the communal lioness, the Leo girl enjoys protecting and nurturing her loved ones, lavishing them with gifts and goodies. She's got a big appetite and loves to be spoiled, but she gives as good as she gets. "Party over here!" Leo is the princess of celebration, and lives to plan elaborate birthdays, sleepovers, and fun outings. Exuberant, dazzling, and downright unstoppable, your Leo daughter can be incredibly self-directed. As long as you provide admiration, attention, and an audience, she's good.

To Leo, life is too short for regrets and what-ifs. And besides, what's the point of what-ifs when she's so good at getting what she wants? It doesn't hurt that many Leo girls are stunning beauties. With her sunny smile, trademark mane of hair, and radiant charisma, Leo may never even have an awkward phase. If she does, it will probably pass quickly. Fortunately, most Leo girls aren't the "don't hate me because I'm beautiful" types. Sure, they can be a bit vain with their primping, carefully choosing their outfits, getting mani-pedis with their mama, and even dabbing on lip gloss before the family goes out for dinner. But the Leo girl knows she has more going for her than her beauty—much more.

Yes, ladies and gentlemen, there *is* a talent portion of this competition, and Leo will probably sweep that, too. Two of the youngest-ever Oscar winners, Jennifer Lawrence and Hilary Swank, are both Leos. She can be the kid doing backflips on the cheering squad, nailing an incredible dance move (à la Leo Jennifer Lopez), or singing show tunes in the hall. At times, her cutesiness can be a little *too* much (cue Leo Soleil Moon-Frye as Punky Brewster or Amy Adams as the cloyingly sweet princess in *Enchanted*). Without meaning to, Leo can come across as Little Miss Perfect. She's a good girl, often the teacher's or her parents' (not so secret) favorite. Even Madonna, the superstar Leo, was a straight-A student and a cheerleader who earned a dance scholarship to the University of Michigan.

Some Leo girls can be quiet, more the haughty and regal lioness types. Still, even the more retiring Leo girls eventually find a place to leave a mark and shine. This sign has strong leadership traits. The Leo girl loves to take charge and even to shamelessly win. Some Leo girls may be called bossy or criticized by people who can't handle girls who are openly competitive. Should that happen, intervene right away. Ask yourself, if she were a boy, would people have an issue with her confidence? Probably not. One Leo we know was called a show-off by her dad when she was young. Years later, she still apologizes or affects a false modesty before performing her kickass feats.

The Leo girl is a star, and she needs permission to *own* it. She should never dim her lights so that others can shine. At the same time, you don't want to pump up her ego or teach her to hog the spotlight. Make sure your Leo daughter is also involved in service work: Girl Scouts, volunteering, or mentoring younger kids. Leo doesn't realize when she's being self-centered, so she may innocently come across as egotistical when she talks a mile a minute about herself or whatever's on her mind. Just as the eye rolling is about to commence, though, Leo will interrupt you midsentence with a gushing compliment or an impromptu tribute to your talent, kindness, or beauty. ("Mommy, you're just so much prettier than the other mothers at school.") Suddenly you realize, *Oh, she did notice there was someone else in the room after all.*

Crafts, fashion, and decorating are favorite Leo pastimes, and this girl's creativity can keep her occupied for hours. Given the chance, sparkle-loving Leo will bedazzle any unadorned surface with sequins, gemstones, glitter, or fake fur. Soon enough, your little lioness could have a thriving cottage industry making T-shirts for her friends' teddy bears or redecorating their rooms. Ophira's Leo stepdaughter Clementine built her own kids' astrology website at age eleven and began selling mugs and other merchandise to classmates. Like Leo Martha Stewart, this enterprising kid could build an empire.

Innocent and earnest, the Leo girl just wants everyone to be happy—and to have fun! Although she won't compromise her own needs, Leo strives to please. It could be a rude awakening when Leo learns that not all of her friends share her extreme loyalty. Leo Demi Lovato, a talented child actress and singer, was bullied as a teen. After seeking therapy for an eating disorder, Lovato made a huge, Leo-style comeback, campaigning for girls' self-esteem and antibullying measures, appearing as the youngest judge on *X Factor*, and joining the cast of *Glee.*

To borrow a phrase from Ophira's Leo mother-in-law—a tiny Dutch fireball who drapes herself in so much gold that her grandkids call her "Oma Bling-Bling"—this sign is like steel: you can bend her, but you can't break her. For unstoppable Leo, success is always the best revenge.

BEHAVIOR DECODER: THE LEO KID

WHEN LEO . . .	IT MEANS . . .	SO YOU SHOULD . . .
Cries	Leo needs your attention. He could be angry or frustrated from not being able to reach a toy or get what he wants. Or Leo feels overwhelmed and needs contact with you. Sentimental tears; Leo is easily moved and can be openly emotional.	Assist Leo in getting all child-safe and appropriate needs met. Take a minute to hug or hold Leo. He will quickly return to happy, independent play. Share the Hallmark moment with little Leo, or comfort Leo with a hug.

CONTINUED ON NEXT PAGE

WHEN LEO . . .	IT MEANS . . .	SO YOU SHOULD . . .
Withdraws socially or gets quiet or moody	Leo feels ignored or not the most special person in the room. This could be a ploy for gaining attention by being the "mysterious" one. Or Leo might be feeling out the scene before diving in.	Get Leo engaged in an activity with the other kids. A couple minutes of interactive play melts the short-term shyness away.
	Leo is lost in his imagination, dreaming up a fun creative project.	Spread out supplies and let Leo's inner artiste go wild.
Acts out (hitting, kicking, talking back)	The lion cub has been cooped up too long and needs to be let loose to run wild.	Let Leo roam free, and maybe even loosen up a few rules and restrictions.
	Leo's not getting enough attention or is angry that someone else has stolen the spotlight.	Teach Leo the importance of taking turns and that real stars also know how to be great team players.
Gets clingy	Leo doesn't feel comfortable in her surroundings . . . yet.	Give Leo a minute to feel out where they are and who they're with. Initiate an icebreaker game or activity so Leo can warm up through play.
Won't eat what you serve	Leos know what they like . . . and what they don't.	Get Leo something he will eat, because it's no use forcing him. Or (not recommended), bribe with dessert if Leo eats a "no thank you" portion (i.e., at least one bite).
Can't sit still	Caginess: Leo has a big plan she can't wait to try or a game she's dying to play. She's feeling excited and just wants to get going.	Distract Leo or set a timer to count down to the moment she'll be free to play. Leos like to have something to look forward to, so anticipation works.

THE SOCIAL LEO

*

ROLE IN THE FAMILY

Playtime! Fun-loving Leo brings a sense of wonder and celebration to the family. These kids love parties, gifts (giving and receiving them), and big holiday gatherings. A Leo child can bring sunshine and smiles into an otherwise serious household. This loyal sign might even be the glue that keeps the clan together—the one person everyone gets along with in a feuding or dramatic family. Since Leo rules the heart and spine, these kids can become the backbones of their clans, renewing a sense of pride and heritage. Leo wants to trace the family tree and preserve legacies. Count on Leo to keep those ancestral bonds strong.

FRIENDS AND PEERS

Lions are communal creatures, and so, too, is your Leo child. This sign wants nothing more than to be surrounded by a pack of close cronies for fun and back-slapping camaraderie. Leo can even be a little clannish, starting "clubs" on the school yard, having boisterous inside jokes, or hanging with a posse of theater geeks who sing show tunes in the hall. (Yes, Leo can be *that* kid, too.) Naturally, Leo will be the epicenter of this little cluster. Just make sure she doesn't veer into clique terrain or adopt the unsavory traits of popularity. (Hello, loud and obnoxious one.) Even though Leo is a kindhearted sign, those born under it need occasional reminders not to exclude others.

Brave Leos get their friends to try new adventures and step out of their boxes. The sheltered kid who befriends Leo will have some eye-opening (and magical) experiences. "Let's go horseback riding!" or "Let's turn our backyard into a haunted mansion for Halloween!" Ringleader Leo loves to explore the world with his best friends by his side—and can work his persuasive powers to make an invitation sound irresistible. Leo's bossy streak may overshadow friends at times. But when a Leo insists with complete conviction, "You *have* to try this" or "Omigod, it's the best thing ever," who could say no?

Toast, please! Sentimental Leos are the friends who will later be maid of honor and best man at several weddings. (Take-charge Leo will probably plan the bachelorette party, give a tear-jerking tribute, *and* get the dance floor moving.) You might already notice your Leo's flair for event planning when she heads up a school decorating committee, transforms her bedroom into slumber party heaven, or starts working on handmade birthday invitations and a theme six months in advance.

Friends may be intimidated or jealous because Leo can be Little Miss Perfect or Mr. Golden Boy, outshining and overpowering everyone else. Encourage Leo to be humble and share the spotlight. Leo may irritate peers by bragging or patting himself a little too heartily on the back. Watch out if Leo lapses into "Enough about me, let's talk about you—what do you think of me?" terrain. (Incidentally, we first heard this joke from a twelve-year-old Leo boy, who was only half-kidding.) Or Leo might just win every contest, game, and starring role, making his excellence just seem like an overstatement. At their best, Leos are unflagging champions and cheerleaders for their friends, boosting their confidence with pep talks and convincing them to try new adventures.

BROTHERS AND SISTERS: LEO AS A SIBLING

Family pride is a Leo hallmark, and these kids are devoted and caring siblings. Leos could be like a parent to younger brothers and sisters, helping to raise and, of course, influence them. Affectionate and huggy, little Leo will be a fixture on an older sibling's lap. Older Leos will want to constantly hold and feed the new baby and could discover their first devoted superfan in a little sib. Proud Leos will brag about their brothers' or sisters' accomplishments to anyone that listens, and if a sibling is struggling, Leo will become her personal champion and miniature motivational coach.

While Leos aren't usually competitive with their siblings, brothers and sisters can certainly be jealous of *them*. Leo often becomes the golden child or favored one, and less secure sibs could start to feel like the black sheep when Leo arrives on the scene. Grr! Make sure you're not stirring up rivalry by comparing Leo to their brothers or sisters. If Leo is the one who doesn't measure up, he'll act out to bring the attention and focus back to him. Leo will not be second best! While a sibling may treat Leo poorly, the regal Lion will rarely stoop to that level. Sure, Leos will fight back if they're attacked—nobody pushes them around. But mostly they'll just get haughty and aloof, sidestepping the drama and doing their thing. Or they'll become judgmental and self-righteous, pointing out the virtuous ways they would handle the situation if the shoe were on the other foot.

DISCIPLINING A LEO

*

Paging Siegfried and Roy! When the Lion needs taming, it could take a skillful team effort. Leo's rebellious moments can be rare but spectacular, truly the greatest show on earth. Go easy when you crack the whip with this wild child, and don't try to break his spirit. Remember Leo Patrick Swayze's most famous line: "Nobody puts Baby in a corner." In fact, you might just try to hug it out. A moment of affection will cure what a hundred time-outs or privileges denied cannot. Lions can either rip your head off or eat right out of your hand. Pet the kitty and work the powers of *purr*-suasion (sorry, couldn't resist) to bring Leo's drama down a notch. Once the storm has passed, this kid is usually pretty darn compliant.

When speaking to Leo, remember the adage "Criticize the behavior, not the child." Proud Leo never wants to disappoint you and will take it hard if you attack his character. In fact, Leo's whole meltdown might have started because he feared losing your approval. Our straight-A student Leo mom once ran away from home when she got an F on her piano lesson and didn't want to face her parents. Yes, Leos can be drama queens and kings!

Positive reinforcement works wonders for this praise-loving sign, so heartily encourage Leo whenever she does something "good." You might take a page from *What Shamu Taught Me About Life, Love and Marriage* by Amy Sutherland, a journalist whose book was inspired by observing animal trainers working with killer whales. According to the author, successful trainers *ignored* negative behaviors and applauded positive ones. She tried the technique on the people in her life, and it worked. Never underestimate the power of a shiny gold star to keep Leo on the straight and narrow. With this kid, a compliment a day keeps the principal away! "As much as I hate bribery, it works with my daughter," admits the mom of a Leo. "She's really into these collectible dolls, so if she accumulates enough instances of good behavior and helpfulness, I buy her one. I've had to raise the bar on my standards, though, because she was turning into a Good Samaritan on speed—all so she could get the latest toy in the series. We now have a list of chores that she does 'just because,' with no reward, so she learns that being helpful is a part of participating in a happy, functioning household. I want her to be motivated, not manipulative!"

HANDLING TRANSITIONS: MOVING, DIVORCE, DEATH, AND OTHER TOUGH STUFF

*

Some changes are exciting to Leos. Depending on Leo's age, a new school, home, or community could be an exciting opportunity to make new friends or decorate a new bedroom from scratch. To Leos, that just sounds fun, and therefore they adjust to change pretty well. However, Leo is also a fixed sign that puts down roots, so these kids don't take well to being ripped away from their cherished turf. But if you turn the change into an adventure and add enough incentives, they will adapt soon enough, forming new loyalties, happy memories, and alliances. Fortunately, Leos land on their feet, provided the change isn't *too* extreme. If you switch Leos from, say, a public school to a wealthy private school where there are clear cliques and all the kids have known each other for years, it might take Leo a little time to break into the tight social circles. Even then, Leos will probably find their way to an extracurricular activity or subject where they form friendships around a common pursuit or project.

The challenging transitions for this sign involve loss or changes with a loved one. Sensitive Leo gets very affected, so if a grandparent is ill, for example, it might even be hard for Leo to visit him without weeping. Expressive Leos need to be free to cry and openly release emotions. Don't tell Leo that "big kids don't cry" or to "be brave." Leo has courage, but his heart rules him.

The breakup of a family can hit Leos especially hard, since they have a romanticized, 1950s-style view of an idealized nuclear setup (even if there are two mommies or daddies). If parents divorce, Leos need lots of reassurance that they're still loved and it's not their fault. They may go through an angry or acting out phase until they regain a sense of security.

SCHOOL'S IN SESSION

*

BEST EDUCATION STYLE

For tribal Leos, school is a built-in social hub and community center. Naturally popular, they might eagerly arrive before the bell rings, rushing to gab with friends or hit the monkey bars before the doors open. Even if they grumble about boring topic or a cranky teacher, Leos love to learn and can be quickly engaged with an interactive lesson or a creative assignment.

Bustling classrooms with fun teachers who make lessons entertaining is a Leo's idea of heaven. Leos love field trips and any holiday that's celebrated schoolwide. Leos might quickly become the teacher's favorite, staying after class to help decorate the bulletin boards or feed the class hamster. These are the kids who might raise their hands for every question, waving their arms wildly and shouting, "Oooh! Oooh! Pick me!"

Competitive Leos are motivated by rewards and will go over the top to earn them, standing up fearlessly to give an oral presentation or adding bells and whistles to a project. They'll turn in a prize-winning essay or score a coveted solo at the winter concert. Show-and-tell was practically invented for Leo, and teachers may need to invest in a gong just to cut off Leo's effusive presentations.

Sitting still and being quiet? Not so much. Leos can pull it off, but they'll eventually grow restless and might even begin acting out. Expressive Leos tend to thrive in schools with strong arts programs that hone their creativity. They can be gifted at sports, too. Later, Leo will probably run for student council or volunteer as group leader for any collaborative assignment. If Leos underperform academically, it's usually because they feel ignored or unable to please their teachers. If your Leo is overly reliant on outside praise and validation, you may need to intervene—engage a tutor or mentor to supply Leo with the one-on-one attention that he craves.

BEST HOBBIES AND ACTIVITIES

Leos are big on extracurricular activities, so the school day could extend until dinnertime (or beyond). There's dance class, theater, sports, choir . . . or any of the bonus rounds Leo enrolls in eagerly. Creative and ambitious, little Leo's hobbies could even plant the seeds for her adult profession. Since this sign loves to perform, you could find yourself on the audition or pageant circuit, playing "mom-ager" to your budding child star. Leos are leaders, but they're also joiners who love to be both the stars and part of a fun community. They enjoy youth groups at their temples or churches, scouting and after-school groups like a volunteer club that does community service, such as visiting sick kids in the hospital or helping at an animal rescue. Competitive Leos will probably sell the most cookies, earn all the badges, or raise the most money in the walk-a-thon. They love to conquer new terrain, so a summer camp with hiking, boating, skits, and other outdoor activities will give Leo cherished lifelong memories.

When they're older, Leos make fantastic camp counselors or peer mentors. They're naturals with little kids and might want to spend free time babysitting, reinvesting the earnings into their own cottage industry start-ups. Early entrepreneurship is common for this sign. You may soon be making ice runs for Leo's roadside raspberry lemonade stand, or breaking $20 bills when she sells her beaded accessories at a craft fair. Why not? Leos enjoy making money for their inventions, and as long as your kid doesn't become greedy or materialistic, a little elbow grease never hurt anyone—especially not a Leo!

GIFT GUIDE:
BEST PRESENTS FOR LEO

* Musical instruments or even a karaoke machine
* Games, especially ones that the whole family can play (Monopoly Junior, anyone?)
* Private voice or acting lessons
* Tickets to a Broadway play or a blockbuster movie premiere (Leos love to be first)
* Outdoors or sports equipment for exploring the wild world
* Clothes, shoes, jewelry, and knickknacks for their bedrooms
* Craft or sewing kits or other supplies for their DIY projects
* Video game systems, especially ones that simulate reality or that Leo can control by jumping up and down

THE VIRGO CHILD

(August 23–September 22)

SYMBOL: The Virgin

COSMIC RULER: Mercury

ELEMENT: Earth

BODY PART: Abdomen

GEMSTONE: Sapphire

COLOR: Cream, tan

GOOD DAY: Helpful
Witty
Curious
Hardworking

BAD DAY: Nosy
Fearful
Self-critical
Negative

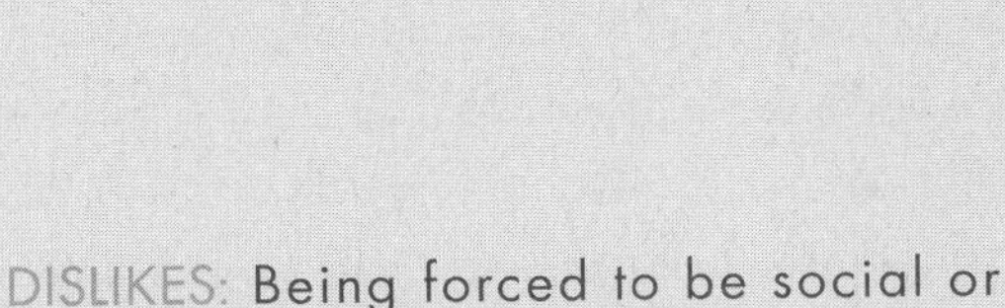

LIKES: Being outdoors
- Nature and animals
- Sports and activities that require skill, practice, and technique
- Mastery, doing things to his own perfecting standards
- Helping others, being useful
- Quiet time alone to read, dream, and scheme
- Good smells, cleanliness, and fresh air

DISLIKES: Being forced to be social or meet new people
- Rushing
- Being indoors for too long
- Sensory overload and noisy places
- Doing things halfway
- Sloppiness, chaos, clutter, and disorder
- Bad smells

* SO, YOU WANT TO HAVE A VIRGO? *

Target Conception Dates for a Virgo Child: **November 25–December 15**

FAMOUS VIRGO KIDS, PAST AND PRESENT

*

Macaulay Culkin, Michael Jackson, Jackie Cooper, LeAnn Rimes, Blake Lively, Rupert Grint, Nick Jonas, River Phoenix, Scott Baio, Ben Savage, Alana "Honey Boo Boo" Thompson, Evan Rachel Wood, Romeo Beckham, Jason Priestley, Ava Phillippe, Chad Michael-Murray, Prince Harry of Wales, Alexa Vega, Jonathan Taylor Thomas, Alexandra Nechita

PARENTING YOUR VIRGO CHILD: THE ESSENTIALS

*

A little help, please! Virgo is the zodiac's sign of service, a natural giver who needs to be needed. Virgo's got a huge heart for anyone (and anything) in need of TLC: an upset child, a neglected animal, even a trampled flower or an abandoned plant. These kids can be quiet and obedient when they're young, but still waters run deep. Their little minds are always working—the Virgo brain does *not* have an off switch!

Ruled by clever Mercury, the sign of communication, Virgos can be curious children who love to learn. Their analytical minds are always sorting, ordering, and classifying. Mischievous Mercury also makes Virgos quite the pranksters, putting a naughty little twinkle in their eyes. They love to tinker and figure out puzzles or solve problems. Virgos are the editors of the zodiac, so these kids are forever rearranging their collections and organizing their toys or clothes. They like everything to have a place and feel most secure when it does.

Sweet-faced and angelic, Virgo kids seem to be born with a halo of light around them. And like delicate little cherubs, they need to be handled with extreme sensitivity. Otherwise, that very halo will turn into a karmic boomerang, tossed right at the folks who brought Virgo into the world. Ouch! Your number-one fan can also be your harshest critic.

Virgo is the sign of purity, meaning their secret wish is to have everything remain in a pristine state—as if to capture that magical moment of newborn bliss forever. Alas, life doesn't quite work that way. Disappointments hit Virgo harder than most. As the zodiac's perfectionists, Virgos hold everyone, themselves included, to impossibly high standards. Their pedestals can turn into prisons.

When people are inevitably human and fallible, little Virgos can grow disenchanted, even bitter. Self-critical and tightly wound, these kids beat themselves up for every misstep—and they're none too quick to forgive yours, either. Kids of this sign can suffer from what life coach Lois Barth calls "one wrong move syndrome"—working up a wicked case of performance anxiety or giving up without really trying in case something goes wrong. (Suggested song for your Virgo child's playlist: Big Bird's classic ditty "Everyone Makes Mistakes.")

Brush up on the child development books, too, when little Virgo comes along. These astute children need you to be a parent and therapist in one. Much of your time could be spent calming their nerves and encouraging Virgos to try, try again. Teach your Virgo critical thinking skills, too, so he can view the world beyond a right-versus-wrong paradigm. Opinionated Virgos can make snap judgments, and they lapse into tunnel vision fast. They need life explained to them carefully, in a way that helps them see the broader perspective.

When Virgos throw a pity party or start to sweat the small stuff, it's time for them to give back. Volunteer work, chores, even small tasks such as gardening or tending to a pet can build their self-esteem. Service-driven Virgos need to make a difference and prove their usefulness in the world. This is not the kid that you should spoil, because when Virgos are handed things on a silver platter instead of earning them, it brings out the worst in them. Industrious Virgos need to pay their dues and earn their keep. It's what makes them feel capable—and therefore safe—in the world.

Virgo children can also be worriers, even kiddie control freaks. If they don't know how to fend for themselves, their minds can concoct some stunning fantasies. *But what if I was stranded on a desert island and I didn't know how to build a fire? Would I starve?* They want you to give them the tools for survival, then let *them* do the building themselves. To adapt the saying, give a Virgo a fish and he'll eat for a day (becoming hungry an hour later). Teach him to fish and he'll feed himself—and the whole family—for a lifetime.

One thing you hardly ever read about Virgos is that they're *funny*—hilarious even! But it's true. Standup comedian Dave Chappelle, whose sharp, satirical wit skewered American pop culture, politics, and racial stereotypes, is a Virgo. These observant kids can also be great mimics (after all, they're watching your every move), nailing your accent, body language, and defining traits. They might be camera shy, but once they claim the spotlight Virgos are gifted entertainers. Michael Jackson, Beyoncé, LeAnn Rimes (the youngest-ever Grammy winner), *Home Alone* star Macaulay Culkin, and Quvenzhané Wallis (the youngest-ever Best Actress Oscar nominee) are all Virgos whose fame arrived early. These old souls truly have the power to make us *feel* something.

However, Virgos' beyond-their-years talents demand a parental advisory. Once kids of this sign begin driving themselves, it's a slippery slope into perfectionism and even self-destructiveness. Many adult Virgos (Amy Winehouse, Macaulay Culkin, Michael Jackson, River Phoenix) have taken a wrong turn into substance abuse, perhaps self-medicating from the pressures of fame or attempting to silence their own inner critics. We don't mean to alarm the parents of Virgos, but the space between this sign's ears can be a dangerous neighborhood if it's not patrolled. So monitor your Virgo for anxiety and perfectionism—and give her plenty of outlets for all that mental energy. Virgos need projects: whether that's a regular list of household tasks (outlined visually on a colorful chore chart); a fish or a small pet to raise; a crossword puzzle book; or a skill-building craft, such as knitting. Technical Virgos like having something to master, so make sure to involve them in activities and games where they can see continuous signs of improvement. Gymnastics, martial arts, and tennis are great for them, too.

Above all, help Virgo remember that we come to this world to make it a better place than we found it. Fan the flames of Virgo's burning desire to help those in need. This self-critical child so easily forgets that his presence matters on earth and that he can be a miracle worker. Tangible results are the best reinforcement for this earth sign. We once knew a Virgo who collected seedpods on a hiking trail and planted a miniature arboretum of trees in his bedroom. Remind Virgo that if he quits or gives up, someone in need won't benefit from his care. Help Virgo see his own role in the cause and effect of something wonderful.

VIRGO: HOW THEY DEAL WITH . . .

*

RULES AND AUTHORITY

Virgos can either be angels or hell-raisers when it comes to respecting authority. When these kids feel safe with the people in power, they'll do anything to please them, even turning into bossy little mini-mes to their peers. Virgos want structure and clear, sensible rules so they know where they stand. This self-disciplining sign may need a few less rules—since they might be too tightly wound to let themselves just play and be kids. Virgos can also elevate their parents or caretakers onto a pedestal that even the strongest adults can't live up to. When the adults in their lives ultimately disappoint Virgo, these kids become disillusioned and even feel unsafe. If authority figures are inconsistent or fickle, Virgo may rebel, hoping to evoke strength from the person in charge. Teach Virgo that "to err is human"—for his own sake and for yours—and that nobody needs to be perfect.

LIMITS

Kids of this perfectionist sign are famous for putting limits on themselves, often way too many. You might hear your little Virgo scolding dolls, pets, or younger siblings—acting out her inner dialogue ("No, no, no—we can't touch that!" or "That's against the rules!"). But too many limits, either yours or their self-imposed ones, can make Virgos paranoid or fearful, and they can be timid about new situations. Be sure to encourage your Virgo child to take some healthy risks. At the same time, being overly permissive can backfire. If you don't outline clear limits for Virgo, they will act out in a subconsciously desperate plea for you to set some.

SEPARATION AND INDEPENDENCE

Virgo kids can be confident little leaders once they're comfortable, but the tricky part is breaking down their walls. Virgos can suffer from separation anxiety; they hate being left to fend for themselves with new people or situations. (This is probably not the best sign for the "cry it out" method, either, nor for the Ferber method, which advocates leaving the child's room or sleep area in gradually increasing increments.) Virgo kids don't always trust their instincts, so they need your approval and encouragement before they venture out. They imagine that the world is a critical place waiting to expose their flaws or a scary setting where they'll be caught unprepared and out of control (big Virgo no-nos). It's all about baby steps, Mama. With your gentle nudges and reassuring presence, you can help your little birdie believe that he can fly.

YOUNGER SIBLINGS

Caretaking Virgo kids might just put you out of a job! This sign loves to help and direct, so with a Virgo child, you've got a pint-sized parent figure who loves to assist you with feeding, diapering, baths, and teaching. Just watch Virgo's micromanaging tendencies, as these kids can get a little *too* controlling with their little sibs.

OLDER SIBLINGS

Virgo's high standards extend to anyone older than them, so big brothers and sisters are viewed through the same critical microscope as parents, caregivers, and other role models. Little Virgos will watch their elder siblings' every move, either worshipping them or disapproving of their actions in an almost self-righteous way. Codependence alert: Virgos can also play the hero role in a troubled family, so they might try to rescue an older brother or sister in trouble—or even become confidants for a parent in need, which can breed sibling rivalry. Virgos can also get lost in the shuffle, quietly escaping into their own worlds and missing out on the attention that a more outrageous sibling demands.

BYE-BYE, BABY: WEANING AND POTTY TRAINING

Virgo is a sensual earth sign, and this kid needs to be held. Affection and touch really matter to the Virgo kid. However, with this sign's sensitive digestion, your Virgo may have been switched from breast to bottle (or even formula) early on to help them digest their food better. When potty-training Virgo, be careful not to push him, as it can become a performance-based issue that he'll talk to his therapist about for years! (We kid . . . kinda.) Virgos are sensitive to criticism and will want to do everything perfectly. This could be your first of many chances to teach Virgo that it's okay if something takes as many tries as he needs and that he shouldn't quit just because he's had an accident. (You might even want to avoid the words *accident* and *mistake* entirely.)

SEXUALITY

Virgo is the zodiac's sign of the Virgin, but this curious kid is not as innocent as legend suggests. Virgo is also an earth sign, so these children are very tuned in to their bodies. They might ask a lot of questions or be the first to sneak a kiss with a little cutie on the playground. Physical and sensual, they can even be flirty when they're young. Curious Virgos know how to find facts and information and may even do so behind your back. Keep the library stocked with age-appropriate books about where babies come from. By the time you get around to the "birds and bees" conversation, you might be surprised to find out how much Virgo already knows (or has been misinformed about—yikes!). Best to be proactive and educate Virgo yourself, letting her know it's okay to ask plenty of questions.

LEARNING: SCHOOL, HOMEWORK, AND TEACHERS

Virgos are either the best students or the absolute worst. It can go either way, but you have to steer them from the first day of school. In the best situations, school can be a wonderful place where Virgos can learn, explore, and flaunt their considerable intellects. This smarty-pants sign can be the zodiac's chicest geek. The downside? School is also a place where Virgos are judged. This sign is hypersensitive to grades, report cards, and performance-based academics, so be mindful if your Virgo starts to fall behind or feels rushed to turn in hasty work. Perfectionist Virgo kids often mistakenly believe, "If I can't do it to A-plus, gold-star standards, why bother doing it at all?" One subpar report card or an embarrassing wrong answer in class (public shaming—the absolute worst thing that can happen to a Virgo) can turn your future magna cum laude into a serious slacker. If Virgo starts to slip academically, chances are one mistake or bad experience has spiraled into a total system shutdown. Virgo needs you (and perhaps a few skilled technicians) to reboot his confidence. "My Virgo daughter is a great writer, but she was overlooked for the 'gifted' English and reading group, and it really rattled her confidence," says one mom. "She stopped writing in her journal and giving me poems, and it was the saddest thing. Finally, I talked to her teacher about it. We arranged for her to do a couple of extra credit stories and reading comprehension work, so she could be reconsidered and placed into the gifted group."

HOUSEHOLD CONFLICT

Helpful Virgos hate conflict, yet when it arises they can't help but get smack in the middle of it. The zodiac's therapists, Virgo kids will attempt to mediate, fix, and restore the control this orderly sign so craves. While some Virgos can shut everything out and disappear into a book, for example, these observant kids see and hear everything. And since Virgo is a sign that needs to be needed, the kids born under it can take on the role of savior, hero child, and helper, becoming the codependent go-between for feuding relatives. *Ay, dios mío.* Should a parent fall from grace or dysfunction befall their homes, Virgos may shoulder an unrealistic sense of responsibility for what's happening, trying to save the day by being "good." Or, since they're such empaths, they'll swing to the opposite extreme and act out an exaggerated version of the dysfunctional behavior—a subconscious attempt to identify with the troubled person so they can understand what's really going on. Handle these kids—and your issues—with extreme care so as not to burden Virgo with adult problems.

THE VIRGO BOY

*

The wheels are turning! The Virgo boy is a mental machine whose thoughts are forever in motion. His face is sweetly cherubic, but behind those wide eyes little Virgo is watching. This observant boy doesn't miss a thing. He can also be incredibly particular, even fixating on a few fussy details. From babyhood on, this guy has strong preferences—in food, temperature, colors, clothes, you name it.

Clever Virgo boys bore easily, and they need to stay busy. An intricate game or project can consume him for hours, but without a focus his nervous energy dissipates fast. This kid needs lots of intellectual and physical stimulation. As an earth sign, playing outside is the best antidote. He's deeply connected to nature and living things and can spend hours entertaining himself. While he might be a "good boy" when he's little, mischievous Virgos like to test boundaries, too. You'll need to keep an eye on this kid, no matter how self-contained he seems. There's a whole world happening between those little ears and that can sometimes lead him to create elaborate, and maybe even dangerous, games and experiments.

Verbal Virgo can be much more emotionally articulate than other boys. He may have a lot of female friends as a result, since he likes to talk and analyze people. He's also incredibly protective: nobody messes with Virgo's loved ones! Virgos can also be mama's boys. They love to have surprisingly deep conversations with you, or long talks filled with curious questions.

You'll need to be precise, since Virgo boys can take your words literally . . . or use them to find a convenient loophole. We once visited our Virgo friend Jared, who was eight or nine at the time. Arriving, we found his dirt bike strung up to a tree and Jared beating it, piñata-style, with an aluminum bat. "My parents said they won't buy me the BMX I want until this bike is no good anymore," he calmly explained. "So I have to destroy it." Virgo's sense of logic can be a little *too* strong!

Virgo boys can be technical and strategic, so keep them busy mastering a skill. How do you get a Virgo to Carnegie Hall (or keep him out of detention)? Practice, practice, practice. Whether it's sports, chess, martial arts, music, acting, or computer science, engage him in a subject where he can go deep. Mastery is his muse, and he can be a proud geek. Virgo also likes to help, so put him to work with tasks and chores, and start him young.

Virgo boys are incredible storytellers, and their detailed minds (coupled with long attention spans) can put together epic scenarios with action figures or other toys. This orderly sign has a sense of rhythm (get him a bass guitar or a drum kit!), timing, and placement. No surprise that some of the most famous and exacting movie directors are Virgos: Baz Luhrmann, Tyler Perry, Guy Ritchie, Tim Burton, and Oliver Stone. Authors Stephen King and Roald Dahl were also born under this sign. Whoever said Virgos are boring never experienced this sign's imagination!

The verbal Virgo boy specializes in sarcasm, too, and his humor can be hilariously wicked. Like Virgos Adam Sandler and Charlie Sheen, he mocks himself *and* the world at once. Virgo is the sign of the critic, so his jokes may have an edge, indicting whoever has fallen short of Virgo's lofty standards. Ouch! Like Virgos Keanu Reeves (who was kicked out of school for mouthing off) and Prince Harry, his rambunctious remarks can get him into hot water, too.

Underneath that bird-flipping facade, Virgo is the ultimate sensitive boy. Like Virgos Ryan Phillippe and River Phoenix, this kid can come across as a brooding, slightly tortured soul. He's also an empath, picking up when things are even subtly out of alignment in his world. Often, Virgo will misbehave, go into full tantrum, or turn inflexible when he senses a loss of order at home. He's born with rose-colored glasses, and when life fails to match his idealized vision the Virgo boy can grow a chip on his shoulder. Keep tabs on his psychological state, especially during major transitions such as divorce, a move, a new baby, or starting school. Systematic Virgos like control and structure and often need extra time to adapt to changes. Patience is a virtue—for both you and little Virgo.

THE VIRGO GIRL

*

Mothering a Virgo daughter is a high-stakes job. After all, you're the primary female role model for the zodiac's perfectionist. No pressure there or anything! Your Virgo girl needs your approval as much as she needs oxygen, and she may tag along at your heels, wanting to please and help you.

She'll study your every move, learning, imitating, and yes, critiquing. At times, you may feel she's sizing you up, even disapproving of your actions. Who's the mom here, anyway?

Virgo can't get enough mother–daughter bonding time, especially if it includes long, conspiratorial conversations. Dishy Virgo loves to analyze people, and she can be quite the little yenta, so try not to fuel that gossipy streak in her! Steer her into talking about her dreams, or take her for special outings to redirect her energy. This kid has the stamina for a museum or a long hike (Virgos love nature). Sharp as she is, Virgo is also innocent, and she will idealize you. You'll need to model high self-esteem around this impressionable kid. This can help avert body image pressures and social anxiety, to which Virgo girls are especially sensitive. Another trait to show your Virgo by example? That you can make a mistake and clean it up, survive, and recover—even bouncing back higher than before.

Virgo's shadowing presence can be both adorable and exhausting, and at times you may feel burdened by your daughter's strong dependency on you. (Hello . . . Mama needs a minute to herself! *Please.*) As a little girl, Virgo can be fussy, needy, and clingy. She's timid about the wider world, but with you as her steady anchor she'll emerge from her shell. And what a debut it can be! Virgo girls can be skillful performers, excelling at music, dance, martial arts, or gymnastics. Earthy Virgos can also have some serious pipes: Lea Michele, LeAnn Rimes, Pink, and Jennifer Hudson are all born under this sign. Prepare for the performance or competition circuit—or even pageants, like Virgo Alana "Honey Boo Boo" Thompson. Your Virgo girl might be uptight at moments, but she can also have flawless comedic timing. When she's not lost in her head, she loves to laugh and entertain you.

Virgo rules the hands, and your daughter can be gifted with hers. Crafts and DIY projects are often favorite pastimes. The rhythm of detailed handwork can help to soothe her worrisome mind. When she's little, Virgo may enjoy puzzles, stacking games, or toys that have to be organized by color or shape. When she's old enough, buy her journals and pretty blank books, as this girl can be a prolific writer. Let her work by your side, too; she wants to feel useful. Bring her into the kitchen with you and let her mix ingredients (or chop them, once she's old enough to handle a knife). Set up a little desk for her in your home office. Like Virgo Beyoncé did with her mom, Tina Knowles, you and your young Virgo might one day start a business together.

There will be times you wish Virgo was a little more outgoing or independent. Other times—like when she talks to a creepy stranger because "he looked so sad and lonely"—you'll wish she were a little *less* friendly. Virgo girls may start out shy and self-conscious, but they can become queen bees once their social hives are established. Stand by.

Those apron strings can weave a tangled web of codependence, though, so tie and clip them with care. Sensitive and thin-skinned, Virgo girls are quick to feel rejected, especially by you. Shirley MacLaine's Virgo daughter, Sachi Parker, wrote a scathing memoir, *Lucky Me*, insinuating that her famous mom chose her acting career over motherhood. Ouch! In typical observant Virgo style, Parker didn't seem to forget a detail—or to have forgiven her mother— even at the age of fifty-six.

Words are a weapon for verbal Virgo. When she's hurt, Virgo may cut off communication while slandering her so-called enemy behind his back. A natural giver, Virgo can keep score, even though she performed her kindnesses without being asked. But hell hath no fury like a Virgo (seemingly) scorned. The Virgo girl will need firm reminders that love does not come with strings attached. Learning to be unconditionally accepting of herself—and by extension, of others—is an important lesson for judgmental Virgo. Teach her to share without expecting anything in return, and to communicate her needs directly. *No* is a complete sentence, so let your caring Virgo know she doesn't have to do anything that feels uncomfortable to her.

BEHAVIOR DECODER: THE VIRGO KID

WHEN VIRGO . . .	IT MEANS . . .	SO YOU SHOULD . . .
Cries	Frustration, usually with himself. He failed to meet his own lofty standards, and he's pissed!	Praise him sincerely, let him know he doesn't have to be perfect to be loved.
	A plea for sympathy. Virgo is hosting a pity party and everyone's invited.	Talk to him like a life coach and parent in one, letting him vent but also taking care not to get sucked into his victim story. Take Virgo out for a treat and distract him with decadence.
Withdraws socially or gets quiet or moody	Virgos can be introverts and may need quiet time alone more often than other kids. They might just be recharging their batteries.	Make sure Virgo isn't brooding, and give her some space to read, draw, journal, tinker, or watch TV.
	Virgo is upset and is overwhelmed by the environment. She may be feeling anxious or uncomfortable about something.	Take Virgo aside (privately!) or even out for a healthy treat somewhere special and let her talk it out. She needs one-on-one attention and understanding to calm her nerves and fears.

WHEN VIRGO . . .	IT MEANS . . .	SO YOU SHOULD . . .
Acts out (hitting, kicking, talking back)	Verbal Virgos can throw daggers with their words. They've been hurt, so they want to hurt you back.	Remind Virgo that you're not a mind reader and to use his words in a different way, to tell you honestly what's bugging him.
	Sensitive Virgos can "cry wolf," so when they're genuinely upset, you might not believe it because of all the crocodile tears. Now they've raised the stakes to send an SOS.	Even if you think your Virgo is being a crybaby, stop and attend to him. Invalidating him is the worst thing you can do. A short time-out followed by a long one-on-one talk can help.
Gets clingy	Tentative Virgo can have a lot of fears and social anxieties. She may not be ready to immerse herself in a new situation or environment.	A gentle separation process can help. Virgo likes to measure, so give her a timer or stopwatch that will count down the minutes until you come back. Virgo is the sign of service, so giving yours a task or responsibility helps her break the ice.
Won't eat what you serve	Virgo rules the digestive system so your kid may have a sensitive stomach, gluten intolerance, or a fussy palate.	Suck it up, Chez Mama: you may need to serve a special menu to Virgo. Fortunately, this sign is often talented in the kitchen, so eventually, you can give her an apron and let her be your sous-chef or prep cook.
Can't sit still	Mental overload! Analytical Virgos can't shut off their minds, which can overwhelm their little bodies. When this happens, Virgo needs to move!	Get this kid to a gymnastics class, dance studio, or onto a sports team, stat. Physical activity is one of the best ways for Virgo to release stress!

THE SOCIAL VIRGO

*

ROLE IN THE FAMILY

Integrity check! Virgos are the purifiers of the zodiac who can restore the family to a state of health and balance. Like any good detoxifying agent, however, they have to dredge up the "gunk" first. Want to know where your family is out of alignment? Observe Virgo. This sign is often the dysfunction-o-meter for their clans, acting out an exaggerated version of whatever's off balance. For example, we knew a Virgo whose family was in major denial over his father's alcoholism. In high school, this Virgo totaled his car driving drunk. The shake-up was a wake-up call, and his dad entered treatment.

Virgos are astute at solving problems and finding flaws, even catching that hairline fracture that can later turn into a huge fault line. Speaking of faults, though, Virgos can become quite the finger pointers and blamers. Though their intentions are noble, they might create *more* chaos in their quest to help, inserting themselves into other people's conflicts or enabling a troubled relative. Virgos need the occasional reminder to butt out—and that no family is perfect. Make sure their attempts to help don't turn into enabling or codependence.

FRIENDS AND PEERS

A friend in need is Virgo's friend indeed. Kids of this helpful sign love to play the helpmate, sounding board, and voice of reason among their pals. Virgos can also instigate plenty of mischief, and they're often the first to crack a sarcastic joke or tease a buddy. Although they might talk smack among friends, most Virgos are scared to get into "real" trouble by breaking the rules. One curmudgeonly little Virgo was nicknamed "Grandma" by her friends. However, that fear can quickly turn into temptation for this curious sign. Monitor Virgo's playmates carefully, because he can also end up as the wingman for a true troublemaker. Your Virgo might be an angel, but his savior complex can draw him to the little devils. Boredom is the most likely reason Virgo will stray from the straight and narrow path. Get Virgo involved in enriching activities that really capture his attention and imagination to ensure that his peer group isn't a bunch of thugs!

Is there a new student in Virgo's class or neighborhood? Caretaker Virgo will shepherd the "new kid" under her wing, thrilling at the chance to show this person the ropes. Not that Virgos can't form cliques—this sign can be gossipy and insider-oriented. Since Virgos prefer having a couple close friends to a whole superficial gaggle, they might need to be gently pushed into new situations where they can expand their social circles. Discourage your Virgo from talking behind people's backs, an offshoot of self-critical Virgo's insecurity.

Should a friend be upset or struggling, Virgo will rush to his aid. When everyone else abandons an underdog, Virgos stand by this person. They can even be a bit self-righteous about it, pursing their lips with disapproval toward anyone who dares to judge. Of course, Virgo kids can be the harshest judges of all, holding their friends to impossibly high standards or keeping score. Virgos are extremely giving, but they're not very *forgiving*. Virgo suddenly might "not be speaking to" a best friend. Children of this sign keep so much in their heads, but they often expect friends to read their minds. A playmate might not even realize Virgo is upset until Virgo marches past her as if she were a stranger.

While intervening in children's friendships should be done with care, you may need to step in occasionally. Validate Virgo's hurt feelings, but encourage her to resolve the matter with her friend. You might even do a "mock" conversation with Virgo to help her express her feelings without being confrontational or accusatory. "My son is very well meaning, but maybe a little too much so," says one Virgo boy's mama. "He doesn't see that he can be overbearing or that even when he has good intentions not every kid wants what he's offering them. He gets his feelings hurt, so I try to teach him not to take things so personally. I tell him, 'Just because your friend doesn't like what you're doing or want to play with your toy, doesn't mean that he doesn't like *you*.'" It's a good distinction to explain to your eager-to-please Virgo, who is quick to feel rejected or rebuffed. These are skills that will serve sensitive Virgo for a lifetime, building confidence and healthy perspective for a sign that tends to blow things out of proportion fast.

BROTHERS AND SISTERS: VIRGO AS A SIBLING

Methodical Virgo likes to know where he stands in the pecking order—and that goes for his family, too. While Virgos can be helpful and loving siblings, they will definitely compare themselves to their brothers and sisters. It's this sign's nature to classify everything, after all. Since Virgos love to make lists, they'll always wonder where they rank on yours.

As perfectionists, Virgos' preference is the role of "golden child." However, because of birth order, personalities, and family dynamics, Virgos can get overshadowed. Perhaps a sibling already occupies the favorite spot—as in the case of firstborn royal Prince William and his roguish Virgo brother, Prince Harry. In other cases, a troubled sibling acts out and consumes her parents' attention, leaving Virgo feeling sidelined and forgotten. Jealousy and rivalry can flare. If they're mad enough, Virgos can even stir up conflicts between different family members, inserting themselves as the savior or go-between to shore up a feeling of importance. Parents should never, ever compare this kid to her siblings. The question "Why can't you be more like your brother/sister?" is a dagger through Virgo's tender, self-critical heart. Make sure to remind your Virgo that she's seen, heard, loved, and special . . . perfect just the way she is.

DISCIPLINING A VIRGO

*

Discipline is an interesting concept for a sign that can be so self-regulating and tightly wound. Some parents might even wish Virgo *would* act out a little—no kid can be *that* good. As a communicative sign, dialogue is always your best first move with Virgo. However, this clever sign does know how to "yes" you to death and sneak around behind your back. Just look right at them; the eyes don't lie!

Virgos want to please their parents and will get frustrated when they can't. They often get upset over a very specific issue (one friend's Virgo toddler freaks out when he outgrows his shoes and is über-picky about each new pair). They may even hammer on the topic until you listen to them, driving you crazy and acting out more openly if you ignore their pleas. When Virgo wants to deliver a message, they make sure to be thorough—and oh, can their sharp words wound.

Some Virgos find trouble out of sheer boredom, as this sign is smart and curious and needs to keep busy. They may be acting out because they have too *much* freedom and are begging for boundaries. Other times, the issue coincides with a traumatic event, such as a divorce, death, bullying, or some sudden change. Virgos crave consistency and hate surprises. Sudden behavioral issues may be Virgo's outward expression of inner chaos. Some Virgos can develop a rebellious streak out of resentment for forcing themselves to be "good" all the time. Because they place so much pressure on themselves to perform and please people, they swing to the opposite extreme and act out.

Like little trial lawyers, Virgos are always prepared with a good defense. They can argue their way out of a sentence or avenge a punishment. One Virgo remembers knocking down his family's Christmas tree (and blaming the cat) when he was upset about being grounded. A consistent course of tough love—reinforcing boundaries and not giving an inch—might be the only thing that keeps this too-smart-for-his-own-good sign in check.

HANDLING TRANSITIONS: MOVING, DIVORCE, DEATH, AND OTHER TOUGH STUFF

*

Orderly Virgos don't cope that well with sudden transitions, unless everything is explained in granular detail. They hate to feel out of control, so unexpected shifts can throw them for a loop.

If possible, tell them what's happening every step of the way, so Virgos can regain a sense of order and adapt to their new reality. Encourage them to express or talk about their feelings. Little Virgos can be very private about their breakdowns and struggles. They might worry that they're bothering you by speaking up. Many Virgos will suppress their feelings, taking care of everyone else. Or their stress will come out in compulsive ways: bed-wetting, crying, organizing, sudden appetite changes, fighting. During traumatic times, Virgos need an extra dose of unconditional love. A pet can be especially therapeutic for this sign, as can some healing time in nature.

SCHOOL'S IN SESSION

BEST EDUCATION STYLE

Virgos can be excellent students—or they can be the kids who are actually smarter than everyone else but refuse to apply themselves. The smarty-pants Virgos are much like Virgo Lea Michele's "Rachel" character on *Glee*—grade-grubbing goody two-shoes. For other Virgos, school can be excruciating, driving up their social and performance anxieties. They're hard enough on themselves, and now they have to stand in front of the class and give an oral report or hand in homework for the teacher to grade? These stubborn Virgo kids may just create a self-fulfilling prophecy, purposely flubbing an assignment or test because they can't stand the anticipation of waiting to hear whether they've passed or failed. Virgos with these issues might do well in an independent school that doesn't give formal grades or lets children learn at their own pace.

Virgo is also the sign of the perfectionist, so these kids will want to do everything the absolute best or not at all. They may feel rushed through assignments and projects and need to be reminded that schoolwork sometimes just has to be "good enough." Many Virgos need hands-on support before they can really fly. If need be, sit down and do school projects together or help them with homework. Once they're confident that their ideas are good enough, Virgos can soar.

The best environment for Virgos is one in which they can learn for enjoyment without the pressure but are still inspired to be their best. Too much independent study leaves Virgo adrift, at risk of underperforming. However, tough grading policies or rabid standardized testing can overwhelm perfectionist Virgo. A supportive teacher can make or break Virgo's love (or hate) of school, too, so make sure your child is being taught by encouraging and sensitive teachers who draw Virgo out of her shell and inspire this sign's love of learning. This can be tougher to pull off in a large classroom setting, so if possible, find a school with smaller class sizes or breakout groups. Personal attention from an afterschool tutor can also boost Virgo's confidence and comfort levels.

BEST HOBBIES AND ACTIVITIES

Little Virgos often have a few specific hobbies and interests. They're the zodiac's craftspeople and love to master new techniques. They excel in extracurricular activities that allow them time to practice, run drills, and perfect a skill, building up a body or work and knowledge. Many Virgos are physically gifted and graceful. They can be talented at activities that require rhythm and precision: martial arts, dance, cheerleading, gymnastics, or sports like soccer and tennis. Others can be adept with their hands and will enjoy drawing, writing, crafting, and building.

Since Virgos are talented mimics, they might come out of their shells onstage, delivering a surprisingly strong performance in the school play. Chefs whites in extra-small, anyone? Today's fussy eater can become tomorrow's foodie. (Celebrity gourmands Mario Batali and Rachael Ray are both Virgos.) Enroll your Virgo in a cooking camp or class if he shows an interest in mixing ingredients or dabbling with pots and pans.

Although Virgos can excel at competition (who else practices as much as they do before the big event?), they might lose their steam when they don't win that coveted blue ribbon. Remember that these kids are famous for beating themselves up. If they want to drop out or quit, they're likely being too hard on themselves and need your encouragement. Don't force Virgos to stay in something they genuinely hate, but urging them to give it one more try or to talk to the coach for some encouragement can renew their spirits.

Virgo is the sign of service, so this kid might enjoy volunteer work with animals, at a nature center, or in a community garden plot. Outdoorsy Virgos love camp, nature hikes, and opportunities to be helpful in the community. Let results-driven Virgo grow and nurture something from scratch, whether it's a pot of flowers or a tomato plant. Bonus points if they can add their cultivation to a recipe or make a table centerpiece out of it later. A packet of seeds and some sunshine could spark a lifelong green thumb—and stoke your Virgo's creativity.

GIFT GUIDE: BEST PRESENTS FOR VIRGO

* Remote-controlled vehicles or planes that precise little Virgos can maneuver around or even a kiddie car that Virgo can drive
* Magazine subscriptions or a gift certificate to their favorite bookstore
* A book of crossword puzzles, word search games, or a Scrabble board
* A beautiful journal with lock and key
* A musical instrument and lessons
* Decorative boxes and bins for organizing their toys
* Anything DIY: a small hobby kit (such as woodworking, model airplane building, or printmaking), a sewing machine, knitting needles and yarn
* A play kitchen—or real kitchen supplies, such as a set of stacking bowls, spoons, and a kiddie recipe book
* A yoga mat and kid-appropriate yoga DVD or lessons to help Virgo relax

THE LIBRA CHILD

(September 23–October 22)

SYMBOL: The Scales

COSMIC RULER: Venus

ELEMENT: Air

BODY PART: Lower back

GEMSTONE: Opal

COLOR: Rose, deep blue

GOOD DAY: Charming
Lovable
Fair and generous
Compassionate

BAD DAY: Scattered
Uptight or perfectionist
Manipulative
Melodramatic

LIKES: Beautiful clothes, music, environments, and people
Socializing and making friends
Gifts (giving and receiving)
Pastel or fun colors (or any shade of pink)
Art, music, dance, and culture
Sugar and sweets

DISLIKES: Sensory overload: loud noises, harsh lighting, and chaotic crowds
Cheap or scratchy fabric
Being alone
Cruelty
Being ignored
Saying good-bye

* SO, YOU WANT TO HAVE A LIBRA? *

Target Conception Dates for a Libra Child: **December 25–January 15**

FAMOUS LIBRA KIDS, PAST AND PRESENT

*

Zac Efron, Will Smith, Serena Williams, Hilary Duff, Avril Lavigne, Kirk Cameron, Barry Williams, Mario Lopez, Alicia Silverstone, Karyn Parsons, Nick Cannon, Kieran Culkin, Jonathan Lipnicki, Lourdes Leon, Angus T. Jones, Lacey Chabert, Ashlee Simpson

PARENTING YOUR LIBRA CHILD: THE ESSENTIALS

*

Love, sweet love! Kindhearted and sensitive, the Libra kid exudes charm from day one. It won't be long before the whole family is wrapped around Libra's chubby little finger—and the baby-model scouts come knocking. Ruled by Venus, the planet of beauty and love, Libras can be exceptionally adorable kids. They may have dimples or just a sweet disposition that's pleasant to be around. Watch out, because you could be spoiling Libra before you know it.

Tasteful Libras can be little aesthetes from early on, too. They love pretty things, so beware a bent toward materialism. Sensitive to light, color, noise, and ambience, Libra needs a beautiful and calm environment. One Libra remembers running out of his noisy elementary school cafeteria sobbing, because the din was too harsh for his ears. Aww! These are the kids you can take to fancy restaurants, and they'll happily dress up or put a cloth napkin on their laps. It won't be long before Libra reaches for the polished silver and shuns the plastic utensils. Skip the mashed peas and baby-food jars while you're at it—Libra would rather eat delicate bites of whatever you're having. They can be artistic and cultured, the kids you can take to a museum as easily as you can to a baseball game.

Don't let the smooth taste fool you, though: Libras are made of sugar *and* spice. Agreeable as they can be, these kids don't just roll over. When something feels unfair or extreme, Libra becomes outspoken or simply refuses to budge. Tenacity (and yes, even stubbornness) is a lesser-known trait of this sign. Gandhi, a Libra, liberated India using *passive resistance*—a nonviolent refusal to cooperate with unjust policies. It's the ultimate "you can't make me"—and it's a Libra specialty.

Symbolized by the scales of justice, Libras need to weigh and measure everything. They like to carefully consider all options before making a choice. It may take Libras forever to make up their minds, but once they do, the deal is sealed. As much as Libras hate to have their own decision making rushed, when they finally settle on an option or direction, they're ready to pursue it full throttle. (Can you say "tunnel vision"?)

Unfortunately, our fast-paced world isn't set up to accommodate this sign's thoughtful process or the desire of Libra to savor each moment when you're in a rush. Any parent of a Libra knows not to present this child with too many outfit choices or breakfast options if trying to leave the house before noon. Libras want to stop and smell the roses: Every. Single. Freaking. One. If you're a working parent or an on-the-go person, plan to set the alarm clock an hour early or to woo Libra out the door with bribery.

Yes, Libras can be maddeningly indecisive, but perhaps a better word is *discriminating.* This sign has an incredible ear and eye for quality. Libras can be downright type A with their exact natures, refusing to settle for anything short of perfection. Thanks to his brutally honest opinions, Libra Simon Cowell has become television's most famous (and feared) judge. This sign can deliver painfully sharp criticisms. Ouch!

Of course, Libra's judgment is soundest when given due time. Hurried along, Libras can make some stunningly bad decisions. Case in point: Cowell eliminated contestant Melanie Amaro from the first season of the US version of *X Factor*. Two weeks later, he flew to her home and announced he'd made a mistake, inviting her back onto the show. She subsequently won the competition and a $5 million recording contract. Although Libra moves like this one make them seem indecisive or fickle, there's often a bigger motive when Libras change their minds (such as fairness or a realization that they've acted in haste). Parents of Libras will have to carefully suss out whether your vacillating child is being considerate—or is just plain confused!

Fortunately, most Libra's people skills can be unparalleled, so even when they drive everyone crazy, you can't help but love 'em. They're fantastic schmoozers and social butterflies, often popular among peers. Libras need people like the rest of us need oxygen, and they adore interactive play. Their network of childhood friends is deeply important to them. In fact, if you want to know what's up with Libra, you might listen to how they talk about their friends. Tuning into other people's emotions is how Libras get in touch with their own.

The only downfall is when Libras learn how easily their charms work on people. Their powers of persuasion might be *so* effective that these kids can become manipulative. Their Venusian appetites for pleasure can make them self-indulgent, too. At age four, our Libra sister, Leora, would push in front of our dad at McDonald's, and before he could order she'd tell the cashier, "I'll take a Big Mac, a twenty-piece Chicken McNugget, and an extra-large Coke!" Fortunately, our father intervened. Otherwise, the film *Super Size Me* could have been based on our family.

Eventually, most Libras channel their negotiating skills into acts of kindness, championing their friends, families, and social causes. With their flair for the finer things, Libras make sure to *look* good while they *do* good. They're the best-dressed philanthropists in town.

Sure, Libras might drive you crazy with their long-winded way of doing everything (like their habit of delivering a simple answer as an epic poem). You may occasionally need to remind them, "Get to the point!" Heck, you might wonder if they even *have* a point to begin with. But the fairy tale that is Libra's life always ends with a "happily ever after," even if she has to slay a few dragons or take a few forest detours to get there. Meantime, Libra invites us to enjoy the journey, instead of just focusing on the destination.

LIBRA: HOW THEY DEAL WITH . . .

*

RULES AND AUTHORITY

Little Libras aim to please and love to make people happy. As such, they can be pretty angelic and might even idealize parents, teachers, babysitters, and other authority figures. Hello, model citizen. However, Libras have a few strong preferences and will revolt if forced to compromise. Don't even bother trying to change their minds. Libra is the sign of justice, so rules must also be fair. Otherwise, you could experience gentle Libra's assertive side—this kid will speak up against anything unjust.

LIMITS

Libras are happy to comply with limits, unless they *really* set their sights on something. Then there's no stopping their willful ways. Libras are masters of charm and will butter you up to get what they want. Or they'll sweetly tell you what you want to hear, then turn around and do whatever they want. A future in politics could be in your midst.

SEPARATION AND INDEPENDENCE

Libra is the sign of relationships, so these kids might never want to cut the cord with their parents and loved ones. Fortunately, Libra is one of the most social zodiac signs. Once Libras form friendships, they'll forget you even exist until you pick them up or call them home for dinner. One mother dreaded dropping her Libra daughter off at day care each morning, until she realized how adaptable her little girl was. "When it was time to leave the house, she'd look up at me with these wide, tearful eyes and say, 'Mommy, I don't want to go to the sitter's,' and I would feel *so* guilty," confesses Mama. "I'd wonder if I was making a mistake by leaving her with someone else, but I didn't have the luxury—or the desire—to be a stay-at-home mom. Once I got her in the door, I hovered while she eased her way in with the other kids. Within a couple minutes, she was always fine. The babysitter would text me a picture of her whooping it up so I would quit worrying!"

Gentle separation works best when you introduce little Libra to a new environment like a nursery school or day care, at least for the first few days. They hate saying good-bye—so coming and going anywhere will take extra time.

YOUNGER SIBLINGS

Patient and protective, Libras can make loving older siblings who appreciate the companionship. However, they might not always want to share the spotlight or give up the spoils of being the baby. Libra might also be the family golden child, especially if he's the oldest, leaving big shoes for a younger sibling to fill.

OLDER SIBLINGS

Libras put their older siblings on a pedestal and crave their approval. However, they can also be infuriating, helping themselves to the older sib's clothes, toys, and possessions without asking. Tagalong alert: when Libra idealizes someone, she wants to copy that person or hang around all the time. The constant shadowing can annoy an older brother or sister, so be sure to steer Libra toward her own individual hobbies and interests. Find ways for her to develop leadership skills, perhaps being team captain, running for student council, or heading up a household project (even something as simple as taking care of a pet or making school lunches). Since Libra is the zodiac's most companionship-oriented sign, kids born under it can get too caught up in togetherness, adopting other people's identities (all the way down to clothes, speech, and mannerisms) rather than cultivating their own personal style. Imitation is the highest form of flattery, sure, but at a certain point it just irritates Libra's older sibs. Encourage Libra to blaze her own trail!

BYE-BYE, BABY: WEANING AND POTTY TRAINING

Libras take their sweet time to do most things. They may resist your attempts to push transitions before they're ready. Then one day Libra might just sit down on the potty himself or drink from a cup and that will be that. Libras hate to be pressured—unless, of course, it's peer pressure. When their little friends start using the potty, group-oriented Libras may want to do so, too!

SEXUALITY

Just the facts, and keep the shame out of it. Libras don't like to feel "bad" or "dirty" (who does?), and since they're ruled by pleasure planet Venus, they need to understand that sex is an adult expression of love. Teach Libra the proper names for body parts, for example, and don't make a big fuss. Little Libras will take it all in stride.

LEARNING: SCHOOL, HOMEWORK, AND TEACHERS

Instant social life? Yes, please. Libras love to be around their peers and will make lifelong friendships early on. Of course, they can get *too* caught up in the fraternizing and become distracted in class. Libra is an intellectual air sign and can be a great student, even a type

A perfectionist who will work diligently on a project until it's done to his exacting standards. These kids are great with creative problem solving, with a wide capacity to be thoughtful and deliberate. Rote schoolwork (math equations, spelling drills) can be mind-numbing—Libra prefers assignments that require his carefully considered opinion.

HOUSEHOLD CONFLICT

Peace, love, and harmony are the Libra virtues. These gentle spirits absolutely abhor conflict. When your household becomes more divided than the Middle East, in steps Libra, the family's own UN diplomat. Masterful mediators, Libras can stay calm and objective, helping everyone see everyone else's point of view. However, if Libra's negotiating skills fail to work, or things become the opposite of "fair and balanced," watch out. Libra can become incredibly rebellious, acting out to the extreme—even becoming the so-called black sheep of the family. Remember: this is Libra's way of expressing his inner turmoil, a reaction to something that's out of balance in the home environment.

THE LIBRA BOY

Make way for the ladies' man. The Libra boy is a suave Casanova from the get-go, a sensitive metrosexual in the making. Charming and photogenic, he can tune into emotions and read people quickly, making them putty in his hands. While Libra can have a scrappy, rough-and-tumble side, he's a cruelty-free kid at heart, a caring friend who always has his buddies' back. In fact, the Libra boy can be downright dreamy, even if he masks it with a stern or uptight demeanor.

Libra is a visual sign ruled by beauty-loving Venus, giving him a taste for the finer things. The Libra boy can be a stylish little clotheshorse who keeps his clothes neat and even dresses a bit more formally than his friends. (Fashion designer Ralph Lauren, a Libra, epitomizes this sign's clean-cut, classic flair.) One mom of a Libra reports that her teenage son religiously polishes his white sneakers with a toothbrush every week. "If only he'd keep his room as spotless as his shoes," she laments. Even Libras who try to be badass—Eminem, Michael Douglas, Will Smith, Tommy Lee—are still foiled by their own symmetrical, "pretty boy" features. Don't hate him because he's beautiful!

What Libra really has going for him, though, are his words. This expressive sign can be a prolific writer and speaker, a poet with incisive wit and a touch of highbrow haughtiness. Many literary lions were born under this sign—Oscar Wilde, F. Scott Fitzgerald, and Truman Capote, to name a few. Even Libra Eminem was the first hip-hop artist to win an Academy Award for his lyrics to "Lose Yourself."

This guy is in touch with his feminine side, too, and not (usually) ashamed to admit it. (Who else but a Libra man could create a character like Holly Golightly from *Breakfast at Tiffany's*?) He might even be vain or snooty, fussing over his outfits or flaunting his cultural literacy. One Libra guy we know shamelessly carries a "murse" (man purse) with stain remover, breath strips, and travel-sized grooming gear inside. He's prepared for anything, that's for sure.

At times, the Libra boy can get a little *too* lost in his head, intellectualizing everything and giving himself a case of "analysis paralysis." His perfectionism can be his downfall, and his type A tendencies can make him a little tightly wound and angst-ridden. Even Libra Oscar Wilde said, "I am so clever that sometimes I don't understand a single word of what I am saying."

Fortunately, Libra has his friends—both male and female—to balance his scales and help him keep it real. Libra is the sign of partnership and collaboration. Without his posse, the Libra guy can get lost at sea. Even if he has a million acquaintances, Libra sticks closely to his BFFs, sharing inside jokes and deep talks. Indeed, you might rarely speak this boy's name without mentioning his sidekick, too. Libra men in famous dynamic duos include Matt Damon (with Ben Affleck), Snoop Dogg (with Dr. Dre), and John Lennon (with Yoko Ono). Little Libra is quicker to pair up than Noah's animals in a flash flood. "My son tries to act tough, but he's a total softie when it comes to his best friend," says one Libra's mama. "I wish he'd actually be a little less loyal at times, but you can't say anything critical about his buddy without him getting all defensive. He's got him up on a pedestal. They're together so much that I feel like I have a second son—and his friend even calls me Mom sometimes."

Many Libra boys are late bloomers, too. It's part of their whole "taking their time" shtick, which could lead you to wonder if this kid has commitment issues—or perhaps will never be satisfied. At some point, you may have a vivid premonition of your Libra son, twenty years from now, still living at home as an eternal bachelor. Libra can be as picky about dating as he is about his after-school snacks.

Not to worry. Libra might have a few false starts and missteps as his scales swing wildly toward equilibrium. His skeptical sign needs to test, try, and even rebel against everything first. But don't give up on him—it's all part of the Libra process. He knows that the best things come to those who wait, so why settle?

THE LIBRA GIRL

*

Vive la femme! Libras are among the girliest girls around, gravitating toward all things pink or princessy without prompting. If you hoped to raise a modern-minded daughter immune to gender stereotypes, Disney may have the last laugh. This girl never met a Barbie, tutu, or dollhouse she didn't like. Angelic in her disposition, this Venus-ruled child can be a beauty from birth, all the way down to her dimples, perfect skin, or long lashes. Then there's her total adoration for the folks who brought her into the world. Libra is both a daddy's girl *and* mommy's little shadow, most content in the company of her loved ones.

Say cheese! Libra can be a ham, striking a pose for endless photogenic snaps. This girl craves attention and affection in large doses. She loves to play dress-up in your shoes and jewelry and will adore big-girl outings like mother–daughter shopping excursions or going out to tea. At age two, Ophira's Libra daughter Cybele slipped into a pair of Marc Jacobs stilettos and clomped around with perfect balance. Libra can be quite the little lady!

Don't mistake Libra's girlishness for weakness, though. She's a lover *and* a fighter. This pretty powerhouse is a true "iron fist in a velvet glove" who knows how to kill 'em with kindness—and get her way through sheer will. Libra Margaret Thatcher, the first female prime minister of the United Kingdom, was even nicknamed "the Iron Lady" for her uncompromising politics. Libra may be a damsel, but she *ain't* in distress! Thatcher herself once sniped, "Being powerful is like being a lady. If you have to tell people you are, you aren't." Boom! Libra TKO.

Thatcher also said, "I am extraordinarily patient, provided I get my own way in the end." Truer words were never spoken of a female Libra. She can outlast anyone in a battle of wills, unleashing her considerable weapons of charm, tenacity, and persuasion. In grade school, we dispatched our Libra sister, Leora, to sell Girl Scout cookies for us every year. Box in hand, she'd march right up to people, flutter her lashes, and coo, "Excuse me, ma'am, would you like to buy some Thin Mints?" The same people who'd hurry past us would hand Leora a crumpled bill and gush, "Of *course*! You're just too cute to resist!"

The Libra girl has a strong moral compass (even if there are occasional outages) and will stand up for her beliefs. One delicate Libra girl we grew up with took down a neighborhood bully when she caught him trying to destroy another family's Halloween decorations and toilet paper their house. Turns out she had a heart of gold—and a mean right hook! As the sign of relationships, Libra is tuned into everyone's feelings, the first to comfort a friend in distress. Her little buddies mean the world to her, and this sentimental girl forms cherished lifelong friendships. Libra is the girl who will be in several wedding parties later in life, delivering the teary-eyed toast that makes everyone cry. She wears her heart shamelessly on her sleeve.

Do be mindful, though, Libras can get *too* dependent on her friends or caught up in her social circle, losing sight of her own goals and obligations. While it's normal for girls to fuss with their looks, you may also need to limit Libra's primping time and make sure she finishes her schoolwork. (Mirror, mirror on the wall, which girl's grades are about to fall?) Don't give Libra a phone too soon, either, unless you want to pay for an extended plan. Once a Libra girl starts gabbing, she can outlast Duracell.

Of course, it *is* all about who you know, so by the time this social butterfly graduates, she'll have amassed quite a social network. Hopefully, they'll be upstanding citizens, since Libras can sometimes gravitate toward questionable characters. They have a soft spot for troubled souls from rough circumstances, since they're sensitive to injustice. However, Libras can fall for a sob story or get taken for a ride by an underdog turned con artist, so keep tabs. In other cases, the Libra girl can be a teensy bit of a snob. While Libra's heart is kind, her words may not be. Make sure your Libra doesn't lapse into mean-spirited gossip or even bullying. Libra is the sign of the judge and the critic, and she can turn her nose up at kids who are awkward or unfashionable. In her desire to bond and fit in, she might gain her place in the group at another kid's expense.

Much like Libra Alicia Silverstone's character in *Clueless*, your Libra may need to be prompted into deeper, less superficial waters. Once she realizes the power of love and kindness, she can become the *least* judgmental person on the planet, a friend to everyone she meets. One day, she could be standing in her Jimmy Choos, thanking her friends and family for the person she's become today. Stick around for your ovation.

BEHAVIOR DECODER: THE LIBRA KID

WHEN LIBRA . . .	IT MEANS . . .	SO YOU SHOULD . . .
Cries	Libra didn't get his way and now he's pissed.	Use the power of distraction and move Libra away from the tempting environment or object.
Withdraws socially or gets quiet or moody	Sensory overload: Libra's circuits can only handle so much stimulation before he needs to rebalance.	A nap, quiet time, or soothing music can help. Transfer Libra to a calmer environment, turn off the TV, or go outside for fresh air and a change of scene.

CONTINUED ON NEXT PAGE

WHEN LIBRA . . .	IT MEANS . . .	SO YOU SHOULD . . .
Acts out (hitting, kicking, talking back)	Libra's reaction to some imbalanced energy in her home, school, or environment. Sensitive Libra picks up on anything that's out of harmony.	Investigate and see if you can remedy the situation.
	Libra didn't get her way.	Frankly, it's easier to give in because Libra can throw a fierce tantrum otherwise. But stay strong, mama, or you'll set a precedent for years of emotional blackmail.
Gets clingy	Libra is just being Libra. Kids of this sign love to be around their closest peeps.	Take a few minutes to connect with Libra, or at least stay within Libra's sight. Parallel play works well with this sign. Libra may also need a transitional object, such as a piece of your clothing, like a scarf, or perhaps a picture of you.
Won't eat what you serve	Libras are particular and fussy about food—and the way it's presented.	Add some variety, garnish, or color, since visual Libras love a beautiful plate. (We know, we know: what is this, a restaurant?)
	Sugar cravings.	Libras have a notorious sweet tooth, so be careful not to fill them up with sugary snacks.
Can't sit still	Boredom. Libras can be patient with some things but have a total short attention span with others. They want your attention or a new form of entertainment.	Play and interact with them, or let them run around freely in a safe area.

THE SOCIAL LIBRA

*

ROLE IN THE FAMILY

As the sign of relationships and balance, Libras are the family fulcrums. These natural diplomats can be the peacekeepers of their families. In harmonious and tolerant homes, Libras can be like Switzerland, getting along with everyone. Their arrival can usher in a golden era of harmony . . . or it can expose where things are out of alignment. When a home environment is dysfunctional or intolerant of certain values, Libras may go to the extreme opposite in an attempt to bring balance or fight against injustice. For example, in an ultraconservative home, Libra could become an outspoken liberal. Or, if education is emphasized at the expense of everything else, Libra might "casually" decide to take a couple years off before college. If there is addiction or dysfunction, Libra may become the "bad" kid for a while whose misbehavior forces the family to heal and deal with the problem. Your astute Libra might be a prophetic messenger in black sheep's clothing.

FRIENDS AND PEERS

Libra is the ultimate "people person," and this affable, fun-loving sign lives for friendship. Libras would socialize around the clock if allowed! Spirited and up for anything, they love having activity buddies who enjoy being out and about. Bonding and sharing are fun for Libra, and they'll love having sleepovers, trading clothes, taking pictures, or exchanging tokens of camaraderie. Sweet and considerate, they love to spoil their friends with special gifts and teary-eyed tributes.

Balance can be an issue in Libra's friendships. At times, they may lean too heavily on their peers for approval and direction. Or they can exhaust friends with their needs and demands. Many Libras even briefly lose themselves in friendships, getting way too caught up in politics and loyalties. Some Libras even go through a phase where they try to fit in by adopting a different group's accent, cultural mores, values, and style of dress. Libra's curiosity and desire for connection can veer into chameleon terrain. They can be pretty experimental as they form their identities—even mingling with friends from a vastly different background than theirs. One Libra we know, born to a Baptist family, attended a synagogue during high school in her predominantly Jewish hometown. Since all of her friends were part of the youth group, she felt like she was missing out on the fun, so she accompanied them on outings and community service work. "I even used to tell people that I was Jewish for a while," she recalls. Over time, as Libras become more self-assured and accepting of themselves, their friendships will become stronger.

As much as Libras can drive their friends crazy with their constant vacillating and indecisiveness, their charm always soothes the savage heart. At the end of the day, it's hard to stay mad at Libra, if only because they're the perfect sidekicks. They'll usually try anything once (even twice). And if a friend is hurt or struggling, Libra will be there with a reassuring hug or a soothing shoulder to cry on.

When two of Libra's friends are fighting, Libra will play mediator, making every effort to restore peace. This sign hates conflict! Of course, this can get Libra, who doesn't want to be dragged into divided loyalties, in hot water with friends, but eventually Libra will learn how to navigate around drama and stay neutral—letting other people work it out for themselves.

BROTHERS AND SISTERS: LIBRA AS A SIBLING

The more, the merrier? In the best cases, a sibling supplies Libra with an instant BFF and constant companion, right in the comfort of his own home. Libras can make proud and protective brothers and sisters. In fact, they could be oblivious to sibling rivalry—even if it's happening right under their noses. They'll just keep killing their sibs with kindness, trying harder and harder to win their approval with charm and adulation.

It doesn't help that Libra is often the "golden child" of the family, though, so parents must be sensitive not to pit other kids against Libra. Our Libra grandfather had a giant oil painting done of him as a curly-haired, adorable child. None of his three siblings had portraits commissioned—and as adults, they never forgot to mention this fact when they visited his home (where the portrait hung at the head of his dining-room table).

If Libra falls on the other side of the favorites spectrum, it can be an ugly scene. Libra doesn't mind sharing the love, but there'd better be enough left over for him. If this kid feels displaced or compared to a sibling, Libra may act out, hoping to regain your focus.

DISCIPLINING A LIBRA

*

Contents are fragile: handle with care! Sensitive Libra has a strong sense of justice, so the punishment must fit the crime. Be careful not to blow your top. These gentle souls do *not* respond well to yelling or any kind of hands-on discipline. Libra needs to feel connected to you and is terrified of losing your approval. Touch is a powerful bridge for this sign. You might need to wrap him in a hug while Libra cries it out. Later, be proactive and make positive behavior into a fun adventure ("Let's dress up like fairies and put the toys away together!") to lighten the mood.

Remember, Libras would rather beg forgiveness later then ask permission first. As the zodiac's charmers, they can be sly, feigning innocence and then disobeying you on the down-low. Once Libras fix their minds on getting something, they can become ruthless in their quest—even when they know better. Later they'll "think about it" and realize the misstep (after getting what they want, of course). Then Libra may come around with a sincere apology or make it up to you with sterling behavior. One mom of a Libra caught her young son about to shoplift a toy he'd been demanding. Apparently, he was tired of being told to wait until his next birthday, so he tried to tuck it into his shirt. Fortunately, it was bulky and conspicuous enough for her to notice *before* they passed through the security sensors! Libra kids need to learn that manipulative actions add up, earning them a rep for being sneaky—or worse. Nip that kiddie-con-artist behavior in the bud by teaching Libra that no means no.

In extreme cases, Libra can become incredibly rebellious, acting out when they sense that the household rules aren't fair or that the emotional energy is off. Often this will happen if there is abuse, addiction, or dysfunction in the home, since Libra is particularly sensitive to imbalance—not to mention tension and power struggles. In the words of Libra John Lennon, this sign wants you to "give peace a chance," and if that need goes unaddressed Libra will wreak havoc until you pay attention. Don't shoot the messenger! Libra's misbehavior is never the problem but rather a symptom of a greater issue. Follow Libra's smoke signals to the true problem and address that. This fair-minded sign also demands mutuality, so remember that parenting a Libra is a two-way mirror. You must be willing to look at yourself, too. With Libra, "Do as I say, not as I do" will never fly.

HANDLING TRANSITIONS: MOVING, DIVORCE, DEATH, AND OTHER TOUGH STUFF

*

Libras move at a slow and steady pace, and sudden change throws their delicate scales off balance. In fact, they can get so distressed that it causes a behavior breakdown. (Book that family therapy appointment, stat.) Divorce is especially hard since Libra is the sign of marriage and relationships and may feel forced into the middle of his parents. Libras are deeply sentimental and nostalgic, especially about loss. If there's a death in the family, make sure Libra is surrounded by loving friends and family. During stressful times, Libras crave human contact more than ever and should never be left alone to make sense of an overwhelming or traumatic situation.

SCHOOL'S IN SESSION

*

BEST EDUCATION STYLE

As students, Libras seem to fall into two categories. Some are type A kids who want to do everything to perfection and can be competitive about grades. These Libras respond well to structure and are neat, organized, thoughtful students who become the teacher's pet year after year. Since Libra is the sign of the scales, Libra kids like to weigh and measure. They might especially like essay questions, compare-and-contrast papers, and assignments that draw upon their critical thinking talents. They could have precise handwriting or tuck school reports into beautiful presentation covers and decorative folders.

Note to teachers: seat assignment is important, since gregarious Libras can be easily distracted by note passing, giggling, and side conversations. The second type of Libra student would earn straight A's . . . if only schools graded them on socializing, popularity, and interpersonal skills. This Libra child excels in an interactive school setting that doesn't pressure them to rush into deadlines or competitive testing measures. Since Libra can be a late-blooming or dependent sign, these kids might need academic hand holding and shouldn't be left with too much self-directed learning. After school, they lose track of time daydreaming, want to lounge before cracking a book, and need you to constantly ask, "Did you bring your backpack home?"

Although it's important to be involved in their schoolwork, don't let them con you into doing it for them! Libras can get lazy when they don't want to deal, but if you coddle them they'll never learn the fundamentals. They need a little tough love and lots of patience. Never underestimate the power of a beautiful environment with this sign, either. Some Libras hate school just because the vibe is ugly, industrial, and uncomfortable. At home, set up Libra's workspace with chic patterns, a comfy chair, and colorful pencils. An incentive program also helps since Libras love material rewards. Special treats when they finish a big project or study successfully for a test can motivate Libra mightily.

BEST HOBBIES AND ACTIVITIES

You know that kid in the yearbook who lists one of his hobbies as "people"? He's probably a Libra. Friends and socializing are what it's all about for Libra, who will put the "extra" in extracurricular. Save up for sleepaway camp and summer programs—and book those playdates—because Libra barely tolerates alone time. (Of course, if you do send Libra off to camp, prepare to send care packages aplenty and come up for Visitors' Day so that he knows you're thinking about him while he's gone.)

Libra is creative and visual, often skillful at drawing with a strong sense of color and balance. You might invest in professional art supplies or enroll your talented Libra in a still life course at the museum. Sartorial Libra may have an early love of fashion and style, putting together sophisticated little outfits or wanting to spend hours at the mall. Libras can also be musical, excelling at dance or an instrument. This discriminating sign can even develop exquisite tastes early. Galleries, musicals, spa treatments, tea at a fancy hotel—Libra might be into all things high end and highbrow from a young age.

Graceful Libras can be athletic, though they're more likely to enjoy interactive games like basketball than solitary sports like track. Part of the fun is the camaraderie, and as the sign of relationships Libras have a great sense of timing for when to, say, pass the ball to a teammate. Since they love to bliss out, little Libras might be the youngest person in their yoga classes. With their innate balance, they can pull off some tougher poses!

Libras love a lively discussion, so later on they can be the kids dressing up and traveling with their school debate team. Playing devil's advocate or arguing a point is something Libras might do for fun. At the very least, you'll hear them engaged in long, sometimes loud conversations with their friends, going back and forth ad nauseam about a topic. Libras take pride in having well-cultivated tastes and do well in activities where they can leave a creative, personal stamp.

GIFT GUIDE:
BEST PRESENTS FOR LIBRA

* Clothes, accessories, or kid-oriented grooming kits (nail polish, lip gloss, sparkly barrettes)
* Room decor, preferably a matched set or a theme
* Art supplies, such as a sketchbook and colored pencils
* Musical instruments and a series of lessons
* Tickets to a Broadway play or to see their favorite sports team
* Books of fiction, poetry, or beautiful illustrations
* One-on-one time with you, doing something special for just the two of you, such as a day of shopping, a trip to the children's museum, or even preparing a special meal and setting a beautiful table for two.

THE SCORPIO CHILD

(October 23–November 21)

SYMBOL: The Scorpion

COSMIC RULERS: Pluto, Mars

ELEMENT: Water

BODY PART: Reproductive system

GEMSTONE: Citrine

COLOR: Black, red, hot pink

GOOD DAY: Magnetic
Passionate
Sharp
Intuitive

BAD DAY: Obsessive with a one-track mind
Possessive
Jealous
Manipulative

LIKES: Knowing how things work
Music and culture
Spicy or flavorful food
Being at home
Staying up late (Scorpios are night owls)
Books, puzzles, crosswords, and problem solving
Winning and being the best at what she does

DISLIKES: Not finishing what she starts
Enforced group activity
Sharing his most cherished possessions or space
Noisy places, big crowds, and overstimulation
Surprises and invasions of privacy
Simplistic or unimaginative people

* SO, YOU WANT TO HAVE A SCORPIO? *

Target Conception Dates for a Scorpio Child: **January 25–February 15**

FAMOUS SCORPIO KIDS, PAST AND PRESENT

*

Anne Hathaway, Jodie Foster, Leonardo DiCaprio, Ryan Gosling, Willow Smith, Joaquin Phoenix, Winona Ryder, Kelly Osbourne, Jack Osbourne, Chloë Sevigny, Kevin Jonas, Kendall Jenner, Christopher Knight, Lisa Bonet, Ralph Macchio

PARENTING YOUR SCORPIO CHILD: THE ESSENTIALS

*

All eyes on you! Keenly observant Scorpio is the zodiac's detective, and from day one that sharp little gaze doesn't miss a thing. Scorpio is the sign of transformation, and these kids feel everything deeply. They might go through intense highs and lows—from euphoria to rage—in a short window of time. Scorpio is the sign of extremes, so these kids can be loud and brash in one place (usually around close friends or family), but eerily quiet, even mute, in another.

Pluto, god of the underworld, is the celestial body that rules Scorpio—and this water sign certainly runs deep! Even if you've given birth to a Scorpio, your child may remain something of an enigma to you. Scorpio is, after all, the sign of mystery. Speaking of which, your little Scorpio might be drawn to all things esoteric. Brace yourself for an early introduction to tarot cards or a fascination with what happens behind the scenes of everything: how babies are made, how fire trucks work, and whether there's life on other planets. (Alert: little Scorpio can also be a future conspiracy theorist in training.) If there's a mystery to uncover, Scorpio is on the case.

Paging the psychic friends network! Your Scorpio's line to the divine can be crystal clear. You'll often wonder how your intuitive little peanut just *knows* things—or can read people like large-print books. Mainly, it's because few details escape observant Scorpio's awareness. Even if you have an expert poker face, you can't hide anything from Scorpio. He's on to you!

If you're the kind of mom who needs her "space," don't expect to get any from this child. Attachment parenting was practically invented for Scorpio, the sign of intimacy and bonding. Because of their keen sensitivity, Scorpio kids may need extra comfort and security from you. Book that La Leche League membership: you may find yourself nursing Scorpio through nursery school or cuddling up in the "family bed" while the gorgeous hardwood crib you splurged on goes unused.

Of course, your Scorpio might not want the crib for other reasons: these kids are notorious night owls. As they get older, lights-out time may become either a flexible matter or the source of frequent power struggles. Creative Scorpios come alive after dark and may do some of their best studying, artwork, or soul searching under the light of the moon. Even if you're firm about bedtime, you may still catch Scorpio sneaking a tablet or book under the covers.

On the subject of attachment, Scorpios will cling to more than just your apron strings. With the memory of an elephant, this sign can hold a grudge like no other. Scorpios are a little *too* good at keeping the past alive. They barely forgive, and they certainly don't forget any perceived slights. Deep down, Scorpios trust very few people, so when they do open their hearts, it's an all-consuming affair. Best friends are sworn in by blood oath, and anyone who gains Scorpio's hard-won confidence becomes a lifetime member of *la familia*. Any slights or wrongdoings cut Scorpio to the core and can bring out the stinging scorpion's vengeful streak. Tread lightly, or little Scorpio will put *you* in time-out, icing you out with the silent treatment or burning you with a mind-melding glare. These kids can even get aggressive if they have too much pent-up emotion, so hide the china—or give them a pillow to punch.

To prevent your Scorpio child from becoming a miniature mobster—or from getting overwhelmed by floods of intense feelings—find a few good channels for their energy. Scorpios need creative and even spiritual outlets to keep them balanced. Music, art, and writing can be therapeutic for this sign, so convert their rooms into little sanctuaries where they can get as messy and inventive as they want. Martial arts hone their natural capacity to focus. Scorpio is never too young to join you for meditation, chanting, or yoga—even if he Zens out by osmosis, sleeping in his stroller. Tunnel vision alert! Working with animals or volunteering with children in need can prevent myopic Scorpio from getting too self-absorbed. It's not that they mean to focus so intently on themselves, but since Scorpios are so easily captivated by the tiny nuances and details of everything, they tend to get lost in their own obsessive little worlds. At times, you might need to remind Scorpio to connect with the world beyond his nose.

Still, the muse for Scorpio is always within. Get this kid a guitar, a sketchbook, or a journal once the angst-ridden preteen years begin. Or how about a karaoke machine? As private as this sign can be, there's an inner rock star in every Scorpio. Once it comes out, forget it: you'll witness lead singer magnetism as your Scorpio unleashes a tsunami of charisma and power. Scorpios might not want their weaknesses exposed, but when idol status is guaranteed Scorpio will gladly take center stage.

Just don't mistake Scorpio's expressiveness for extroversion. This kid is not a joiner (hold back on the enforced group activities!) and will never be a true "people person" at heart, even if he memorizes the name and vital stats of every kid in school. Too much social contact will send Scorpios scurrying back to their private chambers. Like slightly mad scientists, you never know what Scorpio is cooking up in that lab. Just don't storm the fortress or pry into Scorpio's business unwarranted. A little privacy, *please*!

SCORPIO: HOW THEY DEAL WITH . . .

*

RULES AND AUTHORITY

Obviously, Scorpio can't run the show as a child, but he'll certainly try! From a young age, tiny Scorpio can exert serious will, making his influence known. As the sign of power, little Scorpio is keenly aware of "who's who" on the metaphorical chessboard and will strategically position himself to curry favor with the key decision maker (e.g., his mom or dad). This systematic sign likes to know where everyone stands, particularly in relation to him. If he could map out an "org chart" he would—naming himself executive vice president of children's affairs, perhaps, or senior counsel for stuffed animals. Caution: ruling with an iron fist or being overly permissive can lead to a power struggle, as Scorpio doesn't trust anyone he perceives as either weak or domineering. You'll need to strike a balance between patiently explaining why certain rules exist and holding your ground when Scorpio tries to steamroll you.

LIMITS

Scorpios hate to feel out of control, so limits can help this security-seeking sign feel safe. Knowing what to expect if they touch a hot stove (burn!) or pull the cat's tail (scratch!) minimizes their chance of an unwelcome surprise. Whew! Of course, many Scorpios need to learn the hard way first. Scorpio might look you straight in the eye (with the famously intense Scorpio glare) and flagrantly disobey you. "I dare you to stop me" is this kid's MO. That's when you need to be extra firm with limits; otherwise, Scorpio will keep pushing the envelope.

SEPARATION AND INDEPENDENCE

Scorpio is the sign of bonding and has a strong need to be attached—often through physical closeness—to the (very) few people this little one trusts. Heading back to work or dropping off Scorpio at day care? Not so fast, Mama. Scorpio could have some powerful emotional outbursts when you first leave her side. You may need a transition period while slow-to-trust Scorpio warms up to a secondary caregiver.

YOUNGER SIBLINGS

Scorpio is the sign of jealousy and possessiveness. One day, the little brother or sister may be "mine!" Other times, Scorpio may get a touch of the green-eyed monster, especially if he feels displaced or one-upped by a scene-stealing sib. Should this happen, Scorpio will maneuver things—or act out—to regain his stronghold.

OLDER SIBLINGS

Sensitive Scorpio loves to be adored, so if a brother or sister is attentive, Scorpio will soak up the adulation. Babying aside, though, Scorpio doesn't want to be treated like a flighty little kid who doesn't know anything. This sign demands a respected seat at the big kids' table—even if she's a head shorter than everyone else there! If an older sibling teases or taunts, Scorpio will quickly become wary and even competitive. Verbal warfare can be brutal, as cutting Scorpio knows how to strike back right where it counts. "My Scorpio sister and I got in the hugest fight over a pair of jeans that we both liked," recalls a friend. "We were in the middle of the store, and suddenly she's accusing me of always dating guys that *she* likes. The jeans, in her mind, were more evidence of how I supposedly stole everything from her—and that I 'had no mind of my own.'" Ouch!

BYE-BYE, BABY: WEANING AND POTTY TRAINING

Scorpio is the sign of bonding, so weaning can be a tricky process for these attachment-driven little ones. Scorpio is loathe to give up anything that provides comfort and security. Potty training, on the other hand, can be relatively easy for this sign if explained as a calm, step-by-step process. However, Scorpio will rebel if it becomes a power struggle or she feels forced to make too sudden of a switch. This sign likes to be in control, even of when (and how) she uses the bathroom!

SEXUALITY

Scorpio is the sign of sexuality so you'll be explaining the birds and bees to this kid at a young age. Or you could find her conducting "amateur research" on herself. Keep an eye on the Scorpio kid who suggests playing doctor with friends. This is also the kid (and adult) most likely to ditch his clothes and run around starkers. Anyone else remember Scorpio Matthew McConaughey's naked bongo drumming incident?

LEARNING: SCHOOL, HOMEWORK, AND TEACHERS

Scorpio's powers of concentration are unrivaled, and this observant kid can be a sharp little student. This sign may have one or two subjects that they pour all their energy into, since they like to focus. Because Scorpios can have such great memories, they often do well on tests and quizzes and can be early talkers. They're also competitive and will want to be the strongest, fastest, and smartest kid in class. If they don't make top billing, these unrelenting kids won't back down. A strong rival just fuels their resolve to crush the opposition—even if it takes them from K to 12 to do it.

HOUSEHOLD CONFLICT

Private Scorpios want no part of the ugly airing of feelings that don't involve them. They'll hide in their little sanctuaries, tuning it all out as they disappear into a book or TV show. Of course, Scorpio will often be the reason there's conflict in the first place, especially if she has siblings. When Scorpios fight, they fight dirty. A brother or sister who invades Scorpio's turf without permission could provoke a vicious backlash! Parents aren't immune to Scorpio stings, either. Even if it costs a month's worth of privileges or allowance, angry Scorpios *will* attempt to have the last word in an argument with mom and dad.

THE SCORPIO BOY

*

Hello, little man of mystery and magnetism. The Scorpio boy is a cannonball of intensity, blasting into life with extreme impact. Whether he's quietly soaking up the scene (those eyes!) or shattering the sound barrier with his shrieks and hollers, Scorpio's presence is palpable. As a deeply feeling water sign, he's a bottomless wellspring, too. The Scorpio boy's emotional energy can go one of two ways: inward or outward. This kid has the capacity for deep silent spells (where you wonder just *what* he's pondering) and the grandest of fireworks.

We've heard it said that emotion is "energy in motion." So think of yourself as the traffic director for Scorpio's self-expression, and make sure there are no bottlenecks, sharp U-turns, or spectacular crashes. You *could* try to control him . . . but we wouldn't advise it. Rather than suppress Scorpio's obsessive nature, help him find a worthy passion. It could be dance, music, sports, acting, computers, the stock market, taking things apart—whatever consumes his vast attention span. This fanatical sign needs a focal point. Once he's found his niche, you're golden. Then your job becomes answering his detailed questions, restocking his supplies, or finding venues for Scorpio to display his precocious talents.

Scorpio boys can be light years ahead of their peers in awareness and ambition. Pablo Picasso was a famously intense kid, and this description nails his Scorpio nature: "A serious and prematurely world-weary child, the young Picasso possessed a pair of piercing, watchful black eyes that seemed to mark him destined for greatness."

Boys of this sign need their own turf, and your home might be his first stage or laboratory. Prepare for a takeover of your *Architectural Digest*–inspired dining room or the family salon as he transforms it into Scorpio Central. Where *else* is he supposed to practice his break dancing or set up a drum kit, after all? (Now, instead of watching TV, everyone's watching Scorpio. Mission accomplished!) To reclaim communal space, you may find yourself doing the unthinkable, such as giving *him* the master bedroom to turn into his own little studio, just so you can have company over again. Damn, he's good.

Here's some great news for you (but not his future girlfriends): Scorpio is the ultimate mama's boy. (Scorpio actors Ryan Gosling and Leonardo DiCaprio frequently bring their mothers as red carpet dates to awards ceremonies.) Psychologists agree that as early as eighteen months, boys start to separate from their moms to begin bonding with other males. Not Scorpio. Later in life, the mother–son dynamic can get a little complex. More than a few of his adult therapy sessions could address his inner conflict about cutting the cord. ("I guess my mom is such a powerful figure it's hard for me to get close to a woman without feeling smothered.") Um, okay. One Scorpio's mother breastfed him until the age of five. No judgment, but she claims he showed zero interest in weaning even then. So be warned: if you ever want to walk Scorpio down the aisle, begin the "gentle separation" process while he's young!

Not that he'll lack options for female attention. Scorpio is the zodiac's sex symbol, and you may see early signs of it. This charismatic kid can have a veritable fan club of girls go gaga for him. Fortunately, Scorpio is an intuitive guy who's interested in what makes people tick. He'll also have a flock of female friends with whom he genuinely connects. His sensitivity, mixed with his striking presence, makes this kid downright bewitching.

Some Scorpio boys are embarrassed by their sensitivity, but most of them eventually learn how to own it—turning their vulnerability into an asset. After all, being so in touch with their intuition allows Scorpio to size people up and stay a few steps ahead of the competition. Oh, and it also helps him steal the ladies' hearts by knowing how to be one of the girls without *really* being one of the girls. Unpopular in school? Not to worry. Scorpio will just create his own inner circle and have the last laugh. To this guy, success is the best revenge. Just ask Scorpio Bill Gates, the "geek" who founded Microsoft. Or cue Scorpio P. Diddy, who after being fired from Uptown Records, created his Bad Boy label and later, a multiplatform music, fashion, and entertainment empire.

Still, you'll want to keep an eye out if Scorpio gets too withdrawn. Since depression is really anger turned within (and as we said, Scorpio's energy goes either inward or outward), boys of this sign can be prone to it. If he grows up in an environment where he's told that "boys don't cry" or "be a man," this can adversely impact him. Some Scorpios can even come across as pent up or a tiny bit tormented (cue brooding Scorpio Ethan Hawke in *Dead Poets Society*).

Remember that Scorpio's connection to the feminine (or yin energy) is his lifeline. It's what channels his creativity, intuition, and powerful instincts. Trying to stamp this out in Scorpio only leaves him vulnerable and unarmed. So the next time you fret because he's so thin-skinned, don't try to "toughen him up." Let Scorpio be. Otherwise, you could be crushing the spirit of a future Picasso!

THE SCORPIO GIRL

*

Make way for your pint-sized power broker. With her all-seeing gaze and cutting wit, your Scorpio girl is four years old going on forty. You'll see it once you lock eyes with her and *you* blink first: this girl doesn't miss a beat. From an early age, the Scorpio girl knows who she is and what she likes, from clothes to music to people. And once she sets her mind on a goal, she's unstoppable. As a child, one Scorpio friend had already planned her education (Yale law) and her fairy-tale wedding (a massive scrapbook of bridal magazine clippings). She manifested both.

Scorpio can be a quiet force of nature or an in-your-face tornado, but there's no ignoring her presence. There's something about Scorpio's intensity that stops people in their tracks, making them want to study her or stare right back. Striking Scorpios Julia Roberts, Lauren Hutton, and Chloë Sevigny all possess unusual but captivating beauty.

Scorpio is an incredibly creative sign, and these girls love to turn their rooms into sanctuaries of self-expression where they can read, lounge, and rejuvenate. They're often drawn to vivid, deeply saturated hues or even black, offset by pops of red and hot pink. Scorpio could be the teen that toughens up her look with black nail polish or punk-inspired accessories. A "vintage" girl, she might also enjoy trolling through the attic or for old clothes, furniture, and castaways, which she'll repurpose into something totally unique. Get this DIY diva a sewing machine and voilà—a design star is born (to wit: eponymous fashion lines by Scorpios Calvin Klein, Zac Posen, and Lilly Pulitzer).

Scorpio doesn't merely have her finger on the pulse—she *is* the pulse. The Scorpio girl doesn't let the trends define her. Instead, she sets her own. While it may *seem* like Scorpio is putting it all out on the table (cue Scorpios Willow "Whip My Hair" Smith and rebellious rock-royal Kelly Osbourne), don't be fooled. This girl is strategic about what she exposes. Her fearless expression is both Scorpio's shield and her sword.

An abrasive or intimidating front protects Scorpio's vulnerable heart, which lies beneath the barbed wire. Deep down, she's incredibly sensitive and compassionate and takes rejection like a stab to the heart. As the sign of power and control, she's reluctant to show her "weak" spots. She may have just one or two close friends—and she even remains a mystery to them. Getting this girl to show her feelings isn't easy. However, when the emotions emerge, watch out. The storm can be fierce!

Scorpio is the sign of focus, and when she's in deep concentration, she's impenetrable. Scorpio can be silent, but she is never submissive. The wheels are always turning in that little head of hers. Even when she works behind the scenes, Scorpio's influence reaches far. *Vogue*'s Anna Wintour and *Sassy* creator Jane Pratt, both Scorpios, inspired cult followings with their magazines. No surprise: exclusive Scorpios like to know who's "us" and who's "them" and can roll as tight as any Mafia ring. (Wintour's Met gala is reportedly harder to get into than Fort Knox.)

Because Scorpio is so easily threatened, you might need to monitor your daughter for any bullying tendencies. She can also end up on the social sidelines because she's such a closed book—or an intense personality that doesn't mesh with the masses. For the CliffsNotes, just watch any movie starring Scorpio Winona Ryder. *Beetlejuice* and *Reality Bites* will help you understand your Scorpio daughter's indie/gothic side. For a primer on Scorpio's cunning streak, watch the black comedy *Heathers*, where Ryder plays a Scorpio-like geek-turned-popular girl who avenges the clique leaders and has the last laugh.

That, in a nutshell, is Scorpio. Even when she's an insider, Scorpio is always an outsider. She might form short-term alliances with the petite elite, but only Scorpio's true-blue homies share her boundless depth and devotion. That concentrated, hawklike energy can take her far, so help her channel it for good. She didn't come to this planet to mess around! There's work to do.

BEHAVIOR DECODER: THE SCORPIO KID

WHEN SCORPIO . . .	IT MEANS . . .	SO YOU SHOULD . . .
Cries	Intense feelings have been stirred and Scorpio is overwhelmed.	Talk to Scorpio right away. Festering feelings quickly build up into a volcanic explosion. Scorpio is never really upset about what she says she's upset about, so get to the core issue and address that.
Withdraws socially or gets quiet or moody	Intense Scorpio craves privacy and needs to retreat within herself, especially after being "on" or around people a lot. However, Scorpio could be brooding about something, too.	Touch base and take an emotional temperature reading. If all is good, just let Scorpio do her thing!

CONTINUED ON NEXT PAGE

WHEN SCORPIO . . .	IT MEANS . . .	SO YOU SHOULD . . .
Acts out (hitting, kicking, talking back)	Turf war! Someone has messed with Scorpio's property or gotten in the way of Scorpio on a mission. This is Scorpio's way of "peeing on his fire hydrant" and establishing his dominion.	Time-out chair! Scorpio needs to reel in the emotions. Give him a pillow to punch or send him out for physical activity where he can safely release the rage.
Gets clingy	Scorpio feels vulnerable and threatened by a new environment.	Gently help him feel at ease and secure. Don't push Scorpio to let go before he's ready.
Won't eat what you serve	Sensitive Scorpio is incredibly detail-driven and may be picking up on a subtle flavor or ingredient that doesn't agree with her palate. Or the dinner table may not be a relaxing space for Scorpio.	Change up the recipe, or ask Scorpio to describe in detail what she doesn't like. Observe the meal environment. Is it rushed or fraught with stress? Scorpio may be absorbing those emotions. Make meals calm times to connect and bond, and Scorpio could "mysteriously" regain her appetite.
Can't sit still	Scorpio is bored. He needs something that can truly absorb his attention.	Channel Scorpio's attention into a worthy outlet—intricate toys and games to take apart and put back together, puzzles and problem solving, or pop-up books that consume Scorpio's full attention.

THE SOCIAL SCORPIO

*

ROLE IN THE FAMILY

Children can bring the family together, and Scorpios are often the "binding ingredients" of their clans. Has everyone gotten scattered and too busy with their own lives? Scorpios give their families a focal point, for good and for bad. With their high vibration and magnetism, people just want to be around them! Scorpio is the sign that rules reincarnation, and these children are often born after a significant family member has passed away. Since Scorpio is so astute, you might get the sense that she's a little messenger sent over from your departed loved one as if to say, "I'm okay here."

FRIENDS AND PEERS

Trust isn't something that Scorpios hand out like Halloween candy. Anyone they consider a friend must pass a battery of loyalty tests or penetrate Scorpio's thick armor. Rule number one: any friend of Scorpio must keep her secrets . . . or else! Once someone makes it past those maximum-security emotional gates, it's a life sentence. Sensitive Scorpios usually have one or two enduring best friends, and these are the few people in whom they confide. Scorpios can be amazing listeners who remember everything their friends tell them. Betrayal devastates little Scorpios, who never quite grasp the ever-shifting loyalties of children. With their indelible memories, Scorpios never forget a slight—which is why they're reluctant to trust in the first place.

Although Scorpios can be loud and showy in the hallways, even bragging obnoxiously, it's often a defense to cover vulnerability. As the sign of power, Scorpios are competitive and aware of hierarchy (hence, beware of those bullying tendencies). Still, fitting in or becoming student council president is never Scorpio's goal. Not that most Scorpios would mind taking over the school. However, they prefer to rule based on merit, not popularity—displaying an incredible talent or earning awards for their grades and academic achievements.

Scorpio kids are not big "joiners," nor will they shamelessly court the spotlight. They'll just quietly resonate at their own vibration, making everyone wonder, *Who's that girl or guy?* If they do become part of a group or club, it's often a fringe or slightly geeky one, such as fencing, debate, A/V, cooking, or even a group they invent themselves. Scorpios are not mild-mannered kids who blend into the crowd—they tend to have strong passions, with personalities to match. Among peers, Scorpios might be an acquired taste, their intensity serving as a screening device. Scorpios don't mind. At least they know who their real friends are.

BROTHERS AND SISTERS: SCORPIO AS A SIBLING

Possessive Scorpios will either be extremely close with their siblings or they'll feel like their personal space is at constant threat of invasion. This sign is territorial, so sharing a bedroom, toys, and other "marked" turf can be a rocky path. However, if Scorpios consider a brother or sister *their* property, all is fine—at least until the other kid wants breathing room!

As an older sibling, Scorpio might keep the little one close and under his control, molding and shaping a miniature minion to do his bidding. Once the younger child forms an identity and wants to break away, tension can erupt (cue the Lesley Gore song "You Don't Own Me"). Scorpio is the sign of bonding and may feel betrayed or abandoned by the normal separation process that happens among brothers and sisters. You might need to encourage Scorpio to form friendships outside the family.

Younger Scorpios have a habit of taking over, well, anything they want. They could anger their older siblings when they make a land grab for the elder's friends and toys. Jealousy can also be an issue if littlest Scorpio feels left out or overlooked. And hell hath no fury like a Scorpio sister or brother scorned—their revenge can be cruel and calculating, striking a sensitive spot or icing the other child out. You've not witnessed sibling rivalry until you've seen a bullying Scorpio in action. Prepare to intervene firmly and quickly before things get ugly.

DISCIPLINING A SCORPIO

*

Scorpios remember every rule you tell them, but that doesn't necessarily mean they'll obey. Power struggles can be common with this sign. Here's a kid who will look you dead in the eye and openly challenge you. Whoa! When Scorpio tries to outsize you, you'll need to grow a couple inches (or a metaphorical "pair") to let Scorpio know who the real boss is here. Never back down with Scorpio, or you'll regret it for the rest of your life. Take a loving but firm approach that respects Scorpio's intelligence. Don't sugarcoat, either, because Scorpios can read between the lines. Get to the point and make yourself *very* clear.

Remember, though, that sensitive Scorpio is a deeply emotional sign. These kids are thin-skinned under any bluster or bravado. You must choose your words and actions carefully with this unforgiving sign. Unless you want to hear about that spanking you gave Scorpio twenty years ago for the rest of your life, spare the rod—and the rage.

Scorpio is the sign of control, so these kids hate surprises. Rather than constantly try to wrangle them, let systematic Scorpios be privy to the inner workings of their rules and schedules, and they may become self-discliplining. Our friend Abby, the mom of a Scorpio, keeps a large poster-board chart of her son Henry's daily activities—bath, lullaby, story, nap time—at his eye level. Henry can visit the chart anytime, giving him the sense that he's participating in his own routine. The methodical Scorpio brain likes puzzles and patterns, so work with their natural strengths.

Some Scorpio children never act out, but that could be a different cause for concern. Since this deeply private sign doesn't always express feelings, your Scorpio could be bottling up emotions like a dormant volcano. This could lead to depression later, so watch that ticking time bomb. Perhaps intuitive Scorpio senses that you're stressed, distracted, or unavailable and doesn't want to upset you. Or maybe it's a case of "once bitten, twice shy" and Scorpio fears your wrath after an episode of harsh discipline. Be careful not to give Scorpios a polarized sense of being "bad" and "good" when you correct their behavior. Remember the adage "Criticize the action, not the person." And if you find yourself on the verge of a meltdown that will lead to regrettable ranting or losing your cool around little Scorpio, it's time to get more support—even to delegate some caregiving. Keeping yourself sane and balanced is good for everyone involved, so don't skimp on the "me time"—especially since intense Scorpios can absorb so much of your attention and energy. Scorpios' emotional security must be preserved at all costs.

HANDLING TRANSITIONS: MOVING, DIVORCE, DEATH, AND OTHER TOUGH STUFF

*

Scorpio is the sign that rules life cycles: birth, death, and renewal. In some ways, your Scorpio might be eerily calm about a loved one's passing or perhaps will even have clairvoyant dreams after a loss. Mystical Scorpios may seek answers in reincarnation stories or by asking you about life after death. If there's a divorce in the family, intuitive Scorpio may already have picked up on the discordant vibes long ago.

Just because Scorpios know something's up, that doesn't mean they can handle it. Despite their old souls, Scorpios are emotionally fragile and their scar tissue never fully heals. These kids are deeply affected by a broken bond, especially if it means leaving a secure home or school abruptly. Scorpios take a long time to warm up in new situations, so the thought of starting over can be terrifying for them. They may begin to act out with aggressive behavior, a way of exorcising their intense emotions. Or these kids could turn inward. Tune in: your quiet little Scorpio might be private about grief or struggle. Still waters run deep, so it could be wise to put Scorpios in therapy to ease a transition, even if they don't show signs of distress.

SCHOOL'S IN SESSION

*

BEST EDUCATION STYLE

Focused Scorpios can be excellent students who rise to the top of their classes. Their attention spans can stretch longer than other children's, and since Scorpios have steel-trap minds, they tend to do well on rote memorization tests. Scorpios are the zodiac's specialists and may thrive in one or two specific subjects, moving on to an accelerated track for, say, science or composition. Your child's "one-track mind" might actually serve her well one day.

Scorpio rules research and these kids can be gifted at discerning patterns, quickly grasping the inner workings of a complex concept. For this reason, they may excel at math, computer science, programming, or languages (verb conjugations, anyone?). Later, you might find Scorpio behind the scenes as publisher of the school newspaper or running the lights for the theater production. From a young age, many Scorpios know what they want to be when they grow up. These kids can be very type A in pursuit of those goals. Summer science camp, studying abroad in high school, music, or acting intensives will put Scorpio on the fast track or give them the inside knowledge this sign craves.

Private schools can be a great fit for Scorpios, since they feel safe in smaller environments with a lower teacher-to-student ratio. These children thrive with as much one-on-one attention as possible. Scorpios can easily get lost in the vast halls of a public school, where they're treated like just another number or standardized test score. Many Scorpios dislike being forced to raise their hands or speak in front of a large classroom. In the security of a small school where everyone is more like a family, Scorpio's talents and charisma can shine.

BEST HOBBIES AND ACTIVITIES

Passionate Scorpios have boundless creativity and will dive deep into their interests. These are no mere dabblers: all-or-nothing Scorpios are supergeeks, fanboys, and rabid enthusiasts. They enjoy hobbies that require concentration and fine attention to detail—preferably ones they can do alone or with only one or two other people. These kids are often serious homebodies, preferring to lounge solo and read, watch TV, or hang out with family.

Scorpios can be musical (it's all about patterns, which is their sweet spot) and could play instruments or sing in the choir. Physical Scorpios can be amazingly flexible and even acrobatic, too, excelling in dance, gymnastics, cheerleading, or martial arts. They might even be early adopters of yoga, joining you on the mat or for a little meditation. Not a bad idea, since this could help diffuse some of Scorpio's intensity.

Other Scorpios are more limber in the intellectual department, getting absorbed for hours in puzzles, crosswords, strategy games, and multiplayer competitions on their computers. They might teach themselves computer programming or make their own beats on a laptop (DJ equipment, anyone?). Since this sign loves mysteries, Scorpios could have a collection of Agatha Christie books or quirky graphic novels. They could also be fascinated by the paranormal and sleight of hand. Get this kid a magic set or a deck of tarot cards. Or let them funnel their focus into crafts. Our Scorpio friend Debbie Stoller sparked an international knitting craze with her Stitch 'n Bitch series. Bonus: zoning out in handwork like crochet, sewing, or DIY projects can relax this overwrought sign.

GIFT GUIDE: BEST PRESENTS FOR SCORPIO

* Crafting or DIY supplies, such as a tie-dye kit, an ice-cream maker, or an elaborate train set that Scorpio has to construct and even decorate—handy Scorpios like to make things from scratch and personalize everything
* Musical instruments, DJ equipment, a karaoke machine
* Diary/journal—with a lock, of course
* Books in the genres of mystery, fantasy, and suspense—especially series such as Harry Potter, Beautiful Creatures, or the Hunger Games (Scorpio will devour them all!)
* Puzzles, crosswords, Sudoko, or any strategy game (chess, Battleship, Clue)
* Tickets to see anything Scorpio loves (hello, little superfan)
* Anything that lets Scorpio peer behind the scenes: detective kits, doctor's bags, chemistry sets, microscopes, or telescopes

THE SAGITTARIUS CHILD

(November 22–December 21)

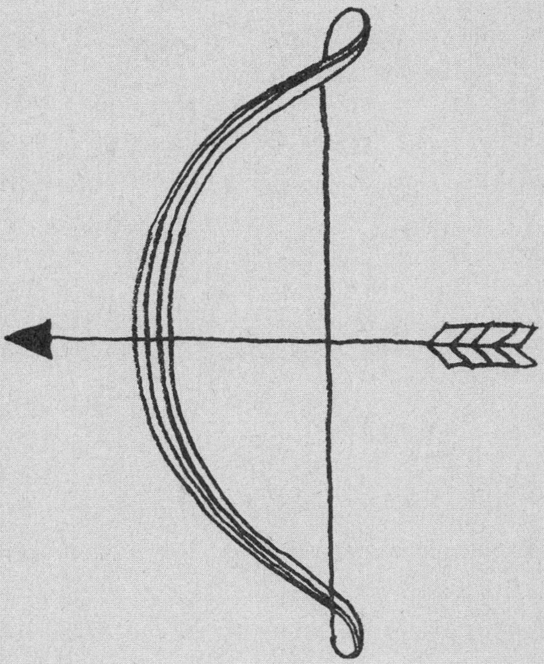

SYMBOL: The Archer/Centaur

COSMIC RULER: Jupiter

ELEMENT: Fire

BODY PART: Hips, thighs

GEMSTONE: Turquoise

COLOR: Purple

GOOD DAY: Wise and insightful
Funny
Free-spirited
Determined
Open-minded

BAD DAY: Blunt or rude
Scattered
Stubborn
Overconfident
Hyperactive

LIKES: New adventures
Vacations and travel
Playing outdoors
Learning and reading
Friends of many backgrounds
Doing things his way
Getting absorbed by a creative project that interests him

DISLIKES: Being told what to do
Sitting still
Following someone else's rules and agenda
Being cooped up indoors
Too much routine or sameness
Uptight or authoritarian people
Boredom and having nothing to do

* SO, YOU WANT TO HAVE A SAGITTARIUS? *

Target Conception Dates for a Sagittarius Child: **February 25–March 15**

FAMOUS SAGITTARIUS KIDS, PAST AND PRESENT

*

Jaleel White, Britney Spears, Christina Aguilera, Pax Jolie-Pitt, Mason Disick, Alyssa Milano, Zoe Kravitz, Vanessa Hudgens, Miley Cyrus, Christina Applegate, Raven-Symoné, Frankie Muniz, Violet Affleck, Taylor Swift, Mayim Bialik

PARENTING YOUR SAGITTARIUS CHILD: THE ESSENTIALS

*

Fasten your seat belt and prepare for adventure! You've just given birth to a dreamer *and* a doer. From babyhood on, this sign is on a quest for freedom—whether fidgeting in a car seat, ditching her diapers, or jailbreaking from a high chair. Sagittarius is a feisty fire sign with a huge appetite for life, the globetrotting Marco Polo of the zodiac. Sagittarians are smiley, happy kids, and many of your snapshots will feature your Sagittarius with an ear-to-ear grin. (Then there will be the occasional photo with an unabashed scowl, since this honest-to-a-fault sign can never hide his feelings.) While your Sagittarius child's lust for life won't leave you much time to put your feet up, there won't be a dull moment, either. These children are adventure seekers who love to laugh. They're the class clowns who keep the whole family entertained.

To fully grasp your Sagittarian child's nature, consider the Archer or Centaur that symbolizes this sign. Like the mythic half-human/half-horse creature, Sagittarius is both a lofty philosopher and a wild child. This sign is known to be clumsy, often tripping over their little "hooves" as they rush between activities, sponging up all the action. Keep your bags packed and carry a stash of snacks, because you could be running among playdates, lessons, and activities for hours. Ruled by abundant Jupiter, this sign wants more, more, more. Hello, exhaustion!

Sagittarius is a strong sign, ruling the hips and thighs, and can have boundless physical energy. These kids are highly active, even athletic. Kiss your couch potato days good-bye, because Sagittarius will want to spend hours in the great outdoors, biking, climbing, running around, and playing sports at the park.

Sagittarius is also the zodiac's scholar. This sign is capable of grasping mature conversations and ideas at a young age. At times, these kids can even seem older than their years, talking and reading early. Keep your video cam at the ready to record their precocious and witty moments. Watch what you say around Sagittarians, too, because *nothing* gets past them. These kids will ask *why* a million times until they get a satisfactory answer. Born with sharp b.s. detectors, little Sags know when you're feeding them a phony line—and they'll call you on it. With strangers or casual friends, however, they can be so trusting that they veer into gullible terrain. There may be a few rude awakenings for little Sagittarians when they realize that not everyone's intentions are as pure as their own.

Sagittarius is the zodiac's truth speaker, and your child's honesty can definitely cut close to the bone. It's never mean-spirited, but Sagittarians are known for their trademark bluntness. Even their compliments can be accidentally backhanded: "Mommy, you really have a lot of friends for someone so bossy!" or "Wow, you know a lot of songs on the radio for an old person." Just when you thought you were hiding or covering up some unfavorable trait, Sagittarius will point it out. Talk about a cure for embarrassment—you'll have to give up self-consciousness to survive with this kid around.

Hoping for a child you could hug and cuddle? Better start cooking up a sibling. Wriggly Sagittarius isn't known for sitting still and will squirm out of your grasp or even wipe away your kisses. This independent sign doesn't want to be coddled beyond a certain point—they'd rather dazzle you with their feats and wit and be showered with genuine compliments for that. The best way to show a Sagittarius your love is by laughing at their jokes and applauding their audacity.

If your family is part of a long legacy—for example, they've lived or summered in the same town for generations—prepare for Sagittarius to break the mold. As global ambassadors, Sagittarius kids itch to leave city limits and see the rest of the world. Traditions are followed on an à la carte basis, so don't pin your hopes on Sagittarius keeping all the family customs alive—at least, not without adding an original twist. The karmic role of cross-cultural Sagittarius is to spice things up by introducing new ideas, not cleaving to the same-old same-old. They're curious about people from different backgrounds; they might even want to learn another language or travel abroad as high school exchange students. Your Sag could ask for a passport before she even gets a driver's license!

Sagittarius is ruled by jovial Jupiter, the merry god of the feast, and these kids have hearty appetites. They can even be built a little stockier or put on weight easily, so a few lessons in healthy body image and self-acceptance will probably be in order. You might also need to teach your Sag how to fill up on healthy snacks instead of junk. This sign *will* belly up to the buffet for second and third helpings and might choose sugary and starchy foods just for a quick feeling of fullness. Add creative salads as a side dish, or jazz up plain veggies for Sag's worldly palate with Thai, Mediterranean, Indian, and Moroccan spices. Sometimes what Sagittarius kids mistake for hunger is really just a craving for more exciting flavor. You might need to go around the world in eighty dishes before Sagittarius discovers a regional cooking style or two that he really loves.

The Sagittarius appetite for life is just as healthy. Amateur anthropologists, Sagittarius tests limits out of sheer curiosity. *No* and *enough* are not in this kid's vocabulary. When Sag hears "You can't . . ." it's not the end of the story but rather an opportunity to creatively prove that he indeed *can*. Telling these kids it's impossible or can't be done will only fuel them onward. Walt Disney and Steven Spielberg were both born under this larger-than-life sign. The Sagittarius motto: "Go big or go home."

Attention, helicopter parents: park those propellers. Your little Archer *will* stumble and misstep many times, and there may be a few injuries along the way. It's bound to happen when they put their hands in so many cookie jars (and on the occasional hot stove). Yet no sign bounces back quite like resilient Sagittarius. The young Archer can be impatient, stubborn, and pulled in too many directions, but when this sign sets her mind on getting something, she's unstoppable. Much like the Archer shooting arrow after arrow until he hits his target, your Sag child will aim for his goals until he reaches them. Hurry up and put your shoes on, Mommy—Sagittarius is already out the door.

SAGITTARIUS: HOW THEY DEAL WITH . . .

*

RULES AND AUTHORITY

Respect is a two-way street for Sagittarius. This kid will likely befriend grown-ups, talking to them like peers. If an authority figure respects him enough to speak to him like a capable human being, Sagittarius can be a model child. If Sagittarius senses condescension, dishonesty or iron-fisted autocracy, he will revolt. Feisty Sagittarius is an independent spirit who doesn't like to be fenced in. Rules weren't necessarily made to be broken, but for Sagittarius, they are subject to interpretation and should be followed on a case-by-case basis. For example, if bedtime is 8:00 p.m., Sagittarius will find a perfectly valid reason to extend it until 9:00, arguing his point so persuasively that most parents will cave. It's hard to stay mad at this upbeat sign for long, if only because they'll make a joke that cracks your stern demeanor. Oh, Sag! You're too much!

LIMITS

All boundaries are negotiable to Sagittarius. *No* is just a two-letter word she has to hear a few times until she gets to *yes*. Keep your wits about you, or your Sagittarius salesperson will convince you to change the rules—and even think it was your idea! You don't want to put excessive limits on this freedom-loving sign, because the Archer needs to explore. However, this kid's intrepid adventures often leave him dancing on the edge of danger. With inquisitive Sag, it helps if you take the time to explain why you set a specific limit, even discussing the possible perils associated with pushing the envelope (in slightly gory detail if you must). While you don't want to scare your Sagittarius, a newspaper story about a kidnapping or a fire started by someone's carelessness, for example, could be the last resort that makes her pay attention to safety.

SEPARATION AND INDEPENDENCE

Little Archers often take time to grow into their independent sides and can be downright shy in new situations when they're little. However, once young Sagittarius gets a taste of freedom, watch out! There's no retying those apron strings after they've been clipped.

YOUNGER SIBLINGS

Sagittarius may see younger siblings as a burden, especially if they feel saddled with the responsibility of looking after them. If the age difference is close enough, they can be perfect playmates and best friends. Otherwise, Sagittarius doesn't want to be tied down by a littler tyke.

OLDER SIBLINGS

Explorer Sagittarius always wants to be ten steps ahead, so an older sibling gives her a glimpse into the exciting world of big people. Hello, mini-tagalong. Still, Sagittarius will have his own independent interests and talents, so don't force this kid to do everything an older sister or brother does, or to wear hand-me-downs if he wants to cultivate his own style.

BYE-BYE, BABY: WEANING AND POTTY TRAINING

Sagittarius is in a hurry to be free but can hardly sit still. The motivation to be a big girl or big boy is there, but the self-discipline might not be. Sagittarius kids may lack the patience for potty training, so it could take a few extra tries before liftoff. Plus, once this sign gets busy playing, they often forget to use the bathroom . . . before it's too late. Keep a change of clothes handy.

SEXUALITY

Curious Sagittarius is full of questions and might ask a few blush-worthy ones so be prepared. But this honest-to-a-fault sign won't accept any lame stories about storks, so prepare to chat about the birds and bees pretty early.

LEARNING: SCHOOL, HOMEWORK, AND TEACHERS

As hyperactive as Sagittarius can be, this kid loves to learn. Sagittarius rules the zodiac's ninth house of higher learning and education and can be a gifted student. They especially love independent study projects and any chance to display their natural creativity.

HOUSEHOLD CONFLICT

Truth-teller Sagittarius isn't one to sweep things under the rug. However, when this action-oriented sign senses trouble brewing, he may rush to fix it, either mediating or taking control of the situation by jumping into the fray. In a dysfunctional family dynamic, Sagittarius would be most likely to take on the role of hero child. Little Archers can even get pushed aside if another sibling or family member is volatile or dominating and might even drift toward spending time at friends' and relatives' homes to avoid dramatic scenes.

THE SAGITTARIUS BOY

*

Unga-bunga! Your junior Tarzan swings from the vines, swooping from one thrilling adventure to the next. Catch him if you can: this restless boy has tons of physical (and mental) energy. Most of your parenting duties will consist of finding appropriate outlets for this force to be reckoned with. A varied schedule is a must, since the feisty Archer gets agitated when he's cooped up for too long. His true home may be the great outdoors, where he can run around and commune with nature, preferably shirtless. His Neanderthal leanings are cute when he's little, but you may have to forklift him into the bathtub when he comes home muddy and stained.

Hoping for a chip off the old block? You might not find your heir apparent in the Archer. Sagittarius marches to the beat of his own tribal drum. He prizes his individuality, so be careful not to pressure him to conform to a family mold. He's a leader, not a follower. Unafraid to voice a controversial opinion or diverge from the crowd, he's not going to carry on anyone's legacy but his own. Among his friends, the Sagittarius boy tells it like he sees it and might gain a reputation as rude for his straight-arrow remarks (a few lessons in tactfulness and manners won't hurt). As Sagittarius Bruce Lee once said, "Mistakes are always forgivable if one has the courage to admit them." Your Sag boy's friends and family might not completely agree.

While he might not be Mr. Popularity now, Sagittarius boys are often late bloomers who grow into their cuteness and charisma in their later teens. Sagittarius boys will have a range of friends, both male and female, who like to geek out over the same things that he does. Speaking of which, geek chic may have been perfected by the Sagittarius boy, who could take a few interesting style risks: vintage clothes, paisley shirts, suspenders, bow ties. Or he might just be more on the awkward side, preferring a uniform of well-worn T-shirts, jeans, hiking boots, and a jacket from his favorite outdoor sporting goods store. Mobility is important to this claustrophobic kid, and he may always look like he's about to head off on a camping or backpacking trip.

Your Sagittarius son could be athletic, excelling at sports that use his powerful leg strength. However, he might not care to commit to the grueling practice schedules of organized sports, which cut into his spontaneity. But hiking, bike rides, Frisbee, a pickup game of anything? He's in. When your Sagittarius is little, buckle him into a seat or trailer on the back of your bike and go. Of course, it won't be long before this restless kid demands a set of wheels for himself.

With his short attention span, the Sagittarius boy changes hobbies frequently, but once he finds an absorbing project, nothing can tear him away. You might eventually just let him skip dinner or dash from the table as soon as he's cleaned his plate. Better he should be editing his first documentary at age ten or building a tree fort from scratch than running the street with punks, right? Sagittarius is the Archer—the zodiac's hunter—and your boy needs a goal worthy of his pursuit.

While some supervision is essential for this untethered sign, Sagittarius boys need lots of independence, too. Forcing Sag to participate in too many structured activities—especially ones that involve sitting still through long dinners, plays, or religious services—will make him chafe. The Sagittarius boy is not a family guy in the typical sense, either; forced participation in family "moments" is not his thing. Sagittarius loves a barbecue or big gathering with his clan, especially if laughter, food, and revelry are involved—and he's allowed to roam free with the other kids. One mom of a Sagittarius realized the futility of trying to force her son to be traditional. "I let him add his own stamp to customs, like making a playlist for holidays or a funny birthday video that has some special meaning to it." Her curious son also likes to play cultural ambassador, so they celebrate as many different holidays as possible, trying out food and traditions from around the world and inviting friends from other backgrounds to their home for multiculti-potlucks. (Empanadas and latkes, anyone?)

Later in life, Sagittarius might become a devoted and dutiful son—but that all depends on how much rope you give him when he's young. If the Sagittarius boy feels suppressed or suffocated by his clan, he'll choose a ZIP code far away from yours when he turns eighteen. (Well, he might do that anyhow, but at least it won't be personal.) And if you have any hopes of meeting his future dates and partners, don't pry. The Sagittarius boy is downright repelled by the idea of you poking in his business. Don't go snooping in this kid's room or organizing his stuff or you'll break his trust. On the other hand, feel free to toss that mountain of dirty clothes in the laundry anytime. The outdoorsy Sagittarius boy loves to rough it—camping, touch football, biking—and might not notice how much of the, er, wilderness he's trekked back into your home.

THE SAGITTARIUS GIRL

*

Well, hello there, Miss Independent. The Sagittarius girl is a spitfire with strong opinions she'll fearlessly voice from a young age. This chatty Cathy can talk your ear off once she gets going! Your Sagittarius may even act like a little adult, comfortable and confident mingling with grown-ups. (One friend nicknamed her Sag daughter "Class President.") Showbiz can be her calling, as this girl has a real funny bone and loves to make everyone laugh. At times, the Sagittarius girl can be a little too much, exhausting everyone with her boundless energy and attention-grabbing antics. Get this girl a sold-out stadium, stat! No surprise, pop megastars Britney Spears, Christina Aguilera, Taylor Swift, and Miley Cyrus were all born under this sign.

In her early years, Sagittarius girls can be somewhat timid in public, perhaps even irrationally fearful of things like dogs or strangers. At home she may be a ham, but in new situations Sagittarius retreats until she feels totally comfortable. Fortunately, most Sagittarius girls shed this hesitation as they get older—especially when they find a talent or platform to express their bold personalities. These girls are leaders, and when they connect to a cause or discover their calling nothing can stop them. In fact, your daughter may be a young entrepreneur, turning her hobbies into profitable little cottage industries.

Sagittarians are girlie in some ways, tomboyish in others. They might play baseball on the street or ride bikes until sunset, then retire to a room decorated in hot pink and Hello Kitty. From early on, Sag girls could have a lot of male friends, since they tend to be active, outdoorsy, and straightforward—not exactly the "delicate flower" types. Among their female friends, Archers champion sisterhood and rail against gender bias. Girl power! This freedom-loving little feminist totally refuses to accept the notion that boys are any more capable, smarter, or stronger than she is.

The confident Sagittarius girl isn't scared to be ambitious or outspoken. If she's brainy, she's proud of her geek-chic cred. Her communication style can be masculine, and she might even express controversial opinions openly. Conservative pundit Ann Coulter is a Sagittarius, and so is child actress turned attachment parenting advocate and neuroscience PhD Mayim Bialik.

Precocious as Sagittarians can be, girls of this sign are emotional late bloomers. Much to their parents' relief, Sagittarius girls might not start dating as early as some of their friends. Physically, though, Sagittarians aren't as slow on the uptake, so don't let the apparent disinterest or naïveté fool you. Curious Sagittarius wants to know everything and anything about sex, and she makes it her business to find out, if only by reading up on it. Once she does start dating, her "coming of age" may be more experimental than you wish, so make sure she's armed and educated. If you don't teach your Sagittarius daughter the facts of life, she'll find 'em out herself. Fans were shocked when Miley Cyrus morphed from her mild-mannered Hannah Montana character to recording racy songs like "I Can't Be Tamed" and "twerking" away her squeaky-clean Disney Channel rep at the MTV 2013 VMAs. (These moments were reminiscent of a pigtailed teen Britney Spears seductively informing us, "I'm not that innocent.")

Your best bet is to keep your Sagittarius daughter savvy and well informed. Rather than shelter her, teach her critical thinking skills and media literacy from an early age so that she can make proper sense of the world she's so eager to experience. One friend allowed her Sagittarius daughter to dye a few strands of her hair pink and purple, recognizing the girl's strong need to express her personality. Give her enough room to be free but not so much independence that she gets into trouble. Cultivate leadership by involving your Sagittarius daughter in hobbies, arts, and programs that expose her to the wider world. A bored Sag can drift into trouble, but keep this girl busy and she'll build an empire.

BEHAVIOR DECODER: THE SAGITTARIUS KID

WHEN SAGITTARIUS . . .	IT MEANS . . .	SO YOU SHOULD . . .
Cries	Sagittarians are sensitive to criticism and your words have cut too deep or your reprimand was too harsh.	Take less of a stern tone. Give Sagittarius a hug and express some unconditional love. He didn't mean to upset you!
	You said no or set a limit, and Sag is upset. He wants more and feels frustrated that he can't have it.	Stick to your guns. Sagittarius will get over it. Divert his attention elsewhere.
Withdraws socially or gets quiet or moody	Sagittarius is tired or depleted. She needs to nap or lounge and reboot.	Hand her a book or a non-electronic toy and send her to relax in her room.
Acts out (hitting, kicking, talking back)	He's trying to express something and doesn't feel heard, so he needs to get your attention.	Sagittarians hate to be ignored; he needs you to listen *now*.
	Sag feels one-upped or overpowered. Someone has stolen his limelight.	Sit him down to talk it out and get to the root of what's upsetting him.

CONTINUED ON NEXT PAGE

WHEN SAGITTARIUS . . .	IT MEANS . . .	SO YOU SHOULD . . .
Gets clingy	He feels shy or awkward in a social situation.	You or someone else needs to introduce him to the other kids, helping him break the ice and warming him up to the scene. Have a friend or teacher give him a glowing intro—Sag wants to be known!
Won't eat what you serve	She may have gorged on snacks between meals. She may need you to make her try a bite, since she can jump to hasty conclusions.	Stock up on healthy snacks or send her out to play while you prepare dinner. Create a "no thank you" portion (i.e., at least one bite). Later let her participate in preparing and planning the menu.
Can't sit still	Typical day for a Sagittarius, who needs lots of hobbies, variety, and activities. Your antsy Archer could feel confined or claustrophobic, since this sign loves wide-open spaces.	Let him burn it off with a dance break or a five-minute wild spree. Your Sag might also be bored, so mix up the activities or give him a detailed project to absorb his attention.

THE SOCIAL SAGITTARIUS

ROLE IN THE FAMILY

Truth serum, anyone? Raising a Sagittarius can be like living with the paparazzi. These kids can and will expose all the family secrets, dirty laundry, and embarrassing mistakes you make—usually by accident. Don't try to make this outspoken kid into your coconspirator, because she will just blurt everything out. Oops! Your Sagittarius can even be confrontational if he senses injustice or that something is off, creating a dramatic scene. As the saying goes, though, you're only as sick as your secrets. The Archer's aim is not to cause trouble but rather to get everything out into the open for the greater good.

Astrological ambassadors, Sagittarius kids have diverse friends and interests. If your family is cautious or sheltered, Sagittarius breaks down the walls of your comfort zone. Prepare to see how the rest of the world lives. Your Sagittarius will have you sampling foods, cultures, and activities you never dreamed you'd try. Keep an open mind!

FRIENDS AND PEERS

Sagittarians are the zodiac's travelers, and they like to have friends from all walks of life. While Sagittarius will have a few lasting, loyal friendships, these kids are seekers who crave new people and experiences. Their best friends may rotate weekly. Since the Archer's interests span such a range, your child might have several friend groups: a theater crew, sports friends, a school newspaper geek squad. This adaptable kid can hang with diverse social circles and loves the variety. Their birthday parties can look like a UN summit!

Among close friends, Sagittarius needs a post of importance. These kids don't like to feel left out or sit on the sidelines—they want to be known for their talents and distinct personalities. Friends rely on Sagittarius to make them laugh or to introduce them to creative new activities and outings. If the group's energy starts to wane or a whiny Debbie Downer is dominating a playdate, Sagittarius will quickly step in and get everyone back to having fun.

Optimistic Sagittarius is born looking on the bright side and as a result can become the cheerleader among friends. If a playmate is upset, little Sagittarius will try to make him laugh or smile. Comic relief is this sign's specialty, though they may sometimes annoy friends by being *too* over the top. This wise-beyond-her-years sign can even become the go-to advice giver in her circle. However, don't lean on Sag for sympathetic hugs and coddling. Sagittarians can be blunt, with little patience for crocodile tears or friends who play the victim. "Don't sweat the small stuff" could be this sign's motto. (Of course, when *Sagittarius* is upset, it's a national crisis, but that's another story.)

Jealous or possessive friends will be shuffled into low-priority status, as loyalty tests and pettiness turn the Archer off. Watch for gossip, as Sagittarius kids can be judgmental and downright insensitive. Teach your foot-in-mouth kid to think before he speaks, and to try to walk a mile in other children's shoes.

BROTHERS AND SISTERS: SAGITTARIUS AS A SIBLING

Siblings are a mixed bag for little Sag, who enjoys the companionship but not the obligation. On good days, the Archer loves having a playmate and partner in crime—someone to join their adventures, to laugh with, and to share inside jokes. Other times, free-spirited Sagittarius doesn't feel like including a brother or sister in their plans and will resent having to do so. A poor little tagalong sib could be treated like persona non grata when Sagittarius isn't in the mood.

When push comes to shove, there's no greater ally than a Sagittarius, especially for a more tentative sibling. Sagittarius will deliver motivational speeches, inspiring sibs to think positively, try new things, and dream big. He can deliver tough love and unsolicited feedback at times, but it's all in the spirit of encouragement. However, you'll need to intervene if Sagittarius is getting too bossy or acting like he knows best. Teach Sag to "live and let live."

DISCIPLINING A SAGITTARIUS

*

Philosophical Sagittarius follows the spirit of the law but not necessarily the letter of it. "Because I said so" is not an adequate answer to this authority-testing sign. Sagittarius is famous for asking *why*, and if a rule feels too constraining the Archer will relentlessly attempt to overturn it or find a loophole. You may cave just because little Sagittarius has worn you down.

When your Sag is caught in a moral dilemma, talk it out. Sagittarius kids respond to the Socratic method: you ask them a series of thoughtful questions that help them arrive at their own answer. This kid feels most empowered when he discovers the ability to find his own creative solutions. It's not that Sagittarius kids want to get in trouble, but when they're curious about something they can't stop until their mission is complete. Author Mark Twain, creator of the impish Tom Sawyer and Huckleberry Finn characters, was a Sagittarius.

Sometimes experience is the best teacher for know-it-all Sagittarius, who often needs to learn things the hard way. If your lectures and lessons don't seem to be getting through, let Sagittarius hit a (gentle) rock bottom. It might take a little scare or shake-up for Sag kids to realize that you were right all along. Mark Twain famously quipped, "When I was a boy of 14, my father was so ignorant, I could hardly stand to have the old man around. But when I got to be 21, I was astonished at how much the old man had learned in seven years."

HANDLING TRANSITIONS: MOVING, DIVORCE, DEATH, AND OTHER TOUGH STUFF

*

Sagittarius kids have a lot to say, and while they are more adaptable than other signs they need to thoroughly understand the motives and reasons when change is sprung upon them. Honesty is the best policy with little Sag, who knows when you're giving them a party line. That's the equivalent of empty calories to them, and Sags won't be satisfied until they understand *why* something difficult has happened. Sit down and tell them the truth and also let Sagittarians express how they see things. They might just surprise you with their wisdom and thoughtfulness. You may need to explain mature subjects like sex, divorce, and death to this sign early or to stock your young Archer's library with informative, age-appropriate books that help her understand the harder facts of life.

SCHOOL'S IN SESSION

*

BEST EDUCATION STYLE

Paging the nerd crew! Inquisitive Sagittarius loves to learn and can be a voracious reader. When a subject or assignment grabs this kid's attention, Sagittarius is rapt. Taking directions or following an unchanging routine, however, can be a challenge for Sag. This impatient sign doesn't like to stay on any topic for too long. During "boring" lessons, Sagittarius might begin to doodle in the margins, or morph from wise to wisecracker. He'll play the class clown to milk his peers for laughs—and pass the time. This will either amuse or annoy his teachers to no end. But Sag usually redeems himself by raising his hand and asking an insightful question, proving that he was paying attention all along.

A school with an interactive curriculum and lots of creative, independent study projects can suit the Archer's temperament. Short attention span Sag needs to get up for a drink of water or a lap around the classroom—something traditional classrooms probably frown upon. In some cases, a gifted or accelerated program might be a good fit.

Sagittarians learns best when they can apply the material to their own lives or with interactive, play-based learning. Imagination and "edu-tainment" make the lessons stick. When they're older, they might want to learn another language or even do a study abroad exchange to experience another culture firsthand.

BEST HOBBIES AND ACTIVITIES

Ready, set, go! Energetic Sagittarius kids love to move around and would happily play outside from morning until sunset. Take them to swimming or skating lessons, or go horseback riding (the sign of the Centaur can have a special connection with horses). While many Sagittarians are natural athletes, they might not enjoy organized sports as much as just being active.

Outdoorsy Archers love nature, so rent a canoe or kayak, plan a fun hike (their powerful legs can handle the climb), or set up a huge trampoline in your backyard. When your Sagittarius is little, invest in a great bicycle seat and strap her in for an adventure. Whether it's on a nature trail or an urban commute, Sagittarius will enjoy the fresh air and changing vistas. Family vacations at an all-inclusive resort suit the Archer's need for variety—and friendship, as your social Sag becomes especially outgoing when organizing a game of beach volleyball or splashing in the kiddie pool with new friends.

Scouting, service work, and other acts of giving back help cultivate this sign's generous nature. It's a great way for your little cultural anthropologist to meet people from new backgrounds, too. A lively scout troop with camping and field trips will thrill this travel-loving sign, who is always eager for new experiences.

Sagittarius rules publishing and your little Archer may be eager to spread her message with a blog, a DIY magazine, or some creative writing project. From an early age, Sagittarius's scribbles or rhymes can turn into crudely bound books that she proudly displays on her shelf. A post on the school yearbook could keep your Sagittarius occupied and out of trouble when she's older. Sagittarius loves telling stories and performing, and could become a junior filmmaker the second you hand him a smartphone, recording witty observations or comedic shorts. An after-school class in digital video editing could pave the way for a career in media for this savvy sign.

GIFT GUIDE: BEST PRESENTS FOR SAGITTARIUS

* Karaoke machine for clowning around
* Climbing gyms, playhouses, or trampolines
* Outdoor equipment and camping/hiking gear
* A bicycle or scooter for getting places faster
* Colorful clothes and accessories, such as boots and backpacks

THE CAPRICORN CHILD

(December 22–January 19)

SYMBOL: The Goat

COSMIC RULER: Saturn

ELEMENT: Earth

BODY PART: Knees, skin, bones, teeth

GEMSTONE: Garnet

COLOR: Dark green, gray

GOOD DAY: Calm
Persistent
Grounded
Wise

BAD DAY: Narrow-minded
Perfectionist
Lazy or stagnant
Repressed

LIKES: A small group of loyal, lifelong friends
Long stories, legends, and elaborate plots
History and tradition
Music—of almost any genre
Structure
Trophies, medals, and other awards that confer status upon her
Being in charge
Name brands, expensive labels, and status symbols

DISLIKES: Huge crowds
Flighty, flaky, or indecisive people and people of "weak" character
Making mistakes and being unprepared
Outdoor sports: biking, hiking, and rock climbing
Doing anything without a larger goal or agenda
Being the center of attention unexpectedly
Asking for help

* SO, YOU WANT TO HAVE A CAPRICORN? *

Target Conception Dates for a Capricorn Child: **March 25–April 15**

FAMOUS CAPRICORN KIDS, PAST AND PRESENT

*

Jason Bateman, Blue Ivy Carter, Danny Pintauro, Gabby Douglas, Shawn Johnson, Zahara Jolie-Pitt, Joey McIntyre, Liam Hemsworth, Kate Bosworth, Aaliyah, Danica McKellar, Seraphina Affleck, Jodie Sweetin, Dustin Diamond, Eliza Dushku

PARENTING YOUR CAPRICORN CHILD: THE ESSENTIALS

*

Who's the parent here, anyway? Wise little Capricorns are old souls who lighten up later in life. They're ruled by taskmaster Saturn, the planet of ambition and maturity—not exactly the makings of a carefree, idyllic childhood! From a young age, Capricorns can be serious and determined, following a straightforward path. Once they make up their minds, they rarely deviate.

Capricorns' steely determination can be tough for parents to handle at times. These stubborn little Goats will dig in their hooves and never budge! Later their tenacity will pay off. Capricorns eventually reach their destinations, no matter how rocky the climb or numerous the setbacks. Capricorn Martin Luther King Jr. changed the world with his words "I have a dream." Of course, the dream is just the beginning for Capricorn. These master planners move quickly from vision to action. Why sit around and talk about it? As Capricorn Benjamin Franklin put it, "Well done is better than well said."

Franklin also said that "an ounce of prevention is worth a pound of cure." Truer words were never said, since Capricorns hate to be caught unprepared. These little workaholics need maps, plans, and objectives. "What's the point?" is their eternal question. Capricorns don't trust anything that comes too easily. These hard workers prefer to pay dues and earn their keep. They won't waste effort unless there's a big payoff at the end. This long-term focus can make Capricorns a little too results driven, though. Teach them to enjoy the process, celebrating milestones instead of just the grand hurrah. Living in the moment doesn't always come naturally to these kids

Silver spoon? Tuck it away in that heritage china cabinet. Spoiling Capricorns only brings out their worst, turning them into entitled little elitists. These kids can get incredibly lazy and stagnant when nothing is expected of them. They need a strong coach, mentor, or leader—someone who demands more of them than they do of themselves. If Capricorns don't have a goal worth getting out of bed for, they'd rather just sleep all day. Our Capricorn friend Kristi was the top violist in her school orchestra with little effort. Since nobody could challenge her, she soon lost interest and stopped practicing all together. When Capricorns reach the number-one spot, move them up to a new, championship-level league. Otherwise, their plateaus can take a sharp drop into lazybones terrain.

Just make sure your Capricorn's competitive spirit doesn't overtake her human spirit. Because Caps can be so hard driving and self-denying, they can form harsh judgments of other people, too. Talk-radio hosts Rush Limbaugh, Dr. Laura Schlesinger, and "shock jock" Howard Stern are all Capricorns. They may not share viewpoints, but they're all certainly opinionated. (And pretty unsympathetic to their fellow man at times. We've heard of tough love, but whoa, people!)

Stoic Saturn is the sign of duty and self-discipline, so this also fuels Capricorn's strident (and at times emotionally suppressed) nature. Of course, every reaction always has an equal and opposite reaction. The harder Capricorns try to be "good" and "normal," the more weirdness comes out. In fact, these kids may start to develop little OCD-like tics or hidden behaviors (lying, stealing, hoarding) if they don't take the pressure off. Capricorn Jim Carrey's edge-of-insanity antics probably stem from being so tightly wound. If your Capricorn starts to seem like a dormant volcano, intervene! (Cue Ben Franklin's wise words about an ounce of prevention . . .)

Teach Capricorns to embrace their humanity. As an earth sign, Capricorns are ruled by their senses; yet they can feel guilty and haunted by their desires. Rather than suppress their feelings, Capricorns need to balance between head and heart—and let themselves be human! Case in point: *Twilight* author Stephenie Meyer, a Capricorn, is a Mormon who eschews drinking and smoking. Her vampire love story was a glorified plug for virginity, with heroine Bella "saving" her moral (and mortal) virtue for marriage. Yet *Twilight* played a massive part in sparking global lust for the sexy undead, inspiring a string of paranormal copycats (involving werewolves and zombies) and even the *Fifty Shades of Grey* phenomenon. Mission *so* not accomplished.

Once they embrace their relationship to the physical world, Capricorns can become deeply mystical in an "earth wisdom" kind of way. It was Capricorn Isaac Newton who gave us the laws of gravity—and Capricorn J. R. R. Tolkien who took us deep into Middle Earth with his Hobbit series. The zodiac's Goats have vivid imaginations, coupled with a rich sense of history, ancestry, and lineage. Capricorns can be some of the best storytellers, with a flair for sequencing and plot. Just make sure they know that their adventures can be just as fulfilling in the everyday world, too. Life is a journey, not a destination!

CAPRICORN: HOW THEY DEAL WITH . . .

RULES AND AUTHORITY

Capricorn is ruled by authoritarian Saturn, giving these kids a strong need for structure. They want to know the rules, spelled out in black and white, and become anxious when they break them. Traditional Capricorns don't mind hierarchy; in fact, they crave it. Respectful parent–child boundaries help these security-minded kids feel safe. Without them, Capricorns often become "their parents' parent," stepping into adult roles and responsibilities before their time.

LIMITS

Capricorns appreciate limits, but maybe a little *too* much. Kids of this sign can be "good little soldiers" for fear of getting in trouble or upsetting their parents and role models. Their fear of making mistakes and coloring outside the lines can be paralyzing for them. You might need to encourage your Capricorn to take a few *more* risks. Help him understand that it's okay to occasionally follow the spirit of the law, not just the letter of it. Otherwise, his fears and anxieties can get the better of him. Or his repressed self-expression can come out in strange quirks and awkward behaviors.

SEPARATION AND INDEPENDENCE

Dutiful Capricorn is the sign of history, and Goats feel a strong family allegiance. These little worriers will try to take care of *you*—and might be afraid of hurting your feelings if they venture off on their own. Hide your teary eyes at back-to-school drop-off, or Capricorn might interpret your sentiment as sadness, somehow thinking that they've done something to make you cry. If your Cap is struggling to separate from you, bring her around a small and consistent group—such as an intimate home day care or a loving babysitter. Because Capricorn is an earth sign, these kids are greatly reassured by touch and physical presence. Give them time to form enduring bonds with a couple of friends and a caregiver, and they'll be fine.

YOUNGER SIBLINGS

Mini-moms and diminutive dads, Capricorns adopt a parental role with their little siblings. They take pride in their job as role models, protecting a younger brother or sister and setting a good example.

OLDER SIBLINGS

Most Capricorns look up to their older siblings, even putting them on a pedestal. If that sibling gets into trouble or follows a path Capricorn disapproves of, he might judge, maybe even harshly, but will usually keep opinions to himself. This sign is a hard-core realist and tends to accept most human behavior with a bemused shrug—and at most a wry remark. "It is what it is" could be the Capricorn motto. If an older brother or sister falls from grace, Capricorns may distance themselves a bit. However, if a sibling is in need, loyal Capricorns won't turn their backs on family. Blood is always thicker than water!

BYE-BYE, BABY: WEANING AND POTTY TRAINING

Shiny gold star, anyone? This overachieving sign responds to incentives and enjoys a challenge. The lofty goal of moving from diapers to the potty could be an exciting conquest for Capricorn. Persistence is one of this sign's virtues, so Capricorns may try and try again until getting the hang of it. Just make sure they don't feel pressured to be perfect—these kids can be hard on themselves, leaving no room for mistakes. Let them know that accidents happen—literally! As for weaning, Capricorn is a sensual earth sign and might not be too eager to break the physical connection with mama (or even a pacifier). The best bet is to transition these creatures of habit into a new pattern they enjoy—perhaps a special bubble bath with washable crayons during the time you'd normally nurse them. Don't underestimate the power of an incentive program for these achievers. A reward for being a big boy or big girl—even a special party or ceremony—could convince Capricorn to make the leap.

SEXUALITY

As the sign of repression, Capricorns could be embarrassed by any talk of sex—at least, when it comes from an adult. However, Capricorn is a sensory earth sign, so understanding the body (and its impulse for pleasure) is important to them. They can either squirm or just be totally cool about it—it's natural, after all. These kids are "touchers," so there could be some, er, hands-on exploration when they're little. Teaching Caps about the birds and bees? Give 'em the facts, all the way down to proper names for body parts. Leave room for a few giggles!

LEARNING: SCHOOL, HOMEWORK, AND TEACHERS

Ambitious Capricorns can be high achievers, but their success often depends on who leads them. If teachers are blasé or classes are too easy, Capricorns can become lazy or disenfranchised. After all, why strive for excellence when (a) nobody cares or (b) they can ace this with their eyes closed? Capricorns are motivated by a worthy challenge, so educators must raise the bar high enough to inspire best performance from them. Believe in Capricorns and they'll believe in themselves. Prizes, trophies, scholarships, and elite memberships (Phi Beta Kappa, anyone?) can also motivate this honors-driven sign. Capricorns are goal-oriented, and they might know what they want to do with their lives from an early age. An aspiring young astrophysicist might blow off her French homework, for example (unless it affects her grade point average).

HOUSEHOLD CONFLICT

Cappy to the rescue! These heroic kids are the patient peacemakers who calm the warring factions. Capricorns can be the voice of reason in an otherwise frenzied household. With their earthy composure, they can rise above the shouting or fighting, helping charged-up family members cool down. If they can't restore everyone's sanity, they might just wash their hands of the whole thing, disappearing into their own little worlds or even creating an alternate reality as a means of escape. Caution: your Capricorn may swallow anger or bury feelings inside. Repression can lead to depression, so make sure Capricorn isn't burdened with being the one who has to hold it all together.

THE CAPRICORN BOY

*

Hello, Mr. Man-Child. Capricorn is the sign of masculinity and fatherhood, and from an early age, your little Cap may have a paternal way about him. At home, he's mommy's little helper, forever wanting to please and serve you. With dad, he's a chip off the old block in best cases or in fervent search of a strong male role model otherwise. Quietly loyal, he sticks with a small "band of brothers" for life. Many of these guys look up to Capricorn, and he takes the responsibility seriously. Being a young man of honor and integrity is important to this kid. His word is his bond!

The Capricorn boy may play quietly, drawing, constructing LEGO towers, uttering few words. Don't mistake him for humorless, though. Just when Capricorn seems incurably stoic, he delivers a flawless zinger, a dead-on impersonation, or a booming laugh. "My teenage daughter was acting all dramatic, ranting on and on, while my Capricorn son was sitting quietly in the corner, playing with his phone," says one mom. "I figured he was tuning out everything, until he looked up, crossed his eyes, and repeated something she said in such a funny way that all of us—including her—just cracked up. The whole mood changed after that!" Capricorn might sometimes take his goals, and himself, way too seriously, but when he sees someone else getting all wound up, he's suddenly able to see the big picture. In fact, Capricorn could become the go-to advice guy among friends and siblings, bottom-lining their issues and getting them to lighten up (if only he could do that for himself . . .).

Since Capricorn rules the teeth, jaw, and bone structure, boys of this sign might look ripped straight from the Marvel Comics pages: chin cleft, chiseled jawline, superhero smile.

This kid can disarm you just by flashing his pearly whites! Like Capricorns Elvis Presley, Denzel Washington, and Bradley Cooper, Capricorn guys often have strong, classically handsome features. Other Capricorn boys can be tall and gangly with hollowed-out cheekbones, and long, serious faces. They might have thick lashes and creamy skin, almost like little woodland creatures. Think of the mythical man-goat (satyr) Pan playing his flute, and there you have it.

Speaking of satyrs, in mythology these randy little goats were fond of revelry. Indeed, the Capricorn boy can swing from self-denial into pure hedonism. On the one hand, Capricorn is ruled by Saturn, planet of restriction and repression. But as an earth sign, Capricorn's physical and material desires drive him, too. He loves his earthly pleasures! This is the teenage boy who will want to earn money to buy himself a nice car or bike—and for whom you should probably stash some "no questions asked" condoms.

The epic hero's journey from boy to man is a major deal for Capricorn guys. Essentially, this process requires a male to leave his comfort zone and face the unknown—struggling against challenges, temptations, and obstacles in order to find his true nature. In fact, the men's movement—the "dudes beating drums on the mountaintop" group that rallied men to reclaim their masculinity—was founded by Capricorn Robert Bly. The movement was Bly's response to his belief that our modern world has "feminized" males.

From early on, your Capricorn might want to try things that seem out of his league. And he'll usually persist until he gets it right, no matter how many tries it takes! His motto could be "Winners never quit, and quitters never win." The hero's journey, after all, is about persevering in the face of obstacles—and that's what Capricorn is all about.

The Capricorn boy manages to instigate trouble *and* keep his hands clean at the same time. He plays the role of amused bystander while his "crazy" friends act up. Even in *The Hangover*, Capricorn Bradley Cooper's character epitomized his sign, playing a groomsman who was somehow at the center of every caper. Indeed, Capricorns have often been the former golden boys defamed by public scandals: Richard Nixon with Watergate, Tiger Woods with his mistresses, Mel Gibson with his drunken, bigoted rants. Yikes! These are extreme examples of what can happen when Capricorns become imprisoned by their own legacies and weighty responsibilities.

A part of Capricorn aches to break out of his "good guy" persona. As author Margaret Mitchell said, "Until you've lost your reputation, you never realize what a burden it was." Well, when a Capricorn boy liberates himself—even through trouble—watch out! There's no putting that genie back in the bottle. You could get the likes of Capricorns David Bowie and Marilyn Manson or some other alter-ego version of Capricorn unchained.

One of your biggest jobs with a Capricorn boy is helping him let loose. Even if he's an academic genius or a champion athlete, give him the freedom to just be a kid once in a while. Capricorns can be incredibly artistic, musical, and imaginative. Give him space to play, express his talents, and enjoy life. Still, know that the Capricorn boy ultimately longs for self-sufficiency. He may take a summer job years before his friends do or find ways to earn his own pocket money.

It's fine—actually, it's great—to give a Capricorn boy chores. This is the zodiac's "provider" sign, and he will enjoy contributing to the household. Without some measure of responsibility, he can become insufferably entitled. He enjoys the finer privileges that life can offer, but it's best if he plays a role in earning them. Coddling Capricorn is a disservice to both you and him, because if you do everything for him he never develops the self-sufficiency that helps him become a great provider. As one of the zodiac's three stable earth signs, he can get inert unless he's given a worthy challenge and a push to be productive. So kiss some of his boo-boos but not all. Teach him that real men *do* cry, but they don't whine. Then send him off on his Hero's Journey: The Junior Edition.

THE CAPRICORN GIRL

*

Pack away the tutus. If you dreamed of putting bows and sparkles on a delicate little creature, get yourself a teacup Yorkie. Capricorn is the sign of masculinity, and this ain't no girlie girl. Loyal, ambitious, and strong, she's the son you always wanted . . . only prettier.

Even a feminine Capricorn is more like a countess than a princess. She prefers panache to flash. (For further study, see Capricorns Michelle Obama and Duchess Kate.) Capricorn is the sign of sophistication, and this girl can have great taste from an early age. Like Capricorns Kate Moss, Sienna Miller, and Christy Turlington, she's got a fresh, earthy elegance. Natural does the trick for the zodiac's minimalist. Or, like Capricorn Melanie "Sporty Spice" Chisholm, she could be a jock who prefers her team uniforms to regular clothes!

Capricorn is the sign of achievement and status. Since unspoken "girl code" dictates a flat, democratic playing field, Capricorns could have more guy friends than female ones. This girl might follow the words of Capricorn comic Steve Harvey and "act like a lady, think like a man." She's not afraid to openly compete or show her strength. Capricorn won't obnoxiously toot her own horn, but if credit is due she will take it. And why not? Modesty is overrated, especially when she's worked hard to earn her stripes.

Capricorn's resilience is a virtue, but make sure this girl has fun, too. Happy-go-lucky as she might seem, the worrisome Capricorn girl carries the weight of the world on her shoulders.

She can be a perfectionist who drives herself mercilessly, and at times she can be incredibly hard on herself. Loyal to her clan, she may spend her free time with parents or other adults rather than playing with peers. Deep down, she might not even relate to kids her own age. Capricorns are old when they're young, and young when they're old—like vibrant octogenarian Caps Betty White and Eartha Kitt.

Winter storm alert! Your Capricorn girl might be quiet at times, but her willpower and determination are intense. You'll feel her forceful nature whether she's communicating through stony silence or a blustery bellow. Perhaps entering the world during December and January, when the ground is frozen and the trees are bare, gives Capricorns a stronger survival instinct. Hale and hearty is fine, but Capricorn girls can also be domineering. At times, you'll need to push back, establishing yourself as a capable authority figure. Weak and wishy-washy parents will have to up their game. Capricorn needs her mama to be a powerful female role model. Otherwise, she'll step in and try to run the show.

Although she keeps a lot inside, the Capricorn girl can have a serious set of pipes. When she opens her mouth, prepare for impact. She can be a girl of many words! Public speaking and music can be powerful platforms for Capricorn girls. Dolly Parton, Donna Summer, and Mary J. Blige (respectively known as the Queens of Country, Disco, and Hip-Hop Soul) were all born under this zodiac sign.

With her impeccable timing, she might also channel her intensity into comedy. Capricorn girls can be masters at deadpan humor, delivering their zingers with an unflinching poker face. The list of Capricorn funny girls is endless: Kirstie Alley, Zooey Deschanel, Diane Keaton, and Julia Louis-Dreyfus. Coincidentally, both Deschanel and Louis-Dreyfus played the lone girl allowed into the boys' club (on *The New Girl* and *Seinfeld*). Talk about art imitating life—at least for this zodiac sign!

If anything, Capricorn girls might need a touch of sensitivity training. Even if they never fully embrace the feminine or froufrou, they could probably stand to soften up—on other people *and* themselves. Remind your Capricorn daughter that the years are long but the days are short. It's not just about getting that lifetime achievement award. Teach her to take things one day at a time, even as she plans for tomorrow.

BEHAVIOR DECODER: THE CAPRICORN KID

WHEN CAPRICORN . . .	IT MEANS . . .	SO YOU SHOULD . . .
Cries	Sensitive Capricorn can be a big crier when he's little, getting easily upset or scared.	Provide physical comfort: a reassuring hug or a hand on his back soothes the distress. He might be in actual physical pain, too, so check for boo-boos.
	If older than age four, something could be genuinely wrong, because this kid is not big on showing emotions.	Sit Capricorn down and find out what's really bugging him. It could take a little digging.
Withdraws socially or gets quiet or moody	Not much. Capricorn can be a kid of few words until she's comfortable. She might just be checking out the scene.	Let Capricorn be. When she has something to say, she'll say it!
Acts out (hitting, kicking, talking back)	Self-defense . . . or revenge! Capricorn is a physical sign and might not realize his own strength.	Give Capricorn a time-out and a firm, direct briefing on the rules. No fancy explanations—just "No hitting allowed." If behavior persists, increase their physical activity. Capricorn may have some pent-up energy and emotions to release. Get this kid a uniform, coach!
Gets clingy	Social anxiety? Capricorns can be slow to feel at ease with new people or situations. Fear might also be the culprit, especially if Capricorn has put too much pressure on himself.	Baby steps! Break the intimidating task or situation down into bite-sized actions. The journey of a thousand miles begins with a single stride for Capricorn.

CONTINUED ON NEXT PAGE

WHEN CAPRICORN . . .	IT MEANS . . .	SO YOU SHOULD . . .
Won't eat what you serve	Capricorn isn't hungry. (Yes, it often is *that* literal with this kid, so don't read between the lines too much.)	Waste not, want not. Give Capricorn smaller portions and let him ask for seconds if he's still hungry.
Can't sit still	A plan is brewing! This goal-oriented kid gets excited when she's set her sights on something big.	Empower Capricorns to pursue a dream and give her the tools of the trade: LEGOs, art supplies, whatever basic materials she needs.
	Intimacy overload: your Cappy can get awkward with too much one-on-one engagement, and may become twitchy and restless.	Let her move around and disperse the energy. Or step in and help break the ice a little so Capricorn can get more comfortable.

THE SOCIAL CAPRICORN

ROLE IN THE FAMILY

Chip off the old block? Proud Capricorn kids want to follow in your footsteps or those of a relative they admire. Even when they wear a different shoe size (and style!), Caps bring a sense of continuity to their clans. Capricorns rule history, and they're often the sturdiest branches on their family trees. This is the kid who could inherit the family business or proudly preserve the treasured traditions of his ancestors. Steadfast and serene, Capricorns are the rocks of their families, standing firm when loved ones fall apart. Parents of Caps must make sure these kids experience an actual childhood! With everyone leaning on them for support, Capricorns carry heavy burdens on their little shoulders. Lighten their loads by helping them lighten up. Avoid saddling Capricorns with adult problems, and resist the urge to confide too much in them, as wise as they may be. You may need to firmly say, "I've got it covered" or "I'm handling this"—and let your actions show that you mean it. Make sure to have fun for fun's sake, since Capricorns can turn even a round of Monopoly or a game of tag into an occasion to self-criticize.

FRIENDS AND PEERS

Friends till the end—that's what Capricorns are. Loyal and highly selective, the zodiac's Goat prefers quality to quantity when it comes to BFFs. Capricorns may fraternize with just one or two cronies, keeping these people around through the years. Clubby Caps don't let just anyone into their exclusive inner circles and may even choose friends on a "who's who" basis. Once you're deemed fit for admission, membership doesn't expire: friendship with a Capricorn is a life sentence!

Minimalists at heart, Capricorns can have a monklike quality to them. They enjoy spending time alone and might play independently for hours, building, plotting, and figuring out how things work. Boredom is rare for a sign that's always busy with goals and plans. Your little Cappy could be an entrepreneur by elementary school, enrolling his trusty sidekick as director of sales and marketing. Friends of Capricorn should prepare to go along with their schemes—and bring a few adventurous ideas of their own. Capricorns need friends to pull them out of their heads when they get too serious or fraught. Bring on the laughter and levity!

Who's your daddy? Capricorn is the zodiac's "father" sign, and these kids can sometimes play a paternal role with pals. Like Cub Scout den leaders, they make sure everyone is safe and prepared. They might even try to toughen up buddies by giving them hard-core advice or teaching school yard survival skills. One Capricorn we know shared an "epiphany" with his mom that maybe bullying wasn't such a bad thing. After all, it could force kids to develop backbone and stand up for themselves. This "end justifies the means" policy is so Capricorn. You might need to remind these kids the difference between tough love and just plain-old harshness, though. A little empathy, please!

BROTHERS AND SISTERS: CAPRICORN AS A SIBLING

Blood is thicker than water, and Capricorns take family ties seriously. Loyal and devoted siblings, they often step in as a secondary parent—whether you ask them to or not. Naturally protective, they'll look out for their brothers and sisters, enforcing the rules when necessary. At times, they can be a little *too* bossy, giving stern orders and directives. (Dial it down, little drill sergeant!)

Is a sibling cranking up the drama-rama? Capricorns will step back and let them have the stage. They're not big on competing for attention. If anything, they'll end up playing the "hero" or golden child while their sib becomes the family's problem child. If Capricorns experience any kind of rivalry, it's not because they've purposely instigated it. However, their brothers and sisters might feel jealous of them, especially if Capricorn happens to be really good at everything or obedient while the other sibling rebels. Capricorns can unwittingly set a lofty standard—bringing home straight A's, lettering in a varsity sport, or being an obedient, "good" kid—that siblings struggle to match. Parents of Capricorns should be careful not to compare them to their brothers and sisters, even if you secretly wish Capricorn's sibs would be a little bit more like him.

DISCIPLINING A CAPRICORN

*

Capricorn is the sign of rules and authority. These kids crave structure, clear boundaries, and sensible policies. With those in place, they can be incredibly self-disciplined and well behaved. Capricorns need powerful leaders who are strong enough to guide them but unafraid to push back during willful moments. When little Goats challenge your authority, they need to see your strength, so show no fear!

Just remember: strength and force are entirely different. Forcefulness stems from weakness and fear, which Capricorns can smell a mile away. With Capricorns, might does not make right. If you rule with an iron fist or blow your stack, you can be sure that Capricorn will begin to imitate that behavior or lose respect for you. Keenly aware of hierarchy, Capricorns take their cues from the top down. You must "be the change you want to see" in your child, to paraphrase Gandhi's famous quote. Preserve your dignity, integrity, and self-respect. It's okay to say "because I said so" when Capricorn tests your boundaries.

Forget about coddling and free-range parenting with Capricorn. If your disciplinary style is "kid guided," you'd better simplify to the bottom-line basics. In the animal kingdom, goats butt heads in order to determine who the alpha is. If you don't step into that role, Capricorns will dominate you—and that's when things can go seriously awry. Behind any Capricorn rebellion is usually a lackluster leader or a pampering parent. Or maybe you've gotten so hysterical about something that you've piqued Capricorn's curiosity. ("Hmmm, if it bothers Mom that much, I'd better see what the fuss is all about!") With Capricorn, that which you resist persists.

When in doubt, raise the bar. Capricorns are the "heroes" of the zodiac, and they strive for excellence. These kids need a worthy mission to keep them out of trouble. They *want* to be held to the highest possible standards—it shows that you believe in their capabilities. At the risk of sounding hard-hearted, these are the kids who might benefit from a taste of boot camp. Not in a punitive way but to provide them with the structure and discipline they crave. Now drop and give me twenty, kid!

HANDLING TRANSITIONS: MOVING, DIVORCE, DEATH, AND OTHER TOUGH STUFF

*

As the zodiac's historians, Capricorns get nostalgic and deeply attached to the past. They may not even seem that excited about something in the moment. But the minute a friend, loved one, or experience enters the faded archives of time, Capricorns add a sentimental sheen to the bond. As rooted earth signs, Capricorns aren't fast to adapt to change. Leaving a childhood home can cause them to temporarily lose their sense of place in the world. Nor does this traditional sign fare well when parents split up. All change must be introduced as gradually and gently as possible.

Stoic Capricorns may keep a stiff upper lip during hardships. Getting them to show their emotions can be like drawing water from a stone. They may just get quiet and pensive, lost in deep reflection. Capricorns can have a melancholy vibe in general, even when they're smiling and joking.

SCHOOL'S IN SESSION

*

BEST EDUCATION STYLE

Capricorns can be academic all-stars, or else they're the kids who "don't apply themselves." Whether they push themselves to earn straight-A report cards or underperform depends on several factors. Goal-oriented Capricorns need to be challenged but in the right proportions. They like to build skills incrementally, with lessons that become progressively harder but not so hard that Capricorn falls behind. Patient and persistent, Caps need time to master each step before being pushed to the next one.

Are you the parent who's dreamed of giving your kid an alternative education at a private school founded on humanist philosophies and noncompetitiveness? Well, you might want to have another child, then. Structured Capricorns seldom thrive in an open-classroom setting. They need clear instructions, well-planned assignments, and yes, competition. As the sign of status and honors, Capricorns love medals, trophies, and shiny gold stars. Public school or a more conventional private school might be a better fit for this by-the-numbers sign. Keep their creative spirits alive through extracurricular activities.

Capricorns tend to be systematic thinkers, often good at science, math, and music. They also enjoy history (especially lessons on epic battles won by strategy and cunning), and since Capricorn rules government, they might enjoy learning about civics—or running for student council. This sign's leadership traits can be fostered through posts of responsibility: team captain, class treasurer, science club president, section leader in the band.

Is your Capricorn a top honors student, a star athlete, and popular to boot? Congratulations . . . with a caveat. While it's great to encourage their ambition, make sure Caps leave time for fun and relaxation, too. These overachievers can easily take on too much responsibility, turning life and school into a burden. They might also take criticism personally, since they're so hard on themselves. An occasional B or C is not the end of the world, but to Capricorns, it might feel that way. Try to get your Goat to lighten up and see the big picture. Curb their worrying impulse and remind them that everything is going to work out fine.

BEST HOBBIES AND ACTIVITIES

For many Capricorns, work and play are interchangeable. Kids of this productive sign like to feel like they're actually *doing* something—even if they're building an impressive LEGO tower or tinkering with a gadget to make it work better. Capricorn rules the zodiac's tenth house of career. Get this kid a chemistry set, a kid-friendly microscope, or a doctor's kit. You could be planting the seeds of a future career!

Athletic Capricorns can have great stamina for distance sports like cross-country running, football, and swimming. Whether stocky or wiry, they can be incredibly strong and nimble. Lace up the boxing gloves! Heavyweight champion Muhammad Ali is a Capricorn—as is his daughter Laila, who became a professional boxer, too. Graceful Capricorns can be talented gymnasts, like Olympic gold medalists Gabby Douglas and Shawn Johnson, both born under this sign. They can also be musical. Whether they play music or appreciate it, Capricorns can curate huge playlists of their favorite songs, often spanning many genres. Soon enough, they could be saving their allowances for DJ equipment.

Paging King Arthur and the Knights of the Round Table? Ruled by timekeeper Saturn, some Capricorns seem to have been born in the wrong century. These kids might be fascinated by another historical era, especially medieval days. Fencing, role-playing games, Renaissance fairs, Dungeons & Dragons—your little "page" or "fair maiden" might love a trip back in time, so be prepared to spend lots of times in museums, or save your pennies for a trip to Europe to see the historical sights of yesteryear.

Capricorns work hard and rest hard. During downtime, these kids love to sleep past noon, lounge in front of the TV, and spend a lazy day playing games with the family. At the end of the day, Capricorns just enjoy being around their small circle of loved ones—doing absolutely nothing!

GIFT GUIDE:
BEST PRESENTS FOR CAPRICORN

* Clothing or accessories from their favorite top-of-the-line brand (since Caps can be label snobs)
* Outdoor sports equipment, especially for rugged terrain: hiking boots, rock-climbing gear, mountain bikes, skis
* Music, instruments, or DJ equipment—this sign can have a natural sense of rhythm and rich vocal skills
* Tickets to a championship game of their favorite sports team
* Hand-knit or cashmere sweaters—a comfy piece Capricorn can cozy up in every day

THE AQUARIUS CHILD

(January 20–February 18)

SYMBOL: The Water Bearer

COSMIC RULERS: Uranus, Saturn

ELEMENT: Air

BODY PART: Calves, ankles

GEMSTONE: Amethyst

COLOR: Violet, indigo

GOOD DAY: Funny
Easygoing
Original
Open-minded

BAD DAY: Anxious
Unpredictable
Rebellious
Destructive

LIKES: Freethinking people who aren't afraid to be themselves
Group events: parties, sports games, music festivals, and concerts
The latest gadgets, cameras, and tech toys
Sci-fi and futuristic topics
The company of good friends
Spontaneity
Sunshine and outdoor activity: running, biking, and walking on the beach

DISLIKES: Injustice and closed-mindedness
Being alone for too long
Sitting still and being quiet
Being "needed" or depended upon too heavily by others
Rules and restrictions
Cold, dark climates
Sentimentality and dwelling on the past

* SO, YOU WANT TO HAVE AN AQUARIUS? *

Target Conception Dates for an Aquarius Child: **April 25–May 15**

FAMOUS AQUARIUS KIDS, PAST AND PRESENT

*

Justin Timberlake, Christina Ricci, Mena Suvari, Rachel Crow, Emma Roberts, Tatyana Ali, Sara Gilbert, Matthew Lawrence, Beverly Mitchell, Elijah Wood, Bobby Brown, Tiffani Thiessen, Molly Ringwald, Mary Lou Retton, Gary Coleman, Ariel Winter, Nick Carter, Lisa Marie Presley

PARENTING YOUR AQUARIUS CHILD: THE ESSENTIALS

*

Welcome, baby bohemian! There's something about your little Aquarius that stands out from the crowd. A lightness, a sparkle, a twinkle of something unique—you just sense that Aquarius is different. And to that end, this kid will rarely disappoint. Ruled by unpredictable Uranus, the planet of nonconformity, Aquarians can be some of the most unique individuals around.

Although fresh-faced Aquarius might *look* like the girl or boy next door, make no mistake. As the sign of surprises, these kids can be shockingly avant-garde. Just when you think an Aquarius is totally cookie cutter, out comes a remark or an action so eccentric, you realize she's from another universe. (Lewis Carroll, creator of *Alice's Adventures in Wonderland*, was an Aquarius. Trip down a rabbit hole, anyone?)

Aquarius is the sign of the future and doesn't like to dwell on the past. Why bother looking back, when each new day holds so much potential? Little utopian citizens, these kids can be incredibly progressive and fair-minded. Many an activist has been born under this sign: Rosa Parks, Yoko Ono, Susan B. Anthony, and Oprah Winfrey, to name a few. (Just keep sci-fi-loving Aquarians away from conspiracy theories, as they can easily veer into on-the-fringe terrain.)

As the sign of teamwork and friendship, Aquarians are forever putting everyone else's needs first. They might save their favorite toys and outgrown outfits for a younger sibling. On the playground, Aquarius will offer a stranger her turn on the slide, even if she's been waiting forever. These earnest kids want to rescue every abandoned animal, heal sick children, and stamp out injustice. Their hearts are always in the right place, even if their heads are, well, who knows where!

Nomads by nature, Aquarians like to wander, finding friends in every port. This is the kid who can hang seamlessly with the popular crowd *and* with the freaks and geeks. One minute, he's a free spirit marching to his own beat; the next, he's migrating with the herds. An intellectual air sign, these kids see right through sloppy sentiment and nostalgia. Don't be surprised when they reveal, for example, that they never really believed in Santa Claus or the Tooth Fairy, anyway.

Aquarians also have a mischievous streak and will go to great lengths for a laugh. With their hilarious observations, sarcastic zingers, and edgy pranks (think Aquarians Ashton Kutcher and Chris Rock), their comedic timing is stellar, though a tiny bit mean. However, Aquarians are usually "cruel to be kind" and never target the underdog. They love to skewer people who've gotten too big for their britches, taking them down a notch. Altruistic Aquarius is here to remind everyone that we're all human!

At times, these kids' equality-minded stance makes them hesitant to claim the spotlight, which often beckons. Charismatic Aquarians can be gifted at sports, dance, acting—or just blessed with natural good looks. They might contend with jealousy from their peers, which is the last thing the zodiac's BFF wants. Other Aquarians can make weirdness seem cool—even when they dye their hair teal, change their names in fourth grade, or keep a bearded dragon lizard as a pet. Aquarians manage to fit in *and* stand out all at once—not an easy feat!

As self-assured as Aquarius might seem, this sign can be insecure and anxious, too. Aquarius is the sign of emotional detachment, so these kids don't always stay with their feelings long enough to process them. Uncomfortable with heavy sentiment, they'll turn serious topics into a joke or give stiff, awkward hugs. Or they may burst into sudden tears at a slight provocation. Their nervous body language betrays their cool facades: restless tics, jerky movements, and darting eyes. Are they hiding something or trying to hold it together?

For clues to their behavior, study the Aquarius symbol, the Water Bearer: a figure holding an urn of water (or emotion). Like their icon, Aquarius kids keep a fountain of feelings inside. They may smile and insist, "I'm fine," while they hold it all in. Then the urn fills to the brim and everything spills over in tears, tantrums, and white-lightning rage. Aquarians' outbursts may seem to come from left field, but their vessels are just at capacity. (Build yourself an ark, fast. Even placid water can do great damage when it all rushes forth at once.)

Parents can help by encouraging Aquarians to share their feelings—or by giving them a few good emotional releases (yoga, outdoor activity, tear-jerking movies) if they get too bottled up. That way, they can "empty the vessel" and release suppressed emotions before they crescendo to an explosive state. Consider it "flood insurance" for their future—and yours. Then you can surf the waves that this fun, fascinating child brings up to shore.

AQUARIUS: HOW THEY DEAL WITH . . .

*

RULES AND AUTHORITY

Up with the people! Aquarius is the zodiac's rebel, famous for fighting the power and sparking revolutions. In short, expect mischief. Aquarius kids often break rules as fast as you can make them. These kids can be incredibly cooperative and easygoing, but if they feel that their rights are being encroached upon, watch out. This spirited sign will go toe-to-toe with any iron-fisted ruler. (It was Aquarius Abraham Lincoln who signed the Emancipation Proclamation, freeing the majority of slaves in the United States.) Aquarius kids want to be talked to like equals, which can be tricky, since *some* degree of hierarchy is essential. Settle for talking to them like human beings.

Aquarius is the sign of groups, and these kids are susceptible to peer pressure. A naughty friend can easily lead them into trouble, convincing Aquarius to break the rules or try something they shouldn't. Take extra care that your Aquarius plays with the "good" kids, since they will be a heavy positive influence. Natural comedians, these hilarious imps can also land in hot water for mocking an authority figure, often with a dead-on impersonation. A future in performing arts—or detention—awaits.

LIMITS

To free-spirited Aquarians, limits are negotiable. With their smooth-talking ways and affable personalities, Aquarius kids can and do charm their way past most parameters. Curiosity is often the culprit of these kids' misdeeds. ("I know microwaves are for food, but I wonder what would happen if I put my toy in there . . .") One mom of an Aquarius toddler was summoned into the bathroom, where she found her daughter smeared in shaving cream and clutching mama's razor. "Look, Mommy—I shaving my legs!" Keep close tabs on your little mad scientist. Aquarius is a cerebral air sign, which means kids born under it can get lost in their imagination and thoughts. This distracted tendency can make them oblivious to safety risks. Plan to keep those corner cushions on the coffee table and plastic socket covers in the outlets for a while. Let Aquarius explore in safe zones, such as a padded playroom or climbing gym with lots of stimulating activities and toys—and plenty of adult supervision. Enrolling Aquarians in organized sports also develops discipline and focus, which can counteract their spacey tendencies.

SEPARATION AND INDEPENDENCE

Mommy *who*? Social Aquarius is the sign of friendship, and while they love hanging out with you, they're just as content to spend quality time with fifty of their closest little buddies, cousins, aunts, and uncles.

YOUNGER SIBLINGS

The more, the merrier! Aquarius kids are great mentors and teachers to younger sibs. Usually not the jealous type, Aquarians become BFFs with little sisters and brothers. They will cheerfully share a bedroom, toys, clothes, and attention with their little sidekick. They can be incredibly protective and giving, even putting their younger sibling's needs above their own.

OLDER SIBLINGS

No matter the birth order, Aquarius kids just want to be best buds with their siblings. Although Aquarians crave companionship and camaraderie, their arrival may spark jealousy from an older sibling who feels displaced. Fortunately, Aquarius kids let it roll off their backs, and usually triumph over the green-eyed monster. Just remember: Aquarius is the sign of individuality, so don't compare your Water Bearer to her siblings or expect her to follow in anyone's footsteps, because she won't. The question "Why can't you be more like your brother/sister?" could stir competition where none existed.

BYE-BYE, BABY: WEANING AND POTTY TRAINING

Easy-breezy Aquarius is the sign of detachment, so your child might not mind letting go. However, some Aquarian kids struggle with anxiety, so make sure to do any training in a relaxed, low-pressure setting. This unpredictable sign might just surprise you: one day your Aquarian might just quit nursing or wearing diapers, and that's just that. Fun-loving Aquarians respond well to anything you make into a game—or even team toilet training at nursery school or day care. Since peers are a strong influence, just let Aquarius admire the big-boy or big-girl pants a little friend is sporting. Soon enough, they'll want a pair of their own!

SEXUALITY

Awkwaaaard. Heavy-duty topics and emotions make Aquarius kids uncomfortable. (Who's squirming more when you reveal how babies are made?) This is the sign famous for bathroom humor and joking about any sensitive topic. Yet Aquarius kids are also hyperrational, so stick to the facts and don't candycoat the information. They can't deal if you present sex in a lovey-dovey way or try to sell them some phony line about a stork.

LEARNING: SCHOOL, HOMEWORK, AND TEACHERS

School is Aquarians' social hub, where they quickly find and form their tribes. They might be the popular jocks scoring seats on student council and homecoming court. Or they can be geeks involved in the after-school chess club and marching band. There's a type A side to many Aquarians, and they can be driven about their grades and goals. Other Aquarians may need reminders that they're in school to learn, not to constantly socialize. (For a cautionary tale, watch Aquarius John Belushi play a very Aquarian character in *National Lampoon's Animal House*. Two words: food fight!)

HOUSEHOLD CONFLICT

Can't we all just get along? Team-spirited Aquarians hate conflict, especially at home. When relatives fight, they'll try to crack jokes to lighten the mood, and if that fails, they'll disengage, scurrying off to their rooms to avoid the drama. Only when things are really unfair do they offer their natural diplomatic skills and mediate. Other times, Aquarius can be the one stirring the pot, playing pranks, breaking rules, or making smart remarks that provoke an argument. When they get into a funk, Aquarians can even be sarcastic and sadistic, externalizing emotions they don't want to process. Duck before you end up the target of their wrath.

THE AQUARIUS BOY

*

Encore, encore! Entertaining and one of a kind, the Aquarius boy can bring a smile to anyone's lips. With his quirky insights, devilish pranks, and unique worldview, this kid can crack you up without trying. Of course, he usually is trying, since this charmer loves to make people laugh. Like Aquarians Chris Rock, Bill Maher, and *Simpsons* creator Matt Groening, there's intellect behind his wit—he's a born cultural commentator who laughs at the world *and* with it. (Warning: while Aquarius might poke fun of himself, he can be thin-skinned about someone else teasing him. Dishing it out is easier than taking it!)

Flirtatious and fresh-faced, Aquarius boys are a mash-up of the brooding "bad boy" (think Aquarius James Dean) and the harmless boy next door. Open and irresistibly impish, he's the cutie that all the girls swoon over. The fellas love him, too. (One Aquarius we know was nicknamed "the Mayor" at his middle school.) Aquarius is the sign of teamwork, and he might be the social director for his buddies and "bros," who rely on him to supply schemes and adventures. He's also the star player of any team, whether he's geeking out with the "mathletes," running student council, or dunking basketballs like "his airness" Michael Jordan, an Aquarius.

With his contagious charisma, Aquarius manages to be naughty and nonthreatening all at once. Perhaps that's why so many boy bands have Aquarius stars: Justin Timberlake ('N Sync), Nick Carter (Backstreet Boys), Bobby Brown (New Edition), Harry Styles (One Direction) . . . even Axl Rose (Guns N' Roses). Any girl who grew up in the *Grease* era probably had Aquarius John Travolta's iconic black "muscle shirt" poster taped to her bedroom wall, too.

Of course, the Aquarius boy might be the last one to recognize his own appeal. An intellectual air sign, he's often lost in his thoughts, cooking up new ideas and plans. Future-focused Aquarius is zodiac's mad scientist and the ruler of technology. He can often be found with the latest gadget in hand, tinkering away or turning his laptop into a laboratory. (Thomas Edison, inventor of the lightbulb, was an Aquarius.) He might be into computer programming, video games, sci-fi—even stories about government conspiracies and extraterrestrials. In fact, he might be something of an alien himself, all the way down to his quirky, robotic movements. The Aquarius boy might not be touchy-feely (sorry, Mom), but he shows his love by making sure everyone around him is happy.

While he might be coolly rational and dismissive about some topics, the Aquarius boy can get worked up about his fascination du jour. He can go through hobbies like water, and as an air sign his attention can shift with the winds. Because Aquarius will try anything once, you might need to keep tabs on his social group, too. The Aquarius boy's friends can heavily influence him, and peer pressure will start young. He can be the instigator of mischief or the enabling wingman to a troublemaking punk. The pursuit of thrills can lead him down the wrong path. Don't let him entirely off the leash, even if you give him a long one.

Not that he's out to destroy property, but this kid bores easily and craves amusement. Our Aquarius friend David procured copies of the master keys to his school. A theater geek, he and his friends just snuck in to climb up to the bell tower "to make sure the lighting and sound would be perfect for the school play." Lucky for him, he was never caught. Boys of this mischievous sign will toe the line to see what they can get away with!

To keep your Aquarius son out of trouble, make sure he's busy and involved. This isn't the boy you want to keep out of day care or put with a nanny. He needs to be around peers, and the sooner, the better. Sports, marching band, student council, academic clubs—anywhere he can be his idiosyncratic self and keep his active mind occupied is good. This kid can also benefit from having a mentor when he's older. Since the future is so important to this sign, a great role model will help Aquarius ensure a bright one for himself.

THE AQUARIUS GIRL

*

Earth to Aquarius! This otherworldly girl is cut from her own mold. On the outside, Aquarius might be the quintessential girl next door (think Jennifer Aniston or Denise Richards). But as the sign of surprises, there's always more than meets the eye. Casual Aquarians aren't the girliest of girls. They can be gangly, geeky, or sporty—but delicate princesses they're not. Even while traipsing around in tutus and tiaras, they have a tomboyish way about them.

The Aquarius girl is sweet, but don't mistake her ingredients for sugar and spice. More like sugar and ice. Her huge heart swells for human suffering, abandoned animals, and strangers in need. On a one-on-one level, however, this air sign blows a little cooler. As the sign of social justice and emotional detachment, Aquarius can be a bit of a "fembot"—fun and friendly, but far less passionate about the small stuff than she is about her worldly ideals.

If you want to see an Aquarius girl's true feelings, don't ask her about herself. "So, what's new?" is the worst icebreaker to use with Aquarius—and might be more of an ice maker. "Um, not much," she'll reply, casting her eyes down and filling the room with awkward, chilly silence. Take two: "What have you been working on lately?" or "Have you ever seen a real komodo dragon?" Engage her with an unexpected question. Talk about her favorite animal. Listen to her rant about an unfair school policy or a classroom injustice. *Now* you've got her attention.

Since the Aquarius girl doesn't like small talk, she can come across as distant or disengaged. In truth, her mind is always working. She's not absent; she's *busy*. She doesn't always have time for deep, heart-to-heart talks. Aquarius is a conceptual sign that prefers discussing big ideas, not the latest gossip. Sure, she can enjoy a laugh about human foibles—but when it starts to get catty, she retracts her claws.

Aquarius is the sign of friendship and popularity, and her sign mates cover the spectrum from Paris Hilton to Sarah Palin to Oprah Winfrey. Aquarius is a trendsetter who marches to her own beat. During the 2008 elections, Palin's stylish updo and eyeglasses incited a copycat frenzy. Socialite Hilton sparked the "celebutante" craze, and you can't say "book club" without thinking of Oprah.

Many an iconic pop-culture blonde has been an Aquarius: Farrah Fawcett (*Charlie's Angels*), Florence Henderson (*The Brady Bunch*), and Zsa Zsa Gabor (*Green Acres*). With their fresh-scrubbed looks, Aquarius girls can also be pageant queens and pop stars. Even *Wheel of Fortune*'s Vanna White is born under this sign. Make no mistake, though: the Aquarius girl is not a ditz. You might "buy a vowel" from her, but she'll sell you the whole alphabet. She uses her charm to disarm.

Perhaps that's why Oprah Winfrey and Ellen DeGeneres (also an Aquarius) are such gifted interviewers. Accessible and engaging, they make everyone feel like a best friend—from the viewer to the celebrity sitting beside them. These women also broke huge mainstream media barriers for black and gay people. Aquarians are the great unifiers of the universe, bringing everyone together by blending cutting-edge ideas with their mass appeal.

Aquarians have many activists and avant-garde thinkers in their ranks: feminist Betty Friedan (author of *The Feminine Mystique*), civil rights pioneer Angela Davis, and peace advocate/artist Yoko Ono. There's also Ayn Rand, whose oh-so-Aquarian objectivist philosophy trumpets the virtues of individual happiness and free-thinking.

While the Aquarius girl flaunts her bold opinions, she also likes to make everyone happy and sometimes goes too far "for the good of the group." In this way, Aquarius is a paradox—she's ruled by liberator Uranus, but she's also the sign of teamwork. She's a protestor and a people pleaser all at once. Her communal nature leads her to constantly seek a "tribe" of misfits to, well, fit in with. Bouts of conformity can be mixed with radical rejections of a friend or clique. This is the girl who gets lost in a crowd in order to find herself again. Underneath the free-spirited facade, Aquarius can be a bit of a control freak. She may struggle with anxiety and can be incredibly hard on herself. Keep close tabs on the Aquarius girl during puberty, especially. The body changes, hormone spikes, and fluctuating emotions can freak out this otherwise cool-and-collected kid. Monitor her stress levels and body image, as she can be at risk for eating disorders (an attempt to control her developing body as a response to feeling out of control in the world).

Although she will need to work on self-acceptance, finding a tolerant, forward-thinking crew of friends can help Aquarius embrace her unique personality and views. This girl needs to let her freak flag fly in her own ".alt" kinda way (cue disenfranchised teen icon Molly Ringwald in just about every John Hughes movie). From an early age, she can benefit from alternative schooling, hip mentors, and involvement with a social issue (animal rights, the endangered oceans, running for student council). As Winston Churchill said, "We make a living by what we get; we make a life by what we give." The Aquarius girl's true spirit shines when championing a cause. Encourage her to be true to herself. The world is waiting!

BEHAVIOR DECODER: THE AQUARIUS KID

WHEN AQUARIUS . . .	IT MEANS . . .	SO YOU SHOULD . . .
Cries	His feelings are hurt or he's having a sentimental moment. Aquarians are sensitive, even if they sometimes act jokey or laid-back. As the sign of surprises, their emotional floodgates can open suddenly and without warning.	Tone down the tough love—you're being too hard on Aquarius.

CONTINUED ON NEXT PAGE

WHEN AQUARIUS . . .	IT MEANS . . .	SO YOU SHOULD . . .
Withdraws socially or gets quiet or moody	Something is really bugging her, since this social sign rarely goes "offline."	Calmly check in and ask her what's up. Don't make a huge deal out of it or get all worked up, or Aquarius will shut down.
Acts out (hitting, kicking, talking back)	Temper alert! Aquarius emotions can strike like lightning, in fast, unexpected, and destructive ways.	The time-out chair was practically invented for this sign. Give this air sign a few minutes to cool down after the storm.
Gets clingy	Aquarius doesn't yet feel comfortable socially and is turning to you as his primary "friend." Or, he may assume that the group he's about to enter doesn't share his interests and won't "get" him	Initiate an icebreaker to get Aquarius settled into the scene and mellow his social anxiety.
Won't eat what you serve	Power struggle—Aquarius just feels like being a brat for her own entertainment.	Ultimatum time. Calmly tell her it's fine if she doesn't eat what's on her plate but that it will cost her a privilege. Then let her decide how to proceed.
Can't sit still	Just another day in Water Bearer paradise—antsy Aquarius is full of nervous, kinetic energy.	Send Aquarius outside to move the energy around. Find out if there's some anxiety brewing that Aquarius needs to talk about. When Aquarians are upset or obsessing, they can't sit still for a second.

THE SOCIAL AQUARIUS

*

ROLE IN THE FAMILY

Comic relief? Light and airy Aquarius arrives to bring levity back to the family—along with a few good laughs. Kids of this sign simply don't take anything *that* seriously for long. Even Aquarians' intense or earnest spells can disappear—poof!—as fast as their onset. Before you know it, a tragedy has turned into comedy, with Aquarius leading the laugh riot. One mom enjoyed this comic relief when she dropped her husband off at the airport for a trip. As her daughter wept because daddy was leaving, her two-year-old Aquarius turned to his sister and said simply, "Save the drama for your mama." Aquarians' ability to see things from a singular perspective or an unconventional angle can broaden the whole family's view. As a futuristic sign, Aquarius can shake up a clan that's gotten too entrenched in past problems or high on its own legacy. This kid is no "chip off the old block," but he *will* take a chip off your shoulder. Radical Aquarius introduces something totally new that breaks the mold, reminding her kin not to take everything so damn personally. Evolution by way of revolution is the Aquarius MO.

FRIENDS AND PEERS

Free to be . . . you and me? Aquarius kids are happiest in harmonious but eclectic groups where everyone is treated with fairness and equality. Hierarchy is not their thing, and they hate gossipy, insecure little coteries. Even when they're part of a "tribe" (drama club, a sports team) these kids loathe the restrictiveness of any clique. Aquarians are the zodiac's free spirits, and in their eyes friendship shouldn't come with strings attached. These spontaneous kids want to come and go as they please sans binding, pinky-sworn obligations. If they want to have a playdate with someone new next Saturday, don't even try to act jealous or lay on the guilt. Live and let live!

Of course, because they're so easygoing and up for anything, young Aquarians often end up in the clutches of a possessive or domineering friend. Parents may need to intervene, steering Aquarius toward healthier BFFs who are more egalitarian. Enrolling Aquarians in camp or clubs focused around a specific topic (science, performing arts, animals) can keep them out of these intense power plays. With a soft spot for the underdog, your Aquarius can be an antibullying crusader from an early age.

As the sign of popularity and friendship, Aquarians are rarely lacking for buddies—unless, of course, they happen to live in an elitist environment where they feel alienated. They could care less about fitting in with the cool crowd, but they *do* crave a sense of belonging. Even the Aquarius still wants real-world friends to hang out with. Finding a like-minded tribe is a primary goal for Aquarius, and they may belong to several disparate groups—for example, cheerleading and show choir, or football and physics club. Got a problem with that? They don't.

Because they appear so confident, Aquarians can end up with friends who latch on and benefit from their talents. Or, in a desire to be liked, Aquarians may tone down their own star power by letting someone else get all their applause. Problems arise when the friend takes credit for something Aquarius has created. This can be the wake-up call Aquarius needs, reminding her to value herself instead of dimming her lights so someone else can shine.

BROTHERS AND SISTERS: AQUARIUS AS A SIBLING

Bring on the brethren! Communal Aquarians thrive in an oversized clan—the more, the merrier. This kid knows the power of numbers and works it to his advantage. Who else, after all, is going to help Aquarius form a human pyramid, build a tree fort, or perform the awesome dance routine he choreographs? Brothers and sisters of Aquarius are forever being recruited into this sign's experimental schemes. (Any sentence that Aquarius begins with "What if we . . ." could set off a day of familial adventures—or a month of revoked privileges.)

Fair-minded Aquarius is often the kid who gets along with everyone, rising above petty dramas. In a family fraught with rivalries, coolheaded Aquarius is the Switzerland of his siblings. Somehow, Aquarius remains neutral and on good terms with everyone. At most, this sign will get involved peripherally, commenting on the absurdity of his relative's behavior. But getting all worked up over whatever is going on? Nah. Why waste time on drama when there's fun to be had?

DISCIPLINING AN AQUARIUS

*

Aquarius is both a pleaser and a protester. These kids want to make their parents proud but also impress their friends, which can lead them down two contradictory behavioral paths. When Aquarius acts out, you should first examine his inner circle. Who has your child been hanging around? Aquarius may have fallen under the spell of a rebellious friend, imitating another child's aggression as a way to feel cool or powerful. As much as Aquarians like to prove their autonomy, they also need to learn the difference between being a "rebel *for* a cause" and just being plain destructive. When you discipline your Aquarius, it's important to suss out her motives. Perhaps she thought was fighting against something unfair—try and teach her how to do a better job of it next time. However, it's just as likely that she got caught up in the thrill of disobedience, which is something you'll want to nip in the bud fast. Take it easy on the tough stuff, though. If you're the "stiff upper lip" type, don't tell Aquarius not to cry. You'll only unleash a torrent as the Water Bearer spills out her whole emotional vessel at once. She may sob hysterically or lash out with a sarcastic, hurtful remark. She might even get aggressive—so prepare to interrupt disciplinary sessions for a needed time-out.

Stay cool when correcting Aquarians' behavior. This sign does *not* respond well to huge displays of emotion from a parent or authority figure. Whenever possible, begin sentences with "I think" rather than "I feel." If you cry, yell, or drop bombs like "How could you do this to me? After all I've done for you?" Aquarius will ice you out. Guilt trips fall flat, since this fair-minded sign is ultrasensitive to manipulation. Aquarians want to be spoken to like adults, not juvenile delinquents (even if their actions put them in the latter class).

Aquarians are sensitive to feeling disrespected or oppressed, so try to engage in dialogue rather than lecturing. Employing the Socratic method—asking your child insightful questions and letting him arrive at the answer—can really win this kid's respect. It also builds confidence, since free-spirited Aquarius craves self-sufficiency. When he knows that he can rely on his own judgment and decision making, he will usually do the right thing. You might even let him come up with his own suitable punishment or consequence to fit the crime.

During truly rebellious phases, Aquarians may suspect that *all* adults have an agenda. In some cases, a dose of tough love—or an outside influence—might be the only way to get through. Peer-driven programs can be helpful, since Aquarians can be positively influenced by group therapy (just don't call it "therapy" to them) and talking openly with other kids their age. When all else fails, you might wrangle a mentor or even a life coach who works with young people. Someone slightly older—but still cool by Aquarian standards—can reach them in ways that you can't.

HANDLING TRANSITIONS: MOVING, DIVORCE, DEATH, AND OTHER TOUGH STUFF

*

Aquarians are the zodiac's nomads, so change is an inevitable part of life's journey to them. They're more adaptable than many signs and quickly rebuild friendships if they change schools or adjust to a new postdivorce lifestyle. As one Aquarius we know likes to say, "The past is history; today is a mystery."

When they're upset, Aquarians might not let you see them sweat. They might insist that they're fine, and one day burst into heaving sobs without provocation. With emotionally clunky Aquarius, you either get a full-on hysterical display or a shrug. One friend remembers her six-year-old Aquarius cousin calmly reacting to news of an elderly neighbor's death by saying, "That's the way the cookie crumbles." It's good that Aquarius is able to move on, but make sure that she isn't glossing over true emotions. As the saying goes, you've got to feel it to heal it.

SCHOOL'S IN SESSION

*

BEST EDUCATION STYLE

Aquarius kids dislike hushed hallways, strict hierarchies, and any educational system that leads with fear instead of passion or imagination. Aquarians thrive in interactive classrooms where they can raise their hands often, collaborate on projects, and be friendly with their teachers. An independent or private school founded on progressive principles can suit their temperaments. However, Aquarians like to branch out and meet new people, so if the school is too small or insular, they may feel claustrophobic.

While these kids need freedom, they also require structure because they can be space cadets or just get lost in their heads. Deadlines and clear assignments keep them from floating off into the ether. And a little bit of authority is necessary; otherwise, Aquarius can spend the day goofing off with a seat mate and never learning a thing!

Some among this sign have a competitive, type A side. They *want* to earn high marks so they get into good colleges and ensure an inspiring future. Under all that pressure, tests can freak them out, and they become anxious or panicked. Trying to get through to Aquarians when they're in deer-in-the-headlights mode is impossible. Their stress response (fight, flight, or freeze) kicks in fast, overwhelming their senses. They go from calm to catastrophic at warp speed.

As an air sign, Aquarians can benefit from using breathing techniques, yoga, and even hypnosis (why not?) to help with their irrational fears. One Aquarius we know tries EFT (Emotional Freedom Technique) tapping before standardized tests, a process that involves drumming on meridian points with her fingertips to release stuck energy. Sometimes Aquarians need to create a self-fulfilling prophecy—failing a test, bombing an assignment—to see that the world hasn't ended. Learning to slow down and live in the moment is important for this future-focused sign. You might get your Aquarius a wristband with the mantra "one day at a time" that they can wear during high-stress times.

BEST HOBBIES AND ACTIVITIES

Active Aquarians may have busy extracurricular lives. Whether they're good at something or not doesn't matter so much—they just enjoy the company of other people in a collaborative setting. Some Aquarians are athletic, with long and lean bodies that make them great at basketball, soccer, football, or any team sport. (Others might just enjoy watching, their mathematical minds keeping tabs on the stats and, later, winning the betting pool.) Since Aquarians often excel at technique, they can also be competitive cheerleaders, track-and-field champions, or karate stars.

Since this sign enjoys competing, your Aquarius could bring home new martial arts belts or trophies each week. (Caution: this sign can be controlling and hard-driven, so keep them out of dance or any sports where they feel pressure to be thin or "perfect.") Paging the talent search! Natural entertainers, many Aquarians can be amazing on stage, singing and dancing like pros from an early age, like Aquarians Mikhail Baryshnikov and Gregory Hines.

Aquarius rules technology, and these kids can be computer geeks, science club stars, web designers, or digital photographers. Set up a video camera or a mic and they may just start their own bedroom-based broadcast networks. Their systematic minds can also make them great at strategy games, chess, and cards. One Aquarius we know makes thousands each month playing poker and online Texas Hold 'Em, which he started at age eighteen after barely graduating high school.

Since some Aquarians are anxious, channeling their nervous energy into service work can be healing. These kids love animals and their souls can be soothed spending time at a pet rescue, walking the neighbor's dogs, or caring for a furry critter of their own. Giving back to other kids is also a great pursuit. One Aquarius girl we know helps her mom with a charity that raises money for children without access to clean water. Another overcame her own social anxiety by mentoring a younger child, which she did every year until graduation. Aquarians need hobbies that connect them to the greater whole, instilling a sense of making a difference. You never know: a career in social justice could await.

GIFT GUIDE: BEST PRESENTS FOR AQUARIUS

* Electronic equipment, cameras, tech toys, and the latest gadget
* Sporty clothes, such as a denim jacket that Aquarius can customize or funky ankle boots she'll wear with just about everything
* Funky accessories (stacks of silver or metal bracelets, clip-on hair pieces in vivid colors) to give outfits a personalized twist
* Bikes, skateboards, or surfboards—anything that helps this air sign enjoy adventure sports where she can feel the wind whipping by
* Books about astrology, science fiction, or any cutting-edge or obscure topic, such as the lost continent of Atlantis or even a *Guinness World Records* book to sate his curiosity about all things strange
* Tickets to a concert, show, or party emporium for Aquarius and ten of his closest friends

THE PISCES CHILD

(February 19–March 20)

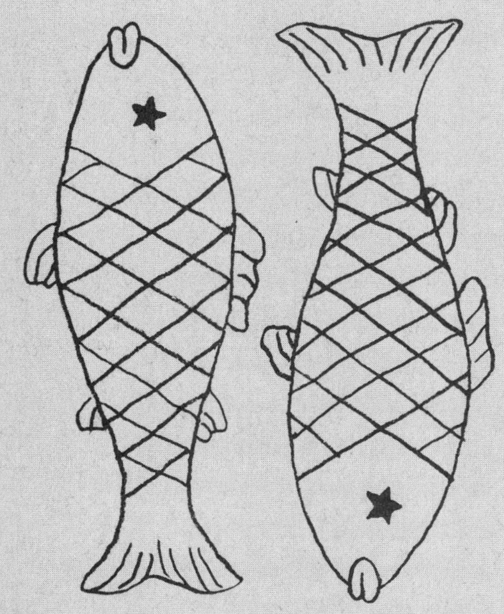

SYMBOL: The Fish

COSMIC RULERS: Neptune, Jupiter

ELEMENT: Water

BODY PART: Feet

GEMSTONE: Aquamarine

COLOR: Sea green, aqua, lavender

GOOD DAY: Compassionate
Artistic
Mesmerizing
Supportive

BAD DAY: Manipulative
Self-pitying
Overwhelmed
Mean

LIKES: Music and dance
Water, water everywhere: bathtubs, pools, oceans, and streams
Photography and film
Fairy tales and make-believe
Beautiful craftsmanship, attention to detail
Spirituality and all things New Agey: angels, divination cards, candles, silk throw pillows
Living a little bit on the edge and the thrill of danger
Helping people and pets in need

DISLIKES: Dealing with reality and being told to "be realistic"
Sensory overload: too many tall buildings, loud noises, crowds, and harsh lighting
Ugliness: cheap fabric, bad design, and poor taste
Feeling exposed
Cruelty to animals
Visionless people who take everything at face value/ hardcore "realists"
Any "-ism" in society: sexism, racism, and so on

* SO, YOU WANT TO HAVE A PISCES? *

Target Conception Dates for a Pisces Child: **May 25–June 15**

FAMOUS PISCES KIDS, PAST AND PRESENT

*

Drew Barrymore, Justin Bieber, Dakota Fanning, Chelsea Clinton, Jennifer Love Hewitt, Ellen Page, Ron Howard, Bryce Dallas Howard, David Faustino, Kesha, Ashley Greene, Kim Ung-yong, Bobby Fischer, Jessica Biel, Bow Wow, Rob Lowe, Thora Birch, Charlotte Church, Cruz Beckham, Brooklyn Beckham, Haylie Duff, Prince Michael "Blanket" Jackson II

PARENTING YOUR PISCES CHILD: THE ESSENTIALS

*

Dream on, little daydreamer. Pisces is ruled by Neptune, the planet of fantasy, healing, and the subconscious. These creative kids prefer the playground of their imaginations to reality and can spend hours lost in their musings. Like the ocean that Neptune presides over, the Pisces depths are vast and mysterious. These little mermaids and mermen will enchant you with their siren songs. You can see the depth of many lifetimes in their wide, luminous eyes.

Pisces are a riddle, a paradox. Symbolized by two fish swimming in opposite directions—one toward security, the other toward freedom—they can run hot and cold. One minute your fragile little Fish is clutching at your skirts, too frightened to leave your side. The next, he darts off to play confidently or faces off with someone twice his height who's bullying a friend. Are Pisces scared of the world or just pretending to be?

A little of both, perhaps. The zodiac's true artists, Pisces are sensitive to every subtlety. Like little sea sponges, they absorb everything deeply—the good *and* the bad. A beautiful song can move Pisces to tears. A slight can keep them brooding for days. Deeply nostalgic, these romantic souls want to witness every rainbow and sunset, capturing the aching beauty in words, music, and art. Seminal nineteenth-century poet Elizabeth Barrett Browning (of "How do I love thee? Let me count the ways" fame) was a Pisces who began writing her verses at age four.

Pisces is the last sign in the zodiac, and these kids are quintessential old souls. Pisces have a sixth sense and may just "know" things, getting clues through their dreams and intuition. Pisces are believed to have lived many lifetimes. Whether it's reincarnation or something else that can't be explained, these children may exhibit talents and abilities that seem to spring from an unknown source. In college, we had a

Pisces friend who could sit down at any piano and play complex sonatas by ear. Yet he'd never taken a lesson in his life. Others on the Pisces genius list: Albert Einstein, Steve Jobs, Quincy Jones (who speaks twenty-four languages and counting), and chess champion Bobby Fischer. Pisces exist in their own dimension—perhaps in Einstein's quantum field, where time and space are elastic—channeling from divine sources.

Pisces is also the sign of karma and reincarnation. Their veil between the earth plane and the spirit world is thin. In their younger years, many Pisces are sick or frail. It's almost as though these old souls are reluctant to leave the blissful spirit world and enter into a body. ("This *again*?") You may become a well-known figure at the doctor's office when your Pisces has yet another ear infection or sprained ankle. Yet these Fish have nine lives and spring back every time.

Born with tremendous compassion, Pisces identify deeply with the underdog, the sick, and the unloved. Pisces is the sign of the nurse and the healer. Their hearts swell for abandoned animals, terminally ill children, or people in abject poverty, and they want to *do* something about it. Sometimes you'll wonder why Pisces want to think so much about the heaviness of human suffering. They're children, after all! But these kids must dive to the bottom of the well in order to come up full again.

As a result, Pisces come to know human suffering; these kids are the ultimate empaths. However, be careful not to burden Pisces with your troubles, as their codependent tendencies are strong. They can get sucked into the undertow of someone else's emotion ocean, losing touch with reality. Pisces need to be encouraged—and sometimes pushed—to develop their own identities. As lovely as their constant companionship can be, self-sufficiency can be a struggle later in life if you don't start 'em young. Pisces also have a tendency to feel helpless or play the victim, and their parents can get sucked into bouts of emotional blackmail. This is a disservice to all. Emphasize direct communication with Pisces. Just because *they're* mind readers doesn't mean you are!

Although Pisces love globally, they aren't always so nice locally. (We told you this sign was a paradox.) When these kids feel insecure they can become gossipy, snarky, and passive-aggressive—even bullies in some cases. Born under the sign of illusions, they imagine that others are judging them harshly, so they deliver a preemptive, self-protective strike by putting that person down. In other cases, Pisces will project their own insecurities onto a weaker subject and target that person. For example, when Pisces' own neediness plagues them, getting a whiff of it in someone else can threaten them. It's like seeing their insecurities in a magnifying mirror, which can make their skin crawl.

None of this is conscious behavior, of course. If it were, Pisces would be deeply ashamed. Any bullying or aggression stems from the Piscean tendency to disown parts of themselves they dislike—which are usually the sensitive parts that society deems as "weak." If only little Pisces realized that their sensitivity is actually their greatest strength! Parents of Pisces might read Brené Brown's book *Daring Greatly* to learn about how our society breeds a culture of shame, especially around being vulnerable. Teaching Pisces to have compassion for themselves will steer them out of mean-person terrain.

To understand Pisces, just look at water, their governing element. Water is at once the softest and the strongest thing on earth. We bathe in its gentleness and drink it to sustain life. Yet water can be forceful enough to destroy rocks (never mind the tsunamis, hurricanes, and floods). You can put water in anything . . . and you can put anything in water. Water can be liquid, solid (ice), and gas (steam). In that same way, Pisces children are a force of nature, making waves but also taking many forms. Teach them to respect their powers and to embrace their own healing properties.

PISCES: HOW THEY DEAL WITH . . .

*

RULES AND AUTHORITY

Ah, the many sides of Pisces. These kids can be innocent angels in your face, slippery fish (or sharks) behind your back! Don't let the sweetness fool you: enchanting little Pisces can be master manipulators. It's not that they're *trying* to get into trouble. However, these curious souls learn through experience—and sometimes they insist on touching that hot stove even when everyone has warned them it will burn. Yes, they can be stubborn in a passive-aggressive way and often to their own detriment. But that's the karmic journey this sign has chosen.

Identifying with the underdog is a key part of the Pisces nature. These kids will stand up to any bully and fight oppression—even if it takes becoming bullies themselves. Born under the sign of compassion, these wee empaths may subconsciously court trouble. They believe that, in the final analysis, humanity is good. Thus, they need to psychologically understand the so-called bad kids and their motives. Later in life, your Pisces could make an incredible healer, counselor, or rehabilitator. When everyone else has written someone off, Pisces still believe in redemption. Perhaps we could all learn a thing or two from this sign! However, you also need to make sure your Pisces isn't being gullible or open to being taken advantage of by people who need to be "saved" and drain Pisces' energy. Teach them the difference between compassion and codependence as they get older.

LIMITS

Pisces is ruled by foggy Neptune, the planet of illusions and blurred boundaries. Limits are a tricky proposition for this sign. Often, their curiosity and imaginations seduce them down yellow brick roads—and they can't stop until they find their Oz. As Pisces Albert Einstein said, "Anyone who has never made a mistake has never tried anything new." To Pisces, rules weren't necessarily made to be broken, but certainly to be questioned.

SEPARATION AND INDEPENDENCE

"Mommy, don't go!" While Pisces crave independence, too much separation can frighten these sensitive souls. They need room to roam, but they also must know that you're nearby to lend, if necessary, a helping hand. Because Pisces aren't the best at boundaries, these kids can get overly wrapped up in your (or a caregiver's) life, neglecting to forge their own identities. Even if they are wise old souls, don't confide in them too much, because they will absorb all your worries and fears.

YOUNGER SIBLINGS

Can you say "ma-ma"? Nurturing Pisces will take a little sibling under their wings and help to raise 'em right. Occasionally, you may need to remind Pisces that you're the mom because they can become bossy and officious with younger brothers and sisters.

OLDER SIBLINGS

If the older sibling protects your Pisces without trying to control him, the relationship can be a tight-knit one. However, Pisces may occasionally resent his older siblings if they're overprotective and restrict him from doing what he wants. The Fish needs space to swim and explore, too, so don't hand the disciplinary reins to an older brother or sister. One mom is more than enough for Pisces, thank you!

BYE-BYE, BABY: WEANING AND POTTY TRAINING

Dreamy Pisces hate to be rushed, and they're not eager to leave a caregiver's comforting embrace. With this sign, attachment parenting could be a never-ending saga! But all good things—the "family bed" and nursing included—must come to an end, even if you have to do it slowly. Take gentle steps and do everything in a calm, soothing setting. Pisces are sensitive to ambience, so playing your Fish's favorite music when she's trying the potty may make the process less overwhelming for her.

SEXUALITY

Pisces is the sign of fantasy, and your Fish needs to preserve a romantic view of sex—or at least, some specialness around it. Harsh reality doesn't go over well with this sign. Even if you teach your Pisces proper terms for his body parts, he might still make up funny nicknames anyhow. Also, since Pisces can have difficulty with boundaries, teaching them a sense of ownership around their bodies is extra important. Make sure your Pisces kid has a clear sense of his personal space and is able to trust his intuition if anyone or anything ever makes him feel uncomfortable.

LEARNING: SCHOOL, HOMEWORK, AND TEACHERS

Structure, please! These daydreamers can get lost in their imaginations, doodling during lessons or drifting off on their own quirky clouds. Some Pisces can be naughty little troublemakers who crack everyone up without trying. There's definitely a mischievous twinkle in these kids' eyes. That very gleam can also be the light of genius and creative inspiration. Don't try to rein in your Pisces *too* much or you could break her wonderful spirit!

HOUSEHOLD CONFLICT

Pisces kids are emotional sponges who pick up everything in their environments. When there's fighting, they freeze. When there's dysfunction, Pisces can't function. Their bodies break down along with their emotions, and Pisces may develop behavioral issues, food sensitivities, or even manifest a mystery flu. Keep petty conflict far away from Pisces and increase the peace!

THE PISCES BOY

*

Life is but a dream! The Pisces boy arrives full of wonder and mischief. Some of the world's wildest imaginations belong to Pisces—including storytellers Dr. Seuss and Lemony Snicket, as well as Mister Rogers with his Neighborhood of Make-Believe. Albert Einstein, Alexander Graham Bell (inventor of the telephone), and Steve Jobs, all Pisces, changed the world with their ability to "think different." From linear to quantum time, and from point-and-click to swipe, the Pisces male is guided by his own quirky navigational system. There's never a dull moment with this daydream believer, so sit back and enjoy the show. As Dr. Seuss wrote, "Oh, the places you'll go!"

Some say the world has a decided lack of good men. Obviously, they've never rifled through the stacks of Pisces biographies. This guy is the original Mr. Sensitivity. And while the people he dates later on might disagree—can you say "drama king"?—the Pisces boy is a lover, not a fighter. From balladeer Michael Bolton to rom-com king Billy Crystal, this guy wears his heart on his sleeve. He might also be a bit of a tortured artist, like Pisces Kurt Cobain and Johnny Cash. Of course, the ladies love him for it. Don't be surprised if your Pisces has a trail of adoring little fangirls following him like the Pied Piper.

Perhaps the reason he's so squirmy in one-on-one relationships is because, by nature, Pisces belong to the world. Astrologically tasked with ending human suffering, they have a big job to do. Their big ideas can plant the timeless seeds of a social movement, so kindly excuse them if they don't have time for dinner and a movie. Take Pisces W. E. B. Du Bois—he was the first African American to earn a Harvard PhD and a cofounder of the NAACP, and his 1903 book *The Souls of Black Folk* shaped the way America thinks about race. Then there's gender studies expert Michael Kimmel, also a Pisces, who cofounded the National Organization for Men Against Sexism. (Swoon!) His books expose the real psychological pain that males experience trying to fit into society's constricting version of masculinity.

In mythology, the sea god Neptune used his trident to cause earthquakes. Similarly, Pisces boys like to stir things up, often using their hypnotic, Svengali-esque powers. Like Pisces motivational speaker Tony Robbins, he might convince you to walk across hot coals as the path to personal liberation. Or he'll inspire rabid legions of "true Belieber" superfans à la Pisces Justin Bieber. This guy knows how to bend physical and universal laws to his will. While he might be spooked by his own sensitivity, this kid is breathtakingly fearless in other ways. Pisces daredevils Johnny Knoxville (of *Jackass* fame) and *Crocodile Hunter* Steve Irwin never met a risk they wouldn't take. With some Pisces boys, it might take everything in your power to keep them from gravitating to danger.

Since the Pisces boy is often ashamed of his own sensitivity, some of his crazy stunts might just be shows of bravado. You might need to help him embrace the fact that he's in touch with his "feminine" side. One mom of a Pisces enrolled her graceful son in a coed dance and theater troupe, making sure he wasn't the only boy involved. Sure, he might enjoy having a lot of female friends, but he wants to fit in with the fellas, too. Pisces rules the feet, so keep your Fish moving—playing soccer, dancing, surfing, skateboarding. His fancy footwork could win the guys' respect and admiration.

To keep your Pisces boy out of turbulent, angst-charged waters, he needs to connect with something bigger than himself. One mom of a Pisces took her son on a trip to Africa, where he was deeply moved by seeing the lives of children in a developing country. Pisces also needs the tools to express his feelings—a musical instrument, a camera, art supplies. From there, he can make magic. When the Pisces boy is plugged into his imagination superstation, things happen quickly. You can't keep him out of trouble entirely, but you *can* make sure he gets into the "right" kind of it—making waves and turning the tides.

THE PISCES GIRL

Move over, Ariel—the *real* Little Mermaid is here. Enchanting and nurturing, the Pisces girl will capture your heart and reel it in hook, line, and sinker. With her sweet face and loving disposition, your Pisces might seem more like an adorable little doll than a daughter. Ethereal creatures, this sign can radiate a halo of glamour, like Pisces Cindy Crawford, Jessica Biel, and Vanessa Williams. Or they can be eternal sweethearts, like Pisces Drew Barrymore and Dakota Fanning.

Don't let her fragile facade fool you, though. The Fish may be tender, but she's also tough. The Pisces girl knows how to get her way, whether it's through charm, a world-class guilt trip, or just plain old bossiness. (You might see early signs in her imaginary games, when her teddy bear orders the stuffed penguin to take a time-out, or Barbie sternly reprimands Ken for his bad manners.) Pisces rules the feet, and when this girl puts her foot down, watch out—nobody can budge her! Still, even in her resistance, Pisces never loses her girlie touch. Those stamping feet might be shod in sparkly pink Mary Janes for her protest march. Even Pisces chicks with swagger (like Queen Latifah and Ke$ha) manage to exude femininity. She's an iron fist in a velvet glove—or maybe a fishnet one.

And, oh, how enchanting others find her to be. The Pisces girl does an alluring "come here, now go away" dance, reeling you in and then casting her line back out. Like a mermaid darting into the depths, the Pisces girl is accessible yet remote, maternal but mysterious. Her paradoxical persona will make other girls want to be her and little boys go gaga. It's why Pisces Elizabeth Taylor had seven husbands and Rue McClanahan, also a Pisces, had six. Pisces may be the Fish, but she's also the bait. (The *Golden Girls* actress even wrote a book called *My First Five Husbands . . . and the Ones Who Got Away.*)

The Pisces girl can be indecisive and even wishy-washy about her commitments. She's into ballet class today, wants to switch to tap tomorrow. Or Sophie is her "best friend in the whole wide world" one week—only to be replaced by Lily the next. The zodiac's Fish doesn't want to get caught on the line, but it can lead to folks finding her flaky. She might also want to be coddled and taken care of to excess. Parents of Pisces need to reinforce her self-sufficiency—even when you're tempted to join the Pisces pity party or "just do it for her." Enabling Pisces will block her from developing critical survival skills. Whenever you feel guilty drawing boundaries with Pisces, think of the mythical siren, whose hypnotic songs lured sailors out to sea and left them shipwrecked. If you fall for her femme fatale routine, it will be to everyone's detriment.

Mean-girl alert! When the Pisces girl feels threatened, she can mask it with harsh or bullying behavior. Insecurity can be toxic for this sign, bringing out some unsavory habits: gossip, emotional blackmail, playing people against each other. Monitor that passive-aggressive streak. Like Pisces comedian Chelsea Handler, she might get her laughs with some close-to-the-bone insults. Her humor can definitely be snarky. Or she may be indirect, smiling in your face but spreading rumors behind your back. Parents will definitely want to teach Pisces how to say what they mean and mean what they say. Or Pisces may need to learn the hard way when a he-said, she-said scenario comes back around to bite them. Nothing like losing a friend to give Pisces the wake-up call she needs.

Some Pisces girls run in cliques to ease social anxiety. While Pisces might create her girl gang for self-protection, it begs the question, what does Pisces need to be protected from in the first place? By becoming the bully she's trying to avoid, the Pisces girl ends up walking down the completely wrong path. Like Pisces Rihanna, she might cover her inner turmoil by playing the aloof, untouchable rebel—then box herself into this limiting role, burying her vulnerability.

Fortunately, Pisces is a mutable (adaptable) sign, and she *can* be steered back in a healthy direction when she drifts. Helping those less fortunate—sick children, abandoned animals, the poor—can give Pisces purpose and perspective. (This girl never met an animal or a baby she didn't love.) When she feels the victim, the Pisces girl can become moody and self-absorbed. But when she taps into her compassion and healing powers, this girl can change the world.

Parents of Pisces girls would do well to cultivate their artistic and creative talents. Like Pisces singers Liza Minnelli and Nina Simone, she might express her powerful emotions through music. She's a romantic at heart, and her softness is compelling. A butterfly, a sunset, the way light refracts through a prism—Pisces feels the aching magnificence in every cell. She can be a gifted writer, too, like children's author Megan McDonald (creator of the popular Judy Moody series), or humorist Erma Bombeck, whose column At Wit's End was a nationally syndicated favorite.

If she's more comfortable behind the scenes, a camera, paintbrush, or sketchbook could be her Pisces power tool. Just give her some raw materials—beads and string, a sewing machine, art supplies—and let her imagination do the rest. Once she connects with her intuition, she'll discover that her strength lies in her openness. "My daughter was incredibly shy in school, and would cling to this one friend who was much more outgoing," says the mom of one young Pisces. "Then, one of her drawings won a school poster contest, and it was blown up and exhibited in the entrance hall. She was even given an award in front of the whole school at an assembly. After that, she became a local 'celebrity' for her creative talents, and she began to show more of her personality." The electromagnetic field of the heart has been found to reach several feet outside of the body. By expanding her heart, rather than shutting it down, the Pisces girl allows the universe to whisper its magic to her. Plugged in and divinely guided, she can be vulnerable and invincible all at once.

BEHAVIOR DECODER: THE PISCES KID

WHEN PISCES . . .	IT MEANS . . .	SO YOU SHOULD . . .
Cries	Anything. This kid tears up at the drop of hat!	Don't overreact and make a big deal out of it. At the same time, don't ignore your Fish's tears or he might develop a "poor me" complex ("You don't care about my feelings!").
Withdraws socially or gets quiet or moody	Pisces is lost in his imagination.	Don't interrupt the dreamscape! Pisces need time to wander and let the muse sweep them away.
	Pisces is brooding. Uh-oh, her imagination's gotten carried away again!	Check in with Pisces and find out what "movie" is playing between those cute but suspicious little ears. If necessary, give her a reality check. This sign can come up with some outlandish suspicions and insecurities!
Acts out (hitting, kicking, talking back)	Pisces may be responding to tension in the environment.	Just add water: a bubble bath, tea, or a soothing drink can be the liquid balm for their souls. Or dial down the atmospheric tension: turn off the TV, dim the overheads, light scented candles. Meditation, breathing, and yoga can help Pisces, too—they're never too young.
	Emotional overload.	Dance break! Get Pisces to move the feelings creatively, by drawing, journaling, singing, or cranking up the music.
Gets clingy	Another typical day with Pisces . . .	Don't clip the apron strings abruptly, but help Pisces become comfortable and secure enough to venture away from your side.

CONTINUED ON NEXT PAGE

WHEN PISCES . . .	IT MEANS . . .	SO YOU SHOULD . . .
Won't eat what you serve	The mind-body-soul connection is strong for Pisces, so something could be "eating" at him, even manifesting as an allergy or food sensitivity.	See a doctor and request some allergy testing, but also find out what's happening with Pisces emotionally, too.
Can't sit still	The muse is present! Watery Pisces needs to let her creativity flow, so physical movement can help her channel the creativity from her imagination into tangible form.	Give her the tools of the trade. Hand Pisces some art supplies or clear a space for dancing.
	Anxiety alert! Pisces might be preoccupied with worry or guilt.	Help her talk through her concerns and reassure Pisces that all is well. Brainstorming solutions can help when Pisces gets overwhelmed.

THE SOCIAL PISCES

ROLE IN THE FAMILY

As the sign of karma, Pisces can be the soul and conscience of the family. These tender spirits arrive to heal hearts, mend fences, and bring compassion back to the household. In some cases, they can stir up unfinished business or reveal issues that have been veiled in secrecy. Relatives should be mindful not to make Pisces into scapegoats when this happens. Only when troubling matters see the light of consciousness, after all, can a difficult family dynamic be transformed.

Pisces may be wise beyond their years, but beware: they're also emotional sponges. These kids soak up everything, which can leave them overwhelmed and resentful. Because they never want to say no or hurt anyone's feelings, they may agree to things they don't actually want to do, then silently seethe or punish you later. Remember that Pisces are spiritual messengers, so they need extra protection and support. But remember, too, not to let them lapse into playing the helpless victim. These "miniature martyrs" might take on other people's issues (even yours) as an excuse to avoid personal responsibility or living their own lives. When your Fish's compassion turns into caretaking, remind him who's the parent and who's the child!

FRIENDS AND PEERS

Dualistic Pisces might have two distinct sets of friends: one for insecure days, another for when they feel experimental. Blending these two groups together is a bizarre mash-up, but Pisces have been known to try! One Pisces friend of ours went to an elite boarding school where she competed in equestrian dressage, but she was also into underground music. "After a horse show, I'd go out with my team to celebrate, and then I'd sneak out in the evening to listen to a band in town with my other friends."

When Pisces feel fragile, they can form cliques for protection—just as fish huddle into safe little schools. Or they may "swim with the sharks," borrowing their bravado from bullies. Insecurity can even bring out a bit of a mean-girl/mean-guy side of Pisces' personalities. When these kids feel disempowered, they can turn catty and gossipy, not realizing that their words have actual power to wound. They might even prey on a slightly weaker link, projecting their wrath onto a scapegoat. Yikes! Parents should keep tabs on Pisces' emotional state and instill confidence in them. Teach them to embrace their vulnerability. That way, Pisces won't overcompensate for their sensitivity by playing the tough guy.

When Pisces feel secure, they branch out and hang with some, er, interesting characters. Freaks and geeks, misfits, loners—the weirder, the better. There's an artsy "underground" side to Pisces that's drawn to all things indie and avant-garde. They can span the highest heights and the lowest depths of humanity. The compassionate side of Pisces makes them want to champion the underdog. Thus, the very people they picked on during today's self-hating moment could be the ones they defend on the school yard tomorrow.

Who can keep up with Pisces and their ever-shifting allegiances? Friends of Pisces might come to see them as fickle or untrustworthy, especially since they're often quick to gossip, make fun of people behind their backs, or even reveal information sworn to secrecy ("I promised her I wouldn't say anything, but if you swear not to tell a soul . . ."). As the zodiac's most illusory sign, their fluctuating fidelities help them stay shrouded in mystery. Pisces may always keep a little bit of distance in their friendships. That way, they can dart off and escape at a moment's notice. Like fish, they don't want to be caught in anyone's net. And like mermaids, they might come ashore to enchant you, but they will always swim back to the solitude of their own mysterious depths.

BROTHERS AND SISTERS: PISCES AS A SIBLING

Is blood thicker than water? Not when you're ruled by Neptune, the god of the sea. Like the tides, Pisces relationships to their siblings can ebb and flow. They can get sucked into family dramas and alliances, becoming codependent with siblings or taking sides with one against the other. Detaching is a real struggle for this sign, but it's a skill these kids need to learn. Otherwise, they can get pulled into the undertow of other people's issues, drowning in the drama. Life preserver, please!

Pisces' shifting moods can often muddle relationships with their siblings. The Fish likes to be nurtured but not controlled. When Pisces need their space, they want to be left alone—and it can be hard to break away from omnipresent brothers or sisters. Yet Pisces also want to be babied. Their MO with anyone older than them is "Take care of me, but don't tell me what to do." Unfortunately, this doesn't always work out so well. Since Pisces kids can seem fragile or vulnerable, an older sibling's protective instincts may naturally emerge. And since they often turn to an older sister or brother for help ("Tell me what to do!"), it can be confusing when the Fish pulls a bait-and-switch, demanding autonomy—or resenting the very support they asked for in the first place. "It's complicated" could certainly describe the dynamics of any Pisces sibling relationship!

DISCIPLINING A PISCES

*

Who, *me*? Seductive Pisces are masterful at pulling the wide-eyed, helpless act. There's something so fragile and sweet about them, you can't believe they'd hurt a fly—much less commit a crime. And when you raise your voice even half a decibel, their huge, luminous eyes fill with tears so quickly that *you* end up feeling like the criminal. Tail tucked between your legs, you slouch off, guilty and ashamed for suspecting Pisces of being anything less than perfect behavior. What kind of monster are you, anyway? One Pisces' mom realized this ruse when she found herself making excuses for her son's cranky behavior to another parent. "I started giving this elaborate explanation about him being extra sensitive because his big sister had recently started kindergarten, and then I said, 'Wait! Do I want to be the kind of mom who feels sorry for her son? What kind of lesson is that teaching him, anyway?'"

None, actually—but you've been conned by Pisces, the zodiac's most adept emotional blackmailers. Yes, the Fish has given *you* the bait this time, and now you're caught. Untangling yourself can be a messy process, but once you fall into the Pisces "poor me" trap a couple of times, you'll start to catch on. Still, Pisces will forever find new ways to reel you in—so don't get too comfortable. These clever kids can outsmart you when you least expect it!

Pisces can also be passive-aggressive, lashing out when they're wounded or expecting you to read their minds. You need to encourage direct and open communication to flow both ways. While you don't want to go *too* tough on the tough love, it's important to set clear limits, since Pisces have such fluid boundaries. That's a dicey matter, since boundaries are what help kids feel safe. If you have to repeat the rules like a broken record, don't be surprised. Trying to control Pisces is like keeping water in a sieve—your grasp on these kids will be slippery at best.

If anything, you might need to borrow some of Pisces' own persuasive tactics. Instead of chasing, reel your little Pisces in. Be the bait that *he* wants to take. Make life into an enchanting adventure, and the Fish will gladly swim along by your side. It might sound like a lot of work, but hey, at least you'll have a trusty companion and the reassurance that Pisces is staying out of trouble! In worst cases, you might need to instill an extra dose of fear in Pisces. It's not a great method, but it works—and when your dreamy Pisces wanders down one too many metaphorical dark alleys, pulling the alarm bells might be the only way to snap them out of their hazy reveries.

HANDLING TRANSITIONS: MOVING, DIVORCE, DEATH, AND OTHER TOUGH STUFF

Feelings, nothing more than feelings. Poignant Pisces react to most changes emotionally though not necessarily with tears or big displays. Their tiny psychic radars just pick up on everything that's going on. Pisces rule the zodiac's twelfth house of closure and endings. Inside, these old souls have a quiet understanding of life's natural cycles, including loss. If a relative is sick or even dying, Pisces will bring healing energy to their bedside. These are the zodiac's nurses and shamans.

Fortunately, because Pisces is a mutable (adaptable) sign, kids born under it won't be traumatized if they have to move or change schools. It gives them a chance to reinvent themselves, which they kind of like. Or they'll escape into their vivid imaginations to cope. Divorce can be upsetting, especially if it shatters a fantasy your Pisces has about the family. In other cases, wise Pisces already knows something is off and isn't really surprised by the news. Parents must also be mindful not to suck Pisces into adult drama or force their child to choose sides.

For some Pisces, the only constant in their lives is change. While they will adapt and "go with the flow," make sure your Fish isn't keeping feelings inside. Since Pisces rules the subconscious mind, these kids aren't always aware when changes affect them. You may see it in your child's artwork, music choices, style, or the books she reads. She might even have nightmares or recurring symbolic dreams. Often it's what Pisces *isn't* saying that will give you the most clues.

SCHOOL'S IN SESSION

*

BEST EDUCATION STYLE

Any takers for a cozy little enclave that looks more like a playroom than a school? A place where teachers go by their first names and kids design their own curriculum? Yes, please! Pisces thrive in creative environments that nurture their imaginations. Drop these kids into a Waldorf-style wonderland and watch them became the next artistic or musical prodigy. Put them into a high-pressure school that emphasizes grades and testing, though, and they'll flop, starved for the air to breathe. Even if they get the grades and ace the tests (which they might), Pisces do best anywhere with a strong arts program or an emphasis on creative problem solving.

The only caveat is that Pisces need *some* structure or they can float off into the ether. Preparing them for the "real" world is essential, since these sensitive souls tend to avoid the harshness of reality. With Pisces, there is a fine balance between letting them flow and giving them essential survival skills. Tempted as you are to shelter or coddle them, Pisces also need to be pushed past limiting self-beliefs. They can be insecure about their own abilities or easily frazzled by a complicated assignment. Help them calm down and cheer them along with a "You can do it!" A serene space for homework keeps them on track, too. Since Pisces soak up the vibes of any environment—especially a chaotic classroom—they might need a transitional after-school chat to clear their emotions. Fix a cup of tea or cocoa and let your Pisces unload. After that, he should be ready to hit the books.

BEST HOBBIES AND ACTIVITIES

On your toes! Pisces rule the feet, and these kids might be graceful on theirs, gifted at dancing, skating, and soccer (like Pisces pro player Mia Hamm). Keep Pisces twirling, tapping, kicking, springing, and spinning like little electrons around an atom's nucleus. Solitude is also important for this reflective sign to recharge. At times, Pisces may need to retreat into their sanctuaries to do nothing—and to detox from any negative energy they've picked up. As Pisces George Washington said, "It is better to be alone than in bad company."

Is your Pisces shy but observant? Give this kid a camera. Pisces is the sign associated with film, and these kids can be gifted photographers who have a beautiful sense of color and light. Renowned photographers Ansel Adams and Diane Arbus were Pisces. They might enjoy capturing what they see with watercolor paints or oil pastels, too. Sign this kid up for a museum class! Pisces can also be scientific. They might be drawn to chemistry sets or anything else where they can mix ingredients and elements into their own little potions. They might enjoy concocting things by cooking, baking, or making their own teas and soaps.

The gentle souls of animals resonate with Pisces. Your child may want to adopt a menagerie of pets or even help with an animal rescue. Begin with an aquarium, and then let her graduate into greater pet responsibility (gerbils, snakes, birds, cats, dogs, lizards). These little daydreamers can lose track of time, forgetting to feed and walk an animal on a regular basis. So unless you're prepared to share in the duties, keep it low maintenance.

Volunteer and service work should be imperative for this sign, and the younger these kids start, the better. Their huge wells of compassion need an outlet. If you notice your little Pisces getting into mischief or going into "victim" mode, it's time for a close-up look at what underprivileged really looks like. In the zodiac, each sign rules, or is associated with, a different set of traits or industries. Pisces rules hospitals, institutions, and old age, so helping the sick or elderly can give them a sense of divine purpose. As Pisces Einstein said, "Only a life lived for others is a life worthwhile." While Pisces shouldn't skip out on forming their own identities, there's definitely truth in Einstein's words—especially for his fellow Fish.

GIFT GUIDE: BEST PRESENTS FOR PISCES

* Arts and crafts supplies—especially watercolor paints
* Any DIY or home decor kit: stained-glass window hanging kits, beading supplies, an ice-cream maker
* A chemistry set or fun science experiment kits
* Camera equipment
* A saltwater aquarium stocked with colorful tropical fish
* Ballet or dance lessons
* Sports equipment, especially for "foot" activities like soccer, hockey, roller derby, or ice skating
* Books about magic, sorcery, spirituality, and the mystical—even a starter deck of tarot cards
* Tickets to a local children's museum, the ballet, or a costume/historical institute

PART II

Mom Signs

THE ARIES MOM

(March 21–April 19)

MOMMY MAGIC - Your Strengths:

Confidence
Self-awareness
Strength
Fearlessness

MAMA MIA - Your Challenges:

Competitiveness
Anger
Tunnel vision
Obsessiveness
Vanity and self-centeredness

FAMOUS ARIES MAMAS:

Reese Witherspoon, Jennifer Garner, Sarah Jessica Parker, Sarah Michelle Gellar, Kourtney Kardashian, Kate Hudson, Mariah Carey, Celine Dion, Victoria Beckham, Kate Gosselin, Claire Danes, Fergie

YOUR PARENTING STYLE

*

Hello, warrior mama! Because the Aries mother does everything with a fierce signature style, you'll charge into parenthood headfirst, intent on leaving your mark. Ruled by red-hot Mars, Aries approach everything in life as if going into battle—alive, alert, and in it to win it. Motherhood's not for sissies, and good thing *you've* never fit that description. There's a diva in every Aries woman, and your confidence never leaves you for long—even if that diva happens to have a milk stain on her Fendi jacket or Ritz bits in her blowout. Like Aries mum Victoria "Posh Spice" Beckham, you could probably even make graham cracker crumbs look glamorous!

In the zodiac wheel, which is divided into twelve houses (each representing a different part of your life), the fourth house influences your mothering style. Depending on your sign, the fourth house will be ruled by a specific zodiac sig that colors your parenting approach. If you are an Aries, the ruler of your fourth house of motherhood is Cancer, so no matter how tough and independent you are, there's maternal instinct in there. You can morph into quite the domestic diva when it comes to your family. Cancer is symbolized by the über-protective Crab, giving you the tendency to shelter your little ones. You won't want your kids inheriting *your* daredevil tendencies. (Cross that mini–motor scooter off the Christmas list, stat.) Motherhood will also bring out your sentimental side—perhaps to your own surprise. Didn't think you were the type to tear up at a ballet recital or to take up scrapbooking? Surprise! Cancer is an emotional sign, so whether it's joy, anger, or sadness, your feelings can run to the extremes when it comes to your children.

The strangest part of motherhood, especially in the early years, is experiencing another human being's total dependence on you. Aries is one of the most self-directed signs, and you're comfortable putting your own needs first. But ranking another person's agenda before your own—and a tiny person's at that? Well, that takes a bit of an adjustment. No matter how much you adore your little chickadee, one thing is clear: you are two distinct and separate human beings.

Frankly, that is a healthy attitude for the most part. Although you may be guilty of expecting *too* much self-sufficiency from your kids, you're great at modeling that very trait for them. Aries never asks for permission to be yourself or to pursue your goals. A martyr mom you ain't! Forever achieving and striving, you're a powerful role model of lifelong learning, a one-woman accomplishment machine—the ultimate glass-ceiling breaker.

"My mom was a black single mother in Detroit making six figures—and that was in the 1980s," says Brandon, the Pisces son of an Aries mother. "She drove a Porsche and lived separately from my stepdad. My mom was beautiful, but she was so serious that she didn't even go to her prom. She graduated from high school a year early, went straight to beauty school, and later ended up buying her own salon, which she still owns."

That's the kind of unbreakable determination Aries women bring to everything. A small identity crisis may ensue when you launch into motherhood, especially as you realize that you can no longer come and go as you please. Ms. Independent now answers to someone, and around the clock at that!

Hopefully, you've got a great partner—or a tribe of folks heavy on the maternal instinct—lined up to help. You'll need the backup, Aries! You may be better playing the stereotypical "dad" role: roughhousing, coaching Little League, making the primary paycheck, enforcing the rules. In your family, you may be the tough disciplinarian, whereas your partner handles the cuddles, bedtime stories, and boo-boo kissing. (Finally, you realize what a genius you were for choosing that human marshmallow of a mate. Hello, on-demand nurturer!) Even if you still play the stereotypical "mom" role, your strength and boundless energy permeate your every move.

Eventually, you also realize that motherhood is a skill set that can only be learned through experience. Even if your bulletproof confidence slips for a bit, you'll embrace the challenge and work hard to regain a firm feminist footing. In fact, you might enjoy ascending to the herculean task of raising a child and even bringing home the bulk of the bacon all at the same time. Like a she-panther, you'll stalk the information and resources you need, planting yourself at the front of the preschool admissions line, orchestrating a fleet of nannies, in-laws, and mother's helpers to help juggle your packed lifestyle. You'll style your kids perfectly, enter them in contests, push them to be the best at everything they do. And . . . you'll make it look *easy*.

That said, Aries is a competitive sign, and even in motherhood, you're in it to win it. Here's a hard truth, though, if you're an alpha-female Aries: other moms may not like you until you take less of a saber-toothed approach. Much to your feminist chagrin, women are still being schooled that they have to be "nice"—or, in your opinion, fake—pretending that everything is a perfect democracy then gossiping behind each other's backs. (Men are so much easier, but let's not even *talk* about what would happen if you started to pal around with all the dads.) You may spice up that playground rumor mill with your unapologetic bids for PTA presidency or your shameless bragging about your child's amazing standardized test scores.

While scrapping for the top spot has done you well in the workforce (how *else* was your family going to afford that private school tuition unless you became chair*woman* of the board?), competitive mothering can be a slippery slope. No way should you dim your light so a bunch of jealous haters can feel better about themselves, of course. You're a star and that's just how it is. But examine your motives if you find yourself always needing to one-up and outshine the other moms around you. Maybe . . . just maybe . . . you're talking about yourself a *little* too much. Cue Aries mother of eight Kate Gosselin, who fell from fans' grace when she began to seem a bit too self-serving in her public image.. One Aries mom we know recently posted an infographic on social media that read, "Competing with yourself makes you better. Competing with others makes you bitter." Good point. Dole out some compliments to the other moms or give them the spotlight, and you'll find it much easier to form friendships.

Aries is the sign of individuality, so you'll definitely need solo time, where you answer to nobody but yourself. We repeat: you *must* have time for yourself. This is the hardest part of motherhood, so keep a fleet of trustworthy overnight sitters and nannies around when you decide to leave the children at home and jet off to Aruba for a week of "me time" or head to the spa for the massage/facial/pedicure package. We know Aries moms who keep a standing weekly spa appointment and a happy hour date with girlfriends. Others unapologetically have locks on their bedrooms doors or home offices, and even rent a pied-à-terre so they can spend a night or two away from the kids once in a while.

While you may raise eyebrows or be called "selfish," consider it an important dose of prevention. The Aries mom who forgoes her decompression chamber can become a seething rage monster, taking her stress out on the kids. Most Aries mothers could use a little anger management at some point in the parenting process. As an impatient sign, you're already a quick burn. So when motherhood tests your limits, you'll need to temper that, er, temper of yours. Hotheaded Aries mamas can fly off the handle a little *too* fast. (Joan "no wire hangers" Crawford, aka Mommie Dearest, was an Aries.)

Finding the healthy midpoint between disciplining and terrifying your kids will take work. In fact, if you're trying the "scared straight" approach, consider that you may need to process some of your own paranoia and irrational fears. A dose of therapy can stop you from projecting those onto your children. You may also be pulling the whole "do as I say, not as I do" number on your children. After all, you left home at sixteen with a bus ticket and $20 to your name—and now your own kids can't stay out past 9:00 p.m., date, or wear makeup until they graduate. What's up with *that*, Aries?

While you can be a world-class listener with your clients, colleagues, and friends in need, you may need to clean out your ears, shush yourself, and learn to really hear your kids. In other words, talk less and listen more. Aim to cultivate the Buddhist version of "beginner's mind" rather than finishing your child's sentences or lecturing him. Monologues and diatribes will only anger your children—even if later in life, you may get the satisfaction of hearing them say, "You were right, Mom."

IF YOU HAVE A GIRL

*

PROS

Girl power! Aries is the sign of the individual and a fierce fighter at heart. You'll definitely want your daughter to follow in your can-do footsteps (even if she's shod in Manolos and Jimmy Choos). You manage to mother with glamour and flair, and if your daughter is a fashionista in the making, she'll certainly enjoy shopping in your overstuffed wardrobe. You'll cheer your little girl on every step of the way, encouraging her to become self-sufficient and ambitious—just like her mama. Whether she's kicking the winning soccer goal or donning pink pointe slippers, there's no greater champion for goals and dreams than the Aries mom. With your own competitive spirit, you'll certainly lead by example. The Aries mother makes sure that her daughter knows anything boys can do, girls can do, too.

At the same time, nobody knows how to demand—and command—queenly respect quite like the Aries mother. Although in extreme cases it can veer into diva territory, the balanced Aries mom teaches her daughter the highest meaning of "ladies first." Pass the crown and scepter! Your daughter will never diminish herself to pump up a man's ego or grab the check on a date. Not under your watch, anyway.

CONS

Easy does it! Just because *you* can conquer the world without breaking a sweat doesn't mean your daughter wants the same high-octane lifestyle. In fact, your own supermom tendencies can have an accidental dark side, making your daughter feel like she has to keep pace with you. Teach your little girl to bring her A-game, but remember that some zodiac signs (particularly water and earth ones) move at a much slower speed than you do. For example, if you're active and fit, your talk of your great metabolism and your dedicated elliptical sessions might make your daughter feel inferior if she lacks the same dedication. As a result, a competitive vibe may spark up, creating a tense rift or giving your daughter a complex.

Watch your Aries tendency to be self-referential, using your own experiences as a barometer for how your daughter should live. Yes, your opinions are thoughtful and wise, but they're still just that: opinions. If your values clash, especially as your daughter gets older, your famous temper can flare. But rather than grapple for iron-fisted control, agree to disagree—and encourage her to think for herself. Better that your daughter should question everything, including *your* beliefs, on the road to becoming an individual. Her fierce self-awareness, after all, may be her greatest tribute to you.

IF YOU HAVE A BOY

PROS

Does a Y chromosome spell . . . relief? There's a big part of you that relates better to boys than to girls. You're "masculine" in your approach to many things, so you can dish out the kind of no-nonsense directness that boys stereotypically need. A wishy-washy doormat you ain't! Your son will learn how to respect authority from you. Although you won't cramp his style, you'll make your boundaries clear, establishing yourself as the alpha in the relationship. As time goes by, he'll learn how to treat women with reverence, growing into the chivalrous man-child of your dreams.

As you continue to maintain your own busy life, you impart an important message: your son may be the prince of your world, but Mama's the queen. He gets a primary female role model who's independent and confident. He learns that his mommy's world doesn't only revolve around him. Later on, after he's explored life on his own terms, he may choose a partner who's also autonomous and self-respecting. And while there may be a diva duel or two in store, hopefully you'll be flattered that he's picked a mate in your image.

CONS

Capable as you are, Aries women still know how to play the diva in (faux) distress. Your boy will learn to pull out your chair, fetch your coat, and steady your elbow when you're in six-inch heels. Despite your ultramodern politics, you'll hammer old-fashioned values into your son about the way he treats the ladies—starting with you, of course. While it's cool to revive the dying art of chivalry, just make sure you don't break your boy's spirit in the process. In other words, back off when you catch yourself micromanaging his every move or trying to mold him into "mommy's little helper."

You're an opinionated mama, and your son will have no vagueness about your values or views on his choices. However, he's entitled to create his own belief system—yes, even under your roof. Otherwise, he may shut you out of his personal life to avoid your meddling and unsolicited feedback. Give him some breathing room and try to supervise from a healthy distance. You may not approve of every hobby he picks up, the friends he makes, or the people he dates. Or you may be *too* approving, adopting his girlfriend as your BFF and becoming a fixture at all of his school events. Check yourself: are you doing this to force your way into his life? If your base motives are territorial ones, exit his turf. And if you're encroaching because you're worried about him, vent your concerns with friends or a therapist to make sure you haven't lost perspective.

PARENTING THROUGH AGES AND STAGES

INFANCY (THE FIRST YEAR)

The newborn phase can be one of the tougher times for Aries moms. As a highly visual, take-charge person, you're used to things going your way. Even though pregnancy gave you a taste of being out of control—hello, complete body takeover—there's nothing like a newborn to send your inner warrior princess to her knees. Even the toughest Aries woman may be unprepared for the sleep deprivation, ceaseless wailing, and assorted indignities that come along with caring for a brand-new babe. And let's not even *talk* about your skin/hair/nails that seem, overnight, to have lost their prenatal vitamin glow. You're *so* not ready for your close-up—and you've already booked a sitting with the best family photographer in town.

Accustomed to springing back quickly from, well, everything, you may be stunned at how long it takes you to recover from birth—physically, emotionally, and mentally. The loss of independence can be a big blow for your on-the-move sign. Remind yourself often that this phase only lasts about a year—which might seem like a century now, but it will pass quickly. Here, Aries mama, is your golden ticket: slow down and give yourself a break! (It may be the first and only time in your life that you do.) Savor the daily and weekly changes. Your baby will never have so many milestones in a single year's time. In hindsight, you'll be so happy you didn't miss them.

Your own competitive nature can be a culprit here, too. Aries are take-charge people by nature, but there's no place for an aggressive approach in the nursery. You may need to soften that "masculine" energy of yours down a bit now. And still, you will realize your own limitations at moments—for real. When all the singing, cooing, and doting in the world fails to soothe your upset infant, you may start to feel like a failure. When your child doesn't instantly respond to your best baby-whispering techniques, your frustration can reach critical mass.

Bonding with your babe, especially the firstborn, may take longer than you expect as a result. You might even be shocked or caught unprepared by the extreme contrast between your dreams and the person actually sleeping in that cradle. You'll need to remind yourself repeatedly that your child is your best teacher. As a stubborn sign that rarely takes direction, the Aries mom may resist being schooled by her tiny, squalling professor. But school is indeed in session. Lesson number one: how to adapt to another person's rhythms when you've spent your whole life marching to your own beat.

If you're in a relationship, parenthood also means compromising with your partner and collaborating on the decision-making process. Balance is not your strong suit, but you'll need to embrace it in order to adapt to this massive lifestyle change. Even single Aries moms will still have a proverbial village of sitters, relatives, and caregivers chiming in and offering to lend a hand. Our advice: take whatever support you can get! Don't try to be the hero and do it all yourself, unless you want to end up depressed and overwhelmed. Remind yourself: I've got nothing to prove here.

"The first five weeks were a bit of a roller coaster," says Rose, the Aries mom of a nine-month-old son. "I felt like my son and I weren't meshing. My husband, on the other hand, was a natural. He knew when the bambino was hungry and how to wrap him in a perfect swaddle. And me, I was a freaking mess. I just felt like I wasn't *getting* this whole motherhood thing."

Encouragement from her own mother made a huge difference for Rose. "The first week alone at home with this fragile little thing was hard—he just wouldn't settle down and then the crying seemed to peak," Rose recalls. "What it came down to was a phone call and the wise words of my mum: 'Believe in yourself. The baby and you are one. He feels what you feel, so be confident and it will get better.' From that day on, I picked myself up, released the feelings of failure and haven't looked back since."

Now that's the Aries spirit! Ironically, if you want to reconnect with your true courageous nature, you have to admit to your own weakness and shortcomings. So take off that "brave face" and allow others to support you. Infancy is not a time to be goal-oriented, and we understand that this is an interruption to your true nature. But trying to prove that "I'm still me" by launching a business or defending your doctoral research while your sugarplum's still in swaddling clothes? That's a recipe for a breakdown. Better to deal with the shifts in your identity—or to embrace motherhood as a new frontier for your intrepid sign to conquer.

Funny enough, Aries is the "infant" of the zodiac. You're the first sign of the cosmic calendar, making you the astrological newborn. So if you think about it, you can probably relate to your babe in ways you hadn't considered: the demand for immediate gratification, abandonment issues (in your case, well-disguised ones), extreme sensitivity to your surroundings (Aries rules the nervous system), and at times, a lack of awareness about anyone's needs but your own.

Yep, you share some of those traits. That means *you* still need to be babied, too. So get that pedicure or facial. Sneak out for a date night, even if you still only fit into maternity clothes (just accessorize to get the glam, and go). Have a quickie while the baby naps. Let your sister sit while you go to yoga. Take a kid-free couple's minivacation. Otherwise, you may secretly start to resent your infant for having so many needs—which will slow down the bonding process even more. Don't neglect your own desires, Aries, even if you have to dial them down a tad, or put them on a more structured schedule.

As the saying goes, "The mother is born with the child." And it's true. Pay homage to your own "birth" during this phase. Aries is the sign of individuality, so rather than feel like you've lost yourself, make an adventure out of finding yourself in this new role. Enjoy witnessing your own milestones right along with the baby's. Create adventures for two. If you're athletic, get a jogging stroller and take the baby for a run. Host a "ladies' night out" for yourself and some savvy mom friends. Before you know it, an "aha!" moment about yourself could turn into a multimillion-dollar invention that parents can't live without, a maternity-wear line, or a best-selling book that inspires other mamas everywhere.

And if you're simply too damn tired to take the world by storm, use this year as a rare chance to practice the fine art of patience and to do some serious mom-baby bonding. A year of intense self-discovery will lead you down new paths, making you a richer, more evolved human being along the way.

TODDLERHOOD (TWO TO FIVE YEARS)

The toddler phase can be both joyful and frustrating for the Aries mom. On the upside, you've got the energy to chase your little speed demon around the park—at least on the days you're not consumed by work or traipsing around in six-inch heels. But with your youthful spirit, you'll enjoy the adventures and active pace of this phase. You and your toddler may even share the same short attention span and love of physical play. Hide-and-seek, anyone?

Still, the Aries mom itches to have her own *thing*, so you may continue to struggle to regain your independent groove while your little one is so dependent on your attention and care. And while you love being *numero uno* in your child's life, this role can leave you frustrated. "There just aren't enough hours in the day!" one Aries mom of a two-year-old sighs. Certainly not if you're juggling Mommy & Me classes *and* a master's degree program, like she is.

But what other option is there for an independent Aries? You need your own life and hobbies, so you'll need to embrace your sign's so-called selfish nature. At least you're modeling independence and self-sufficiency. Your child will learn that Mommy isn't always there as an on-demand provider, which in the right proportions can encourage healthy separation. But during this stage, there will be moments when your child will accept no substitutes, and you'll need to give a lot more attention than you want.

If you can't beat 'em, join 'em. Make sure to have lots of fun activities planned that *you* actually enjoy, too. Don't force yourself to take a baby swim class in that chilly YMCA pool (Hypothermia? No thanks) or to visit the petting zoo (where your germophobic side goes haywire). If you'd enjoy a dance class, drumming, or doing mom–baby yoga together, then for goodness' sake, do that. At this age, it's more important to your child that you're sharing quality time, even if you're finger painting or banging spoons on pots and pans.

On that note, your competitive side might think this is a good age to start your child on the Suzuki violin method, to sign your budding athlete up at an elite karate school, or to put your diva-licious daughter on the pageant circuit. Tread carefully here, Aries. Not only can this damage your kid's psyche if he or she isn't ready for the leap, but you might be creating a time-zapping trap. Picture yourself in two years: schlepping your kid to martial arts tournaments and national music competitions, or spending a fortune on spray tans, pageant coaches, and sequined gowns. The "mom-ager" circuit is a surefire way to become the kind of martyr mother who lives for (and through) her kids—unbefitting of an Aries.

If your tot is truly talented, then cultivate those gifts. But don't steal his childhood because you're trying to prove what a great mom you are or to instill an early competitive spirit in your kids. You may be in go-getter mode, staking out the best activities and organizing the preschool's annual fund-raiser. Just take it down a notch every now and then—you don't always have to be in charge of the mommy meet-ups and playdates. The toddler years are a time when a lot of mothers feel incredibly frustrated and overwhelmed, and your tolerance for hearing other women complain can run thin. While you don't have to sink down into constant commiserating, make sure not to brag, either. Nothing good can come of telling that half-asleep mom "I have the best babysitter" or "My kid falls asleep right away." Modeling confidence and competence is one thing, but don't forget to validate other moms' emotions and experiences, even if you offer them sage, pick-me-up advice.

Besides, the "terrible twos" can be tough, even for you, Aries. When you're in the hot seat, you'll be glad you didn't alienate your new support network by trying to look perfect. This phase only lasts a couple years, and it's the perfect time for solo-flying Aries to learn the power of teamwork. Your toddler *will* misbehave, defy you, and make you look like a terrible mother to judgmental observers—no matter how strict or intimidating or by the book you are.

On that note, your natural discipline style can be a little aggressive, which you'll want to monitor. You may struggle to keep your cool when your toddler throws a public tantrum, or darts out toward the street, scaring the daylights out of you. The question looms: how do you teach a little one the necessary "fear" that prevents dangers and life-threatening situations? Maybe it's *you* who needs the training, Aries. Rather than splurge on pricey music classes your tyke will barely remember, take a parenting workshop instead. It doesn't mean you're weak or bad at the job of being a mom; in fact, it takes real strength to admit that you don't have all the answers. Cultivating the patience and perspective this phase demands can make you a better person all around.

Also remember: when an Aries mama's happy, everybody's happy. If you're not finding enough quality time to relax, you may need a total change of environment. Yes, that might mean a new address, one in a calmer place than you imagined for your pre-child self. Have you always been a city slicker? The burbs might look appealing for the first time ever. You might shock yourself (and your friends) by relocating to a different part of town—if not to another state or country. Or you might plunk down for that lakefront cabin, country house, or time-share condo just to have a regular escape. Now more than ever, you need that balance between "mommy time" and "me time." If that means rearranging your priorities and lifestyle, it could be well worth it to you.

EARLY CHILDHOOD (SIX TO ELEVEN YEARS)

For whom does that (elementary-school) bell toll? You, Aries! It's the sound of sweet freedom, when you can shepherd your little ones safely into the capable hands of a schoolteacher—and get back to your own pursuits. For the last five years, you've been chomping at the bit to launch your online boutique, finish your PhD, or regain your status as top real-estate salesperson in your county. Or maybe it's time to ring that executive recruiter who's been hot on your heels with a senior VP opening. You'd be perfect for it . . . wouldn't you?

There may be a few misty-eyed moments

after breakfast or school drop-off: how did they grow up so fast? After all, you *just* got used to this new identity as a mother, and now the game is changing again. But those tear ducts will dry up quickly once you realize how much free time you've regained. Besides, there are plenty of opportunities to leave a fancy footprint at your child's school. *Someone* has to plan a school district fund-raiser that people actually want to attend (picture a circus theme complete with live animals and striped tents, catering by local restaurants, a toy auction—you're gonna blow them away). And who else will boldly champion the integration of technology in the classroom when your child comes home with a ten-pound backpack? Get set to mobilize a team who can convert textbooks into digitized data and downloads. Boom! Who's a better PTA president than you, Aries?

At this phase, your child starts to individuate a bit more, and you like that. It's certainly easier to deal with than a defiant toddler. At this impressionable age, your little one may outright idolize you, which you secretly love. Don't be surprised if he brings home hand-drawn stories and essays about his amazing mom. (Grab those refrigerator magnets, stat!) Time together becomes fun instead of frustrating, because you can actually engage intellectually with your child. You enjoy the earnest questions, and teaching him to achieve and think for himself. This could very well be your "golden era" of motherhood.

However, you'll face a different set of challenges during this phase, too, mostly related to time management. You may be working a lot now, so between after-school activities, homework, and your day job, finding quality time to accomplish goals, exercise, and pamper yourself can still be tricky. If you overschedule your kids, you could find yourself stressed and harried, feeling more like a chauffeur than a mom (and probably snapping at your daughter en route to ballet). But it's better than dragging them to your errands, meetings, and appointments. You want them to have proper supervision and outlets all through the day, even if you can't be the one delivering it. And, if someone else is providing that attention, you can pay some attention to yourself!

As Brandon, who grew up with a single Aries mom, says, "My mom worked as a hairdresser Wednesday until Saturday, from seven a.m. until the night. She was so type A that when she got home, it wasn't like she poured herself a glass of wine. She wanted to know about my homework, my friends, my projects. She made dinner, and then we watched *Cheers.* She was always 'on.' " Amazing and capable as you are, Aries, even you can burn out if you try to do it all during this phase. This is the time to stretch out of your superwoman comfort zone and get communal: swap babysitting, carpooling, and other must-dos with fellow moms. Maybe you have the whole kiddie crew over on Mondays for board games and spelling drills, and then another family handles Tuesday gymnastics pick-up and drop-off, and so on. Get creative, Aries.

If you own a retail business, set up an area of the shop for your little ones to draw, play games, and do homework. Since kids this age still aim to please, put them to work. Give them little tasks and even a small allowance as a reward. At age eleven, Brandon was hired to sweep his mom's salon and work as a shampooer. "To this day, if I need some extra money, I'll go into her salon and shampoo some heads," he laughs.

If you can't beat 'em, join 'em seems to be the Aries way. "My mom ran a day care and a cake-baking business out of our home," recalls one daughter of an Aries. "It was just expected that we help out. My sisters and I watched those kids and we mixed ingredients for her cakes—we ran her business right along with her. Although I resented it sometimes, she showed me a good work ethic and probably kept me out of trouble. I'm grateful for that now."

Single-focus Aries doesn't like to stray from a target. And now you need to compartmentalize life more than ever: free time for yourself, fun time with your kids, work, school, activities, romance, and so forth. How do you survive? You bring your full attention to whatever it is you're doing, Zen Buddhist–style. When you're working, you're working. When you're playing, you're really playing. You might want to carve out a regular "family day" or nonnegotiable together-time traditions. Ban cell phones from the table and have distraction-free dinners. If you observe a religion, there could be a day at church or temple followed by a special family lunch. Maybe there's an adventure afternoon every Saturday where you all go skating, hiking, or to an interactive event at the museum. Combining enrichment and affection will go far: your kids will love to explore the world with their cool, capable mom!

Getting involved at the school is another great way to share quality time—and hopefully make some cool new mom friends. However, this isn't something Aries moms do easily. You're a solo-player sign who tends to start and lead communities—you're not an eager joiner of groups that already exist. It can take a minute to adjust to the school scene, so ease in gently. Brandon's mom actually sent in her friendly Sagittarius sister as an auntie ambassador, since she was often too busy to attend the PTA meetings but still wanted to keep tabs on what her son was learning and doing.

Here's a hot tip: many Aries have two speeds in new social settings. You either come in guns blazing (fire the principal; there's a new sheriff in town!) and overwhelming everyone with your directness, or as a hawklike observer who can seem snobbish and standoffish. Easy does it! Push yourself to be warm and friendly, rather than sizing up the other parents—otherwise, you'll earn a reputation as aloof, or worse. In this environment, humility is the key. Ask questions ("How many kids do you have? Do they both go to school here?") rather than bragging about your child or talking about yourself too much. And don't forget to smile! Aries rules the face, so your expression says a thousand words. A pinched appearance might accidentally communicate "I'm too good for this place" when you're really just feeling uncomfortable or looking for a niche.

As you get more comfortable, you'll enjoy having your kids' friends over for the occasional sleepover or playdate, keeping a watchful eye on their interactions and taking them out for fun, over-the-top days on the town. If your career is superbusy, make an extra effort to get to know the parents of your kid's closest friends. Aries don't trust people easily, but you don't want to constrict your child's social life just because you haven't subjected other caregivers to one of your CIA-style background checks. Invite the whole family over for dinner. As you serve your world-famous chicken cacciatore (okay, so you reheated a dish from Whole Foods—who needs to know?), you can ask important questions that help you secretly size up their values and parenting styles.

Above all, remember to enjoy the sweetness of this stage of your child's life! Don't get so caught up in the "doing" of everything that you forget just to connect with your kid. Is it really imperative that your daughter be a prize-winning "mathlete" or that your son learns Mandarin Chinese to prepare for the changing first world powers? Not if you never see each other. Through trial and error, you'll learn how to prepare them for life while still being present.

ADOLESCENCE AND TEENS (TWELVE TO EIGHTEEN YEARS)

Willful. Headstrong. Wants to come and go as she pleases. Thinks she's invincible and has an answer for everything. Wait, are we talking about your teenager . . . or you, Aries?

Adolescence is no picnic for any parent, but you of all signs have the chops to handle this impulsive, identity-shaping era. Teenagers are funny creatures: one minute, they want to flaunt their independence; the next, they want to be babied. So stop and ask yourself, am I not the same way?

You're also fearless about holding your ground and setting firm limits. No smart-talking teen can intimidate or bully *you*, Aries. As much as it may seem otherwise, adolescents actually crave boundaries because it helps them feel safe to know what's expected of them. The key is to make sure your rules are reasonable. You're not afraid of your kids—but you *do* fear the destructive influences around them. So how do you set limits without crushing their individuality?

"Consistency is everything," says our Aries friend Terri Cole, a talent agent turned therapist who inherited three out-of-control teenage boys when she married a widower fifteen years ago. "When I walked into that house it was insane. The kids were running the place. At our first dinner, the youngest yelled, 'Shut up!' at his brother across the dinner table. I took a deep breath and calmly said, 'From now on, there's no more yelling in this house.' He looked at me like I was crazy. Then I put the whole family into therapy. There was a lot of healing that needed to happen—and it did."

Smart move, especially since Aries can have famously short fuses. Frustration builds up quickly, especially when you feel out of control. You need to feel like you're steering the family ship, and you don't fancy wrestling for the wheel with a defiant fourteen-year-old. Terri's own therapist training helped her understand the underlying emotions—anger, frustration, insecurity—beneath the surly teenage communication style. "At one point, my youngest only wanted to talk about cars and rims. So that was how I related to him—we talked about rims," says Terri. "To this day, and he's now grown and a father himself, he comes to me for advice."

If you're not an Aries with such keen listening skills, you might want to develop some now. Otherwise, you can lapse into lecturing, or having intense reactions/explosions triggered by your fear of losing the upper hand. Believe it or not, your kids desperately want your guidance, but you have to make yourself approachable enough for them to confide in you. That also means dealing with your own bruised ego or disappointment when your child pulls away. When your number-one fan suddenly turns into your public enemy number one, you need to remind yourself that the teen years are a temporary stage and that her distancing is how she forms her identity.

"The thing to remember is that you're always the parent," reflects Terri. "You always have to be the adult for them." Of course, that doesn't mean that you'll *look* like a grown-up. Forever youthful (and dare we say it, smokin'), you may remain glamorous, trendy, and even a sharper dresser than your kids. This could make your teenager simultaneously proud and embarrassed, especially when your outfits veer into edgy or sexy terrain. Save those for your girls' nights out, Aries—the last thing you need is a wardrobe malfunction at a PTA function.

You'll be busy and on the go with your own life by this time, which is also a mixed bag. You may overinvolve your teen in extracurricular activities to keep him out of trouble, especially if you're not around to supervise. Warning: this could also pile on the pressure, leading to a revolt. Let your child have a balanced life. Expose him to things rather than sheltering him, but don't push too hard, either. You'll inspire him to want more for himself by showing him the exciting possibilities waiting in the wider world.

"Kids rise and fall to your expectations," says one Aries. "If you enable them by rewarding bad behavior, it's like telling them that you think they're losers, or incapable." Just don't forget that teenagers' bodies and brains are still developing, so your expectations need to match their developmental level. Need a reality check? If you're in a couple, your mate can help you determine whether you're being unnecessarily harsh. Not that you'll always listen. The visionary Aries mama imagines a brilliant future for her progeny, and she's not afraid to push or follow through on consequences.

Something to be mindful of is that while most Aries moms know how to keep their romantic relationships intact, this phase could threaten even the most bulletproof partnerships. You may be polarized as the "tough" parent while your mate is cast as the softie. While you're perfectly comfortable handling the discipline or being the "bad cop" if it keeps your kids off the streets, you also need to create a united parental front.

Even if you only have time to show up at their important events (tournaments, school concerts, award ceremonies), your teenagers will know that Mama's got their back. If they don't? Just let them come home crying about a bully or some other adolescent injustice. You'll go into full-on warrior mode, teaching them tactics for overcoming adversity and outwitting their enemies. You're a pro at not taking crap, after all, and your unbreakable spirit—yes, the very one they just railed against unsuccessfully last night when you wouldn't extend their curfew—gives them the confidence to walk the harrowing halls of high school with their heads held high. Just like their mama would do.

BYE-BYE, BIRDIE: LEAVING THE NEST (EIGHTEEN-PLUS YEARS)

Sweet surprise! The day your child leaves home can be the beginning of a beautiful relationship—a friendship even. It's kind of like a "see no evil" situation: without your kid under your watchful eye, you can indulge in a little bit of healthy denial. Your fears ease up and you can really enjoy your son or daughter as a fellow adult. For the first time, you can allow yourself to truly be pals with your offspring, showing your fun side instead of your strict one. Not that you won't still express your opinions or attempt to guide them. But now you just may wait until you're asked to butt in. Once you're no longer legally responsible for your child, it's easier to view them as separate people who make their own mistakes.

The tough love you've dished out over the years could pay off, too. As hard as you've pushed your kids to achieve, and as often as you've dropped clichés on them like "Winners never quit and quitters never win," they should be ready for the competitive world of adulthood. You've modeled self-sufficiency and taught them about the crueler realities that await them in the wider world. If you haven't given them too much of a complex (you can be a bit controlling), you've probably prepared them to earn a living, pay bills on time, and handle grown-up responsibilities.

Of course, if you have a fragile or late-blooming child who's not quite ready to leave the nest, this could be a tough time. News flash: just because *you* think independence is the greatest thing since sliced bread, doesn't mean your kids are ready to leave home. And though you might not ship them off to the army or leave their bags on the curb, you'll lay on the pressure. Your child will certainly feel unwelcome when you remind him that he's a legal adult or demand rent if he wants to live under your roof. Naturally, you don't want your kid sponging off you forever, but some just aren't ready for independent living, college, or to pick a lifelong profession just because they're old enough to buy beer and vote.

Another secret factor, especially for the

Aries moms of boys: how quickly they move out depends on their usefulness to you. If your son doubles as a handyman or an instant tenant for your multifamily home (a rent-paying tenant, of course), you don't mind if he stays around. And if he's within driving distance, you'll keep him on speed dial anytime you need some heavy lifting or household help—especially if you're more the divalike Aries mum. No son? No problem—your daughter will do. Sure, you're strong enough to move a midsized appliance or paint the pantry yourself. But you figure you've paid your dues by raising these kids, so you reserve the right to rely on their help.

Adulthood might also be an opportune time to reconnect with your child. Unlike other moms who've sacrificed their identities for their children, you've likely maintained a full life throughout their school years. There shouldn't be much of an empty-nest period for you—in fact, you might convert your child's bedroom into a home office as soon as she's out the door. Sentimentality has its merits, but you need personal space! You also need time to yourself, which you'll have loads of now that you don't have to cook, drop kids off at band practice, and map your schedule around someone else's. Ahh, you could get used to this! (Wait, you already have.)

With all this extra room to relax, you'll enjoy more quality time with your kids when you do see each other. You can plan special outings, shop together, have a real conversation—then kiss 'em good-bye and go back to your own turf. If only it could have been this easy all along! Well, consider this your reward for putting another person's needs above your own for nearly two decades. No small feat for a me-first Aries!

THE TAURUS MOM

(April 20–May 20)

MOMMY MAGIC - Your Strengths:

- Stability
- Good taste
- Common sense
- Hard worker

MAMA MIA - Your Challenges:

- Indulgence
- Materialism
- Mood swings
- Vanity

FAMOUS TAURUS MAMAS:

Tori Spelling, Jessica Alba, Tina Fey, Sherri Shepherd, Cher, Megan Fox, Teresa Giudice, Lily Allen, Penélope Cruz, Uma Thurman, Adele, Kimora Lee Simmons, Elisabeth Röhm, Cate Blanchett

YOUR PARENTING STYLE

*

Taurus is the original "mullet mama"—business in the front, party in the back. Some days, you lead with a stern demeanor that puts the fear of God, traffic, and creepy strangers in your kid. But once you're sure everyone's safe and sound, it's party time! The Taurus mother is selectively staunch and, yes, downright rigid on a couple of key issues. There's an old-fashioned girl in every Taurus, and you simply won't budge on a few of your standards. But behind that firm facade is a bawdy nature goddess who's refreshingly down to earth. You're the mom who might force your kids to stay in Sunday school until adulthood but will also let them witness a home birth or ride a motorcycle when they're twelve.

The ruler of your fourth house of motherhood is regal Leo. This gives you a queen-mum/lady-of-the-manor air—and makes you fiercely protective of your little cubs. You're classy and sophisticated, and you know how to present well in public. Keeping the family name in good standing matters a lot to you, Taurus. At times, this Leo aspect of your chart can make you a little *too* concerned with being admired (and, taken too far, can add a touch of narcissism). To Taurus, reputation matters—a lot. After all, it's what opens doors and ultimately allows you to provide a secure, wonderful life for your family.

Taurus is the zodiac's budgeter and wise spender. You believe in return on investment. So if you devote years of your life to raising a child, you expect to be acknowledged for it! You'll raise your kids to have good manners, respect authority, and if possible, to idolize you. At the very least, you intend to occupy a VIP pedestal marked MOTHER for the rest of their lives. While you hope to be close with your children, you won't sacrifice respect to be their best friend. There's a (well-manicured) iron fist in that Italian leather glove—even if it takes a lot for you to raise that fist. As long as your kids don't embarrass you publicly, violate one of your core values, or outright disrespect you, there shouldn't be any problems. Simple enough, right?

Motherhood makes great use of your managerial qualities, which most Taurus women come by naturally. With your flair for practical details and businesslike nature, you're the COO of your clan. You love to run people's lives—heck, you've been doing it for your girlfriends and family long enough. The structured rhythm of child rearing feels natural to you, unlike for many other zodiac signs. Even Taurus moms who run late for social engagements (and we know quite a few) will never be tardy applying for an elite arts camp scholarship, getting on the private school waiting list, or planning a posh first birthday party for their little one (and his seventy-five closest aunts, uncles, cousins, et al.). When it comes to your top parenting priorities, you're as precise as a laser. Everything else is secondary and rarely gets the white-glove service you give to whatever you deem truly important. Caution: you might need to consider the impression this leaves on people when you, say, show up for the last fifteen minutes of a bar mitzvah or christening, missing the whole ceremony and reception because your daughter had a dance competition that day.

Since Taurus is the sign of daily routines and habits, you stick to consistent bedtimes, meals, after-school pickups, and chores. You know how to find pleasure in the "mundane" details of life: fixing dinner, changing diapers, reading bedtime stories. And with kids, there's no shortage of those! You also enjoy instilling your values in your children, teaching them your favorite traditions or sharing your spiritual beliefs.

The down-home moments are mixed with decadent ones, though. As practical as you insist you are, there's an undercover diva in every Taurus. Your sign is ruled by Venus, the planet of love, beauty, and sensuality. The Taurus mom is a lusty goddess and makes no secret of her need to be wined and dined. There will be date nights that you get dressed up for, and you probably have an amazing king-sized bed in your room.

You might even talk openly about sex. Your kids can be a little confused by this (or grossed out), but you take more of a European-style approach than a puritanical one. Besides, you work hard, so you like to enjoy life. A glass of red wine with dinner, lounging in your satin robe, a walk-in closet designed by a professional decorator—you refuse to stop feeling like a goddess just because you're a mom.

You'll indulge your children aplenty, too. For starters, you love to shop—and you can sniff out quality in a bargain like no other sign. Taurus rules the material world and the senses, so a plush environment is extremely important to you. You put a lot of thought into dressing your children well or creating the right ambience in your home. You're a natural at curating spaces that feel tasteful and lived in at once. There may be some off-limits zones for your finer furnishings, but there will also be comfortable and stylish family areas and bedrooms. You may become your friends' favorite home goods supplier when you periodically redecorate—generously donating the art, sofas, and dining-room sets you no longer want.

Toys, clothes, and other kiddie stuff will require extra storage systems, because you can seriously accumulate. We know one Taurus mom who starts her annual Christmas shopping every July, and she's always the first person in the hottest Black Friday shopping lines. *C'est la vie.* Spoiling your kids is a right, not a privilege, as far as you're concerned.

Not that you're just plunking down credit cards all over town. Because many Taurus moms love a bargain, and a good DIY project, you'll probably express your sophisticated taste the homespun way. Our Taurus friend Tanya won a Pottery Barn Kids Halloween contest when she dressed her son, Kainoa, as a piece of sushi. Tanya's handmade costume was clever and done to professional-quality perfection. The following year, Pottery Barn released its own baby-sushi Halloween costume. Coincidence? We'll never know, but in our opinion, Tanya's ten-dollar creation (complete with seaweed-wrapped sashimi) was far more artful and authentic.

That's the Taurus touch: when it comes to putting your stamp on anything, you go all the way. Pride is a Taurus trademark, but too much of it can make you dogmatic and stubborn to a fault. Your intensity about your beliefs can even alienate a child who doesn't share your worldview, making her feel like an outsider in her own family. For Taurus, there's no "I'm okay, you're okay." It's more like "I'm okay, and you're not."

Tolerance is not always your strong suit, but it's a skill you need to learn. Getting stuck in a right-versus-wrong paradigm will only alienate you from your kids. Besides, they'll probably just sneak around and defy you behind your back. Better to teach your children that opinions evolve and change over time (yes, even yours). You'll never resolve family conflict when you frame situations in an oversimplified good-versus-bad context. Respect your kids' self-expression, politics, and choices—even if you make it clear that you don't agree.

Taurus is an earth sign, so you might just be the everything-organic kind of mom, like Taurus actress Jessica Alba, who created an eco-friendly baby line called the Honest Company, or Rachel Sarnoff, whose website Mommy Greenest reports on all aspects of eco-conscious parenting. From chlorine-free diapers to DEET-free bug spray, you'll monitor what your child eats, wears, and touches with an all-natural eye. Yet you're still very discerning, even snobbish, about your consumer choices. Oh well, the high-end markets and boutiques probably have *you* to thank for keeping them in business, economy be damned.

For another set of Taurus moms, your earthy nature just means you're, well, down to earth. You have neither the time nor the interest to forage for gluten-free children's snacks or to splurge on detergent made without a certain dye. You might keep things stylish on the surface, but skip the whole eco-conscious parenting part. It's simply not in your nature to be that cutting edge. *Your* mother raised you on Kool-Aid and Kraft macaroni, and *you* turned out fine.

There are definitely some material mamas among the Taurus ranks, and they don't hesitate to let people know where they bought everything (and the great deal they scored). Maybe you're the mother who splurges on kiddie couture. One Taurus friend of ours pays a fortune for a horse and stable so her daughter can compete in equestrian events. Sometimes that's just how you roll. But if you're trying to keep up with the Joneses—or more likely, to one-up them into oblivion—check that status-oriented side of yourself. You don't have to prove that you're a great mom by how many pairs of shoes your little fashion plate has or by getting your kids into the "right" schools with "good" families.

Taurus moms can get so caught up in providing for their children's material security that they fall out of touch with their kids' emotional needs or miss clues that the kids are in distress. Alas, you'll find that tossing an expensive toy at problems won't make them go away. Nor will bellowing at the top of your lungs like an angry Bull. "I never hit my kids, but I *have* thrown things at the wall in anger," confesses one Taurus.

In a bumpy patch of parenthood? Spend a little less time putting on a show. Giving your kids the space to be themselves—even if you find it embarrassing—will form a more enduring mother–child bond. And if you're the type of Taurus mother who rushes in too quickly for the save, stand back. Sure, you can fix just about anything for them, but sometimes it's best to let your kiddos struggle and develop character along the way. Give your children the tools to form their own opinions and to make solid decisions in life—ones that leave them happy, healthy, and self-sufficient.

IF YOU HAVE A GIRL

*

PROS

Ruled by sensual Venus, the Taurus mom knows what it takes to be a goddess. You're eager to train your little girl in the art of femininity and hopefully to have a sidekick for indulgent escapades. You have a formal side and a relaxed one, and you'll groom your daughter with manners while also encouraging her expressive side. You want her to have every opportunity, and that comes with knowing which fork to use for the salad course and how to write a proper thank-you note. Since you can sniff out a sample sale like no other sign, you'll teach your daughter how to be a smart consumer, getting the best of everything for a great price. Your take-charge side will love helping her get dressed, decorate, and find her personal style. If you're a domestic goddess, you'll pass on your homespun recipes, decorating tips, and flair for entertaining. Or you'll teach her the fine art of high-end shopping and how to make *your* favorite thing for dinner: reservations!

When your down-to-earth side kicks in, you can speak frankly with your daughter about the birds and the bees. Taurus rules the five senses, so you're in touch with your body and the importance of pleasure. At the end of the day, you want your daughter to feel in control of her life, her body, and her choices. Although your old-fashioned side hopes she'll wait until adulthood to have sex, you're also practical and realize that hormonal changes and sexual urges are a biological reality. Better that your daughter is informed than left to navigate these confusing feelings herself. In fact, the Taurus mom works hard to make sure her daughter doesn't take any guff from anyone. She knows you've got her back, and if anyone messes with her, they'll have her mama to deal with!

CONS

Though you might not admit it, you can be a teensy bit competitive with your daughter. There's an alpha side to the Taurus nature, and if your girl happens to inherit your headstrong pride, trouble can brew in your household as the two of you butt heads. You may need to remind yourself (repeatedly) that imitation is the highest form of flattery. So lead by example and dial down a few of your high-maintenance tendencies. Your impeccable dressing, perfect meals, and prize-worthy interior decorating can be inspiring or intimidating to your daughter, especially if she's not as gifted in these areas as you are. Be careful that you're not setting the bar too high by doing everything to exacting perfection.

You want your daughter to be able to talk to you about anything, but there may be a few topics that push your buttons, and these are best avoided. Generally, you could disagree around politics, her work ethic (as evidenced by her grades and how she treats her possessions), her friends, and any hot-button social issue that you have strong views on. When a Taurus mama starts to preach, it's fire and brimstone. But don't expect your daughter to tune in for the soapbox sermon. If you simply can't be open-minded enough to live and let live, you might need to outsource touchy topics to a more laid-back aunt or godmother. And while you're a great problem solver, your protective side can become enabling if you try to fix everything for her. Practical Taurus is gifted with an ability to cut through the crap and find simple solutions, "bottom lining" every issue. But your tendency to oversimplify can block her from going through a necessary emotional process. Telling your daughter "he wasn't good enough for you, anyway" won't ease her first heartbreak, for example. Rather than be handed a prescription or a magic pill, she probably just wants you to *listen*. Make it safe for your daughter to screw up a little and be sure she knows that you love her anyway. One day, you might get the satisfaction of hearing her say, "You know what, Mom? You were right." Until then, bite your tongue, oh bossy Bull.

IF YOU HAVE A BOY

PROS

A star is born! The Taurus mother brings her boy into the world with a hero's welcome and keeps the red carpet rolled out for years. You make no secret of the fact that you're raising a star, and you just hope he cooperates with your plans. Oh, do you have plans for him, Mama Bull. Your son—especially if he's the oldest boy—is your showpiece. You'll brag about him, blog about him, mine his funny moves and stories for material.

Your son may cultivate some metrosexual tendencies under your stylish influence. However, you'll still let him be a stereotypical boy, involved in sports and competitions. A proud mother if there ever was one, you'll show up at every event to cheer your little guy on. When your son is young, you'll enjoy introducing him to your hobbies and cultural interests, sharing your love of music, dancing, cooking, and creativity of all kinds. On her Offbeat Mama blog, Ariel Meadows-Stalling wrote about taking her two-year-old son, Tavi, to a four-day camping and music festival in Oregon.

Of course, while you're the ultimate soccer mom *outside* of your well-appointed home, you're no fan of indoor Wrestlemania sessions that threaten to break your cherished possessions. You might need to (sniff) pack up your pretty things for a few years—or barricade your gorgeous salon to prevent the inevitable boy breakage. Oh well! You'll find the perfect "fabulous fakes" at IKEA or Target, raise the chandelier a few inches, or even restore a secondhand dresser that you don't mind having knocked over once in a while with clever sanding and painting. Voilà—a tasteful home that can still survive the wear and tear of a Y chromosome!

CONS

Snuggling with your little man-child is your affectionate sign's favorite thing. But as he grows up and wriggles out of your clutches, you may have a touch of heartache. Taurus is a consistent sign, and you don't like change—especially in your cherished relationships. However, you'll need to evolve your mother–son bond to create some age-appropriate boundaries, and that can be hard. Your territorial side might make a showing, and you'll try to mark your turf with possessive moves. You'll weigh in with unsolicited advice on his choices of hobbies, dates, music, and clothes. Keeping your son on too short of a leash can backfire, though, especially if the tone turns emasculating. One friend remembers his Taurus mom conspiring with his high-school girlfriend during a turbulent teen fight. He picked up the phone only to overhear his mom saying, "If my son doesn't get his s*** together, he's gonna lose the best thing that ever happened to him." Whose side are you on, anyway, Mama? Treating him like a demigod one minute and putting him in his so-called place the next will confuse everyone.

As much as you like to keep the *familia* tight-knit and under one roof (yours, of course), your job is to train him to be a self-sufficient mensch who will carry on some of your traditions while creating a few of his own. Sure his choices and actions reflect on you, but at a certain point, your job is done. Live and let live—that's the hard-core advice you dish out to everyone else, after all. If your prince prefers a greasy slice of pizza to your lovingly-prepared boeuf bourguignon once in a while, chillax. You haven't failed to instill good breeding in him, and it's not his job to help you win Mother of the Year. Turn your attention elsewhere for a while rather than trying to control his every move. Make it safe for him to spread his wings and you'll see—he'll be back.

PARENTING THROUGH AGES AND STAGES

INFANCY (THE FIRST YEAR)

Baby bliss? The sights, sounds, and scents of your newborn can certainly transport you—or make you jarringly aware that, well, you aren't in Kansas anymore. Taurus rules the five senses, and with your heightened attunement, you can soak up the sensory pleasures of this fleeting phase. Tactile Taurus moms love affection, so you'll savor the touchy-feeliness of infancy. You'll lose track of time nuzzling your newborn protectively, making up silly songs and nicknames, nibbling tiny fingers and toes. And there's nothing like that new-baby smell perfuming your nostrils (although on the downside, a bad diaper *can* activate your gag reflex).

Even industrious Taurus moms planning a speedy office return can be completely overtaken by newborn fever. Surprise—you no longer care about the twenty-five hundred emails sitting unchecked in your inbox! You'd rather spend your days in a cuddle puddle with your brand-new bundle of joy. And if you don't take to mothering instantly, there's nothing that a little practice can't improve for your persistent sign. Chances are you'll welcome the excuse to slow down, simplify, and take life day by day—the optimum Taurus pace.

The regimented mother Bull can shine during her child's infancy—at least once she gets the hang of things. While infants don't come with instructions (besides their sign, of course), there are a few baby-whispering basics that you may come by naturally. Eat. Sleep. Self-soothe. Repeat. Yeah, that's kind of how you roll, too.

Not that you'll be elevating your legs and eating bonbons like you did as a pregnant goddess. Motherhood is a job, and you harbor no illusions about that fact. Some Taurus women have a rep for running late socially (your glamour process *can't* be rushed). However, when duty calls, clocks can be set to your movements. Thus, you probably won't mind the predictable pace of your baby's first year. Naps at ten and four o'clock, feedings every two hours on the dot—you fall easily into a pleasant daily rhythm.

Newborns, after all, can sleep for sixteen hours a day. (Finally, someone who can outsnooze you!) That leaves plenty of time to puree homemade organic baby food, catch up on your favorite shows and reading, or book a home visit from your favorite masseuse. Nap time for baby can mean pampering time for you. Who says Bellinis and breast-feeding don't mix every now and then?

Of course, if you happen to have a colicky newborn who won't follow a routine, the first year of motherhood can be challenging. Simply put, you don't like the stop–start pace. The zodiac's Bull operates at two speeds: totally on or completely off. You work hard, but you relax with the same gusto. Once you've powered down for the night, hands wrapped around a stemless glass of Malbec or a mug of lavender chamomille tea, you're off the clock. If you don't have a mate who's willing to play night nurse—or the capacity to tune out your wailing baby—you may suffer through this first year mightily. You'll also want to schedule in regular sex dates with your partner—a must for the lusty Taurus mama. A sensual sign, you need a physical release for stress, and there's no better way for you than in the boudoir. (Just take precaution so you don't end up with "Irish twins"!)

"The first year was really hard for me," says Taurus mom Michelle. "I need my self-care routines to stay sane. When the baby was crying while I was trying to give myself a manicure, I could get really frustrated. My husband would tell me to go to the nail salon, but I didn't trust him to watch the baby or do anything the way I wanted it done. It was rough!"

This stage is often when the Taurus woman who considers herself easygoing discovers the limits of her own flexibility. "Babies are unpredictable—and, therefore, scary!" insists Sam, the Taurus mom of a five-week-old and a toddler. But what really spooks your sign isn't the fragile new life in your charge. It's being caught unprepared. Your sign craves the security of knowing what to expect—before *and* after you're expecting. When you've read every manual on the shelves, and you *still* can't stop the crying, reduce a fever, or express your milk, there can be some tense moments, fraught with feelings of failure and frustration. Taurus is a natural provider, and when you feel like you can't supply instant comfort for your baby, a rare sense of helplessness can kick in.

"I didn't schedule anything when my son was an infant," says Jill, a Taurus mom who learned the hard way that motherhood was *not* the time to experiment with being laid-back for the first time in her life. "I wanted to be 'go with the flow,' but it was a huge mistake. I just ended up having to impose a schedule way later, which was so much harder than it would have been."

It doesn't help that Taurus can have massive amounts of pride. You may have self-righteously judged other moms before the shoe was on your (still-swollen) foot. But—and there's no way to say this delicately—it's best that you start pumping your breasts instead of your ego now. There's no place for bullish bravado in the nursery. Better to admit that you're overwhelmed and out of your league, and allow some loving friends and family to support you.

Luckily, the Taurus mom is an ultrarealist at the end of the day. You'll soldier through sleepless nights with your sign's unflappable determination. You're also an earth sign, which helps you stay grounded. For this reason, the natural mama vibe really suits you once you embrace it. In fact, you might just extend "barefoot and pregnant" into "barefoot and postpartum" if you can. Latham Thomas, a Taurus doula and author of the natural parenting handbook *Mama Glow*, describes her son Fulano's idyllic infancy: "We lived on a friend's property in Bridgehampton with a garden to tend and an outdoor shower," Latham recalls, making us jealous of her *Town & Country* baby bliss. "Fulano was immersed in nature. We had a hammock in the middle of the room and I spent a lot of time lying there with him."

While this might sound like your very fantasy, reality may be pretty different, especially if you're a single mom. There's a good chance you're the breadwinner or at least a contributing provider to your family's income. So do yourself a favor and ease back into your old routines gently once baby comes. You'll only jar your system if you swing from baby bonding to workaholic mode.

Remember: Taurus is ruled by Venus, the planet of beauty and sensuality. You need to honor the pleasure-principled part of your nature. Be sure to structure in some date nights and self-care as soon as you can. Exercise does wonders for you, too, although you may need to push yourself to start. The Taurus mother can get a little *too* inert after pregnancy, and baby weight can come off slowly. While you need to be patient and loving with your body, do pay attention to when you're indulging yourself out of frustration. Being a creature of habit, once you stop moving around it's hard to start again. Push yourself to stay active and to make healthy food choices, even if you begin with a daily walk around the block then build up slowly to more, or force yourself to drink lots of water all day. Taurus rules the zodiac's second house of routines, so for you the journey of a thousand miles (or thirty pounds) begins with a single step.

While you're at it, stimulate your senses. Window-shop as you power-walk (with or without bébé) to and from your favorite bookstore, cafe, or gourmet grocery store—and pick up fresh flowers while you're out. Add a spa treatment to your package of postpartum Pilates sessions. Drizzle essential oil into the air mister. Turn on music and dance in your living room. Get your sex life back into the swing.

Savor your baby's every milestone, too. There will be more growth spurts packed into this year than at any other time in your little one's life. While you can get as busy and distracted as the next person, few other signs can really be "in the moment" like yours, Taurus. Embrace this amazing ability to be present and try to, er, milk this phase for as many great memories as you can.

TODDLERHOOD (TWO TO FIVE YEARS)

Welcome to chaos beyond your wildest imagination! Fun chaos but chaos nonetheless. For a practical sign that likes to keep things in relative order, having a toddler on the loose can test even *your* ample patience. Most kids this age have the attention span of a gnat, meaning just as you get that block tower or clay sculpture under way, they lose interest and want to do something else. Hello, exhaustion!

Multitasking is not your specialty—you like to do one thing at a time and do it well. Unfortunately, your singular focus is no help during toddlerhood, when juggling seems to be part of the job. Consistent Taurus doesn't like change; yet change is pretty much the only constant now.

If you planned to be a work-at-home mom, best of luck—you may quickly find this setup far from ideal. If you need a paycheck while your child is young, you might be best off leaving the house to earn it. "I'm not great at focusing on two priorities at once," admits Taurus mother Sam. "I just focus on work while at work, and home while at home. It has to be one or another or I get stressed."

Although you may feel a pinch of guilt about leaving your little ones with a caregiver, you also like to be productive. Make your life as efficient as possible so you can avoid the frustration of work–life overlap. There's nothing worse than trying to meet a deadline or answer emails during a tantrum.

Coparenting is especially important during this stage, so if you're in a relationship be sure to coordinate strategies. This can be a time when many couples fight, because you realize you have vastly different approaches to discipline, routine, and the like. Play to your strengths and divide up duties (you handle breakfast; your partner does bath and bedtime), or else adhere to a few simple family guidelines (no TV after 5:00 p.m., sugar-free snacks only).

"Having a great nursery for child care, a supportive team at work, and a *very* hands-on husband helps loads," says Sam. Capable as you are, trying to do it all now is a recipe for a breakdown. You need to be able to delegate to your partner and/or caregivers—if only to keep your sanity intact. Let your mate be part of the parenting process, even if you've "got it handled." It's not just about how quickly and efficiently you can cross things off of your list; it's about everyone being involved in the process of raising your child.

Fortunately, you're a regimented sign that likes routine. So go ahead: design the daily rundown and then hand off duties to your troops. You relish being the family manager, setting a schedule and sticking to it: wake up at 7:00 a.m., eat a healthy breakfast at 8:00, arrange the bath and bedtime story to be at the same hour every evening. You can get pretty innovative with your routines, too! One hard-working Taurus mom keeps several prepacked bags handy, each filled according to activity: overnight, playdate, preschool, swimming, and so on. The labeled bags hang neatly in the closet so she can just grab the appropriate bundle and go. Not a bad idea!

The other benefit to being so efficient? Your "quality time" with your child truly *is* high quality. You know how to leave the office and call it a day. Your distraction-free zone allows you to focus on your kids, getting down on the floor for a romp, mixing up cookie dough, cuddling, and giving each other nose kisses without sneaking glances at your BlackBerry. Since you enjoy routine, you also don't mind the repetitiveness of watching the same Elmo DVD fifty thousand times or going to the same playground over and over again.

You'll be game for engaging in the hedonistic pleasures of toddlerhood as your child gets a little bit older (and more obedient): ice-cream sundaes, visits to your favorite toy store, pizza parties, and carnival rides. You'll snap away with your trusty camera, capturing all the adorable moments.

Watch out for spoiling, though. Sure, distracting your kid with stimulating games, presents, and activities works as a tantrum-calming technique. However, retail therapy does not make for an appropriate long-term behavior modification strategy. You might also be teaching your child some manipulative tricks: "If I scream really loud, Mommy will buy me a stuffed animal! Awesome!"

Since you like to look good in public, it's possible that you'll be embarrassed by your kid's raucous meltdowns. Taurus women like to be well regarded, so you may fear that toddler screamfests, biting, and defiance make *you* look like a "bad" mother. You might even secretly believe that yourself. Oh, Taurus! While there are many things you can control in this lifetime, toddler meltdowns are not included.

If you're still feeling like a failure, read a parenting book like *The Happiest Toddler on the Block*, which has great methods for soothing an upset child. (We like this one because it likens your toddler to a primitive little caveman—frankly, not far from the truth!) Children this age have no real reasoning skills; they act on instinct and raw emotion. It's kind of like you, Taurus, when you get angry and turn into a raging, charging Bull. Almost nothing can stop you when you're in stampede mode, and your toddler is the exact same way. So have a little compassion for yourself, and your little guy. You've certainly walked a mile in those tiny light-up sneakers.

Positive reinforcement is a great trick every Taurus mama should master. Instead of buying your toddler that ice-cream cone or lollipop to calm his tantrums, treat him for good behavior instead. This is not bribery and shouldn't happen for every good act. However, there's a certain measure of bargaining that has to happen with kids this age. Think more in terms of delayed gratification: "Yes, you can have a cookie, sweetie, but only after you put on your coat and shoes." Once the right action occurs, heap on the praise and rewards. Toddlers have no conscience, but they live to please their parents!

Despite the hassles of this age group, your inner manager feels purposeful and fulfilled now. You have the important job of running someone else's life, and that gives you meaning. If you haven't already hoofed it to a hip suburb, you may be perfectly thrilled to ditch your downtown digs for home ownership now, complete with lush lawn, swing set, and great public schools. You've probably fantasized about having a big home, a garden with fresh vegetables, perfectly decorated rooms and lots of space for entertaining. Toddler time is the perfect life cycle for that kind of nesting.

Some of your Martha Stewart dreams may need to wait, though, since your kid's kamikaze crashes could destroy your pretty things. But hey, it's just stuff, and some of it can be replaced. Right? Hmmm. If it can't, it has no business being within your babe's reach. Pack it away safely and bring it out again in a couple years. Then set up the biggest, plushest, most colorful toy area you can—and enjoy getting down and dirty in playland, spilled milk and all.

EARLY CHILDHOOD (SIX TO ELEVEN YEARS)

Let the fun begin! Because Taurus works hard and plays hard, you enjoy the liveliness of this age . . . most of the time. Taurus is a single-speed machine, so when you put your full focus on your child, the time together can be unbelievably rich. Santa Claus is comin' to town—or at least being channeled through you. You'll plan a full slate of weekend activities, from a decadent hotel breakfast to indoor rock climbing followed by a shopping spree, ice-cream sundaes and a live show. It might be hard to tell who's enjoying the entertainment more.

Of course, when you're in deep relaxation mode after a long day, the kids' energy levels can be exhausting—especially if they want to do something interactive while you've already burrowed into your favorite sofa spot. "Can't we just watch a movie together?" you'll beg—and toss in a bribe for good measure. Your den may rival an FAO Schwarz showroom as a result of all your attempts to sneak in "me time" during family hours.

Modeling a great work ethic is your specialty, Taurus. If you have a career, your children see a mama on a mission, since you go full-stop with everything you do. Attention, attention! Make sure to set up another source of after-school activity and homework help if you can't clock out when the school bell sounds its dismissal. "Being a small business owner who works from home has been a tremendous blessing for my family in so many ways," says Ariel, "but there's no denying that it means my son has a *lot* of experience at feeling ignored by his mom. Sometimes Mama's just gotta work—and that means I have to shut the door while he's in the living room with his dad, yelling for me."

Fortunately, you're a natural project manager, so juggling homework, sports practices, and meals isn't hard for you. You're great at prioritizing, so you'll make sure your home is run like a tight ship. However, this stage will still require a lot of planning, especially since you'll want to maximize productivity while your child is in school. Being a creature of habit, your big adjustment will be to not having your kids around all the time or the switch from day care to a potentially shorter school schedule. Your time management strategies will need yet another switch-up—but fortunately, you'll create a basic routine you can stick with until they graduate high school.

Soon enough, you'll be involved in their school, too. At this phase, you'll begin to be more of a fixture in the school community, seeing the same parents every day at drop-off and pickup, PTA meetings, and concerts. Most Taurus mothers relish the soccer-mom role; whether you're rocking tasteful "vegan leather" boots and a dainty diamond nose ring or decked out with a Louis Vuitton handbag and Jimmy Choos, you're cheering on your children with the same ferocious pride.

Caution: your need to be well thought of by society can kick into high gear now. Deep down, every Taurus woman harbors a fear of being judged. It's not that you really care what people think of you—you stand behind your opinions and choices and are pretty damn vocal about them. However, you turn into a walking PR firm when there's any kind of threat to your livelihood or your children's happiness. You know that the school gossip mill can be a cruel and condemning one, with parents forming cliques and alliances as often as kids do. So you'll leave nothing to chance, planting yourself firmly in the mix to make sure that your family's reputation—and access to opportunities—remains stellar. It's a way of unconsciously protecting your kids: you instinctively know that if they're well thought of, they'll meet the right people, be given the best opportunities, and set themselves up for lifelong security.

"I raised my kids in a pretty affluent area where most of the moms didn't work," says Taurus mom Maria. "I worked full-time, but I didn't want them to be treated differently. So I was the class mom every year and really involved in their school. I'd let them get name-brand stuff because I didn't want them to feel different or left out."

Just watch the line between maternal and material. Otherwise, your need to impress people can trigger a competitive side of your nature—one that could backfire and turn people off. While you may love your Gucci bag or the Mercedes coupe you bought with your own hard-earned cash, you run the risk of passing along superficial values to your kids by name-dropping or acting as the unpaid brand ambassador for your favorite luxury label.

Be mindful not to spoil your kids during this phase. It's okay—smart, actually—to start making them do chores to earn privileges and even their allowance. It's a great, gentle way to start the inevitable separation process that could come on like gangbusters during their teen years. Secretly, you may hope that coddling your kiddos will make them want to follow in your footsteps or spend more time with you. You might have even dreamed about sharing one of your favorite childhood hobbies with them: coaching your son's soccer team or bequeathing your pint-sized pointe shoes to a prima ballerina-to-be.

"I really wanted my daughter to be into dance like I was, so we could share that," says Michelle of her eleven-year-old. "But I put her into competitive dancing and it was too much—she's a Cancer, so she was way too sensitive—and the instructors were so mean! It turned out that she loves horses, because she needed something to nurture. So I bought her a horse and pay to keep it in a barn. It's costing me a fortune, but I feel really strongly about my kids having a passion. You have to have a passion in life."

That's the Taurus mama's way. Nothing is too expensive for your children if their happiness or future success is involved—and you'll work your fingers to the bone to provide that. But is that always healthy? Check to see if there's some underlying sadness or worry driving you to provide for your child's every want (and then some). At this stage, you may need to develop a greater capacity for coping with some inevitable disappointments, such as your child's realizing there's no Santa or Easter Bunny. Deal with the sadness of realizing that your little boy or girl is growing up, preferring to spend "mommy and me" time with friends instead of with you and stop trying to keep them trapped by "stuff." (Fortunately, many kids this age still want to cuddle, and you'll be able to sneak in the affection here and there.) Remind yourself that you're doing your job of preparing a self-sufficient future citizen.

Soon enough, you could come to really enjoy your free time. Those must-have manicures? You can enjoy them uninterrupted; even throw in a ten-minute foot massage. "I remember when my kids could bathe themselves and brush their own teeth and I didn't have to bend over the tub anymore," says one Taurus mom. "It was such a relief—it was like they had graduated college or something!"

Gather the other mothers for some goddess-like indulgence while the kids are off at swim practice or a birthday party. You'll probably cultivate a little posse of mom friends that you roll with, meeting for drinks, power walks, or a little retail therapy.

Now is also a great time to be less of a habitual creature and to try a bunch of new things you might not otherwise. Yes, Mama Taurus, you might just go camping with the Girl Scouts or learn the finer points of floor hockey so you can relate to your son. "I would read magazines like *Family Circle* and *Woman's Day* for ideas," recalls Maria. "We'd have Wednesday-night dinner picnic-style on the carpet, and we'd have game and movie nights. I would plan themed birthday parties for my daughter."

Soon enough, your kids might not want to be seen in public with you (sniff), so take advantage of bonding opportunities now. Time together will dwindle—or at least, you'll have some stiff competition from their peers. Feather the nest, but be sure to nudge them out of it, too.

ADOLESCENCE AND TEENS (TWELVE TO EIGHTEEN YEARS)

Two is definitely *not* company when your once-adoring child turns into an angry angst-ridden, acne-covered adolescent. Suddenly, there's another stubborn, willful person in your house—someone who's always right and thinks he knows everything. Wait, isn't that *your* job? Your mini-me is now a magnifying mirror of sorts, and it's not always comfortable for you.

Speaking of mirrors, Taurus is ruled by beauty-planet Venus, and because of this your own vanity or insecurity could flare up now, especially if you have a daughter. This may be the first time you feel "old"—how is it that you're the mom of a *teenager*? You might cope by trying to relive your own youth, bonding with your kid through judgmental and sarcastic jokes. You have a snarky side yourself, so you may find some of your kid's surly remarks amusing—as long as they aren't directed at you. But soon enough, they will be, Taurus, so brace yourself before you blow!

Although your temper can get triggered, your earth sign nature helps you remain stable. Many days, you're the terra firma that your teen runs (or skulks) home to; other times, your firmness is a barrier your limit-testing child butts against. Taurus, you're not the most flexible person—not, that is, when it comes to your most prized values. Whether you expect your child to perform well in school, spend time with family, keep her room tidy, or respect her mama (this one's nonnegotiable), you simply won't budge on your bottom line. And your teen may seem to have a sixth sense about that, knowing how to flagrantly disregard that which you hold sacred.

So . . . what's a Taurus to do? It's a tricky dance, like any good bullfight. But even though you're the Bull, you may need to take a page or two from the matador. He doesn't run straight at the charging beast, which is what happens when you parent with an iron fist. The bullfighter waves his cape but knows how to gracefully step out of harm's way when necessary. That's the real art of parenting, Taurus. The more you dig in your heels and resist your teenager's efforts to flaunt his shaky independence, the more likely you are to be trampled. Letting your buttons get pushed too easily will only lead to a regrettable showdown that you will probably lose.

One thing that can help? You may need to learn how to read between the lines better—and to soften your own style, since you tend to be über-direct (ouch!) and rigid rather than nuanced and compassionate. Your kid certainly knows where you stand—you've made that all too clear. But respect is a two-way street. Sure, you're entitled to it as a mother. But are you also being empathetic and seeing it from your kid's point of view?

Listening isn't always the Taurus strong suit. You have strong filters and a flair for "selective hearing," keying in on what you *want* to hear and tuning out the rest. This skill makes you incredibly productive at work and efficient when you need to focus on a task at hand. This particular skill is not so effective when you need to decode teen-speak, which tends to be in veiled grunts and shrugs.

"I've learned to criticize the behavior, not the child," says one Taurus mother. Wise choice. There's also a fine line between validating your kid's emotions (something you should always do) and being overly permissive. Understanding *why* your teenager smoked a cigarette—the painful pressure to fit in, wanting to be thought of as cool by a certain person—well, you can certainly get how he would feel that way. By admitting that, you're not telling your child it's okay to smoke. You're empathizing, which can set the stage for an honest talk about dealing with all kinds of peer pressure and may actually lead to self-correcting behavior the next time cigarettes are passed around the party.

The key is to catch yourself *before* you go ballistic. Chances are your own reaction is based in fear—including anxiety about what other people will think of *you* as a parent. (One adult daughter of a Taurus recalls being grounded for making her mother look bad in public—but hey, reputation is everything to your sign and can make or break your family's future opportunities.) After years of rewarding your kids with material stuff, you may attempt to punish them by withdrawing their privileges around the car, computer, and other possessions. Or you might decide that it's time they pay dues and earn their keep. Unfortunately, your children may now be a bit, shall we say, spoiled—used to having their mama provide—so prepare for some backlash until they get used to the new work ethic you've established.

In the end, though, the payoff can be great. "I encouraged my kids to work and do chores for allowance," says Taurus mom Maria of her now-adult children. "That way, if they wanted something, I'd pay for half. I helped them make budgets. We set up coffee cans for different funds: long-term and short-term goals. My son was able to buy his own guitar that way."

You may also find it helps when you set clear expectations for your kids. "One semester, I told my son, 'Just do the best you can,' " recalls Jen, the Taurus mom of an early teen. "So he came home with a B-minus on his report card, which was a drop for him. His response was, 'Well, you just told me to do my best.' I said to him, 'You've been blessed with a great brain. This is not your best. Straight-A's is your best.' "

Administer the right dose of tough love so that you're preparing your children for independent, self-sufficient living at the next phase—adulthood—rather than enabling them to think you will handle or bankroll everything. Examine your own motives if you're playing financier. (DJ, one more round of "Can't Buy Me Love," please.) Deep down, you're a sensitive soul, and you may feel rejected when your kids pull away during these years. But attempting to keep them closer by buddying up or buying their affection is a big no-no, Taurus—which could stunt their developmental growth.

Kids need to separate now and know that it's safe to do so. If they feel like they're somehow hurting you by individuating, they'll stage their rebellion in private, doing stupid things with the wrong crowd while you sit by clueless, patting yourself on the back for having such an angelic child.

"My freshman year of high school, I would sit in my parents' pool house and drink beers," remembers the son of a Taurus mom and dad. "They didn't notice because they were so busy working and paying attention to my little brother. I was having a really hard time fitting in at school and I was in my first relationship, which was kind of dramatic. Looking back, I was probably depressed. But I didn't want them to worry about me, because they were working so hard. I think I just wanted some attention, so one day I drank so much that they caught me."

Remember, Taurus, the teen years are a tricky time no matter what your sign. When all else fails, repeat the mantra "This, too, shall pass." Your steadfastness is one of your greatest traits, so keep holding the space of love, encouraging your mini-adult to do his best, and instilling your stellar work ethic in him. Guide your child, rather than enable or intimidate him, and lead by example. That's the best you can do, Taurus!

BYE-BYE, BIRDIE: LEAVING THE NEST (EIGHTEEN-PLUS YEARS)

Shock alert! Change is definitely *not* on your list of favorite things. After more than a decade of shuttling your child between school, extracurriculars, camp, and sleepovers, the departure from familiar daily routines can be a bumpy one. Life as you know it is over, and your empty nest can feel like a death of sorts, complete with a mourning process. After all, you've built so much of your identity around your child, and now there's nobody to nurture, structure, or project-manage. As much as you might have complained about your role as designated schlepper, you'd give your right arm to chauffeur you kid to and from swim meets or band rehearsals now.

"I went into a tailspin," recalls one Taurus mother of sending her daughter off to college. "Since I was divorced, I was suddenly in this big house alone. I left suburbia, rented out my home, and moved into an apartment in the city."

Since Taurus is a creature of habit, you'll need to fill your time with new routines. If you're spending your days misty-eyed, curled up with your daughter's first teddy bear or polishing her competitive skating trophies, it's time to get a hobby. "I started taking voice lessons, because I didn't have anything to do outside of my kids," says Brenda, a Taurus who revived a passion for singing once her children left home. "I was so used to being busy with them! I didn't want to turn back the hands of time, but I had to make a plan for myself."

Wise move. Otherwise, you can turn into a *teensy* bit of a mommy-stalker, which happened to Maria. "When my son was first in college I drove up every weekend," she laughs. "I drove forty-five minutes to pick up a huge laundry bag. I took it home and washed it, and drove it back all clean and folded on Sunday. I might only see him for ten minutes in total, but it was my way of checking that he was doing okay."

In all fairness, this *was* before the advent of video chat, but still. Taurus is a visual and sensory sign, and seeing is believing, so you won't rest until you truly experience your child doing okay on his own. Just keep your standards reasonable, Bull-mama. It's understandable that you want them to feel comfortable. However, you will need to curb the impulse to whip out your debit card and *zhush* their barebones dorm rooms or starter apartments with fancy furnishings. Yes, your daughter is actually using a plastic milk crate as a nightstand (*quelle horreur!*). Uh-huh, your son has propped his mattress up on cinder blocks because he was too lazy/busy/clueless to get a proper bed frame (and may have spent the check you mailed for one on pizza and beer instead). Is this about them . . . or you? Who cares what the neighbors think, Taurus! Especially when the "neighbors" are twenty-year-old Grateful Dead groupies whose prized living-room accessory is a giant water bong propped against a hand-me-down South American tapestry. (Viva Garcia!)

"With my daughter, I tried something different," says Maria. "While she was in college, I went to her house every Sunday and cooked dinner for her and her friends. I'd make big trays of ziti so they had food for the whole week. It served my need for a routine and we got to spend quality time. It worked so well that we started meeting during the week for a girls' dinner at a restaurant, too."

Great idea, right? Regular contact with your kids can definitely help ease the transition; just do it in a noninvasive way. Soon enough, they'll be coming home for the holidays—toting their own laundry bags—and eventually, bringing their own rug rats to enjoy the traditions you so lovingly upheld during their childhood. Then you'll get to do it all over again with grandchildren, spoiling them in style—the way only a Taurus can!

THE GEMINI MOM

(May 21–June 20)

MOMMY MAGIC - Your Strengths:

- Versatility
- Youthfulness
- Curiosity
- Open-mindedness
- Originality
- Creativity

MAMA MIA - Your Challenges:

- Inconsistency
- Lack of boundaries
- Tendency to contradict self
- Impatience
- Talking or lecturing instead of listening

FAMOUS GEMINI MOMS:

Angelina Jolie, Joan Rivers, Heidi Klum, Courtney Cox, Brooke Shields, Natalie Portman, Nicole Kidman, Alanis Morissette, Elizabeth Hasselbeck, Barbara Bush, Kendra Wilkinson, Josephine Baker

YOUR PARENTING STYLE

*

Ah, to be a mom of many personalities—complex and even contradictory at times but certainly never boring. Such is the way of the Gemini mama, ruled by the zodiac's Twins. Varied and versatile, you keep your family guessing what you'll say or do next. There's never a dull moment under your roof—even though some household members wouldn't mind one every now and then!

You can be free-spirited and bohemian in some aspects, following the Euro-chic model of treating your child like a mini-adult who sets his own bedtime or sports a kiddie mohawk. Yet, since nothing in a Gemini's world occurs without its equal and opposite, you also launch into motherhood with a certain need for control. As laid-back and groovy as you can be, there are also rules—of your own design, naturally—that you adhere to from day one.

For some Gemini mamas, that means an eco-chic nursery (complete with biodegradable diaper bags), cosleeping (since your favorite earth-mother baby guru insists it quells separation anxiety), and a strict diet of breast milk and pureed organic veggies for the tot. Your greatest baby-gear wish is that Mobi wraps came in funky stripes and colors so you could add custom flair to your favorite new accessory.

Other Geminis might go to the complete opposite pole, starting immediately with formula, firm bedtimes, and a full-time nanny. No way you're giving up your individuality—you *will* have it all. After all, you were midway through pitching a sci-fi movie script/opening a yoga studio/running a digital marketing firm/touring with your band when the pregnancy test revealed those two unmistakable lines.

The urge to micromanage your life is partly astrological, of course. Your fourth house of motherhood is ruled by Virgo, the reputedly uptight sign of health, well-being, and organization. Parenting may bring out a stern or regimented side of you. Control issues can also be a reaction to shock. After all, motherhood is a major life change, no matter how much you gush to your friends. Somehow the universe has decided to make you—wild and crazy *you*—responsible for another human being's life. Whether through birth or adoption, two souls have intertwined in a mother–child dance, and you're not yet sure of the steps. So you might quell your nerves by banishing everything nonorganic from your home or by keeping your baby under constant watch. "We were pretty much attachment parents, instinctively," says one type of Gemini mom.

Of course, since your standards can be subject to change without notice, your rigidity is tempered with a bold streak of the opposite. You'll scour the ingredient list of your baby wash but take the kid to a jazz club or raise her in a smog-filled metropolis. Let's face it: you can't help but contradict yourself at times. If you were totally principled, you wouldn't be an airy, unpredictable Gemini. So you might just buckle that rear-facing car seat into a Prius (adorned with peace-symbol and NAMASTE bumper stickers), and drive your babe to an elite Mommy & Me group in the nicest part of town. Or your tightly run ship happens to be on an actual *ship* . . . because you've decide to spend your child's first year living on a houseboat. With Geminis, you just never know.

While Geminis have a rep for being breezy and hard to pin down, they can actually be quite anxious. Your sign is ruled by Mercury, planet of communication and the intellect, so your brain simply never shuts off. As a result of all this mental energy, you might just be the most eccentric mom on the block—or the most opinionated. Hey, your brand of maternal instinct is a unique concoction.

While you might drive your kids nutty or sometimes talk their ears off, there are also times when your advice will be golden. You have a special way of cutting through the bull and just nailing a commonsense zinger that hits the mark. Are you opinionated? Sure. There's a strong "mother knows best" streak in every Gemini. You can't help it: you're a trivia hound, always reading another book or article, unearthing obscure facts from the most random corners. And you have a zillion hobbies and interests. So even if your kid is your number-one priority, she will probably have to compete for your attention with your start-up business, book club, Canyon Ranch girls' weekends, fund-raiser committees, or the folk–pop album you're finally recording at age thirty-seven.

Some Gemini moms may have a measure of guilt about having so many balls in the air. "My challenges?" says Gemini blogger and author Danielle LaPorte. "Patience, a constant sense of guilt, and a seemingly black vortex of not having enough time to do what I want for myself, my career, and my kid."

All that Gemini multitasking can create a steeper learning curve when you become a parent. Until you hit your stride, you may be overinvolved one minute, then absent the next, swinging between wildly inconsistent styles. If you happen to have a grounded partner, this can help balance things out. However, there are times that children won't accept a mommy substitute. Some days they just need your undivided attention—and you may find yourself frustrated having to supply that, especially in their younger years.

"When my kids were little I gave up everything for them," says Yael, the Gemini mother of two boys who owns an independent record label. "And I hated who I was. Now I've accepted that I'm not that kind of mom—I can't put my focus on them all the time. So I spend all day on my business. At six thirty, I eat dinner with them, read them stories, and play and then put them to bed and go back to work on my business until two in the morning. I'm much happier and I think it makes me a better mom because I'm not angry and yelling all the time."

If all else fails, follow your Gemini sisters Angelina Jolie and Heidi Klum and have a large brood. Or take a page from Gemini Josephine Baker, who adopted twelve children from all over the world (Korea, Japan, Israel, Colombia, and Finland among them) and married four times. Give your kids their own posse. Can you say "sibling power"? At least the kids can entertain each other while you're off building a school in Malawi, running for mayor, or taking a six-week certificate course on ancient goddess culture.

You'll be back soon enough—and with a vengeance. Making up for lost time is a Gemini mom's specialty, and oh, the places you'll go! Gemini is the sign of the Twins, so you'll really want a playmate and a child in one. Unrealistic? Maybe at some stages but not if you take the long view of motherhood. Although you may need to grit your teeth through endless readings of *Goodnight Moon* when your kid is young, think of yourself as investing in a lifelong friendship. Strange as that sounds, that thought might just get you through the more demanding days.

Besides, Geminis often treat their friends better than anyone. So flip the switch in your brain to "future BFF" when times get tough. Get out of your head and stop, connect, reengage. Slow down and savor the moment as you make memories together. Geminis aren't "lifers" by nature, but parenting is a permanent gig. As Angelina Jolie said, "[Children] remind you every day what matters in life." Motherhood is a gift, because it's teaching you how to commit without having an exit strategy (which isn't really committing at all). Yes, this is a life sentence, but one you will thoroughly enjoy.

IF YOU HAVE A GIRL

*

PROS

Shrinking violet? Not under your watch! With a Gemini mama as primary role model, your daughter will grow up with a voice, opinions, and a healthy respect for her own creativity. Your daughter won't be afraid to raise her hand in class or, later, to compete in a "man's world." After all, she's watched *you* win every battle of wits—so she's learned from a pro.

Since Gemini is the sign of the Twins, you and your daughter might be attached at the hip—at least, when you're not fighting. Yes, occasional squabbles are de rigueur with a Gemini mama and her girl. Fortunately, you'll balance that out with tons of fun, making you a dynamic duo. Our Gemini friend Regena dons costumes and records homemade "music videos" with her teenage daughter. Gemini comedian Joan Rivers worked the red carpet for years with her Aquarius daughter Melissa. You might be more like sisters than mother and daughter! With your youthful spirit (and in some cases, a wardrobe to match it), you'll probably share clothes, music, and makeup with your little gal. Prepare to have a blast painting the town red.

CONS

Being a role model is a weighty responsibility, and there will be days when it feels more like a burden then a blessing. You're a free-spirited, experimental sign and you don't want to tone that part of yourself down. With your short attention span, it's hard to keep focused on the tasks at hand that come with mommying. If your daughter is shy, clingy, or moody, you may grow impatient with her neediness, doling out tough love when she needs tenderness. Although you're quick with an answer to every problem, sometimes your daughter will just want to be *heard*. Learn how to listen and "mirror" back her emotions rather than just talking at her. (Or, call upon an honorary auntie, especially a more patient earth or water sign like Capricorn, Virgo, or Cancer.)

Challenges can arise when your daughter hits adolescence and turns into a mini-know-it-all. Mirror, mirror! After all, you're prone to playing the devil's advocate and even contradicting yourself—a recipe for disaster with teenagers. Geminis have a hard time looking at themselves beyond a certain point—or maybe it's just tough to keep track of all those different personalities! Your daughter may call you out on what she sees as inconsistency, whereas you simply view it as the right to change your mind on a moment-to-moment basis. You'll need to work harder to give a clear and consistent message, even if you have to write down what you told her in a datebook in case you forget! Say what you mean, mean what you say, and be vigilant with yourself on this.

IF YOU HAVE A BOY

*

PROS

Most Gemini moms have an easier time with boys than with girls. After all, you don't mince words. You're direct, opinionated, and unapologetic—a more stereotypically "masculine" way of communicating. This will be especially useful in your son's teenage years, since you probably won't take his grunts and rebuffs of your affection as personally as other moms might. You'll know how to guide him with cool-headed logic, helping him talk through difficult decisions objectively.

Leading by example, you'll instill a grand sense of adventure in your son, exposing him to all kinds of people, classes, cultural experiences, and travel. Like Gemini mom Angelina Jolie and her first son, Maddox, you might be joined at the hip when he's younger. You genuinely enjoy planning fun activities for your little man and sharing his childish delight. While you might find his boyish antics exhausting at times, they mostly amuse you. You tend to "let boys be boys" and won't mind if your son roughhouses with a friend or plays with toys that make loud, exploding noises. And if he happens to prefer Barbies to G.I. Joe, that's okay with you, too. It's "free to be . . . you and me" for the Gemini mama's son.

CONS

Closeness may spark togetherness, but too much familiarity can breed contempt. At a certain point, you've got to create a healthy emotional distance from your baby boy, and that can be tough. Gemini moms don't do well with separation unless they're the ones initiating it. But at a certain point, your son will want to branch out beyond your mom-o-sphere to create his own world. After years as each other's favorite conversation buddies, it will be time to find a new BFF (or three). Otherwise, your nonstop Gemini chattering can become nails on a chalkboard to him, and your need for his attention can even feel oppressive. If you've been a full-time or single mama, especially, it's vital that you channel your energy back into hobbies, classes, work, and community involvement once he reaches school age.

Gemini moms aren't huge on iron-fisted discipline, and if this describes you, you may pay for it later when the boundaries you didn't set for your son when he was little soon give rise to a wild child. Suddenly you might find yourself losing patience, even yelling or trying to "get him in line"—so push yourself to have a few more rules when he's young. You may also need to relax the control in other areas, such as his eating habits. Even if you raised him gluten- and dairy-free through grade school, your best efforts may be no match for that "Boy Meets Pizza" preteen moment. Choosing appropriate battles is a learning curve for Gemini moms.

Since Gemini is ruled by Mercury the messenger, you're always up on the latest news and gossip. Be mindful of oversharing, though. One friend's Gemini mom called him whenever a high-school friend got into Harvard, sold a script, or passed the bar. While he was struggling to break into the film industry, her updates made him feel like a failure. So filter yourself a little, Gemini. While it's great to be a strong woman with opinions, make sure that you're not crowding out his right to have a different viewpoint than yours. Remember, boys are sensitive, too! He might feel under the microscope if you blog about him or comment on him constantly ("He's so touchy!") in front of other people. Temper the teasing and sarcasm, too, if that's your style.

PARENTING THROUGH AGES AND STAGES

*

INFANCY (THE FIRST YEAR)

Welcome to the world, mini-me! The sign of the Twins now has a permanent companion, someone who makes your scattered sign slow down, focus, and be in the moment. Foreign as that might feel, it's a good thing, so enjoy this fleeting year of enforced Zen Buddhism for what it is. Bliss out in the timeless, meditative moments (cuddling, breast-feeding). Find your center during the sleepless and disorienting ones. Think of this new lifestyle as a spiritual discipline, and eliminate as many distractions as you can.

While infancy might not be your favorite stage—you're a verbal sign who loves the interactive years—you never met an adventure you didn't like. And caring for an infant is indeed an adventure. You love to figure things out, then to share your copious research results with other moms. It makes you feel useful (and kinda cool) to be the go-to resource. "Vigilant research about health, nutrition, chemicals, child psychology, et cetera has been a lifelong interest," says one new Gemini mother. With your quick thinking and speedy search engine skills, you could be the neighborhood go-to expert in no time. Can't get the milk to express or the baby to latch? You've bookmarked the instructions on lalecheleague.org. Swaddling not coming together? Ping that friend of a friend who runs an infant day care. Thank you, Google!

As the sign of the Twins, you're accustomed to collaborating. So unlike other signs, you're not too proud to ask for help and advice. If anything, you'll err on the side of soliciting *too* much information, driving yourself into analysis paralysis in the process. At a certain point, you have to stop the web researching, book reading, and opinion polling, and just get out of your busy little head. Not all of your new-mommy questions should be crowdsourced, Gemini. At a certain point, you have to just own that even you—the former rock groupie/all-night partier whose first "date" with your baby daddy was supposed to be a one-night stand (oops!)—have that implacable thing called maternal instinct. So use it! Of course, it might take some time to fully embrace this part of your identity and lifestyle, but the outcome is the sweet sight of your affectionate side emerging. Some Geminis, it turns out, are major cuddlers—at least with their offspring. You enjoy rocking, talking, singing, and making funny voices. You're a sucker for the undeniable, heart-stealing cuteness of newborns. And secretly, you might even have moments when you think, *Wow. I was born to do this.*

The slower pace of life with a baby may be the hardest thing to adapt to, since Geminis don't do boredom well. Sitting around while your tiny one sleeps eleven hours a day could have you climbing the walls. You could be simultaneously savoring the sweetness of this phase and counting the minutes until your kid is old enough to hold court about why the sky is blue.

Even if you're utterly sleep-deprived, you still definitely need a hobby or two. One Gemini mother held a sold-out workshop on flirting when her daughter was only one month old! Staying engaged in your "other" life is key, even now. Otherwise, you might just fill your day with errands just to have something to *do.* "I'm a stay-at-home mom . . . but I'm busier than ever!" says Giada, a Gemini mother who ran a prestigious photo studio in New York City before her son was born. Another Gemini mom bemoans: "It's difficult to manage all my other responsibilities and motherhood. I barely find time for myself, my hobbies, my art, and even for my husband."

If you can relate, you might need to check your calendar: is it stuffed with "filler" activities and appointments? Try to create some meaningful outlets in which to channel that anxious energy, and cut the fluff that is crowding your calendar as much as you can.

As the sign that rules local events and communication, you might want to turn your living room into a (toy-scattered) hangout/salon, throwing together a few hors d'ouevres and inviting friends to stop by. While your pals take turns cuddling and rocking the baby, you can indulge in chitchat about milk, sleep schedules, and vaccinations mixed with banter about the latest incendiary blog you found while your tot was napping, some local gossip, or your pet project du jour.

If you get really lonely—say, none of your friends have kids, or their children are a totally different ages—you could even attend a new mothers' group just for the conversation. Even if you just sit around nursing together in a daze (or yeah, talking about baby stuff ad nauseam), at least you can trade tips or make a few connections. Who knows? One of those zombie moms could be your "in" at that private preschool in a couple years.

And if you're really bored, take a class or get back to work sooner than you planned, even part-time. Our hairdresser Jo, a Gemini mom who runs the busy downtown New York City salon Dop Dop, let her newborn snooze in a car seat beside her station while she clipped and colored hair. Her dutiful Capricorn husband handled the diaper runs and changes; she handled the nighttime parenting. Whatever works for *you* is what works best for the family!

TODDLERHOOD (TWO TO FIVE YEARS)

Prepare for the most fun *and* frustrating time of your life. Your little one is becoming more interactive and verbal, which means it's time to read, teach, and play together. On days when you have the patience for it, your animated sign will enjoy sharing the wonders of childhood with your kid. Gemini is the zodiac's mimic (it's that Twin thing), so you naturally understand how to mirror a toddler's exaggerated expressions, a great technique for development. Since you love language, you might even raise an early talker or reader. And while too much clinginess can drain you ("Whining zaps my patience," says one Gemini), you also love having a worshipful sidekick to share fun times.

Most experts advise setting regular regimens for toddlers, but that can be hard for your spontaneous sign. "I am the most unstructured person—and sometimes I like that about us," admits Desiree, the Gemini mom of a three-year-old. "A regular dinnertime, a bedtime, and a routine would be nice . . . but then we wouldn't be able to do anything that we want."

While some Gemini moms may just choose to wing it like Desiree, you may find it easier to put your toddler to bed right after dinner ("bath, brush, book, bed") so you can have precious evening hours to yourself. With greater demands on your time and energy, you may be forced to schedule, even against your nature. Whenever possible, though, you'll find it fun to include your toddler in one of your many projects.

Heading up the decorations committee for your temple's holiday fund-raiser? Hand your tot some nontoxic glue and glitter. In charge of cooking dinners? Give your little one some beans to mash or pots to bang on with a wooden spoon. Knitting a scarf? Get a little ball of yarn and some cardboard for your kiddie. Play music while you work. Gemini mom Regena Thomashauer, headmistress of Mama Gena's School of Womanly Arts, uses "dance breaks" as a required tool to help harried women return to a state of pleasure. Crank up the Beyoncé and bop around together with your toddlers. It will do wonders. Fortunately, you're not a sign that needs clearly demarcated "grown-up zones" or gets anxious about your furniture. Rather than put plastic on the sofas (never!), your home might look like the love child of Pottery Barn and a Toys "R" Us showroom after a one-day sale.

One thing you and your toddler may share is a supershort attention span. This can lead to clashes, unless you keep your days busy and varied. While you might be guilty of overbooking your calendar, your impatient Gemini self feels more comfortable hopping from art class to playground or running errands while the baby naps in the stroller. If you have the luxury of staying at home full- or part-time, being a homebody shouldn't be an option, since cabin fever will only get you both into trouble. Of course, we're not suggesting that you drag your child around from morning until night. Just keep enough variety in your schedule.

Luckily, the social aspect of the toddler phase is tailor made for your sign. For Gemini, there's strength in numbers, so gather your fellow mamas and head to the climbing gym, children's museums, or any place with padded floors where the kids can run around while you catch up on gossip, vent about preschool admissions, or trade organic lunch recipes. You're constantly researching and trying things out, so you've got loads of information to share with the other moms, too. Since you tend to get overwhelmed by too many choices—weaning, day care, potty training—it's good to have a mom posse to help you talk things out.

The ever-curious Gemini mom honors her children's desire to learn, especially through play and discovery. (After all, that's how *you* like to learn!) Your child's education will be of prime importance to you. While your tyke is still in the womb, you'll be busy researching all the different methodologies—from Rudolf Steiner to Montessori to homeschooling—and the best educational toys for healthy socialization and neural development.

Some Geminis will experiment with more "radical" parenting techniques, alternative forms of discipline (or nondiscipline), and extreme diets. There is such as thing as having "too much information," especially in your case. One late-night watching of a documentary like *Fast Food Nation* or *Hungry for Change*, and you might be clearing your cabinets of anything that contains refined sugar and white flour. There may be power struggles when the preschool passes around animal crackers and apple juice from the supermarket.

"We practice attachment parenting. We do not praise and do not punish," says Jenn, who runs the Montreal-based website Mama Naturale. "Our daughter is very free. We choose our battles so that she understands no really does mean no. She really is free to do what she wants, and we keep the dangerous stuff away from her so she isn't tempted. I am pretty great at making sure that no matter how busy we are, my daughter eats nutritious, homemade food, often organic, sometimes grown in my backyard." While the other eleven zodiac signs bow to Jenn's unusual abilities in awe (and might even raise a skeptical eyebrow after reading this), the über-energetic Gemini mama somehow *does* manage to pull off feats that can make other moms feel like chicken nugget microwaving slackers. Fortunately, this talkative sign is more than willing to share her multitasking secrets.

Gemini is one of the zodiac's "teacher" signs, so finding the teachable moments of toddlerhood can be a smart survival strategy. Why is the sky blue? Why is the grass green? While other moms would brush off these questions with a distracted "Because they are, dear," you're on Wikipedia, answering with facts, teaching your four-year-old terms like *chlorophyll* and *photosynthesis.*

Gemini is an intellectual air sign ruled by verbal, rational Mercury. One Gemini mom told us that baby talk was a big no-no in her house. Like Sergeant Joe Friday, you want just the facts, ma'am. You might insist upon calling the body parts by their textbook names—and the sooner you can dispel those myths about storks and tooth fairies, the better. You might even benefit from learning about brain development and the science of a baby's mind. The more something makes sense to you, the better able you are to relax and go with the flow of how your child is developing.

And remember, just because a "village" of personalities lives within you, it still takes an actual village to raise a child. You've got nothing to prove by trying to do it all yourself. Your other relationships could suffer. "I spend so much of my energy on being a mom that I am not always the best partner," says Desiree. "My man comes home sometimes, and I'm so stressed out that if he says one thing wrong, I snap."

For some Gemini moms, insecurity can lurk in the background. Remind yourself that your child will still love and adore you, even if you don't spend every minute together. Sometimes a secret jealousy or competitiveness can be the culprit. You want to ensure your alpha status in your child's life, sometimes even over your partner. You might even take it personally if your little one runs to Daddy or Grandma instead of you. Was it something you did? Were you not a good enough mom? Does he love them more than you? No, no, and no. The more rich and varied your life is—and yes, that includes date nights with your partner, the pottery class you're yearning to take, and time alone devouring a novel—the better mom you'll be. So share the love, and the duties, and remember that your relationship with your child is a unique and irreplaceable one.

EARLY CHILDHOOD (SIX TO ELEVEN YEARS)

Welcome to your mommy zone! As an eternal child, you deeply understand kids this age. In fact, you've got a lot in common now. You and your child are both curious, eager to explore the magic of life, and often painstakingly honest. Now that your son or daughter's cognitive development allows more logic and reasoning, you'll enjoy engaging in dialogue. You might even have some fascinating philosophical conversations as you tuck your kid into bed or drive home from school. Geminis are gifted storytellers as well: you might even have a children's book or two in you!

"What I do best as a mother is I listen and I really fan the flames of his creativity," says Gemini mom Danielle of her eight-year-old son. "I'm really mindful about not pushing him to be someone that he isn't but pushing him to believe in his true nature. For example, my kid is not into team sports. He might be someday, but right now, he's resisting it with every fiber of his being. But if I let him do what he wants, which is swim, or take a cardboard box and turn it into a condo, that's where he shines."

This is also a time when you become a major advocate for your kids—using that big Gemini voice of yours. When our friend Lois was bullied as a child, her Gemini mom, Edie, took control. "My four-foot-eleven Gemini mother met with the teachers and principal," recalls Lois. "It scared the mean kids so much that everyone was really nice to me after that—in a creepy, Stepford kind of way. When my sister was physically bullied, she actually went after the kids and threatened them. Years later, even a six-foot-four jock was afraid to walk down our block!"

Of course, Edie had grown up as the only Jewish girl in a rough Brooklyn neighborhood, so, like many Geminis, she had street smarts to spare. "My mom survived by charming the gang members and befriending the leader of the toughest bunch, Dynamite Tony from the Lords of Flatbush," recalls Lois, laughing. Only a Gemini! You're certainly a colorful mom, and you'll do what it takes to ensure that your kid is protected—even if that means fighting on the stoop!

Jo, a Gemini salon owner, somehow found the time to become PTA president at her children's school. "I came in and took over," says Jo. "It was a hot mess! People were just sitting around eating. The computer in the parent room was ancient. I let them know we're not running a kaffeeklatsch here. We replaced the computers, and now there's no eating until after the meeting is over."

While you can be stern about discipline on some issues, you'll continue to be a free-range parent in other ways. "I believe that children know what's best for them to a vast, deep extent," says Danielle. "So our child has a ton of latitude but a lot of firmness around values that we do not waver on: respect, safety, and kindness. We say that if you have those three things, you can do whatever you want."

In times of trouble, Gemini moms do best when they talk it out with their children. However, remember that just because your child *sounds* mature doesn't mean he is. "If my kids can make a compelling argument in support of something they've done wrong, I cave," admits Gemini mom Christie. Children at this age can grasp right and wrong, but their moral code is still wired to see what they can get away with—and they will often lie to avoid punishment. Setting sensible boundaries helps to instill important values and reassure your child that he's safe. A set of simple rules will help your kid know what's expected of him. Otherwise, he could end up walking on eggshells, never knowing what's going to get him in trouble—which can be confusing for a kid to figure out on his own. Or he might expect that he can talk his way out of any punishment if he is clever enough.

Children need consistency, but for ever-changing Gemini too much routine can feel like torture. Since much of your life is staged in the short-attention-span theater, you have a hard time following through with all of the hobbies, activities, and projects that you start. In your thirst for variety, you may unwittingly destabilize your family's routines. (High-profile example: Gemini Angelina Jolie is a fascinating parent . . . but will her kids become weary little citizens of the world after changing schools and home bases so many times?)

This tension between routine and wanderlust can be eased by hiring a good babysitter (especially an earth or a water sign). Or you might outsource the mundane tasks that make you restless: shopping, cleaning, meal prep, school pickups, and drop-offs. Work the barter system with other parents, too. Perhaps another mom drives the kids to soccer practice, and you take them out for milkshakes afterward, which you happily pay for. One Gemini mom we know has a private chef come prepare and freeze a week's worth of meals. Another sent her daughter to boarding school—possibly an extreme choice but one that improved their relationship and the quality of time they *did* share.

Or, launch like Ellie—the Gemini mother of three daughters, Raven (fourteen), Cedar (eleven), Twilight (five), and the owner of Bootyland—a shop featuring modern, eco-conscious kids' clothing. The shelves house wooden toys, cloth diapers, and edgy onesies that pronounce THEY'RE RAISING ME GAY and MY DAD IS A HIPSTER DOUCHEBAG.

When we spoke to Ellie, her daughter Twilight was busily stamping stars and owls on the brown paper bags used for customer purchases. Another visit to the shop, and Cedar helped to ring up our order. The girls are regular fixtures at the shop, by Ellie's design. "When you're younger, helping out is so exciting. Plus, it gives them a cool experience and skill. And they are pretty confident about it!" she insists. "And it is helpful to be able to bring the kids to the store, because I still get to be social with people while raising them."

You may fiercely protect your kids, but you don't shelter them. Of course, this could lead to a few moments of overexposure to an adult world. A little censorship is okay, Gemini. Monitoring your speech is also über-important for Gemini moms at this stage. Since you're constantly changing your mind, you can accidentally talk out of both sides of your mouth, which can be confusing to your kids. They don't understand why Mommy was campaigning for animal rights all winter but is eating grass-fed beef in the spring. The whole "do as I say, not as I do" thing doesn't pass children's finely honed b.s. detectors. It can also breed rebellious teenagers who act out in an effort to test where you stand. Consciously pick a few key values and stick with them—both in your word and deed.

And if you find your time divided between a gazillion outlets, pick *one* thing that you and your child love to do together. Whether it's taking digital photos and uploading them to a family website, making a signature dish for Sunday dinner, or reading a book before bedtime, those special shared moments make a difference at any age. Soon enough, your kid will want to go to the mall instead of hanging out with you—so enjoy these times of togetherness while they last!

ADOLESCENCE AND TEENS (TWELVE TO EIGHTEEN YEARS)

Put on your battle gear, Gemini—you're heading into the trenches. The teenage years can be tough for the all-knowing, all-seeing Gemini mom. On the positive side, you're an au courant mommy who's hip to the latest trends. You're up on the latest pop culture and celebrity gossip. You share eye shadow with your daughter, guyliner with your son, and you know more about obscure bands and indie films than any of their hipster friends. You're genuinely intrigued by the school yard dramas and interpersonal dynamics your kids are experiencing, and you'll help them talk through social struggles. You might not mind if your kid sports a faux-hawk or even gets a discreet tattoo or naval piercing. Heck, you might have a "sleeve" full of ink yourself! Individual expression? You're all for it.

Even though you're a lot like a teenager yourself—whether in your fashion choices or your need to question everything—that doesn't mean that you can handle raising one. At this phase, your child needs you to be the *least* like him, more of a parent than a peer, a steady base camp rather than a BFF. You may resent this because it makes you feel "old" or tied down. No way are you gonna quit teaching burlesque workshops or demonstrating outside the grocery store that buys from factory farms or coming to PTA meetings in a pink wig just because your kid feels *embarrassed* by it.

If you're a more traditional Gemini mom, it can be hard not to get overly enmeshed in your teenager's highs and lows, taking the mood swings personally and unwittingly making it all about you. You're the sign of the Twins, so you may unconsciously assume that you're joined at the hip with your kid. This overidentification can be troublesome now, since the fundamental purpose of adolescence is separation. Your child *needs* to individuate and create her own identity. You may need to work through some of your own private anxieties so you can shorten (or tighten) the leash appropriately.

You're okay with a good amount of teenage self-expression: letting your daughter paint a mural on her bedroom wall or converting the garage into a man cave for your son's drum kit and band practices. The limits of your comfort zone are when your child starts talking back to you. You hate anyone thinking that he's smarter than you—above all, your own kid. After all, you pride yourself on your intellect and sharp wit. So, when your number-one fan morphs into public enemy number one—unleashing sarcasm and a know-it-all attitude on *you*—all hell can break loose. Who does this kid think he's messing with?

Gemini, you could be doing more harm than good by engaging in a battle of wits or taking an "I'll show you" stance. Your teen is testing your boundaries because she either *wants* to know your limits or thinks that your limits are unfair. The more you react, the less she respects you. Biting your tongue ain't easy—Gemini is, after all, the sign of communication. So if you must respond, you'll need to learn a better way than lashing out with a killer comeback or a cutting zinger.

One of the best books we've read on this topic is Dr. Haim G. Ginott's *Between Parent and Teenager.* This guide explains the subtext behind a teenager's rebellious actions and how to read between the lines so you can respond appropriately—with compassion and composure. One of the main dilemmas is that a teenager is caught in a limbo state between wanting to be a child and longing for the privileges of adulthood. Hey, can't you relate to that, Gemini?

You might notice backlash in areas where you've been too lax as well as overly controlling. It will show up in your teenager's habits and chosen rebellions. If your child does get into trouble—body image issues, drinking, or drug experimentation—you could struggle to appropriately address the issues. If and when a child is in this kind of distress, it can be hard for the Gemini mom to look at herself. Since Virgo—the perfectionist sign—rules your fourth house of motherhood, deep down you're really hard on yourself. Secretly, you blame yourself for everything that goes wrong with your child while outwardly pointing fingers at everyone else: the school, the other parent, your own parents. You may be afraid of being attacked and called a bad mother, thus taking the "best defense is a good offense" route and going on the warpath. "How could she do this to me, after all I've done?" Or "I don't know who's teaching him this stuff—this world is so dangerous and scary these days."

Gemini, if that happens, slam the brakes. Blaming and shaming accomplishes nothing. An ounce of personal responsibility, though, is worth a pound of cure. Perhaps your child *has* been adversely affected by one of your choices in life—a divorce, a lack of consistency, that year you moved four times, whatever. Maybe you've been too much of an open book about adult subjects and need to be a little more private, so your child feels safer. Or perhaps there *are* some areas where you've lapsed into an all too familiar (to Geminis) "do as I say, not as I do" mode.

"I left home at sixteen because of my mom's extreme reaction to my eating disorder," says the daughter of one Gemini. "She had her own body issues and couldn't separate mine from hers. So I had to get away for a few years."

It doesn't make you a bad person or mean that you've totally screwed up. It just means new skills are needed and that it's your job as a parent to build those skills so you can meet your child halfway. Don't be afraid to look into the mirror. Be grateful that your kid is a messenger, because it's an act of love to help someone see where she needs to grow.

The good news is that curious Gemini is an eternal student of life. Once you give yourself a little objective distance (and forgive yourself for being imperfect), you can become a masterful mama. You'll probably be inspired to help other moms, too, with your new treasure trove of tips and expertise. So dive into those child psychology classes, parenting workshops, and dialogue groups. Bring your friends. And don't make it too much of an intellectual process, even though you love a good idea or theory. As the seventeenth-century English poet John Wilmot said, "Before I got married, I had six theories about bringing up children; now I have six children and no theories." Applying these ideas to real life is where the magic happens. Remember, practice makes perfect!

BYE-BYE, BIRDIE: LEAVING THE NEST (EIGHTEEN-PLUS YEARS)

Although you may have spent the last eighteen years secretly wishing for more time to yourself, some Gemini moms find themselves panicked at the idea of a child leaving home. As the sign of the Twins, you might find yourself feeling a case of astrological separation anxiety—no matter how much you fought with your kid for the last few years.

Our friend Tina's Gemini mom was dead set against her going away to college and wanted Tina to live at home through her college years. Finally, she relented—or pretended to, anyway. "We got to my dorm room and unpacked, decorated, set everything up," recalls Tina. "Then my dad suggested we take a walk around the campus to explore. My mother told us she had a terrible headache and needed to lie down. So we left her in my room and went for an hour. When I got back, my entire room was packed up! It looked like I hadn't even moved in there. My mom says, 'Okay, you went to college. Hope you liked it. Now let's go home!'"

Fortunately, Tina managed to talk her mom out of this momentary madness. Because truthfully, Gemini, absence can make the heart grow fonder between you and your child. Your child will learn to rely on her own strength rather than expecting you to have all the answers. And since you can be a larger-than-life personality, it will help your kid to step out of your spotlight for a few years and claim his own.

Don't be surprised if she follows in your footsteps anyway. Gemini supermodel Isabella Rossellini's daughter Elettra Wiedemann became a high-fashion model herself—but she also has a master's degree in biomedicine and has dabbled in the restaurant business. Hey, you've taught your kid to be a trailblazer by example. Now you have to let go and allow that magic to happen!

Soon enough, you could come together as true friends—a relationship you can savor even more than the dependent mother–child one.

Now you're both adults, and the playing field is more level. You can talk frankly about any topic, trade ideas, and give advice that's (finally!) well received. This is actually easier for you. Your role of provider can morph into one of caring confidante and friend, and you can just enjoy each other—taking vacations, watching indie films, trading books, and talking politics.

Of course, you'll always be mom, and you'll love spoiling your child when he comes home to visit. "My Gemini mom would drive me crazy when she'd buy me red peppers to take home anytime I visited—and I'd have to carry them home for twenty blocks," says Lois. "But my partner, Charlie, really helped me with that. Charlie and my mom adore each other, and he explained that she was just trying to show love."

You'll also continue to have strong opinions about whom your child chooses to date or marry and where he wants to live. Keeping those to yourself won't be easy, and you might irritate your children by dropping unsubtle hints ("You know, my *friend's* daughter decided to take that LSAT after college . . . just in case she wanted to pursue law").

Resistance is futile with a Gemini mom, though, and eventually your kids will realize it—even if they have to become parents themselves first to understand. The good news is you get funnier and more endearing with each passing year, as your Gemini wit mixes well with wisdom. (Now you're less the argumentative know-it-all and more the gutsy person who's not afraid to say what everyone else is thinking.) So the Gemini mom that drove her kids nuts in their youth could end up being the most hilarious source of comedic material ever created. Our family friend Miriam Samson, a 101-year-old Gemini with her full faculties, travels internationally, campaigns for political leaders, and sends email. She's been known to saunter out of her nursing home on the arm of a 26-year-old friend. Hey, you're the timeless kind of mother—and you get better with age. How many people can say that?

THE CANCER MOM

(June 21–July 22)

MOMMY MAGIC - Your Strengths:

- Sensitivity
- Comfort and hominess
- Good taste
- Devotion
- Sentimentality

MAMA MIA - Your Challenges:

- Overprotectiveness
- Mood swings
- Fearfulness and clinginess
- Jealousy

FAMOUS CANCER MAMAS:

Princess Diana, Gisele Bündchen, Pamela Anderson, Courtney Love, Selma Blair, Jessica Simpson, June Carter Cash, Edie Falco, Nancy Reagan, Nadya Suleman ("Octomom"), Ariana Huffington, Liv Tyler, Sofía Vergara, Kristen Bell

YOUR PARENTING STYLE

As the sign that rules all things matriarchal, you're the zodiac's mother superior. For most Cancer women, maternal instincts are hardwired into their cosmic DNA. From an early age, you've been a nurturer—to friends, siblings, dolls, pets, anyone needing a maternal touch. Some signs are ambivalent about children, but most Cancer women feel they were born for the job. You're the mom who could have an at-home birth, train as a doula, and breast-feed your kid until it teeters on unnatural. Hello, La Leche League president!

Kids are often a nonnegotiable item in your search for a spouse. You might even marry a starving artist or someone with less education than you as long as his eyes get dreamy when he talks about raising a family. Whether you dress in head-to-toe Catherine Walker like the late Cancerian royal mum Princess Diana or you're an edgy rocker like Crab Courtney

Love, you still can't wait to pack those little peanut butter and jelly sandwiches and bounce a baby on your knee.

Your fourth house of motherhood is ruled by balanced, beauty-loving Libra, the sign of relationships. This gives you an idealistic approach to family—and a flair for creating a pretty, comfortable home. You're deeply invested in your relationship with your children and will likely be their lifelong confidante. Even if you're a pierced and tattooed parent—like Cancer Ariel Gore, creator of the Hip Mama enterprise—you're still the ultimate mom on the inside.

Since relationships are so important to you, some Cancers will even break all the so-called dating rules and discuss children on the first date. Does it send potential partners fleeing? Sure. But you might as well screen out those Peter Pans—lest you become *their* mommies and waste your childbearing years raising *them*. (Admit it: it's happened before.) If you can't imagine yourself blissfully coparenting by the time appetizers arrive, you might as well walk. There are plenty of folks out there who will appreciate your old-fashioned respect for family and your burning desire to procreate.

Your relationship with your own mother is a central theme in your life. If you were lucky enough to have a healthy mother-daughter bond, you could be lifelong best friends. While other signs eagerly cut the cord at adolescence, you want your mom nearby—at least within frequent-visiting distance. Once she becomes Grandma, closing the geographic gap could become a top priority. While pregnant, our Cancer friend Anna bought her widowed mom an apartment two floors above hers. Now her mother shuttles between Anna's childhood home in the Midwest and the New York City pied-à-terre, which is just an elevator ride away from the grandkids.

Shy Cancers were often clingy kids—or else wildly emotional and hyperactive in a bid for attention. Either way, much of your childhood temperament stemmed from a desire to feel secure in your parents' love. Since you know what it's like to need your mommy, you're supersensitive to your own children this way. While you don't want to overprotect them—every kid needs a dose of street smarts—you're keenly aware when trouble's brewing, and you're always on standby for soothing. (Our Cancer grandmother swore by the healing properties of chocolate and cherry Kool-Aid.)

Cancer women who claim to lack "maternal instinct" may have had a tough, neglectful, or narcissistic mom who failed to properly parent her. Or perhaps your mom passed away when you were young, a blow that Cancer girls take harder than any other sign. Either of these challenges is enough to make you overcompensate in your own parenting. In reaction, you may try to create a perfect, 1950s-style family, giving your kids everything you didn't have. Or you could second-guess your every move, for fear that you'll cause them the same pain you endured. This can become constricting for you and confusing for your kids, who need you to show more authority. Remind yourself that clear boundaries help your children know where they stand with you, which builds their sense of security. You won't scar a kid for life if you say "no" or have a full life that doesn't completely revolve around your child. If you find yourself projecting your own past pain onto your kid, sort that out with a therapist or some wise mom friends. Consider the words of author Jill Churchill, who said, "There's no way to be a perfect mother and a million ways to be a good one."

Becoming a mother has healthy side effects for your social life. Since Cancers can be a little shy or reserved upfront, your kids provide the perfect excuse to engage with other parents. Your budding social circle could be filled with the moms of your children's friends or with families you meet through nursery school outings, PTA, and your children's sports teams. Talking about your kids lets you quietly screen people before deciding that they're worthy of your trust. When you hear their views on schooling, discipline, dietary limits, and the like, you get a keen sense of their values and whether they're compatible with yours. Eventually, you'll open up and start talking more about yourself with a few of them, allowing a genuine friendship to unfold. A true sign of trust is often when you invite someone into your home. There's no casual (play)dating happening in your household. Not just anyone makes it into a Cancer's sanctuary!

Can you be a tiny bit of a snob? Yes. But Cancers are true-blue friends whose bonds become as close as family over time. You don't let people into your world easily—but once they're in, they're in. You expect a high degree of loyalty when you've opened your heart. Becoming your friend is a life sentence, and you'll cherish the bonds you form even more once children are in the picture.

IF YOU HAVE A GIRL

PROS

When the ultrasound tests double X, it's a joyous day for the Cancer mom. Tutus, tea parties, and traditions dance in your head. You can't wait to introduce your daughter to the spoils of girlhood. Shopping, cooking, crafting, gardening, and decorating, plus books, museums, and culture, are all vehicles for passing on your great taste to your daughter. Even when the only white garments she's wearing are cloth diapers and onesies, you could be mentally designing her wedding dress and planning the reception.

At the same time, you remember your turbulent teen moods, the uncontrollable emotions, and the bumpy path to womanhood. Gulp. Are you prepared for *that*? More than you realize, Cancer. When her period comes, you'll be inspired to create a special ritual.

And since Cancer rules the chest, you know exactly where she should go to get fitted for a proper (and pretty, of course) bra. While some parents dread teaching their kids about the birds and bees, you take a more natural approach to this. Part of you loved developing into a woman. The shared blessing and burden of the menstrual cycle can be a common bond with your daughter, and cramps will be a valid excuse for skipping school or sports practice in your book—and afford time for a nice cuddle or to watch your favorite Jane Austen adaptation together.

Your deepest desire is that your daughter sees you as a compassionate confidante and best friend for life. Your own mom could occupy the top spot on your speed dial, and you'll hope to replicate this closeness. Cancer is ruled by the intuitive moon, and your sensitivity—when used correctly—can make you a wonderful and nurturing mom, the kind every daughter dreams of having.

CONS

For some Cancer women, daughters are a sigh of relief—no baseball bats swinging near your shabby chic vases, no hyperactive wrestling matches breaking your Depression glass vases, no muddy shoes on your velvet chaise lounge. Close call, chromosomes! But should you have birthed a spirited jock or future class president with a mind and tastes of her own, your dreams of high tea at the Plaza Hotel will vanish faster than you can say "Eloise." (Cancer mom Jessica Simpson once said she would "croak" if her daughter asked for Nikes instead of Louboutins.) Remember, your job is to create a secure base for her to become her own person. If she doesn't follow in your well-heeled footsteps, it's not a rejection of you or a failure on your part.

At times, subtle competitiveness can lace your mother-daughter relationship. You don't fancy being upstaged, even by your own flesh and blood. And when your daughter pulls away to form her own identity, thin-skinned Cancer mamas can feel hurt or rejected. You might start to make snarky or sniping little remarks to or about her out of jealousy (and hurt feelings). Cancer moms are famous for the "Oh, she's such a [insert subtly unflattering adjective here]" side comments. Even when they're said with affection and play, an undertone of control is brewing with these comments. You might need to do some healing around your own mother-daughter relationship. If you lived in your own mom's shadow or never clipped the apron strings, the unresolved residue can permeate your own parenting. Becoming conscious of those issues and triggers can make you a happier mom, less dependent on your daughter to validate you.

IF YOU HAVE A BOY

*

PROS

So you're having a boy, Cancer. Admit it: your heart breaks a little at the news. Tea parties tainted by testosterone! Dress-up dreams denied! Yet, once the reality settles in, you may actually feel relieved. In some ways, it's easier for Cancer women to raise boys. With a girl, you relate a little *too* personally and also feel the pressure of being their primary role model. When boys mess up, you can just blame their dad—or distance yourself from culpability in some other way. But you can only be so hands off before you rush in for the save. As the zodiac's quintessential helicopter parent, you never really park your propellers.

If your son is athletic, you'll like that, too, since Cancer women can have a sporty side. Your own competitive streak will come out as you cheer on his softball and soccer games—and woe be to the kid from the other team who messes with your precious boy. There could be a serious postgame showdown with his mother . . . followed by a bake sale where you upstage the other moms with your prize-winning brownies (a secret family recipe, natch).

Fortunately, all babies start out dependent on their mothers, so in his infancy you form the same bond with your son as you would with a little girl. You get to experience all the sweet moments before gender socialization kicks in. No, you may never be as close as you would with a little girl, and he might always feel like a bit of an interloper in your girlie-girl world. But you can learn to deal with the rhythms of a little boy, encouraging him to develop his sweeter side.

CONS

Caution: just because you've loosened your Crab-like grip, doesn't mean you should swing to the permissive polar extreme. For the Cancer mama, your little boy quickly becomes the apple of your eye and he can do no wrong. You'll cherish being the primary woman in his life until he's married. (And let's not even discuss the "hazing" his betrothed might go through to curry *your* favor as a mother-in-law. Sheesh!) One Cancer mom we know made a big show of befriending her son's standoffish girlfriend once she got wind of an impending marriage proposal. She turned on the warmth and charm, getting the unsuspecting young woman to share some deeply personal confidences. "We have a close-knit family, and I was worried she wouldn't fit in—or that she might even try to distance my son from us," this mama confesses. "If that was the case, there was going to be an intervention. But once I got to know her, I learned that she was really just shy. She was an only child whose parents were teachers, and our noisy family was a little too much for her. Fortunately, my snooping worked out for the best, and she and I are extremely close."

While it's great to make your son feel special, you could turn him into an entitled little prince who doesn't have to do a thing to earn his keep. Exclusive private nursery schools, elaborate gifts, even pulling the lame "boys will be boys" card—we've seen Cancer mothers do it all. Not only does this reinforce icky gender stereotypes (and potentially turn him into a cad), it's a wasted opportunity. With your sensitivity, you can train your son to be a mini-mensch—one who's caring and considerate with the girls (or boys) he'll date.

It only requires setting a few limits to make sure he gets the message that women can be strong authority figures. Park your inner pushover—and your easily wounded feelings, too. Because emotional Cancers are quick to bruise, you may fear your son's rejection if you come down too hard on him. He may kick, scream, and throw things when you lay down the law, but sternly remind yourself that he still loves you—and knows you still love him even if you're stern. Bottom line: Cancer is a matriarchal sign, and you're the boss. So quit acting like *you* work for him! It's downright confusing to both of you.

PARENTING THROUGH AGES AND STAGES

*

INFANCY (THE FIRST YEAR)

Cancer moms crave closeness, so infancy might be your all-time favorite stage. There's zero separation between you and your babe, and this tiny, helpless creature is utterly dependent on you. It's pure elixir to your sentimental soul, and you'll be framing photos as quickly as you can snap them. If you breast-feed, you might just get addicted, especially since oxytocin (the feel-good "bonding hormone") is released when you nurse.

While you may not cosleep at night (if only for your partner's sake—or your fear of rolling over on the baby), you'd be wise to invest in a great rocking chair, where you can enjoy afternoon snoozefests with baby curled on your chest. You could sit with your nose pressed to the baby's skin for hours, inhaling the newborn smell, crooning lullabies, and giving soft kisses to your sweet one.

Fussing over the baby is your greatest delight, and you love shopping for tiny clothes, educational toys, and organic food. With your fancy tastes and frugal budgeting, you're the first in line (or online) for high-end kiddie sample sales (Petit Bateau hoodies at half price? *Mais oui!*) and bulk discounts on chlorine-free diapers. A baby-food processor is a great asset, since you'll only want the purest ingredients going into your child's body.

Privacy, please! Cancers can be paranoid, so you might not be the mom plastering your kids' faces all over Facebook or the Internet. You shudder to think of some creepy stranger gazing at your albums. A password-protected brag blog? That's another story. With the security of an invitation-only barrier, you can record every coo, gas bubble, and milestone, with a montage of digital images to illustrate.

If you're heading back to work while your wee one's in onesies, you'll prefer if your mom or another close female relative steps in as nanny. Again, it's a trust thing. You like the idea of one parent staying home with the kids, but if your partner's not available, the next closest person will do. Or you might just opt to be a work-at-home mom for a while, even if that means leaving your current job. Possessive Cancers aren't too fond of just anyone being around their children—or in their homes. You may be reluctant to leave your kids with a sitter, even if it would do you some good to have a little free time. Whenever possible, try to interrupt the lovefest here and there and go out with your girlfriends, get a pedicure, or see a movie. Remember, just because you've gained a family member doesn't mean you have to lose yourself!

You might also want to save a little lovin' for your significant other—or a potential mate if you're a single mom. Romance is often the first thing to go out the window for many Cancer moms, since you're so consumed by your newborn duties. Try to get a night away from home together or go where adult conversation takes place—and no, not about the hassle of picking preschools or the merits of pureeing your own baby food. Of course, you happen to find the whole topic of child development fascinating, so it can be hard to rein in the impulse to share stories all night. You might even need to issue a baby-talk ban a couple of times a week, so you can remember who you were as a couple in the BC (before children) era.

The Cancer mom can get *so* absorbed in this new role that her home starts to resemble a day care center or baby goods store. Remember: motherhood is not an excuse to bypass developing your own identity. Shy Cancers like to hide behind their friends and children—and you now have a socially sanctioned excuse to do just that. But think twice before you take advantage of this opportunity to hide. In the long haul, your children will benefit most from seeing mama have a life and an identity of her own. While you don't have to rush off and do that yet, be sure to maintain some space in your home, life, and schedule where you come first. Cultivate your hobbies and interests, connect with old friends, and keep a sense of self alive.

TODDLERHOOD (TWO TO FIVE YEARS)

Toddlerhood is still a joyous time for you. The emotional cord hasn't been cut yet, and your little one still needs you. That more than makes up for the manic moments: public meltdowns, playground biting, and blowout diapers in a bathroom-less cafe. Besides, as the zodiac's moodiest sign, you understand this stage implicitly. How can a child go from delirious joy to pure seething rage in a nanosecond? Easy—you just did that an hour ago.

While you may still pine for the days when your babe slept eleven hours (seven of them curled on your bosom), toddler time is great for your social life. In fact, you might make some of your dearest lifelong friends at the park, music class, or swim class. Activities give your sign an instant icebreaker, helping you get past those awkward first (play)date moments. Yes, there's a whole courtship ritual among moms, too—and talking about your toddlers is a way of sussing out suitable sisters. Since you value culture and education, take your kid to children's activities at museums, libraries, and nature conservancies. You're more likely to meet someone with similar interests when you head to thoughtfully curated spaces.

If you haven't discovered your inner elitist, this side of you could emerge as you start the preschool search. You want your child to be safe, nurtured, and yes, a tad sheltered—and you'll grill the faculty about education methods, credentials, arts programs, and the type of families it attracts. "I know it sounds awful," confesses one Cancer mom we know. "But I just want to make sure my child is around the right people and opportunities from day one."

You fervently want your child to be safe and happy at all times, and that's natural for any mother. Yet the more you worry, the less secure she'll feel in the world. The best message you can model is that everything will turn out okay. Of course, *you* have to believe this, and that's your work to do. Cancer moms have a tendency to act out of fear. However, fear-based parenting only creates anxiety for both of you. Regular reality checks (hello, mommy support circle) will remind you that the human spirit is resilient. Relax, Cancer. It's a lot harder to mess up kids than you think.

You might be accused of overprotectiveness during this stage, and certainly, you're a guilty-as-charged toddler coddler. A little helicopter parenting isn't the worst thing, though. At least your kids know you care—as long as you don't constantly invade their airspace. Deep down, you don't really believe that kids can be spoiled. How can a human being possibly get too much love?

Still, this *is* the age where kids need to start learning discipline. You might not be the one to give it to them, as you find their antics—even the ear-splitting tantrums—utterly adorable most of the time. Hopefully, you have a partner who's good with boundaries or a caretaker who enforces routines. You'd rather not be the one who has to play the "bad cop."

"I have a tendency to constantly accuse my husband of being too hard on the kids, especially our daughter," says Cancer mama Carrie. "I think it's me wanting to bring the kids into my 'shell' and keep them safe. I have to focus on not telling him to stop when he's correcting her."

If you breast-fed, the hardest part about this stage could be weaning. You could be the mom who pumps until pre-K or nurses until nursery school. While many doctors would high-five you for it—and it's a personal choice—just make sure separation issues aren't stopping you from closing the milk bar when it's time. To make it easier for you, create a transition ritual, a closing ceremony for the last feeding (even one where you let yourself shed tears). Invent some new ways of bonding *without* the boob that are equally satisfying. For instance, maybe during the pre-bedtime hour when you'd normally nurse your tot to sleep, you cuddle with a favorite book and a warm sippy cup of milk—assuming your child will accept substitutes. Also, many lactation consultants are also experts at helping mothers wean, so dial one up and book an appointment. You may just need a pro to show you the ropes.

You might also ask yourself, am I trying to wean because I genuinely want to or because I think I'm supposed to? Some Cancers may just feel self-conscious about being judged by family, friends, and society overall. If you're still producing milk and your kiddo finds it comforting, then maybe the best answer is to go with the flow—literally and figuratively. "I just decided to nurse until my son is finished or I don't have any more milk," says Abby, the Cancer mom of a toddler. She laughs and adds, "Of course, I sometimes worry that he'll be one of those 'outliers' who nurses until he's five. But I think it will all work out."

EARLY CHILDHOOD (SIX TO ELEVEN YEARS)

Dial the therapist! The elementary-school years can be a bumpy ride for you. For the first time, you're forced to cut the cord and let your child individuate, which is always tough for the sensitive Cancer mom. As those baby sparrows start flapping their wings, your heart will break a little—and any attachment issues that have been bubbling under the surface will flare up big time.

That's where a mommy support group or good friends can pitch in. You'll need to get those hurt feelings under control so you don't project them onto your kids or smother them with emotional neediness. Taken too far, your kids could feel like they've abandoned you by having their own tastes and opinions. They might feel "punished" when you become aloof toward them, even if you're just nursing your wounds. Take extra care to hide this emotional process from them, Cancer.

Of course, there's only so much separation you can bear. You'll remain as involved as possible by volunteering at school, heading up the Brownie troop or offering your home for sleepovers and playdates. The closer you can keep your birdies to the nest, the better. When all else fails, remember: we're spiritual beings having a human experience here. Your child has a unique soul mission, and it's your job to support that. By clinging too tightly, you can interfere with your kid's finding his own path.

Plus, once you stop taking things so personally, you can have a lot of fun during these years.

This is the perfect age to pass along your love of culture and to nurture your children's hobbies. Share your favorite music, do art projects together, play around in the kitchen. Cooking and baking can be a perfect way to bond as a family. Many Cancers love yoga, so why not roll out a matching mat for your little one and teach her a few poses? Cancers have a sporty side, so go to baseball, football, or soccer games. This is also a great stage to join a YMCA, a country club, or some kind of recreational center that has activities for all ages. Now is when you'll solidify family traditions, like making holiday recipes every year, hanging special child-made Christmas ornaments, or returning to a favorite summer vacation spot.

School is a primary concern for you during this phase. You want to shelter your kids from growing up too fast, even if that means paying megabucks for private school tuition. Moving to a cheaper neighborhood or downsizing other expenses can help you swing it—and you won't mind. You'll do anything to protect your kids from harmful influences that make them grow up too fast.

You'll also need to be a little less hands-on with their interpersonal conflicts. You can be overprotective, but this is an important time to teach your children how to fight their own battles and develop a code of ethics. Don't go marching into school to confront a bully or take a teacher to task in front of your child or her classmates.

Another thing to watch at this age is your tendency to genderize, especially with toys. If you have a daughter, go easy on the kitchen sets, dolls, and playthings that scream "Women are caretakers." Not that there's anything wrong with that, of course, but throw in a few puzzles, work benches, and gender-neutral art supplies. Making things from scratch together can be empowering, and so can creative problem solving, such as figuring out how to construct an elaborate toy or learning basic guitar one step at a time.

If you have a boy, nurture both his masculine *and* his feminine side. Don't just toss him into team sports and G.I. Joe–ville. Let him play a musical instrument, learn a language, help out in the kitchen and with chores. Doing volunteer work as a family develops his compassionate side—so he can turn out more mensch than macho.

The other consideration: are *you* expressing your own individuality enough? Push yourself to have a life separate from your kids, Cancer. Bake cookies for the school fund-raiser, sure. But consider the other options and balance it out. Go back to work (even part-time), steal away to write that novel, or launch that cottage industry. It will keep you from resenting your kids for having a life while you (unnecessarily) sacrifice your own.

And if you want to be a mommy mogul, go for it—without an ounce of guilt. There's actually an alpha female in every Cancer, though this is a lesser-known trait. Cancer is one of the four cardinal signs—along with Aries, Libra, and Capricorn—which makes you a strong leader. This is why some Cancer girls are dubbed "bossy"—but don't get us started on the gendered unfairness of that one. (Would a boy be insulted if he took charge? Never!) You're setting an excellent example for your child by following your dreams. So, as your kids take a bigger step into the world, join them with one of your own.

ADOLESCENCE AND TEENS (TWELVE TO EIGHTEEN YEARS)

It's time, Mama. Let the little birdies make their own beds, pick up after themselves and take on more mature responsibilities. Yep, your coddling cutoff date has arrived. Your kids now need a different kind of parenting: clear boundaries, compassionate understanding, and wise guidance as they navigate tough decisions. Dry your tears (or save them for your therapist and Martini Mamas happy hour group), because your kids need to see your strength now.

You might enter this phase with trepidation, but soon enough you'll find that you're pretty damn equipped to parent a teenager. Who else could understand the emotional highs and lows better than the zodiac's most sensitive sign? As hard as you imagine the teenage years will be, the reality isn't as bad as your fears. Your firsthand experience with fluctuating moods comes in handy here. Plus, you remember well what a nightmare you might have been for *your* mom at this age. (Cringe!) The teen years might be your karmic debt to settle.

Because you can remember simmering with adolescent angst and intensity as though it were yesterday, not much will shock you about your kids at this age. Sure, you have some old-fashioned, homespun personality traits, but when it comes to your kids' growing up you're pretty hip. One Cancer mom we know was a pink-haired confidante of her cheerleading teenage daughter, sharing the same taste in pop music and graphic novels. Another, a women's health educator, made a point of teaching her son and daughter about sex early on—all the way down to proper anatomical names and functions. (Those humiliating sex-ed films about "nocturnal emissions" and menstrual cramps were no biggie for her children.)

If you have a daughter, you're probably eager to play concierge and introduce her to the world of classic femininity—teaching her how to dress, do her hair and makeup, accessorize, and so on. If you have feminist leanings, like many Cancer women do, you'll also be eager to impart your critical thinking skills and teach media literacy. (Hey, if you're a domestic goddess, it's because you genuinely enjoy it, not because you think women should be stuck in a 1950s housewife time warp.) In this regard, you're pretty versatile, at ease in both feminist and feminine realms.

With your son, you'll want to remain on close emotional terms, making it safe for him to open up about his first crushes, peer conflicts, and general life experience. You're not above feathering the nest in order to entice him and his buddies to hang out almost exclusively at your home. At least you can keep an eye on them—and continue instilling a "home is where the heart is" ethos into your not-so-little guy.

While it might be all festive bonding to you, though, you need to be careful not to make your kids too self-conscious at this age. The Cancer mom will point out her daughter's budding boobies or her son's deepening voice in a lightly teasing way—perhaps you do this to deal with your own discomfort about your baby's growing up. But the way to taint their trust is to let them overhear your conversations with friends or their grandma: "I think Max has a girlfriend" or "Lily's been so moody. I think she may get her period soon." Just remember how self-conscious *you* were (and still are). You'll need to regularly remind yourself to respect your children's privacy during this phase. Don't blab confidences or blog about embarrassing stories that you find "cute."

Worried about how your preteen will deal with the onslaught of body image issues, extreme gender roles, and peer pressure? If you have a daughter, read the work of pioneering researchers like Carol Gilligan (*In a Different Voice*), Joan Jacobs Brumberg (*The Body Project*), and Peggy Orenstein (*Cinderella Ate My Daughter*). For moms of boys, we recommend Lisa Bloom's *Swagger: 10 Urgent Rules for Raising Boys in an Era of Failing Schools, Mass Joblessness, and Thug Culture*. As a concerned Cancer mom, you want to be sure you're doing everything you can to impart the right values on your children, even as they're exposed to influences outside your control. And you want to be informed of everything that might, and quite possibly will, happen to your child as he or she matures.

Still, even the best preventive measures can't stem the tide of hormonal moments that are par for this developmental stage. There will be times when your kid ices you out, shuts down, or mouths off, and your tender feelings will get hurt. The last thing you want is to be treated like your child's enemy.

While your kids' bratty back talk can sting, remember that teenagers swing quickly from bravado to neediness. You'll be on the frequent texting plan with your teen, secretly relishing every demand to pick your son up from practice or to plan your daughter's elaborate Sweet Sixteen. At least you're involved in their lives! You want your kids to be safe, even if that means keeping them a little dependent on you.

Unless you have a truly headstrong teen who just *has* to assert some independence—or who lapses into the wrong crowd no matter how much guidance you've offered—you could be unusually close with your kids at this age. You'll listen with genuine sympathy to their after-school angst and rush to their sides in a crisis. Just remember that there's a thin line between empowering and enabling them. Don't get overly involved in their dramas and fan the flames of their teenage torment, even if it keeps them and their friends gathered around your kitchen table after school.

Our own mom and aunt would call their Cancer mother monthly to say, "I got my Auntie M" (their pet name for period). When we finally figured out that they weren't talking about *The Wizard of Oz*, we couldn't believe grown women would ring their mom for mother-daughter menses chitchat. But that's the kind of lifelong bond you can establish with your kids, Cancer. With your keen emotional sensitivity, you're a safe space for them to come home to, even when they insist on learning about life the hard way. Although you can be tough when your child gives you attitude, that shell cracks when you see that they're hurting. Once you realize someone needs their mommy, you snap into action. Out comes your soft side to dry tears, whip up some comfort food, and talk about it.

Old-fashioned as you can be, you're a with-it mom in many ways. Years ago, our friend Ariel Gore, a hip, tattooed Cancerian writer who became a mom at age nineteen, founded the Hip Mama brand, which includes books and a website with witty parenting stories and advice. You relish the challenge of interweaving motherhood with your own unique tastes and personality. With your savvy style, your daughter will raid your closet and makeup bag, and you'll love to take her shopping. The Cancer mom is a culturally literate lady, too. You might listen to the same music as your kids—or in some cases even introduce them to obscure bands, indie filmmakers, and avant-garde artists. Sure, you're still Mom at the end of the day, baking cookies and tucking them into bed—even if you whip up vegan gingersnaps and hum an obscure Ramones tune as a lullaby.

Your deepest desire is to be best friends with your child, and there's a good chance you'll achieve that. But to pull it off, you must keep your own emotions in check during this angst-ridden, turbulent phase—and be selective about what you share. You don't have to hide your feelings, but don't expose your adult and personal issues to your kids, no matter how wise or mature they seem. It's okay if they see you cry at a touching moment, like a wedding or at a family gathering. But weeping over a fight with daddy or fuming over a friend's selfishness should be done out of their earshot.

The key to surviving this phase? Keep a welcoming and accepting space at home and trust that your kids will circle back after their adventures. Holidays and traditions will usually happen at your house, so make them fun and let your teenagers invite their friends and significant others, and allow them to contribute new customs to the family fold. Let them decorate their rooms without your input (unless it's requested) and encourage them to express their creativity in their own domains. With your flair for home decor, it might be a fun bonding project to spruce up their spaces together if they want you involved, or to revamp a communal area of the house, such as the den or living room, together. As long as your home is a safe haven, it will always be the heart space of your family. They'll be back!

BYE-BYE, BIRDIE: LEAVING THE NEST (EIGHTEEN-PLUS YEARS)

In your heart, you hope that your kids will always need you—and they will as long as you don't force them into closeness. When it's time for them to head out and make their own way in the world, you'll get overemotional (surprise, surprise) and might even hang on too tightly. Heaven forbid they should spend the holidays at a new college friend's or with the family of someone they're dating. You can get some serious empty-nest syndrome now, especially if your identity has revolved around being a mom.

If you catch yourself mailing out weekly care packages, driving to your kids' college or apartment to pick up dirty laundry or change their sheets, commenting on their daily Facebook updates, and forcing your way into their personal lives, it's time to slap the cuffs on yourself. You may never have fully individuated from your own mom, but that doesn't mean your kids don't need to carve their own path. Back off for a couple of years. With any luck, you'll get to do it all again with grandkids.

Think of your home as a welcoming harbor for your children, a port in the storms they'll inevitably face. However, this is the time for them to learn the skills of self-sufficiency so that they can create their own homes and families in the coming years. Be mindful not to infantilize them, lest you end up with a grown child who reoccupies his childhood bedroom, dines at your table, and expects an allowance for eternity. Need a wake-up call (and a laugh)? Watch the Will Ferrell movie *Stepbrothers*, a story of two immature fortysomethings who refuse to leave home. You might just recognize yourself a teensy bit here. Separation is one of the hardest tasks for the zodiac's clinging Crab. In fact, it might be something you have to learn right along with your kids during this phase. While the process can have its messy moments, it will ultimately set the stage for a healthy relationship in the long run.

THE LEO MOM

(July 23–August 22)

MOMMY MAGIC - Your Strengths:

Playfulness
Leadership
Creativity
Confidence

MAMA MIA - Your Challenges:

Self-centeredness
Drama
Too much energy
Pollyanna tendencies

FAMOUS LEO MAMAS:

Madonna, Halle Berry, Jennifer Lopez, Soleil Moon Frye, Martha Stewart, Whitney Houston, Jacqueline Kennedy Onassis, Kate Beckinsale, Sandra Bullock, Rebecca Gayheart, Mary-Louise Parker, Kathie Lee Gifford, Giuliana Rancic

YOUR PARENTING STYLE

*

Lights, camera, action! The creative and dramatic Leo mama leaves her signature stamp wherever she goes. Parenting is the ultimate personal expression for you, Leo—a job you throw yourself into, heart and soul. Leos tend to be hands-on mothers, involved in every aspect of their children's lives. You take pride in raising capable, successful citizens who will grow up and do great things in the world.

Motherhood suits the Leo woman in so many ways. It allows you to be an eternal child yourself! You're the mom who has the patience to get down on the floor for "tummy time" and relate to your infant at eye level, to sing the ABCs with your toddler ad nauseam while making swooping, animated gestures. The lively Leo mama loves to have fun and views life with kids as one long playdate. As your children get older, you want to do as much together as you can. Shopping, bike rides, crafting, cooking, camping, jet skis—your boundless energy levels are unmatched. Forget about chasing after your kids; they probably have a harder time keeping up with you!

Leo's fourth house of motherhood is ruled by Scorpio, the sign of power and control. As fun as you are, you can also have overbearing and intense moments here and there. Leo moms tend to micromanage or direct their children's lives and can be selectively strict. Madonna, a Leo, may be a champion of free expression, but her little ones weren't allowed to watch television or read magazines. While married to Guy Ritchie, Madge even canceled Christmas one year; another season, they rang in the Yuletide cheer with a macrobiotic meal and a three-gifts-per-child limit.

And Madonna's not the only famously extreme Leo mama: just peek behind the Dupioni silk curtains into Leo Martha Stewart's life. In her tell-all memoir *Whateverland*, Martha's daughter, Alexis, reveals that her famous mom would turn off all the lights on Halloween so no trick-or-treaters knocked on their door. "Martha does everything better!" Alexis gripes. "You can't win. If I didn't do something perfectly, I had to do it again. I grew up with a glue gun pointed at my head."

While you're not a mean mom by any stretch, Leo, you *can* be stern about your standards. You're a tough act to follow, since you tend to be a high achiever. Our Leo friend Patricia Moreno kept her fitness brand Sati Life thriving—training teachers, giving classes, filming workout videos—while juggling a toddler and infant twins. You hold yourself to very lofty standards (and meet them effortlessly), so you may not realize when you're pushing your kids too hard. Or maybe you do. And when your kid grows up to be a successful doctor, lawyer, businessperson, artist, or whatever, he'll thank you. The return on investment is worth it! Besides, your innate sense of entitlement can work to everyone's advantage, gaining your family access to exclusive schools, arts programs, and elite summer camps. Nothing can sway you when *you're* on a mission, and even if your kids turn out to be your polar opposite in career, lifestyle, or beliefs, you'll still have played a strong role in their upbringing.

Not that you won't play as hard as you work. Madonna may have called off Christmas, but when a Leo mom decides to celebrate, she goes all out! You're a consummate event planner: no party or pile of presents can rival a Leo mother's lavish layout. Giving gifts is a grand occasion, and you shine in this area. Maybe some people think you're spoiling your children. To you, presents are a way of acknowledging that you *know* someone and took the time to find something beautiful to show it.

Let it be noted that you happen to love receiving gifts, too. Visual Leos adore tangible, heartfelt expressions of love—especially when a sentimental card is enclosed. After all, Leo rules the heart, so you can be quite the mushball. Our condolences to the Leo mama with a more laid-back child (say, an Aquarius or a Sagittarius) who doesn't treat Mother's Day like the national celebration that it is. Not that you'd complain aloud—you have too much pride for that—but your feelings are definitely hurt if special occasions go unmarked.

As proud and protective as Leo is, you can also be dramatic and (dare we say it) a wee bit self-centered, putting the "me" in "mommy and me." You're the zodiac's most expressive sign, but your theatrical style can be amusing and exhausting in equal parts. One adult friend has taken to answering the phone with "Who died?" when her Leo mom calls, so accustomed is she to her mother's overblown expressiveness. You gasp when you hear someone's news—good or bad. Your excitement meter goes from zero to ninety in seconds. And when you love something, you can make it sound like you've just ridden bareback on a unicorn: "Oh my God, I just had *The. Best.* Hamburger. Of my entire life." Or "You *have* to see this movie—I was sobbing through the whole thing." There is no middle ground with Leo.

When you're in drama-mama mode, even a mundane traffic jam can become a show-stopping experience, retold with grand embellishments. "I was stuck behind this trailer . . . and we were gonna be late for Amanda's soccer game . . . and I was *so* stressed that I was drenched in sweat!" You may not even be aware of the amount of attention your drawn-out stories demand, since Leos can get so caught up in recounting a tale that they forget to come up for air. (Yes, you can be a wee bit self-centered at times, Leo, even if you don't mean to be.) Or maybe you're the "strong, silent type"—the long-suffering Leo who will give and give and give. Although you don't complain, your sighs are especially heavy, the stories milked for praise and flattery, just so everyone knows how hard you work for your family's happiness. (It's all drama—just depends whether you happen to be playing the bubbly rom-com heroine or the long-suffering Joan of Arc character.)

Remember, nobody has ever won an Emmy for being a mom, so dial back the performance art. Channel more down-to-earth Leo mothers, such as Sandra Bullock, Charlize Theron, or former *Punky Brewster* star Soleil Moon Frye, who created an eponymous parenting brand and website to help new moms embrace the "happy chaos" (as she puts it) of raising kids.

And if you must be dramatic, use it to have some fun! The Leo mother is often glamorous and radiant, a style icon in her own right. Even if you're low maintenance, there's probably a lipstick in your purse (red, in many cases) or a striking wrap that you can toss over your shoulders for a little day-into-evening transition. While many Leos rock a trademark mane of flowing locks, you'll find a big contingency of Leo moms with close-cropped dos, which manages to look stylish rather than asexual (think Leo Halle Berry). Says one Leo mom, "I'm aware that a happy mom makes happy kids, so I make sure to take good care of myself."

Although Leo is an independent fire sign, it's also of fixed quality, meaning you have a traditional side that likes to build: legacies, families, businesses. You might be busy running an empire—or at least plotting one out—while your kids are young. You're often the stereotypical supermom, making the rest of the world look like slackers. Our own mother, a Leo born July 31, fulfilled her lifelong dream of becoming a rabbi in her midfifties, even moving to New York City for rabbinical school and other urban adventures (picture a fifty-three-year-old midwestern mom biking through Manhattan). This was after years as PTA president, Girl Scout leader, and part-time college student earning her master's in counseling, all while running our household. (Anyone else need a nap now?) To this day, our mom has never hired a housekeeper, cook, or any other serviceperson to make her life easier. The idea of asking for help rarely occurs to the Leo mother. Even if you're a stay-at-home mom, you're the commander in chief of your home, the family COO, busy keeping your family in A-list form.

Although the typical Leo mom is warm, loving, and protective, we must say a word about a small but significant subclass among these royal mums: the ice queen Leo. These narcissistic mothers are steeped in the haughty, regal, and imperious side of the Leo nature and can even be competitive with their children and judgmental of others. They establish dominance with chilly elitism and grandiosity. One friend's Leo grandmother did this for years and even now plays the queen bee of her retirement home, snubbing other seniors in the dining hall. "We don't want to sit near *those* people," she told her visiting family at lunch hour. "They're not like us."

Of course, these self-important Leo mothers probably wouldn't even pick up this book. If you're reading this, you probably fall into the ranks of the warm, capable, and devoted Leo mom. In part, you can blame the cosmos for these Leos' behavior. Leo is ruled by the sun, which is the center of our solar system (and *the* sustainer of life, thank you very much). Because you are your own first reference point, you may unwittingly compare your children to yourself, struggling to see them as separate people with their own values and identities. One Leo mom admits to being embarrassed by her grown son's staunchly opposite politics. She was running for local office on the Democratic ticket and he planted a campaign poster for the Republican runners in his front lawn (they lived in the same town). "Doesn't he know how this makes me look?" she complained. Recognizing that your children are not here to be your ambassadors, foot soldiers, or personal PR team can be a rude awakening for some Leo moms.

Whether you lavish your kids with hugs and kisses, or express love by faithfully showing up for every important moment, there's no question: your children are truly your pride and joy. So go forth: cuddle and coddle your lion cubs. Just don't forget to teach them how to hunt and forage for themselves. They need survival skills as much as they need your fierce matriarchal protection. While a tight-knit family is a blessing, you also need to loosen the reins, letting your progeny go off and explore the wild world on their own.

IF YOU HAVE A GIRL

*

PROS

It's a girl! At last, someone to love, spoil, and mold in your image. You dream of sharing everything with your mini-me: telling her all your childhood stories and introducing her to your favorite pastimes and vacation spots. You love shopping together, buying presents for her and dressing up. You might be constant companions! You encourage your daughter to be creative, to express herself, and to pursue her dreams. The Leo mama will never raise a doormat!

And you walk your talk. The Leo mom is an amazing female role model—a shining example of loyalty, independence, and living life from the heart. She honors her femininity and desires, but she's also a hardworking achiever and an unapologetic go-getter. No doubt your daughter will follow in your ambitious footsteps. In your home, every day is Take Our Daughters to Work Day, especially since you probably have a cottage industry or two up and running. Who knows, you and your little girl might just set up shop together someday!

CONS

A little breathing room, please! It's great to be close, but you might be a little *too* enmeshed with your daughter. Where does your life end and hers begin? Does she really need to know the name of your childhood street or the first boy who kissed you? Figuring out where you begin and she ends can be a challenge for Mama Leo. You might even take it personally when she takes a different path than yours.

The Leo mom can be a teensy bit vain, so you might find yourself projecting your own body image issues onto your daughter when she hits her awkward teen years. Be careful not to give her a complex by nagging her about her weight, her skin breakouts, or the way she dresses. Remember, it's not her job to be your junior representative.

While you're deeply involved in her life, you can get distracted by your own drama, too. Single Leo moms who get back into dating can make iffy choices, exposing their daughters to turbulence. It doesn't help that your sign is often attracted to charismatic men who could fit the "bad boy" or "heartthrob" mold and whose strong personalities might clash with yours (cue Leo moms like Halle Berry, Sandra Bullock, and Jennifer Lopez). Remember, you're setting an example for your daughter's future relationships, so don't mix her up in any messes.

IF YOU HAVE A BOY

*

PROS

Where's mama's little huggy bear? Who's that handsome guy? There will be no lack of love in your little boy's life, Leo. In your relationship with your son, there's none of the competition or projection that can happen with a daughter. You'll fuss over your son's clothes and what he eats. A wall of fame will be dedicated to his stellar report cards, trophies, and accomplishments. Just as you "stand by your man" in love, you'll remain your son's number-one cheerleader and champion.

He'll also have a strong female role model, since the Leo mom takes pride in all she does. You might clock into a day job where you cut sheet metal, run a major corporate division, or decorate epic wedding cakes (all jobs held by Leo mothers we know). Or perhaps you consider maintaining a beautiful home and family life your main gig and keep a lavishly appointed nest for your royal clan. Either way, you'll teach him to treat a lady like a queen—starting with the first woman in his life: you!

CONS

Spoiler alert! Yeah, we're talking to you, Leo. As you groom little Simba into a mighty king, his ego could grow to be outsized. "My Leo mom favored me over my sister, no question," says Jeffrey. "I never had to do any housework—and I wasn't allowed to touch the dishes, because my mom was afraid I'd break them." Another guy remembers his Leo mother cleaning his room every day while his sister was in charge of tidying up her own quarters. That's not the only such report, either. "The girls in my family had to make the boys' beds," recalls Dina, who grew up in a large Italian family helmed by two Leo parents.

Today's mama's boy could turn into tomorrow's mensch . . . or *monster*. As much as you cherish your matriarch role, you can be a little *too* hands-on with your son, refusing to loosen your grip. You're aware that the clock is ticking closer to the day when another person becomes more important in his life than you. Your warm "welcome to the family" embrace of his girlfriends may be heartfelt, but are you also subtly claiming your turf? Your need to feel needed and appreciated can go too far, and you might even unwittingly prevent your son from growing up.

PARENTING THROUGH AGES AND STAGES

*

INFANCY (THE FIRST YEAR)

All hail the queen mum! The Leo mom shines during this phase. With your brave and protective nature, a cub in need is your cub indeed. Babies amaze you—and now you have a living, breathing extension of yourself to fascinate you all the more. You rise triumphantly to the challenge of sleepless nights, diaper rash, and the grand new responsibility you've just taken on, with all its ups and downs.

The doting, awestruck Leo mama will track your baby's every move, diligently recording each milestone. (One-month checkup! Lost umbilical cord! First full night's sleep!) Our Leo mother kept an exhaustively detailed baby diary for our first three years; another Leo mom we know faithfully posts her updates on a blog. The art of scrapbooking was practically invented for you—and you might even have a fully stocked craft room, like one Leo mom we know.

Your natural urge to be close to your baby is healthy, too. Dr. Harvey Karp, author of *The Happiest Baby on the Block*, wisely advises parents to treat a child's first three months as a "fourth trimester," mimicking the conditions of the womb with swaddling, shushing, and the like. So there you have it: a built-in excuse to keep your baby in your arms as much as possible.

Of course, there's a good chance you may be the family breadwinner, so hopefully you've planned for a proper maternity leave—or at least have managed to scale back from your typical over-the-top professional pace. While you like to feel productive, Leos can find plenty of ways to turn motherhood into a full-time job (which, frankly, it is—even if society doesn't see it that way). As a superwoman type, you might not be comfortable outsourcing duties to your much needed team of nannies, grandparents, or teenage sitters, especially not while your babe is so young.

As a result, the newborn phase can be a time of major lifestyle adjustments in your family. This might be your first time realizing the limitations of trying to do it all—and your need to ask for help. Chances are you've assumed that you could handle this like everything else—no sweat!—and you may have a rude awakening.

Fortunately, there's a golden opportunity here. When Leo mom Soleil Moon Frye brought her first baby home, she felt overwhelmed, like she was doing everything wrong. In her book *Happy Chaos*, Soleil writes about struggling to open her stroller (while other moms did it with a flick of the wrist) and leaving the house with spit-up in her hair and her clothes on inside out. Finding advice for "real" moms in short supply, she used social media to ask questions, vent, and connect with other parents. Soon a community of perfectly imperfect parents was born. In true Leo empire-building style, Soleil leveraged her million-plus followers to create a baby brand called Little Seed, and Target named her its first "mommy ambassador." Ah, a day in the life of a powerhouse Leo mother.

Ruling the world comes naturally to you, Leo, but sharing control with a partner doesn't always. "I'll just do it" can become a catch-phrase that strains your relationship during this crazy first year. Because you're so capable, you might think it's inconvenient to delegate tasks like diaper duty to your mate. After all, you can warm up a bottle in half the time, so why let the baby cry longer than necessary? But in nonurgent moments, try to pass the baton. You'll get a well-deserved break and your partner can enjoy bonding moments with the baby, too. Share the love, Ms. Independent!

The other adjustment of this phase affects the Leos who love to be the center of attention. While you were pregnant, you were the star, with people fawning over your belly and complimenting your lovely mama-to-be glow. Yeah, you milked those thirty-eight weeks, Leo. Now everyone's focus shifts off you and onto the baby. What are you, chopped liver? It doesn't help that you probably feel less glamorous than ever right now. It's not that you begrudge your babe an ounce of love. You just wouldn't mind getting some of that yourself!

As Leo megastar Jennifer Lopez told *InStyle*, "[Parenthood] totally changes your perspective on everything. You don't come first anymore. There's somebody else you care more about than yourself." For Leos who tend to get a little too self-focused, this shift can be a fringe benefit.

Leos are the queens of reinvention, so you might also artfully weave your children into a glamorous new identity as a mom. Go ahead and reclaim the spotlight—and show off your miniature masterpiece while you're at it. Leo mom Kathie Lee Gifford inspired a love-hate relationship with viewers for effusively sharing about her children Cody and Cassidy on *Live! With Regis and Kathie Lee.* J-Lo modeled with her twins Max and Emme for the Gucci children's collection. Madonna's daughter Lourdes launched a 1980s-style clothing line called Material Girl, inspired by her famous Leo mom. Nobody rocks a mother-child tag team effort quite like you do. Make it a family affair!

TODDLERHOOD (TWO TO FIVE YEARS)

Toddlers are exhausting, but for you this could be one of the highlights of motherhood. You love the wide-eyed wonder, the breathtaking discoveries, the nonstop playtime. Leo, you have a lot in common with your child during this adorable but exhausting phase. You certainly share the desire for instant gratification. When you want something, you want it *now*—so you understand the emotional immediacy of this phase firsthand.

With your expressive style, the Leo mom loves to teach. You don't mind the endless repetition of the alphabet and counting, reading books in an animated story-time voice, playing dress-up and making silly faces. Toddlers learn by mimicry, so when your child starts copying your go-to phrases and body language, you'll get a kick out of it. Imitation *is* the highest form of flattery—and the Leo mama never turns down a compliment! A toddler's primary concern is pleasing his parents, and you'll find this heartwarming, too. You don't even mind when your cub gets clingy or cranky.

"I love the so-called terrible twos," says Leo mama Stefanie. "They're still baby-cute, but already starting to act and talk like bigger kids. They have such a great sense of humor, but don't know how to lie or deceive. They come to you for protection and cuddles. Even their tantrums are kind of cute!" Only a Leo could find the charm in a meltdown, we imagine. The rest of the zodiac's mamas? Not so much.

When it comes to discipline, Leo moms can also be remarkably creative, devising clever ideas to keep your kids on their best behavior. "I've started sounding a Tibetan singing bowl when it's noisy to get their attention," Stefanie says, referring to a gonglike bowl that emits a vibrating sound from its rims and sides. "It's much more calming than shouting!"

Not that you're a huge disciplinarian, in the strict sense. The Leo mama leads with love, taking most toddler antics in stride. As long as your child's safety isn't being compromised, you save the sternness for appropriate moments. Plus, with enough structure—and outlets for their boundless energy—many toddlers don't need to act out. You understand that those pint-sized diva moments are just a toddler's way of expressing frustration. Redirecting their attention into a new focus or game helps Leo moms prevent many a meltdown. Leos are great at setting up a warm and inviting space. You've probably constructed a fabulous play area with lots of different activity centers to keep your toddler entertained.

Fortunately, Leos can also be consummate planners. "Always be one step ahead!" says Leo mom Cecilia, explaining her favorite survival strategy. "There is time for everything and everyone—but it's easier if you plan in advance."

However, Leos tend to overschedule, filling every waking hour with activities. On any given day, you can be found running from preschool to dance class to the park—possibly even while launching your own start-up or multidivisional company. It's just a day in the life . . . when you're a Leo. "I am an amazing multitasker," says Janice, a Leo. (Hey, modesty isn't your strong suit—but it's overrated anyhow.) "How else could I handle being a stay-at-home mom to three little ones and manage the household?"

As a social sign, you love to be around people, too, so outings and classes with your toddler are the perfect opportunity to meet other moms and bond over shared experiences. Loyal Leos might even make lifelong friends while your children are young. Still, don't forget to take some "me time" here and there. Even you have limits, Leo! You can't say yes to every outdoor concert, parade, swimming lesson, and birthday party—especially since your love life needs some care and feeding, too. Overbooking yourself and your toddler can leave you short on time for yourself and your relationship.

Remember also that spending quality time with your child is more important than being a supermom. As much as you want to turn every event into a Hallmark moment, it doesn't have to be done to DIY perfection. Will your three-year-old remember the difference between a hand-sewn Halloween costume and a store-bought one? Nope. And does a four-year-old need a circus-themed birthday party, complete with live zoo animals and professional clowns? You get the idea.

Fortunately, your more sensible side kicks in eventually. After one or two extravagant fiestas, you might just save those funds for your *own* over-the-top birthday bashes (or for your children's college funds). For her twins' third birthday, Leo Jennifer Lopez threw a cartoon-themed bash with a VIP guest list, cotton candy machines, and moon bouncers under a giant tent. But when her "coconuts" (as she calls them) turned five, Lopez celebrated simply by baking and frosting cupcakes for their school. Of course, even her understated kitchen prowess, documented on social media, made the typical mom look like a total slacker. How can any mother now justify a store-bought cake when she doesn't judge televised talent shows, run a clothing and fragrance empire, act, record albums, and dance? (We kid—our party hats go off to her, even if we can't keep up.)

Your heart is in the right place, Leo, but too much of a good thing is just too much. Unless you plan to join your child for nap time, learn to pace yourself. This isn't a competition, and you're not being graded on your performance. The toddler phase demands many lifestyle changes, even for the best multitaskers. Don't do the false cheer routine, where you rah-rah yourself into having a positive attitude, sweeping your conflicted feelings under the rug. It's okay to have days when you miss your old life and freedom or need to indulge a meltdown. Allow yourself a few rock-bottom moments—and let yourself be supported. Leo is ruled by the radiant sun, but remember that a few storms and cloudy days are an inevitable part of the process of life.

EARLY CHILDHOOD (SIX TO ELEVEN YEARS)

Loosen up those apron strings, Leo. Your little one is heading out into the world, creating a social orbit that's broader than your little tribe of two. You might feel a few empty-nest pangs while your child's away at school, enjoying summer camp, or sleeping over at a friend's house. Like it or not, your mini-me is forming a separate identity now, and you'll need to shift into the role of facilitator/chauffeur/organizer instead of constant companion.

While the individuation process can be hard, children are still interested in pleasing their parents during this stage. Even if there's a little less cuddling, the interactive energy is fun and exciting for you. With a plethora of parties, sleepovers, and vacations to plan, your inner cruise director will have a field day—and you'll love making memories through all the shared playtime.

"I love explaining how the world works and answering my kids' questions," gushes Leo mama Stefanie. "Realizing how new and exciting everything is for them is great. I love going to playgrounds, where I also climb and swing with them. We enjoy cooking together—they can be productive and see all that they can accomplish when I trust them to do it! Basically, I love being with them as they grow, learn, and develop."

So go ahead, proud Lionness: admire your handiwork. You're not above a little bragging, either. Sure, other people's kids might be amazing, but you know yours are pretty damn special and you like to tell the world about their talents. Your stairwell or foyer could be a veritable wall of fame, with family photos, trophies, art projects, and awards on display. Why pass up an opportunity to gush about your pride and joy?

The school community is also fertile ground to leave your lady-lion footprint. You won't hesitate to mark your turf, signing up to helm the PTA or fund-raising committee, to chaperone the sixth-grade campout, or to sew Broadway-worthy costumes for the school production of *Annie.* For Leo moms who tend to be more standoffish (the proud and regal lioness), taking on a leadership role at school is a great icebreaker. Once you're running the bake sale or coat drive according to your lofty event-planner standards, you'll feel right at home in those hallowed K–6 halls. (Can someone say "boss lady"?)

The Leo mom's pride and showiness guarantees she'll take on too much. On any given day, you could be organizing a huge sleepover birthday party, working your full-time job, and making cupcakes for the entire school district. (Yes, you really *did* rent a commercial kitchen and make hand-cut fondant toppings for eight hundred people. What's the big deal?)

Our friend Dina Manzo, a cast member on Bravo's *Real Housewives of New Jersey,* is the youngest of eleven children, and her Leo mother ran the household with trademark Leo resourcefulness. Dina shared a funny story about her Leo mom making grilled cheese with a household iron. "Because there were so many of us, she would line up bread and cheese on the ironing board, cover it with foil, and iron it to melt the cheese," Dina laughs. "We never had anything store bought, either. We made our own clay out of flour and water, and we went into the woods to collect branches for crafts. It taught me to be creative instead of lazy."

Like a truly stylish Leo, Dina's mother had a huge craft room and even changed her decor seasonally—everything from pillows to throws to chandeliers. "She would make these huge flower arrangements and tell me she was 'building a story,'" Dina recalls. "At the time, I thought she was crazy. But now that I'm a designer and event planner, I find myself telling my team, 'You have to build a story.'" That's the kind of legacy a Leo mom wants to leave!

Can you set the bar way too high for your children? Yes—especially if they happen to enjoy being "normal" or "average" kids instead of hyperachieving superstars. But you simply don't like doing anything halfway. When you tell your slacking kid, "You're better than that," you mean it!

You also lead by example, constantly going above and beyond the call of duty. Our childhood friend's mom is a Leo who made weekly trips to an off-price fruit stand, poring through bins of bruised produce to find what was salvageable. Afterward, she'd spend a whole afternoon cutting out the bad parts and making giant tubs of fruit salad that she could serve all week long. After Girl Scout summer camp, she would greet the entire bedraggled troop in the parking lot, serving a spread of fresh bagels, cream cheese, and orange juice. Other parents just showed up empty-handed, ready to toss their campfire-scented kid and her dirty duffel bag into a station wagon and peel off. Not this Leo mama, who coolly shrugged off any praise for her efforts. It was just what a mom *does* . . . at least, if she's a Leo!

The Leo mom is equal parts frugal and extravagant, sniffing out sales on her family's favorite things. Your love of bargain shopping, for the most part, is more about the thrill of the hunt than actually saving pennies, since you'll splurge without blinking elsewhere. Your competitive side comes out, and you also love to show off what a great deal you scored. With your love of the lavish life, you also tend to overspend in some areas, balancing it out by swinging to the other extreme.

That competitive edge often gets passed down to your progeny. So maybe you push your kid to be above average, but so what? You know that children are impressionable now and that it's your job to teach them standards. What really burns you is when you buy your kids nice things and they don't seem to appreciate it. Respect is a must! When her daughter Lourdes was nine, Leo Madonna cracked the whip about dirty clothes left on the floor. "We take all of her clothes and put them in a bag, and she has to earn all of her clothes back by being tidy," Madonna told a reporter. "She wears the same outfit every day to school until she learns her lesson."

Another priority is to preserve your children's innocence. You hate when kids grow up too fast and miss the wonders of childhood. However, as much as you shelter your children, you may also expose them to other topics earlier than most moms. Leo doesn't shelter her kids from the facts of life. (The "vagina monologues" may start early in your home.) Thanks to our Leo mother, we knew the proper anatomical names for every reproductive organ before kindergarten, as well as how babies were made—information we happily passed along to other children. Were their parents thrilled when they came home saying "penis" instead of some childish nickname like "pee-pee"? Or that Ophira told her second-grade class that Santa Claus wasn't real? Oh, probably not. But the Leo mom values honesty, so you keep your kids well informed.

There may be a few misty-eyed moments as you realize that your baby's growing up. Once you adapt, though, you can enjoy the fringe benefit of reclaiming your independence. Leos like to keep busy, and you'll soon enough find plenty of ways to occupy your time. And you'll be glad you did just in time for your child to become a teenager, which comes with a whole different set of rules.

ADOLESCENCE AND TEENS (TWELVE TO EIGHTEEN YEARS)

Welcome (back) to the jungle, Leo. Sure, your sign might be queen of the wild, but even the mama lioness can't survive this phase without a scratch or two.

The biggest challenge occurs when your teenagers pull away or take a different path than yours. You've groomed your cubs to continue a legacy, and you will very likely take it personally when they don't want to follow your teaching and traditions anymore. You've invested so much in raising 'em right, exposing them to the best possible experiences and opportunities. And still, they insist upon walking a harder path than the one you've paved for them. What happened to the closeness and love?

It's not that you suppress your kids' individuality. In fact, you love when your children are creative and self-expressed. While we were in high school, our Leo mother let us dress in vintage clothes from the Salvation Army and paint our car from bumper to bumper with 1960s-style artwork. We drove around town in the Psychedelic Chariot (as we named our wildly painted jalopy) and our mom didn't raise a single objection.

When we wanted to drop out of Sunday school, however, that was another story, since our mother's identity was deeply invested in religion. She even became a rabbi after we finished college, a lifelong dream of hers. The Leo mom has a few untouchable standards, and you may be shocked when your kids seem to go right for the jugular, rejecting the very things you hold sacred. (Repeat after us: This is a test. This is only a test.) Naturally, you'll take it all personally, feeling like it's a rejection of you and everything you hold dear.

Traditional as you can be—even to the point of babying your children forever—you also believe in giving them real-life experiences. If necessary, you'll perform miracles to make sure your kids have them. Our Leo friend Jennifer, a single mom, works long hours at a full-time job to send her daughter to costly voice lessons and an elite performing arts high school in New York City. While Jennifer shelters her daughter from the seedier side of city life, she also brings her along to Sedona for meditation retreats and to meet a group of Native American elders called the 13 Indigenous Grandmothers. (Ask Jennifer and her girl about the crystal skulls or the Mayan end of days.) It doesn't hurt that the Leo mom may harbor her own showbiz fantasies. You don't mind having a spotlight kid or even playing stage mother.

The Leo mom is also a trailblazer, and while your kids might not appreciate it now, they will someday. Our friend Nicolle, a Leo mom who lost her husband of fifteen years to a sudden heart attack, decided to sell her possessions, buy an RV, and homeschool her three teenage sons for a year as they motored across America, seeking a city where they all want to settle down. "Hey, I just got my master's in education," says Nicolle matter-of-factly. "I guess this is what I'll use it for."

That resourcefulness and strength in the face of adversity makes you a safe harbor for your children. Even if your teenagers push you away and talk back at the moment, they still know that you'll be there in a pinch. Despite your flair for drama, the Leo mom doesn't fall apart in a crisis—especially not when your child is having one. You have reserves of steely strength for them when they go through breakups, bullying, and other teen tribulations. You'll remind your kid to value herself and fight back! You're a wonderful anchor for your teen, and you can also relate personally to her feelings. You might even be mistaken for your kid's older sister because you look, dress, and act so youthfully. Just make sure that you don't end up enabling your teens or fighting their battles. Know when to take a step back and let them figure things out themselves a bit more.

During this phase, you might push your kids into extracurricular activities, which you believe can keep them out of trouble. However, not every child wants to move at your turbocharged pace. Teenagers actually need more sleep for their development. So while you don't want a household of lazy bums, you might need to relent on a little more lounging. They don't have to be busy 24/7, even if you are.

Remember, Leo: just because you starred in the school play doesn't mean your daughter wants to try out for the lead in her high-school production. And if your son is a swim team star but has no desire to be the next Michael Phelps, it doesn't mean he lacks drive. Put your stage mothering tendencies and Olympic medal fantasies in check. Ask yourself, is it really about them, or is it about making me look like a good mom? Don't try to extend your kid's childhood (and your own) by making him feel guilty.

Still, the Leo cocktail of dreams and dogged determination isn't the worst thing to pass on to your kids. It certainly works miracles for you. Just try not to fall back on comparisons, using your own teenage years as a reference point. Your child may be completely different from you—and that will become more pronounced than ever now. If you were wild as a teenager—and many Leos have done their share of exploring—you might be afraid that your kid will be as defiant and reckless as you were. You might remember your own insatiable curiosity and your need to experience everything firsthand—and the narrow escapes from danger that produced. Or, if you were more of the "good girl," you recall the rocky paths that your troublemaking peers went down and will fight to make sure your offspring doesn't go that route. As a result, you may be extra strict, which could feel unfair to your child.

Remind yourself that your child is a separate human being now and that as a parent it's your job to guide your teenager safely into adulthood. That means offering *guidance*, not doing it all for him. At a certain point, you've got to let go and trust your kids to learn from their own experiences. You might as well start practicing now, bit by bit. Think of how much you cherish your own independence, and pass those self-sufficiency skills on to the next generation, Leo.

BYE-BYE, BIRDIE: LEAVING THE NEST (EIGHTEEN-PLUS YEARS)

Say it isn't so! Your baby is heading out into the big, bad world, and the mama lioness is feeling mighty protective. Out come the homemade cards, the baby albums, and a tidal wave of sentimental memories as you try to sustain the feeling of a full house even after the kids have moved away. You might even keep cooking your son's favorite meals, even if he's not at the dinner table anymore.

You're not the mom who will turn your child's bedroom into a home office the second he ships off to college (though you *will* clutter up the closets with all your paraphernalia and projects). Those empty-nest feelings can be tough for the Leo mom to deal with at first. One Leo mom on the verge of menopause even started talking about having another baby when her older child moved out. Heck, if you could put your child back into the womb and do it all over again, you would.

Meantime, you'll probably send cards, emails, care packages, and gifts to keep the connection alive. However, watch that thin line between mothering and smothering. When we asked one grown man how his Leo mother acted when he left the house, his response was blunt: "Completely overbearing and unwilling to let go."

To prevent your well-meaning gifts and gestures from feeling like emotional blackmail, make sure to dive back into your own full life, Leo. It shouldn't be hard, fortunately, since you probably have a million interests and involvements. You might go back to school—if only to identify with your kid and compare notes. And since you're a nurturer, you could adopt a pet and have someone around to spoil until the grandchildren come. The Leo mom needs to be needed, so get involved in civic duties, volunteer with the elderly, or even run for office. Mayor Mom kind of has a nice ring to it . . .

Funny as it sounds, getting your kids to come home is sort of like dating. The way to keep them interest*ed* is to remain interest*ing*. In other words, have a life that doesn't revolve around them. Chances are you'll remain feisty, colorful, and independent well into your golden years. At this writing, Dina Manzo's Leo mother Nettie has an active Twitter account, which she uses to send funny shout-outs to her clan and have chitchats with her several thousand followers. Our "honorary grandma" Hannah, a Leo, read political biographies and kept up on current events well into her golden years. She was hip, hilarious, and even a little naughty. One day, she passed out handmade pot scrubbers that she'd fashioned out of colorful mesh. "They clean your dishes beautifully—and you can even take them into the tub for a delightful orgasm," she quipped. Only a Leo!

The day before she died, Hannah called Ophira from her hospital bed, naming every family member that she was sending regards to and asking about each of them. That's the bighearted way of the Leo mom, warm and invested in everyone she meets.

And since home is where the heart is, you can bet that your house will be a holiday hub, where you can roll out your party planning talents and bring the family back together. Soon enough, there could be grandchildren and you'll have a chance to relive your child-rearing years all over again. Someone new to spoil: a dream come true! Just lay off the well-meaning procreation pressure, Leo. You'll have your chance to don that ASK ME ABOUT MY GRANDCHILDREN sweatshirt one day if you're lucky. Just remember, it's got to happen on their timeline, not yours!

THE VIRGO MOM

(August 23–September 22)

MOMMY MAGIC - Your Strengths:

Organization and structure
Common sense
Healthy habits
Intellect

MAMA MIA - Your Challenges:

Judgmentalism
Worry and neuroses
Self-righteousness
Tendency to overanalyze

FAMOUS VIRGO MAMAS:

Salma Hayek, Faith Hill, Jennifer Hudson, Ricki Lake, Shania Twain, Beyoncé, Michelle Williams, Jada Pinkett-Smith, Rachel Zoe, Nicole Richie, Michelle Duggar, Amy Poehler, Pink, Sophia Loren

YOUR PARENTING STYLE

Uptight mommy/free-spirited mommy. The Virgo mother is a curious mix of contrasts. In some ways, motherhood plays to your orderly Virgo tendencies, giving you an excuse to plan, direct, and micromanage. At other moments, it brings out your fun, down-to-earth side. It's your free pass to let loose and play—whee!

While some Virgos take to motherhood like fish to water, swapping your indie rock playlist for Yo Gabba Gabba! jams, others require an adjustment, especially if they're a bookish or introverted Virgo who cherishes personal space. The invasion of privacy that comes along with children, not to mention the land grab on your intellectual time, well, let's be honest: the rewards don't always balance out the loss. The downshift from PhD to ABC can be tough for brainy babes of the Virgo persuasion.

Still, even resistant Virgos may grow to

love motherhood. Sure, you'll get a live daily showing of your fussy and neurotic tendencies, which can get triggered by motherhood's many surprises. It may require a shift in context: rather than recoil at the sticky, grape-jelly fingerprints on your cheek, you learn to savor the fact that your adoring child just took your face in her hands and said, "I love you, Mommy." Unwrinkle your nose, unpurse your lips, and pucker up for a peanut butter and jelly smooch, would ya?

Almost every Virgo mom we spoke to expressed great pride in her ability to discipline, set firm boundaries, and guide her children. Even if you live by just a couple nonnegotiable rules, you'll impress those onto your progeny. Proper table manners, a no-television policy, time-outs for hitting—kids are never too young to learn values in your book. Your list of how to raise a child right probably includes a great education, cultural exposure, and plenty of fresh air. Virgo is an earth sign, so it's important to you that your kids spend time in nature.

Virgo is the sign of health and wellness, so you may be staunch about eating habits, sneaking fresh fruit onto your kids' plates at every meal or opting for a gluten-free diet for them because of research allegedly linking wheat, rye, and barley to autism. It also makes things easier for you, frankly: Virgo rules the digestive system and you may have a host of food sensitivities yourself.

Despite your obsessive nature, you also have a relaxed side. Your fourth house of motherhood is ruled by Sagittarius, the sign of travel, adventure, wisdom, and the higher mind. This bohemian effect offsets your anxiety and tunnel vision. It helps you see the bigger picture and trust that your kids will turn out okay. Sagittarius is an advice giver, so its influence in your chart makes you even more prone to be a walking mommy search engine among your friends. It also awakens your humorous and philosophical side, helping you see motherhood as a grand adventure. While some women suddenly feel "old" and weighted with responsibility as mothers, your children can lighten you up. "I am proud that my kids laugh all the time and they laugh with me, at me," says Virgo mama Karen. "We have fun."

If you're married or partnered, this playfulness can extend to your relationship. With your stellar planning skills, you manage to make time for date nights and adults-only getaways. "Finding the time to do things you enjoyed before kids is the key," says Karen. "My husband and I have been together since we were eighteen, so that's twenty years. We always enjoyed going to concerts, and finally we snuck in two concerts [recently] and spent three weekends away without the kids. It renewed us. Even having a half hour for coffee in the morning before the kids wake up works for us, too!"

Not that your controlling side doesn't make itself known. There's a hidden alpha female in every Virgo. As the sign of the critic, you can get a little "mother superior" at moments, judging other women's parenting styles—even if you don't admit it. With friends, you're a champion and cheerleader, though you may secretly snipe behind their backs. "Allison's a great mom, but I just can't understand how she lets her son eat peanut butter out of the jar and put it back in the cupboard," you say with a sigh. "What about the germs? I guess *my* kids won't be having lunch dates over *there.*"

With strangers, all bets are off in the compassion department, especially when you're feeling a little threatened and clannish. You might eyeball the way they manage their kids with a strained or disdainful expression. At the playground, you could march over to a lax caregiver, demanding to know why she's not telling her child to stop throwing sand or to take turns on the tire swing. Although you claim to hate the Mommy Wars, you may be partly responsible for fueling them.

Virgo, we know you're only trying to help. Just remember that when you get on that soapbox, your principles can feel like a judgment of other people's choices. Besides, what's really going on behind those strident beliefs? Quite likely, it's your own Virgo perfectionism. You've set such a high bar for yourself, that you may judge yourself the harshest of all. While having a parenting style and philosophy is great, you may need to question whether you're trying to "measure up" to some ideal mother mold or if this is genuinely your joyful self-expression.

Comparing yourself to other mamas not only makes you needlessly insecure, it can prevent you from forming a supportive community. As it turns out, that's not good for your mental health. Research shows that women's brains have a more advanced stress response than men's. We go beyond the "fight or flight" pattern into what's called "tend and befriend." Translation: under stress, women will start cleaning, nurturing kids (or pets), and gathering with other women. This prompts the brain to release oxytocin, the "bonding hormone," which reduces fear and makes you relax. So there's your replacement for the Xanax prescription, Virgo. Quit worrying about other people's opinions and join that mommy meet-up.

Your perfectionism isn't exactly great for your kids, either. It can turn into smothering more than mothering, so seek support if you start acting like a helicopter parent. It's entirely possible you have something valid to worry about: maybe the school system or neighborhood isn't a great fit for your child and you need to make a change. By all means, do that. Just shield your kid from your fretful overanalyzing process. If your kid senses your anxiety or neuroses, he may grow to feel unsafe in the wider world—and that's the last thing you want.

The classic child development book *The Magic Years* defines *neurotic* as having constant harsh self-judgment. And, Virgo, this means you. One Virgo mom we know took her depressed son to a therapist and was told that *she* had the issue. Another friend's Virgo mother once left the family alone for five days and had a near-nervous breakdown, which she later blamed on a food allergy. In this state, you can easily forget that the purpose of having kids is to facilitate independent, self-sufficient human beings and deliver them safely into adulthood. Information is a great antidote for the Virgo mom. You need to understand the mechanics of each developmental phase and have strategies for coping. When your analytical sign knows how things work, you can feel prepared, which allows you to relax and be present.

But as the zodiac's ultimate helpmate, your biggest new frontier is allowing others to help *you*. Motherhood is best enjoyed as a communal affair. So get creative about how you spread the duties around. Big family? Take a page from Virgo mom Michelle Duggar, matriarch of the TLC show *19 Kids and Counting*. She raised her children with a buddy system, appointing one older child as the overseer of two or three younger ones. While her methods are obviously way too extreme for most of the population, it definitely shows the Virgo mom's flair for problem solving. Remember: giving your kids a measure of responsibility teaches them self-sufficiency and survival skills.

You might read up on the work of the late pediatrician and psychoanalyst Donald Winnicott, who developed the theory of the "good enough mother." As he believed, the way to be a good mother is to be just that, a good-enough mother—human, three-dimensional, providing a safe and nurturing environment, but not catering to your child's every need, treating her like the center of the universe, or depleting yourself. That can be a challenge for Virgos, who like to do everything perfectly. But if motherhood can teach you anything, it's how to ease up your self-critical tendencies and cut yourself some well-deserved slack.

IF YOU HAVE A GIRL

*

PROS

At last, you have an outlet for your psychological nature. With your daughter, you can be mommy, therapist, and ultimate confidante in one. When the chips are down or your girl is upset, there's no safer harbor than you. You're one of the most thoughtful people on the planet, attentive and supportive. "My Virgo mother could freak out about the littlest things, but when one of us was in trouble, she knew exactly what to do, who to call, and how to fix it," says Suzie.

You're interested in child development and will probably read up on it, familiarizing yourself with all the experts and their theories. You'll read up on girls' self-esteem, the effects of the media on her body image, and so forth. But you'll also want to make sure that your daughter feels confident in her appearance. You might take her to get her makeup done professionally or splurge on a pricey haircut (even highlights) when she's still in high school. You understand that sometimes looking good and feeling good *are* symbiotic—and if a little twirl of mascara boosts your spirits, so be it. For self-denying Virgo moms, a daughter is also an excuse to be "bad" (much as we wish you'd nix that word from your vocabulary). You'll make indulgence into an all-day event—shopping, going out to eat at expensive restaurants, throwing lavish birthday parties—letting your daughter know just how special she is to you, even if you only go all out once a year.

CONS

When you're the zodiac's biggest self-critic, spawning a mini-me can present an existential crisis. "What if she turns out like me?" fretted one Virgo mother-to-be. Instead of being hyperaware of your own "flaws," you now need to build a healthy storehouse of self-love. Join a women's circle or meet up regularly with a couple of supportive friends so you can have a safe outlet to vent and to embrace your own humanity, too. Don't sacrifice your interests and talents to be a mom. Even if you quit working for a while, you need to stay engaged with the wider world and feel like you're making a difference, which boosts your self-esteem. One Virgo mom we know built herself an artist's studio in the basement, decorating it beautifully. Lastly, don't skimp on the self-care: your Hatha yoga, Pilates, morning green smoothie, and evening organic skin-care regimen should not fall by the wayside just because you're a mother. When you don't take care of number one, your mood and self-image dip, and you start beating yourself up. Then you're likely to project some of your own hang-ups onto your daughter. While being someone's primary female role model is no small job, you're more than up to the task, Virgo. It's you who has to remember that—and to remind yourself daily!

Since many Virgos have difficult mother-daughter relationships that never get resolved, you might worry about how you'll get along with your own girl. Some forgiveness work may be in order, especially if you idealized your mom or condemned her for being a fallible human being. As Oscar Wilde sagely wrote, "All women become like their mothers. That is their tragedy. No man does. That's his."

Remember, Virgo, just because your childhood had its rocky moments doesn't mean your daughter will inherit the same angst. For all you know, she could be unflappably confident or have an entirely different constitution than yours. Yes, the world can be cruel to girls, and you want to shield your daughter from all the bullying, body image issues, and awful mean-girl politics. But, Virgo, don't "feed the dragon"—creating a self-fulfilling prophecy by overly focusing on what you *don't* want for her. Take a proactive approach: arm your daughter with knowledge of who she is and what she needs to succeed in life, in advance, and keep an open-door policy when she has questions. Your calm, wise responses instill amazing confidence. Do what you've gotta do to stay out of that fretful, panicky state.

IF YOU HAVE A BOY

*

PROS

Enter the prince! Though you may never admit it, Virgo moms can have a double standard when it comes to raising boys versus girls. Because he's a different gender than you, this relieves some of your perfectionism and the pressure to be an ideal role model. You feel freer to love, adore, and idealize him—and you will. One Virgo mom we know waited *twelve weeks* before naming her son. She wanted the "perfect" name to come to her and wasn't willing to settle for anything less. Although it meant calling her son "baby boy" and "boo bear" for three whole months—and enduring endless inquiries about when she would just pick a name already—there was no settling for this Virgo. When the name "revealed itself," she and her partner did an elaborate outdoor baby-naming ceremony.

You want your kid's childhood to be free, fun, and adventurous, and with a son your worrywart side doesn't come out quite as much as it does with a daughter. Because you're so self-critical, you tend to see your own "flaws" magnified more in your daughter—or to compare her to yourself, which is tough since you're already your own biggest censor. With boys, you're better able to see them as individuals. You also trust boys to be resilient and to bounce back emotionally and physically, so you enjoy indulging their whims. One Virgo mom we know let her son build a hideout under a tall counter in her otherwise pristine chef's kitchen. She even placed a little table and chair in the nook for him, so he has a cozy hideaway during moody moments when he wants to be left alone. In addition to honoring his emotions, you'll also instill good values and respect in your son. Your deepest desire is that he grow into a man of solid character, walking evidence that you raised him right. You pay close attention to his moves, guiding him carefully to do the right thing, talking to him like the intelligent and capable person that he is. Even when life deals your son a rough break, he'll always know that Mama believes in him.

CONS

You're a great listener and a natural therapist, which makes you awesome in a crisis. However, the "mother knows best" role you cherish can infantilize your son, preventing him from developing his own critical problem-solving skills. You may need to force yourself to let him struggle a little—and push yourself to separate for your child when he needs room to grow. You may be the kind of mom who willingly ships out to the suburbs, planting yourself in the best possible school district and making a million sacrifices for your son's happiness. But giving up too much of your identity could give him the wrong message, shaping a future expectation that women will cater to him.

Speaking of women, you might get a little too involved in your son's romantic choices, too. Is any girl good enough for your little boy? A slim few, to be sure. You may hone in on her "flaws," expressing your reservations vocally. There can even be some jealousy and competition, since Virgo moms like to be the queen bee in their families. This lack of boundaries can certainly cause issues between you and your son. We've seen otherwise sane and sensible Virgo moms get downright wacky when they felt possessive over their sons. One Virgo mother always leaves a territorial red lipstick kiss on her grown-up son's cheek when she kisses him good-bye. Another friend's Virgo mom posted the comment "Who's that handsome boy?" when he displayed his new headshots online. This would be fine . . . if he weren't thirty-two years old. So even if a part of you would like to keep him close forever, you'll eventually need to deal with the sadness of separation. Make sure to keep a full, balanced life of your own as the best prevention.

PARENTING THROUGH AGES AND STAGES

INFANCY (THE FIRST YEAR)

Welcome to your sweet spot: baby's first year. For most Virgo moms, the newborn phase is their absolute favorite. As the zodiac's "virgin" (symbolically, of course), you groove to the innocence of this phase. Virgo is a natural-born helper who needs to be needed, and your cautious sign loves the responsibility of handling a delicate newborn. What feels daunting to some mothers feels like destiny to you.

Just as women dream of their weddings, you've lived for the day you could hold your newborn in your arms. The miracle of birth is not lost on you, and you'll want to savor every development of your baby's first year. If you have other kids, you may need to reassure them that this special newcomer hasn't replaced them. Include them in the responsibilities, but don't forget that they might need to be "babied," too.

Even if you're not a people person, you may still be a baby person. (Yes, you separate the two. As one Virgo put it, "Babies are still partly with God. They're not jaded, cynical adults. Uck.") After Ophira gave birth, the first friends to visit the hospital were Virgos. One even spread a picnic on Ophira's hospital bed and joyfully rocked the baby in her arms while Mama scarfed down dinner. Another offered her "expert swaddling services"—and she didn't even have children of her own. And for a full week before the baby arrived, our Virgo friend Abby administered daily acupuncture treatments—at her insistence—in an effort to help speed up Ophira's labor and avoid an induction.

So, the baby's here and chances are you're prepared. Overprepared is probably more like it. Your stash of diapers and onesies could clothe a small nation. Doctors' appointments have been scheduled six months out. Your iPod is stocked with soothing Beethoven and Mozart symphonies. And your inner circle has witnessed every excruciating detail, from Facebook rants about the price of doulas and strollers, to your near-breakdown choosing the perfect nursery color scheme.

Hey, it's not your fault. Virgos tend to be structured and organized (though not always neat—you have a few secret hoarding tendencies). You enjoy little tasks, and mothering an infant is full of chores that make you feel pleasantly productive. Whether it's scrubbing out a sinkful of cloth diapers, pureeing organic sweet potatoes, or reading product reviews of educational toys, you love it all, even if you complain.

Virgo rules the digestive system (lucky you), and you may be not so secretly fascinated by everything that shows up in your baby's diapers. Or, like Virgo mom and psychology expert Andrea Olson, there might not even *be* any diapers. Yup. Billing herself as a "diaper-free baby mentor," Andrea started a successful business after researching and using a method called "elimination communication" with her newborn son. Apparently, babies signal when they need to go potty, and their natural timing can be learned. Andrea's own son has been diaper-free since nine months old, pooping and peeing hovercraft-style over a toilet since birth. Sure, that might sound weird to some folks. But according to Andrea's website over *half* the world practices this method. It's worked for centuries and it's practiced in many countries to this day.

As a health- and eco-conscious sign, you might just find this fascinating enough to try—even if you live a rattle's throw away from a big-box baby store. The stats on diapers, landfills, and their environmental toll are enough to rack you with guilt. And let's face it, Virgo, you do *not* need one more thing to get neurotic about.

Still, the inevitable neuroses creep up, largely as a result of your sign's tendency toward overanalyzing and worrying. As in the zone as you are with a newborn, you'll still find something to freak out about—a news story about kidnapping, a horrifying report about SIDS, or toxic toys manufactured overseas. There could be bouts of perfectionism about which kind of diapers are best and when to introduce solid food. You might try to diagnose every little sniffle on the Internet or rush to the doctor "just to be sure" it's not pneumonia. And when your partner or a caregiver is on duty, you can be a nightmare, micromanaging his every move.

Virgo, you may need to be stern with yourself and calm down. Take a power nap. Walk away. Go shopping (even if you check a nanny cam once or twice remotely). The baby will be fine when you return—and you'll be a much better mother when you've taken a well-deserved break. Plus, you'll realize how resilient your child truly is—without your constant helicoptering. Your romantic relationship will also improve if you can curb your impulse to control everything. Should your partner have a different agenda or views (and likely will, since you've had different upbringings), this time could put a strain on the relationship, since you don't naturally compromise well on the child-rearing topic. You'll need to stretch into some new coparenting skills and involve your mate in the decision making.

Your own perfectionism can also meddle with your baby mama bliss, so you'll want to be conscious when you head down that slippery slope. And heed this warning sign—when you start to get all mother superior on the woman who gives her squalling infant formula instead of the breast or post a rant about the psychological hazards of enforced sleep training, consider these smoke signals. Chances are the mother you're looking down on is reflecting something you need to examine—or she's exhibiting a fear you have about your own inadequacy. To paraphrase your fellow Virgo Michael Jackson, start with the "mom in the mirror."

Chances are you haven't wanted to look at her—especially because she may still be carrying some pregnancy weight. Virgo mothers may have a hard time with the postbaby effects on your body and how you feel physically in general. As a healthy sign, you'll be eager to get back into top form and frustrated when even your best planning skills still can't prevent a missed workout. But you won't go down without a fight. One Virgo friend trained for a marathon by running for miles with her sleeping daughter in a jogging stroller. Instead of focusing on how you look, just ramp up the self-care and emphasize *feeling* great. Our Virgo friend Abby hired a postpartum doula to make meals for the first week after her delivery so she could rest and know that all in the family would be well fed.

Your best defense may be a good scrapbook or baby blog site. Since you're going to be this attentive, you might as well document the details in some kind of permanent form that you can share with your child someday. What cute thing did she do on the play mat? How did the two-month checkup go? When was the first smile? With all the research you've done, you're an encyclopedia of knowledge—you really love knowing the best stroller, for example, and giving advice to other moms.

Remember that the first year goes fast, and it's filled with exciting milestones. You don't want to miss the joy of experiencing these moments because you're caught up in trying to "do it right." If your standards for yourself or the baby are too high, you may have to deal with some disappointments and learn how to let go. Meditate, breathe, get into Downward-facing Dog for a minute—whatever brings you out of your head and back into your body, so you can be present, which is all your baby really needs you to be. The rest, Virgo, is optional.

TODDLERHOOD (TWO TO FIVE YEARS)

Welcome to your walk on the wild side—especially once your little one takes those first steps! It's an exhausting but adorable time, one that makes fantastic use of your flair for structure and planning. Chances are you'll be the parent who overschedules her child: music appreciation class, toddler tumbling, possibly baby language classes. Hey, why shouldn't your child be a multilingual citizen of the world—which you've read will give her a competitive edge before college. (Grrr . . . do we hear a tiger mom roaring?)

And let's not get started on the preschool application process, which seems to have become a necessary evil of parenthood in many parts of the country. You'll be armed and ready, having scouted out the best schools and the inside scoop on admissions. You might even have a relocation planned to a top school district, and you've scoped the census data to help identify your perfect ZIP code. Suburbia, here we come!

Verbal Virgo is ruled by Mercury, the planet of communication, and you enjoy talking with your toddler, charting her language development and milestones. You might spend hours on interactive games that teach the alphabet, animal sounds, and body parts—or at least you'll stock up on educational toys and videos approved by your go-to child-rearing expert (you're discerning about your gurus, too). You know how to be stern about rules, and your toddler will be well versed on how to use his "inside voice" even if he doesn't always remember to use it.

You can be unwavering in your quest to raise 'em right, and you're not afraid to play the firm authoritarian when your kids are young. Not that you're hard on them—more of a stern schoolmarm reinforcing the rules. "My son's father and I both share the discipline," says Sosefina, a Virgo mom. "However, I'm probably more of the stickler when it comes to correcting behavior. I don't stand for tantrums, back talk, or any attitude. I like to show my son that there are other ways to express yourself and what is more effective."

When things are good, your playful side comes out, and you'll enjoy singing, dancing, and frolicking outdoors with your toddler. Virgos love to teach, and you'll view the world through their kaleidoscope of wide-eyed wonder. There's nothing sweeter to you than a little one's fascination with a dandelion, flying geese formations, or spotting the moon every night. With your love of routine, you won't mind reading *Goodnight Moon* over and over again, either, even if you've invested in a well-stocked library that's largely going unappreciated.

You can also benefit from the social opportunities of this stage, which are more comfortable for your selective sign when centered on learning. You'll enjoy going to classes and commiserating with other moms about the everyday trials you're both experiencing. Once you get used to seeing the same moms at playgroup, art class, or day-care drop-off and realize they're not judging you, it's easier to relax into a supportive new social circle.

At times, you can take a left turn into self-righteous terrain, so beware. Red flags: you share exhaustively about why you chose an alternative educational method for your child, citing research on the ineffectiveness of standardized testing. Or you post an article extolling the psychological benefits of attachment parenting. When books like *Bringing Up Bébé* (CliffsNotes: the classy French moms do it better) and *Battle Hymn of the Tiger Mother* (CliffsNotes: no, the hard-driving Chinese moms do) made national news, one smart Virgo we know shot back, "I have nothing against parenting books, but I prefer mine by developmental specialists, not Francophiles or mothers who identify with big cats."

Your safety worries can also go onto high alert, turning you into an anxious basket case. "The worst stage for me was fifteen months or so," recalls Karen. "They're walking, running, grabbing things, and you just can't stop following them." Let's be real, it doesn't take much to bring out the worrier in you, especially if your kid isn't a normal eater or in the "right" percentile on the height-weight continuum. You fret that your kid will be screwed up and, worse, that you've (gasp) made some kind of irreversible mistake, for which you'll be publicly shamed and condemned. As a result, your compulsive oversharing is actually your attempt to convince yourself that you're a good-enough mom.

If anything, the toughest part of toddlerhood for you is the chaos. By nature, you dislike the lack of predictability and impulse control. The brain development of toddlers is such that they simply don't take orders, and even the sternest discipline might not avert a meltdown. Your children's antics will mostly amuse you—that is, as long as those antics don't happen in public.

"I must say I prefer the newborn stage versus the toddler stage," says Virgo Sosefina. "My son as a newborn was gentle and easy. He was on a natural routine and was never fussy. Now, as a toddler, he's a wild man—a total California beach boy whose clothes and toes are always sandy!"

If you're not a stay-at-home mom, your control issues can really rage for a while. Virgos tend to worry when you're not in charge, spreading your anxiety like an epidemic. One Virgo mom remembers (gratefully, in hindsight) that her day-care provider even started screening her calls. "I would ring her at lunchtime, asking if my son had pooped or if he'd eaten the healthy snack I packed." Like this mom, you'll need to learn how to trust that your child will be okay, even if the sitter gives her Jif instead of natural peanut butter, or he sits in a soggy diaper for a couple extra minutes.

Then, of course, you have your germ paranoia, especially if you live in an urban area. While you have no aversion to dirt and grass, you're on high alert for contact viruses on the playground or at nursery school. "I always keep a 'mom kit' in my purse," admits Sosefina. "It's a superchic cosmetic bag that is large enough to carry anything from Neosporin spray to a travel Febreeze, wipes, Advil for mom, sanitizer, and so on."

The silver lining of the toddler phase? It's when many Virgos finally realize that it takes a village—and not a village with one chief and a bunch of slacker citizens, either. As the sign of the helper, you're not exactly quick to ask for support. Hopefully it won't take a near nervous breakdown or serious burnout to convince you to spread the load around. Remember, humanity has survived for aeons by treating child rearing as a communal task. Only in our modern, Western culture that prizes "rugged individualism" has motherhood turned into some kind of competitive solo sport.

Earthy Virgos always thrive when you do things the natural way. If that means nursing until your kid is three and a half, cosleeping, or even living in an extended family setting where everyone pitches in to make meals and put the kids to bed, so be it. One Virgo we know was actively looking to invest in a large property that could be shared by several families in a communal arrangement. The best "rules" for parenting are the ones that you make yourself—remembering, always, that they were also made to be broken.

EARLY CHILDHOOD (SIX TO ELEVEN YEARS)

Next to the newborn phase, early childhood might just be your favorite part of your children's development. They're old enough to understand everything you say and too young to talk back—at least not too much. At this age, kids still want to please their parents instead of defy them. You'll enjoy teaching them about life, introducing them to books and activities, spending time in nature, and fostering their intellectual growth. Let the adventures begin!

Some Virgo mamas could get a case of early empty-nest syndrome now, worrying how your kids will do without you supervising every move. As a chronic worrier, you're so tuned into their needs that you overdo on the preventive measures. Now's the time you have to remind yourself that they'll be fine if they have to struggle or problem solve a little on their own. (This little witty redefinition from satirist Ambrose Bierce sums up the Virgo mommy MO: "Sweater, n.: garment worn by child when its mother is feeling chilly.") Your need to be needed will have to be tempered a bit now.

That said, Virgo mothers make great advocates for their children's rights. After all, you may have struggled socially as a kid, or at least you remember what it felt like to be misunderstood by a teacher or authority figure. If your son or daughter is floundering in school, you'll be a fixture on the scene until the problem is solved—whether that means lobbying for an antibullying policy, engaging a tutor, or even switching your child to another school. As the zodiac's ruler of natural health, you're not above trying progressive remedies, either. For example, if your child is diagnosed with a learning disability, you'll research like crazy and perhaps even experiment with dietary, sleep, and environmental changes. Perhaps it's a gluten intolerance or an allergy—and you'll willingly test your own intuitive theory.

Sometimes bigger changes are needed—and you'll step up to the challenge here, too. One Virgo friend put her extroverted son into an elite private elementary school founded on an "alternative" philosophy, where competition was discouraged and utopian ideals were upheld. Unfortunately, there was a serious personality clash between her boy and his teacher. "I even hired a private social worker to come in and observe him in the classroom setting, to see if the problem was his behavior," she admits. It turned out that the teacher, who identified as a "pacifist," was really just afraid of conflict and her classroom was out of control.

Her son is now thriving in a public school—a lesson for this Virgo mama that sometimes the best fit for your child is an environment that matches *his* personality, not yours. As scary as it is to send your kid out into the big, bad world without you each morning, there's only so much control you wield. You can do your best to cultivate a conscious attitude and expose your children to experiences that bring out their best.

"I am most proud when I see my kids being compassionate and kind toward another person," says Virgo mom Sally. "Then I know they are absorbing all the positive books, quotes, and energies that I keep floating around the house."

You will stress good values during this impressionable time, and your Pollyanna side can come out full force. Hey, you know your kid is a stone's throw away from adolescence, when peer pressure will most certainly trump your influence. So you want to leave as much of a mark as you can now, in the hopes that he'll hear your wise words echoing in his head when, say, he feels pressured about sexual activity or a joint gets passed around at a high-school party.

Virgo, you've got no shortage of smart strategies, and this phase is a great time to implement them. You enjoy matching your kids up with extracurricular activities that fit their personalities—cello lessons, soccer, nature camp—and you're keenly attuned to their progress. Like a stern but loving librarian, you quietly observe and guide them. "I'm always trying to find the tools, resources, and materials for their expression," says Virgo mom Beth. "Whether it's classes, art supplies, or even clothing for my son. It's so important to be flexible with children and to try and see each of them as an individual."

Not that your flexibility doesn't have its limits—let's just say that the Virgo mom is adaptable within a controlled range. "In other ways, I'm pretty structured," admits Beth. "I force my kids to eat good food and restrict sugar to some degree—though every day they get dessert. We use a reward system and try positive reinforcement all the time. Both Ethan and Cecily have had 'point charts' and they get a point when I catch them being good. This is highly effective for them."

While schooling and grades are important, what really matters to you is your child's attitude about education. Is your kid enjoying the learning process and digging the material? You have a deep love of learning, and are on a lifelong path of self-improvement, and it's a trait you hope to share with your kids. You want them to find their passion and paths, and to have a life filled with doing things they love. "I stress the 'freedom to be who you are meant to be,' " says Sally. "I put focus on having respect for your work and trying your best."

Introverted Virgos may struggle with the enforced community element of this phase. Inevitably, there will be classroom duties, field trips, school concerts, or sports events, where you'll have to interact with the parents of your children's peers. As selective as you are about your inner circle, you may need to chill with the mom-snob tendencies, which are rooted in shyness or insecurity.

"Being a solitary person who loves nothing more than reading and writing can be hard," says Beth. "I realized that parenting is best done in groups. Ultimately this has been great for me and I find I don't love being alone as much as I thought I did."

So go ahead and sign up for that fundraiser committee or lead a kid's yoga class. It will keep you from getting isolated, especially since you'll now have a lot more time on your hands while they're in school. Even if you've been working the whole time, there's a new rhythm with their school days and activities (possibly an even busier or more stressful one than before—much to your dismay).

Still, you have most of your brain cells back now—and you can channel your attention back into your own pursuits again. Whew! And when your kids aren't in school, you may prefer having playdates with friends where you only need to peripherally supervise instead of providing the entertainment.

"When the kids were babies and toddlers I can honestly say I did not read a book for years!" recalls Sally. "Then Oprah did a show on journaling and mentioned a book called *Simple Abundance.* This book changed my life. It's a daily devotional book, so I could read one page a day and it was something that fed my soul. I began to keep a journal and really create a dialogue with myself. It helped me awaken to *me* again."

This period may be the calm before the approaching adolescent storm, so savor the balmy skies while they last. Enjoy bonding with your child and identifying activities and interests you both enjoy. You may need to call upon these as peacemaking tactics in the years to come.

ADOLESCENCE AND TEENS (TWELVE TO EIGHTEEN YEARS)

Awkward. Self-conscious. Never fits in or feels understood. Wait, are we talking about your teenager . . . or you?

The painful feelings of adolescence may still be a fresh memory for you as your kid turns the corner into the teenage years. And as your sweet little angel morphs into a magnifying mirror of your own neuroses—with a streak of sadism or a touch of torment—you may be caught unprepared. It's a time when your kids are being excessively hard on themselves. If anyone can relate to that, it's you. So this raises the bar: you have to get past your harsh self-criticism both for your sake *and* the sake of your children.

Few parents would call the teen years their favorite time, but for Virgo mothers they can be a very rough ride unless some solid resources and support are implemented. That could mean going to family therapy, dealing with your own fears around losing control, or experimenting with the right amount of strictness versus permissiveness.

"As they grow and become teenagers, they sort of disappear and need privacy," says Sally. "This phase brought up two emotions for me: abandonment and freedom. I felt sad and abandoned because they wanted to hang with friends instead of snuggling on the sofa. All of a sudden, I'm not the center of their universe; pop culture is."

She continues, "Then came the realization of freedom! I have more time to take a class, get back to my career and have lunch with girlfriends. It's so wonderful. But even in all its glory, that freedom is limited because someone always needs a ride somewhere, or takes your last twenty dollars out of your wallet."

As a zodiac sign that needs to be needed, you may feel rejected as your child pulls away and rebuffs your attention. And at the same time, you've never felt quite so burdened by worrying about her emotional state, or who he's hanging out with after school. Plus, you may see all your control—and the years of painstaking investment in your child's upbringing—seemingly topple like a house of cards.

Giving up everything for your kids is usually a bad idea for Virgos. When your identity becomes too wrapped up in theirs, there's no space for either of you to grow. You're already hypersensitive to feeling hurt and betrayed. If your children feel pressured to validate you as a mother, the relationship goes askew. And frankly, when you don't have enough hobbies and interests, you can stir up some real mama drama. Suddenly, there are friends you're not speaking to or family members you've cut off—a famous wounded Virgo move that can leave your kids feeling confused and divided in their loyalties.

Back talk and surly attitudes can push your buttons, too, especially since you may feel hurt by it. "I don't do well with conflict, disrespect, or not being appreciated—all characteristics of teenagers," admits Virgo mom Kristin. You invested so much in raising them better than that. Where did *you* go wrong? (Hint: you didn't.) And how can they treat you like this after all you've *done* for them? (Hint: it isn't personal, even though it feels like it.)

All the same, you're sensitive to the adolescent turmoil and compassionate about how painful it can be—even as you wring your hands about the terrible choices your teenager could make (not to mention the awful consequences). You may feel helpless during this phase, keeping your child on a short leash out of fear.

Your efforts to keep your kid "scared straight" can occasionally go too far. In an attempt to prevent your kid from doing stupid, life-threatening things, you might use fear tactics or criticize his choices: showing a picture of a blackened smoker's lung side by side with a picture of a healthy one, making your daughter listen to a panel of *real* "teen moms" talk about how hard raising a child really is, or forcing your son to volunteer at a hospital rehabilitation wing with teens who were injured while driving drunk.

Yikes, Virgo. Watch out for polarized good-versus-bad moralizing—being overly black and white or teaching your child that there's only one way to do things correctly (a tactic that will guarantee a rebellion). Since you can't control whom your kid interacts with as much as you'd like, you might resort to making judgmental or critical comments about this person, hoping your child will take the hint.

"I knew from the minute my son started dating his high-school girlfriend that she wanted to get pregnant as fast as she could," says one Virgo mom. "I could smell it on her. And I told him that. Of course, she got pregnant while he was in college and she was still in high school. I'll never forget the day he came to tell me that she was expecting. Before he opened his mouth, I just looked him in the eye and said, 'She's pregnant, isn't she?'" Ouch! Because you're such a keen observer of people, you may correctly sense their motives. The dilemma: do you jump in and say something when you suspect things could take a wrong turn? Learning when to speak up and when to let teens make their own mistakes is a tricky line for Virgos. You know that an ounce of prevention is worth a pound of cure. At the same time, you can't always force an adolescent to take that preventive medicine, and that's hard for you.

While your mama-knows-best role might give you the dubious satisfaction of saying "I told you so" someday, it's probably better to learn practical strategies that you can impart to your kid. "I'm big on critical thinking skills," says Brenda, a Virgo who's raised a son and is now helping to raise teenage grandchildren. "I teach them: consider the outcome of your actions before you take them or of your words before you say them. They need to learn to see the bigger picture and to look at things from a broader or long-term view. I tell them, 'That's your perspective, and now let's take a look at some other ones.'"

When and if your kids actually *do* come to you for advice, they get a solid dose of wisdom and some much-needed levity. If only they'd do that more often! They'd realize that you only want to help, protect them and prevent them from hurting.

"In high school, my mom once caught me crying over a bad grade," recalls the now adult daughter of a Virgo. "She made me go to the beach instead of to my classes that day, because she felt like I was taking school too seriously. It was awesome."

"We have a system that works out really well," says Sally. "When the kids are feeling overwhelmed by school and peers, I allow them to take what we call a mental health day. When they come to me and tell me they need one, I clear my schedule and I know we are going to get a good bonding day having fun! I allow them to choose what they would like to do, whether it's going into the city to shop or see a show, going to a movie, lounging around in pj's, or doing some crafts. The key is that they get to forget about everything for the day and spend it with Mom."

A word of warning, though: make these exceptions in limited doses or else your kids can take advantage of you. Teenagers are master manipulators, and they need firm yet flexible boundaries to feel safe. If you aim for a little more balance between rigidity and relaxation, they may not get stressed out to the point of needing a day off—at least not because of you.

Since you're a fixer and a problem solver, you may accidentally invite a crisis—perhaps as a way of unconsciously connecting to your child by reverting to the comfortable old role of being needed. However, this will backfire, because you may give your kid an incentive to have meltdowns or the notion that "Mommy will fix it." This thwarts your child from learning personal responsibility, so don't shield her from the consequences of her choices. Learning to connect the dots between cause and effect is a necessary life skill your child must learn now. Guide from the sidelines instead of jumping in for the save.

BYE-BYE, BIRDIE: LEAVING THE NEST (EIGHTEEN-PLUS YEARS)

Your child's departure into independent living can be tough for you, Virgo. You're out of a job in a sense—or so you worry, and you'll hope that your child remains nearby. A college drop-off can be tearful and dramatic, with lots of remarks like, "I can't believe my baby's all grown up and leaving home!" Of course, if you didn't get along that well in their teen years, there may be secret relief, too, which you'll feel (needlessly) guilty about.

For some Virgo moms, your kid's exit from the nest may only be a partial or temporary one, especially if you've unwittingly tried to slow down the separation process. You might even convert part of your home into an apartment or just put off the inevitable by letting your child linger on until he's "ready" to move out. (Tick-tock, he's creeping into his late twenties, Mom . . .)

A handful of Virgo moms may be openly singing "hallelujah" about reclaiming your home and life, making no secret that you're overjoyed to ship 'em off. With your perfectionist tendencies, you may have exhausted yourself as a high-achieving parent for all these years, sacrificing your own need for solitude so that your kids would want for nothing. Although (and maybe because) Virgos are the ultimate givers, you cherish your personal space.

Now you have a guilt-free pass to put yourself first. You can decorate, read fiction, turn a child's bedroom into a yoga room, do Sudoku with your morning coffee . . . and simply enjoy the silence.

"I celebrated!" says Brenda about her son's departure to college. "I couldn't understand people who were sad. It was great . . . it was freedom, which is one of my favorite things. Whenever he came home, I instantly become the mother again. I started worrying if he was okay. So I was always glad when he went back to school."

But if your child moves out before you feel ready (yes, we said *you*), you'll maintain strong matriarchal ties, bringing over dinner, sending care packages, taking her on lavish shopping trips or vacations, making sure you're needed at all times. Or you may stake out your turf on more of an emotional level, establishing yourself as the go-to daily confidante whom your kid calls for advice on love, life, and laundry.

Once you do let go, you may actually discover that you love having your space back. Rituals like redecorating a worn-down or lesser-used part of the house can help you carve out the kind of sanctuary Virgo women thrive in. Revamp your home office into a Zen-like study with your books and spiritual objects. Refresh a walk-in closet for your shoes and handbags. Remake the kitchen and bring out the good dishes and gourmet cooking supplies. Fix special meals for yourself and your partner—or if that worsens the empty-nest pangs, have a weekly dinner with a few close friends, so you can still nurture and connect with others through a meal. No, it doesn't beat the family dinners you're missing, but it helps soothe the hurt.

You also enjoy connecting to younger generations, so feel free to make dinner for other kids from the neighborhood or pay them to help you with household projects. Help a friend with a young child, even babysitting once a week. (That alone may cure your baby blues when you remember how much work it is. Plus, you've got a novel to finish!) If you're a business owner or in an executive position, take on a fun intern you can nurture and groom—mentorship can also give you a "mother energy" fix. If your child is away at college, let him bring new friends home for a fun weekend or invite his buddies along on a family vacation. The bonding moments may be fewer and farther in between, but you can still aim to get the most out of them.

And now that you have all this time to yourself, you can refocus on your many interests, Virgo. You love to master a detailed skill or craft, and now you have the attention back to do them. If you never got around to taking that eighteenth-century literature class or touring California wine country, you can dust off those deferred dreams, guilt-free. Still in a relationship or married? If the trying teenage years didn't tear you apart at the seams, it's a great time to rekindle the spark.

Fortunately, with your expert Virgo planning skills, you've probably preserved your romantic bond through date nights and little getaways. Now you may want to use said skills to create new hobbies and big projects together that don't center around the kids. (Hey, honey, want to buy and restore a seaside cabin/grow organic vegetables/travel around Europe for six weeks/open a gourmet cheese shop?)

Adult conversation, as it turns out, is underrated. You'll enjoy getting back into it with your partner and friends—and hopefully transitioning into more of it with your now grown kid. Of course, you'll always be Mommy, and that's just that. But as Nancy Friday wrote, "When I stopped seeing my mother with the eyes of a child, I saw the woman who helped me give birth to myself." This, really, is the job you were made to do. As you transition into more of an adult-to-adult relationship, remember that your child's independence is not abandonment but true evidence of a mother's job well done. Shiny gold star for you, Virgo.

THE LIBRA MOM

(September 23–October 22)

MOMMY MAGIC - Your Strengths:

Patience
Refinery
Good taste
Fairness

MAMA MIA - Your Challenges:

Inconsistency
Snobbery
Vanity

FAMOUS LIBRA MAMAS:

Gwen Stefani, Gwyneth Paltrow, Kate Winslet, Kim Kardashian, Naomi Watts, Alicia Silverstone, Ashlee Simpson, Catherine Zeta-Jones, Hilary Duff, Sharon Osbourne, Kelly Ripa

YOUR PARENTING STYLE

*

You know that elusive "balance" that Libra, the sign of the swinging scales, is forever seeking? Motherhood might be the very thing that helps you find your center point, bringing you out of self-induced chaos into the calm "eye of the storm." Well, some days, anyhow. Born under a languid sign famous for procrastinating and stopping to smell every single rose (not that there's anything wrong with that), you suddenly become structured and even downright type A as a mom.

Libra is the zodiac's sign of relationships, and—as much as this defies any self-help book written since 1982—you're happiest when you live for another person. Children give you the perfect excuse to do just that. Organizing your life around, well, organizing *their* lives, is a habit you take to like a mermaid to water.

For the most part, living for your child is a lot healthier than living for a romantic partner, pet, or adult family member, which you may have been doing for years (with the added baggage of codependence). Yes, you can become enmeshed and overidentified with your kids (more on that later), but during their early years your steady presence helps little ones feel secure and loved. Knowing *when* to cut the cord—or perhaps a more fitting word is *whether*—well, that's another issue—especially when you might not have done so with your own parents yet.

So, how does this extreme case of attachment parenting happen, anyway? Regimented Capricorn—the sign of structure, discipline, and long-term plans—rules your fourth house of motherhood. As a parent, you take on traits of this five-star general sign, morphing into a stern and goal-oriented taskmaster.

At times, your standards can even be a little *too* high, as you push your kids to compete with the elite or worry about their futures to the point of inducing anxiety. Our Libra friend Denyse followed a practice of reading her two-year-old daughter, Syann, *twenty* books a day, which she built up to book by book (yes, Libras have saintlike patience, we're convinced). This was all in preparation for impending preschool applications, which Denyse hoped would lead to private school admission and, inevitably, a shared Ivy League legacy (Denyse was a Yale alum). You may be a gentle sign, but your willpower can be unmatched when you set your sights on a goal—especially when it involves the ones you love.

Anyone who's read Gwyneth Paltrow's "Goop" newsletter has been privy to the Libra mom's overdrive and exacting standards. But underneath the perfect veneer can be roiling fears that you'll fail miserably at (arguably) the most important gig of your life. Although you might make motherhood look easy-breezy, deep down, you feel more scattered than ever, especially when you're forced to rush and multitask. As one Libra mom, a hairdresser at a major TV network, put it, "I aspire to be type A—but that's because I feel like I'm always failing at everything."

As a Libra mom, it's important for you to question your motives if you get swept into the kiddie rat race. What's really going on here? It's usually one of these:

a. Fear of being judged (and looking bad in the eyes of those you admire)
b. Fear that something terrible will happen to your child if you don't, say, feed her a diet free of processed foods and white flour or start her Suzuki violin lessons at age three ("I would rather die than let my kid eat Cup-a-Soup," Lady Paltrow once said)
c. A belief that you're "not enough" as a mother and thus need to overcompensate

One of Libra's main life themes is the struggle to feel like a "whole" person on your own. Partnership oriented by nature, you may yearn for someone to validate your decisions or show you the way. While this can make you an excellent coparent who prioritizes family life, it becomes detrimental when a choice has to be made. Motherhood challenges you to gain the confidence that you've got everything it takes to be a great mom. Most Libras could benefit from reading up on Dr. Donald Winnicott's theory of the "good enough mother." In short, you start out with total attachment to the baby but gradually separate, moving into a role of guide rather than provider of every need.

As Libra mom Kelly Ripa once joked, "I think children are like pancakes: you sort of ruin the first one, and you get better at it the second time around." Of course, she has three kids, so it may have taken her lots of practice to gain such levity.

Fortunately, children are resilient, and you grow together. Once you embrace this fact, you shine—and your strident efforts to raise 'em right will stem from love rather than insecurity. Libra moms enjoy being part of the nurturing process from start to finish. As a beauty-loving sign ruled by aesthetic Venus, you enjoy exposing your kids to the arts, culture, style, and all the finer things. From an early age, your child may know how to identify an Impressionist painting, be able to say "thank you" in flawless Italian, or discern which fork to use for the salad course. Your baby might even clock time on the modeling circuit. Hey, why not sock away college funds *and* capture their cuteness in a Baby Gap ad?

You love all the stereotypical trappings of childhood—from oversized dollhouses and trucks to elaborate tea parties and train tracks. Tasteful toys may litter your well-appointed parlor when your kids are young. Libras don't like to rush, and you have a strong ability to really be in the moment with your kids. You're amused by their antics and in love with their quirks and questions—happy to spend hours explaining exactly *why* the sky is blue or helping them pinpoint the exact location of heaven when a pet goldfish dies.

Libra moms may romanticize or idealize parenthood, too. One Libra we know stayed up all night to create photo books of her daughter's first two years; another has a long-running blog that's essentially a love letter to her three children as they've grown from babies to school age. Yes, you can get downright sincere and sappy when it comes to your children, and you're not ashamed of it!

Interestingly, we've noticed a high number of Libra moms who've adopted children—even when they're able to conceive or already have a biological child. Perhaps it's your sign's innate sense of justice: you simply can't stand the idea of an innocent child growing up feeling unloved. Heck, if you could take in a whole orphanage, you probably would. And if you happen to inherit kids as a stepmother, you'll treat them as your own. (Picture Libra actress Julie Andrews as governess turned stepmom Maria Von Trapp in *The Sound of Music.* Play clothes made of curtains, anyone?)

Libra *is* the sign of fairness—and that's also why you're great at creating rules that make sense rather than enforcing punitive measures. "My kids never acted out," recalls Dr. Christiane Northrup, the Libra mom of two now grown daughters. "I never expected that they would, and they never did."

While stricter parents might argue this is a case of denial, naïveté, or conflict avoidance, some Libra moms are actually just naturally skillful enough to guide their kids without force. Perhaps there's no need to raise your voice when you respect your children and treat them like human beings with free will—rather than possessions you control. Most Libra moms would agree . . . in theory, anyway. Pulling it off is another story, but as with all things Libras thrive when they have a great support system. One Libra mom tells us she's a devoted follower of a movement called the Orange Rhino Challenge, an initiative started by the mother of four boys who swore off yelling at her kids for a year. The creator has defined a Yelling Meter on a scale of 0 (the everyday voice) to 7 (the raging scream) and challenge takers must stay in the realm between 0 and 4 (4 being the "oopsie" snap, when you start to get nasty but catch yourself). If Mama yells, her whole 365-day cycle resets to day one, and she has to begin the entire challenge again. The Orange Rhino website even sells plastic bracelets, key chains, and stress balls (in orange, of course) for cute visual reminders to stay cool.

As long as they learn healthy boundaries and respect, why not make the discipline process as pleasant as possible? Of course, there are indeed times when you can slip into denial, casting too much of a rosy glow on the world. It's okay to make your kids a little afraid of certain things because there are definitely real-world dangers out there. You also want your children to trust their intuition, even if their expression of it can embarrass you. For example, if your son shrinks away when the nice old man from next door tries to pat him on the head, don't force a "But Billy, Mr. Jones is our friend! Be polite and say hello." Motherhood sometimes means skipping the rules of decorum and honoring your kid's rights and boundaries. Hey, how would *you* feel if you were forced, in the name of so-called good manners, to sit on someone's lap or hug a person who scared you?

Save your social graces (and lap sittings) for date nights with your partner instead. If Libras are good at anything, it's keeping the romance alive—or at least a fun sense of play, even if you bring the kids along on a few of those so-called dates. You'll use any excuse to get out of the house and back on the scene, social butterfly that you are.

In that regard, Libra moms model self-care for your children, dressing well and refusing to "let yourself go" just because you've had a baby. Sure, you may still be carrying a few postpartum pounds, but that won't keep many Libra moms away from Chanel lipstick and cute shoes (with as much of a heel as you can tolerate). And if you do get a little frumpy for the first couple years, you'll make sure your children are as well-appointed as you'd like to be, dressing them in adorably stylish outfits. You can be more than a touch vain at moments, also making your kids part of your personal vanity project at times. Remind yourself periodically that they weren't born to be your showpieces or personal ambassadors. Strive for a healthy state of *interdependence*—where individuality and separateness are respected, just as deeply as times of togetherness are cherished.

IF YOU HAVE A GIRL

*

PROS

There's no denying it: your heart skips a joyful beat when you hear the words, "It's a girl!" You've barely outgrown your own tutu-clad, fairy-princess fantasies and now you have a chance to relive them all. Even if you ditched your Barbie doll days for an anthropology PhD, you'll allow your daughter to enjoy the full spectrum of all things feminine—from deep mauve to neon magenta to ballet slipper pink.

Your sense of fairness guarantees that you'll teach her how to be thoughtful and tolerant. No mean girl will be raised in your home! You take the time to explain things and to hear her point of view. "My biggest strength with my daughter is that I come from a place of always trying to see her side," says Tanya, a Libra writer and life coach.

Although you can definitely be a "mother who loves too much," there's no question that you're devoted to your daughter's success, even if some of your actions are a tad controlling. You'll encourage her creativity and will patiently engage in developmental activities that build her skills and confidence. You'll teach her how to cook, decorate, dress—whatever your particular gift—and hope she'll follow in your oh-so-talented footsteps.

CONS

You're an idealist who wants to see the world through rose-colored glasses, and that includes your relationship with your daughter. This can add pressure to your relationship, though, especially if your need to see the world with childlike wonder doesn't match your daughter's experience. Life is not a fairy tale, Libra, not even with kids. Giving your girl the space to be upset or fight her own battles is important. "My husband said to me the other day, 'I think you might be *too* present as a mother,'" laughs Tanya. "If my daughter is struggling, I'm like, 'Stop everything! What are you *really* feeling now?' I go into coach mode with her."

The beauty-loving Libra mom can also veer into vanity or materialism, using retail therapy as a crisis cure-all instead of getting to the root of the issue at hand. The line between caring and control can blur for you at times, making your selfless acts seem selfish. As much as you think you're showering your daughter with love by giving, you can also be saddling her with guilt. One friend's Libra mom paid for her daughter's entire wedding and took out a $70,000 loan to buy the newlyweds furniture for their starter home. The marriage fell apart, but the daughter felt so guilty it took her almost twenty years to replace the couches and tables that symbolized her failed relationship. She was too scared to hurt her Libra mom's feelings.

Libra mama, your heart and intentions are always pure. Well, mostly. There's definitely a part of you that hopes your daughter will remain a lifelong best friend. As a cautionary tale, rent the film *Grey Gardens*—either the actual documentary or the HBO remake—and learn what *not* to do by watching Libra mother "Big Edie" Beale. When her wealthy husband divorced her, Big Edie dashed her Scorpio daughter's dreams, and the two became wacky shut-ins together out in East Hampton, New York. Granted, this is an extreme scenario, but you might just recognize traces of your own fears in this plotline. It might be best to have an outlet—such as a journal, a blog, a support group, or one of your own hobbies—that becomes a cherished place for you to express your more intense feelings.

IF YOU HAVE A BOY

*

PROS

Patient and loving, you find the antics of little boys amusing. While you may not be the mom to get down and dirty on the floor with him (hello, fresh manicure), you'll set up thoughtful projects that stimulate his imagination or host playdates that double as an impromptu cocktail garden party with a friend's mother. A lover of the arts, you'll enroll your son in classes that cultivate a Renaissance sensibility, encouraging him to play an instrument, take acting lessons, or develop his creativity. You'll also spoil him with silly fun: trips to the fairgrounds, movies with popcorn *and* candy, birthday parties that showcase your event-planning skills. Fortunately, you do know how to be firm when necessary—but for the most part you welcome the chance to enjoy the trappings of childhood a second time around.

The Libra mom knows how to put the "gentle" in gentleman. As the zodiac's fairest sign, you stress the importance of good manners and courtesy—and take full advantage of the privileges that affords you: opened doors, coats checked and fetched at restaurants, chairs pulled back for Mama. Chivalry will be alive and well in your family. You'll also uphold a strict policy that your son treats women with respect. Sure, some of this might be old-fashioned (and even counterintuitive to your gender equality ideals), but so what? You want your son to be the kind of man that understands the true meaning of "ladies first."

CONS

Gird your loins, Libra, there's a Y chromosome in da house. Visions of Tonka trucks ramming into your Wedgwood-stuffed china cabinet can strike fear into your gentle heart. Even though you love men and might very well be a daddy's girl, the task of raising a boy into a man can seem daunting at first. You might even veer into denial. Surely, your little prince is perfect, incapable of committing such crimes as, say, whacking a fellow sandbox dweller over the head with a plastic shovel! Right? You might just end up with a wild boy simply because your conflict-hating sign doesn't want to go into the "masculine" state that's required to effectively discipline him.

Yes, sitting down and talking it through is great, but sometimes boundaries and real-life consequences are more effective. If you overemphasize etiquette over ethics, you may just teach your son how to be manipulative. Your son could learn to act like Mr. Perfect to your face and Mr. Shady behind your back. The key is to learn the right balance (that key Libra word) between being overly stern and too permissive. Consistency is the ticket, but it also happens to be a tough act for Libra moms to follow. The only way to master it? Practice, practice, practice.

PARENTING THROUGH AGES AND STAGES

INFANCY (THE FIRST YEAR)

Prepare for a balancing (and rebalancing) act. Life as you know it has changed permanently and there may not be time to adjust. Libras hate to rush, and suddenly your whole life feels frenzied. Amid the euphoria of blissful bonding and cuddling your newborn, you may feel more frazzled and overwhelmed than ever. In fact, Libra moms can even be prone to postpartum depression because of this unnervingly fast new pace.

Your expectations—and their oft-sharp contrast to reality—can also complicate the adjustment process. Maybe you've cast an idealized fantasy on your baby's arrival—all soft focused, sepia-tinted, and trimmed with scrapbook ribbon. If so, get ready for a rude awakening as you plummet into spit-up, sleepless nights, and stained onesies. Many Libra moms, especially first-timers, might experience what psychologist Leon Festinger coined "cognitive dissonance." It's that weird, imbalanced in-between state of disequilibrium as you move from a familiar reality to a strange new one. Yeah, your first few weeks (or months) might feel like you're living in an altered state, Libra.

It doesn't help that our society elevates pregnant women to saintly status—a prenatal perk you've surely milked to the fullest. Strangely enough, the same people who once leapt to offer their bus seats are now the same ones clucking judgmentally as your newborn wails in a cafe or you struggle with a stroller and block the door to Starbucks.

Rude awakening number two: mothers may

be sanctified in theory, but in real life they're often shamed, blamed, and scapegoated when they fail to be less than halo worthy. What a difference a delivery makes! For you, this may be especially hard, as Libras want most of all to be liked and admired by others. You're a lover, not a fighter, and you'd never willingly cause conflict. So the idea that you're making people uneasy by, say, nursing in public, can really rattle your cage.

Of course, this might just bring out the justice fighter in you—especially as you notice other new moms being treated with disregard and disdain. Libras may occasionally let people walk all over them, but when you see your sisters being steamrolled, it's impossible to stay silent. You'll be the first to post incendiary articles about, say, why the Europeans breast-feed without covering or how some doctors advocate nursing until age two—or older. While some friends may tire of your opinionated rants, you don't care. Getting some fire in your belly is a great way to transition into your new mom status, frankly. *Viva la mama!*

A healthy dose of social consciousness, even righteous anger, will also help you avoid the comparison trap. For example, if everyone in your mommy meet-up claims her baby sleeps through the night, you might tell a white lie just to fit in. Meanwhile, the bags under your eyes should make it glaringly obvious that your munchkin wakes up every two hours and demands a feeding. Seriously, Libra? These women are probably too busy worrying that *they're* doing everything wrong to think about what you're doing.

Ironically, you'll gain *more* social capital once you get the guts to keep it real. Libras are wonderful at bringing balance back to a group. So make like Libra Fran Drescher in *The Nanny* and blurt out a raw, inappropriate remark that's undeniably true. ("My nipples feel like they've been rubbed with sandpaper," vented one Libra mom we know when talking about nursing.) You'll liberate yourself *and* everyone else, setting your fellow mamas free to be the support system you all so desperately need.

Community and companionship are your saving graces as a new mom, so why taint the experience by pretending to be perfect? You need to feel like you're not alone now. Those baby music classes are as cathartic for you as they are for your infant. Science even confirms this fact, showing that women have a unique coping style under pressure called "tend and befriend." In stressful moments, many women will start cleaning, bonding, and caretaking, which bathes their brains in relaxing oxytocin, aka the "love hormone"—and what Libra couldn't use a dose of that? One calming neurochemical cocktail with a twist of (sub)lime, please!

Once you get your groove back, Libra, you can focus on what's *really* great about this phase: the million milestones waiting to be captured on camera, in a journal, or the creative format of your choosing. While you might not be ready for *your* close-up, you'll snap away as your babe coos, smiles, and holds his head up for the first time. Libras can be incredible documentarians, and you'll diligently record every detail of baby's first year.

"I was so annoyed that my wife made us constantly take pictures," recalls the husband of a Libra mom. "But now that our daughter is getting older, I'm just so thankful that she captured those special times."

If you have more than one kid, you could feel spread too thin and guilty about dividing your attention as you struggle to juggle. Remember, you can also cultivate a lot of great sibling bonding (and a proud mommy's helper), by including your older child in the caretaking of the little one. If you take special time with each kid, that can help to ease jealousy. Be patient and gentle with the process—and with yourself.

The best thing you can do is to savor the sweetness of this fleeting phase. Let yourself get all sappy and earnest. Dress your baby up and paint the town together—stroll the museums, coffee shops, and your favorite waterfront promenade. If you're in a relationship, you'll love taking outings as a family, too: picnics, county fairs, petting zoos, posing with Santa at the mall. Even though your little one is too small to appreciate the big world around him, you can still enjoy the anticipation of next year—and snag some cute photos in the meantime.

While it might take a village to get you back to your social butterfly ways ("When I finally got out of the house, I celebrated," recalls one Libra), you'll be *so* glad you pushed yourself that extra mile. Sure, you might lock your keys in the car or forget to pack the burp cloth, but embrace this mile-a-minute time as a chance to lighten up. Curb the multitasking, too, lest you swing from inertia to overload. You don't have to sign up for every single class or activity the local YMCA offers. Everything in moderation!

TODDLERHOOD (TWO TO FIVE YEARS)

Curveball alert! Just as you finally adjusted to new motherhood, a whole different chapter begins. Alas, it's not *Infancy: The Sequel* . . . or even close. Thought having a newborn was challenging? You may yearn for the time when your babe snoozed in a sling or cried for cuddling. Ah, the good old days: before he was banned from playgroup for biting or throwing the tantrums that made you persona non grata at your favorite department store.

Still, there's a golden opportunity in this phase, especially for conflict-averse Libras. Mothering a wily toddler helps you discover your inner disciplinarian. Reach deep—she's in there! Of course, it will take lots of experimentation to find the right balance. You're likely to be too lax about some things and too rigid about others. It might take a time-out for *you* to regain perspective.

One big question to ponder: am I getting upset because my child is in danger or because

I'm worried what others will think of *me* when she acts out? Libras hate to be embarrassed in public and can be overly concerned with what others think of you. As a result, you can overreact when your toddler does something defiant—for example, hitting another child. You might even resort to bribery or keep your kid on a short leash, just to avoid being mortified.

But you know what? Screw what the neighbors think—and the other parents, too. While social ostracism may seem akin to death for a Libra, nobody's gonna oust you from music class if your toddler acts like . . . a *toddler*. Children this age are scarcely capable of understanding right from wrong, so expecting them to have a fully developed conscience is downright unrealistic. In truth, toddlers are largely motivated by a desire to please their parents. At age three or four, they respond to very few behavior limits. So use lots of positive reinforcement rather than freaking out or holding your toddler to unrealistic standards. One shiny gold star for good behavior is worth a thousand time-outs. Perhaps some of dog whisperer Cesar Millan's techniques might work, too, such as his recommendation that you use a calm-assertive tone to establish your alpha status.

Necessity is often the mother of invention. For example, our Libra friend Denyse discovered her inner mama bear on a New York City playground. When an older child purposely spit on her two-year-old daughter, Denyse stood in the middle of the playground and bellowed, *"Whose child is this?"* This primal howl emerged from a normally elegant woman who never raised her voice.

While you're on this tear, Libra, pitch a few more rules of decorum, too. You don't have to return every call, handwrite thank-you notes, or buy gifts for everyone on the planet's newborn child. You'll also probably run later than you already normally do, and you might even (gasp) need to leave the house without your "face" on. Give yourself a moratorium from playing Miss Manners now.

The upside? You'll have a lot more time to enjoy fun activities with your toddler, something Libra moms love to do. And oh, the places you'll go! Dynamic Libras have endless energy for being out and about, children in tow. All the better if you can meet up with other toddler mamas at a park or indoor playspace, where the little ones can run around together while you chitchat on the sidelines.

"I don't really like to play," admits Katie, the Libra mother of three young children. "I like to go places and do things more than getting down and playing on the ground with them."

You also love shopping for cute little outfits—even more now that they're walking and talking. (Your pregnant friends are already putting dibs on future hand-me-downs.) You might book some professional portrait sessions just so you can rock your kiddie-stylist skills. One Libra mom professed her love for Borrow Baby Couture, a website that allows moms to rent designer duds in miniature sizes—Cavalli, Fendi, Dior—for less than $100 a week. Hey, you never know when your toddler will be invited to a black-tie gala or high-end photo shoot . . . right?

Fine, so you can be a little over the top in this department. And in a few other places, too. During toddlerhood, your lack of Libran balance will probably be most evident. You'll tend to overschedule your toddler and constantly have to adjust between "too much" and "not enough." Such is the life of a Libra mom!

Are you a Libra who's weak on structure and punctuality? Surprise: you could find that parenting a toddler forces you to stick to routines. While this is tough at first, it's actually a blessing in disguise—one that will have a positive ripple effect in your own life.

EARLY CHILDHOOD (SIX TO ELEVEN YEARS)

It's party time! Outgoing Libras love an "activity buddy," and at this stage your child is a willing little wingman. This is a lively phase tailor-made for the social butterfly Libra mom—with school committees, field trips, birthday parties, and other fun things you can do together. And like the Pied Piper, you may have a roving band of merry munchkins trailing behind you, as your children's friends will love being around you.

Among the other parents, you're the hostess with the mostest, forever flinging open your doors for weekend slumber parties and after-school playdates. While you can be a tiny bit elitist or showy (you don't *really* need to serve homemade dark chocolate chunk and dried cherry cookies when simple Chips Ahoy! will do), that usually eases up once you get to know the other parents and realize they're not judging you. So put away your grandmother's china and tea service, which is more likely to intimidate than impress.

Is your house too small to be party central? That won't stop your socializing. You'll arrange to meet another family at the playground, letting your kids run around while you catch up on gossip and swap stories. It's all about relating. A fixture on the school scene, you hang out after drop-off to chitchat, or to rally other moms for a Pilates class. The more, the merrier!

"I'm the room parent for second grade and superinvolved in my other son's kindergarten class," says Maysan, a Libra mom of three. "I don't like the mentality that as soon as your kid goes to school, you can just check out and let the teacher do all the work. You have to get involved, get to know the teacher. It's a way to stay connected with your kid so that when they're retelling what happened in school at dinnertime, you know what they're talking about."

Because you know that school is prepping them for "real life" on their own, you can be pretty stern about homework and behavior. This is the time that you really ramp up the investment in your child's future, paying premium rates for private violin lessons or an exclusive club membership. Savvy Libras understand: it's all about *what* you know and *who* you know in life. You may go a little over the top, though, packing your child's schedule with one too many activities. Remember to let your kid be a kid, too!

"I worry that my daughter is a little bit of an underachiever," admits Tanya, the Libra mom of an eight-year-old, "but she's like *the* most content kid ever. So it's funny: I wish she had a little more hunger and drive, but I also know that she's happy. I recognize that I micromanage relationships—and that I might be doing that with her."

One friend remembers bringing home an elementary-school report card with straight A's and one B. His normally doting Libra mom decided to be stern that day, and said, "Wouldn't it be nice if there were all A's on there?"

Although you might not be *that* extreme, be mindful not to project your own perfectionism onto your child. (Fortunately, this friend's Sagittarius aunt jumped in and lavished him with enthusiastic praise.) Positive reinforcement really works with kids this age, and so does dialogue. Making your kid's report cards and achievements all about you places unfair pressure on your child ("Oh no—I've disappointed Mommy!"). Perhaps this Libra mother's concern should have been the story *behind* the B. If you find yourself in a similar situation, don't fall into the good student/bad student trap. Rather, investigate any inconsistencies for what's really going on.

Get granular, Libra. For example, perhaps a low grade is a sign that your child needs more help understanding a certain subject. Maybe he feels nervous with the teacher or sits next to a distracting classmate who lures him into goofing off during lessons. Simple hunger or dehydration could even be the culprit. The excellent book *Yardsticks: Children in the Classroom Ages 4–14* reports that allowing kids to drink fresh water boosts their concentration throughout the day.

Maybe your kid needs special permission to eat a small midmorning snack. Even better, perhaps you can rally for the school to set up fruit and water stations, and allow students to break for a pick-me-up. If you get the standard "the school district doesn't have a budget for that" response, then put on your party planner's hat and hold a fund-raiser or collect petition signatures from other parents. Where there's a will—and an injustice-fighting Libra mom—there's a way. Trust.

If you're the utopian type of Libra who doesn't "believe" in competition, this might be an area that you need to rethink, too. Children this age *will* have conflict. Your tendency might be to intervene too quickly—you're not the mom who lets your kids work it out on their own. And that might be wise at a certain point, given that bullying is on the rise. So if you've gotta swoop in like a mother hawk, so be it.

"There's nothing that sets me off more than seeing my sons in conflict with each other," says Maysan. "If I see them being unkind to each other, I go from zero to banshee in a millisecond. I don't let them sort it out themselves; it is a forced reconciliation. But it's paid off. They call each other the snuggle brothers. They're each other's number-one fan and best friends."

Tanya recently used her professional coaching skills to intervene when her third-grade daughter clashed with a classmate. "The Libran part of me is able to see that neither kid is wrong," says Tanya, "but they need to find a different way to communicate. So they're going to start writing letters to each other about how they're feeling. I'm able to give them contained space—and to manage without micromanaging."

As long as you don't encourage your child to "keep the peace" at the expense of dignity or personal safety, that's fine. You can still teach them to fight for what's right without using physical violence and help them to understand how bullying works, even on a psychological level, so that if it happens to them they're not afraid to report it.

As your children remind you, life isn't always perfectly equal and fair—as much as you wish it was. But while they're under your roof, you can still preserve the sweet parts of childhood. At this age, they still want to snuggle, hold hands, be tucked in, and talk about their days over dinner. Libra, you're always ready, willing, and able to show up for that.

ADOLESCENCE AND TEENS (TWELVE TO EIGHTEEN YEARS)

Breathe through it, Libra. Just breathe. These may be the years when you have to reach deep to stay composed. As a peace-loving sign, the nearly inevitable chaos of your child's teen years can definitely throw you off center.

At the same time, you have an innate sensitivity toward teenage turmoil, since your own adolescent years are probably still a fresh memory. Libras tend to be the "balancers" in their families, which can cast you into all kinds of fun archetypes like scapegoat or hero child during your young life. If there was any sort of dysfunction or extreme viewpoints in your household, you might have intuitively acted out as a sort of familial self-correction.

For example, if your parents held ultraconservative religious and political viewpoints, you may have ditched college for the Peace Corps or become an environmental activist. Or, if there was addiction in your household, perhaps you got in trouble with the law, forcing everyone to confront their denial.

If that was you, Libra—then you'll probably have a keen radar for emotional turbulence in your own teen, as well as his friends. You know when a meltdown is brewing, and which kids are bound to be a bad influence on your child. Not that you won't take that disenfranchised punk under your wing, too. Libra moms know that the power of love can break down angry walls. You might just be the adult who turns this poor, confused kid's life around—sharing your own experiences in a heartfelt, nonjudgmental way. Your teenager may feel safe opening up to you about her troubles, knowing that you'll validate her feelings and experiences instead of blowing up.

If your balancing role in your nuclear family was to be the "good girl," there's a chance that you may never have rebelled. Well, don't get too fond of that shiny halo just yet, Libra. The downside here is that you may have skipped healthy, necessary parts of the separation process. It's vital for teens to pull away from their parents to some degree and form their own identities. If you didn't do that, there's a chance you never developed the confidence to become your own person, formulating opinions, goals, and values different from those of your family. In a pinch, it might be hard for you to make a decision (which is already difficult for Libra) or to step into an authority role and confidently discipline your child. In your perfect scenario, someone else would do the rule enforcing, and you could be the good guy. You might even be stuck in a state of dependence with a spouse, friends or family, playing more of a childlike role than an adult one. So just as your teen is learning how to individuate, you might be taking your first wobbly steps in this arena, too.

Perhaps you were afraid of falling from a parent's grace. Maybe you felt guilty because a parent was sick, hardworking, or consumed with a difficult sibling. One Libra we know became the dutiful child after her sister was killed in a car accident; it was her attempt to compensate for her parents' grief. Such well-intentioned acts are valid and often develop unconsciously.

Still, if you suppressed the urge to separate, be warned: your own teenager may rebel with double the strength. This will effectively force you to find your voice, and even some of the anger that you never unleashed as a teen. "I get too worked up and yell too much," admits the Libra mom of three teenagers. "I tend to overreact to little things."

The lack of serenity that comes with parenting a teen can definitely throw your delicate scales out of whack. All you want is some peace, but that seems like too much to ask for some days. "One Christmas break, I was woken up one too many times on a work night, and I went to the living room and threw the remote," confesses one Libra mother of teens. "I normally *never* lose my temper, but I did, felt better, and went back to bed. The house was quiet after that."

This phase might be a good time to acquire some new skills around boundary setting. You might want to train in nonviolent communication, (NVC; aka compassionate or collaborative communication), a technique that was developed by (surprise, surprise) a Libra: psychologist Marshall Rosenberg. Used in conflict resolution worldwide, NVC adopts a three-part method: *self-empathy* (being in touch with your own valid feelings and experiences), *empathy* (listening with compassionate respect to the other party), and *honest self-expression* (communicating so authentically that it inspires compassion in your listener).

Methods like these can make all the difference now. Some Libra moms just check out mentally and emotionally during this period, at least until they learn other coping mechanisms. No, you don't have to become a raving lunatic, nor does your child have to be a hulking, sulking presence that ruins every family dinner and holiday. But without some sharp new tools, you can lapse into a deer-in-the-headlights state, pretending the unpleasant things aren't happening, or hoping they'll go away on their own. (Some will, but others won't.)

You might try to pass the disciplinary buck to your partner or another relative. "When I was a teenager, my mom would always say, 'Ask your dad,' and then let him be the one to say no," recalls Laura, the daughter of a Libra. "My older sister was often the one setting limits, too, because my mom didn't want to be the bad cop. She even yelled at my sister once for overdisciplining me!"

Denial prevents you from being the healthy authority figure that your teenage child needs now. Some kids act out as a way of almost asking for an intervention. Boundaries, though they may rail against them, actually make your kids feel safe. Sure, you might plunge into despair when your previously worshipful daughter first lashes out at you, or your once adoring son posts a KEEP OUT sign on the door of his man dungeon.

If you start taking it personally, get to a therapist or support group. You may be afraid your kid will hate you if you set limits, a dagger to the heart of any Libra. Well, Mama, he may not *like* you—but he'll love and respect you. Remind yourself that you're training your child to become self-sufficient. Once he leaves your nest, he'll hear the word *no* aplenty, so it's your job to teach him that he can't bully or manipulate people into doing his bidding.

Mirror, mirror. And speaking of the looking glass, you might also need to confront some of your own issues around aging and beauty now, too. It's not easy having a daughter come into that youthful glow just as you line up your first wrinkle-eliminating facial or start covering your grays. For beauty queen Libra, this transition can prompt insecurity, jealousy, and even a midlife crisis.

You may try to relive your youth through your kid—perhaps (gulp) shopping at the same stores, flirting with younger guys and sharing clothes with her. If you have a son, you'll befriend his girlfriends. Perhaps you were a young head turner back in the day—or maybe you're hoping to experience those debutante dreams through your daughter. (Careful: your own focus on appearances can give your daughter a complex, especially if she's going through an awkward phase.)

Our friend Laura will forever be known for the Sweet Sixteen party her Libra mother planned and "probably took out a loan for" even though Laura didn't really even want it to happen. The affair was Cinderella-themed and held at a real castle—and no expense was spared. Laura even wore a crown and a custom-made dress embellished with Swarovski crystals.

"It was like a wedding," Laura recalls. "My mom even ordered the wedding menu from the caterer. We had a dais with eight boys and girls—like a bridal party—and my mom bought everyone their dresses. I was so embarrassed, but still to this day, people talk about it like it was the party of the century, which makes my mom all proud. She's like, 'See?'"

When your daughter starts dating, you'll be so excited. Unlike other moms who are scared of this phase, you can't wait to help her prep for her prom or an evening out. By now, you'll have told her the (romanticized) story of how you and your partner met many times. Or, if you didn't live the fairy tale, you'll want to help craft one for her.

Again, you'll want to be careful not to project your own fantasies onto her process or to overidentify with her. There's a need in every Libra to be validated as a mom by seeing yourself reflected in your daughter. If you find yourself saying things like "She's exactly like me!" take a step back. She needs the space to explore and become her own person. It doesn't mean she's abandoning you or rejecting you. Like a rubber band, she'll stretch and spring back—so loosen your grip just a little bit, Libra. You'll see.

Your own relationship with your mom may be superclose, the apron strings still securely tied well into adulthood. It's not uncommon for Libra women to describe their mothers as "my best friend," and for the relationship to veer in and out of codependent terrain. Libras tend to either idealize their moms, hoisting them onto an untouchable pedestal, or to demonize them, focusing on their fatal and unforgiveable flaws (and vowing that you'll make up for her awfulness by being the best mother ever). Because of this, you may expect to have a tight lifelong bond with your own child even during the teen years—and fear any signs that they're pulling away. Once again, the struggle is to see yourself and your child as two separate people. Where do you end and they begin? For you, it's a hazy line at best, one that can veer into emotional blackmail if you're not careful.

One daughter of a Libra remembers her mom rotating the "favored child" role between her and her two siblings regularly. Whichever one was the most adoring and cooperative would receive special treatment. As a result, they'd all compete for what felt like their mom's scarce and conditional love. "I never figured out what *I* wanted or liked until much later in life," she recalls, "because I was so busy vying for my mom's approval of everything I did."

Remember: two people can still maintain a close emotional attachment even as they go through the separation and individuation process. It might feel like your child is rejecting you—or all that you've taught them. In reality, you probably need more support than ever navigating this unfamiliar terrain. Remind yourself that your child loves you no matter how they act—and make a point of showing your teen that you love them unconditionally, too.

BYE-BYE, BIRDIE: LEAVING THE NEST (EIGHTEEN-PLUS YEARS)

For many Libras, there was never a true separation process from your own parents. Even if you acted out in your teens, you still may have remained dependent on Mom and Dad well into adulthood: for emotional support, housing, a few extra bucks when you were short on rent. So if you have a child who's raring to break out on her own, you could be caught unprepared.

You may even try to keep the connection intact through financial dependency. And while that may not be a problem for you, consider that you might be saddling your own child with some handicaps or preventing him from learning self-sufficiency. Sure, (not so) little Jimmy might enjoy having a roof over his head and home-cooked meals while he commutes to college. But it might be even *better* if Jimmy went away to school and learned how to prepare his own meals and pay some of his own rent. Nothing inspires maturity like Maslow's hierarchy of needs—so when the food, clothing, and shelter aren't a given, your child will get downright resourceful.

You may feel a little better about all of this change if your child has a sibling. "I'm their number-one idol for twenty years," says Libra mom Maysan of her two young sons. "But they'll have each other for the next eighty years. So I figure if I invest in their relationship now, I've given them this magical gift of having a great sibling for the rest of their lives."

Smart move. Nonetheless, you may need to deal with your fears of being alone. Chances are you have a tendency to surround yourself with people so that you never have to really "be" with yourself or to face those shadowy fears that you're not enough on your own. Consider the empty-nest transition a great opportunity to confront these anxieties. Being forced into independence can be the best (albeit the hardest) thing that ever happened to you, Libra.

Not that you'll be lonely for long. Social Libras have a knack for filling their dance cards swiftly. Before you know it, your home will become the go-to spot for dinner parties, women's circles, and holiday open houses. Libra mom Dr. Christiane Northrup fell in love with tango dancing and once even moved the furniture out of her living room to make a de facto dance floor once her daughters moved out. Another Libra mom we know got deep into social activism. After her daughter entered the military and came out as gay, this mom launched a civil rights support group for other families in this situation.

Once you and your child get through the adjustment process, you'll probably become great friends who genuinely enjoy each other's company. Since you tend to be eternally youthful and fun, your child will probably love inviting you along on their adventures. Our friend Laura's Libra mom insisted on going to a stadium concert with Laura and her cousins—then called Laura's aunts and convinced them to come, too. "She stayed up later than everyone because she refused to leave before the concert was over," Laura laughs.

And that's the magic of a Libra mom—that is, it will be if you finally let your hair down. Admittedly, you can be uptight, especially when you stray out of your comfort zone. But once you get over feeling "old" because you have grown children, you might just realize how young your spirit really is. We once had a postcard that said HOW OLD WOULD YOU BE IF YOU DIDN'T KNOW YOUR AGE? Pick a number, Libra.

THE SCORPIO MOM

(October 23–November 21)

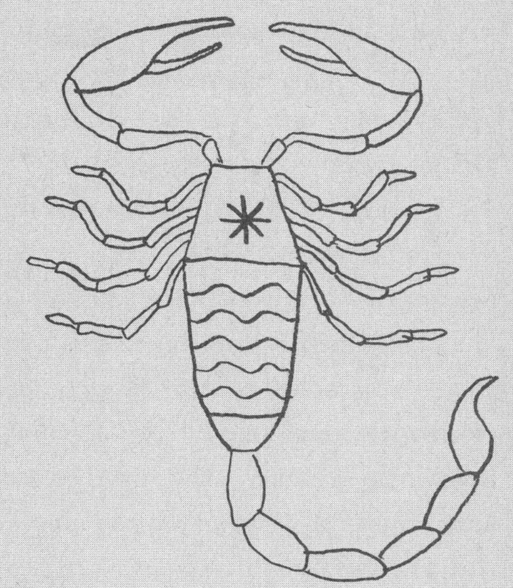

MOMMY MAGIC - Your Strengths:

Strength
Resilience
Intuition
Willpower

MAMA MIA - Your Challenges:

Control
Paranoia
Emotional unavailability
Obsessiveness
Intensity to a fault

FAMOUS SCORPIO MAMAS:

Demi Moore, Bethenny Frankel, Jenny McCarthy, Hillary Clinton, Kris Jenner, Kelly Rutherford, Ivanka Trump, Julia Roberts, Calista Flockhart, Ramona Singer, Maggie Gyllenhaal, Vanessa Lachey

YOUR PARENTING STYLE

The Scorpio mother is a magnetic mama—a curious mix of quirky and controlling, inspiring and intimidating. Depending on your mood, your kids may cling to you—or scurry away from your wrath. Not that you'd ever turn the full wrath on them. One "death stare" from a Scorpio mom is all it takes to keep a willful child in line. Fiercely protective, you guard your children with irrepressible spirit and strength. You've got a streak of Carmela Soprano in you: a mafia matriarch (in stilettos) that nobody dares to cross twice.

Equal parts tiger mom and cougar mom, sizzling Scorpio manages to be both maternal *and* sexy—no easy feat in a culture that loves to polarize women as either Madonna (the virgin mother) or Jezebel figures. Truly, Scorpio women are among the zodiac's most misunderstood. While you may have a barbed exterior, the few who really know you understand the vast depths of your devotion. Beneath that Scorpion stinger, there's softness, an intense loyalty and compassion reserved for those on Team Scorpio—especially *la familia*.

Scorpio is the sign of intimacy and permanent soul bonding. When you're in, it's for a lifetime ("till death do us part" is a vow you take literally). "The depth of my love is one of my strengths as a mother," says Meggan, the Scorpio mom of three-year-old Shai. "Some people are a little scared by how fiercely I can love, and it comes off as being way too intense. I had this relationship with a man where it seemed like my personality sort of sizzled his face hairs off. I'm not sure how much he loved himself, so the intensity of my love overwhelmed him. But when it comes to my son, for the first time in my life I get to love as much as I can and it's actually received and appreciated."

Perhaps this is why Scorpios approach motherhood with a mix of joy and trepidation, especially the first time around. To be *that* attached to someone is a scary prospect. However, once you hold your child in your arms and feel the bond, it's too late to turn back. Luckily, most Scorpios take to motherhood quickly. You're an emotional water sign, after all, and your nurturing qualities are automatic. Although Scorpios can be slow to warm up to the rest of the world, your child will melt your defenses in a heartbeat. Soon enough, the hard part isn't getting attached—it's letting go.

In the meantime, though, you'll work hard to ensure that your child's life is crafted with precision. Like Scorpio "mom-ager" Kris Jenner with her Kardashian kids, you'll work hard to ensure that your clan has a rock-solid future—whether that means sending them to an elite prep school, buying an "investment property" they can live in someday, or (ahem) scoring them hot product endorsement deals. Scorpio rules the zodiac's eighth house of wealth, joint ventures, and long-term finance. Fiscal security is extremely important to you, and motherhood makes you work that much harder to lock it in for your children. "I had my daughter's college fund set up before she was born," says Meredith, the Scorpio mom of a seven-month-old. "I'm the one who brought up that we needed to put money aside and make sure that her college is paid for—no matter what."

Intuitive Scorpio is fascinated by what makes people tick, so kids are an endless curiosity to you—the ways they can be molded and the ways they come in fully formed. You're an observer by nature, but you're not so comfortable when the lens is turned on you. There's a deeply private side to every Scorpio, one that maybe even your own children and partner don't get to see. Scorpio is the sign of mystery, intimacy, and spiritual transformation. You wear some emotions on your sleeve and lock others away in an impenetrable chasm.

However, you can read people like an X-ray scanner. Your maternal instincts might be downright telepathic. "I don't just know what my kids are thinking," says Nina, a Scorpio. "I know what they're *feeling*—even though it might seem overbearing."

"My mom has a way of saying everything in

just a couple of words," says Krista, the twenty-five-year-old daughter of a Scorpio. "I'll show her an outfit and ask if she likes it. She'll say, 'I *guess*.' That's when I usually go change—because I know she doesn't!"

Not that you're worried about being domineering. You'd rather shelter your kids from the crazy world out there than let them fall prey to its dangers. And yet you have a quirky side to you, too. Your fourth house of motherhood is ruled by Aquarius, the rabble-rousing sign of rebellion, cutting-edge ideas, and counterculture. Try though you might, you're just not a mainstream mother. Aquarius is free-spirited, so this adds an interesting twist to your parenting style. One minute you're an iron-fisted matriarch, the next you're a laid-back BFF with your kids. You'll encourage your children to express their individuality but remind them that "Mommy sees everything." You allow them to be unconventional and self-expressed—within a controlled environment.

Both Scorpio and Aquarius are signs that are drawn to New Age ideas. You'll feng shui the nursery, consult a psychic while your babe is in utero (if only to make sure she's not reincarnating as your hideous great-grandmother), and even bury the placenta in your backyard under a tree seedling. It's funny: while Scorpios rarely trust another human being, they tend to have absolute faith in the mystical. So you'll be inclined to turn your worries over to a storefront tarot reader or palmist, hoping for some divine reassurance that you're doing this motherhood thing right.

Aquarius is a youthful sign, and its influence helps you stay hip and in touch, pairing well with your Scorpio sexiness. Even if you don't dress like a dominatrix demigoddess (and many Scorpios do), you'll still exude a head-turning magnetism. Your family also knows to expect the unexpected with you—your shock tactics can leave people's jaws on the floor. Did you really just say that? Oh, yes you did. Scorpio comedian Roseanne Barr, the mother of five, has joked, "I figure that if the children are alive when I get home, I've done my job" and "Experts say you should never hit your children in anger. When is a good time? When you're feeling festive?" Dark humor is a Scorpio trademark.

Home is your sanctuary, and you'll create a beautiful space for your clan. You love to curl up on a comfy sofa and watch movies, cook together, or (if you're an affectionate Scorpio) cuddle with your kids. Doing things together as a family is so important to you. Like Scorpio Julia Roberts, who traded her big-city life for the quiet of Taos, New Mexico, you might even move to a more low-key location once you become a mom. You couldn't care less about the rest of the world once you have your tight-knit dynasty around you. And you'll do everything in your power to make sure they feel the same way.

While your outspoken nature can be jarring at moments, your kids also learn to be bold and self-expressed by your example. You might not be a stage mom, but if you know your kid's got star quality, you certainly encourage it. You love when children have strong, even flamboyant, personalities. And when your child gets in trouble at school, you'll defend him to the end. You're not the parent who screams at your kid, "What have you done?" Nope. Your naturally protective instinct (and clannish tendency) is to assume your child is innocent until proven guilty . . . and even that's subject to interpretation.

Life with Scorpio moms may be an exhausting game of chess, but the queen trumps all in the end. Your plotting, controlling, maneuvering, and sidestepping are part of a divine dance between you and the universe, which whispers a little more loudly in your ear than any other sign's. Scorpio is one of the zodiac's most intuitive (and even psychic) members, and you tend to faithfully trust your own inner guidance system. After all, it seldom steers you wrong. Everything you do is deliberate, as your calculating sign rarely speaks or acts without a strategic master plan—even if nobody else is privy to the details. Sometimes *you're* not even entirely sure of why you're acting on instinct; you simply feel compelled to do so. The Scorpio mama is a force of nature, but she's got her children's backs! What could be better than knowing that?

IF YOU HAVE A GIRL

*

PROS

The world has a shortage of empowered women, and in your opinion that counts as an endangered natural resource. Thanks to the Scorpio moms of the world, however, the headcount of future female world leaders is going up! You raise your daughter to be fierce and feminist, aware of herself and her power, and to never take crap from anyone. If your daughter wants to wear a tutu and sneakers to school on Field Day (as one Scorpio's little girl did), you let her. You'd rather she have bad taste than no taste at all!

Once she's old enough to develop better fashion sense, she'll undoubtedly "shop" in your closet. With your impeccable eye and ability to sniff out great quality for a bargain, you'll teach your daughter how to be a savvy consumer. (Beware: your own online shopping addiction can get a little out of hand, especially when you constantly spot cute items in her size.) But you'll do more than make sure your daughter knows the value of a dollar or a high-end clearance rack. The intuitive Scorpio mom can read her daughter like a large-print book. Unless you willingly bury your head in the sand, you'll spot danger on the horizon before it happens. If she's facing bullying, self-esteem breakdowns, or body image issues, you'll hone in and eviscerate the problem before it can become a full-blown crisis. While you'll eventually teach her to fight her own battles, she'll always know that Mama's in her corner.

CONS

Dial it down a notch, Scorpio! You take hands-on parenting to a whole new level. Scorpio is the sign of intimate bonding, so it can be hard to cut the cord with your daughter—and yes, the fact that you're the same sex *does* matter. Because you see so much of yourself in your daughter, you may project some of your own issues onto her. Realizing that you're two separate people with distinct personalities can be a challenge for you. Remember: what's good for the (mother) goose isn't always good for the gander!

Scorpio moms tend to be tougher on daughters than sons. While you'll totally baby a boy, still coddling him when he's old enough to make his own bed (and decisions), you push your daughter to be strong and independent. Sure, this will pay off in self-sufficient spades later. But sometimes you might slather on the pressure too thick, which could give her a complex. If your daughter genuinely hates the swim team, for example, she doesn't need to "build character" by toughing out a season. Just because you push yourself to extremes doesn't mean others have to keep pace. Quitting isn't always a sign of weakness, Scorpio.

Jealousy can also flare between Scorpio moms and their daughters. Embarrassing as it is to admit, you might feel slightly competitive if you have a daddy's girl who vies for your partner's attention. (Don't you have enough of this rivalry with your mother-in-law? Jeez!) Catch yourself when you're feeling possessive—and remember that there's enough love to go around. Looking at things the other way, your ability to look hot and pulled together at any age might be a little intimidating to your daughter as she hits her awkward teen years. Make sure your girl doesn't feel like she has to compare herself to you in any way.

IF YOU HAVE A BOY

*

PROS

Paging Mama's Boy Central! The Scorpio mother swoons at the sight of her son, the golden prince who can do no wrong. Will your little man know that he's loved to pieces? In spades, Scorpio. There's something about his sweetly vulnerable little boy energy that just shreds your heart—and melts the tough, no-nonsense demeanor you show to everyone else. Cuddling and coddling is the order of the day. You're also sensitive to his feelings, respecting his sentiments and making sure he grows up emotionally literate.

Although you may be too soft on him, you still set a great example as a primary female role model. Your son will be attracted to powerful women because of you, no doubt—especially since Scorpio moms are often the family breadwinners. Even if you're not, you exemplify fierce willpower and determination. While he might be a little scared to cross you, he will learn to respect women . . . or pay the consequences of their anger! Not that you would turn yours on him, Scorpio.

CONS

Enabler alert! As loving as you can be to your son, you can also accidentally emasculate him by solving his problems instead of letting him learn from his struggles. Yes, it's hard to set aside your protective instincts as you watch him fumble his way from boy to man. But while your inner mama bear wants to leap out and make it all better, it's best to march that she-grizzly back into the cave. Trust that your son knows you're there for him—but don't do all the hard work for him, or you could accidentally breed a slacker who lacks initiative and confidence. Children rise to your expectations, so if yours are too low, start challenging him a little more.

Jealous much? You might harbor possessiveness of your baby boy that can turn toxic. Deep down, you know that one day he'll "leave" you for another woman (or for a lovely man—which you wouldn't mind), and this isn't easy for the Scorpio mom to process. But tame that jealous instinct, especially when he starts dating. His girlfriend probably already knows you're the alpha female, so don't make her quake in her fleece-lined boots by being unfriendly—or aggressively interested. Boundaries, please!

With your strong personality, you have to be mindful not to embarrass or eclipse your son as he gets older. Sure, it's flattering that his friends think you're hot (and he might even secretly be proud of it), but you don't need to wear those lace-up boots or leather pants to his soccer games, Scorpio. Your inclination toward the spiritual might also go a little too far for him. Don't be offended if he doesn't want your sage wand passing his doorframe or if he turns down an offer for a crystal chakra healing once he's older. Just wish him "love and light" and do your thing, Scorpio.

PARENTING THROUGH AGES AND STAGES

*

INFANCY (THE FIRST YEAR)

Let the bonding begin! Scorpio is the sign of intimacy, so being "as one" with your newborn is something you take to easily. The hours of nuzzling, nursing, rocking, and cuddling during this phase can be downright blissful for you. You might be surprised by how quickly you click with your baby. After all, Scorpios tend to be paranoid, imagining everything that could possibly go wrong down to the last detail. "I was anxious about everything up until my daughter got here," says Scorpio mom Meredith. "I wondered, who's this person gonna be? What if my baby doesn't like me or I'm a crappy mom?"

If you've adopted, you'll bond just as readily with your wee one. Scorpio is a spiritual sign that rules the zodiac's house of karma and reincarnation. You probably believe that this soul has picked you to be her mother—and that you've shared many past lives. (Your psychic told you as much, anyhow.) So this is just a reunion, really! One Scorpio we know even attended the birth of her adoptive son, coaching his biological mother through the labor.

Of course, if you have a colicky infant or a child you can't hold right away, this can be emotionally tough at first. After all, you're a capable sign who can always make it all better, and this may be your first taste of helplessness. "When my daughter was born, she had a little problem gaining weight, and she was constantly hungry because she wasn't nursing," says Meredith. "The first six weeks were tough because I wanted so much to feel close to her, but she was struggling to be happy, so it gave us a slow start. I couldn't fathom why I couldn't make it better on my own."

Since you're a private sign, you may be relieved that the attention is focused more on your baby than on you now. All the idolizing and glamorizing of pregnant women can be uncomfortable for Scorpios, even creepy. Having strangers touch your belly? Being fawned over just because you got knocked up? It was probably all you could do not to whip out the pepper spray.

Not that you won't be ready to rumble if people get too close to your newborn. Strangers peering into your carriage and invading your personal space is a big no-no for you. Fiercely protective, you're not the type to hand your child to anyone who wants to hold him, either. If someone gives you a bad vibe, you'll make an excuse before you let them touch your babe: "She didn't sleep much last night" or "I don't want you to get spit-up on your nice outfit—he's been a little queasy today." When you're a Scorpio, you can never be too careful.

Since Scorpio rules the reproductive system, you'll want to take special care of your hormonal health before, during, and after pregnancy. You may be particularly susceptible to postpartum mood swings or jarring emotional shifts if you decide to wean during the first year. It's especially important that you stock your diet with nutritious "superfoods" such as avocados, blueberries, and dark leafy greens that help you rebalance—along with exercise and even meditation.

"Yoga, yoga, yoga . . . and more yoga!" says one Scorpio mom of her saving grace. "I crave silence and space." You might even try exercise with a spiritual element, like Kundalini yoga or Nia, a sensory-based movement class that combines dance, martial arts, and healing. Or limber back up with a little pole dancing. Nothing like finding your "erotic creature" (as S Factor creator Sheila Kelley calls it) to feel like your sexy self again. Speaking of sexy time, the Scorpio mom will probably be the quickest sign to get back on the metaphorical saddle after giving birth. (Maybe *that's* why so many of the Scorpio moms we spoke to had children less than two years apart!) At the very least, you'll attempt to put yourself together so you don't get stuck in a "schlump slump." You're not the mom who leaves the house in sweats—but even if you do, you manage to look fetching!

When it comes to sharing the parenting duties with your partner, you may struggle to adapt. Scorpios are possessive—and not always collaborative, since you like things done a very specific way. As a result, you might snap or bark orders at your partner, especially when your patience wears thin. You'll need to watch your tendency toward extremes, which can be damaging for your relationship. "I threw myself into parenting, to an extent that was harmful to my relationship," recalls Nina, Scorpio mom of four and creator of the organizing company momAgenda. "I didn't strive for balance at all; I just unequivocally put the kids first. This was great for the kids but not for my marriage."

Too much attention on the tykes can be overwhelming and a recipe for imbalance unless you call in the troops. We know several Scorpio moms who even hired a night nurse or live-in baby nurse for their children's first year. Although you can be a night owl, you still need your beauty sleep—and your brain cells, since you may be running a small empire, like Scorpio mom and Skinnygirl creator Bethenny Frankel. What might seem like an extravagance could be worth some carefully allocated funds.

Or you can learn to work as a team with your partner, which can really strengthen your "us against the world" bond. Sure, it might seem easier to divide into distinct roles—your partner works, you handle the parenting—but this dichotomy can leave you feeling even more alone and estranged. Just remember that your goal isn't to force your partner (or any caregiver) to do things exactly the way you would. As long as your baby is safe and happy, that's the point, Scorpio. "I'm more intuitive and instinctive and end up just doing things—while my husband wants to consult a manual," says Meredith. "I'm always listening to my daughter and watching her and trying to interpret what she's doing . . . and he literally checks progress charts." To each his own, Scorpio!

It's also important to let others know when you're struggling instead of trying to act like you've got it all figured out. During this phase, you'll feel more vulnerable than ever—much like a newborn yourself. Don't lean too heavily on the same handful of people for support. In fact, your tendency to isolate yourself could be strong now, putting you at greater risk for postpartum blues. Push yourself to get out of the house and meet other moms. You need a bigger support network now than you normally allow into your life. If you find yourself in a snarky or judgmental mood, that's your cue that what you really need are some girlfriends, stat.

"I've never felt more vulnerable in my life," says Meggan. "I experienced for the first time how much I need people—and how much I couldn't do this on my own. It took me a while to finally start saying out loud to people, 'I can't do this. I'm drowning.' I only got to that point because I was desperate: I was so incredibly exhausted and wasn't able to write or do much work. The response was amazing, but that was a huge lesson for me. It was a challenge to get to the point where I could admit that I can't do this all my way."

Of course, you'll still be fiercely private during the new motherhood phase. We know many Scorpio moms who tightly control the baby pictures they post online, and we know others who refuse to post at all. If you finally relent to sharing a few images, you might set up a photo shoot that you can creative direct. Even then, you'll opt for the highest privacy settings possible when you put them on the Internet.

Once you regain your equilibrium after this absorbing and surreal first year, your whip-smart humor saves the day. Because Scorpios specialize in hyperrealism, it's likely you'll see the divine comedy in your bodily functions (and malfunctions) and other indignities of new motherhood. That's reason enough to get to that mom circle—if only to find an appreciative audience for your hilarious jokes and colorful tales. Soon enough, you'll realize you're not alone. In fact, you'll probably form lifelong bonds with a couple of the women you meet. It's well worth leaving your comfort zone for that!

TODDLERHOOD (TWO TO FIVE YEARS)

Ready, set, decompress! Kiss the control you crave buh-bye once your kid starts crawling, running around, wriggling out of your grasp, and dashing into danger. You don't want to suppress your child's freedom, but you're also paranoid about safety. So bring on the outlet covers, corner cushions, webcams, and baby gates. You might even pack up your city slicker lifestyle and head to the burbs—or a few acres of land—where your child can freely explore without giving you a nervous breakdown.

The difficult part of this age is that Scorpio is such a focused sign. Whatever you're doing at the moment, you give it 110 percent of your attention. So if you're trying to work and mother a toddler at the same time, good luck. Switching between "mommy brain" and "mogul brain" will exhaust you. Scorpios tend to get absorbed by the tasks in front of them, and you really enjoy being in a state of deep focus. The short attention span of a toddler can leave your nerves frazzled as a result. Just as you're really getting into building a LEGOs tower or sand castle, your little one loses interest or throws a tantrum. Or you want to read *Vanity Fair* while your toddler demands another round of *Curious George*. Pure frustration!

"When my daughter Annie was two, I remember lying down in her room while she crawled all over me—and I felt like a mother dog," recalls Scorpio mom Kate. "I would play with her, but I looked forward to independent play. I was not someone who loved to play games. I preferred to *experience* things with Annie. Back then, I was one of the only mothers in New York City who had a seat on the back of my bike. I would take her on car trips as young as age four."

After a while, you might actually check out

and become inattentive—just because your brain needs a break. Or you'll start inventing household tasks (cooking an elaborate dinner, for example) just so you can say "Mommy's busy now" without feeling guilty.

SOS! It's time for some help, Scorpio. You *could* delegate to a babysitter or a relative. However, that presents a challenge: the Scorpio green-eyed monster. Yep, you've got a jealous streak, especially when your child starts to bond with the caregiver. "I couldn't work at home—I was too attached to my kids," says Scorpio mom Nina, who attempted to set up a home office while her kids were in a nearby room. "If I heard them playing with the nanny while I was working, I'd be seething."

If you're heading back to work or just taking a few hours of "me time," you might need to reckon with your own jealousy. If your partner is the primary parent at home, you might feel the same envy. And if the nanny takes your tot out on the town, well, throw in some paranoia for good measure. "I would sneak over to the park and peek through the bushes to see what my son's babysitter was doing," confesses Carol, a Scorpio mom. "It took me forever to even *get* a babysitter. My husband and I would take our son on date nights, to restaurants in New York City—he came everywhere with us."

Another Scorpio set up strategically placed spyware when she went back to her office job. "Without a nanny cam, I couldn't have functioned," she admits. (Note to nannies of Scorpio mothers: Big Mama *is* watching.) Another Scorpio mom used to stand outside her apartment door every morning until her son stopped crying. "At that point, I needed the support so much that it was a huge relief to have a sitter," she says. "But I would wait until I heard my son laughing before I left the building."

Hard as it is to let go, you need to ignite your career or get back into a personal groove. Consider it prevention—or "obsession management"—that will benefit you as the years pass. More than any other sign, the hyperfocused Scorpio mom can lose herself in her children, which can set her up for an identity crisis in the next ten to fifteen years when they are no longer completely dependent on her.

Of course, you can also go to the same extreme with your career—which is probably why you dialed back in the first place. This can be a bit of a dilemma for Scorpio moms. Taking a ho-hum job you're not passionate about just to pay the bills can really grind you down. Even if you're not quite ready to return to the full-fledged workforce (should you have the luxury of a maternity leave), you should probably plan to do something productive with your time when your child is in school. You may want to work with a life coach to help you find your next path—especially if you left behind an intense, high-powered job and have no desire to go back to running the world from your smartphone.

"My mom gave up her job to raise us," says Lily, the adult daughter of a Scorpio. "She's the perfect mother on paper, but I always sense there's this deep unhappiness, even a subtle depression. Now that the youngest in our family is in high school, she seems really lost. I worry about what she'll do when the house is empty. She hasn't really worked in her field for years."

Consider that a cautionary tale, Scorpio. This demanding phase has a silver lining, though: it can force you to seek balance and moderation, possibly for the first time ever. Fortunately, Scorpio moms are good at prioritizing and choosing which details to focus on. You won't sweat *all* of the small stuff. But your tendency to obsess and fixate may need to be managed or at least redirected. Funnel that energy into research. You can find the best prices online for diapers, strollers, and other essentials. You'll also carefully scout out schools, and even move to a new district if it positions your kids for the best educational opportunities. As a water sign, you might consider living near a lake, river, or ocean if you relocate.

Once you settle in, find your tribe—even if that's just one or two people who become your close confidantes. Although you may act like an open book with some of your blunt jokes and comments, you tend to divulge your most intimate self to very few people. Scorpios don't tend to be "group" girls. Why would you willingly be vulnerable in front of strangers?

Instead, find a community that feeds your soul. For many Scorpio mothers, a spiritual outlet is a great antidote to the frustration that builds up during this phase. Regular exercise, retreats, or a meditation group can be your saving grace. One Scorpio mom we met lives on a communal piece of land with a few other families, where she holds monthly full moon ceremonies—creating "sacred space" for women to gather monthly and get in touch with "the goddess within."

The loss of peace and quiet can be tough for your internal, reflective sign. Whether your favorite escape is a spin class or a Wiccan workshop, don't feel selfish for needing "me time" now. Scorpios absorb other people's energy easily, so you'll need to get away and recharge your mind, body, and soul. It will make you a better mother all around.

And if you can't beat 'em, join 'em. Get in the bathtub with your kid and soak in the bubbles. Take day trips to the beach where you can both enjoy the healing effects of sand and surf. Grab your favorite (and maybe only) mom friend and let the kids run around together while you bond. Replenishing your tanks can mean the difference between exhaustion and elation.

EARLY CHILDHOOD (SIX TO ELEVEN YEARS)

Welcome back to *you*, Scorpio. With your kids in school and more independent, you can take a deep breath and resume your own life again. You can read books, work on a business, renew a spiritual practice, or develop a creative passion. You've finally got time for yourself! You might even feel comfortable leaving your kid with grandparents or a close relative while you and your partner go off for a romantic weekend together. Ah, date night: a forgotten pleasure!

You might get your first taste of empty-nest syndrome during school hours. While the separation can be hard at first, your child is now at an age where you can trust him on his own a little more. If you have younger kids or teenagers, you may shift your attention onto them now. These could very well be the golden years of your mother-child relationship.

"My favorite stage was between ages five and eleven," says Kate. "You can go out to eat with your kid. They're in a latency period, so they're just completely unself-conscious and free. And they still care what you think. I lost my life for a while, so I was eager for my daughter to go to other people's houses so I could have some 'me time'—as much as I hate that phrase."

For Scorpio moms returning to work, there's a chance you might also be the breadwinner now. We've known many Scorpio women whose mates play the stay-at-home parent role or whose partners manage the household, dinners, carpools, and so on. You're a powerhouse, Scorpio, and it might just make more financial sense, especially if you want to send your kid to costly private schools, summer camp, and activities.

When it comes to discipline, you're not afraid to work your natural powers of intimidation. "With Scorpio moms, there's no 'wait until your father gets home,'" jokes Amanda. "I feared my mom's sting; I would never cross her." Disrespect can push you over the edge. When you talk, you expect your kids to listen, and your tolerance for being ignored is paper thin. "I rarely get angry, but when I do I get *really* angry," says Nina. "What sets me off is when I ask my kids to do something and they blatantly don't do it."

Fortunately, one look or pointed remark from a Scorpio mom is all it takes to get your kid back in line. Laura recalls her Scorpio mom's go-to disciplinary tactic at the grocery store. "She would say, sotto voce, 'Are you going to embarrass me? Because I can embarrass you right back.' It was enough to make me and my brother stop acting up—*instantly*."

When it comes to teaching your kids about the birds and the bees, the Scorpio mom can be pretty frank. Although some Scorpio moms said they left that job to their kid's sex-ed teacher, most preferred to make sure their children were properly informed. Hey, you're the zodiac's "sex sign," so you embrace it as a fact of life and don't try to hide your own sensuality. You'd rather teach your children about mature topics than leave them in the dark—which will only tempt them into experimentation and potentially irreversible mistakes. So you'll set aside your own embarrassment if it means protecting your kids from becoming candidates for a *Teen Mom* casting call.

The enforced community aspect of this phase might be a challenge. Now that your child is in school, there's no more begging off the mandatory, interparental group activity. There will be PTA meetings, school membership committees, sports teams, and concerts. You will be forced to commune with people you may not like—and to prevent that distaste from showing up on your face. "My Scorpio mom doesn't suffer fools," says Matt, "and she's not good at hiding it."

Your solution might be to turn your home into Playdate Central. "My mom didn't do any of the outside mommy stuff," says Amanda. "She didn't get down on her hands and knees and play with us—but I always knew she was there. She wasn't a helicopter mom, but when people played they played at our house. There were always twenty kids over, and my mom would just oversee it like a preschool."

You do need personal time, so try to get enough of it so you can be "on" when truly necessary. Scorpios tend to crash, burn, and rise again. Because you're the sign of extremes, your emotions can run hot and cold. Sometimes you're totally friendly and outgoing; other times you can withdraw into your own world. "When my siblings and I were little, we all had to go into our rooms or outside for an hour every day to entertain ourselves," recalls one Scorpio's daughter. "My mom needed her own time to recharge. She'd read books while we played in our rooms."

Make sure you have a go-to haven—even if it's just the bathtub—so you can release emotional buildup when your moods get too dark or intense. Just make sure your kids know that *they* haven't done anything wrong. Otherwise, when you withdraw, it can be a little scary for them. You probably don't realize how intimidating you can actually be!

Although you can deliver tough love, you're still emotionally attuned to your kids and vigilant about their development. You may push them to do well academically, but you're also compassionate about any struggles. If your kids are having trouble academically, you don't blame them—you investigate. Maybe the school or the teacher isn't a good fit. Perhaps your child is dealing with a bully or his desk is placed in a spot where he can't hear. You'll hone in on those issues and get to the bottom of things.

One Scorpio mom we know homeschooled her kids for a couple years and then switched to a more cutting-edge approach. She "unschooled" them—meaning they went to the "school of life," as she explained it. In unschooling, the child's curiosity is the guiding force of her education, and learning occurs through play, household work, and her own exploration. (Bonus for a Scorpio mom: it keeps your kids under your roof all day.) Of course, this woman's children got into great colleges as adults, so maybe she was on to something. Trendsetting Scorpios often are!

In fact, educational reform is a passion for many Scorpio moms, as you may have felt deeply misunderstood in your own school years. Your sign also rules psychology, so you're keenly attuned to child development. Scorpio actress Goldie Hawn, a practicing Buddhist, created a cutting-edge curriculum through her nonprofit, the Hawn Foundation. The MindUP program, as it's called, trains school-age kids in Buddhist techniques of "mindfulness," which helps them manage stress, regulate their own behavior, concentrate, and develop greater empathy. Pretty cool!

ADOLESCENCE AND TEENS (TWELVE TO EIGHTEEN YEARS)

Welcome to the perfect storm of puberty: Your moods. Their moods. Your iron will. Theirs. All under one roof. Yeah, this could get intense.

The teen years can challenge any parent, but you actually may be better equipped than you realize. After all, you know what it's like to have intense mood swings and emotional tsunamis. (Never mind the sarcasm and surly attitude—yep, you've got that, too.)

Still, it could take a while before you get a handle on watching your sweet child morph into a hell-raiser. Up until now, you've been close confidants, more like friends in some ways. At the very least, your kid has been obedient, complying with your firm rules instead of challenging them. Now he starts to turn on you—or so it seems—pushing you away despite your best efforts.

When the rejection begins, you might wonder what you've done wrong. After all, you've been practically clairvoyant when it comes to your kids. And you're tuned into your kid—it's not like you don't listen. You've never been deliberately embarrassing or, worse, uncool (like other moms). In fact, you've probably been mistaken for the younger, hipper (and hotter) babysitter on many occasions, thank you very much.

But now motherhood can feel like a thankless job. It's not that you mind being an authority figure—you just don't appreciate being seen as no fun. You're still the awesome rock 'n' roll mom who dressed your kid in camouflage pants and a Ramones T-shirt when he was five, after all. Now your child just sees you as one thing: old.

You might even be accustomed to being the head turner in the family, only to find that your teenager is getting all the looks now. You could secretly feel a little jealous, taking pains (and other means) to keep your youthful appearance. But *gawd*, you never want to be the mom who looks forty going on twenty-one—at least not in an obvious way.

At this point, it's time for a change on a deeper level, oh controlling one. You'll need to back out of your kid's business, Scorpio, difficult as that is. This is a fundamental time for children to individuate, and if you stall their process you'll regret it in a few years. (Picture this: your twenty-three-year-old arrives at your doorstep, suitcases in hand, announcing that he's moving back in.) If you don't give your kids that space, your feelings are bound to get hurt when they lash out fiercely in an attempt to claim sovereignty. It's tough not to take it personally when your child pulls away, especially when you've tried to be cool and understanding all along. "It was hard when my kids stopped snuggling and cuddling and holding my hand," admits one Scorpio mom.

Your teen's disrespectful outburts could also awaken some angry demons within you. As impenetrable as you may appear, Scorpio *is* a deeply sensitive and emotional sign. When your feelings get hurt, your temper turns white hot . . . and hell hath no fury like a Scorpio scorned. Although you may not fall into this category, we've heard tales of "intense" and "scary" Scorpio moms going into full-fledged rages with their disobedient teens.

As the sign of power and control, your fears can definitely get out of hand during this period. Keeping a therapist and several confidants on call is probably essential (and beats the Pinot Grigio you might otherwise reach for). You also need to remember your own headstrong teenage years—nobody could tell *you* anything, either, Scorpio. Perhaps you're afraid that your child will follow in your own extreme footsteps, experimenting with anything she can get her hands on. Perish the thought! Or, perhaps your tunnel vision becomes so laserlike, you lose perspective, blowing things out of proportion.

Fear, in fact, is probably at the root of anything that upsets you. You're a worrier, Scorpio, often to the point of paralyzing. You trust no one, least of all your teenager's impressionable peers. Competing with them for your child's attention feels like fighting a (losing) battle of wits with unarmed rivals—who happen to be wearing too much eyeliner and Axe body spray. Helplessness: *not* a feeling any Scorpio can handle for long.

You may go to great lengths to make sure that your family remains close—reminding them, Mafia-mama style, that they really can't trust anyone 100 percent except their family. And hey, if taking them on great trips, hosting lavish Sweet Sixteens, and buying them nice clothes reinforce your "blood is thicker than water" credo now, you might occasionally resort to such tactics. When bribery keeps 'em off the streets, the end justifies the means, right?

Sensing how difficult the teen years can be, you could take a preventive approach, too. Our friend Nancy Gruver, a Harvard-educated Scorpio mother of twins, created the girls' coming-of-age magazine and online community *New Moon Girls* when her daughters were eleven. She was deeply influenced by the pioneering work of gender scholars like Carol Gilligan, who found that girls often lose their unique voices and identities at adolescence. Like a true Scorpio, Nancy researched extensively for magazines and resources that would help her daughters with this transition. Finding none, she (along with her husband and daughters) decided to create their own. The result is an empowering magazine written by and for girls that's been around since 1992.

Keeping your kids educated and informed is a great strategy, one you'll want to employ now. Rather than limit their exposure by sheltering them, push yourself to be frank about the realities they'll face. As the zodiac's "sex sign," you may not mind teaching your kid the nitty-gritty facts of life. Better they learn from you than be misinformed by their peers. Raunchy as you can be, you might even joke about sex with your kids. Your hope is that by being open and casual about it, they'll know that they can come to you with questions.

Since Scorpios like rituals, you can even

turn their developmental milestones into occasions. When puberty hits, why not celebrate with them? If you have a daughter, you might take her to a Red Tent ceremony or treat her to a special lunch when she gets her period. If you have a son, you can encourage him to ask you advice about girls—or you'll make sure he has a go-to male role model at the ready. This open-door policy will be good when they face the inevitable teen tribulations. Scorpio moms, after all, are great in a crisis. While your own freak-outs can reach epic and irrational proportions, you remain steely and clearheaded when your child is in distress. The second you sense trouble, you're on the case.

Your children know how powerful you are, Scorpio. Perhaps that's exactly why they rebel so intensely sometimes. It's not because they think you're weak. Rather, they want to find their own strength—to know that they can stand up for themselves without needing Mama. "In her teenage years, my daughter *had* to get away from me because I'm strong-willed," says Scorpio mom Kate. "So by the time she was going to college, her dad and I were like, 'Good . . . go!'"

Once your kids find their wings, don't worry: they'll be back. It might be hard to trust this, especially if you clash during this period. Since you're so psychologically minded, reading up on the behavior patterns of this age group can be a lifesaver. One Scorpio mom credits a book on teenagers called *Get Out of My Life, but First Could You Drive Me and Cheryl to the Mall?* as helping to turn her turbulent relationship around. Who knows: learning about human motivations, neuroscience, and development can become a new fascination. Your research might even lead you to an intriguing new path, one you can pursue when your kids go off into the world.

BYE-BYE, BIRDIE: LEAVING THE NEST (EIGHTEEN-PLUS YEARS)

Scorpio mothers can shine with adult children, especially once you transition to a less codependent relationship. Your piercing insight and emotional strength can anchor your child as she heads out into the big, bad world alone. "When you need your mom, it's nice to have a Scorpio mom," says Amanda, thirty-five, who became closer to her mother after leaving home. "My mother is the wisest, most emotionally intelligent person I know. When I call her, she'll talk to me as long as I want, and she always has the perfect thing to say. I didn't appreciate that when I was younger."

But letting go is hard to do, especially when you're a Scorpio mom. While you might want to act cool and copacetic when your child goes to an out-of-state college or moves abroad, you feel deep emotional pangs—especially if you're left with an empty nest. Serious abandonment issues can flare up. And even though you know they're irrational, it can be hard to stop yourself from projecting these onto your child. Once a Scorpio has staked an emotional claim on another human being, it's for eternity. So you can't help but take it personally when they choose to move out of a radius where you can drive and deliver care packages—or help them furnish their starter apartment in a style that meets your hard-won approval.

"I recently bought furniture that looked just like my mom's style, and she was so happy," says thirty-six-year-old Kirsten. "She was like, 'See, you inherited my taste!' The only difference is that she's a Scorpio, so hers is all muted, and I'm a Leo, so my couch and chairs have the same frames, but the cushions are in all these bright colors."

You can't help it: you need to see evidence that the connection between you and your child is still there. And yes, you need to be needed, Scorpio. So you'll keep the nest feathered and comfortable—baiting the (parent) trap so that your children just *want* to come home. Because Scorpio is the master seductress, you'll use all your secret weapons however you can. "My Scorpio mom is always calling and asking, 'When are you coming home?" says Krista, twenty-five. "She doesn't ask what I'm up to for the weekend, even though I live in New York City and have a boyfriend. She just asks if I'm bringing him home with me and what we want to eat."

Amanda's Scorpio mom Judy was happy to reclaim her space after raising three children. "She was done," Amanda says, laughing. However, Judy's home remains the hub for all family dinners and holidays. "My mom didn't want the bird to leave the nest and never come back," Amanda explains. "She wanted us to move out of the nest and come back often."

While *la familia* is gathered round your table, you can scan everyone's face, posture, and body language, intuitively assessing if they're doing okay. Scorpio is the zodiac's observer, an all-seeing hawk. If you sense something's off, you'll pull that child aside and interrogate (or politely but pointedly ask) what's going on. It doesn't take more than a few carefully chosen words before your kid is confessing everything. The penetrating gaze of a Scorpio mom is like an X-ray scanner and a lie detector machine all in one. You won't hesitate to weigh in on your children's choices, either. One Scorpio's daughter recently called her mom, excited to share that she and her boyfriend were thinking of moving in together—in a year. Rather than get swept up in excitement, Mama issued this subtle-yet-direct inquiry: "Do you think he'll be making a large *purchase* before then?"

Hey, Scorpio moms know how to command power and respect, and if you have a daughter, you'd rather her beau "put a ring on it" before she gets too serious. Or you might discourage your child from rushing into anything permanent before finding a solid career path. As Scorpio mom Kate jokes, "When my daughter was little, she said to me, 'Mom, let's pretend I'm fifteen and having a baby.' I said, 'Let's pretend you're thirty-five and *thinking* about having a baby.'"

You know how to use your approval and disapproval to mold your children—and you won't stop just because they're adults. Nine times out of ten, you're right. However, sometimes you need to let your kids learn things through a few tough experiences before you rush in for the save. One adult daughter of a Scorpio confesses that she has a lot of anxiety making her own decisions—largely because, growing up with her capable mom, she never had to before. "I recently stopped calling my mom every day," she says. "I would call her whenever I got anxious, but I realized that I was relying too heavily on her strength. I was always wondering, 'What would my mom think?' or 'What would my mother say about this?'"

When you feel like you're out of a job as your child's ultimate advisor, it can sting. And so, you may sting back. Scorpio is the sign of revenge, so be careful that you're not passive-aggressively punishing your child for striking out on his own. One friend recalls telling her Scorpio mother that she wanted to shed a few pounds by eating healthily. Her mom showed up a couple days later with a huge pan of fettuccine alfredo. "I felt like she was trying to sabotage me," says the daughter, "and then I felt guilty for thinking that at all, because she's so supportive of me in other ways." Oh, the mental chess you can play, Scorpio!

Although some boundaries may need to be established, your kids always know that you can be counted on for solid advice and guidance, even if you get intense at times. Like mother-daughter actresses Goldie Hawn and Kate Hudson, or Kris Jenner and her Kardashian crew, Scorpio moms can become their adult children's best friends, too. If you have a son, chances are you've got a lifelong mama's boy on your hands. (Good luck dealing with his future wife there. Eh, you can handle her. She's the one who will need the luck!)

Yes, you'll always be molding your kids—it's your job, after all, and you don't plan to take an early retirement. The recipe for success is to have a life outside of your kids, Scorpio. Since you tend to microfocus on your child, the move away from this can be tough, and you can even slip into a little bit of a depression if you don't have other outlets.

There are midlife crisis tales from the Scorpio trenches, too. Scorpio Demi Moore, once superclose to her daughters, went through a difficult public divorce just as her three girls were all grown up and she turned fifty. Indeed, you may want to bring sexy back when you no longer have to play the dutiful mom role. Even if you tell people you're glad to have your life back, it's hard not to be needed anymore!

If you've sacrificed your sensuality over the years, then we urge you to reawaken that passion. But take note: Scorpio is the sign of extremes, so you might find yourself going from zero to cougar a little too fast, rushing to the tattoo parlor or the plastic surgeon in an attempt to fill a void. Make sure you deal with underlying sadness, even grief, before you ink on a regrettable "tramp stamp" or let a scalpel touch your face.

The key is to learn how to trust your children even when you're a sign that pretty much trusts no one. Their efforts at independence are not a rejection or an abandonment of you. You don't have to keep them on a short leash or infantilize them to keep them coming back (okay fine, maybe a little). Remember, you're a powerful force of nature—and your children are probably too scared to let you down. Make sure they know it's okay to blaze their own trails . . . and that you'll always be there to cheer them on.

THE SAGITTARIUS MOM

(November 22–December 21)

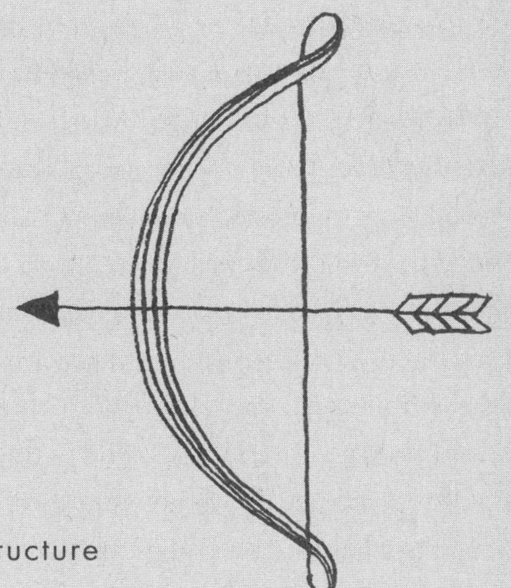

MOMMY MAGIC - Your Strengths:

- Adventure
- Wisdom
- Humor
- Perspective

MAMA MIA - Your Challenges:

- Impatience
- Crudeness
- Bluntness
- Too much spontaneity and lack of structure

FAMOUS SAGITTARIUS MAMAS:

Britney Spears, Bette Midler, Katie Holmes, Julianne Moore, Kim Basinger, Mayim Bialik, Christina Aguilera, Jane Fonda, Katherine Heigl, Christina Applegate, Jenna Bush Hager, Mo'Nique, Alyssa Milano, Anna Nicole Smith, Nicole "Snooki" Polizzi, Jennifer Connelly, Jamie Lee Curtis, Joan Didion, Nelly Furtado, Teri Hatcher, Sonja Tremont-Morgan

YOUR PARENTING STYLE

*

As the zodiac's freest spirit, parenting is an interesting adjustment for you. Spontaneous Sagittarians live in the moment, acting on impulse and instinct. You cherish your independence, and this new level of permanence can feel surreal. Who, you—a disciplinarian? An authority figure? Parenting is a big lifestyle change for a sign that includes Britney Spears, Nicole "Snooki" Polizzi, and Anna Nicole Smith among its ranks. While you can be wonderful with children, treating them like real people instead of patronizing them, kids also demand a lot of time and energy. Your pencil-it-in-now-and-see-how-we-feel-later lifestyle just doesn't cut it anymore. Even if you're great at planning, your own life may already run on a packed schedule. Now you have to integrate another person's needs and demands into this active routine.

Getting the proportions right could take a minute. Ruled by Jupiter, planet of excess and abundance, Sagittarians tend to either overcommit (and work until exhaustion, doing it all yourself) or to avoid commitment altogether. You're famous for shooting first and asking questions later. This daredevil spirit is a double-edged sword when it comes to motherhood. On the upside, your spontaneity makes life fun. You'll toss the kids in the car and drive to the next state to buy fireworks or see a traveling circus. You'll serve pancakes with whipped cream for dinner and leftover Chinese for breakfast (hey, at least they ate, right?). And you can pull together an impromptu vacation or slumber party like no other mom. But when it comes to planning and structure . . . not so much.

On the zodiac wheel, Sagittarians' fourth house of motherhood is ruled by dreamy Pisces—the sign of healing, illusions, and compassion. Although you're a go-getter out in the world, motherhood can bring out a softer side of you. Pisces is notorious for blurring boundaries, and that may be your parenting challenge. Without realizing it, you can dole out a guilt trip or get way too involved in your kids' personal problems. You can even turn into a "martyr mom," sacrificing beyond your limits, then feeling resentful and overextended.

Discipline may be tough for you, too, as you have a hard time setting limits, perhaps as a result of your own unresolved childhood issues. "I've tried to keep my daughter away from the TV, but it turns out she enjoys media as much as I do," says one pop-culture-loving Sag mom. Enforcing too many restrictions just isn't your thing. After all, you're a curious soul, so you don't want to block your child from experiencing the world, either.

Being the "bad cop" might not be fun, but kids need structure, so give yourself time to adapt—and yes, even mourn the temporary loss of your pre-mom freedom. Some Sagittarians have a thin tolerance for the "boring" and mundane details of motherhood (and life in general). It might feel as if some evil Diaper Genie stole your identity away in a poof of Pampers and preschool applications. More than any other sign, you need to make sure you preserve your own autonomy and "me time." It just makes you happy . . . and a better person to be around. No guilt allowed!

Since motherhood *is* a life sentence (though a wonderful one), your best bet is to turn it into an adventure. In fact, we advise that you do. Ask questions, get advice, take in the outside counsel, and then synthesize it with your own personality and beliefs. The independent Sagittarius woman does it her own way, and nobody can tell her otherwise. In fact, you might be the sign most likely to have an accidental pregnancy or to raise a baby on your own—a card-carrying member of Single Mothers by Choice. You leap without looking, assuming it will all work out in the end. It does but not without some serious tests of will. And since you may have arrogantly shunned any advice or help, you often end up swallowing your pride and hearing an "I told you so" or two.

The Sagittarius mom is also famous for her short attention span and endless multitasking, which can get tricky when your kid becomes a walking monologue machine. "Mommy, why is the sky blue?" is an adorable conversation thread when you're not rearranging the entire living room to resemble an *Elle Decor* feature. But while you're busy spackling the walls and restoring the original crown moldings, it's hard (and frustrating!) to host a kiddie Q&A session. At times, you may have to forcibly pull yourself away from tasks and be present for your child. Kids are intuitive, and the more you ignore them, the more they strive for your attention.

So how *does* the zodiac's party girl morph into the PTA president? Hello, existential identity crisis . . . or maybe not. The best strategy a Sag mom can take is the "if you can't beat 'em, join 'em" approach—or what the experts call parallel play. Repainting the kitchen for the ninth time? Hand your babe a brush and a little bucket of color, and give him a corner to coat. Planting an English garden? Get a pint-sized watering can, a couple of small pots, and cultivate a young green thumb. Bonus: you'll foster a sense of leadership, build skills, and enjoy a shared sense of accomplishment from completing a project together. Remember, your kids just want to be with their mom, feeling close, and connected. Integrate them into your adventures, and presto—you have an intergenerational win-win.

Modeling healthy relationships can also be a challenge for some Sagittarius mothers because they're so independent. You march to your own beat and bristle at the idea of asking for permission to do, well, anything. Coparenting can be difficult for you. If you're bringing up *bébé* with a partner, you might want to find a group of friends to lend support and an ear, so you can talk about the things your partner does that make you crazy. This way, you can air your struggles in a safe setting. Your candid comments will entertain the others (and occasionally shock them). Plus, you'll get creative solutions and new skills that can save your relationship.

Remember, it's not that you don't love your child or have what it takes to be a great mom. But when "freedom" is your middle name, dealing with a dependent child and a tight schedule could require new muscles. As our Sagittarius friend Amanda likes to say, "I'm a person who happens to be a mother—not a mother who happens to be a person." When all else fails, remember: there's not always much dignity in motherhood, so use your innate sense of humor to see the divine comedy in it all.

IF YOU HAVE A GIRL

*

PROS

Meet your new future BFF! As the sign of wisdom, you can't wait to impart all that you've learned to your impressionable mini-me. You're eager to shape a future feminist or a spunky, self-sufficient little leader. Unlike some moms who treat their daughters like showpieces, you may issue a household ban on anything overly feminine: cake-topper hair bows, frilly Communion dresses, infant ear piercing, and anything that restricts your little girl's movement or makes her look like she belongs in a bakery window has no place in your house.

As an independent woman, you can be a positive role model for your daughter, teaching her to be outspoken and self-sufficient. Never one to act helpless, you'll model confidence for your girl, and you'll encourage her to speak up for her beliefs. While you might not love to do all the hands-on kiddie arts and crafts, you'll expose your daughter to other adventures—travel, avant-garde ideas, and perhaps even entrepreneurship. You want to create a "citizen of the world" who's comfortable expressing her own opinions and thrives among people of all cultures.

CONS

Your attention, please! It can be hard for the restless Sagittarius mom to break routine and go into Little Girlville, especially if you have a superfeminine daughter. While the teddy bear tea party makes an adorable photo op, the long, drawn-out motions (". . . and now *this* bear gets a cookie . . . and *this* one needs a cup of tea . . .") can provoke a full-on outbreak of mommy ADD.

When your daughter starts to face those painful adolescent issues, you may rush in with tough love or quick solutions, which won't be helpful. Your personality can fill up a room, so you may need to dial it down at times to prevent a future alpha female battle. Instead, try the Socratic method—asking a series of thought-provoking questions that help her draw out and arrive at her own conclusion.

Your own competitive—and yes, masculine—energy can feed into antimale sentiment, which won't serve your daughter in the long run. While you may be a fierce feminist, remember that the real enemy here is gender inequality, not boys and men (or, as your college sociology course put it, "the patriarchal, male-dominated, capitalist hegemony"). Be careful not to make disparaging remarks about the fellas or to create a "girls' club" in your home.

IF YOU HAVE A BOY

*

PROS

The "typical" male responds to direct communication, and your Sagittarian straightforwardness can play well with a son. Because you're respectfully honest with him, he'll learn to see women as smart, self-expressed people with valuable opinions. You teach your boy the more civilized stuff: how to be a kind person who's respectful of the opposite sex, the environment, and people from different backgrounds. As a lifelong learner, you'll foster a sense of curiosity in your son by enrolling him in special programs. Many Sagittarians are outdoor adventurers, too, so you'll enjoy hiking, picnics, and camping trips together.

The vulnerability of little boys is adorable to you, and you manage to stay cued into your son's sensitivities throughout the years. In your care, he feels understood. You may try to maintain a connection by giving him advice, shoring up his self-esteem, and talking to him about everything. He always knows you're there to be a sounding board. By holding him to his highest potential you give your son the message "I believe in you!" With Mama's faith and encouragement, he's destined for success.

CONS

It's great to be the cool mom who can talk to her son about anything, but being your son's best friend isn't always the greatest idea. At a certain point, a boy has to separate from his mama (experts say this happens as early as eighteen months) and become his own man. That means learning to make decisions without checking in with you—no matter how sound your guidance may be. And while it's good to relate to him, at a certain point it's okay if you don't. You can joke around like the best of 'em, and you may be a bit of a jock yourself. Just stay out of the metaphorical locker room, puh-leeze. Even if you've had your share of male friends and you're fluent in "guy talk," Mama Sag doesn't belong in the man cave.

The Sagittarius mom is incredibly capable, with reserves of strength that can be accidentally emasculating. You don't want to breed the world's next mama's boy (or slacker . . . or thug) by figuring everything out for him, weighing in on his romantic choices, or relating to him like he's still your little "chubby choo-choo" when he's actually a high-school senior. Your son could actually benefit from the tough love you shell out to everyone else on the planet, too.

Nearly every Sagittarius woman has reckoned with an arrogant man who underestimated her capabilities, and your sign's tolerance for male chauvinism is tissue thin. Be careful not to project these personal conflicts with men onto your son, though. Plan on doing a little inner work around any residual father issues, perhaps with the help of a good therapist.

PARENTING THROUGH AGES AND STAGES

*

INFANCY (THE FIRST YEAR)

Welcome to the surreal world—there's another human being completely and utterly dependent on you. You've spent your entire lifetime avoiding this kind of attachment with people, and now there's no turning back. As trippy as your new mom status is, there will be moments of pure bliss. The tiny creature in your arms, blinking up at you . . . the new baby smell . . . the beautiful moments of bonding.

While a newborn may force you to slow down, this isn't such a bad thing for your on-the-go sign. And although there may be sleepless nights, most infants sleep up to sixteen hours a day (or so the parenting manuals claim). You can still check email, work remotely, or catch up on your favorite TV shows while recovering from delivery or adapting to an adoption. Plus, there will be plenty of visitors, which your social sign loves—even if you're too exhausted to really engage with them.

One big challenge is getting out and about. You hate to be confined, but the hassle of dragging a stroller or changing diapers in a public bathroom can be enough to make you a shut-in. And a confined Sagittarius is a miserable Sag, who can drag everyone around her down with her nonstop complaining.

While hormones are a factor in postpartum depression, isolation can be just as much of a downer. Get proactive. Spend a little extra on a high-end stroller or buy a great one secondhand—then combine baby's nap time with your exploration time. Many an infant will sleep peacefully while you troll the bookstore, get your hair cut, hit a funky flea market, or even meet your friends for a ladies' lunch. Integrate your lives as much as possible, and make the hours work for you. You don't have to be held hostage by new motherhood!

As Ophira found during her Sagittarius new-mom days in New York City, a sleeping baby has never been persona non grata in an unexpected place—like a slightly upscale tapas bar or oyster happy hour—as long as you don't show up during the rush. In fact, your little one might even get extra doting from the staff (who doesn't love a baby's smile?), and you'll have a few sets of arms to cuddle your cherub while you scarf Spanish omelet and chorizo . . . or enjoy a nice 3:00 p.m. glass of Rioja.

Visiting favorite haunts from your pre-mom life is important for Sagittarius, because you can easily feel like you've lost your identity once your little one comes along. Remember, motherhood is a new facet of yourself, not a personality transplant. Yes, you may have moments when you feel frumpy, dumpy, old, and inert—but don't freak out over it. This, too, shall pass.

Another adjustment of this phase is allowing people to support you. Sagittarius women are the "sisters are doing it for themselves" breed, so relying on the kindness of family and friends isn't easy. You're not great at asking for help, being such an independent DIY-er, but during this phase, you'll need to cultivate that skill—that is, if you want to shower more than once a week. You like to do things your way, but loosening that control a little will leave you time to rejuvenate.

One of life's biggest paradoxes is that commitment can actually set you free. Once you actually commit to something, you have clarity, focus, and purpose. It's the avoidance and vacillating that wastes so much precious energy. A new baby might actually make you more productive and self-assured in the end.

TODDLERHOOD (TWO TO FIVE YEARS)

Toddlerhood can be the hardest stage of all for Sagittarius mothers. Why? You're confronted with someone *exactly like yourself*: a human being who refuses to take direction, has zero patience, demands instant gratification, and has no sense of her limits. A person who seems to have a filtering device that blocks out the word *no* and who constantly tests the rules. Sound familiar?

Mirror, mirror on the wall. You're exactly alike, so now what? Every hour is another existential meltdown that leaves you mentally spent. Do you say no when your babe wants the boob and you're trying to wean? What if she screams herself blue? Is it better to cave? Will she remember and hate you when she's older?

The restrictive nature of toddlerhood doesn't jibe with your wiring. You're an independent soul who usually has a ton of friends, hobbies, and interests. Suddenly, all of your creative energy is going to making sure your two-year-old doesn't run out into traffic or snack on a choking hazard. You're not used to being this focused on another human being, and it's downright disorienting.

This is the time to call in the reserves! Delegate, delegate, delegate. You may find peace in admitting that you're out of your league, and you just need to get through these years. Don't bother trying to change yourself too much (although you'll surely benefit from scaling back and simplifying your life a little). By the time you learn to stop negotiating with your tiny terrorist, he'll be done with this stage . . . and you might be hauled off in a straitjacket.

The trouble is moms are so often shamed for not doing everything perfectly. Thanks to the so-called Mommy Wars in the media, we're told that we're not good enough or that we're neglecting our children if we don't hover over them constantly, catering to their every need. Forget the guilt: let the babysitter put your eighteen-month-old to sleep every night if you can't deal. You're not a bad mother, a failure, or a fraud. There will be plenty of years to make up for it with meaningful bedtime stories that the kid will actually understand and even remember. The helicopter parent thing—no thanks!

And if you insist on doing it all yourself, turn to the power of the group. You need community during this phase like never before. But here's the rub: the whole mommy group scene can make a Sagittarian's skin crawl. You simply can't fathom choosing friends on such mundane grounds: "You were pregnant? Wait, so was I—let's be friends!" Um, no. For Sagittarius, life is too short to spend time with boring people whose conversation is limited to burp cloths and private preschool admissions. But you may need to get over a bit of snobbery and force yourself to attend a new mom circle or two. The payoff? You'll get the resources and innovative ideas you need.

Misery loves company—yes, we said it—and sometimes this exhausting stage can only be survived by banding together with other cool moms who are also into creative child rearing. Eventually, you can handpick them selectively. As Sagittarius mom Amanda says, "You only need one friend." And if you can't find her on your own, fine—suck it up and open your mind. Try several mom groups until you find one that fits. People are people, so give them a fair shot if you're really feeling lonely. Isolation is the enemy now.

In addition, pack your posse with lots of child-free friends who love kids. Anoint them honorary aunts and uncles. They're the ones who aren't too wiped out to chase your manic toddler down the street or play peekaboo for five hours straight. Still overwhelmed? Apply the principles of *The Four-Hour Workweek*, which is all about creating freedom through outsourcing. Have someone come in and handle the afternoon nap time and then have them fold the laundry while your little guy sleeps. You'll get a few hours to yourself and a pile of clean clothes.

Hanging out with single or child-free friends serves another useful function. To avoid turning into an automaton, you must keep vestiges of your pre-mom life alive and kicking. Shut down the milk bar once in a while and head to the wine bar. Take an hour a day (minimum) to do whatever you want, on your own agenda. Find a cool preschool or drop-off music class and take those hours back.

Once you've revived yourself with a run of vintage shopping, reading magazines at your favorite French cafe, or an "afternoon delight" in the bedroom, you'll be totally up for another round of ring-around-the-rosy and finger painting. A little baby-proofing goes a long way, too, so pack up that shabby-chic furniture that screams "splinter hazard" for a year or two. Eliminate the things you have to say no to, and you'll be free to say yes to the cuteness of this adorable but overwhelming stage.

Sagittarius is the seeker, so read up on child development, psychology, and cutting-edge parenting methods. You'll feel hip and in the know—and it will help. Pore through the What to Expect series or the classic tome *The Magic Years* by Selma Fraiberg, which explains the mentality of the eighteen-month- to three-year-old set. You'll learn that children this age have no conscience and are motivated only by parental approval and disapproval. That will do away with the fears you have that strictness and structure will leave scars. If anything, you'll be preventing your child from inheriting some of your most challenging traits—impatience, a quick-rising temper, and bouts of bullheadedness.

When Ophira's daughter Cybele morphed from a docile infant into a wild one-year-old, she found great relief from the book *The Happiest Toddler on the Block.* The author, pediatrician Harvey Karp, explains how to speak "toddler-ese" and outlines the four stages of brain development that toddlers go through from ages one to four. Karp likens an upset toddler to a miniature caveman and suggests mirroring the child's emotional reaction as a way of validating that you've "heard" what your preverbal little one is trying to communicate by way of a meltdown. When Cybele shouted "No no no no no!" Ophira would do her best imitation, throwing herself on the floor and shaking her head vehemently (hoping nobody witnessed the indignity). While it didn't work every single time, a few instances stopped Cybele in her tantruming tracks.

Because knowledge is power for Sag in particular, you'll want to arm yourself with information. Since you love to give advice, you'll become the playground oracle and go-to resource before you know it.

EARLY CHILDHOOD (SIX TO ELEVEN YEARS)

You made it! The hardest part is over, and you've got a real, live human being to interact with now. This might be your favorite stage of childhood. If only you could have put your babe into a time machine at nine months and zapped him here.

Sagittarius is an interactive sign, so you may find the preverbal years frustrating, even mind-numbingly boring at moments. Not that they weren't adorable, too, but chasing a squirmy toddler or trying to reason with a screaming, overtired child with a ten-word vocabulary (good luck with that) isn't really your idea of fun. Now your child can actually tell you what he wants. She possesses a measure of self-sufficiency now that frees up your attention span.

Well, kinda. During this phase, your child has discovered language, a blessing and a curse. There could be endless questions and demands of a different sort. However, philosophical Sagittarius moms are happy to answer an adorable litany of thoughtful questions, since you're interactive by nature. You can also teach lessons on manners, patience, waiting turns, and the like—buying yourself time instead of being held hostage by a brewing public meltdown. You can now give simple instructions like "Let's use our inside voices" or "It's cleanup time" and get an actual response. Amazing!

At this age, kids like to be on the move, which jives with your on-the-go personality. At the playground, you don't have to be hypervigilant anymore—they can make it up and down the slide independently and might even negotiate sharing with another kid. You get more space and breathing room, especially once your child goes to school. And since Sagittarians are good teachers, you may enjoy being the primary parent in charge of homework now. This is also an easier time for communal playdates with like-minded moms, where you can send the kids off to entertain themselves while you kibbitz over coffee or a glass of wine. You might even cut babysitting costs by hiring a local teen to be your mother's helper for a few hours after school. Or you'll get your child involved in a bunch of activities outside of the house, freeing up some time for yourself.

As you start feeling more like your own person again, this stage could also be when you shed that last bit of baby weight, or get back to your hobbies and goals. You might even love including your child in those activities. While your kids are this impressionable, eager-to-please age, you'll be able to impart your ideas, skills, and values to an enthusiastic audience who hangs on your every word. You might even be surprised by a few empty-nest pangs when your kids go off to school.

The only potential drag may be your new role as chauffeur—for sleepovers, day camp, swimming lessons, and the like. You'll still need to be a lot more structured as a parent than your personality would dictate. This might also be the first time you really feel your age, as you become part of the community within your child's school. Youthful Sagittarius will not go quietly into mom jeans, a shapeless haircut, or a minivan. Nor should you. As a fierce individual, you need to feel like yourself—and during this phase it's all too easy to get absorbed in PTA meetings, class mom duties, and club fundraisers. While you may need to push yourself to be a little more open to this kind of thing, you still need to maintain friendships with those who share common interests. The fact that you've both procreated is not enough to form an enduring bond with another mom. You might just feel like you live in two alternate realities now—mommy world and your world.

Erin, the Sagittarius mom of two and a graphic designer, fiercely missed her hip, downtown San Francisco neighborhood, where many of her friends still lived. "For my kids' sake, I moved out to the burbs," she explains. "It was just too cramped and chaotic to stay in my old area, and the real-estate prices were way out of my budget. So we bought a house forty minutes outside the city, and I set up a home office. It was ideal for my kids, but I started to feel trapped in soccer mom hell. Even though the other parents were cool, I really missed my old life."

To remedy this, Erin decided to move her office back to her old Bay Area hood, renting a small studio apartment with another freelancer. "We installed a Murphy bed in case either of us want to crash there," she says. "Now I go in to work a couple times a week, and I stay overnight by myself once or twice a month. I'll see a live show, have dinner with friends, or get dressed up for a fun event. It's the closest thing to the best of both worlds I can get. And my husband knows that I'm a much nicer, happier person if he supports me with this!"

ADOLESCENCE AND TEENS (TWELVE TO EIGHTEEN YEARS)

Turbulence ahead! As your child begins to pull away and take wobbly steps toward becoming his own person, it's tough for you to relax. You're well aware of the ass-backward choices a tween can make without proper guidance and supervision. Yet you also know you can't exactly helicopter around, snooping on your daughter's phone for text messages or forcing your former chatterbox son (now morphed into a mute creature) to recount the day's events on demand.

In some ways, this phase can be as exhausting as toddlerhood, because your child will swing from needy one second to assertive the next. This is a phase of early boundary testing as your child takes the first steps toward independence, then scuttles back to the safety zone with almost babyish behaviors.

As blunt as Sagittarians can be, you're also quite sensitive. It's easy to take the separation process here personally, feeling rejected or irritated by the know-it-all remarks and moody spells that start on the cusp of puberty. You may need to take lots of deep breaths before you engage in a battle of wits with this unarmed person. Set a few clear boundaries and stick to them. Remind yourself again that discipline and rules—in proper amounts—actually make your child feel safe and loved.

Psychologists find that tweens crave both freedom and adult support. It's a great time to bring other adult role models into their lives, like an aunt or uncle, a tutor, even an after-school mentor like a sports coach or a music teacher. Good news, Sagittarius: you don't have to do it all yourself—nor should you! Rather, your job is to curate a council of wise adults who can expose your tween to enriching new experiences and values.

This impressionable age, as your kid transitions from childhood to adulthood, is a great time to employ your Sagittarian wisdom. Kids become mini-philosophers now, asking all kinds of identity questions, seeking to apply more sophisticated moral and ethical reasoning behind their choices and actions. Rather than grow stern and rigid, open dialogue with your tween. You can teach critical thinking and cultural and media literacy, fostering a thoughtfulness that will carry them into adulthood. Rather than preach hard-core values when your daughter wants to start posting suggestive pictures on social media or your son reveals that a classmate is smoking, delve into your kid's psyche through conversation. Use the Socratic method: ask a series of leading questions that helps your child "find" the answers himself. This is excellent groundwork for the teen years, too, and it develops inner strength as your child discovers his own moral compass under your guidance. After all, you don't want your kid to become a sheep who buckles to peer pressure!

The tough truth: if you don't talk to your kids about what they're seeing and experiencing, they'll get their information elsewhere—the Internet, friends, uninformed sources. While you can't shield them from everything or preserve their so-called innocence, you can ensure that they emerge from adolescence savvy and self-aware rather than having lost their voices and identities. Your Sagittarian honesty is an asset and will help you to gain your child's trust, especially since her b.s. detector is especially strong now. Teach skepticism in its truest form: a questioning attitude toward things generally accepted at face value. No need for cynicism to have a role here.

When your child becomes a full-fledged teenager, you get the freedom you've been dreaming of all along. So why do you feel so sad? Some Sagittarius moms could feel like you're losing your best buddy as your teenager gravitates toward friends, after-school activities, or the no-trespassing zone of her bedroom. To your own surprise, you may miss the rootedness of being needed—just as you'd gotten used to it!

Fear not, though. There will be plenty of moments when your teenager reverts into needy mode, pressing you into service for pickups and drop-offs, help with research papers, and yes, even emotional guidance in a crisis. And if you are best friends, it may happen a little too often for your liking. This is a time when your child needs to separate. If she's still clinging to you, it may be an indication that you're not cutting the cord, which could be stunting her emotional and psychological development.

The teenage years can be confusing both for you and your child. On the one hand, you've got a shockingly mature person now living with you, who seems wise beyond his years and possesses incredible insight. Because Sagittarians remain youthful (and are often pop-culture junkies), you might even watch the same TV programs, share books and magazines, and enjoy some of the same activities.

However, you have to be careful not to let your teen get *too* comfortable with your hipness. Watching the same reality shows, shopping in the same stores, or trading music downloads might be fine. Draw the line at asking for love advice, exposing them to your own personal life dramas, or saddling them with excess responsibilities (such as babysitting younger siblings). It's important to keep a balance of being relatable *and* a capable authority figure.

This can be a tricky line for the Sagittarius mom to walk, especially since you hate being too much of a disciplinarian. You've never been a fan of the word *no*, and you remember how important experiences were in your own youth. Chances are you still love a wild night on the town yourself, but you might need to be a little more vigilant about what you let your teenagers see. If you curse like a sailor, as many Sagittarians do, don't be surprised if your teenager's dialogue becomes laced with f-bombs. The whole "do as I say, not as I do" thing won't fly now.

Yes, Sagittarius moms respect the power of rebellion to an extent. You'd rather raise a fiercely independent freethinker than a follower. At the same time, you get what you get (see our kid chapters for more on that), so the trick is to be a loving but firm guide without encroaching on their individual rights. It's a tough line, with the lure of drinking, drugs, body image pressures, and all the horror stories of bad teen judgment gone tragically askew.

The teenage brain isn't fully developed—in fact, its self-regulating parts are the last to mature. Thus, kids this age actually need a lot more sensation to feel the same amount or pleasure that an adult does. In the meantime, you need to fill in the gaps, providing help with planning, organizing, limit setting, and moral reasoning. (Not all of these are your strong suits, so if need be, call in the reinforcements!)

This is a time when a clear no and yes makes an important difference, no matter how much your teen doth protest. You're not limiting your kid's freedom with every no, but in some cases, it's fine if you are. Bolster your efforts with positive reinforcement, as your teen does still desperately crave your approval (even if he doesn't show it). One of our favorite books is called *What Shamu Taught Me About Life, Love, and Marriage* by Amy Sutherland. The author studied animal trainers and noticed that they didn't get the animals to obey by nagging, punishing, or focusing on disobedience. Rather, they rewarded the positive behaviors each time. She decided that if it worked for animals, it might with her resistant husband—and indeed it did. We suggest it for the Sagittarius mother of a teen, too.

Sutherland also tried "least-reinforcing scenario," a Sea World technique whereby rather than freaking out at each infraction, a trainer remains coolly nonreactive. So if your teen shouts "I hate you!" or "You never listen to me!" you simply ignore him or stare blankly while going about what you're already doing. The bad behavior subsides; the rage dissipates when there's nobody to brawl with. It's a more subtle way of letting your kid know that his behavior isn't okay, without getting hooked into a blowout fight. Apparently, it works.

It's also better than getting all preachy, which your lecture-loving sign can resort to at moments. Remember, teens are stunningly sensitive, and tough love can wound them. When your daughter comes to you crying about a friendship rift, your first response might be, "You don't need those girls anyhow" or "You're better than them, so forget about them." But she might just need a hug instead. Give her time to process her emotions and try the mirroring technique, whereby you acknowledge and reflect back her feelings. That way, you give her the safety of knowing that her feelings are legitimate while also training her to trust herself.

If you have a negative, self-doubting, or "dark" kid, you may want to let a mentor or another adult to take your child under her wing. Your sunny, optimistic outlook may not save the day here. While you have faith in your own tremendous abilities to pull through any challenge, if your child might better relate to someone else, then it's best to employ those human resources.

Don't worry about "invading" their space too much. Mandatory family time, including activities you can all do together (like volunteer work, especially involving travel), is an important way to bond with your teenager—and also a good way to ensure that your influence remains strong. You appreciate dialogue, and during these together times—say, on a beautiful hike or while building a Habitat for Humanity home—you may have moments in which your child really opens up to you. Be present and available when the opportunity arises, and share the best of your Sagittarius wisdom.

BYE-BYE, BIRDIE: LEAVING THE NEST (EIGHTEEN-PLUS YEARS)

Switcheroo! For once, it's your kids packing their bags instead of you. The shoe's on the other foot, and it's a strange sensation indeed. By now, a good amount of your identity may revolve around your role as a mom. While you may not ever have an empty nest—you've got too much going on for that—it will be an eerily quieter one.

Now is your time to travel, to dive deep into your "lifelong learner" mode and fill the space with experiences and exploration. You might even enroll in a few classes ("matriculating matriarch" has a ring to it), start a business, or take special interest in what your children are studying at college. And your role as advice giver will be much more appreciated now, as your child begins to navigate the real world.

On the upside, you may now become the cool mom whose wisecracks and easy laughter no longer embarrass your kid. You'll probably talk regularly and see each other often. Your eternally youthful mind-set will be appreciated now, and you may resume best-friend status. Our friend's fiftysomething Sagittarius mother, a wholesome type with a mischievous streak, called her to announce that she's discovered thongs . . . and was wearing one as they spoke! Another friend's Sagittarius mom took off on a pilgrimage to Indian ashrams when her sons started college, and later adopted a new Sanskrit name.

There's a chance you might even work on a family business with your kid, collaborating on a profitable project that employs both of your talents. You're deeply invested in their self-sufficiency now and will do anything to encourage it. This is the time when they're discovering their dreams—or should be, in your book—and you want to cheer them on loudly.

THE CAPRICORN MOM

(December 22–January 19)

MOMMY MAGIC - Your Strengths:

- Planning
- Structure
- Traditional values
- Consistency
- Patience
- Thoughtfulness

MAMA MIA - Your Challenges:

- Worry and anxiety
- Overly dutiful or cautious
- Pessimism
- Self-doubt
- Seriousness to a fault

FAMOUS CAPRICORN MAMAS:

Christy Turlington Burns, Michelle Obama, Kate Moss, Amanda Peet, Annie Lennox, Kyle Richards, Tina Knowles, Katie Couric, Kate Middleton, Sienna Miller, Shonda Rhimes, Diane Keaton, Kristin Cavallari

YOUR PARENTING STYLE

*

Who's your daddy, er, mommy? Since Capricorn is the zodiac's "father" sign, this adds an interesting twist to your mothering style. In stereotypical terms, you may be more of the dad than the mom—or both parents rolled into one. Not that you don't have a sentimental or feminine side, but Capricorn's ruling planet is Saturn, the stern taskmaster associated with authority, masculinity, and structure. You're not afraid to set limits or to teach your kids necessary life lessons. You'd like to be close to your children, but you don't need to be best friends. Hierarchy based on age is fine with you. As a traditional sign, you respect your own parents (even if you don't like them) and may be quietly conventional. In fact, you may have wed young—perhaps a reason many Capricorn women have two or three marriages.

As the sign of the Goat, Capricorn slowly and steadily ascends life's rockiest hills. You may stumble or face setbacks, but you never quit. If you have a child with special needs, for example, you'll stand steadfastly by him. Or you'll preemptively hire a tutor long before standardized testing season to ensure that your child is academically prepared. Capricorn is a master strategist who's always thinking ten steps ahead. If need be, you'll put practical considerations over emotional ones, forgoing pricey Disneyland trips so you can finance private school tuition. As Capricorn Dolly Parton once said, "If you want the rainbow, you gotta put up with the rain."

Capricorn is the sign of public image. Reputation matters to you. You're not just a mother; you're also a twenty-four-hour representative of your family, and you take this job seriously. Admit it or not, you don't want to be "just another mom," and this concern carries into your style, speech, and demeanor. With your earthy, everyday elegance, you exude effortless cool and chic. Cue Capricorn mom Kate Moss and her Topshop line or Michelle Obama, who became an inadvertent style icon in J.Crew. The Capricorn mom is selective, putting thought (sometimes too much) into everything she does. Yet you manage to make it all look *so* easy. That's the Capricorn mama's magic: you know how to edit and prioritize. You revel in the art of simplicity. And when you don't have the energy to put on a show, you don't. Other moms will appreciate your refreshingly down-to-earth ways. Dressed up or dressed down, the Capricorn mama keeps it real . . . and manages to stand out by seeming both approachable and a little untouchable all at once.

Capricorn's fourth house of motherhood is ruled by Aries, so this gives you a bold, badass streak of independence. Like neon lining in a pinstripe suit, you have a quirky side that peeks out when your guard is down. Since Aries is the solo sign, you also need "me time," even if you spend it training for a 5K, surfing, or cheering courtside at an NBA basketball game. Similar to your sign, Aries has a strong masculine (even macho) influence. You might be the mom who picks up her kid in a shiny convertible sports car (rocking aviators and a leather jacket)—or on the back of a Harley. Our childhood friend's mom Jackie, a Capricorn, tooled around town in a blue Corvette, rocking sexy Jordache jeans and frosted hair (it was the 1970s). Still stunning at seventy years old, Jackie remarried recently; she and her husband spend free time riding motorcycles. Capricorns are said to age in reverse, becoming more lighthearted after age thirty-five or forty. Buh-bye Grandma, hello glam-ma!

Under the competitive, Aries-driven influence, you do have alpha mom tendencies mixed in with your hardworking and homespun ways. You might quietly size up other families, wanting yours to be at the top of the food chain. You'll encourage your kids to hang out with children from "good" homes, or to succeed in sports, academics, whatever their passion. It may sound elitist, but you're well aware that success depends on who you know, so you might as well start guiding 'em that way young. There might even be a "mom-ager" in you, like Capricorn Tina Knowles. She helped steer daughter Beyoncé's music career, sending her on auditions at age eight and later designing costumes for Destiny's Child.

The combination of the Aries and Capricorn influences can make you a tough-love type of mom who delivers stern lectures and stiff hugs. You might not be the most touchy-feely person, either, preferring to show your devotion through your actions rather than affection. How this plays out depends a lot on your own upbringing. Capricorns tend to be "old souls" who play the dutiful soldier in their families, keeping a lot of their emotions inside. Your own childhood may have been colored by hard experiences or hefty responsibility placed on your small shoulders (perhaps self-imposed, as many Cap kids are overachievers). Or maybe your parents worked hard to provide for your needs. Now you feel a deep obligation to repay them by succeeding.

Your own mother may have been a strong personality, too, which can fuel your ambition. If you two were close, then you may regard your mom as an iconic figure and strive to follow in her determined footsteps. Or perhaps she was critical, demanding more of you than your siblings. One Capricorn mom remembers feeling mortified by her over-the-top mother, who would dress in fake furs and garish costume jewelry, talking in a booming voice about inappropriate topics. This conservative Cappy vowed never to embarrass her own daughter, but as a result she kept her child at arm's length and missed out on mother-daughter bonding.

Either way, the notion of a fun, carefree childhood can be foreign to some Capricorns, since you probably didn't have one. You might overcompensate for this by making sure your kids never feel lack. Or you'll pass along your dutiful work ethic, stressing the importance of paying dues. You might be the mom whose sentences begin with, "When *I* was your age, we had to [insert unfair, child-labor-law-violating experience here]." Even if you spoil your kids, you won't hesitate to pull the bootstrapper card if they take their privileges for granted.

There's a "steel magnolia" in every Capricorn mom. Like Katie Couric and Michelle Obama, you exude feminine beauty layered over deep reserves of strength. You're the rock of your clan, the force that holds everything together through thick and thin. It was Capricorn Donna Summer who sang "She Works Hard for the Money," and that's certainly true for you. Capricorn is the zodiac's provider sign, and with your solid work ethic you could be the family breadwinner. Or you'll make sure to marry well, choosing a partner who brings home a solid paycheck while you raise the kids. Sure, it might sound old school, but the Capricorn mama does what this line of duty demands—even eschewing her career if it's best for her dynasty, er, family.

While you work hard to hold it all together,

many Capricorn moms struggle with a deep reserve of self-doubt. Your fear of making a mistake can be crippling at times. You may not show this to the world, but it can surface as a heavy demeanor, a serious facial expression, an energetic sigh from out of nowhere. If you had an animal totem it would be Eeyore, the sweet but melancholy donkey and friend of Pooh.

Although your planning skills are unparalleled, Capricorn moms need to learn how to live in the present. With your workaholic ways, you could easily end up being too focused on tasks to experience the joys. Escape from your obligations whenever possible so you don't miss your little one's fleeting moments of cuteness. Pay attention when people tell you that "it goes by so fast." They're not kidding.

Bottom line: you can be seriously hard on yourself, Capricorn. When you get into this mode, chances are you're approaching burnout from taking on too much. You need to lighten up and unburden yourself. Nobody ever won a medal for working herself to death! So follow the Pareto principle—also known as the 80/20 rule. Commit to setting aside at least 20 percent of your time for personal care and family bonding and spending the other 80 percent on your responsibilities. Your ruling planet Saturn rewards you for patience and persistence, so when you find yourself being too goal-oriented—in your parenting and elsewhere—pause and bring yourself back into the present. Remind yourself that everything works out eventually, and let divine timing take its course.

IF YOU HAVE A GIRL

*

PROS

You're a consummate role model, pushing your daughter to develop her talents and strive for high achievements. A hard worker, you will raise a tough cookie who's both book smart *and* street smart. You're a patient teacher who takes the time to thoughtfully explain everything to your girl. If you have a particular skill and own a business, you might even pass your talent along. You certainly lead by example when it comes to teaching her persistence and determination.

With your ability to take the long view, you can keep your daughter from getting mired in mean-girl drama, reminding her of the big world that awaits her if she keeps her eyes on the prize. Capricorn moms know that life begins after high school (it did for you), and you'll encourage your daughter to be confident and proud of her individuality from a young age. When she falls apart, you're strong enough to be her rock. You don't react to her every up and down like some parents. You may come across as a little unsympathetic, but you know how to be the adult, which instills a strong sense of security in her.

CONS

Got an issue? Here's a tissue. The Capricorn mom isn't always the most sympathetic when her daughter is upset. Since you tend to keep a stiff upper lip or hide your feelings, you may not be able to teach your daughter emotional literacy. As a result of your stoicism, she might even act out, displaying the very emotions you've always suppressed. With your tendency to dole out tough love in a crisis, she might feel you don't understand her. Things aren't always so black and white, Mama. Although your intention is to problem-solve and make things all better, you need to validate her feelings before jumping into strategist mode. Hug it out, Capricorn. Remember, you're talking to a kid, not running a Fortune 500 board meeting!

If your daughter is a tomboy, an athlete, or more academically inclined, it might be easier for you to relate to her. A girlie girl could have you at a loss. "I taught my mom more about how to be a woman than she taught me," says one Capricorn's adult daughter. Let yourself show "weakness" (i.e., be human) when you can. Being vulnerable has other benefits. When you deny your feelings or stay in unhappy situations out of duty, you can plummet into burnout and even depression. Remind yourself that moods are contagious (it's been proven) and that your own worrisome energy can filter down to your daughter. You are, after all, her primary role model. Strive for greater work-life balance—for your own sake and for your daughter's.

IF YOU HAVE A BOY

*

PROS

Since Capricorn is the zodiac's masculine sign, boys are much easier for you than girls. You can be straightforward and direct without worrying about hurting their feelings (gender stereotypes be damned). Since you're off the hook as their primary role model, you don't have to burden yourself with such a heavy sense of responsibility. You're freer to be playful and affectionate with your son as a result. "My mom is definitely closer with my brother," says one Capricorn's daughter. "She's like a totally different person with him in some ways."

While you might spoil your son, you still encourage him to achieve. You're more of a coach than a cheerleader, always teaching him life lessons and pushing him to learn self-sufficiency. Since you tend to "think like a man" in many ways, you can probably relate personally to some of his boyish ways. You might even be sporty and active, so if your son is athletic, you'll be there cheering at every game. Even if you have zero interest in his video games, drum kit, or other boy accouterments, you'll respect the boundaries of his man cave, giving him the guy time that he needs.

CONS

The Capricorn mom is a great provider, but could you be breeding a future slacker? You're so capable that you might do *too* much for your son, preventing him from developing survival skills. When you catch yourself saying "I'll just do it," pause for the cause, girl. Use your Capricorn long-term planning skills and remember that if you enable him today, you may leave him less capable to thrive in the real world tomorrow.

Mood alert! When you dip into a melancholy spell (often as a result of worry or burnout), you might accidentally transfer those feelings onto your son. Or he may get the sense that women are generally unhappy—especially if he tries unsuccessfully to cheer you up. This can weave a tangled, codependent web that gets complicated for you both. Watch your demeanor around his father or other key male role models, too. Because you tend to be headstrong and set in your ways, you can sometimes veer into an emasculating tone. You might put some men up on a pedestal and demonize others, making your son feel constantly at risk of losing your approval. Catch yourself when you're about to fire off a critical or belittling comment, and try to make simple and straightforward requests.

PARENTING THROUGH AGES AND STAGES

INFANCY (THE FIRST YEAR)

Earth mama to the rescue! Your calm, unassuming energy is especially grounding to a newborn. The Capricorn mother has a soothing aura that babies adore—and with that, you've won 90 percent of the battle. Even if you feel anxious and topsy-turvy on the inside, your physical presence is never manic. You're steady and deliberate, an anchor for this new life you've introduced to the world. The trendy "slow" movement (slow food, slow living, slow travel, etc.) might be a rising societal response to our fast-paced world, but to Capricorn this is just the way life should be. Slow parenting, anyone?

The regimented Capricorn mom takes a structured and pragmatic approach to new motherhood. You'll aim to get your child on a schedule as fast as you can. It might take a few months before you're ready to wean or sleep train, but once you do you manage to be disciplined about it. "I was on the floor bawling the first night," recalls one Capricorn mother who tried a cry-it-out video series with her young son. "It felt like he was screaming for hours and

I was the worst mother in the world. But by the third night, he went right to sleep."

Your ability to be present but also think long term is a saving grace, too. When nothing but mama's embrace will do, you provide physical comfort to your baby. Yet you also understand that building skills, such as learning to self-soothe, is important for development. Although you're known to make your own rules, you're also not shy about following the time-tested techniques. Pass the *What to Expect* manual, please!

Fortunately, you're a creature of habit—and a patient one. You don't mind the repetitive rocking, nursing, and shushing—although your inner taskmaster *would* like to get a few more things done on any given day. The Baby-Björn might become your new best friend, allowing you to do laundry, grocery shop, and cook as your baby snoozes on your chest. Fresh air and sunshine are also classic cures for any baby blues. As an earth sign, having your feet on the ground is a natural antidepressant. Slip on your favorite comfy jeans, flats, and a T-shirt, and take walks as often as you can. Like Capricorn mom Sienna Miller, you manage to look glamorous grabbing coffee with the baby or strolling the farmers' market, sporting boho-chic basics and a freshly scrubbed look.

One thing you'll enjoy is having the attention shift from you (all those annoying strangers trying to touch your belly—ugh!) and onto your child. Reserved Capricorns like to control their public image, and you're *no*t fond of being fawned over. Not that you'll be all for it with your baby, either. You tend to be private and protective. You won't post every milestone on social media or even a ton of pictures. Of course, you might keep a little notebook charting the baby's progress or a baby blog, but it will be password-protected and shared selectively.

Sensible Cap moms can definitely get into the "green" lifestyle, setting up an air filter in the nursery, using chlorine-free nappies 'n' wipes, even choosing a crib made from untreated beech or oak. You might even make sure the wood was sourced from a conscious company that replants every tree it cuts down. Your local breast-feeding advocacy group could even find an unlikely member in you, once you've read an incendiary article about the conspiracy of formula makers or the long-term benefits of breast-feeding. Once you switch to solids, you might pick only organic greens or sweet potatoes to puree your own baby food.

Sleepless nights? Mounds of onesies to wash? You won't catch the dutiful Capricorn mom complaining. You're well aware that you signed up for this job, so you'll soldier through first-year trials with a gritty "it is what it is" realism. You made your bassinet, so you'll lie in it. Sure, you might sigh when asked how motherhood is treating you—especially when the person expects a rainbow-bright response like "Pure heaven!" You're not gonna lie about it. However, you will never lapse into melodrama (weeping "Pure hell!"), either. As with everything, you'll give a measured, witty little summary, "Well, my left breast is demanding a paycheck and overtime wages. But on the bright side, the baby gained two pounds at his last checkup!"

Speaking of paychecks, you might miss yours now, especially if you've taken maternity leave. In fact, you might have a small identity crisis, since many Capricorns define themselves by what they do for a living. Even if you don't, your profession is the pillar that you organize the rest of your life around. The shift away from that can be jarring. Since being a workaholic is a top Capricorn vice, quitting cold turkey isn't always the best way to break your productivity addiction. You might even continue to work remotely a few hours a week. Look for something part-time, or even take on a virtual assistant type of position, which allows you to set your own hours. Since your maternal instinct might take a little while to kick in, this can help with the transition.

Other Capricorns welcome the built-in excuse to ditch their nine-to-five lifestyle, should they have the luxury (not that motherhood isn't a round-the-clock job and the world's biggest source of unpaid laborers . . . but we'll save that conversation for sociology class). "I was working full-time as a buyer at Barney's, and it was really hard to give that up," recalls Margaret, a Capricorn mom who left her swanky post after giving birth. "It was a prestigious position and I really didn't want to lose it. Plus, I genuinely enjoyed my job. I loved the people I got to work with, and I loved making my own money. It gave me a sense of purpose, and it was a big part of my identity. But it didn't make sense to go part-time and spend my whole check on day care." Your sensible sign will generally let practical considerations trump your desire to keep a Louboutin firmly on the corporate ladder.

Just be aware that once you get out of the habit of clocking in, it's harder for your sign to return to the workforce, as you tend to create a routine more easily than most signs. It's always good for the Capricorn mom to keep some post of responsibility, even if it's being treasurer of the PTA or doing the family's monthly bookkeeping.

Stability and certainty are important to Capricorns, and with the inevitable curveballs that come with this phase even the most prepared mother will be challenged. If you're a rigid or perfectionist type—as many Caps are—you may have a few dark days until you learn to relax. Since your ruler Saturn can be stern and disapproving, you might lack confidence or be especially hard on yourself. Find sources of encouragement that you're doing a good enough job.

Capricorns fear making mistakes, so you need constant reminders that at this phase, all parents make massive and frequent screwups. It's okay to fall off your carefully orchestrated routine, especially if the baby is happier that way. One Capricorn mom shared how she wanted to breast-feed, eagerly reading up on the health benefits. A few weeks in, she got a painful case of thrush and needed to switch to formula. "I felt like a failure at first," she recalls. "I'd set my mind on how it was going to go, and I hadn't even imagined another option.

I was caught unprepared, and I really hate that. When I had to give my daughter formula, I beat myself up, freaking out that I was going to cause all kinds of health issues for her. Now that she's older and perfectly healthy, I can look back and see how hard I was on myself. I wasted *so* much energy stressing like that, and it took away some of my enjoyment of the new mom experience."

When possible, try not to turn everything into a judgment of yourself. You're not being graded, there's no report card—and no, the percentile growth charts at the doctor's visits are *not* a commentary on your parenting. Your child will be fine if she doesn't eat much for a day, or misses a nap. Since you have a tendency to worry, that can be exacerbated now, especially if you're a first-time mom who's freaked out about your newborn's fragility. Watch out for OCD tendencies like compulsive hand (or pacifier) washing or making mountains out of molehills. Although you might not want to join that mom circle, the benefits of membership can make all the difference as you relax into the support of people who can relate.

A surefire sign that you're heading into anxiety-ville is when you lose your trademark sense of wry humor. If you can't even muster a flippant or sarcastic remark, that means you can no longer see the divine comedy of life, and it's time for an intervention—or a break! And who better to give you that than your partner, a grandparent, aunt, or close friend? Don't refuse assistance when it's offered, Capricorn, because this is a team effort.

To use a workplace metaphor (since you are of course the COO of your family): if this were a business, you would delegate tasks to your employees and executive team. The company would fail if you tried to do everything yourself, right? You'd expect chaos during the first year. You would establish a corporate structure, but you'd also let natural trends emerge and allow for change. You might even expect to invest more than you get back in the beginning. Apply the same rules to Motherhood, Inc. and your "start-up" will soon become a thriving venture.

TODDLERHOOD (TWO TO FIVE YEARS)

Welcome to the age of unpredictability, Capricorn. If you thought life with an infant was manic, fasten your seat belt. It might seem like the only thing constant in your life is change. Whether you're chasing your now-upright child through the playground, reciting ABC drills or potty training, there's a lot to manage. Just as you get into one groove, a whole new developmental milestone comes along, demanding that you adapt *again*. No rest for the weary!

Admittedly, this might not be your favorite age, for the sheer exhaustion alone. However, it's a humbling one that forces you to squarely face your own humanity. As Capricorn mother Annie Lennox once said, "Motherhood was the great equalizer for me: I started to identify with everybody."

There's a silver lining to that, as

achievement-driven Capricorns might learn for the first time that life isn't a race or a competition. You tend to judge others (and yourself) on performance. Now you may silently rue the days you rolled your eyes at the struggling mom at the grocery store checkout or sniped about an uncontrollable toddler on your flight. Thought you could do it better? Yikes . . . maybe not.

All the same, your flair for structure will come in handy now. Toddlers thrive on a routine, and once you establish a simple rhythm, this phase will get much easier. "When we go out to eat, we have a system," says Donna, the Capricorn mother of two young kids. "We rotate their toys or whatever they're playing with every twenty minutes so they don't get bored and restless. So if we're out for an hour, I bring along three things for each child." Talk about efficient!

Smart strategies like these are the Capricorn mom's forte. You like rules and enjoy some of the "obedience training" of this phase. Just remember to follow the spirit of the law, not the letter. You may not stick to your nightly sequence perfectly—baths might be skipped here and there, or your child will eat dinner in front of a movie instead of at the table. Be flexible within these guidelines, and it will all be fine.

Pamela, who ran a four-diamond-rated B&B with her first husband and worked in the hospitality industry, says her strong customer service background influences the way she communicates with her daughter, Elle. "I read a book that suggested verbally narrating everything you're doing—like 'I'm changing your diaper now' or 'Mommy's going to take some relaxing time now'—even when your child is an infant," she shares. "It felt unnatural at first, but over time it gave my daughter a lot of security because she understood the how and the why of life. Now at four, she's really gracious and tuned into people's emotional needs."

Capricorns like to stay ten steps ahead and plan for the future. You may have been first in line on the preschool waiting list, for example. One savvy Capricorn business owner donated to a private school's silent auction for years. When she became a mom, her kids were a shoo-in with that school's admission board. You'll do what you have to do to secure a great future for your progeny.

Even with the best of advanced planning, though, the staggering amount of decisions to be made now can be overwhelming to many Capricorns. You don't do well when life gets overcomplicated. Paper or plastic, breast or bottle, yes or no—your bottom-line sign wants clear options and direct answers. You might now decide to simplify your lifestyle, moving to an area with great public schools, or relocating to be near your parents (who may already live close by).

While stay-at-home mom probably never topped the list of your childhood dreams, you might discover you're really good at it once you get your sea legs—damn good, in fact. You'll find plenty of opportunities to apply your managerial talents to parenting, and you'll also learn how to go with the flow, something that may be a whole new (and rewarding) experience for your driven sign. "My second husband offered to support me financially, which was really scary, since I have a strong professional background," says Pamela. "Once I accepted, I didn't look back. Ironically, I had a hard time getting pregnant and couldn't understand why—I'd always followed the formula of doing my homework, trying hard, and getting the result I wanted. I had to learn how to surrender and trust, which was a great setup for motherhood."

If you're the type who likes to plan and control things, remembering to stay in the moment can be a challenge during this phase. Your toddler's needs are very immediate, but your mind may drift from Elmo stories and patty-cake games to wondering if you need to run and restock wipes for the nanny. One Capricorn mom even confessed that she hated the playground and secretly felt like it was a "waste of time" to just "sit there and do nothing" while her toddler ran around. You're not always the most social person—at least not immediately—so breaking the ice with other moms can be awkward. Once you get to talking, however, you could soon become the unofficial mayor among the moms you see regularly. Hello, Chatty Cathy!

Publicly disciplining your kid can also bring up self-consciousness. Capricorn mom Stephanie recalls a particularly rambunctious summer when her son was four. "I asked him to get out of the swimming pool," she says. "He looked me in the eye and said, 'What are you gonna do to me if I don't?'" Not wanting to make a scene, she backed down. Toddler: 1. Mama: 0.

"My daughter would do these things to act out and I would crack up. She needed to have three pacifiers at all times and would have a tantrum if she dropped one. I laughed through a lot of it," recalls Capricorn mom Margaret. "But I cried through a lot of it, too. Living in New York, I would get embarrassed waiting in line while she was screaming bloody murder and people were rolling their eyes. That's why she had a pacifier in the first place."

The Capricorn mom is supportive of her kid's individuality, and you like when your children are expressive or have a little edge. Privately, you might even find their antics hilarious. Usually, any embarrassment you might feel is rooted in fear of being judged as inadequate, so lighten up those supermom standards. A solid support system can help, so you can trade tips and know you're not alone. Push yourself out of your comfort zone and strike up a conversation at the park, or make a family playdate with one of your child's preschool classmates. You need to be proactive now.

Making time for social events can be another challenge, especially since you may very likely be back at work full swing now. Your partner might take on more of the domestic and child-rearing duties, particularly if you're the breadwinner. We know several Capricorn women who own a business with their spouse, which can make certain things easier (one of you is usually free to pick up the kid from day care) but other things harder. (Sex life? What sex life?) Usually, the division of parenting duties is based on financial considerations, not emotional ones. Whichever mate has the more solid paycheck and benefits will probably not do the lion's share of parenting.

You may feel some guilt about this, of course, but the worrier in you just can't leave your kid's college fund to chance. Just fill your child's world with playful people. While they can't replace mommy, they can certainly keep your little one happy and entertained while you're bringing home the bacon.

During this busy time, monitor your martyr mom tendencies. Since you drive yourself so hard, you might skip self-care. Mani-pedis, root touch-ups, and drinks with friends might seem like luxuries, but they're not. And if you don't want to spend hours in a salon, go see a live show or do something outdoorsy, even if you have to schedule the time block weeks in advance. Capricorn mom Stephanie is part of a bicycle club; another Capricorn we know is part of a fun women's networking group that meets monthly for cocktails. If you must do business on your time off, at least combine it with pleasure!

Do you need to have more fun now? Yes. Can that feel like hard work for you, Capricorn? Mmm-hmmm. Being a good mom doesn't have to mean going against your no-nonsense nature entirely. However, think of your toddler as your little *sensei*, a wise teacher. When he starts acting out, it's your karmic cue to come back into your body (and out of your head) and into the moment. Remember that whatever bill you're paying or family issue you're fretting about is less important than *being here now.*

EARLY CHILDHOOD (SIX TO ELEVEN YEARS)

Sitting by the window waiting for your kid to come home? Dabbing at tears when summer vacation ends? Maybe for a minute or two. In your home, an empty nest is a busy nest, though, and you'll make productive use of your child's school hours. Getting stuff done makes you a happy Cappy. If you've been itching to get back to work or focus on a business venture, now is the best time.

It's not that you don't cherish family time. You just hate having your attention spread between a million different tasks at once. Now your life is more compartmentalized, which makes it easier to separate work and play. Your newly independent child also has other sources of entertainment—peers, birthday parties, siblings, relatives, books, and video games. As his little universe expands, you no longer have to be the center of it 24/7. There's a tinge of sadness but also relief. Finally—you have time to focus on your own priorities again!

"Sometimes kids have to come first, and sometimes adult relationships do," says Kristi, the Capricorn mom of two. "I've always felt that kids need to learn that they're not always the most important thing going on at any given time. Adults have adult things to do that have nothing to do with the kids. That's why there are babysitters and day cares and schools. And Disney movies."

Not that you're off duty. With homework, school functions, and extracurricular activities like sports or dance class, you could be pressed into service more often than you'd like. You want your child to do well in school and get into a good college, so you'll make every effort to ensure a solid academic performance. There could be some late nights helping with homework, filling out summer camp applications, or practicing drills for a tournament or competition.

Prepare to part with your hard-earned cash now, too, as you balance your dueling desires to be frugal and to keep up with the Joneses. "I felt pressure to spend money on birthday presents because my daughter would get ridiculously expensive gifts from people," remembers Margaret. "I could easily drop a thousand dollars on a birthday party, just because everyone else did. Looking back, I regret spending that much money. I think I was really trying to fit in."

As a traditional sign, you do like to mark important occasions, though—even if you do it on your budget and terms. "I enjoy rituals, like making dinners, birthdays, and holidays meaningful," says Pamela, the Capricorn mom of six. "I'm a planner and I care about marking those milestones. When each kid turned ten, we did some kind of travel experience. My husband took the two boys on an epic hunt. I took the girls on trips and gave them each of them a small Tiffany necklace to commemorate that we see them as individuals and are witnesses to their journey as they grow up."

In fact, your thoughtfulness is an anchor for children this age, especially if you become part of a blended family. Lisa, an interior designer and architect, won her soon-to-be stepkids over by helping each one organize and decorate a room that reflected their personality. She took time and care, making each child feel special.

You understand that respect is a two-way street, and you'll bring that into your disciplinary style. Although you can be tough about your standards and morals, you try to keep an open dialogue with your child. You'd rather patiently explain why something should be done differently than yell or lecture. Perhaps you remember how hard you were on yourself as a child and want to make sure your kid embraces the self-compassion you never had. Just make sure to model this behavior, too, and stop beating yourself up for mistakes.

Since you're selective about your friendships (and loyal to only a chosen few), you may dislike the enforced PTA meetings and fund raising drives. Reserved Capricorns could feel socially awkward at school functions. You're not much of the small talk type. However, once a Capricorn gets yakking, she usually doesn't stop. Alas, deep conversations can be rare in the afterschool pickup lane, so there's a good chance you'll take a "quality over quantity" approach with your friendships now. Besides, you have far more discerning criteria for friendship than "I'm a parent, you're a parent, and our kids go to school together. Let's be friends!"

"I never connected with many of the other moms and dads," says Margaret. "I'd see them at parties and we'd be polite, but it was weird. I was single at the time, too. I remember going out a few times for drinks with other single parents, hoping to connect, but it didn't happen."

Watch out for competitiveness or getting caught in the "compare and despair" trap now. You may quietly size up other families to see how yours measures up—which can spiral into crippling anxiety and self-doubt. Motherhood is a journey, not a competition. Careful with the grade-grubbing, too, and the "one percent" mentality, or you could end up being the reason that the Occupy Wall Street movement began. And as the saying goes, it's lonely at the top—especially for moms. Relax a little and you'll find a supportive community of friends instead.

Don't let everyday overwhelm convince you that you're not a good mother, either. "Sometimes I feel like I'm more self-centered than I wish I was," says Kristi. "I struggle to do more than the bare minimum: make sure they have food, tell them I love them, then go sit by myself in silence and read. I just feel like I'm always going to drop the ball and bum my kids out."

Capricorns know how to be world-class sufferers, but it can often be self-inflicted. When you've lost perspective, you either need community or a good old-fashioned break. If you've stopped working, get involved with a cause you care about, even if that means taking a post at your house of worship or hosting a semiannual solstice party (as one Capricorn mama we know does). If your days feel like an interminable to-do list, add some mandatory pleasure to the regimen, stat! A little acknowledgment goes a long way, too. Grab a sheet of those shiny gold stars from your kid's classroom, and give yourself twenty of them. You're doing the best you can, Capricorn—and you've earned a playful reminder of that, perhaps paired with a nice massage.

ADOLESCENCE AND TEENS (TWELVE TO EIGHTEEN YEARS)

Let's face it: the Capricorn mom doesn't exactly have a PhD in rebellion. There's a strong chance that you were the "good girl" in your family, the one who responsibly did her homework, earned good grades, and even married her high-school sweetheart. If you did revolt, it was probably by packing up your things and leaving a dysfunctional household, one where you felt like your parents' parent. Even the most outwardly badass Capricorn will have some wholesome skeletons in the closet.

Because of this, you might go through a delayed adolescence—one that's unfortunately timed with your child's teenage years. Or you could struggle to parent a "typical teenager," not knowing exactly how to identify with their angst since you never faced your own. "I was fifteen going on forty," recalls one Capricorn mother of her own teen years. Since you're so self-disciplined, you probably didn't require much parenting then, so you won't have a lot of experience with appropriate boundary setting. You may be confused when to hold 'em and when to scold 'em.

"I give my kids a lot of advice and coaching: how to act on a date, how to eat a balanced diet, dining skills," says Capricorn mom Pamela. "But I have to make sure I'm not giving my kids corrective coaching and overwhelming them with that. Sometimes, I catch myself giving them feedback instead of just being with them and letting them feel loved."

Born under the provider sign, you're a solution-oriented strategist. However, you might need to retire from this post now and let your kid struggle to find his own solutions. It could take a while before you stop reacting to your teenager's mood swings, treating his melodramas like a genuine crisis or jumping in for the rescue with a quick-fix solution. This is a great age to build self-sufficiency, something you'll encourage by letting your teen get an after-school job or do chores for allowance. Remember to guide him toward emotional resilience, too, by encouraging him to come up with creative solutions while you act as a sounding board.

A strong-willed child or one who doesn't follow the path you envisioned for her can be difficult for Capricorn moms. You may be tough, but you're not a fighter—especially not with your kids. So if you have a child who needs a lot of attention, warnings, repeated boundary setting and the like, you may just feel resigned and give up.

"Sometimes, it seemed easier not to fight," recalls one Capricorn mother of her headstrong daughter who left home at seventeen and decided against going to college. "I would ask her three times to clean her room, and then when she hadn't I'd just let it go." Nicole, the daughter of a Capricorn, remembers her mom telling her high-school boyfriend to "just spend the night" because it was too late for him to drive home. "When I talked to my mom about it later, she said she'd rather have us here than in the back of a car somewhere," Nicole recalls.

Many Capricorn moms we interviewed emphasized wanting to give their kids what their parents didn't give them: freedom, a chance to go to college, sex education, or rules that feel fair. That's all wonderful, but remember that children also need clear boundaries to feel safe. If you have an obedient kid, setting a few basic rules helps him stay secure, especially if you compliment him for following them. And if you have a difficult teen who likes to push the limits, you might want to read one of the many books on parenting a strong-willed child, such as *Empowered YOUth: A Father and Son's Journey to Conscious Living* by Michael Eisen and Jeffrey Eisen (which is relevant for moms and daughters, too) or *How to Talk So Kids Will Listen & Listen So Kids Will Talk* by Adele Faber and Elaine Mazlish.

One of the suggested techniques in many of these books is to "break the will of the child, not the spirit." In other words, teach your teen to yield to your authority, but do it with respect (no cursing, put-downs, violence, etc.) so that you preserve your kid's right to be an individual. Obviously, this is a skill that takes practice. But if you apply your trademark persistence, you'll prevail. Don't waste time beating yourself up or blaming anyone if your kid gets into trouble. Just get busy acquiring a new set of skills and a solid support system so you'll be prepared if it happens again.

One Capricorn strength is helping her teen feel comfortable in a developing body. Although you have your share of hang-ups, sexuality isn't usually one of them. "I think sex is like food and it's important," says Margaret, the mother of a fifteen-year-old and the owner of a sensuality company called the Lingerie Goddess. "I know my daughter will want to 'eat,' and I want her to know what it's all about." Margaret started leaving books about body image, periods, and puberty around the house. "My daughter was horrified that I was talking about it, but I didn't give up. I knew her resistance was normal, but I told her I wanted her to feel safe asking questions and that this was a very normal part of life."

Recently, Margaret took her daughter to a 5Rhythms class, which is a free-form movement system created in the 1970s. "I was a little nervous because she was the youngest one there," Margaret explains, "and sometimes they do partner dancing that's kind of sensual. I was sitting there as a mom thinking, 'Oh my God, where have I brought her?' But she thanked me later and said, 'At first I was really uncomfortable, but it's building my self-esteem.'"

While it's great to be close with your teen and even friendly, you don't necessarily need to be best friends, especially not if it goes hand in hand with an attempt to reclaim your lost youth. Since Capricorns are said to age in reverse after thirty-five or forty, you might have a full-blown midlife crisis right as your child hits puberty. Perhaps you've sacrificed all your fun and femininity to be a dutiful parent, breadwinner, and provider. Now your inner voice suddenly bellows, "Party time!"

While you're certainly entitled to (finally) honor your repressed desires, just make sure your kids aren't forced to be your audience. "My mom was a teenager when I was a teenager," recalls Nicole of her Capricorn mother, who had divorced a few years earlier. "She was partying a lot, dating a guy, and was practically living with him. She always hung out if my friends were over, and she even tried to go to parties with us. My friends were like, 'Wow, she's the coolest mom ever' and I was like, 'No, it's not cool.'"

The straw that broke the camel's back happened at a high-school football game. "When I was a senior, one of the football players came up to me," remembers Nicole. "I was so blown away that he was about to talk to me. Then he asked me if my *mom* was dating anybody."

Yikes! The transition from martyr to MILF can give everyone whiplash, so if this happens try to find a community of adults to share your experimental phase. "I signed up for a class called Mama Gena's School of Womanly Arts," says Pamela, who gained access to a two-hundred-plus collective of supportive "sister goddesses." Since you tend to suppress your own feminine energy, your own journey into womanhood—feeling your emotions, opening your heart, facing insecurity as you allow others in—could be as tumultuous as a teenager's progress through puberty.

While you can't prevent yourself from having an "awakening" (nor should you), you can monitor the pace of the process. Rather than having such a strict dividing line between work and play, try to integrate more fun into your life. "After my second divorce, I started doing things like mountain biking and eating healthily," says one Capricorn mom. Another began a tradition of regular trips with a couple new girlfriends. Creating rituals to honor your own desires and individuality is especially important during this phase of your life as a mom. Just as your child is becoming a separate person, you need to permit yourself to do the same.

BYE-BYE, BIRDIE: LEAVING THE NEST (EIGHTEEN-PLUS YEARS)

Free to be . . . you and me! Now that your child is out of the house, you can kick up your heels—or at least pick up all those back-burnered projects and dreams. After years as the family workhorse, you have an expanse of unstructured time stretching out in front of you. Unlike some mothers, you won't waste time figuring out how to fill it. One Capricorn mom we know got divorced, went straight back to school, and swapped her "Mrs. degree" for a PhD in medieval studies. (That's *Dr.* Mom to you, thank you very much.) Another sold the family home and relocated halfway across the country—to a lovely condo that she furnished with tasteful *Town & Country*–style furniture. "It's my time now," she says plainly.

Before you tender your resignation, remember that just because your kids look grown up, doesn't mean their emotional development is complete. Sure, they can legally vote, buy cigarettes, or drink beer, but they still need you—at least for a transition period. The good news is they actually start listening to your wise advice now. You might finally hear them say, "Mom, you were right" (music to your ears) or watch them implement your helpful suggestions. "Now that they're older, I love to have coffee and talk with them," says Karen, the Capricorn mom of two young adults. "We go out to dinner or run errands."

At times, you'll need to stop yourself from micromanaging, pushing your kids to choose a solid profession or properly handle their finances. Old habits die hard for Capricorn, especially the urge to play provider. You might tell yourself that your job is complete but then continue to financially or emotionally support your kids well past their prime. "My Capricorn mom babied my brother for years," says one woman. "Until she remarried, she used to fly out to Colorado for a week every year and clean his house. It's probably why he's fifty and never married."

Then again, your focus on money and security can backfire if you emphasize it too much. One Capricorn discovered that her eighteen-year-old daughter, a former cheerleader, was making beaucoup bucks doing lunchtime lap dances at a gentleman's club—using the stripper handle "Envy." Not exactly the fate this successful mama had in mind for her girl. She decided, in practical Capricorn style, that it was better to keep an open dialogue with her daughter than to judge her. "I took it one day at a time," says this mother. "I figured, at a certain point, she'd either get bored, embarrassed, or sick of it." (She was right.) Adds Mom, "Hopefully one day she'll get a job in corporate sales—since she's obviously good at taking money out of people's pockets." Because this Capricorn mama was able to step back and keep a cool head, the once rebellious daughter eventually ended up marrying her high-school boyfriend and starting a family, settling into a stable and traditional lifestyle.

Whether your child's questionable choices are a short-lived phase or the gateway to a series of unfortunate events, there's only so much you can control. "I wish I was the kind of mom who would drag my daughter out of the strip club and lock her up until she changed her ways, but I'm not," says Envy's mom. You're simply too much of a realist. Live and let live is your motto, and you'll keep your judgments to yourself for the most part. You've shepherded your child into adulthood and the rest is up to him. Or, as another Capricorn mom put it, "It gets to a point where you realize that this person is just like any other person that you *didn't* give birth to."

Still, if you had your preference, your kids would follow a more traditional track, giving you something to brag about instead of something to hide. You may secretly blame yourself for anything that goes awry, even when your kids marry and start their own families. Remember that you've done your best and provided them with the basics. Now it's time to shift into an adult-to-adult relationship, passing the torch and letting yourself have some well-deserved fun.

THE AQUARIUS MOM

(January 20–February 18)

MOMMY MAGIC - Your Strengths:

- Youthfulness
- Open-mindedness
- Originality
- Fairness

MAMA MIA - Your Challenges:

- Boundaries
- Turbulence and drama
- Detachment
- Overly permissive tendencies

FAMOUS AQUARIUS MAMAS:

Sheryl Crow, Minnie Driver, Elizabeth Banks, Camilla Alves, Christie Brinkley, Alicia Keys, Denise Richards, Isla Fisher, Sarah Palin, Shakira, Brandy, Farrah Fawcett, Diane Lane

YOUR PARENTING STYLE

What do you get when you mix the girl next door, a rock 'n' roll groupie, a pageant queen, a fembot, and your childhood best friend? Add a couple tattoos, a karate black belt, or at least one unexpected personal skeleton in the closet (a regrettable piercing, a Trekkie membership) and you've got the Aquarius mom—in all her eclectic glory.

The Aquarius mother is a curious character who's impossible to put in a box. You're affectionate yet aloof, stern yet spontaneous, the world's mellowest control freak. You're a unicorn-riding Pollyanna who sings about rainbows and sunbeams; yet you can be the snarkiest cynic on the block. You specialize in organized chaos, and your parenting can be subject to change without notice. Life with an Aquarius mom can range from adventurous to bats**t crazy, but it's never boring. You view your existence as a grand journey, and you want your children to experience a magical utopia for as long as possible—one fashioned from your own vivid imagination.

Your ruling planet is unconventional Uranus, which is associated with emotional detachment, rebellion, and surprises. "Expect the unexpected" could be your mothering motto, at least until you get your bearings. Your temper, moods, and even romantic partners can be subject to change without notice. Aquarians are known for being uncomfortable with intimacy—you're the sign of casual connections and friendship, so you're more at ease belonging to the world, not just one little person. So one of the biggest surprises of motherhood is the depth of emotion it can bring up. You might weep sentimentally one minute, then put on your game face the next, becoming as steely as a basketball coach during the last thirty seconds of playoffs. Hot and cold are your default settings—even if you give the appearance of being easygoing and agreeable. It could take a while before you find an even keel as a mother.

At the same time, your fourth house of motherhood is governed by traditional Taurus. This cocoons your quirky-cool style in practical, earth sign energy—envision a white picket fence built around a VW bus. In fact, your nomadic sign might just crave security and roots for the first time when the kids come. "Being a mom got me out of my head," says Carrie, the Aquarius mom of a two-year-old, who was married in a roller-disco-themed wedding and now lives on a farm in Washington. Suddenly, you could be sharing online about mini-cupcake recipes and chemical-free bath products instead of your latest tequila-soaked girls' nights out. Another Aquarius mom concurs: "Motherhood brought out a conventional side I didn't know I had."

If you get the urge to play the domestic goddess, have fun—but don't abandon your edgy, pre-mom self. Otherwise, your airy sign may quietly resent the dust gathering on your wings, which could lead to a full-on identity crisis. Mia, mom of a three-year-old, takes herself to the movies as prevention. "I need to be a person, too," she says, underscoring the Aquarian desire for a distinct identity. "I was used to having hobbies and doing things alone that were more highbrow and used my analytical mind. Because I wanted to be a 'good mother,' I felt guilty when I was doing that stuff. But I need some kind of escape."

Because you're so independent, many Aquarius women are ambivalent about motherhood, sometimes waiting until their late thirties and early forties to have kids. Others, like Aquarius Christie Brinkley, have kids early and marry more than once. Although you may not be a young mother, you're always a youthful one. You might seem more like the hip older sister or cool aunt than a so-called typical mom. (Your kids will find this thrilling *and* embarrassing over the years!) There won't be any muffin-top jeans and tacky Christmas sweaters in *your* wardrobe.

Since Aquarius is the sign of humanity, you consider every child in the world yours, in a sense. You're the mom who takes in a runaway or whose couch harbors a tearstained teen who is seeking a safe haven. With your inborn sense of social justice, many Aquarians become proud adoptive parents. As Aquarius Oprah Winfrey put it, "Biology is the least of what makes someone a mother," and you no doubt agree. Perhaps that's why Aquarius Mia Farrow adopted eleven of her fifteen(!) children. (She also lived in a separate apartment from then husband Woody Allen during their entire twelve-year relationship—a classic Aquarian move—to maintain her own identity.)

The Aquarius mom champions freedom on a personal level. Long before you became a mother, you were probably touting some kind of social issue or ideal, and you won't stop just because you've had children. Your sign counts among its (child-free) ranks feminist pioneer Betty Friedan, objectivist author Ayn Rand, and civil rights activist Angela Davis. Aquarians are often outspoken women who march to their own beat. This could mean holding ultraliberal values and raising your kids in a bohemian bubble—complete with Waldorf education, lesbian godparents, and a Parisian lifestyle that includes sips of wine and adult conversation. Or, like Aquarian Sarah Palin, your brand of personal liberty might include an NRA membership, five children, and a platform to rail against big government.

The bottom line is that nobody tells you how to think or believe, even if that makes you a walking contradiction. Palin, for example, made history as the second female vice presidential candidate—for a party that often opposes women's rights. A paradox? Yep, that's you. As an air sign, you blow with the wind and follow your impulses . . . wherever they might lead!

At times, your nomadic ways can be destabilizing for your children. While your wild style may have made you a favorite storyteller with the brunch set during your *Sex and the City* years, too much inconsistency can leave your kids feeling scared and without roots. It doesn't help that you're drawn to narcissistic types as partners or friends who are intense and unstable. You can get easily caught up in relationship (or other) drama, which distracts you from your parenting duties.

Aquarius is the sign of friendship, and you certainly have a colorful cast around you. However, now that you're a mom, you might find it's best to filter out a few of the fringier types. If you're a single mom, "Daddy" might be a questionable character (or an anonymous sperm donor), so your child may meet a few father figures through the years. This is yet another part of your life you might need to shield your kids from. "My mom was always unconditionally supportive of me," recalls the daughter of an Aquarius. "Her boyfriends, on the other hand . . . ugh. Don't get me started."

Although you'll probably want to be friends with your child, you might also find it hard to walk the line between BFF and authority figure at times. One minute you can freak out or crack the whip, but the next you're totally laid-back and permissive. Strive to be a bit more predictable whenever possible.

Since Aquarius is the sign of the future, your controlling tendencies emerge when you're uncertain about what's ahead. Sure, you like spontaneity—when it comes in the form of an invitation to the Paris spring runway shows or tickets to a hot music festival. Being caught off guard is another story. You're a secret worrier and your analytical side needs to process everything before you can see the humor or the fun in it. The Aquarius mother is a mommy blogger waiting to happen—so you'll need to connect, interact, and hash things out with your intellectual equals. Only after you've examined a situation from an objective distance can you glean the wisdom and purpose of it, spinning it into a helpful lesson for others.

Of course, being in the moment isn't always easy. The present and the past are not the Aquarius mom's domain, and you can seem downright unsentimental or checked out at times. The remedy? Make sure you maintain a strong individual identity, even after you become a mom. While this is necessary for any mother, it's especially vital for outgoing Aquarius to nurture your youthful and social ways. If you loved going to music festivals, sports games, gallery openings, or on long girls' weekends out of town, then find a way to keep that up. Ditto for your quirky sense of style. Skip the soccer mom look and keep rocking your cool vintage ankle boots, kitty-eared ski hats, and halter maxi-dresses. If you try to be the perfect Happy Homemaker, you'll only want to rebel, and motherhood will feel like a trap. Find the right balance between honoring your individuality and being a source of consistency in your children's lives.

IF YOU HAVE A GIRL

*

PROS

You're eternally (and maternally) youthful, so your daughter gets a friend and a mother in one. You might even be mistaken for sisters! When she needs advice, you won't lie or sugarcoat the truth. The Aquarius mom respects children's intelligence and doesn't talk down to them. A natural teacher, you prefer to foster your daughter's critical thinking skills. You'll expose her to avant-garde ideas mixed with lowbrow quirk—museum classes, tarot cards, volunteering at a pet rescue, tie-dying. You'll encourage her creativity and teach her kindness, especially to animals and the environment.

The Aquarius mom prizes individuality. You'll challenge your daughter to think freely and question everything. Since most Aquarians have a tomboyish streak, you enjoy being active together: biking, skiing, boating, hiking (possibly mixed with girlier stuff like shopping, going out to eat, and watching movies). You're in touch with pop culture and might be considered the "cool" mom among her friends.

Your youthfulness can keep you connected through her difficult and turbulent teen years.

CONS

Earth to Aquarius! When you're preoccupied, you can be downright checked out. Your daughter will sense your anxieties when you get lost in your head, and she may worry when you flip from cool-as-a-cucumber to a bundle of nerves. You tend to repress your feelings, insisting that everything is "fine" when clearly something is bothering you. Then your Water Bearer urn overflows and out pours a tidal wave of stifled emotions. Life jacket, please!

It's great to be friends with your daughter, but you may blur that boundary and expose her to your adult concerns a little too early, even turning her into your coconspirator. Just because she seems like a wise confidante doesn't mean she needs to witness your experimental lifestyle choices or be forced to choose sides when you fight with her other parent (put away that pint-sized TEAM MOM T-shirt, please). In fact, you might sabotage your desire to be lifelong best friends if you're overly controlling or prevent her from becoming her own person. Froufrou alert: Aquarius women aren't always the girliest girls, so if your daughter is more interested in makeup than marathons, you might be out of your league. Delegate the spa dates to a girlie godmother or aunt.

"Boys are so easy. I honestly have no idea what to do with a girl sometimes," confesses Winnie, the Aquarius mom of two older boys and a younger daughter. "The hair, the clothes, the *emotions*—it's a whole new world, and I'm still not sure if I like it. I wasn't your stereotypical girl. Even though I like having fun with clothes and makeup, I'm really not fussy about my appearance. I didn't do the frilly dresses and tea parties that my daughter loves. And when she has a meltdown, I have to stop myself from thinking, 'My boys were *never* like that.' It's not really fair to her—but I can't help comparing." Winnie and her daughter have found some common ground playing tennis together—although she admits that she wooed her daughter into it with the cute tennis skirts. Hey, whatever works!

IF YOU HAVE A BOY

PROS

Whew! News of a Y chromosome can bring great relief to the Aquarius mom, especially if you're the tomboyish or intellectual type. You won't engulf your son or smother him with too much feminine energy, turning him into mommy's little prince (and a future nightmare to the women he'll date). "I don't do girl things, I don't deal with whining, and I don't know what to do with a girl," says Adi, the Aquarius mom of two sons. "I thank God every day I had boys."

With your active lifestyle, you and your son will share many adventures. "I take my son to brunch and we also go into nature and roll around in the dirt," says Aquarius SunHee Grinnell, *Vanity Fair*'s beauty director and an avid runner. "We do high and low." Aquarius is the sign of the future, so you'll also encourage him to focus on his long-term goals and achievements. Since you have a competitive streak, you might start him in sports from an early age. You'll also encourage him to be open-minded and a freethinker, welcoming his friends from all walks of life into your home.

CONS

Laissez-faire mama alert! The Aquarius mother can be way too permissive with a son, falling into the old "boys will be boys" trap and letting him get away with far too much. You don't want a monster on your hands, so be clear about your expectations and goals for him.

If you have a sensitive son, you might either be overly harsh to "toughen him up" or rush in for the save and enable him. Tread lightly on his tender emotions, and try not to tease him when things get too touchy-feely.

Aquarius is the sign of society, and you want your son to fit in among his peers. However, beware trying to mold your kid into Mr. Popularity or forcing him to be a "joiner" if he's an introverted sign. Just because *you* never met a stranger doesn't mean he can't be discerning in his choice of friends. (Heck, you could probably take a cue from him on that front.)

While his friends will adore you—and you them—you may need to back off a little on the buddy system. You might be inclined to adopt his girlfriends into your inner circle, which could irritate your son. One man's Aquarius mom traded daily text messages with his ex-girlfriend for two years after their breakup. Remember, trying to retain your sense of youth by being the hippest mom on the block could be embarrassing for you both. Ix-nay on the family water bong or mother-son smoke breaks, puh-leeze!

PARENTING THROUGH AGES AND STAGES

*

INFANCY (THE FIRST YEAR)

Aquarius is the sign of casual connections and emotional detachment, which doesn't sound much like the makings of maternal instinct. You're calm, cool, and collected . . . until you hold your brand-new baby in your arms, that is. Suddenly you fall madly in love with another human being, and there's no backing out or escaping. It's a whole new world, filled with intimacy and permanence. Your system might just shut down for a temporary upgrade.

Still, nobody is more surprised than you to discover that you're a natural with newborns!

Who would have pegged you as the local baby whisperer? Yet most Aquarians snap to maternal duty like the flap on a well-made onesie. Motherhood brings out a real take-charge side of you. Sure, you may loathe authority, but when you make the rules, watch out! Now that you have your own domain to preside over, you're a whirling dervish of efficiency. "I love the baby phase because I like to handle everything," says Adi, an innovative Aquarius mom who runs her own virtual small business solutions company from home. Using high-tech equipment and a satellite staff, she's found a way to support her family and spend quality time with her sons.

Not that you didn't have your fair share of freak-outs during pregnancy. You're the sign of the future, which can lead to neurotic overpreparing. One Aquarius woman we met—still single and child-free—socks cash into a fund for a night nurse, so that *when and if* she has a child, she can get a good night's sleep for her nine-to-five job. A lot of Aquarians are animal lovers, so you might worry how the pets will get along with the baby—or even feel guilty not paying enough attention to your cat or dog when the new addition arrives. Then there's the baby-proofing, the detoxing of your home, and the endless research on attachment parenting versus Ferberizing. You truly know how to drive yourself mad at times!

While some Aquarius mothers loved their prenatal glow, others were tweaked by the sensation of a babe growing in their bodies. ("I felt like Sigourney Weaver," jokes one Aquarian, who nicknamed her son "Alien" in the last trimester.) Since your sign is prone to anxious self-doubt, you might have secretly worried if you were up for the task. After all, you may have couch-surfed your way through your early twenties (and beyond). Now you're responsible for another human being's life—when you barely want to be in charge of your own! Even Aquarians who are conscientious and competitive employees are known to shed their type A personas the second they clock out.

So welcome to your adjustment period. As you tumble down the mommy rabbit hole, you might need to pause from your usual activities and friendships or even disappear off the social radar. Baby bonding rearranges your molecules forever. Fortunately, holding an infant can really bring you out of your head and into your body—the perfect, humanizing antidote for the Aquarius space cadet. Since your fourth house of motherhood is ruled by sensual Taurus, you'll enjoy the physicality of this infant phase more than you imagine. "I could coo at babies all day long," laughs publishing veteran Kierna Mayo, the Aquarius mom of two. "I'll be the great-grandmother sitting at someone's orphanage just rocking babies."

Since Aquarius is the sign of collaboration, you might feel like the ultimate tag team when you strap on that BabyBjörn and step outside your door. You'll make faces at your baby in the stroller, pointing out all the exciting sights and sounds. Feeling housebound? Call in the troops. You'll get by with a little help from your friends—or rather, a lot of it. Tap into your sign's communal spirit and join a mom group, or find your tribe of fellow mamas however you can. Bonus points if you come from a large or extended family, since for Aquarius, it's all about having that crew of kindred-spirit parents (often coed) who share your ideals and approach. If the community happens to be virtual, it's all the same to your tech-savvy sign. Camaraderie is what counts.

"I went to some classes on cloth diapering and met about thirty moms from a Facebook group," says Carrie, the Aquarius mom of toddler Sylvie from Seattle. "About half are still strongly active, and they're great. I can say anything to them on Facebook and they can say anything back. There are moms on every spectrum and nobody judges each other. It's a true 'momtopia!'"

Since you're keenly attuned to societal injustices, motherhood can bring out your humanitarian side more than ever. While the baby naps, you might stay busy posting about reproductive rights, the unfair banning of women from public breast-feeding, or the release of hazardous toys by overseas manufacturers. On the flip side, you might staunchly refuse to be "that mom" who loses her former identity, sharing more about your career, political opinions, and social pursuits while keeping the parent stuff separate. You'll work hard to prove you're no glassy-eyed "mombie" who hums Elmo ditties to herself and never showers. "Since my son's birth, I've always talked to him as a fellow human being—no baby talk," says Tiffany, an art professor in New York City. "Now that he's two, we have great conversations!"

The Aquarius mother needs to keep some of her old life intact to feel balanced. Yet this might be tricky to pull off now, especially if you've been busy convincing yourself that motherhood wouldn't change you. Like it or not, an entire lifestyle shift is indeed under way. And since you're the sign of radical change, you might swing to the extreme, deciding to change everything at once. Caution: this rip-off-the-bandage approach may have worked for you before, but casting yourself into unfamiliar waters (especially if this is your first child) could leave you feeling depressed and isolated. Not that anybody can stop you once you set your mind to it! Fortunately, you figure it out eventually—even if your old friends begin to tune out after one too many false-alarm meltdowns.

The people-pleasing side of Aquarius can become problematic now, too, especially if you tend to make too many sacrifices for others. You may try to prove that you're a good friend and answer every phone call or let people drop by when you're exhausted. Remind yourself that this phase only lasts a year or so. You're not losing your edge just because you become more selective about whom you spend time with or let a call go to voice mail when you're putting the baby down for a nap. Friends who don't get it—and you may have quite a few of them—need to step to the left. This may be the time when you figure out who your real friends are. Aquarians have a lot of people around who haven't earned that title. Now, for the first time, you need to set limits and know that it's okay to be selective.

Too many radical changes can impact your romantic relationship negatively, too. You may outright neglect your partner due to your deer-in-the-headlights adjustment process—and you might not feel so interested in sex when your old wild-child self has no outlet. You might even resent that your mate has needs when the baby does, too. There could be far too many people demanding your attention, a big change for your intimacy-averse sign. Be on guard for the looming rage monster. The lightning-bolt Aquarian temper can strike fast and do great destruction, so monitor how much resentment you allow to build up. Couple's therapy might be the best postpartum gift you give yourself.

Of course, you can be your own harshest critic, Aquarius. You may be overly accustomed to seeking validation from peers and society, but second-guessing your instincts or seeking approval will send you into a tailspin. Perfectionism has no place in the nursery! "I'm from the school that beats myself up," says one Aquarius. "I feel guilty that I wasn't able to nurse my kids, couldn't stay in my abusive marriage . . . There's a lot of guilt. I'm very emotional and sometimes my biggest challenge is keeping my own emotions inside to be strong for the kids."

As kind as you are to the rest of the world, please spare some compassion for yourself. Instead of throwing a themed first birthday bash (thinking "it'll be fun!"), for example, just do a casual potluck or picnic. If you need an outlet for your nervous energy, buy a jogging stroller and go for a run. Or take a moment to breathe (important for an air sign), bringing yourself back into your body and the present moment.

TODDLERHOOD (TWO TO FIVE YEARS)

Get ready for fun! While other moms might struggle with this phase, you revel in your toddler's accidental naughtiness and boundless curiosity. There's a natural teacher in every Aquarian, and you enjoy being a hands-on parent during this active and malleable stage of your child's life. You're an overgrown kid yourself, so here's your excuse to delve back into the wacky wonderland of childhood, pint-sized companion by your side.

"I love the toddler years—your child is such a sponge, everything is new, and every day you see them grow," says Hannah, an Aquarius marketing consultant. "They don't have strong personalities and don't talk back, so you get all the joy of parenting without any of the difficulties."

As a group-oriented sign, you'll love the endless opportunity to hang with other families during these years, shooting the breeze while your babes waddle around in an enclosed area. Although you'll sidestep the Stepford moms, you're always down for a playdate with hip parents and their little ones. You might even become the chief organizer, hosting creative little gatherings at your home with yummy snacks and clever art projects you find on an obscure crafting blog.

Aquarius rules society, so you're keenly aware that you're raising the next generation of world leaders—even if your future king or queen's first "throne" happens to be the potty. An idealist to the core, you'll expose your impressionable child to carefully selected influences. As Aquarians like to research and learn, you may geek out on cutting-edge techniques in child development. You might dabble in alternative education, immersing your child in a system such as the Waldorf schools—the world's largest independent alternative education movement that's now in sixty countries. Founded by Austrian philosopher Rudolf Steiner in the early twentieth century, children learn curriculum based on three seven-year developmental stages. Waldorf schools have a strong emphasis on creative play and on fostering critical thinking—many even have a strict no-television policy. While *you* might never be able to forgo your favorite HBO miniseries, ensconcing your child's creative spirit in this kind of a bubble appeals to your idealistic side.

During this phase, your surrounding community becomes of special importance, and you want to make sure it's stocked with everything that matters to you. Our Aquarius cousin raised her two daughters on an Israeli kibbutz for years, where they lived in a communal setting based on socialist principles. One nature-loving Aquarius friend fled the city to raise her children on a farm among goats and chickens. Another chic urbanite poured her nest egg into a Brooklyn brownstone; her handy husband gut-renovated it into a dream home for their family of three.

Whatever your form of utopia looks like, the Aquarius mom can be staunch about keeping her kids in a bubble during these early years. This is partly to quell your own nervous energy, since a lot of anxiety simmers under your cool exterior. You want to be able to enjoy your child as she becomes more verbal and interactive, and if you're constantly worried about your surroundings you'll miss all of her cute and hilarious antics. Thus, you might be the most unlikely neighbor on your well-manicured block—Costco (or organic co-op) membership and all.

Suburbia may seem like a good idea, but once you're landlocked among endless rows of clipped hedges and cookie-cutter strip malls, your Aquarian soul can deflate. You're a creative sign with avant-garde leanings, and you need a cast of colorful characters to flavor your days. While part of you is relieved to give up your former extended youth, don't kid yourself. You still need an unconventional posse for those lifesaving girls' nights out even if it's margaritas at the Macaroni Grill instead of two-dollar shots at your favorite dive bar. Fortunately, Aquarians are great at making fast friendships. Our Aquarius aunt, after leaving her quirky enclave for a nearby town on a military base, began championing public art in her new neighborhood. She was later elected arts commissioner and museum president, leaving her unique stamp on the formerly cookie-cutter downtown district.

If you can't take time off from your job when the kids come along, there's a chance you might be a work-at-home mom during this phase. Adi, a mom of two young boys, runs a home-based business while her toddler Jason is around. "I work from home, but it's important for me to be there for the kids to feel wanted and included and appreciated," she says. "I love having the opportunity to teach and break things down to their level. I like to do real-life things with them. I don't build pillow forts or chase dragons, but Jason cooks dinner with me, runs around with a mini-shopping cart, and he has a toy laptop and phone. The other day, he said. 'Mom, I need my computer. Be quiet, I have a phone call.'"

In fact, you're not too big on babysitters during this phase unless it's absolutely necessary. "I'm not a controlling person, but I'm controlling about letting my kid be around a babysitter," admits one Aquarius mom. "Like, what if that person says or does something that she doesn't like? I know she's more resilient than that, but that's my thing."

The disciplining part of this phase can wear you down at first, too. You find some naughty antics funny and don't get embarrassed by public meltdowns. However, your patience thins when you're trying to get somewhere and your kid procrastinates or tests your limits by hitting and kicking. Whining is also a big pet peeve for your sign. Aquarius mama SunHee broke her son of the habit by pretending not to understand him. "I don't speak Whine," she told him. "So if you want me to know what you're saying, you'll have to speak English."

You promised yourself you'd never yell or spank or shame your child—yet you find yourself treading into "woman on the verge of a nervous breakdown" terrain some days. "My Aquarian philosophy is that while you're disciplining, you must be present," says Kierna. "My kids tend to drag their feet, and last year, I would yell. I just had to check myself and start planning better to avoid the morning stress. I'm learning to be organized, without losing the spontaneity."

Once you absorb a few tricks of the trade, though, you can become quite the Zen mommy. "I learned that being calm doesn't mean being nice," says Carrie. "Early on in the toddler years, I felt like I was either being rolled over, or being overly authoritarian. I read a blog by Janet Lansbury explaining a parenting theory called RIE (resources for infant educators). She suggested saying things in a calm, authoritative voice, like a CEO speaking to her employees. So now, I think, 'What would a CEO do?' Or I use my 'CEO voice'—and it works!"

If you're a competitive or accomplishment-driven Aquarius, you may feel frustrated at moments now, as though you can't get anything done. Set aside your checklists and results metrics if you can. Focus on enjoying your family as much as possible—including quality time with your partner if you're still together. This is a great time for creative co-parenting whenever possible, whether it's just the two of you or a whole gang of friends herding the kiddos.

You might as well soak up all the together time you can with the little ones before the school bell tolls and you have to share their attention with teachers, classmates, coaches, and friends. Until then, enjoy being the mommy, creative director, and chief designer of their little utopian universe.

EARLY CHILDHOOD (SIX TO ELEVEN YEARS)

Prepare for change, again! Just as you got into the toddler groove, your kids go off to school, which introduces a new routine for you to plan your life around. While you may cherish the return of your free time, it could quickly be zapped by soccer practices, sleepovers, and other activities that turn you into the family chauffeur. Of course, you'll enjoy accompanying your child on these adventures whenever possible, and you might just become the favorite "activity mom" among your kid's friends.

If you've isolated yourself for the past couple years, it's time to rekindle friendships and form new communities. Fortunately, school can provide the perfect opportunity, especially if you send your child to a more alternative program where parent participation is strong and you are more likely to find like-minded moms to hang out with. Families from your kids' extracurricular programs can also become part of your ever-expanding social circle.

"My husband and I both work from home, around the clock," says Adi. "We're not a superromantic couple—in fact, romance bores me. Confidence is more of an aphrodisiac than flowers. But our whole family competes in martial arts tournaments, so we all train together. If we have time alone, we have our friends with kids come over, send them all upstairs to play, and hang out downstairs. We'll have thirty people over, host Ultimate Fighting Championship viewings and watch mixed martial arts, and that's just a regular Friday night."

At this stage, your child is developing a personality, and you'll enjoy answering his gazillion curious queries. Since you're a sign that questions everything, you'll encourage critical thinking while continuing to carefully expose your child to influences of your choosing. You're not quite ready for that utopian bubble to pop; yet you understand that he's around his peers all day, and you can only control so much of what he learns on the streets and school yard.

"I never want my kids to be the victims of anything," says Adi of her two sons. "I'm very cognizant of empowering them to make good choices and stick up for themselves. I want them to advocate for other people, too. Strength is important to me, in both personality and conviction."

As your kid develops a stronger sense of separateness, however, you may find yourself having a small existential crisis. For as much as you champion individuality, the Aquarius mom cleaves to a few definitive values and ideals. So if you notice your child veering in the far opposite direction of those, you may have a dilemma on your hands: do you support her right to individuality, or do you intervene?

"My oldest son has a total fascination with the WWE," says Aquarius Kierna. "I'm a girls' girl, and I never imagined I'd be ordering a seventy-dollar pay-per-view of The Rock. I was on him for years, teaching him about nonviolence, telling him, 'Just because you're a boy doesn't mean you need to fight.' But I finally realized that my son enjoys commentating and this was feeding his soul. It's allowing him vocabulary, and since he's dyslexic, he's using words he wouldn't otherwise. So now we talk about how cool it would be if we could create our own league. Sometimes the lessons about how to raise a child are just rethinking what you know. Everything that I thought was negative about wrestling turned out to be empowering for my son."

All the same, you'll want to make sure your child fits in among his classmates and isn't ostracized from peers. "My older son does things that are socially awkward, and I cringe at those behaviors," admits one Aquarius mom. "I get concerned when he's the kid that other children find annoying. I even found myself secretly worrying, 'Do I have an uncool kid?'"

While you want your child to be well liked, your humanitarian sign is staunchly antibullying. Since you're naturally affable yourself, Aquarians often grow up as part of the "in" crowd (even if you were the fascinating rebel in the bunch). Despite being embraced by the cool kids, you probably managed not to be clique-oriented, exclusionary, cruel, or any of the other less savory traits of popularity. Hey, you just happen to get along with everyone you meet—from the freaks and geeks to the homecoming queens and the prom kings of the world. As a result, you'll make sure your child is well rounded and kind to everyone—a leader, not a follower. You'll emphasize standing up for one's beliefs and taking risks. Since you may have been academically or athletically competitive, you might also groom a future science-fair winner or sports medalist.

While this is pretty much the golden era of mother-child fun for your active sign, you might need to watch out for being overly permissive. "I don't micromanage," says one Aquarius. "Bedtimes and chores are flexible." But now is a good time to teach your child responsibility, even if you're too busy having a blast together to force the issue. Unless you want an entitled teen on your hands in a few years, turning chores and other everyday tasks into a game will groom your kid for a responsible entry into the next phase of maturity.

ADOLESCENCE AND TEENS (TWELVE TO EIGHTEEN YEARS)

Midlife crisis, anyone? You never felt "old" as the mom of little ones—if anything, they kept you feeling young and active. Now you may have your first encounter with being the "uncool" person in the room as your teenager tests your boundaries. Aquarius moms pride themselves on being laid-back and fair, so you may quietly resent that your kid doesn't seem to see, or appreciate, that.

Hip and avant-garde, the Aquarius mom is often up on the latest books, movies, music, and slang—and it doesn't even seem weird that you know this stuff. Your kid's friends probably come over to visit *you*, and your daughter will always want to borrow your clothes if you wear the same size. You'll sit around shooting the breeze with your son and his pals for hours, telling them tales of your own rebellious years. You believe that the school of life is just as important as high school and college.

With your bohemian soul, the last thing you want to be is the harsh authority figure who cramps your teenager's individuality or style. After all, your own life may be such a patchwork quilt of experimental moments (and mistakes morphed into lessons) that you don't feel qualified to serve as a role model. You may have spent your entire adolescence "fighting the power" and promised yourself you'd never become *that* parent.

"My mom never wanted to be authoritarian when I was a teenager," recalls one woman of her Aquarius mother. "When I asked to do something, she'd just say, 'You should ask your dad.'"

It's a moral dilemma: of course you don't want to be overly permissive and steer your kid into trouble. Yet, as the zodiac's rebel, you know that if you're too strict your child will just drink/smoke/experiment with sex and drugs behind your back. Is it better to rule with an iron fist, keep an open dialogue, or to let them learn from their own mistakes?

Some Aquarius moms go the overprotective route, turning their teens into best friends and even coconspirators. "My mom and I would have secret shopping trips," says Melissa, the daughter of an Aquarius. "She'd spend money on me that my dad didn't want her to spend, making me promise not to tell my father. It was almost like a girlie sisterhood. My mom could be more herself with me than with my dad. We had inside jokes—and still do."

As your teenager starts to individuate—rejecting you as part of the separation process—you could feel lonely and abandoned. You *thought* you'd be relieved that your kid is growing less dependent on you. Instead, this could be your first real heartbreak—cue the vintage Gwen Stefani: "I really feel like I'm losing my best friend."

When you do crack the whip, it can be disastrous, since you don't always model the behavior you demand from your children. It's not that you mean to, but you're also a multitasking maniac who can get as scattered as the wind. "My kids' room is always chaotic, and it hangs me up all the time," says Kierna. "Yet, when you go into *my* room, which is half office and half bedroom, you can see they get a lot of that from me."

Aquarius is the sign of friendship, and you treat your kids like peers or equals. To a certain extent, this is fine. But when the s**t hits the fan, somebody's got to take control. If it's not you, then your child is left to figure out her own sense of right and wrong, and the results might not be pretty. Setting boundaries makes children feel safe, because it lets them know their limits and also shows that you care enough to protect them. Your own ability to say no also helps them develop a moral compass.

Don't let your desire to be liked interfere with parenting duties. Sure, your ability to (seemingly) relate could lessen conflict during the turbulent teen years. Or . . . it might just confuse your kids. Bethany, the daughter of an Aquarius, recalls her mother serving her friends beer in high school. "Everyone thought she was the coolest mom in the world—except me," says Bethany.

Be careful not to get caught up in reliving your youth through your children. "My Aquarius aunt would take me and her son out late at night for pizza or to the movies all the time," says Laura. "She'd be like, 'I love this stuff!' It was like hanging out with a friend—who could also drive." Another Aquarian's daughter remembers her mother openly having a fling after leaving an unsatisfying marriage. "I was twelve years old and I had no idea what was going on—just that my mother was being totally immature. It was so confusing for me." The daughter ended up acting out even more strongly as a way of regaining her mom's wayward attention, and the situation got worse before it got better.

Some astrologers believe that Aquarius is coruled by two planets: Uranus, the planet of rebellion and youth, and stern Saturn, the planet of maturity and repression. Talk about opposites! This could explain why you're at once rigid and totally laid-back—and why some Aquarians marry so young (we know several who wed their high-school sweethearts). Just know that underneath any old-fashioned values is a quirky freedom fighter, one who can't be held down. Though you may refuse to be a "typical mom," make sure to get yourself some support if you find yourself plunged into turbulence at the same time as your teen.

"I knew I was older, but I didn't expect to feel *this* old," admits Aquarius mother Carla, who's still quite hip for her early fifties, dressing in clogs and sporting a nose ring and a short, spiky do. "I went through a kind of mourning period when my daughter started high school. I was like, 'Wait—that's supposed to be me walking through those halls, trying out for the school play and the softball team! What's going on here?'" You may need to recognize your own Peter Pan inclinations, owning that deep down you'd rather avoid some trappings of adulthood altogether.

Fortunately, Carla shifted her focus to civic duties, and launched a community-supported agriculture program in her community, which sourced its produce from local farms, and began teaching kids in poorer areas how to grow food and eat nutritiously. She attracted volunteers of all ages, including a few of her daughter's classmates. Carla says this gave her a sense of purpose that transcended her fears about aging. "I was connecting with people around a cause. I felt passionate and alive again, like my best 'young' self. I stopped wishing I could turn back time, and fell back in love with my life."

BYE-BYE, BIRDIE: LEAVING THE NEST (EIGHTEEN-PLUS YEARS)

There's letting go in theory . . . and then there's reality. While you intellectually understand your child's need to leave the nest, you may have some deeply mixed feelings about it. Once again, it's as though your best friend is leaving you behind in some way. Your child may be the first and only person you've allowed yourself to feel this attached to—even more than any romantic partner. So naturally you'll want to remain connected and hopefully grow into true friends.

"When I talk to my mom as an adult, she lives for the things I share with her," says Melissa, thirty-nine, of her Aquarius mother. "If I start getting in my own world and don't share, I notice a drift from her, less enthusiasm in her voice. I think she feels left out. But I can tell her anything, and she's not going to interject a judgment. She's really supportive. My mom never asks when I'm getting married and having kids. She's says, 'It would be great to be a grandma, but I understand you have other things going on.'"

If you're an Aquarian of cooler disposition, you might send your child off with a flourish, cheering on his grand adventures. "My mom once told me, 'Go be homeless in New York—it's a great opportunity!'" says one Aquarian's son. Beth, the adult daughter of a rather standoffish Aquarius mom, remembers coming home to visit after not seeing her parents for several months. "My mom looked up from her book, nodded slightly, and looked back down," she recalls.

While these might be extreme scenarios, you'll hopefully go about living your own life, perhaps having a personal Renaissance once you get into your groove. If you're single, you might go on a dating spree, move, or even return to school yourself. Married Aquarians might rekindle the old adventurous spark, taking that second honeymoon you've put off for years. One Aquarius mom in her late fifties even went to the Burning Man festival, camping in the desert among kids half her age. Another started dating a younger photographer, accompanying him on his shoots all over the world. You might meet up with your kids or take trips together. "My Aquarius aunt always wants to double date with me," says Laura. "Now that her son has left home, she just wants to hang out!"

Should you find yourself mourning an empty nest, turn to the preferred Aquarian remedy: the power of numbers. Get involved in a community effort, a charitable cause, or any kind of group effort to reconnect. Don't give in to the temptation to isolate yourself during tough emotional times. Alas, an Aquarian hermit is rarely a happy one. So get back out among the people and rekindle your spirit of adventure. There's so much to look forward to, Aquarius, and when you remember that the rest takes care of itself.

THE PISCES MOM

(February 19–March 20)

MOMMY MAGIC - Your Strengths:

Compassion
Imagination
Nurturing
Creativity

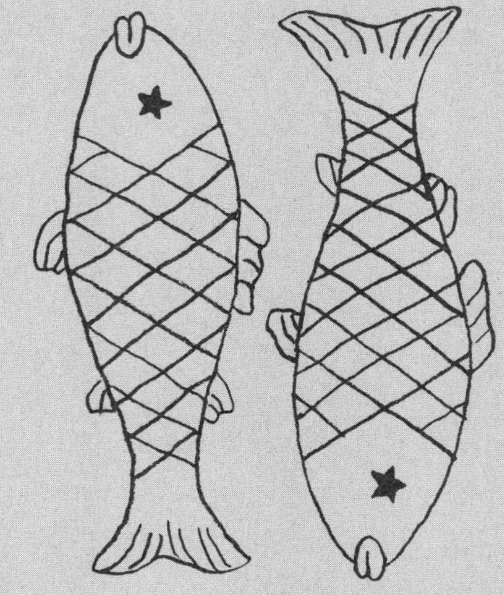

MAMA MIA - Your Challenges:

Kookiness
Manipulation
Instability
Guilt

FAMOUS PISCES MAMAS:

Drew Barrymore, Elizabeth Taylor, Kristen Davis, Camryn Mannheim, Cindy Crawford, Ali Larter, Dina Manzo, Rachel Weisz, Jennifer Love Hewitt, Emily Blunt, Olivia Wilde

YOUR PARENTING STYLE

Hello, mermaid mommy! The Pisces mother is a seductive siren and an earth mother rolled into one glamorous package. You love to ensconce your family in a cozy but luxurious bubble, and chances are you'll have a well-appointed home and wardrobe to match. Even in sweatpants, you manage to look coiffed and ready for your close-up most days. Fortunately, you emanate enough warmth to be enchanting rather than intimidating to other moms. Even if you can be fastidious in your tastes, your door is always open to the world. Watery Pisces is the zodiac's last sign. You're empathic and ethereal, spiritual and sensitive, wise and emotionally intelligent. You know how to treat yourself like a goddess—and you'll encourage the mothers around you to do the same.

The Pisces mother has quirks, and plenty of them. Your heart is always in the right place—even if your head isn't. A walking paradox, you can be totally together one minute and an emotional wreck the next. In zodiac lore, two fish swimming in opposite directions symbolize Pisces, which is why you seem to contradict yourself. If your family accuses you of being hypocritical or inconsistent, this is why.

But you can't help it. You know that people are complex creatures, not one-dimensional droids who fit into neat little boxes. The Pisces mom reserves the right to change her mind—and to change it often. (Perhaps that's why Pisces Elizabeth Taylor had seven husbands and Drew Barrymore has married three times before age forty.)

As a mom, you follow the flow of your feelings and live by your intuition. You may ardently believe something one day, only to champion a totally different philosophy the next. One Pisces mother we know, formerly a grassroots organizer and animal rights activist, became a card-carrying member of the NRA after marrying a conservative Republican. She even traveled with her shotgun in tow to enter clay pigeon shooting contests. Everything is subject to change without notice in your world, which makes you either flaky or flexible, depending on how you spin it.

Another reason you're a multiple-personality mama? Your fourth house of motherhood is ruled by Gemini, the sign of the Twins. Both Pisces and Gemini are dual signs (two fish, two people), giving you an experimental edge. This house ruler also makes you fun, quirky, and youthful. You're a mom about town and you love to expose your kids to creative or progressive experiences. You'll encourage them to be edgy and cultivate their individuality. You're the mom who makes pancakes shaped like monsters or strange animals, takes your kid to see obscure art films and museum exhibits, or brings them on meditation retreats. Since visual Pisces often have a flair for photography and film, you'll have an artful gallery of family photos on display, too.

And then there are your friends. The Pisces mom always has a colorful cast of characters around to keep life interesting, ranging from poets who've taken a vow of poverty to wealthy hedge funders who invite you to sail the French Riviera on their private yachts. Your children could have a band of "guncles" (gay uncles) or offbeat godparents who further enrich their lives. Since many Pisceans have a soft spot for animals, especially rescues, you might have a posse of pets, too. One Pisces mom we know even had a menagerie of zoo critters at her own fortieth birthday party—the "guest of honor" was a sloth!

Pisces is the zodiac's escape artist, and you need an outlet for "me time," especially after you lapse into martyr mommy mode. Keeping that essential balance is difficult for your sign. In fact, this is why some Pisces moms can morph from unconditionally loving into "cold fish" at times. You're not always aware of your limits, so you give and give until you're depleted. Then your system shuts down and you're forced to emotionally withdraw. One man remembers feeling frightened as a child when his Pisces mother locked herself in her room for a day. He pounded on her door to no avail and grew terrified as the hours wore on. What had happened? As a single parent, she had gotten overwhelmed trying to do everything alone and nearly had a nervous breakdown. She stayed in bed for hours and couldn't even get up to open the door for her son. Pisces, let this be a cautionary tale for you: know your limits and respect them.

For the Pisces mom, pleasure is not a luxury—it's a necessity. Remind yourself that well-deserved breaks help you be a better mom. Repair to a retreat center, luxuriate at the spa, or let your hair down at grown-up haunts where adult beverages are served. Keep your tribe of female friends on speed dial to join your flights of fancy—you may not realize how much you crave community, but friendship is balm to the Pisces mama's soul. While you don't book your social calendar months in advance, you're always up for a spontaneous happy hour, lunch date, or girls' night out, so indulge guilt-free.

Like Pisces mom Lyss Stern, coauthor of *If You Give a Mom a Martini . . . 100 Ways to Find 10 Blissful Minutes for Yourself*, you might even turn your high-end mommy escapes into a business. Weaving together the Pisces skill-set trifecta of hostessing, creating gorgeous settings, and helping the world, Lyss created Divalysscious Moms, a networking group for New York's most fabulous mothers. In addition to spa, fitness, and shopping events (some of which are completely family friendly), Divalysscious Moms hosts exclusive book launches, among them a nine-hundred-person blowout bash for *Fifty Shades of Grey* author E. L. James. With your Svengali charms (and your gossipy, girlfriend-to-girlfriend chatter), you know how to make a perfect stranger feel like the most intimate member of your inner circle.

Pisces is also the ruler of charity and karma, so if your decadent events help a good cause, all the better. Pisces mom Dina Manzo, who appeared on a couple seasons of *The Real Housewives of New Jersey* and on her own HGTV show *Dina's Party*, also runs Project Ladybug, a foundation that raises money for kids with cancer. Dina's gallery-style shoe closet and well-stocked wardrobe is bigger than some people's apartments, but she makes a compelling case for marrying style and soul in life. "You can be glamorous and make a difference at the same time," says Dina. "It's all about putting on that fabulous pair of shoes, then going out and doing something good for the world."

It's exactly this *Alice in Wonderland*–type of unreality that makes you such a magical mama, turning family time into a floating Mad Hatter tea party. There are no typical days in your household, and your kids might be in awe of what you pull out of that rakish chapeau. Enchanting vacations, road trips, outings—you can come up with these ideas in your sleep. Will they be decadent or disastrous? You'll find out once you do it. Albert Einstein, a Pisces, famously said, "The true sign of intelligence is not knowledge, but imagination."

(He also said that "a person who never made a mistake has never tried anything new.")

The downside to your freewheeling style, however, can be a lack of boundaries or stability. You can be a little *too* out there, embarrassing your kids as they get older or making them anxious from the unpredictable changes and lack of structure. Since you hate being told what to do and when to do it, you may struggle to get your kid on a regular bedtime and meal schedule or to give them enough of the consistency that kids crave. Your best bet is to have a partner, grandparent, or caregiver help enforce these routines if you feel oppressed by this facet of parenting.

Pisces is ruled by dreamy Neptune, the planet of imagination, illusions, and blurred boundaries. For you, the line between mother and friend is thin and can fluctuate hourly. Pisces mom Elizabeth Taylor, who had four children, reportedly fit this description. "She wasn't a hands-on mother, necessarily," said biographer William J. Mann, author of *How to Be a Movie Star: Elizabeth Taylor in Hollywood*. "There were a lot of nannies and assistants to take care of the kids. She was more of the pal than the disciplinarian. She was the kind of mother who said, 'I'm here if you want to talk to me.' She was only eighteen when she had [her first child,] Michael, they weren't that far apart in age, and she took that approach with all of them."

Not that you can't be surprisingly strict or tough about certain things. (Like we said, you're a walking paradox.) You have a few stern rules that you cleave to, and the rest is subject to interpretation. "I hate to be authoritarian, but I like to be in control," says Pisces mom Tina. "I veer around a lot. I struggle with consistency, work-life balance, and second-guessing myself. We never use physical violence toward our children and would never let them cry themselves to sleep or anything like that. However, we do have bedtimes and we have to write thank-you notes and the like."

While Pisces women can play the "delicate flower" card and even lean too heavily on their kids for emotional support, they're also as protective as they come. Nobody messes with the ones you love! You can go into Mafia mode if you hear of school yard cruelty or mean-girl activity. You might have to stop yourself from taking out your diamond studs, kicking off your stiletto booties, and beating up a bully.

Sure, it might be a little overboard, but that won't stop you. And yeah, you can be accused of codependence, but you're okay with that. Better you care too much than not enough, in your book! Your kids always know that you have their backs, and there's no sacrifice you wouldn't make for their happiness. Your children will definitely grow up with a healthy sense of self-worth as a result of your adoration (in some cases, a little too healthy, but so be it). In your eyes, they can do no wrong, and you're there to soothe them, spoil them, and cheer on their every accomplishment. Some Pisces mothers elevate their kids onto quite a pedestal; you may or may do this yourself, but you cherish every moment that you spend with them. Although you have your own life, you'll maintain closeness with your kids over the years. Mom, best friend, social director, and confidante: you do it all and make it look effortlessly chic.

IF YOU HAVE A GIRL

PROS

You're in heaven with a little girl, Pisces. You can't wait to do girl things like mother-daughter weekend getaways, trips to the spa, and tea for two. You love to cuddle with your daughter and dress her up—can we get a photo shoot, please! With your cultural interests and savvy, you'll enjoy going to museums, films, galleries, and concerts together. You might even share music and clothes!

The Pisces mom is a wonderful role model when it comes to giving back, since you probably do a good amount of charity or volunteer work. Whatever your pet issue is, you'll speak out about it, acting as a great role model for your daughter. Through your own example, you'll teach her to be kind and compassionate—to herself and others.

CONS

Codependent no more? You want to make sure your daughter knows that you're always there for her, but your relationship can get too close for comfort. If you're always protecting her and fighting her battles, it can turn into enabling. Rather than providing constant bail-outs, teach your girl how to stand up for herself and use critical thinking skills. Pisces moms aren't always the best at modeling boundaries and detachment, alas, and you might even have a few toxic people in your inner circle that you keep around out of guilt. Let your daughter be your excuse for breaking free of martyr mode. Teach her to try to change the world, not save it.

Remember, it's your job to train your daughter in the art of self-sufficiency. However, this can be tricky for some Pisces moms, who may be a little wobbly in that area themselves. Since you're prone to getting flustered or freaking out at times, you can play the damsel in distress. You can't tell your daughter to be strong and then act helpless yourself. Watch your "do as I say, not as I do" tendencies or you could lose her respect.

IF YOU HAVE A BOY

*

PROS

Boys will be boys? Not under your watch! Your main priority is making sure that your son is a compassionate person with strong values and respect for his fellow humans. You might even steer him into the arts rather than sports or at the very least make sure he develops a solid cultural and emotional IQ amid his fantasy football games and soccer matches.

Advance warning for your son: he's probably destined to be metrosexual, at least to a degree. Nobody can put the "man" in mani-pedi quite like a Pisces mother. You'll bring him along on all your activities and pampering dates, and he'll learn to love getting his shoulders massaged and his nails buffed. While he might resist you turning him into a softie, he'll appreciate it once he realizes how much the ladies love him for it. His future girlfriends are sure to love you, too, and they might even enjoy spending quality time with you. One Pisces mom received this Facebook post from her nineteen-year-old son's girlfriend: "Shout out to Jane on her birthday! Thank you for allowing my amazing boyfriend to exist." Only a hip Pisces mama could inspire such intergenerational affinity.

CONS

Emasculation alert! The line between mothering and smothering is a thin one for a Pisces mama and her boy. You may treat your son like a best friend and confidant, pouring way too much energy into him. You'll push attachment parenting to its outer limits (one Pisces mom we know breast-fed her son until he was five). Be careful not to emotionally engulf your son by getting too close to his friends and girlfriends or overly involved in his affairs. He needs personal space and a little privacy, please! Your overly intimate teasing might also wound his pride, making him feel self-conscious when you call him by a cutesy nickname or share an embarrassing story in front of his friends.

While you'll teach your boy how to respect women—opening doors, pulling out chairs—you may also need to hide some of your emotional ups and downs from him. The Pisces mom can wear her heart on her sleeve, unwittingly exposing the kids to her trials and tribulations. If your son sees you weeping or falling apart, he may unconsciously feel that he has to save you, which can create a feeling of resentment and helplessness. Dial up the therapist or a confidante when your sensitive side makes an appearance (which will probably be often).

*

INFANCY (THE FIRST YEAR)

Ah, bliss! Your baby's first year is a haze of nuzzling, nursing, and nesting as you connect with this brand-new life. Even better, science shows that your emotion ocean is creating healthy waves. Snuggling causes your brain to release oxytocin, the bonding hormone (or "cuddle chemical")—which can be stimulated by giving birth, breast-feeding, or holding a newborn babe in your arms. Yes, you could soon find yourself literally addicted to love (no rehab necessary!).

Pisces moms are the ultimate attachment parents. You love the touchy-feely sensuality of this phase, you don't mind the diapers, and you'll probably cosleep with your baby. You'll happily breast-feed as often as the little tyke requires. There's nothing you love more than the feeling of being at one with your baby.

"The first month when my daughter just slept was bliss," says Linda, a Pisces mom who took her college exams and earned a degree literally days before giving birth. "We watched movies, slept, and snuggled. Then it all became a blur of sleep deprivation, painfully boring baby playgroups, and endless hours of laundry and musical toys."

But hey, who needs gadgets and enforced togetherness when you already have a soul connection with your wee one? "Babies are the closest thing to God," insists another Pisces mom. "I feel like they're wiser and more aware than the rest of us." Since Pisces is the most spiritual sign, you would know! In fact, you may even have "communicated" with your child in the womb, talking, singing, and dreaming about him.

While your first year of motherhood can be heavenly, it can also be disorienting. With your sign's tendency to lose track of time, your grasp on reality can slip a bit. Your life may revolve a little *too* much around the baby's schedule, which can throw you off. You're already known for disappearing into la-la land for weeks at a time. (Hello, Pisces? Your voice mail is full . . . again.) And now you might go off the grid even more.

"The first six weeks were horrible," says Tara, the Pisces mom of a nine-month-old girl. "She was such a great baby, but the adjustment was really hard. I don't think people talk about how hard that is. They would ask, 'Don't you love being a mom?' I would reply, 'I love my daughter, but I'm not fond of all these new aspects of my life.'"

Part of the issue is confidence. There's a "damsel in distress" in every Pisces. Although you're incredibly capable, you may be the last to believe it. There will be moments of anxiety in which you feel as helpless as your infant. Any bouts of ceaseless crying, colic, or sleepless nights can fray your delicate nerves. You tend to get consumed by your feelings—including the fearful ones. This year could be an emotional roller-coaster ride with pronounced highs and lows.

As much as you love bonding with your baby, you can feel alone and isolated if you get too disconnected from the outside world. Be careful when you start to feel overwhelmed, Pisces. If you tend to be the "rescue me" type, then now is the time to flip the script. A theme of this first year will be developing self-sufficiency. Yes, Pisces, you *can* soothe your baby's gas pains or recover your dignity when your boobs leak through your silk blouse. You've got this. Maternal instinct is more than half the battle—and you have that in spades. The rest you can learn on Google, by grilling the pediatrician at checkups or in your collection of parenting books. ("The sequel to *Your Baby's First Year* was ragged and dog-eared by the time my son was a toddler," recalls Pisces mom Heather.)

If you return to work, you may need to deal with some heavy inner conflict. "The work-mom balance is the hardest," says Tara, a Pisces mom who returned to work shortly after giving birth. "My job isn't superdemanding, but it's a career and there's pressure to perform at the same level as I did before I had Hazel. And I just can't stay at the office until eight p.m. every night. If day care calls and she has a fever, I have to go. There's a lot of guilt on both ends for me as a working mom."

You also need to release guilt over relying on aunts, uncles, grandparents, and friends—the proverbial village—for help. Because you don't want to "bother" anyone (or feel like you owe them), you may avoid asking for support until things approach a near-crisis state. Don't wait until you're in the midst of a meltdown to reach out, Pisces. Remember that people aren't mind readers (okay, maybe *you* are, but the rest of the zodiac isn't quite as attuned). You have to speak up and explain what you need.

Like a good Girl Scout, you'll need to be prepared. Although advance planning may feel counterintuitive to your go-with-the-flow nature, it can stop a minor setback from spinning into a five-alarm drama. Pass out a few spare keys to friends and family and let them know the door is (almost) always open. Even if you're doing the stay-at-home mom thing, you'd benefit from hiring a nanny for a few hours. Or shell out a few bucks to a teenage mother's helper who can hang around and change the occasional diaper or watch the baby while you pee. You'll probably enjoy the company, too!

Speaking of company, if you can drag yourself out of the house to a baby music class, a museum, or a baby/mom yoga class, do it. Bundle your babe in the carrier, and force yourself to get out of the house, if only for an hour or two. Stroll through a museum or your favorite department store while the baby snoozes.

You could also bring the adventures inside. Hire a meditation teacher to teach a private class for you and a few other moms, or host a casual Sip and See for friends to meet the baby. Charity work might be another excuse to get dressed up and back into the world. Join a fund-raising committee or do a Walk for the Cure to raise money and get back into your pre-baby shape.

Your love life will benefit from your return to civilization, too. If you don't connect with the wider world, you might drain your partner by relying too heavily on him or her for emotional support. Or, by creating a little just-us-three bubble, the relationship could start to feel claustrophobic. Break it up a little, and even schedule a date night or two with a no-baby-talk policy. Pisces is a romantic sign, so a little ambience goes a long way now. Reconnect over adult conversation, a gourmet meal, and a glass of wine. Your pre-mommy self needs some time and attention, too.

TODDLERHOOD (TWO TO FIVE YEARS)

Pisces is an adaptable sign, and your natural go-with-the-flow attitude comes in handy now. You won't be an iron-fisted mom who freaks out if her kid flings sand at the playground or drops trou (or diaper) to pee in the sandbox. It happens, right? You find most toddler antics amusing, and your child doesn't embarrass you easily. Congratulations, Pisces. You've already surrendered to one of toddlerhood's immutable facts: you have little to no control over this creature!

"I loved my son during the supposed 'terrible twos,'" says Pisces mom Tina. "Despite a very busy life where I can barely remember what I did fifteen minutes ago, I can remember whole days of that year. Everything is crystal clear in my memory, like a beautiful September day with bright blue skies, golden leaves, and green grass. Everything he did was a joy; every minute was a new and fun experience."

As adorable as your sprout may be, the chaos of this phase can still test your limits. You don't loving playing the rule enforcer, so being consistently firm with your toddler is hard. "I deal with discipline because I can understand my child's motives and psychology more than my partner," says Candace, the Pisces mom of a three-year-old. "I understand children are supposed to try to see how far they can push their limits." Be careful, though, because being so empathetic, you might overidentify with your child, fearing that you'll scar him for life if you're always saying no. Since you resist being the bad cop, you may not deliver the necessary life lessons and "teachable moments" that children this age require.

In fact, you could start to become a stage mom now, egging on a future performer—or spawning an out-of-control diva. You've got no qualms about selling your kid's cuteness to a modeling or talent agency or letting your toddler shoot a cameo in a commercial or a friend's indie film. One Pisces we know listed her religion on Facebook as "Rosie" (her daughter's name). A filmmaker by trade, she often captured her precocious little girl on camera. Unfortunately, she also turned her daughter into an attention seeker who later annoyed her peers by always being "on."

Other times, you swing to the opposite extreme and turn suddenly strict. This usually happens when your toddler does something scary, such as running into the street or drifting away at a department store while you try on a cute pair of peep-toes. When you get frightened, your inner control freak makes a rare but dramatic showing. This whiplash-inducing shift from permissive to rigid can confuse your little one, pointing to a need to teach some clear-cut rules and boundaries.

You might benefit from following a "positive discipline" (PD) philosophy. In this method, the parent focuses on the positive aspects of the child's behavior. It's based on the idea that there are no bad children, just good and bad behaviors, and that it's most effective to reinforce the good ones. Parents who practice PD are kind and firm at the same time. For example, rather than yelling at a toddler for making a mess, you teach him a cleanup song and make a fun ritual out of putting toys away. Or, instead of revoking privileges and shunning your child in the time-out chair, you consistently praise good behavior as it happens. This feels more natural to your loving and compassionate sign.

Another challenge of this phase is structure. Living by the clock isn't exactly a Pisces strong suit, but most toddlers benefit from a routine, even a simple one. Knowing what to expect helps them feel safe in the world and builds their confidence. Toddlers can especially become fearful of the unknown, so having a routine—brushing their teeth, putting their toys away, taking a bath—can build their sense of agency and autonomy. Since they face so many developmental changes at this age, they can better cope with transitions that occur within the framework of familiar daily activities.

For the Pisces mom, though, sticking to a schedule can feel oppressive. You need your time to daydream, relax, and slip into your fantasy world. Alas, the very thing that revitalizes *you* can leave your toddler feeling adrift. Remember, you don't have to be the one (or the only one) enforcing the consistency. Just make sure that someone in your child's life does. If your partner is more regimented than you are, let him or her handle the baths, meals, potty training (your least favorite!), and bedtimes. Or delegate to a caregiver. Your child won't care *who* makes her macaroni and cheese, but she *could* get thrown off if it's served at six o'clock one evening and nine thirty the next.

Sure, you'll probably feel guilty if you're not reading the nightly bedtime story or tucking your baby in. But look past your emotions and consider what's best for your child (and you!). The rule for Pisces moms: don't let your mouth write a check that your ass can't cash. Promise only what you can consistently deliver and nothing more. You might commit to handling the bedtime routine on the weekends (when you follow a different schedule, anyhow), and letting another person read *Goodnight Moon* from Monday to Friday. Or, if your spouse is genuinely better at getting your stubborn toddler dressed, don't act the martyr and force yourself to soldier through. You'll only feel resentful, which will lead to a passive-aggressive backlash and put unnecessary tension into your relationship.

Focus on the quality of time you spend together, not just the quantity. You have so many creative and fascinating things to teach your child. One Pisces mom's list of "saving graces" reads like the culture pages of a highbrow parenting magazine: "I love Miyazaki movies—*Spirited Away*, *Kiki's Delivery Service*, *Cat Returns*," she says. "They're amazing and filled with Japanese folklore as well as heroines with courage and originality." This mama makes a point of exposing her kids to artful animation and stories with more complex narratives, balancing out their standard Western media diet with more substantial fare.

Self-care rituals are particularly important for your sign, and you need them more than ever now. If you're going back to work, have the sitter arrive an hour before you leave (at least), so you can primp for the office in peace. Winding down at the end of the day is vital, too. Pay the nanny to stay later once a week so you can soak in the tub. When you don't take a step back, you can get paralyzed by all the choices this phase demands, making everyone crazy by reacting hysterically to simple decisions. One Pisces mom we know forced herself to return to work while she had two young children, throwing herself completely off kilter. Her outer world soon became a reflection of her turbulent inner landscape: she moved three times in eighteen months, most recently into a one-bedroom Manhattan apartment where she, her husband, and the two boys share a bedroom. Pisces, you need your personal space—and if you sacrifice too much, everything else will suffer.

As Pisces fitness expert Jillian Michaels, mother of two, said, "I come home, and I'm like, 'Okay, let me bathe you, change you, feed you, read you books, put you to bed'—wait, how am I supposed to do all this? Son of a bitch, this is hard!'" She goes on to say, "My new motto is 'As long as I'm winning more than I'm losing, I'm still winning!" Such platitudes and mantras can anchor a Pisces—you may be the mom whose kitchen is cluttered with magnets and mugs emblazoned with uplifting quotes.

You may start to reevaluate your lifestyle at this point. Are the friends in your life energy vampires, or are they supportive? If you find yourself ignoring text messages or procrastinating returning a friend's call, there could be a larger issue at play. If the thought of this person leaves you feeling guilty or anxious, perhaps you've set up an unhealthy dynamic—or you've enabled a needy person to suck you dry. Well, Pisces, now that you're responsible for an actual child, those "adult babies" could become downright intolerable, and it might be time to cut them loose.

You might also reconsider where you live now. Is the area family-friendly? Does the community feel like a welcoming home base now that you're a mom? Do you like the other parents and the general vibe of this town? After all, your child will be going to school in this district, which means you'll have to spend significant time around these people. If you find your neighbors to be bourgeois snobs (or unevolved hicks), it might be time to sink a FOR SALE sign into your lawn.

Friendship, after all, will get you through the next fifteen to eighteen years—so it really does matter if you like the people around you. "If I didn't have my friends, I would have lost it," says Pisces mama Heather. "More than anything else, talking with my BFFs either about their parenting experience or about their own childhood has proven to be the most invaluable piece of raising a child. It truly takes a village."

Research also shows that you're likely to become similar to the company you keep, so make sure you actually *want* to resemble your fellow moms. Are they happy and positive or bitchy and bitter? A July 11, 2012, *Scientific American* article titled "Is a Bad Mood Contagious?" by Michael Lenneville and Gary W. Lewandowski Jr. describes a three-step process, "emotional contagion," whereby a person's mood is transferred to someone else. It all begins when you unconsciously make the same distressed facial expression as the person you're talking to, which triggers your brain to feel the same emotions, and then you begin acting in sync with those transferred feelings (e.g., getting short with your kid when you weren't even cranky before). Because you're a natural empath, your susceptibility to emotional contagion is probably highest among all the zodiac signs. So choose your companions wisely! The Pisces mom needs a cathartic clan with whom she can commiserate, vent, and share funny stories. You see the humor in the daily tribulations and can be a great source of "momedy" (mommy comedy). One Pisces remembers her three-year-old summoning her into the bathroom. When she walked in, her daughter proudly held up a shaving-cream-covered leg and a razor. The tale of the toddler who shaved her legs has since become family lore. Once you're laughing, your levity always returns.

Toddlerhood is filled with trials and tests—there's no question. So in the spirit of PD, focus on *your* strengths rather than where you think you're failing. Yeah, you might have ordered takeout six nights last week (and burned the meal you actually attempted to cook), but you also set up the most incredible stuffed animal fort and shot some magazine-worthy pictures of your peanut. When your toddler got cranky, you cranked up the music and held an impromptu dance party, turning that frown upside down. And when your daughter asked to clomp around in your Louboutins and freshwater pearls, you let her—because couture may be expensive, but cultivating her imagination is priceless.

EARLY CHILDHOOD (SIX TO ELEVEN YEARS)

Dry those tears, Pisces mama. You could feel some serious empty-nest pangs when your kids go off to school. Even when they're just down the block, you feel like they're halfway around the world. You may leap at the chance to be involved in your child's school. "I was the class parent, in charge of the fund-raisers, and at every single field trip," says one Pisces mother. "The teachers had to gently suggest I give someone else a chance."

Yes, you might have a harder time letting go than your kid does. If you have an über-attached water or earth sign child, you'll probably both want to keep the apron strings intact. But a more independent fire or air sign might not want to be babied anymore. Your tender feelings might get hurt if your child wriggles out of your hug or wipes off your kisses in a show of autonomy. "Mom, I'm not a baby anymore!" might be a refrain you'll have to hear a few times until you accept it. Be mindful not to make your child feel guilty or worried that he's hurting your feelings.

In fact, guilt is a running theme for the Pisces mom. "When I can't come through with something my son asks for and deserves because of money, I feel like a failing parent," says one Pisces mom. "I should be working more hours, but I'm terrified of neglecting my child."

So what to do with all of your nurturing energy now that your kid is in school for all those hours? It certainly needs an outlet. Now might be a great time to try work that helps you balance quality time with your child. Sometimes art (and work) just imitate life. You might not need to look further than your own front door to find your calling. If you truly enjoy aspects of parenting such as birthday party planning, making puppets, or filming "vanity videos" of your kid, there could be a cottage industry in the making. Don't overlook opportunities that are right in front of you!

The Pisces mom really wants to impart a sense of civic responsibility in her children—especially at this impressionable age. Volunteering together is a great way to bond with your kids. Whether you organize a park cleanup, visit a hospital ward, or sing Christmas carols at a senior center, some of your most memorable mother-child moments can involve giving back.

You might even throw parties that teach your kids that making a difference can be fun. One Pisces mom we know wanted to book her child's tenth birthday party at an animal shelter or pet rescue center (followed by an indulgent pizza and ice-cream lunch). You balance your guilt about spoiling your child by doing something humanitarian. Invitations to your kid's soiree might include a notation such as this: *In lieu of gifts for Bobby's seventh birthday, donations can be made to the Nature Conservancy.*

Not that your child will feel deprived. Your home will be a well-stocked wonderland of toys, games, and art projects. You're especially sensitive to aesthetics and presentation, something you'll pass along to your children. Gift wrapping, handwritten cards, and old-fashioned tasteful touches really make a difference, especially in this day and age. You'll teach your children not to judge a book by its cover—but to give it a gorgeous wrapper just the same.

Your creativity can save the day now, too. "If everyone is grouchy or misbehaving, I'll try to do something very different and off the wall," says Tina, the Pisces mom of two. "The other day, they were crabby, so I declared that it was a spa night. We lined the bathroom with candles, played soft music, and had a candlelight bath!"

Pisces aren't competitive, although they do care what others think. You're sensitive to criticism and may feel self-conscious among other parents in the school community. You might even be a little cliquey or gossipy at times. However, you won't pressure your kids to perform at the expense of being well-rounded and happy. Spiritual Pisces believe in fate, and you know that everyone has a divine gift that they came here to express. You'd rather your child discover his purpose and be a good human being than ace a standardized test.

To nurture creative potential, you'll expose your child to culture as often as you can. Your outings could include gallery strolls, trips to the museum, music lessons, and *The Nutcracker* ballet at Christmastime. Pisces is ruled by dreamy, poetic Neptune, which gives you the soul of an artist and a flair for music, decorating, food, fashion (especially shoes—since the Pisces-ruled body part is the feet), and originality. You appreciate aesthetics and will help them to value the thoughtful touches and bespoke details of good craftsmanship. Your kids will grow up versed in many artistic styles, fashion trends, and musical genres, and they'll sample the finer things that life has to offer.

Compassionate Pisces moms are hypersensitive to injustice and bullying, and you'll keep a watchful eye out for this. One Pisces mother put her Mensa-smart son in an academically advanced school for this reason. "He would probably end up at the bottom of a locker if he went to public school," she explains.

"I love hard," says Pisces mom Mindy of her son Cayden, seven. "He knows that no matter what he does, he *can* come to me. I may get upset, but he is fully aware of my unconditional love. I believe he is a sensitive spirit aware of others' pain and wants to help when he can. When I see him try to soothe another person who's down, I think, 'What a big, beautiful heart this child has.'"

Just remember that your kid's feelings will occasionally get hurt, and that it often takes two to tango. Don't get up in the principal or teacher's face without getting the whole story. Remember, your child needs to learn to stand up for herself, too. Let her know that she can always come to you with problems and you'll help her work them through. Just make sure she doesn't get the message that mommy will fight her battles. The goal is to empower your child by teaching necessary survival and social skills.

ADOLESCENCE AND TEENS (TWELVE TO EIGHTEEN YEARS)

Fasten your seat belt! You're going for an exciting and exhausting ride now. Among all zodiac signs, the Pisces mom understands the teenage emotional roller coaster best. Since you're so sensitive, you can identify with a child who feels invincible one moment, fragile the next.

You often swing between capable and helpless in a day's time, too.

For the most part, you get along with your teenager and might even be more like a friend than an authority figure. Your home will be a comfortable place for your teen to hang out, and you'll be chummy with the kids that come through your door. Since Pisces always side with the underdog, you're the mom whose couch might harbor an occasional runaway or your child's classmate who's clashing with her parents. With your gift of empathy, you'll know how to validate an upset teen while still giving solid advice.

"My son is my partner in crime," says one Pisces mom of a twelve-year-old. "Really, we spend all our time together. The rules of the house are mine, but I listen if he thinks I'm being unfair or babying him too much. I'm empathetic to his thoughts and concerns and I speak to him like an adult."

While this egalitarian parenting style has its benefits, it can also make things lopsided when it's time to be the authority. "I think I'm a little too much on the permissive side," admits this same mother. "I'm trying to get control of that before we have a huge teenage disaster."

During this phase, you'll really need to hold the line and be tough at moments—even when it seems easier to give your child a hug or cave to her demands. Remember, Pisces: it's appropriate to set restrictions. Certain standards are nonnegotiable, and this may be the first time you pull the "Because I'm the mom—that's why" card. As the experts say, children need boundaries to feel safe. If you're too much on your kid's level, acting like a peer instead of a parent, he may not feel secure. Your teen might even act out to test your boundaries—the adolescent way of begging you to set limits.

Learning to be a consistent authority figure can be a steep learning curve for you now. "My mom is a hypocrite," complains the seventeen-year-old daughter of one Pisces. "Her rules make no sense and she totally contradicts herself." She goes on to explain how her mother bought her an expensive car for her seventeenth birthday when she got her license but didn't trust her to drive it alone for two weeks. "I don't know why she thought two weeks was this magic number and I'd be ready. I wasn't any better than when I first started driving, and she hardly practiced with me." A couple months later, she got into a fender bender and her Pisces mom took the car away.

You may grapple with the question, is it better to be tough and face a rift with your beloved babe (which is painful for your easily wounded sign) or to be overly permissive so you don't lose your child's affection? Now would be the time to take a long-term view into consideration. Some believe there's a bigger cost to giving your teenager more than she's capable of handling. Kabbalah (which we've only studied informally) has a concept called "bread of shame," which is a sort of spiritual heaviness or detriment that occurs when someone receives an undeserved gift. It's the reason that most lottery winners lose all their earnings within three years: they haven't done the "inner work" to handle that much responsibility or abundance yet. So before you plunk down your credit card, consider that you could be spiritually burdening your child!

Often, guilt is your motivator for being the softie. You're aware of your shortcomings as a mom and may feel like you have to constantly make up for them. "I really struggle with consistency," says Heather, an artist who juggles single motherhood with a full-time PhD program. "Making sure I keep on top of my son's home and school duties is a monumental task. Between his tutor, his boys' group, and talking with the teachers on a daily basis, I frequently feel overwhelmed and know I let some things slip."

There's a difference between empathy and enabling, so learn how to validate your child's emotions without rushing in with advice, comfort, or control. One of our favorite books on this topic is child psychologist Dr. Haim G. Ginott's *Between Parent and Teenager*, which helps explain the mind-set of both the protective parent and the adolescent who longs to experience things as an adult. The root of the struggle: parents need to be needed, whereas teenagers want to *not* need their parents.

The simple communication style Dr. Ginott suggests is especially helpful when your teenager talks back, since the sensitive Pisces mom can easily take this behavior personally. Some days, you manage to stay strong and unbreakable in the face of the audacity. "My daughter could be a real bitch," says Pisces mom Katie. "So I learned to give it right back to her." Other times, you might need to excuse yourself while you burst into tears, sobbing to your friend, "Why is she doing this to me?"

While your kids will probably see you cry (there's no avoiding it—you weep at the drop of a hat), they should never be pressed into the role of de facto therapists. Even if your teenager is wise beyond his years, it's okay to set limits on what you share. Save the venting for the psychiatrist's couch and keep it out of the minivan. You're a sensitive sign, but when your own feelings get hurt you don't always stick up for yourself or address it head-on. Rather than communicate directly, Pisces moms can become passive-aggressive or emotionally manipulative. "I'm fine," you'll insist, when it's obvious to your entire family that you're not. Although you're just nursing hurt feelings, this withholding has a detrimental effect. You're showing a disconnection between your words and reality, which could lead your children not to trust their own emotions—or you.

As a parent, you'll need to work harder to be transparent and direct, since teenagers have finely honed b.s. detectors. If they sense that you're giving them a guilt trip or subtly punishing them, it will only drive them away. Want to keep their love *and* earn their respect? Say what you mean, and mean what you say.

Beyond that, you may blur the boundaries and let your kids be a little too privy to your personal life. Pisces moms can be a strange mix of sheltering and inappropriate. When you get on a gossipy roll or go off on one of your tirades, you forget to self-censor. News flash: your impressionable teen might not be the best audience for some of your mature subject matter. Pisces can fall into the "victim" mentality, so be mindful not to do that around your kids. You want to model personal responsibility, not teach them to blame and point fingers.

"I got divorced when my son was twelve, and it was really difficult for a while," says one Pisces mom. "My husband left me for another woman, and I was a wreck. My son saw me crying, heard me venting to my girlfriends and my mom, just basically watched me fall apart. At my low point, my friend and I were laughing at the mistress's Facebook page, making fun of her, like, 'My husband left me for *that*?' When my son started acting out—then blaming his misbehavior and slipping grades on the teachers, his classmates, and on me—I knew I had to pull it together. I had to grow up and realize that nobody was in charge of him now but me, so I'd better start acting like an adult and a role model."

While every teenager feels embarrassed of their parents at some point, you might give your kids good reason to pretend you're a stranger now and then. Pisces is ruled by bohemian Neptune, and you're naturally drawn to all things alternative and underground. If you show up at your kids' school rocking an avant-garde outfit that looks like you stole it from the Met Costume Institute, don't be surprised if they pretend not to know you. The Pisces mom can be a party girl, too. So if you get sloppy drunk at a girls' night out after drowning your sorrows at the martini bar, by all means, sneak in through the back door or stay at a friend's house. It doesn't help that you hate feeling "old" and may become quite aware of the aging process around this time. Being the mom of a teenager can certainly spark a midlife crisis—especially if, like many Pisces, you were once the glamorous ingénue!

So how do you stay connected to your kid in the midst of this tumultuous time? The best recipe for Pisces is a mix of compassion and common ground, firmness, and flexibility. You can do volunteer work together, travel, and encourage individuality. A touch of permissiveness goes far, too, so let your kid be in a band (you might even sub for the bassist or do backup vocals), give him a sip of wine at a wedding, and explore the world together.

You can also delve into your spiritual side or do self-development work, as this phase is rich with personal growth opportunities. Pisces mom Linda prides herself on "being conscious of my own ego, attachment, and upbringing and making sure my daughter has plenty of space to become who she is." While you may not be able to maintain this level of enlightenment around the clock, it's a noble intention. Just leave room for your own humanity in there, too—and remind yourself daily that everyone's doing the best they can with what they have.

BYE-BYE, BIRDIE: LEAVING THE NEST (EIGHTEEN-PLUS YEARS)

Grab the tissues! Sensitive Pisces can have a tough time when their kids grow up. You might even go through a mourning period—or a small identity crisis—when you see the bedroom all packed up or come home to an empty house. After all, your life has been structured around someone else's for the last eighteen or more years. You may have poured all your energy into parenting, so there could be cobwebs to clear!

Fortunately, the physical separation may be instant, but the emotional part takes time. Learning independence is a process—for both you and your kid. Your child likely won't become a stranger overnight, and if you maintain a healthy connection, there's no reason ever to be estranged. For starters, you're young at heart, and you'll probably continue hanging out with your son or daughter throughout their adulthood.

Still, you might be fearful and paranoid about what will happen outside of your watch. Heck, you might even spy on your kids' social media to keep tabs on their behavior. Since you may have intentionally babied your child, there could be frequent texts and calls filled with feigned helplessness. Before you know it, you could become the go-to hotline for every crisis, great and small. ("Mommmm, my roommate has her boyfriend here every single night and I can't study! What should I do?" or "Do I wash my colored clothes on hot or cold rinse?") Not that you mind (secretly, you kind of like it), but you don't want to thwart your child's attempts at self-sufficiency.

You might even subtly suggest that the door is always open if things don't work out and your kid wants to move back in. Be careful what you wish for, though. (Rent the movie *Step Brothers* to make sure your life doesn't imitate "art.") Like one Pisces mom we talked to, you might even consider relocating to be near your child. Don't be too quick to start packing the china, Mama. Kids have to learn to fly on their own when they outgrow the nest.

Of course, if you're busy with your own life—especially with a new or renewed romance—all bets are off. If you're in a longtime partnership, you need to rediscover your relationship again, which can be awkward to say the least! (What *do* grown folks talk about around the dinner table again?) It could be time for a full-on reinvention of your marriage: a vow renewal, a long vacation to Bali, or a shared hobby. If you're single, you might dive headfirst into the dating scene again.

Fortunately, Pisces is a mutable (adaptable) sign. As such, you're resilient and good at reinvention so you'll land on your well-shod feet. Not, of course, without a good amount of emotional drama first. But once the show is over and the curtains close, you'll move gracefully into your next act. Who knows? The kid you raised with such a devoted heart and soul could grow up to be your biggest fan.

PART III

Mother and Child Matches

ARIES

ARIES MOM + ARIES CHILD

WHERE YOU CLICK

Viva la diva! An empowered, independent superstar has arrived in the form of Baby Aries. Your pint-sized star mate will fly out of the womb with a mind of her own. While a bit demanding as a baby, young Aries will quickly match your active lifestyle, showing interest in everything from sports to student council. You might have to hire a driver (or don the chauffeur's cap) to shuttle your wee Ram from activity to activity. Since you're born under the same sign, there's an innate understanding of each other's need for autonomy. You won't have to helicopter parent this kid, but do keep a vigilant watch. Little Aries is a daredevil, just like you, and might think it fun to climb on the garage and learn how to fly. Yikes! To avoid the stitches, crutches, and miniature casts, take extra care to childproof your house.

You're both ambitious. Your Aries child will be more than appreciative of your encouragement as you cheer your kid on to be the best. You'll get the same in return. When it comes to championing your cause, your Aries kid will be right behind you, rallying for his supermom at every turn.

WHERE YOU CLASH

Baby Aries can be demanding, throwing a world-class tantrum when hungry, tired, or just plain bored. You both like to have your needs met instantaneously, but providing this for another human being? *¡Ay, caramba!* You want to be left alone to work on your projects and come and go as you please. The constant (loud, divalike) interruptions of wee Aries can stall some of your bigger ventures. When your Ram's horns lock you're both stubbornly resolute—and you have fiery tempers to boot. The brooding silent treatment is another tactic Aries employs, igniting a cold war that could chill your home for days.

You're the queen bee of your home, but your independent mini-me does not like to follow rules. Iron-fisted parenting only makes little Aries want to rebel even more. If you want your young Ram's cooperation, you'll have to explain the reasoning behind your edicts. Well, why not? You're grooming a leader here, Mom. You'll find that your prescient Ram will cooperate if the logic behind your decisions is clear.

ARIES MOM + TAURUS CHILD

WHERE YOU CLICK

As next-door-neighbor signs, Aries and Taurus share very few common traits, but the domestic realm is where you and your little Bull will bond. Order that oversized sofa, stat! Your Venus-ruled child will evolve into a culture vulture, introducing you to rarefied bands and movies, boosting your status as the cool mom. Taurus loves tradition and the Aries mom loves to celebrate. You'll have a blast planning birthdays and holidays together. The Ram and Bull both have a rough-and-tumble nature and red-hot tempers that can flare up out of nowhere. Set up a pair of punching bags in the rec room or get involved in family sports leagues with your child to burn off that steam.

You both love to be spoiled, but here's hoping you have a good-sized shopping budget for luxe-loving Taurus's teenage years. Since you both value hard work, support your industrious Bull in getting a part-time job at the mall to offset the damage of a back-to-school spree. You're all about the big picture while Taurus loves to analyze the details. You might just learn something from your kid if you can breathe and wait for the slower, measured ideas to flow forth.

WHERE YOU CLASH

You and your child move at fundamentally different speeds! Taurus hates to be rushed while the energetic Aries mom is always on the go. Getting your languid Bull out of her silk pajamas and off for the day will try your patience. While you love to nest, you get incredibly claustrophobic if you're cooped up for too long. Not so for your child. Home is where the heart is for the domestic Taurus child. Get some projects set up around the house, Mom, because you're going to be there more often than you'd prefer with this child. Firecracker Aries moms get excited about trying new ideas and starting big projects. Taurus kids prefer the tried-and-true and may be reluctant to get on board with your adventurous ideas. You both have short fuses, and tempers may flare quickly when either of you sees red. Count backward from ten and take those deep breaths, Aries mama!

ARIES MOM + GEMINI CHILD

WHERE YOU CLICK

You're a brainy mother-child duo both blessed with the gift of gab. It's never a dull moment between you two chatterboxes with plenty of "notable quotables" flying from both of your mouths. (Tweet away!) Warrior Aries and contrarian Gemini love to debate, and this is one kid who can question your line of thinking without infuriating you. That's because inquisitive Geminis come from a place of genuine curiosity, not defiance. When they ask why it's not okay to run into the street, for example, it's because they genuinely want to know. In turn, thick-skinned Gemini will take your unfiltered feedback and run with it. Both Aries and Gemini hate to be bored. When home, you'll always be inventing something together, making crafts, or working side by side. Set up the Play-Doh or model airplane set and let young Gem go to town while you put the finishing touches on a proposal. Energetic Gemini can keep pace with your manic trips about town. Sure, you might have to squeeze in a few extra stops at toy or funky kid clothing stores. But hey, it's only fair, since wee Gemini eagerly helped you grocery shop, photocopy a proposal, and pick out a new pair of midcalf boots. In many ways, you'll have a BFF in your little Gemini, making it harder to be the disciplinarian but lots of fun to be adventure buddies.

WHERE YOU CLASH

Aries is a fire sign, passionate and emotionally intense. Gemini is a cool air sign who needs to pull back and view things objectively. Be careful: you can overwhelm your kid with your larger-than-life personality. The Aries mom is decisive; the Gemini child is indecisive. It's easy for you to steamroll this kid with your executive decisions, but don't! Instead, teach young Gemini practical decision-making techniques like writing out a pros-and-cons list. The Aries mom is fundamentally independent, whereas Gemini is the zodiac's twin and craves constant companionship. You may find your child needy at times, especially when the constant barrage of "who, what, when, where, why?" questions begin around toddlerhood (and never stop).

Gemini shares your impatience and may have trouble sitting still at school. Don't expect your kid to follow in your teacher's pet footsteps—little Gem has an impish streak in him! Two Chatty Cathy's living under one roof can be trying at times, especially to the other members of the household. Create a few quiet zones for moments when you need a break from the prattle of a kid who can definitely outtalk you.

ARIES + CANCER CHILD

*

WHERE YOU CLICK

Cancer is the zodiac's mother sign, whereas Aries is the baby—a bizarre role reversal indeed. Mugs of hot tea will be handed to you as soon as your nurturing Crab is old enough to boil water. This child is an empath to the *n*th degree, willing and able to focus directly on you (something superstar Aries truly appreciates). But wait . . . who's the parent here? Don't forget to ask little Cancer about *her* day, too; you don't want your child developing a Cinderella complex.

Boy Cancers need to have a special bond with dear mama. Heap on the praise and avoid barking orders at your son. Although you might want to toughen him up, his sensitivity is what makes him special. Both Aries and Cancer like to be left alone to putter about in their personal space. You'll enjoy plenty of comfortable silence with your Cancer kid, coexisting under the same roof without interfering with each other's activities. Neither one of you trust very easily, so you can bet that any friends little Cancer brings home will have been put through the same exacting standards and loyalty tests you extend to social contacts. It takes a special person to make it into the world of a Ram or a Crab!

WHERE YOU CLASH

Caution: mood swings ahead! Your Cancer kid rides the emotional roller coaster like it was a ride at Six Flags. Although you've thrown a diva fit or two in your day, you have limited patience for this child's ups and downs. When the storm clouds gather, you'll wish your little Crab could just snap out of these spells. What helps are comforting hugs, hot cocoa, heaps of compassion—*not* the tough love advice you're famous for delivering, Aries. Soften up! As cardinal signs, both Cancer and Aries have an alpha side (though Cancer is more of a mama bear than anything). Who's the boss? This kid could give you a run for your throne, oh queen bee.

Sometimes your sweet Crab's conservative values can cramp your wild style. Don't fall into the trap of kowtowing to your kid's standards of propriety. Just drop Cancer off with the grandparents when you want to indulge in more grown-up adventures. This is one sign that actually prefers to remain sheltered in a bubble of childlike innocence for as long as possible.

ARIES MOM + LEO CHILD

*

WHERE YOU CLICK

Bold and showy, the limelight loves the charismatic Aries mom and your star-powered Leo scion. If you aren't literally working the talent circuit with this child, you'll certainly attract loads of attention wherever you two go. As fellow fire signs, you have an easy compatibility with your little Lion. Playful adventure lovers, you'll paint the town red together, dressing up for movies, plays, and pop concerts. You're both impassioned souls! Your conversations may quickly escalate in volume, earning you both annoyed stares (neither of you will notice) and envious, appraising looks.

Daredevils, too, you'll also adore your shared athletic adventures, trips to amusement parks, and other exhilarating activities that might require safety gear. Praise motivates both Aries and Leo, and with your competitive personalities, you make fierce contenders as a tag team. The trouble is you'll both struggle to remember that the competition is just a game: Aries and Leo are in it to win it!

WHERE YOU CLASH

What happens when there's only room on stage for one diva? You may secretly resent your Leo child's ease at slipping into the spotlight or, worse, inadvertently outshine your Leo, snuffing out your kid's spark in the process. While other parents might see you as the perfect PTA president and scout leader, limit your participation in your Leo's daily life. Your baby Lion needs to rule his or her own jungle, not compete with you for attention and power. You're not a coddler, but Leo's constant need for hugs and compliments could drive you to the brink. Time is no object to Leo, who adores complex games and launches into lengthy and colorful stories every five minutes. Your already short patience could wear threadbare from this child's extended soliloquys.

Leo is zodiac royalty and may challenge Queen Bee Aries for her seat on the throne. Power struggles will erupt when Leo tries to boss *you* around. That said you don't want to snuff out this child's majestic personality. Entrust Leo with leadership and empower your Lion to make important decisions, too. You'll be proudly staring at a mini-me by the time you send him off to college.

ARIES MOM + VIRGO CHILD

*

WHERE YOU CLICK

The Aries mom is particular, wanting things done just so. Meticulous Virgo is cut from the same cloth. Sure, the two of you might drive the average waitstaff to the brink, but you'll be pleased to be raising an independent, assertive child who isn't afraid to custom-order, just like you. Virgo is the sign of service, and this kid will be your happy helper. Give your child tasks and watch him shine! This is a relief for the overbooked Aries mama who always needs an extra pair of hands. Make sure you have a reward system in place or you could inadvertently strengthen little Virgo's martyr complex.

You'll have a clear "meeting of the minds" with this child and may be amazed at the depth of conversation your kid can carry from an early age on. You may ultimately share a bookshelf, too, as neither one of you can get enough of those self-improvement selections at the bookstore. Oh, and pass the hand sanitizer! Both Aries and Virgo are known germophobes. While the neuroses of little Virgo might drive some mothers insane, that's not the case with you. You'll be relieved that you don't have to muck around in that bacteria-laden playland, either.

WHERE YOU CLASH

The Aries mom is the picture of confidence and self-love. Perfectionist Virgo struggles with self-doubt. Tone down the tough love, Mom! Little Virgo needs lots of positive reinforcement and encouragement. Any hint of disapproval (which you'd define as being direct and honest) can send Virgo into a shame spiral.

Investigative Virgo needs to know why and how everything works; yet this child's nonstop questions can drive the impatient Aries mom over the edge. Childproof your web browser ASAP and teach your kid to Google. Either that, or schedule daily Q&A sessions, where you look up the answers to Virgo's vast curiosities in a supervised manner.

The Aries mom can be loud, flashy, and over the top. Modest Virgo may balk at your theatrical personality and your more risqué fashion choices. You could get a finger wagging from your conservative child who is definitely more uptight than you! While you may need to tone it down a bit when visiting Virgo at school, don't lose your free-spirited verve, Aries! One day, your kid will appreciate your spunk.

ARIES MOM + LIBRA CHILD

WHERE YOU CLICK

Sweet Libra idolizes the powerhouse Aries mom, quickly charming her into submission. Yes, you'll be putty in the hands of this child, rare for such a commanding leader like yourself. This peace-loving kid is born with the disease to please, but the Aries mom will ensure that her child develops a backbone. In turn, Libra will help soften her stance, making her more cooperative and less combative.

Wardrobe! Styling! You both love to look your best and will work it like a pair of fashionistas in the public eye. Plus, Libra loves to socialize, which is perfect for your active, on-the-go lifestyle. Wrap this kid in a BabyBjörn and let him accompany you to those power lunches, professional appointments, and dinner dates. Aries is the zodiac's warrior; Libra is represented by the scales of justice. You're a force to be reckoned with when uniting for a common cause. Get little Libra involved in charity work at a young age. Later in life, let your diplomatic Libra charm folks at the fund-raising drive that you spearheaded. They'll open their checkbooks quickly under the spell of your kid's dimpled smile and genuine gaze. Way to make the world a better place!

WHERE YOU CLASH

As the zodiac's baby, you never stop craving coddling from your nearest and dearest. Little Libra, dimpled, divalike, and adorably demanding, could crowd you out of your proverbial crib. Try not to throw any tantrums to get the attention you crave, Aries! Mornings may be the worst hour for this mother-child matchup. Languid Libra hates to be rushed and the Aries mom is crazy impatient. Your sling-backs will pace a hole in your hardwood floors while waiting for your daughter to work through a hissy fit because she wants you to let her leave the house in her princess costume or waiting for your son to painstakingly coordinate his oxford with his socks. Surrender! This child might just teach you to slow down and enjoy the moment.

Aries is the zodiac's warrior; Libra is the pacifist. Your divergent approach to conflict resolution could be the biggest sore spot in your relationship. You simply can't go in with guns ablazing or even be too direct when disciplining this kid unless you want to reduce your offspring to tears or snuff out his developing opinions before he can grow his own spine (Libra would rather fold than fight). Take deep breaths and cool your temper. You have to be firm with the Libra charmer, but you must also be calm when you set those rules.

ARIES MOM + SCORPIO CHILD

*

WHERE YOU CLICK

You never thought of yourself as a hover mother until Baby Scorpio arrived on the scene. Call it karma or a rich past life history; there's a preternatural connection between your signs. You can't get to the portrait studio fast enough to capture every moment of your wee Scorpio's evolution—and odds are you'll be posing right alongside your kid for every shot. Loyal Scorpios will pledge their allegiance to the powerhouse Aries mother. This is not a kid who will question your eminence but rather brag to friends about how incredible you are. What's not to love about *that*?

Neither Aries nor Scorpio trusts easily and you're both prone to paranoia. You have to be careful not to feed your little Scorpion's OCD tendencies, so keep the dramatic, cautionary tales in check.

High achievers, you'll share a thirst for domination, and if you have common interests this could lead to a moneymaking venture. This wunderkind might just take over the family business (the one you built from a labor of love into an empire), working under your wing as a teen and inheriting the scepter later in life.

WHERE YOU CLASH

Because you bond so deeply, you could form an unhealthy "us against the world" dynamic with your Scorpio child. Jealousy is an Achilles' heel for both of your signs. Little Scorpio may become possessive when you're with your friends—and vice versa! Your share a vicious competitive streak and you'll make a formidable pair when you team up on a mission. But if you find yourself on opposing sides, look out! Little Scorpio's stingers have a special way of cutting you to the quick. In many ways, you're no match for your kid's intensity and vengeful ways of punishing when you don't give in.

As an independent adventuress, you proudly regale the tales of your wild days, à la rocker-loving Aries mom Kate Hudson. But beware! Your rebel chapter is just a brilliant flash in the history of a fire sign. Water sign Scorpio, however, is prone to self-destructive behaviors. Steering Scorpio away from trouble will be your biggest responsibility as a parent. Send your child off to Grandma's if you plan to cut loose. Scorpio needs to see an unwavering role model in order to feel safe in the world.

ARIES MOM + SAGITTARIUS CHILD

*

WHERE YOU CLICK

Can you say "BFFs"? Spunky Sagittarius is a chip off the old block: independent and adventurous, just like you. There's no telling when the two of you will come home when you set out for a day of fun. Unplanned stops will be plentiful if either of you sees something that catches your eye. You're both fire signs, but where you're a fierce fighter, Sag is more of a philosophical diplomat. Your little Archer can cool your fiery temper and remind you to look on the bright side before you burn down the village.

Both Aries and Sagittarius are known for being athletic, although your mini-Archer may be clumsy, lacking your finely developed motor skills. Go slowly when introducing Sagittarius to the more coordinated sports you've mastered. Otherwise, you could see little Sag on crutches from that trip down the bunny hill. That said, rough-and-tumble Sagittarius will bring out the tomboy in you, a welcome break from diva-dom indeed! You're both entrepreneurial by nature and your Archer may take an interest in your business ideas, even helping you develop one of your ventures from a young age onward. In turn, you'll happily encourage your Sagittarian's enterprising ways, building the booth for your kid's lemonade stand and even serving as the angel investor for your child's first business after college graduation.

WHERE YOU CLASH

Aries is unnervingly direct, whereas Sagittarius is downright tactless. Things can get ugly if your piercing Ram's horns get tangled with your little Archer's arrows. As fire signs, you both get heated quickly. Indeed, cooling down in your own corners is probably your best hope for conflict resolution. Accept the fact that Sagittarius was born as headstrong as his mother. Impatient much? When either of you wants to go, you want to go *now*! Don't drag this kid along to activities you know she won't enjoy. Better to hire a babysitter, as your vocal Archer will interrupt your good times and tug on your sleeve furiously until you've said an abrupt good-bye and turned the key in your car's ignition.

When it comes to socializing, you have breathtakingly different styles. You, Aries, are highly selective about who you become friends with; remarkably, little Sagittarius bonds with everyone from the picture-perfect teacher's pet to the unwashed troublemaker who hails from a dysfunctional home. You may be borderline horrified by whom your kid invites for a sleepover at times, but your accepting Archer can help you open your own mind.

ARIES MOM + CAPRICORN CHILD

*

WHERE YOU CLICK

Little Capricorn is your long-awaited wunderkind, a high achieving, go-getter who can match your ambition stride for stride. You'll be the beaming parent at every awards ceremony as your little Goat brings honor to the family name. Polite, disciplined, and self-correcting Capricorn is a model child, one who can accompany you on your many high-powered missions.

Country club membership, anyone? You're both rather exclusive when it comes to picking friends—not any Joe Schmo can find his way into the inner circle of an Aries or Capricorn. Together, you may become a tad elitist, so be careful not to encourage your kid toward snobbery. Maybe you're not so fond of her nursery school playmates or the kids on his baseball team, but rather than nitpicking teach your Capricorn tolerance and encourage a less-judgmental attitude. Hey, that means you'll have to walk your talk, Aries, which will force you to stretch your own social boundaries.

WHERE YOU CLASH

Aries is the zodiac's baby, and Capricorn is the sign associated with fatherhood. You could easily fall into a role reversal such that your kid feels more like your parent than your child. Hey, at least you won't have to worry about who will be taking care of you when you're older. Save that for your sunset years and don't foist adult responsibility on this kid too early.

Capricorns are born perfectionists. If you're too quick to criticize—or just sling one of your mindlessly unfiltered, critical observations—you might derail little Cap from the goal of self-confidence. You're both incredibly stubborn. While you might be the louder, more forceful one, strong-arming little Capricorn will backfire. The calculated approach of the Capricorn can rival the strategies of a decorated general. Hello, cold war! Don't talk over your quieter kid or shut down his opinions too quickly. Your Goat will retreat, preparing to do battle from a distance by withholding love and undermining your efforts.

ARIES MOM + AQUARIUS CHILD

*

WHERE YOU CLICK

Your brainy Aquarius child is a chip off the intellectual block, whip smart, just like her mama. You're both full of innovative and quirky ideas: you might invent a product together or start a revolution! Like you, your Aquarius wants to change the world and shares your keen sense of injustice.

Both Aries and Aquarius are future forward. The wee Water Bearer shares your love of discovering the latest and greatest things. Aquarius may be more of a gearhead than you; hand your child your gadgets to program and you'll never have to call the Geek Squad again.

Social butterflies, Aries and Aquarius can work a room like nobody's business. You'll be the mother-child life of the party, the first ones to arrive and the last ones to leave. You're both active and adventurous. From trips to museums to movies to sports events, Aquarius is your ultimate hanging buddy, a child who might turn out to be your best friend. There's a prankster living in both of you. Playing practical jokes could become your favorite pastime. Bring on the whoopee cushions!

WHERE YOU CLASH

Even as a mother, you thrive on recognition—admit it, you like it when your kids admire you. Alas, your dynamo moves won't get the hoped-for ooohs and ahhhs from your cool, aloof Water Bearer. Ouch!

Both Aries and Aquarius have a rebel streak. No matter how hip and understanding you are, inevitably "fighting the power" will mean questioning you at every turn. This is doubly tough to take since it will feel like staring in the mirror. (Is that Grandma snickering from the sidelines? Eek!) Your iron-fisted edicts won't go down well with Aquarius. This is a kid who responds to logic. Explain it like this: if you do *x*, here is the reward; if you do *y*, here is the punishment. When Aquarius feels a sense of choice, he might just become a self-governing body.

Both Aries and Aquarius struggle with anger management. You heat up quickly and often. Aquarius's temper strikes out of nowhere, and then dissipates. For Aquarius kids, there's usually a specific injustice that incites their rage. Unfortunately, they don't always show signs that they're getting frustrated, making it hard for the Aries mom to prevent a meltdown. (For example, if you'd *known* your kid didn't want to do his English homework because he felt the teacher had unfairly graded his last essay, you might have been less stern.) Although your vocal sign may wish Aquarius would give you a clue, don't push him to be more expressive or you could see that flash of destructive rage appear. Not a pretty sight!

ARIES MOM + PISCES CHILD

*

WHERE YOU CLICK

Pisces are known for being passive, whereas Aries moms are aggressive. This child will happily pass you the reins, allowing you to take charge. From the dance classes to etiquette lessons to the young debutante's club, whatever dream you had of molding your child into, mutable Pisces will comply. But is that really a good thing? It's a little too easy to fall into the groove of shaping this child, forgetting to teach Pisces to develop a mind of his own.

Make sure you also nurture your Fish's interests, which you'll only discover by observing your child in action. Both Aries and Pisces adore the arts and can be incredible performers. Enter mother-child dance competitions or charm on the talent show circuit as a dynamic duo. Just remember: little Pisces is less prone to talking and more prone to doing. This kid will wow you without saying a word.

Let's face it, Aries, you don't suffer fools lightly, but sometimes you can be a little too quick to cut people off. Compassionate Pisces will teach you to open your heart. In turn, you'll help your far-too-understanding child to set boundaries and stick up for herself—an important lesson for Pisces to learn!

WHERE YOU CLASH

The Aries mom is all about action and clarity. Life is but a dream for flowy, unstructured Pisces. Your on-the-go lifestyle *will* be slowed, so prepare for a downshift. Languid Pisces loves to linger in pajamas till noon, setting up an imaginary world with doll friends, playing with musical instruments, or just staring off into space, daydreaming about who knows what. Alas, you can't drag your ethereal child along on too many of your errands. Getting her in and out of the car seat alone will try your patience. This child prefers to stay in a safe and cozy bubble, and with good reason. Piscean psychic receptors are stronger than most; your little Fish will absorb every energy in the room.

While the Aries mom is direct, little Pisces can be sneaky, even manipulative. Setting boundaries won't be easy here. You'll find yourself saying yes when you mean no, charmed by this little operator. If you are coparenting, make sure you align with your partner on rules and regulations. The slippery little Fish might go to Daddy for permission when you've denied a request! Write the household guidelines on poster board so there are no (ahem) "misunderstandings" about bedtimes, curfews, and chores.

TAURUS

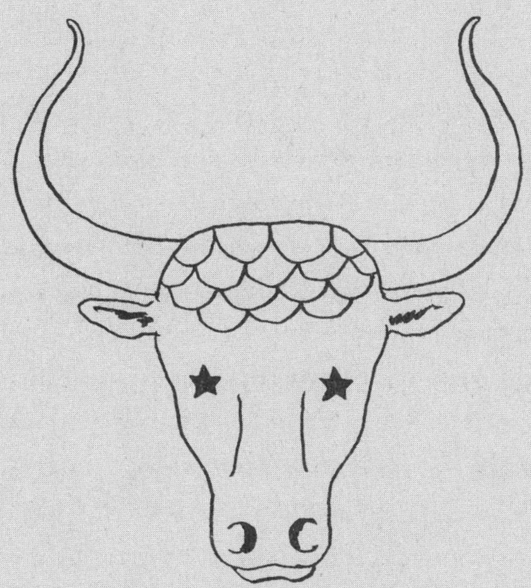

TAURUS MOM + ARIES CHILD

WHERE YOU CLICK

The "strong like bull" Taurus mom and the headstrong Aries kid are both fierce and determined. Extremely passionate about your beliefs, neither one of you has trouble speaking your minds. You'll understand little Aries' fussy tastes, too, and won't mind making a plain hamburger for your picky little Ram when it's boeuf bourguignon night for the rest of the fam.

You're both tinkerers who tend to be mechanically inclined. Break out the LEGOs, complex crafting kits, and model airplane sets. Building things by hand helps you bond. There's a thrill-seeker living in both the Taurus mom and the Aries child. Mother-child sports, trips to amusement parks, even zip lining and skydiving can lure you both. Although little Aries can make your heart stop with his antics, you'll be secretly inspired to push the envelope yourself. Just make sure you set a few limits so your little Ram realizes that "mind over matter" does not give her the ability to fly if she leaps off the roof of the garage.

WHERE YOU CLASH

Frenetic Aries zips around at a manic pace and changes directions at a moment's notice. You're more methodical, plotting your course in a well-designed itinerary and cruising along at a leisurely pace. Trying to keep up with your mini-Ram will be exhausting!

You're more old-school traditional; Aries is a rule-breaking renegade. Just try to make this kid sit still for a religious service or follow a dress code. You could have an all-out mutiny to deal with. Alas, Taurus mama, you can't parent by the books with the Aries child. The Ram does everything according to his own timeline, not the one you read about in all those parenting books. Don't be hard on yourself about this. You're not failing as a mother if Aries weans later than most (or never latches in the first place) or gets more bumps and bruises than most kids. The accident-prone Ram seems to find trouble at every turn. It's better to childproof the house than to expect yourself to be in chase mode 24/7.

TAURUS MOM + TAURUS CHILD

*

WHERE YOU CLICK

Ahh, the sweet sight of a contented Bull and calf. Taurus mom and child are two peas in a pod, lounging in the field of sweet grasses (i.e., your overstuffed L-shaped couches) or charging after a waving red cape (read: the Macy's one-day sale). You're quite an indulgent, affectionate pair, and cuddle time will be sheer heaven.

Tradition, tradition! Your baby Bull shares your family values and love of rituals. Here's the perfect little guardian to whom you can pass down secret family recipes and stories of your ancestors. Holidays are huge with both of you, and you love all the rituals around them, from baking cookies to decorating the house to gathering with the rest of your relatives around the hearth. Afterward, you'll both dive into a scrapbooking project, immortalizing the event with printed photos, decorative stamps, and handwritten liner notes.

Taurus is equal parts pleasure-seeking and pragmatic, so be sure to pass on some of your common sense, too. Before you know it you might have a Bossy Betty on your hands, but hey, your kid will keep siblings and playmates in line, which just makes parenting easier for you.

WHERE YOU CLASH

Now playing: Stubborn and Stubborner. The willful Taurus child is as bullheaded as you are and fights between the two of you can become endless battles for domination. Your line: "Because I said so!" Little Taurus: "You can't make me!" Argh!

Neither one of you adapts well to change. From weaning to potty training to the first days of kindergarten, every transition may come with a bit of resistance. This difficulty in letting go crops up for both of you—abandonment fears can be an Achilles' heel for your sign. You may struggle with sending your little one off, inadvertently stirring up her fears of leaving you for the day.

Trying to get two slow-moving Bulls out of the house can be an exercise in frustration. This kid likes to primp and dawdle as much as you do. Taurus is the sign that rules ethics and values. When the teen years strike, your mini-Bull's rebellious phase could lead him down a different political or religious path than your own. Take a deep breath and let him find his voice—and hopefully his way back home. If you've done your job like we know you have, you've instilled a good sense of right and wrong in your child. Have a little faith!

TAURUS MOM + GEMINI CHILD

*

WHERE YOU CLICK

Chaotic Gemini is like a helium balloon with the air streaming out of it. You'll never be able to keep up with this kid's frenetic flight, and you shouldn't try. What Gemini needs is structure and routine—the very things Taurus excels at creating. Home should feel like a safe harbor for little Gemini, predictable and secure. Good thing you're a hard-core nester! By the same token, couldn't you afford to get out a little more? That's where little Gemini is such a godsend for you. Field trips, playdates, adventurous little jaunts—your wee one will have you out on the town all day! You are both culture vultures, with a special love of music. Little Gem will rock out by your side at that concert in the park, creating many a photo op.

Making things by hand is something you both adore. Can vegetables (the ones you cultivated yourself), brew pots of sun tea, build a play set by hand. Your Gemini will be an eager assistant and is likely to put an innovative spin on your classic formulas. Genius!

WHERE YOU CLASH

"Why, Mommy, why?" is Gemini's favorite query. Oh. No. Questioning every aspect of life is not something the by-the-books Taurus mom has much interest in. You can be rather black and white, whereas little Gemini wants to crack the code on enigmas that just aren't of interest to you. Warning: you'll be doing lots of research to find answers for your child. The upside: you'll stretch your own intellect in the process.

No more pencils, no more books? Gemini is not always a traditional learner, which can be tough for schoolmarm Taurus. Forget the cookie-cutter curriculum that worked so well for you. Little Gemini may require an alternative or magnet school, perhaps Waldorf- or Montessori-style education. It's not ADD; it's just a Gemini thing. So don't let anyone slap the labels on this kid or administer Adderall without exploring other options first. Silence will not be golden with a Gemini in the house. This chatterbox will definitely interrupt your longed-for quiet spells. Soundproofing the kid's room wouldn't be such a bad idea, especially if he picks up a musical instrument as many Geminis do!

TAURUS MOM + CANCER CHILD

*

WHERE YOU CLICK

Pass the milk and cookies! As two comfort-loving homebodies, you'll bless your nest with warm, sentimental vibes. No holding back your zealous maternal style here; Cancer loves to be mothered. If you aren't careful, though, you could be doing this kid's laundry until he's married—and maybe beyond. Rather than henpecking or enabling dependency, enlist this helpful kid on your housekeeping missions by turning him into your sous-chef or gardening assistant. Take Cancer to work with you, too, and encourage your Crab to get out of that shell and into the world.

Insular and family-oriented, you both prefer a tight-knit crew who are either blood-related or have earned family status by sheer loyalty. Just make sure you don't raise an introvert here. Nudging shy Cancer to make new friends may be necessary. Cancers are foodies and you have gourmand tastes yourself. Warning: both signs can use food for emotional comfort so you'll have to be careful not to pass on that bon-bon-binging habit to this child. Keep healthier snacks on hand and point out the nutritional value of vegetables with as much zeal as you have for that box of Mallomars.

WHERE YOU CLASH

Is your Cancer overreacting . . . or is it really *that* serious? The emotional Crab's sensitivity is definitely foreign to the matter-of-fact Taurus mom. Alas, telling this delicate child to "get over it," will only bring on more waterworks. Your patience will be tried as you dry your kid's tears, but you will become more empathetic and less harsh in your delivery.

Your coarser ways may be a bit much for the sheltered Cancer. Keep it G-rated in this kid's presence, even if your friends are a bunch of bawdy babes. Of course, most Taurus mothers have a perfectionist streak, wanting to appear as if you have it all together in front of your kids. But playing the "steel magnolia" can backfire, too. Emotional Cancer needs to see your softer side in order to relate and feel safe opening up in your presence. Try a little tenderness and share your feelings from time to time. Otherwise, your little one can wind up feeling ashamed for being so delicate.

TAURUS MOM + LEO CHILD

*

WHERE YOU CLICK

Viva la diva! Fanciful and fashionable, little Leo shares your love of luxury. Head to an upscale department store and outfit this child in style. Then show off your progeny at the fanciest, kid-friendly places in town. You're the ultimate stage mother and child star, a proud pair indeed! You might even work the pageant or acting circuit with this one. (Go easy on the spray tans, please.) You're both affectionate and love to be preened and pampered. Mommy-kid spa trips may be in the future for you two, so start saving up.

Both Taurus and Leo can be traditional and share a love of history. Here's a kid who will accompany you to prayer services or on the neighborhood architectural tour. Leo brings out the energetic, playful energy in the Taurus mom, too. Bring on the pillow fights, potato sack races, and family Frisbee games. If any kid could get you off the couch, it's this one! You have high standards and little Leo likes to please. Plan on handing out lots of gold stars to motivate your Lion to bring his best. Be careful, though: you want to pass on your stellar work ethic to your royal child, not teach her to expect a prize every time she lifts a finger.

WHERE YOU CLASH

You're a true material girl, but unlike this child you understand the concept of a budget. Little Leo has a huge appetite for life, always wanting more, more, more. Curb your enthusiasm for luxury in the name of teaching Leo to value money.

Leo's creativity and imagination know no bounds, which can strike fear in your pragmatic heart. Warning: you may drive your little Lion harder than necessary in the interest of building his work ethic. Fine, Mama Bull, make him have a paper route, but sending him off to the farm for a summer when he'd rather be playing on the soccer league? That's a bit extreme.

On the flip side, you can spoil little Leo by feeding her ego and heaping on too much audible praise. Teach Leo to share the spotlight and to give props to her peers. Confidence is one thing this kid will have no shortage of. While you're proud to develop a leader, you don't want to groom a megalomaniac. Diva duel alert! If you have a Leo daughter, there could be a competitive under-current at times. You like to be involved in your kids' lives, but give her space to shine among her friends instead of flaunting your cool mom status and accidentally one-upping her in the process.

TAURUS MOM + VIRGO CHILD

✳

WHERE YOU CLICK

Fellow earth signs, Virgo shares your grounded, pragmatic approach to life. You're a pair of perfectionists who like things done "just so." While you're decorating the foyer in the style of an *Elle Decor* spread, this child will be meticulously arranging the dollies on her shelf or lining up toy cars according to year, make, and model.

Virgo is a keen observer of life and you have a blunt call-it-like-it-is MO. You'll love sharing observations with this savvy child, analyzing every nuance like a pair of professional critics. Just be careful that you don't send out the message that it's okay to gossip or trash people. Repetition, rules, and routines help this anxious child feel safe. You're the master of such things, setting up consistent times for dinner and lights out, packing your fussy eater's favorite foods and showing up at every major event. Have little Virgo help you devise the rules, too. What does she think is fair punishment if they are broken? Virgos love the opportunity to set up systems and cultivate a responsible side. They might even put themselves in the time-out chair, without your saying a word!

WHERE YOU CLASH

Your brassy style can be a bit much for modest Virgo. This kid would rather recede into the wallpaper than make a scene. Eek! You might even delight in embarrassing your little Virgo in an effort to get him to lighten up. Bad. Idea. Tone down the loud and dramatic complaints, too, at least in your child's presence. While you may merely be venting, Virgo is a fixer and will rush into rescuer mode trying to remedy mama's woes. No big deal to you but a huge ordeal to your sensitive kid who is an anxious worrier by nature. Unless it's truly an emergency, use your indoor voice and play it cool.

Virgo is a perfectionist, too, and your blunt observations can send him to a dark place. You'll need to couch the critiques with plenty of compliments or perhaps avoid delivering them altogether. Odds are your perfectionist Virgo child is well aware of her weak spots. Positive reinforcement works much better. Praise and encourage the traits you'd like to see Virgo develop instead of pointing out faults.

TAURUS MOM + LIBRA CHILD

*

WHERE YOU CLICK

Relax, relate, release. Leisurely Libra operates at the same mellow speed as Mom. The two of you could turn lounging into a sport. Both Taurus and Libra are ruled by the elegant, romantic Venus, which gives you a shared affection for rich food, elegant clothes, and pretty trinkets. The apple doesn't fall far from the tree when it comes to fashion sense! And you thought you took a long time to pick out your clothes and primp in the morning? Little Libra will be particular about color and style and may start selecting her own outfits from a young age.

As a duo you can be epic dawdlers though, frustrating friends, teachers, and playdate parents by being egregiously tardy for the party. Try to get an earlier start on your mornings and save your Libra child some demerits (and yourself some stress).

Two tickets to the theater, please! Like Mom, Libra is a culture vulture and appreciator of the arts. You don't have to wait for this kid to graduate to invite him along to museums, concerts, and festivals. You might even start a playtime band together, rocking out on the plastic instruments then moving on to real ones.

WHERE YOU CLASH

The no-nonsense Taurus mom sees the world as black or white. Libra loves to ponder the gray areas, endlessly deliberating. You'll grow impatient waiting for Libra to make a choice! In turn, little Libra may resent you for rushing her decision-making process. Harmonizing Libra likes co-operation and partnership. The Taurus mom prefers to barrel in and take charge, and it's all too easy to steamroll this child. Warning: just because Libra is going along with your game plan, don't assume all is well. The peacekeeping Libra child may sacrifice her wishes to keep conflict at bay—a sure recipe for resentment.

Ambassador Libra likes to make friends from all walks of life, which could activate the snob in you. Ditch your predictable groove and let Libra's "one love" attitude open your mind to different cultures, philosophies, and ways of life.

TAURUS MOM + SCORPIO CHILD

*

WHERE YOU CLICK

Because Taurus and Scorpio are opposite signs, they can click and clash in equal measure. Your tough and dependable nature helps anxious Scorpio relax and feel safe. In turn, your kid's sense of loyalty and shrewd strategic moves make you beam with pride. Stay close! Little Scorpio has innate abandonment issues just like you. As such, you'll understand your child's need for extra reassurance, extended hugs, and perhaps your twice-a-week stint moonlighting as the classroom monitor. Since you love to be involved in your kid's life, you'll find these clutchy qualities endearing. Just be careful not to enable Scorpio's belief that the world is a scary place. You're a tough cookie, and you can teach your child to develop a thicker skin.

Neither of you is a fan of change. You'll fall into a natural groove with each other, developing cozy and endearing habits for coexistence. Is that the sound of comfortable silence? You both like to zone out in your own little worlds giving each other plenty of space to dream. With the homey bubble you create, you might have trouble nudging Scorpio from the nest when that day comes.

WHERE YOU CLASH

While you're both prone to mood swings, Scorpio's dark spells last far longer than yours. As your child's bedroom door slams with a cry of "Leave me alone!" you'll feel like barging right in and making your kid deal with it—*now*! That strong-arming tactic won't work here, Taurus. Let this child brood in private. She'll get over it. Eventually.

Matter-of-fact Taurus moms take things at face value, whereas Scorpios are always digging for hidden reasons. Expect to have some complex questions hurled at you, ones that might keep you on your toes. Scorpios are deeply private, but you can be brash and outspoken. Think twice about sharing a "funny story" if it exposes your Scorpio or embarrasses him in any way. Once trust is broken, it's hard to get it back with this kid. Plus, this sign can be vengeful. Young Scorpio might put your most embarrassing moments on the Internet in response. *Très* embarrassing!

Bedtime should be interesting, too. Scorpio is a nocturnal creature, but you? You're a bit of a narcoleptic by nightfall. This kid could get into some misadventures while you're nodding off. Lock up the cookie jar!

TAURUS MOM + SAGITTARIUS CHILD

*

WHERE YOU CLICK

Your keep-it-real signs are on the same candid wavelength; in fact, little Sagittarius could even one-up you in the bluntness department. Fortunately, you'll enjoy hearing your child's bold opinions. High fives and amens will be plentiful between you two, as will the laughter.

Wild-child Sagittarius loves to be out in nature, calling forth the earthy side of you. This kid will get you out of your Calvin Klein and into your camping gear. At home, planting a garden will be a fun way for you to nature-bond with your mini-Archer.

You're both indulgent, especially when it comes to food. Sagittarius is ruled by Jupiter (god of the feast); you, by decadent Venus. Your bake-offs will be legendary, but since neither of you is great as resisting another bite of cake save the Betty Crocker moments for special occasions. Prepare healthier recipes, too, to keep your little Sag in a healthy weight category.

The Taurus mother works hard for her money and the Archer is equally ambitious. Take your Sag to work with you! This mini-entrepreneur will be setting up a lawn-mowing business (and who knows what else) before you know it, making the material mama in you proud.

WHERE YOU CLASH

Ouch! Both of you can dole out truths that hit a little too close to home. Your raw observations can take the wind out of your Archer's sails, and vice versa. You'll have to teach this kid some tact—just try to lead by example! The Taurus mom is methodical, believing that haste makes waste; Sagittarius is Speedy Gonzales incarnate. Good luck getting this kid into those fussy suits or dresses with the bows that you find so adorable. It will be ripped and muddy in no time. Individualistic Archers prefer to pick out their own clothes and find their own friends, but you find it tough not to meddle. When it comes to socializing, the Taurus mom prefers pals with pedigree, while kumbaya Sagittarius bonds with people from all walks of life . . . yes, even *that* person.

You won't be able to foist your values on this child, especially when it comes to religion. Sagittarians are seekers who need to shape their own views and ethics. The best you can do is introduce your child to your beliefs. Be sure to ask your Archer for feedback. You'll be amazed by the wisdom this pint-sized Socrates can spew!

TAURUS MOM + CAPRICORN CHILD

*

WHERE YOU CLICK

Hardworking, dependable, and disciplined, you're a mother-child match made in heaven. Groom Capricorn as mommy's little helper. You never know: the two of you could open the doors to a family business one day. Both signs like status symbols and when your Cap gets old enough to discern Hermès from H&M, you'll have a shopping buddy, too. Uh-oh, this could get expensive.

When it comes to family, you share a deep loyalty to your loved ones. Capricorn kids are known for taking great care of their parents and you're the type of mom who loves to keep her children near. You'll likely remain in close proximity to each other throughout the years. The Taurus mom is a planner and the Capricorn kid comes out of the womb focusing on the future. You'll love imagining your daughter's someday wedding ceremony (while she's still in her christening gown) or planning your Capricorn son's entry into the Major Leagues (while he's just gearing up for his first Little League practice). While it is fun to fantasize about what the future holds, don't forget to enjoy the present, too.

WHERE YOU CLASH

Although you're a toughie, Taurus, you're also quite sentimental. Reserved Capricorns don't show their emotions quite as often. You want to gush and be affectionate, but your child would prefer that you didn't rain the kisses on him, thank you very much.

Like you, Capricorn is a perfectionist, but it runs much deeper with this kid. Your offhanded comments could feel like major critiques, sending Cap into an overachieving, self-flagellating spiral. If you notice your progeny working hard, brow furrowed, it's probably a sign that she's trying to win back Mommy's approval. Avoid this pitfall and use positive reinforcement only. Praise, but not flattery, works well with Capricorn, who prides himself on being a hardworking achiever.

Homebody Taurus won't log enough couch potato time with this kid. Popular, active Caps will be involved in everything from sports to scouts to summer stage theater. Organize a carpooling spreadsheet with other parents or you could burn out from playing chauffeur!

TAURUS MOM + AQUARIUS CHILD

*

WHERE YOU CLICK

Did this child drop down from a different planet? It sure feels that way. Still, you'll enjoy watching your clever, inventive Aquarius develop into a budding mad scientist. You're mechanical, and Aquarius is innovative. Bring on the chemistry sets, model rockets, and musical instruments. Building things by hand is one surefire way you can bond. Planning parties and entertaining friends is something you both enjoy, too. Like you, your Aquarian can be a social butterfly, although you'll definitely be drawn to different crowds of people! Nevertheless, birthday parties, holiday celebrations, and family gatherings can be legendary when your elegant creativity meets your young Aquarius's quirky novelty.

Aquarius is the sign of the humanitarian and you have a huge heart when it comes to the less fortunate. Get involved in a community service group and activate your little Water Bearer's goodwill at a young age. Aquarius can be rebellious and you have a wild streak in you, too. As your kid grows up, you may have a partner in crime for extreme sports and physical challenges—and you'll be happy to be on hand to make sure that your kid wears his helmet!

WHERE YOU CLASH

Space cadet Aquarius is lost in la-la land while you have your feet planted firmly on earth. You'll struggle to understand this kid's offbeat ideas, which can be so left-of-center you are sometimes left confounded. Try not to judge the experimental art projects, punk-rock Barbie haircuts, and strange alien noises coming from the child in the corner, please. This is the zodiac's rebel you gave birth to, after all!

When it comes to people, you are highly discerning, preferring the company of a particular ilk. Anything-goes Aquarius will make friends with the most unusual characters in town and the wildest kids in class—from all cultures and socioeconomic backgrounds to boot. If it's time to open your mind, this child will ensure that you do just that.

Taurus has a teacher vibe; Aquarius is the class clown. You'll have to lighten up a bit and restore your sense of humor. Handing out demerits won't keep the Water Bearer in line. If you want to discipline this child, turn those chores into games. Aquarius kids are as playful as they come, and a little inventiveness will have them rushing to be your happy helpers.

TAURUS MOM + PISCES CHILD

*

WHERE YOU CLICK

Imaginative Pisces shares your artsy sensibilities—and sonic ones. Dancing, singing, and going to concerts together will become treasured pastimes for you two music lovers. You'll be the cool mom who takes your Pisces teen to her first live show. Bring on the rich pastries and frilly, ruffled outfits! This is the kid who won't mind being dressed in a miniature tuxedo or three-layer-cake dress replete with fondant ribbons. You've been waiting for this costume party forever, Mama Bull, and your fairy-tale loving Fish will be all over it. Set the alarm clock, though. You're both major sleepers and your household "slumber parties" could leave you rushing to get your dreamy Pisces to school before the first bell rings.

Has your inner Bossy Betty met her match? Although Pisces kids have their passive moments, they can also be finger waggers and a tad moralistic. Sound familiar? You'll get a chuckle out of watching your Pisces commanding the other kids on the playground to follow the rules. Flashback!

WHERE YOU CLASH

The Taurus mom is a hard-core realist, whereas Pisces is the sign of fantasy. Herein lies the major difference between you two. People rarely have to question where you stand: you've made it eminently clear. Pisces, however, can be major chameleons, adapting to whatever "school" they are swimming in. As someone who is staunch in her values, you'll struggle with your kid's inability to take a firm position. You're tough and Pisces can be gullible—and this brings out your overprotective nature. This overly trusting kid needs positive peers influencing her but may be drawn toward the troubled ones. You'll have to be more hands-on in directing this kid's social life. That said, it's easy for Taurus to bulldoze the Pisces child, who will sooner retreat than fight. Just because your kid seems agreeable, don't assume all is well. Secretive Pisces need to be drawn out of their shyness and encouraged to express their true feelings. But they won't talk unless they feel they have a safe space to open up in. Tone down your judgments if you want to truly know what your child is thinking.

GEMINI

GEMINI MOM + ARIES CHILD

*

WHERE YOU CLICK

The mercurial mommy has met her match in quick-thinking Aries. Your wee Ram is sharp as a tack and can keep pace with your clever commentary and Miz Wizard's World ideas. There's a geeky streak in both of you, and this kid may get you into wiring electronics, building gadgets from individual parts, and otherwise turning life into a science fair.

Stuck in quicksand? Never! Since you both have short attention spans, you'll be in perpetual motions with this child, never staying at any playground or playdate for too long. Like you, Aries is fun-loving with a daredevil streak. Bring on the season passes to amusement parks, snowboarding slopes, and rock-climbing gyms. In many ways, this child will feel like your favorite hanging buddy.

WHERE YOU CLASH

With your finely honed nervous systems, you're both reactive. Aries throws an epic hissy fit when you don't meet her "critical and urgent" need to eat, leave, sleep, or whatever else, and your fuse is short when it comes to her fussiness and outright bratty demands. There will be lots of deep breaths and counting backward from ten to keep your sanity here.

"Me, myself, and I" is a favorite topic of conversation for both the Aries child and Gemini mom. You'll be competing for the spotlight in moments, especially since you're both better at talking than listening. Independent Aries kids need lots of alone time, too, and may get territorial about her room. The on-the-go Gemini mom may have to stay home more than you prefer so that Aries can play with his many half-finished projects that are too big to tote along in the car or stroller.

GEMINI MOM + TAURUS CHILD

✳

WHERE YOU CLICK

There's not a ton of common ground between the air sign Gemini mom and the earthy Taurus child, yet that may be the magic of this pairing. You provide a sweet balance for one another. The little Bull bringing out your more domestic nature making home a fun and lively place to be. Since you're both artsy-craftsy signs, you may soon be giving "Madame Martha" a run for her money with your holiday decor and birthday party spreads, even setting up an Etsy shop to peddle your handcrafted wares.

The experimental Gemini mom gets the stubborn Taurus kid to open up and try new activities, foods, and even friendships that might normally make it past this tunnel-visioned kid's radar. Both signs are music nuts: bring on the dance breaks, concerts in the park, and perhaps, one day, the mother-child jam sessions!

WHERE YOU CLASH

The routine-based Taurus child adores traditions, whereas the Gemini mom is constantly reinventing the wheel. (So much for your plans to ditch Christmas in favor of a family surfing vacation.) Taurus is a planner who prefers to know what to expect rather than being caught off guard. You hate the idea of being predictable in any way, but your gypsy lifestyle (and habit of changing directions and plans at a moment's notice) will need to be toned down if you want little Taurus to feel safe and secure.

Ruled by sentimental Venus, the Taurus child needs *lots* of affection. Hugs make you happy, sure, but when Taurus ties herself to your apron strings, you'll wish you could get *a little* more space. Bulls are big sleepers, and dragging this kid out of bed can slow your manic mommy pace big time.

GEMINI MOM + GEMINI CHILD

*

WHERE YOU CLICK

Extreme field-tripping, anyone? Every day is a madcap adventure and multileg journey for the restless Gemini mom and child. Variety is the spice of Gemini's life, and when the mom-kid duo is on the same wavelength this pairing will be sheer heaven. Hello, playmates! You're both practical jokers who get a giggle out of playing pranks on other family members. Bring on the exploding can of peanuts and other gag gifts!

Your Gemini mini-me will stay on top of trends making it easy to retain your desired status as the cool mom. Little Gem will babble endlessly about bands, actors, and pop icons (like mother, like child) keeping your mental database as modern as can be. Geminis adore games so your household should be lively and entertaining at all times with this little one. Together, you'll keep the whole family in a lighthearted state. Whee!

WHERE YOU CLASH

Information overload! You're both so busy chattering and spouting factoids that you might just talk right over each other. Pause, Mom, and listen, and be sure to teach your mini-me to do the same. Gossiping is a Gemini pitfall, and when the two of you get going you can really tear people down. You'll have to keep your own persnickety ways in check or you could pass on a bad habit to your child. And woe to the Gemini mom who teaches her sign-mate child to kvetch about other family members! Worst-case scenario: you or your child wind up creating rifts among relatives. Bad idea.

"Because I said so" won't fly when it comes to disciplining little Gemini. This kid needs to know *why*, just like you do. At times this parent trap may feel like a mental chess game!

GEMINI MOM + CANCER CHILD

*

WHERE YOU CLICK

This pairing brings a happy role reversal that works for both of you. The caretaking Cancer kid is naturally maternal, whereas Gemini's youthful nature is eternal. Here's a kid who will bring *you* tea, offer reassuring hugs and advice when you're stressed, and quietly step in to help with chores when you're overwhelmed. In turn, you play the role of the cool, exciting mom who helps shy Cancer break the ice with friends and come out of her shell to try new activities.

Cancer is an old soul and may become your BFF and confidant. You might even forget that you're not talking to another adult at times. This kid really knows how to listen and will sit rapt, hearing your stories and monologues. PS: this child will also remember everything you say, which you may find flattering . . . or a double-edged sword. Think before you speak!

WHERE YOU CLASH

Uh-oh. Did you just create a monster? If you let Cancer (boy or girl) mother you once too often, you may have to wrest back control of the household. This is especially true if there are other siblings involved. Your Crab can become a goody-goody or miniature tyrant at home. Gemini is mercurial and Cancer is moody: opinions and emotions will change hourly for both of you. The sensitive Crab's brooding can be too much for you to take at times. Can't he just get over it already?

Private Cancer needs to retreat to his room for solitude and serenity. Your constantly ringing phone and revolving cast of guests can disturb your child's peace. Then there's the fact that Cancers are scared of strangers—a definite downer for your active social style.

GEMINI MOM + LEO CHILD

∗

WHERE YOU CLICK

You prize originality and the Leo child definitely brings it. Your little Lion's creativity will make your heart sing! You're both showstoppers and you'll adore this kid's fearless stage presence. The two of you are sure to attract a lot of attention together. Life's a costume party for the Gemini mom and Leo child. Bring on the glitter, sequins, boas, top hats, and capes. You both love quirky, colorful clothes and any occasion to dress up. Halloween will be a hit at your house. Since you're the kind of mom who encourages fearless self-expression, you won't mind if your Leo wants to wear his Power Rangers suit to kindergarten, either. Live and let live!

You're both über-social: Leo will happily tag along to your many engagements, making fast friends with the other children there. Little Leo loves to invent and play games, just like the Gemini mom—fun the whole family can enjoy!

WHERE YOU CLASH

Does *everything* have to be such a big deal? The Gemini mom is prone to exaggeration and little Leo dramatizes everything. Minor issues get blown out of proportion easily, making for some heated tantrums—on both sides. Praise-hungry Leo needs constant validation, but so does the Gemini mom. The two of you could wind up competing for airtime, talking over each another and giving everyone a headache. Ruled by the sun, Leo may forget that he is not the center of the universe at times. He can demand more attention than the distracted Gemini mother is capable of giving. If you don't take time out to acknowledge this child's hard work, however, your little Lion may act out to get you to notice. For this kid, negative attention is preferable to being overlooked.

GEMINI MOM + VIRGO CHILD

*

WHERE YOU CLICK

Gemini and Virgo are both ruled by the same planet—curious, expressive Mercury. You're both strategic thinkers and trivia hounds who are endlessly fascinated with the details of life. Little Virgo's favorite question is "Why?" just as yours was as a child—and probably still is. How delightful to have an eager audience to whom you can pass your extensive knowledge about so many random things.

Both signs love to analyze people, and you'll be amazed by old soul Virgo's spot-on assessments of the folks that come into your orbit. Just be careful: Virgo is a critic, and you don't want to raise an intolerant or judgmental child. And you're both mutable signs who adapt well to change. Although Virgo is more particular than you, he can also roll with your mercurial moods and ideas better than most.

WHERE YOU CLASH

Your Virgo child has a very different social style than you. Fussy and particular—and at times a wee bit snobbish—your kid won't be so keen on the rotating cast of characters (*serious* characters) that comprise your friendship circle. Virgo has an uptight streak. Even if *he* is a wild child, he doesn't necessarily want his mom to be. The Gemini mother who favors tattoos, piercings, and long dreadlocks might get some unfavorable commentary from little Virgo when she realizes you're "not like the other mommies."

Helpful Virgo goes into fixer mode when sensing a problem. The Gemini mom verbalizes everything! To you, you're just venting, but Virgo hears your complaints as crises. Tone down the kvetching around this child so you don't make her more anxious or neurotic than she already is.

GEMINI MOM + LIBRA CHILD

*

WHERE YOU CLICK

Air sign soul mates, the Gemini mom and Libra child breeze through life with a shared joie de vivre. Libra's loving nature buoys your own mood—you'll feel more optimistic about life in this sunny child's presence. In turn, you can help the slower-moving Libra pick up the pace, edifying this cultured kid in all the wonders of the world. Here is the perfect companion for shopping, museum treks, and live music performances. Little Libra is as obsessed with the details as you are, sharing your love of fashion, art, and music. Like mom, she may be a major trendsetter.

Your child has an intellectual streak, too, and you may spend a good deal of time reading side by side. Patient Libra is a wonderful listener and will listen raptly to your soliloquys. Just try to let him get a word in edgewise sometimes, too!

WHERE YOU CLASH

Making a decision is as easy as winning the lottery for you two. Both Gemini and Libra can be wishy-washy to the extreme. Get an earlier start on your days, as it could take *forevah*(!) to get yourselves out of the house, pick a playground, pack a picnic, or choose an outfit for the day.

Sentimental Libra can get a bit too syrupy for the cool Gemini mom. While you love the hourly hugs and finger paintings dedicated in your honor, you may wish this child would dial back the mush factor just a little. Libra is the zodiac's peacekeeper who wants everyone to get along. Gemini stirs the pot constantly. Your need to debate and question everything can disrupt your kid's sense of harmony. Plus, you're often ticked off at *someone* or *something.* Don't expect little Libra to form alliances with you. This kid might just teach you to rise above—a good lesson to learn!

GEMINI MOM + SCORPIO CHILD

*

WHERE YOU CLICK

There's an intense and karmic bond between the Gemini mom and Scorpio child. You'll feel protective—even possessive—of this child, who won't at all mind your hold-'em-close approach. Intuitive Scorpio has a sixth sense about people and can spot the red flags the Gemini mom often misses. You'll learn to sharpen your sixth sense just from being near this wee oracle.

There's a detective in both Gemini and Scorpio: you'll love playing games that have a mystery element, and puzzles, too. With the eagle eyes you both possess, treasure hunting for rare objects will also be a blast. You may amass quite a valuable stash of collectibles before this child graduates from high school. As your Scorpio gets older, you'll have deep and engaging discussions about everything under the sun—politics, ethics, media—and you'll do a fine job imparting your critical thinking skills to little Scorpio. Although you might not always agree, you make each other think a little deeper. Neither of you suffers fools, and you both like an intellectual challenge. Hello, mother-child meeting of the minds!

WHERE YOU CLASH

Gemini's need for constant change can make fixed-sign Scorpio deeply insecure. Scorpio hates to be caught off guard! You'll need to keep a more consistent lifestyle. Both Gemini and Scorpio can rely on strategy too much, scheming instead of simply being direct. You'll try to fool Scorpio into thinking vegetables are candy; your kid will manipulate you into doing her homework for her. Honesty is the best policy here if you don't want to foster Scorpio's sneaky traits.

Both the Scorpio child and Gemini mom can hold a grudge—and you're equally quick to write people off. The difference is that you run hot and cold, invariably turning frenemies into friends. Once Scorpio declares an enemy, it may take an eternity for her to forgive. Watch who you condemn in this kid's presence or you may forever eat your words.

GEMINI MOM + SAGITTARIUS CHILD

*

WHERE YOU CLICK

Free-spirited and spontaneous, the Sagittarius kid is your ultimate coadventurer. Traveling together will be a blast: your kid's first photo shoot might be at the passport office. Both Gemini mom and Sagittarius child are social butterflies who love meeting new people. Like you, this child will have many acquaintances but few close friends. The Archer is independent and likes to be left alone to work on projects and play with his toys, giving you lots of desired "me time." No hover mothering required here—phew!

With your shared sharp senses of humor, your home may feel like a comedy club; laughter will not be in short supply. Sagittarius inherited your gift of gab and may possess a talent for writing, just like Mom. You might even team up together on a blog or short stories. You both have a way with words!

WHERE YOU CLASH

Sagittarius is your opposite sign and there will definitely be clashes. For one thing, the Archer is the zodiac's truth seeker, whereas you have a reputation for speaking out of both sides of your mouth. This principled child may call you out (and in public, at that) for your ever-changing views. By the same token, you'll find your child rather self-righteous at times. Who's the adult here, anyway?

Sagittarius is a passionate fire sign; Gemini is a breezy air sign. The tantrums this kid throws will send shudders down your cool, collected spine. Both Sagittarius and Gemini are hunters, but what happens when each of you is fixated on a different target? There could be some major blowups when your agendas clash. This is not a kid who likes tagging along with his mom's busy plans. Keep a backpack of Sag's favorite toys on hand at all times so you can occupy the restless Archer.

GEMINI MOM + CAPRICORN CHILD

*

WHERE YOU CLICK

Ambitious and enterprising, little Capricorn loves a complex project as much as you do. This happy helper is your ultimate right-hand kid. You'll come up with the million-dollar ideas and young Capricorn will put in the legwork to help you take them to the finish line. You'll be amazed by your child's tenacity!

Young Capricorn may bring out the rare traditional side of the Gemini mom. You'll feel more centered in this child's presence. In turn, you'll shore up the pessimist Capricorn kid with your silly sense of humor and playful ideas. While your zodiac signs have little in common, this can be a wonderful parent-child pairing if you can accept and admire each other's very different styles.

WHERE YOU CLASH

Patient, persistent Capricorn picks a lane and sticks with it. The Gemini mom is constantly merging from left to right. You'll find your child's single-focused groove trying at times. Can't this kid lighten up? In turn, your quicksilver style frustrates your child who wants to be still long enough to finish what she has started. Word is bond to the Capricorn child who honors his promises like a knight of Camelot. You've made at least three commitments (and forgotten two) before you break for lunch. Don't pull this on your Cap: she takes your pledges to heart!

Capricorn is a worrier, and the boys are especially protective of their mamas. Verbal Gemini moms should be careful not to vent in front of this child or you could stress him out. Call a friend instead and let your kid be a kid!

GEMINI MOM + AQUARIUS CHILD

✱

WHERE YOU CLICK

As a pair of free-spirited, freethinking nomads, you and the wee Water Bearer are two peas in a pod. It's anyone's guess where you gypsy souls will wind up when you set off for an adventure—and whom you'll meet along the way. The hypersocial Aquarius loves people even *more* than you do (yes, it's possible). Neither one of you ever met a stranger; you'll happily encourage your child's garrulous nature.

Gemini and Aquarius are technically and scientifically inclined. You'll totally nerd out over educational computer games, chemistry sets, and other DIY projects that involve wires, motherboards, or secret codes. Enterprising, you're both full of offbeat ideas. One day, you might even start a family business together!

WHERE YOU CLASH

Idealistic Aquarius looks for the best in everyone. The Gemini mama is a fault finder with a gossipy streak—even the ones you adore can't escape your occasional snarky critiques. You'll wish your kid would stop befriending all the underdogs, but hang on, Mom. Little Aquarius is here to teach you tolerance, so open your mind to his "unusual" friends. Aquarius is a team player who loves to be surrounded by a group. As the sign of the twins, you prefer to talk to one person at a time. Your Water Bearer's multiplayer games can exhaust you. All those screeching voices in the back of your SUV—yikes! In some ways, you and this child are *too* alike, both getting lost in your heads. You may need to cultivate warmth and affection in this pairing. How about a hug?

GEMINI MOM + PISCES CHILD

*

WHERE YOU CLICK

Life is but a dream for the Gemini mom and Pisces child. Your little Fish shares your supersized imagination and your love of fantasies and fairy tales. You'll get right in on your child's make-believe games, nurturing his innate creativity. Spontaneous Pisces can roll with your ever-changing flow. Tear up the agenda and itinerary. An unplanned day together will be far more fun: ice-cream sundaes on top of the tallest building in the city, perhaps?

You both respond to visual cues, sharing affection for movies, films, and colorful (and musical) live performances. Sweet Pisces will bring out your softer side, helping you become more compassionate toward people. In turn, you'll help your oft-naive child sharpen his critical thinking skills and develop a thicker skin.

WHERE YOU CLASH

Caution: guilt trips ahead! The brooding Fish is far more emotional than you, Gemini mama. You may underestimate the strength of this child's feelings, brushing them off then ending up in shock when you discover Pisces is *still* hanging on to the pain. Drying tears is not your cool-headed sign's favorite pastime, but this kid requires more coddling than you're perhaps comfortable with.

The Gemini mother is logical; little Pisces relies on intuition. You'll be perplexed by your child's decision-making process at times, which won't be grounded in any measure of common sense. You're both drawn to unusual people, but Pisces can find the serious characters in any bunch. Try to keep your snap judgments in check when it comes to your child's friends, but *do* steer Pisces toward positive peers—especially if you see her trying to rescue all the troublemakers.

CANCER

CANCER MOM + ARIES CHILD

*

WHERE YOU CLICK

Let the games begin! Two alpha signs, you're both sporty and more than a little competitive. Together, you raise each other's energy levels and keep one another from getting complacent or lazy. Aries and Cancer are both leadership-oriented cardinal signs. You're particular about what you like (even a tad divalike at moments), so whatever you're both passionate about, it will be to the extreme. Hello, mother-child superfans!

Cancer likes to spoil, and Aries (the zodiac's baby) is happy to be lavished with gifts and attention. You'll definitely have to keep yourself from turning this precocious kid into a demanding brat. You both have strong emotional reactions to, well, just about everything. You can work each other up into a frenzy at moments, and you're both fiercely protective. No matter how much you lock horns, you always have each other's backs, especially in the face of a common enemy.

WHERE YOU CLASH

Security! Is that your little Aries about to swan-dive off the high board at the pool when he can barely tread water? Yup. This daredevil kid will send the overprotective Cancer mum into hourly cardiac arrest with thrill-seeking antics and gravity-defying stunts.

In the areas where you differ, the differences are often polarizing and can lead to intense power struggles, especially if your values and priorities clash. Independent Aries like being spoiled, but they don't want to be sheltered or coddled, which is the Cancer mum's style. The family-oriented Cancer mama will have a hard time loosening apron strings and letting your little Ram roam free. You're both sensitive signs who take things personally, and you can spend a lot of your time feeling offended and indignant if you don't put your righteous sides in the parking lot. When your Aries bucks family tradition to blaze his own trail, you might feel rejected. You'll need to rein in your urge to cling and control.

CANCER MOM + TAURUS CHILD

*

WHERE YOU CLICK

Pass the remote, honey. Your homebody signs are champion loungers, and your biggest squabbles may be over precious sofa real estate. As two of the zodiac's most traditional and family-oriented signs, you shouldn't have too many values clashes. Nor will you have to worry about your Taurus flying too far from the nest, as you both have a touch of abandonment issues. Tactile Taurus will happily accept your hugs and affection, so go ahead and take that infant massage class or brush your Taurus daughter's hair every morning.

Music and the arts can be a common passion, as Taurus is ruled by aesthetic Venus. Both signs dislike change, and you share a pragmatic side—along with a shared penchant for gourmet treats, designer clothes, midnight snacks, and expensive spa treatments. Ah, the good life!

WHERE YOU CLASH

Cancer is an emotional water sign, whereas Taurus is a hard-nosed earth sign. You're the tender one of the pair, Mama! At times, your blunt little Bull can run roughshod over your feelings. Ouch! It could take all your effort not to crumble or collapse into tears. The Taurus child needs to feel productive, so give this kid a job, even if you'd rather spoil her. Too much Cancer-style coddling and you'll end up with a lazy, entitled Bull who *never* leaves the pen.

You both have strong opinions, so the rare fight can be a long and excruciating battle of wills. Don't bother trying to change this stubborn kid's mind or offer emotional counseling. Practical Taurus learns through hard life experience. You'll need to make extra effort to stay physically active, as your indulgent signs can easily bring out each other's lazy sides.

CANCER MOM + GEMINI CHILD

*

WHERE YOU CLICK

While your signs are quite different, you have some common interests, and you'll have lots of fun exploring those together. Cancer and Gemini are both culture hounds who love the arts and hands-on activities. You'll find your groove with art shows, cooking, crafting, and decorating—or through sports if you happen to share a favorite activity.

Together, you can be extremely talkative, and you love to banter about bands, books, TV shows, celebs, and the latest gossip. You can be a fun pair at parties, too: chatty Gemini eases your social anxiety while you play the perfect mommy hostess, providing awesome decor and food. Experimental Gemini gets you to try new things you wouldn't otherwise; you teach this free-spirited sign the value of putting down roots.

WHERE YOU CLASH

Did an alien abduct your child and bring back . . . this? At moments, you may wonder how a traditional person like you could have spawned the Prince of Short Attention Span or the Princess of Ever-Changing Interests. Trumpet lessons one month, gymnastics the next, scuba diving after that—you can be exhausted by the Gemini kid's fickle flights of fancy and endless hobbies that he starts but doesn't finish. Between Gemini's ever-changing personalities and your shifting moods, it can be hard to find a common beat.

Values can be a sticking point, too. Your Gemini's lack of sentimentality is a downer for your homespun hankerings, and your protectiveness could make this free-spirited child feel smothered. Gemini goes through friends like Kleenex, whereas you have a tried-and-true crew—good luck establishing an ongoing circle of moms for consistent playdates.

CANCER MOM + CANCER CHILD

✳

WHERE YOU CLICK

Home is where your hearts are, and you'll savor each other's company the most in your cozy, love-soaked abode. Cooking, gardening, decorating, doing anything domestic—you'll have a blast together without even leaving the property. Family vacations, game nights, and shared meals are important structures that solidify your bond and make you both feel secure.

Teenage rebellion, wherefore art thou? This is the kid who's so reluctant to leave the nest you may need to push him out with bribes (or a heavy crane). Nostalgia hounds, you'll both look forward to the holidays each year, happily keeping traditions passed down through generations. If you have a daughter, there will be indulgent shopping trips and shared wardrobes. A natural nurturer, the Cancer kid makes a protective older sibling. Hello, mother's helper (without the expensive babysitting charges). You both love hugs, affection, and closeness, and you naturally understand your Cancer kid's sensitivity.

WHERE YOU CLASH

Mood mania! All the emotional ups and downs in one household could give you whiplash if you're not careful. You might need a Costco membership just to keep the family stocked in tissues. Because you're both emotional sponges, you can get codependent, absorbing each other's moods. You can also project insecurities onto each other, leading to ugly bickering. Being your kid's BFF may *sound* ideal, but it has its downside.

The Cancer child tends to idealize her mother, so there could be lofty standards to live up to here. Heaven help the Cancer mom who gets divorced or shatters her Cancer kid's rose-tinted image of the perfect matriarchal figure. Any interruptions to your kid's security will need immediate care, perhaps with the help of a family therapist. Otherwise there could be a bumpy emotional transition and even long-term scars. Can we have some fun here, please? Since Crabs fear change, you'll need extroverted relatives to ignite your latent adventurous spirits and keep you from turning into a pair of recluses.

CANCER MOM + LEO CHILD

*

WHERE YOU CLICK

Move over, Beyoncé and Tina Knowles. You've got the ultimate child star–stage mother setup here. Leo happily performs to the crowds while you swoon at your kid's fearlessness (and control the showbiz profits in your Crab-like "mom-ager" grip). Leo loves to be mothered, cuddled, and cooed over, and the Cancer mom happily obliges. You both want a mother-child bond, and you'll swoon as young Leo loyally sticks by your side.

This outgoing and adventurous kid gets you out of your shell and inspires you to invent tons of fun activities. (Plus, your secret competitive side will relish having the most popular kid in the playgroup.) You share a love of culture, shopping, and the arts, so you have a lifetime companion for film premieres, off-Broadway shows, and gallery openings—plus a wing-kid whose confidence blasts open social doors you might never approach on your own.

WHERE YOU CLASH

Pass the Valium. The nonstop Leo child is like a windup toy that never runs out, talking, playing, and performing gravity-defying stunts that give you heart palpitations. Cancer mama needs some quiet private time, but you might not get it unless you ship this one off to boarding school. You like to be needed, but sheesh! Leo's demands for attention can be exhausting. Your poor little Crab claws will tire of clapping for your pint-sized praise hound. Of course, with your tendency to spoil, you may have created this monster. Make sure you set some clear boundaries and get comfortable saying no. Otherwise, you could turn into martyr mommy, catering to the endless demands of an entitled little lion cub. You could also end up with an out-of-control teenaged thrill seeker whose daredevil antics are downright scary, especially once a driver's license is obtained.

CANCER MOM + VIRGO CHILD

*

WHERE YOU CLICK

Hello, domestic divas. Together, you'll keep the local craft supply store in thriving business. Virgo and Cancer share a love of all things DIY, whether that means ripping open a radio and rewiring it, nursing a hard-core scrapbooking addiction, or creating elaborate tablescapes for your tea parties.

You're both natural caretakers with a soft spot for small creatures. The Virgo child will beg for a younger sibling, and should you grant the kid's wish you'll have a built-in babysitter, prep cook, and all-around household helper—along with a confidant who will gladly chatter about the latest gossip with you. Your signs are wordsmiths, and you may share crossword puzzles, magazines, and favorite television series. Story time can turn into a mother-child book club, and you're both sentimental about the past. Virgo and Cancer are both frugal souls who like to save and collect. The downside? You both have trouble throwing things away.

WHERE YOU CLASH

There's a bossy streak to both your signs. While you appreciate your Virgo's unusual maturity and responsible ways, you may be shocked when your tight-lipped, disapproving little one chimes in with unsolicited parenting advice. Critical Virgo can wound your sensitive feelings, especially since, as an earth sign, Virgo isn't always as warm and expressive as you are.

This kid's refusal to be fussed over could leave you with unrequited cuddling urges, and you might need to adopt a pet or have another child to fill that hug quota. While you're generally simpatico, you're both set in your ways, and can be particular about how things are cooked, served, organized, styled, and so on. You both have an inner drama queen that rears its head when one of you is affronted. ("How could you *do* this to me?" could be a common refrain.) Since you both cherish alone time, you'll need to carve out your own private spaces, lest there be a turf war over the coziest corner in the house.

CANCER MOM + LIBRA CHILD

*

WHERE YOU CLICK

With a Libra, you could have the ultimate girlie-girl daughter or metrosexual son—a late bloomer who's as reluctant to leave the nest as you are to shoo him out of it. You both love pretty things, decor, fashion, and the arts, so it's not hard finding activities to enjoy. You might even cohost classy and sophisticated parties, with your little Libra hand-drawing place cards and arranging the flowers. Together, you can be a pair of culture-hounding shopaholic foodies, enjoying life's finer things with wild abandon.

At times, you can also be downright snobbish together, as you both notice the snarky little style flaws and fashion missteps others make. Meow! Yet you're both sentimental about family and friends—even to Hallmark levels of cheesiness. The Libra child, with his open heart and wide-eyed view of life, keeps you from getting bitter or cynical.

WHERE YOU CLASH

While your mood swings may be necessary and cathartic to *you*, they can throw your little Libra's scales way off balance. You may need to shelter this kid from your bleak spells lest she absorb your darkness and tumble down a rabbit hole of the blues—one that's much harder for a Libra to exit than it is for you.

There's a fine line between sheltering the Libra kid and smothering her. This social butterfly needs to flap her wings, but Libra's "all the world's a friend" attitude can arouse fear in the protective Cancer mom. You may be tempted to snoop just to keep tabs on your impressionable (and at times naive) little Libra's influences.

You can also create a monster: Libra can be lazy, making the Cancer mom work overtime. Can you say "enabler"? Don't be so charmed by this kid's cuteness that you end up doing all of his chores and fighting her battles while he cools his well-shod heels. Otherwise, your Libra may never strike out and form an individual identity, a necessary part of growing up.

CANCER MOM + SCORPIO CHILD

*

WHERE YOU CLICK

You're both water signs who ride the same emotional waves. Trust does not come easy to either of you, and you are both extremely private. There's an understanding between you that doesn't need to be discussed or explained. You can spend hours in each other's presence without talking, each of you absorbed in a book, puzzle, or detailed project, happily grooving along in each other's company. Not that you can't have great, deep conversations, too. Your insightful little Scorpio is often wise beyond his years, though still fragile and in need of your protection. Your heart expands each time your Scorpio child confides a secret or asks your advice, since you know that you're one of the cherished few (if not the only one) allowed to get so personal with this secretive sign.

The kitchen is another bonding place, as both of your signs can be amazing cooks and bakers. Sensitive to complex flavors and textures, you can be quite a pair of foodies! Crank up your favorite indie band and get the Cuisinart rockin'!

WHERE YOU CLASH

While your shared moodiness helps you understand each other, your signs can both be punishing when your feelings are hurt. Between the Crab's pinching claw and the Scorpion's stinger, you can lash out at each other in the most personal way and damaging that delicate trust. Ouch! Even when your rage is fully triggered, be extra mindful not to hit below the belt.

Speaking of such things, Scorpio is the zodiac's "sex" sign, and this kid's sensual energy can make the Cancer mom uncomfortable. You might need to talk about the birds and bees a little earlier than you hoped so as to ensure that your curious child learns proper boundaries and correct anatomical information. Overall, the Scorpio child can be a bit intense, even for you. As a teen, this kid is prone to depression, absorbing the moods of everyone around him. You'll need to manage your own emotional roller-coaster rides, so you don't bum out your sensitive Scorpio.

CANCER MOM + SAGITTARIUS CHILD

*

WHERE YOU CLICK

While your signs couldn't be any more different, that can actually make for a fun connection—as long as you don't try to change each other. Outgoing Sag will rope you into trying campy-but-fun activities like karaoke, dancing in public, and putting on plays for the family. In turn, you teach your Sag kid manners, good taste, and an appreciation for culture. Candid Sagittarius will help you speak your mind (instead of stewing with silent resentment), and you'll teach this kid to be more tactful and compassionate.

You'll also find common ground in the kitchen and the library, as both of your signs love to cook, eat, and learn. It's also easier to get into a conversational groove with the little Sagittarius when you're simultaneously *doing* something productive, like raking leaves, wrapping presents, or making crafts. While this kid won't always take your advice, she'll appreciate the soothing hugs you offer when she brings home scraped knees and wounded feelings.

WHERE YOU CLASH

Sagittarius is a worldly, optimistic sign, overly comfortable with risk and never looking before leaping. Protective Cancer anticipates what could go wrong and tries to shelter her kids from potential bumps and bruises. This is where you clash, as the hardheaded Sagittarius child would rather learn from the school of life than heed your sensible warnings. You'll have to bite your tongue to stop from saying "I told you so" on a daily basis.

Cancer is cliqueish; Sagittarius befriends kids of all walks. Blunt Sag calls it like he sees it, which can wound your tender feelings. You want to shop the Parisian boutiques, whereas the Archer prefers camping and outdoorsy vacations. And if you have a girl, quash your frilly outfit fantasies—this is a wash-and-wear baby who feels confined in anything formfitting or fussy. Rather than push for a supertight mother-child bond, regard each other as curious travelers or diplomats from foreign nations who know nothing about each other's cultures and customs. You both have a lot to offer each other as long as it's presented in the right packaging and dosages.

CANCER MOM + CAPRICORN CHILD

*

WHERE YOU CLICK

You're two of the zodiac's most responsible and family-oriented signs—natural caretakers and providers. With the Capricorn child, you fulfill dreams of creating an intergenerational legacy, handing down traditions and customs from your own ancestors. You both find solace in things that stand the test of time—classic novels (or cars), great antiques, old photos, and family stories told and retold.

You both have a snobbish side and gravitate toward cliques, preferring to roll with a small circle of lifelong friends. You'll never have to wonder whom your Capricorn is hanging out with, because it will probably be the same handful of kids from kindergarten until graduation. This is the child that loves bringing friends home, which will make your heart swell. You happily play the cool (but appropriate) second mom to your Capricorn's crew, letting them raid the fridge or serving them snacks while they cool their heels in your family room. During the turbulent teen years, you might even take in one of those childhood friends who's having a tough time with his own parents.

WHERE YOU CLASH

Cancer and Capricorn are opposite signs on the zodiac wheel, and at times your differences can be polarizing. Water sign Cancer rules the heart, while earthy Capricorn is all about duty, responsibility, and integrity—not driven by emotion like you are. Tone down the protective nurturing vibes here, Mom.

This child needs to be challenged, to have the bar raised constantly so he can strive for new achievements—his main source of pride. Alas, your intuitive parenting style can be way too touchy-feely. It will be a delicate dance here, as you may feel this self-critical and perfectionist child is way too hard on himself. Along with your hugs and reassurances, you'll have to push yourself to give honest feedback and constructive criticism. While you yearn to envelop your child in an embrace and smother him with kisses, you may at best get a one-armed hug and a dry peck on the cheek.

Food can also be a sticking point, as many Capricorns are regimented eaters who'd rather have sunflower seeds or a bland "macro plate" than your lovingly prepared béchamel sauce and flourless chocolate cake. Since food equals love to the Cancer mom, you may feel rejected if your Capricorn kiddie follows a spartan diet—especially when you've spent all day reducing stock or deglazing a pan.

CANCER MOM + AQUARIUS CHILD

*

WHERE YOU CLICK

How your homebody sign birthed this free-spirited bohemian is a wonder, but your differences can be refreshing. Aquarius is a breezy air sign who keeps things light and fun, with comedic timing that leaves you in stitches. Sign this kid up for showbiz, fast—and get ready to play stage mother as the crowds eat up his antics. Add "soccer mom" to the list while you're at it, as the Aquarius kid is often a great athlete, as well as the sign of group activity, which gives you the perfect chance to play den mother. This is fabulous common ground, since many Cancers have a sporty side, and you love to cheer for your child. You like being physically active together: surfing, snowboarding, skiing, boating, playing on the beach.

While Aquarius is BFFs with the world and a naturally popular kid, he's not always articulate in the emotional intelligence department. Fortunately, that happens to be your specialty. You help this child get in touch with his feelings, and he teaches you to lighten up when you get too intense.

WHERE YOU CLASH

You like knowing what to expect, but with Aquarius the only thing you can anticipate is the unexpected. From whoopee cushions on your dining-room chairs to dropping out of college to backpack through India, this eccentric prankster comes up with some out-there ideas. Kiss that picture-perfect family portrait farewell, and quit worrying what the neighbors will think—that is, if you want to keep your sanity.

When it comes to friends, you're more than a wee bit elitist, preferring to roll with a tightly edited and time-tested clique who's passed your many loyalty tests. Aquarius has no such scruples. This free-loving sign instantly befriends the homeless guy sleeping on the curb and might even invite him over for a glass of Mom's "famous" iced tea—much to your horror. Was this naïveté or an attempt to school you? Hard to tell. Aquarius is the sign of social justice and also a rebel. If this kid gets a whiff of closed-mindedness from you, she'll challenge it in ways that make your head spin. And as much as you long to be her confidante, the less you know the better. Just hold the space and offer your best nonjudgmental hug when she comes home bruised from the battlefield yet again.

CANCER MOM + PISCES CHILD

*

WHERE YOU CLICK

Nurturing empaths, you enjoy exploring the lush landscape of human emotions and all its complexities. Your relationship feels like a support group with lots of kitchen table wisdom thrown in. In fact, you may find yourselves gathered there regularly for a soothing cup of tea and a treat. Because your intuition is so strong, you can be downright telepathic with each other. The risk of all this shared sensitivity, however, is that you both absorb the feelings of everyone around you. This can suck you both into the dark cloud, making you feel fearful and hopeless about life. Fortunately, it's nothing a good field trip can't snap you out of.

Artistic and intuitive, your signs dwell in the land of creativity. You'll enjoy listening to obscure bands, hitting exhibits and plays, shopping for artisanal creations, and even taking art or music classes together. You both cherish history and style and may enjoy geeking out over period pieces, elaborate costumes, and highbrow-lowbrow creations like steampunk culture.

WHERE YOU CLASH

Grab a life preserver, because you'll need it to stay afloat in this emotion ocean. Young Pisces may seem terribly fragile, but your Fish needs both security *and* space to swim away into her own private world. This can provoke your Cancerian abandonment issues, especially when your child runs hot and cold or withdraws without warning.

The Pisces child is particularly prone to guilt, so you'll need to be careful not to make him feel bad for individuating or voicing upset feelings. Pisces kids can also have a self-destructive or rebellious side that alarms you. Neptune—the planet of illusions and self-deception—rules this sign. You just can't watch your kid make poor choices about friends, lovers, and life without attempting to intervene. However, the more you try to control, the more Pisces withdraws into an unreachable world. It will be an ongoing challenge to strike a balance between holding tight and letting go—and to teach this child that healthy boundaries are vital to her own safety. Beware a tendency to pass the codependent "hot potato" or stuff down resentments, too, since you're both constantly worried about hurting each other's feelings.

LEO

LEO MOM + ARIES CHILD

✱

WHERE YOU CLICK

Viva la diva! The Leo mom and Aries child are scene-stealers who love the spotlight. This is the ultimate pairing of the stage mother (who's earned her own chops, too, thank you very much) and the child star. With your blessing and encouragement, your Aries may literally perform to sold out crowds or rock her standout talents in another realm. Hello, mini-me superstar!

You both love fanfare and luxury, and if your Aries is a girl there will be plenty of dress-up outings in your future. The rough-and-tumble Aries boy brings out your own playful nature. You *are* the queen of the jungle after all, and your wild streak gets a workout chasing this kid on his daredevil adventures. Aries and Leo are enterprising fire signs who tend to profit from their creativity or rise to positions of leadership wherever you go. This kindergarten tycoon couldn't have a more supportive mama for her start-up ventures and climb to the throne!

WHERE YOU CLASH

Two dominating personalities in the same house? Uh-oh. There could be some major power struggles with this totalitarian tot, especially since you both like to get your way. Sure, you're the mom, but you'll give your Ram a run for her money when it comes to throwing a tantrum. And since Aries is even bossier than *you*, there could be a parent-child role reversal in this pairing.

Leos is a hands-on mama. Independent Aries may feel smothered by your attentive style. Leo moms thrive on praise and like lots of validation from her kids. Self-directed Aries may be too caught up in her own fascinations to remember to tell you that your new dress is pretty, dinner was delicious, and that she really appreciates you taking all her friends to the zoo. A few etiquette lessons are in order to teach your kid the power of "thank you," but don't look to this child to prop up your sense of self-worth. Instead, let yourself be inspired by your Aries' innate sense of confidence. Your Ram knows he's great, no matter what anyone else may think!

LEO MOM + TAURUS CHILD

*

WHERE YOU CLICK

Since both Leo and Taurus are fixed signs, you'll share a love of tradition, routines, and keeping things "as they've always been." Pass down those colorful family stories you so love to share. Little Taurus will treasure these tales and keep them alive for the next generation. Both Leo and Taurus enjoy luxury, especially objects that have a history. Here's a little partner for your symphony outings, architectural tours, and yes, lavish shopping trips.

When it comes to style, both signs tend to be over the top. Dress the Taurus girl in giant bows and the boy in bowler hats. Your Venus-ruled child loves to fuss in the mirror, just like mama. Party planning will be a stellar bonding experience for you creative souls, so collaborate on the menu and decorations scheme. This pragmatic kid might just follow you around with a clipboard or iPad, helping you stay organized and adhere to a budget! If you have a "mechanical Bull," as many are, let them put together a playlist (they are music aficionados), wire up the lights and speakers, and build props. Voilà! A celebration worthy of a magazine spread, just the way the showy Leo mom likes it.

WHERE YOU CLASH

Both Leo and Taurus can be loud, but you are less inclined to turn down the volume. Your effusive energy may zap your Taurus kid's reserves, especially when she is in a mellow mood. Playful Leo moms like to bounce from activity to activity. Languid Taurus needs time to lounge and dream. Let your sleeping Bull lie instead of forcing her to accompany you on your wild rides through town.

Although you're both extravagant, Taurus is far more practical than you. This old soul may admonish you as you're about to blow a paycheck on a pair of designer shoes or order the bottomless hot fudge sundae. Buzzkill! She *has* heard you fret about your spending or stress about your waistline and, alas, won't let you forget the self-improvement pledges you've made. Taurus is the sign of morals and ethics and will develop his own set of values. For the Leo mom, who likes to look at a mirror image, this can be challenging.

LEO MOM + GEMINI CHILD

*

WHERE YOU CLICK

This is the ultimate BFF mother-child combo. Like you, little Gemini is chatty, dramatic, playful, and curious. Finally, someone who can keep pace! There will be many energetic conversation and jaunts around town together. Gemini loves to ask why, and Leo loves to spout off answers. Bring on the "edu-tainment"-style field trips to planetariums and guided nature trail tours! Gemini is quirky and creative and you're the mom who prizes individuality. Your young mad scientist will feel appreciated and encouraged by you.

Both Leo and Gemini love to develop a creative personal style, and shopping trips will be fun and imaginative. But put a lock on your couture! If you have a girl, she may slip off to high school in your sequins and high heels when you aren't looking!

WHERE YOU CLASH

Your sign is ruled by the sun, and sometimes you forget that you aren't the center of the universe. Gemini, who is ruled by expressive Mercury, needs constant feedback and validation. A fine pair of chatterboxes you are, but who is going to zip it and listen? You could wind up shouting over each other at times—and the competitive attention grabs can get exhausting!

Gemini has a short attention span and craves constant variety. The elaborate projects and plans you dream of setting up for your children—like the children's theater workshop in the backyard or live puppet-making demonstration—will frustrate this fidgety child to no end. Don't expect Gemini to sit still through Disney on Ice, either, just because you loved it as a little one. If nothing else, pack some books and games, or prepare to take plenty of intermissions with your mini-multitasker.

As a Leo, you prize loyalty and will try to pass this trait down to your children. Fickle Gemini changes allegiances by the day. Monday, little Susie is her BFF, by Wednesday, they're mortal enemies; on Friday she wants Susie over for a slumber party. It's enough to make your head spin, but don't get involved in the drama. Otherwise, *you'll* be upset long after the kids have moved on.

LEO MOM + CANCER CHILD

*

WHERE YOU CLICK

Go ahead and be as hands-on as you like, Leo. Cancers are the zodiac's mama's boy and girl and will revel in your high level of involvement in their lives. PTA president? Scout leader? Classroom aide? Sign yourself up! Shy and vulnerable, these kids want the protective lioness (you) around. Just be careful not to coddle them *too* much, or they may never emerge from behind your apron strings. The warm hearth you create feels like a safe haven for Cancer, who needs to come home to a stable and nurturing setting.

While Cancers can be reticent, your live-out-loud personality will help this child develop an identity of his own. It's okay to be your emotional (and sometimes dramatic) self around this kid. Expressing your feelings helps your supersensitive child feel safe opening up and accepting his ever-changing moods. While you'll lovingly dry tears, give your kid a nudge and help him develop some backbone. With proper support and a lot of encouragement, Cancers *can* be alphas, too.

WHERE YOU CLASH

Leo ruled by sun, Cancer ruled by moon—you can be literally as different as night and day. You're competing for the same stage here—the sky—so make sure your Cancer has a place to shine, too. With your bold personality, you could easily bulldoze your little one. Just because Cancer is quiet, don't assume he is content. Your Crab can hold a grudge and may be silently seething, waiting for the right moment to give you a pinch with those fierce claws. Check in regularly with a "How are you feeling, sweetie?" and make sure you actually *listen* to Cancer's answer!

Don't make the mistake of turning this insightful child into your confidante. To feel safe, she needs a mother who is solid and self-assured. Cancers are deeply private, and you'll have to tone down the gushing to keep her trust. Also, it's easy to make this kid self-conscious. *You* may have had a party when you got your first training bra, but this little girl won't be so eager to trumpet such tidbits to the world. Shhhh!

LEO MOM + LEO CHILD

*

WHERE YOU CLICK

The lioness and her cub: what a captivating sight to behold! Your mini-me shares your flare for drama, so let the variety show begin. Playtime will be epic with your combined imaginations dreaming up all kinds of fanciful ideas. Help little Leo produce plays, put on talent shows, or ringmaster his own circus while he's still in elementary school (the family dog won't mind dressing up like a tiger . . .). Bring on the feather boas and oversized hats!

Life is a costume party for the Leo mother and daughter. Heads up: those shopping trips could get expensive when she's a teen! The Leo boy is loyal and protective of his mother, which makes your heart sing. Set up the good-deed chart and reward this kid with shiny gold stars. Like you, little Leo thrives on praise and rewards. It's easy to understand what makes this child happy, and you'll have a mutual admiration society on many days.

WHERE YOU CLASH

Who sits on the throne in this house? Your bossy wunderkind can turn into a royal tyrant if you give her too much leeway. Use the reward system judiciously, so she doesn't expect a treat every time she lifts a finger to help you. Be careful about your public boasting, too. Leo rules the ego, after all. Let little Johnny overhear one too many gushing tales of his greatness and it *will* go to his head. You may have to take him down a peg—neither easy nor fun.

Your Leo child shares your large appetite for life, and it's easy to blow the household budget saying yes to her eager-eyed pleas. Learning to set boundaries—especially when it comes to spending—will be your biggest challenge here. Teach your little cub the value of the dollar, and learn it for yourself, too! Delayed gratification builds character.

LEO MOM + VIRGO CHILD

*

WHERE YOU CLICK

The noble Leo mother is a natural helper; Virgo is the sign of service. Being there for loved ones comes naturally to you both. There's lots of family loyalty in this sweet pairing! The Leo mother plays the director role, while Virgo is the producer: what a stellar tag team! Cooking dinner, decorating the house, making crafts—every undertaking will be a fun and elaborate production for you two hands-on signs.

Virgo kids have a parental quality about them, so if there are younger siblings, you'll have a built-in babysitter. Good thing, too, since you tend to overbook your schedule with supermom activities and your own hobbies and interests.

Curious Virgo loves to play Twenty Questions, and the chatty Leo mother loves to give long, elaborate replies. Discovering answers together is fun, too, and makes for a great excuse to take an educational field trip. Both Leo and Virgo love to collect. Although your tastes may be flashier than your modest child's, treasure hunts will be a delightful bonding experience. (If anyone can ferret out valuable Depression glass in a heap of junk, it's Virgo!) Head to an outdoor flea market, sample sale, or consignment district and hunt away!

WHERE YOU CLASH

Leos are eternally youthful—you're the mom who is forever in touch with her inner five-year-old. Old soul Virgo can be uptight and actually *craves* discipline. This relationship could turn into a frustrating role reversal if you are too lax with this child. Leos like to make dramatic entrances; Virgo abhors a scene and may be embarrassed by your theatrical ways. You'll have to develop a thicker skin, especially when your critical Virgo turns those eyes on you. Virgos are also prone to anxiety. You may inadvertently worry your child with your audible sighs and five-alarm responses to minor issues. These keen children hear everything and go into fixer mode when they sense a problem. Tone down your emotional volume when venting within earshot of Virgo. Better yet, don't make this child privy to your problems at all. Let him enjoy childhood!

LEO MOM + LIBRA CHILD

*

WHERE YOU CLICK

Say hello to the material mom and child. Creative and fashionable, you're a head-turning pair, like Leo Madonna and her Libra daughter Lourdes. True to astrological form, the two started a fashion line together! The aesthetic realm is definitely a place where you two will click, poring over pretty things and creating plenty of them yourselves.

Music is another shared love, so pump up the jams. Stylish social butterflies, the Leo mom and Libra child will leave the house "for a couple of hours," and be gone on all-day outings. This good-natured child is an easy companion for you, jumping right into playtime with other kids. Quieter Libras might avoid the sandbox, but they are patient and self-contained. Your child may simply zone out and daydream, read her book, or patiently play video games while you work the room.

Giving gifts is the love language you both speak. Lavish little Libra with presents, and start planning birthday parties months in advance. It's going to be tough not to spoil this one!

WHERE YOU CLASH

Leo is a fire sign, passionate and effusive, whereas Libra is a breezy air sign. Expect your kid's temperament to run a lot cooler than yours. Your effusive nature may be a bit too much for this gentle child, especially if you get fired up and start talking loudly. Dynamic Leo moms are always on the move; languid Libras like to take their sweet old time. Rushing this child can throw off his delicate sense of balance. Grrr. Life is a costume party for the Leo mama, but vanity is not a value that you want to develop in your Libra. It's fine to help your kid cultivate style (not that she will need much assistance), but be careful not to overemphasize appearances. Libras can get a little too hung up on visuals, especially when it comes to their own reflections in the mirror. Teach this child a broader definition of beauty, encouraging him to look for it in everyone and everything.

LEO MOM + SCORPIO CHILD

*

WHERE YOU CLICK

A fascinating parent-child pairing, the Scorpio child has a personality as magnetic as your own. People will be innately curious about the two of you. Leo mom is the more overt showstopper whereas little Scorpio captivates with old-soul mystique. Set up an art room and music studio, stat! Little Scorpio is a talented creative force, just like her mama. Your sing-alongs could turn into epic jam sessions with you on the vocals and Scorpio on guitar, or vice versa.

Loyalty is a quality both Leo and Scorpio hold in high regard. You'll be pleased to see your little one developing a code of honor similar to your own—in *some* ways. You're both a tad possessive, too. Little Scorpio will stick by your side. In turn, you'll always be near, showing up for recitals, swim meets, and school plays, giving sensitive Scorpio the support and assurance he needs to feel loved.

WHERE YOU CLASH

Call off the backup dancers, Mama Leo! Your Vegas-sized personality could chill secretive Scorpio—especially if you share one too many a tale from the family vault. This is not a child you want to embarrass or, God forbid, betray! Little Scorpio can hold a grudge like nobody's business. The equally sensitive Leo mother will have to endure a few heart-wrenching moments when her child ices her out. Develop a thicker skin, fast!

It's your job as a parent to discipline your child and sometimes that means being the bad guy. While Scorpio will resist, you *must* be firm and keep the upper hand. Otherwise, this little operator will play you like the aforementioned guitar. He'll know exactly how to push your buttons. Eek! While you're an open book, Scorpio needs to have secrets. Never read her diary. Ever. Scorpio boys are loyal to their moms, but don't take advantage of this. Otherwise, he may never leave the nest!

LEO MOM + SAGITTARIUS CHILD

*

WHERE YOU CLICK

It's a nonstop playdate for the Leo mom and Sagittarius child. You're both wide-eyed adventurers, keen on exploring every corner of the world. Get your baby Archer a passport right away! Your swaddled or stroller-bound travel companion loves to be on the move like you. "More, more, more!" is your shared mantra. Like you, the Sagittarius child loves to take risks, dream big, and turn her enterprising ideas into businesses. There couldn't be a more supportive mother for such a venturesome child who may have her own Etsy store or blog before graduating from junior high. You're both eager students of life, taking fun classes and workshops together.

Two tickets to Broadway, please! A theatrical duo, little Sagittarius shares your wacky sense of humor. You'll get in on your Archer's jokes and add a few of your own punch lines. Who knows? Your mother-child spunk might even draw the reality TV cameras. You're a wildly fun pair to watch!

WHERE YOU CLASH

The Leo mother thrives on praise and flattery, but little Sagittarius cannot tell a lie. Forget about turning this kid into your personal cheerleader. If anything, you'll have a pint-sized life coach on hand to give you unfiltered feedback and a dose of tough love. Better keep up with the trends, Leo! Sagittarius will point out any lack of cool or poor fashion choices—not that you're prone to making such missteps often. Well, Leo, you'll probably be the better person for it—even if you wish this kid would learn some tact! Try to teach that trait with all your might.

Sagittarius is adventurous but won't be keen on going along with anyone else's itinerary. Agree in advance on your route to avoid meltdowns. Always bring along books, crayons, sports equipment, and the iPad. Otherwise you could weather some tantrums from this child, who won't take kindly to sitting around with nothing to do while you take care of your errands.

LEO MOM + CAPRICORN CHILD

*

WHERE YOU CLICK

Hello, alpha child and mom. Ambition is in the Leo woman's blood. Status-oriented Capricorn is all about achievement, too. Whatever each of you does, you strive to be the best. President of (insert organization here) is a title you'll each hold frequently. You're a formidable tag team in everything from sack races to the family business the two of you may start together one day.

Little Capricorn has a similar code of honor to yours. You'll admire your child's loyalty to siblings, relatives, and playground friends. When it comes to loved ones, you'll both defend 'em till the end. Traditional Capricorns are incredibly loyal to their parents and they adore family traditions. For the mom who hates to let go as much as she loves to celebrate every occasion, this is a parent-child match made in heaven.

WHERE YOU CLASH

It's always playtime for the Leo mom who loves to whistle while she works. The sober Capricorn child is far more serious, scrutinizing her crayon drawings and even ripping them up if they don't pass muster. You'll worry over this, wishing your Cap would lighten up already! Competitive Capricorn may have a different idea of fun than you, so don't foist your games onto this child. If he wants to obsessively practice his jump shot instead of joining you for a picnic, so be it! Hell hath no fury like a Capricorn cut short from his quest!

The Leo mom is warm and gregarious, opening her arms to the world. Capricorn is more reserved, bordering on snobbish at times. Forget about forcing the playdates to go well. If Cap doesn't want to play with your yoga buddy's tot, there's no changing her mind. Capricorn is a worrier, so be mindful of venting within earshot. If he hears you've had a rough day or that someone hurt your feelings, he can become overly protective of you, acting more adultlike than he should be at such a young age.

LEO MOM + AQUARIUS CHILD

∗

WHERE YOU CLICK

Even though Leo and Aquarius are opposite signs, they can complement each other beautifully. Your offbeat Aquarius child adores your kooky ways and shares your silly and playful sense of humor. In turn, you'll be awed by your little Water Bearer's unconventional view of the world. You're sure to learn lots from this innovative child! Originality is a calling card for both of you, from your outrageous clothing choices to your scene-stealing ideas. You won't mind if your Aquarius child wants to wear rainbow leg warmers and a unicorn hat to a school concert. Suppressing self-expression is not your style!

Social butterflies, you both love to flutter about and talk to strangers. Aquarius might even outnumber *you* in the friend department. Since you both love parties, this is just more reason to celebrate. Put your heads together on that Halloween costume bash, and plan on baking a ginormous cake!

WHERE YOU CLASH

The gushy Leo mama can be a bit overbearing for the cool, detached Aquarius kid. Don't take it personally when the little Water Bearer wipes away your kisses or doesn't want to do extended cuddle time. You've given birth to a free spirit here, and Aquarius needs lots of personal space in order to think and grow.

Leo has a teacher's pet personality, whereas rebel Aquarius is the class clown. Your child's refusal to follow the rules will infuriate, and even embarrass, you. You have a short fuse compared to your child, but when angered your Aquarian's temper can be quite explosive. Doors will slam and should probably stay shut. Cool downs and time-outs will be necessary in this pairing. Leo is the solo star, whereas Aquarius is the team player. Your egalitarian kid will be frustrated by your constant need to be the best. Let her teach you the fine art of cooperation, Mom!

LEO MOM + PISCES CHILD

*

WHERE YOU CLICK

A fairy-dusted duo, there's an enchanted dynamic between Leo mom and Pisces child. Set up the craft room, musical instruments, finger paints, and magic castle playrooms. Like you, little Pisces is dreamy and artistic with a supersized imagination. Don't forget the dance classes! You're both light on your feet and will have fun rocking out together at home or concerts in the park. Sensitive Pisces feels vulnerable in the world, but the über-protective Leo mom is there to create a safe haven. Little Pisces loves to be lavished with the gifts the generous Leo mom can't help but give. In turn, you'll have a gallery exhibition of crayon drawings devoted to "My Mommy."

Both Leo and Pisces are people pleasers and need a good deal of validation. Fortunately, you'll have a mutual admiration society in each other. Here's the kid who says, "Mom you look beautiful" before you even asked. Awwww!

WHERE YOU CLASH

Leo mom is a confident, take-charge kind of mom. This can push your Pisces toward his more passive demeanor or do the exact opposite by bringing out his bossy streak. Wait . . . who's the mom here? Leo tends to have the bigger (or at least louder) personality. Be careful not to outshine your Pisces in the public eye. The little Fish needs lots of encouragement to cultivate her own strength. While Leo is sunny and optimistic, Pisces is more the brooding-worrier type. This kid can cramp your free-spirited style with phobias and anxieties. Keep a good babysitter on speed dial. Pisces might dig in the heels of her patent-leather buckle shoes just as you're both dressed and ready to leave for a family celebration.

There's a lot of love between you, but sometimes it can tread into codependent terrain. Give your child space to be (and remind him that it's okay to do the same with you) instead of fussing and fretting over each other endlessly.

VIRGO

VIRGO MOM + ARIES CHILD

*

WHERE YOU CLICK

Can we get that special-ordered, please? The fussy Aries child is as particular as his Virgo mum, and while it might be a tad inconvenient to cater to this kid's tastes, you'll be proud that your little Ram has his own mind. You're both thinkers—Aries rules the brain and Virgo is governed by mental Mercury. Pass your progeny the books, crosswords, and strategy games that you adored as a child. The Virgo mother loves to fuss over her children. Being the zodiac's baby, Aries will enjoy all the added attention you pay to her . . . as long as you're not *too* smothering.

Aries boys tend to be tinkerers (the girls are less patient for that sort of thing), the perfect helper for your many DIY undertakings. Aries girls are hardworking hustlers who will match the business-oriented Virgo mom stride for stride. You'll have fun being productive together, so set up an ongoing shared project: construct a giant jigsaw puzzle, paint a bedroom wall mural, or tend a vegetable garden. Keep the chessboard open, as your matches could stretch on for days. You both love a mental and physical challenge, so let the games begin!

WHERE YOU CLASH

Quicksilver Aries is ruled by impulses—just *try* to wrangle this child into your rigid routines and timelines! You're going to have to loosen up the restrictions a bit here, Mama, for the sake of your own sanity. Daredevil Aries fancy themselves X Games athletes, turning stairwell banisters into monkey bars, leaping off the roof of the toolshed, flying down a steep hill on their dirt bikes at top speed. This child's antics could send the anxious Virgo mom into near cardiac arrest!

With their short attention spans, your Aries will leave half-finished projects and games all over the house, forgetting to pick up the mess. This infuriates the neatnik Virgo mom! Start training early by singing cleanup songs and giving gold stars for tidiness. Although you enjoy catering to your children, fussing too much over Aries could turn your Ram into a spoiled brat. Back off a bit, and make your kid work for the special treats!

VIRGO MOM + TAURUS CHILD

*

WHERE YOU CLICK

Earth sign soul mates, little Taurus has a similar disposition to your own. This child thrives in a structured environment with clear-cut timelines and routines—sheer heaven for the organized Virgo mama! Family traditions are a big deal to both of you. Taurus will listen rapt as you share stories from your childhood and eagerly absorb instructions for preparing the secret marinara recipe passed down from your great-grandmother. How sweet it is to know that these customs will live on through your Bull!

Set up the craft room; keep the toolbox handy. Like you, Taurus kids love domestic and mechanical projects, from sewing to playing guitar to wiring the whole house with a speaker system. Since you're both earth signs, get a garden going, too, and pass down your love of fresh, homegrown food. The particular Virgo mom is keenly visual. Though the Bull's tastes can be a bit more elaborate than your pared-down style, your kid's aesthetic sense will be close to your own. You both like things that are clean, natural, and freshly scented. Decorating and shopping for fine (organic/natural) goods is a love you'll both share. Field trip to the craft show and farmers' market, anyone?

WHERE YOU CLASH

Taurus is ruled by decadent Venus and loves to indulge. The Virgo mom is a health nut who would happily keep a sugar-free, wheat-free, dairy-free (and so on) kitchen. Those kale chips you lovingly pack in your child's lunchbox may be swapped for an M&M cookie (if any kid will take 'em) or tossed in the trash faster than you can say vitamin C. Enforcing rigid dietary rules will be an uphill battle here.

Virgos love to serve and languid Taurus loves to be served—on a silver platter, at that. You can raise a lazy child if you go overboard with the chicken soup brand of nurturing. Taurus loves the finest of everything while the oft-frugal Virgo mum knows how to cleverly mix high and low into a perfect pastiche. You'll shudder during shopping trips with the bullish preteen who may demand clothes that outprice anything in your own wardrobe!

Your Taurus kid needs lots of time to lounge, take long naps, and stare at the cumulus clouds. Scale back your lineup of culturally edifying activities or you could overwhelm this leisurely soul who needs about half of the stimulation as you.

VIRGO MOM + GEMINI CHILD

*

WHERE YOU CLICK

Virgo and Gemini are both ruled by expressive, intellectual Mercury. Little Gemini's mind is as inquisitive as your own! You're both trivia hounds who love to learn little factoids and share them with other people. At times you can be know-it-alls, too: like mother, like child. You'll enjoy solving puzzles together, playing strategy games, and taking wee Gemini to "edu-tainment"-based activities like the planetarium or a famous historical figure's home for a guided tour. Conversations will be lively and stimulating with this kid.

You're both nonstop talkers who share a love of gossip. Be careful here, Mom, or your snarky words could be repeated at the worst possible moment—a huge embarrassment! Still, you can't help but giggle at Gemini's cheeky commentary. This kid sees *everything*, just like you. Oh, behave!

WHERE YOU CLASH

The Virgo mom is a caretaker who can't walk by a wounded soul without stopping to dab tears and offer words of encouragement. Restless Gemini hates to be saddled with other people's problems. You'll need to teach this child a little more compassion; by the same token, does your Gemini have a point? Carrying the weight of the world on your shoulders isn't always necessary, as this child knows.

You're a creature of habit and you need routines in order to feel grounded and centered. Mercurial Gemini kids crave constant variety. "Why are we going to *that* park/restaurant/friend's house again, Mommy?" your little one will whine. You may become a less-frequent fixture at your favorite haunts after Gemini is born and your go-to rituals will last for five minutes instead of thirty. Safety always comes first for the anxious Virgo mom, but little Gemini can be a daredevil who chases after danger. Your heart will definitely race with this child! Being a perfectionist, you'll also struggle to watch Gemini's sometimes-slapdash approach to life. Your child simply loses interest faster, but take heart: when Gemini finds something that fascinates her she can be as painstakingly obsessive about the details as you!

VIRGO MOM + CANCER CHILD

*

WHERE YOU CLICK

How sweet it is! The nurturing Virgo mom and sentimental Cancer child are the warm and fuzziest pair around. Home is where the heart is for both of your signs and there will be domestic bliss aplenty with this child. From baking cookies to decorating for the holidays to preparing a special Sunday-night dinner for the family, you both love spoiling your nearest and dearest.

Little Cancer is as particular about people as Mama: only the truest of friends will enter your sanctums and you both prefer to keep your circles tightly knit. Little Cancer is as protective of you as you are of him. (Swoon!) This caring child will brew you tea and dry your tears in those moments when you're feeling frustrated by the world. Cancer kids love a hands-on mom. Go ahead, get as involved as you'd like in this child's life—you'll get no objections from the wee Crab!

WHERE YOU CLASH

Comfortably close or codependent? Anxious worriers, you can enable each other's worst traits here, with the Virgo mom becoming the bossy busybody and the Cancer acting like a helpless baby. Step back, Virgo, and encourage your cautious Crab to take more risks (glug) and stick up for herself instead of hiding behind your apron strings.

Sentimental Cancer likes to hold on to objects and craves familiarity—even rearranging the furniture can disrupt her sense of security. The minimalist Virgo mom is all about decluttering. Prying treasured objects away from your child may faintly echo an episode of *Hoarders*. Let your Crab in on the mission instead of bagging up "unused" dollies or action figures for Goodwill while your kid is at school.

Virgo is the sign of the critic and you can't help but point out areas in need of improvement. Alas, your "helpful hints" can wound the soft-bellied Cancer child who learns best through positive reinforcement.

VIRGO MOM + LEO CHILD

*

WHERE YOU CLICK

Hollywood, here we come! Leo is the superstar and Virgo is the proverbial stage mother. Should your child show signs of prodigy-like talents (as little Lions often do), you'll have Leo enrolled in lessons with a master teacher, on the competitive circuit, or auditioning for parts in no time. It's all about being supportive—and you'll need to keep Leo's ego in check and teach your kid the power of humility. In other instances, little Leo plays the director and the Virgo mum producer. From elaborate pageants to locally grown, organic strawberry lemonade stands, you'll take your enterprising kid's ideas to the next level. What a team!

You're both goody-goodies who love praise: it's a mutual admiration society here for sure. Little Leo is a happy helper and a wee bit nosy, too. When you race off to support friends, neighbors, relatives, and near-strangers in crisis, this bighearted child may tag along or send a crayoned "get well soon" card. Melt!

WHERE YOU CLASH

Chatty Cathy has entered the building. You thought *you* were talkative . . . until this garrulous child arrived on the scene. Not only does Leo gab nonstop, but he also demands a rapt audience for his running monologues. The quiet, meditative moments the Virgo mom craves will be hard to come by. Set up a silent zone in the house and reward Leo for using his indoor voice. (And plan on popping a lot of Advil or wine, whatever your poison.)

Theatrical Leo is creative and flamboyant and this can make the modest Virgo mom shudder. Teach little Leo what is socially appropriate, but don't squash your child's imagination. No one throws a tantrum quite like the zodiac's Lion—and he'll do it in the checkout line, during church services, while you're visiting friends. Since perfectionist Virgos strive to be supermoms, this is doubly embarrassing. Don't beat yourself up: those stormy tears and flailing little fists do not connote failure on your part.

VIRGO MOM + VIRGO CHILD

✱

WHERE YOU CLICK

Here's the happy helper you always dreamed of! This child likes to sit beside you and learn as you plant a garden, strip and stain an antique armoire, change the oil in your own car, and follow other crafty, DIY inclinations. Curious trivia hounds, little Virgo will be a collector of factoids, just like Mama.

Here's to efficiency! You run a tight ship. There are clear-cut rules and regulations at Château Virgo. Your pint-sized star mate will thrive in this structured environment and may even take on the role of rule enforcer with siblings. (Be careful not to overempower this bossy trait, even if you find it secretly endearing.) Your Virgo child can be fussy and particular and may have a sensitive stomach like yours. Fortunately, you'll know firsthand how important it is to custom-order to your needs. Unlike other mothers, you won't give this child a hard time for making special requests.

Little Virgo is a keen observer, especially when it comes to people. You may be amazed by how insightful your child's commentary is, especially when discussing classmates and peers. One warning: gossiping is a Virgo pitfall—and you can be rather critical of people yourself. Tone down the judgments so your little one doesn't grow to be intolerant of others.

WHERE YOU CLASH

Pick, pick, pick. You fussbudgets can really get under each other's skin. Who's the kid and who's the parent here? You might wonder when little Virgo starts wagging a finger at *you*, even repeating your own advice. Or you may notice young Virgo nagging classmates and trying to impose some of your household rules on them—the mirror is definitely held up to you in this pairing! Are you being a bit too stern, Mom? If your selective tastes clash, things can devolve into a special-ordering nightmare. Making a second dinner for your picky eater every night? Who has time for that!

You may also see your own perfectionist tendencies reflected in your child. Take care not to make self-deprecating remarks about yourself in front of this child. The last thing you want is to see little Virgo criticizing her reflection or tearing up a precious craft project because it's "not good enough."

VIRGO MOM + LIBRA CHILD

*

WHERE YOU CLICK

Virgo is the zodiac's critic; Libra is the sign of judgment. Your child is equally keen on details, although you'll examine most situations from different angles. Libra sees the bright side and you are a troubleshooter. You'll find your kid's perspective refreshing (if not a tad Pollyanna-ish); in turn, you can imbue flighty Libra with your common sense. You are both culture vultures. Pass on your knowledge of art, music, and film to your child, who appreciates an indie gem, too; in fact, you both have a knack for sniffing out what's cool, long before the rest of the world catches on.

Young Libra is sensitive to color and detail, as is his Virgo mom. Let your child weigh in on home decor and perhaps your clothing choices. You'll be amazed by this child's innate sense of style. The mellow Libra will love the peaceful, well-ordered home you create. Both of your signs can be health nuts (we know many Libras who went vegetarian in their teens). Bring on the raw food dinners and green smoothies!

WHERE YOU CLASH

Analysis paralysis alert! Obsessing over the details can go to extremes in this mother-child pairing. This can lead to squabbles and stalled timelines as you each fuss about what the other one is wearing, or you insist that little Libra rewrite a one-page essay with neater penmanship, or you get into an argument about some other trivial matter. At some point, it's probably wise to adopt a "live and let live" motto here instead of constantly nagging. Though you are fearful of your child making a mistake, head-in-the-clouds Libra might have to learn a few things the hard way. Let the teacher correct her sometimes, too—every lesson doesn't have to come from you, Mom.

Ruled by decadent Venus, your tastes, Libra, run toward the expensive. You never met a sale rack you didn't like (although you do adore the finer things, too) and will have to work harder to teach this child the value of a dollar. Languid Libra operates on his own timeline: don't rush this kid or overschedule him. He needs time to zone out and daydream. Busy yourself with a DIY project so you don't pace a hole in the floor waiting for Libra to get in gear.

VIRGO MOM + SCORPIO CHILD

*

WHERE YOU CLICK

The Scorpio child is a kindred spirit who may feel as much like your best friend as your offspring. You view the world through a similar lens: curious but cautious and ever alert of what might go wrong. You're the dynamic duo of damage control, hovering over the other members of the household to make sure they are safe and sound. Even if Scorpio is the youngest child, she will still be protective of her siblings, so you can relax knowing there's an extra pair of eyes watching, well, everything.

Little Scorpio is an investigator; you're the ultimate researcher—and you can both be obsessive collectors. Bring little Scorpio along to the antique district and teach him to distinguish Shaker-style furniture, French mattress ticking, and other valuable collector's items. This kid can find a needle in a haystack, and cultivating hobbies like these will keep the Scorpio occupied and away from trouble.

Serious, intense, and analytical, you'll both feel at home in each other's presence, even when you're sitting together quietly, reading books, tinkering with projects, or solving crossword puzzles. Hello, comfortable silence.

WHERE YOU CLASH

Secretive Scorpio needs lots of private time and space. The Virgo helicopter mom can be rather nosy at times. It may be tough for you to respect your Scorpio's need for closed doors and locked drawers. Don't even think about reading tween Scorpio's diary (okay, we know you've already peeked at a page) unless you want to permanently break trust.

You're going to have to rely on faith in many instances, since there's no way to keep this edgy kid completely out of trouble. Your helpful nature can border on nitpicking, and if you cross into critical terrain, look out! Scorpio's stinger is sharper than your tongue, Mom. This little one can cut you down to size with an acid-laced truth bomb about one of *your* shortcomings. Ouch! Modest Virgo moms will have to get over a few hang-ups, too. Since Scorpio is the sign of sexuality, this child can be unabashedly curious about the body, grilling you about the birds and bees at an unusually young age. Have pamphlets and the book *How Babies Are Made* ready so you can deliver the facts to your child. Better she should hear it from you than some playground raconteur!

VIRGO MOM + SAGITTARIUS CHILD

*

WHERE YOU CLICK

Le geek, c'est chic! The knowledge-hungry Sagittarius kid and the erudite Virgo mom love to learn together. The world is your workshop! Young Sag will love tagging along for your studies, from your conversational French class to ceramics (*avec* kiln) to the shamanic drumming circle. The great outdoors is a shared passion, too, although the earthy Virgo mom can be a bit fussier than her wild Centaur child. Forget about the pristine picnics in the park. This kid is going to get muddy, scraped up, and completely mussed before you've finished unpacking your gluten-free spread. Bring lots of wipes and just roll with it.

Class clown Sagittarius will definitely help you to lighten up, breaking through your austere MO with ridiculously clever jokes. This child shares your love of language, and you'll giggle over puns, coin funny household terms, rename the pets, and one day enjoy passing books back and forth between you. Your world feels broader and a lot more fun with this child in it.

WHERE YOU CLASH

Paging Dear Abby! Little Sagittarius loves to dole out unsolicited advice, just like the Virgo mom. But when you turn those preachy beams on each other, look out! Young Sagittarius may take it upon herself to weigh in on your style and friendship choices, giving you an uncomfortable taste of your own medicine. This kid will definitely teach you tolerance. The less you judge, the less he will. The unfiltered Archer sometimes suffers from "open mouth, insert foot" syndrome. This is incredibly embarrassing for the polite Virgo mother who might whisper about someone's shortcomings but likes to keep up niceties in public. Beware your gossiping tendencies, Virgo mom! The unfiltered Sagittarius will invariably repeat them to the wrong people. "Well, my mom said that I shouldn't stay for dinner because your mom doesn't know how to wash dishes." Eek!

Sagittarius is a wild child who is ruled by expansive Jupiter. Limits and boundaries are not in this child's lexicon. Your rigid restrictions will be challenged at every turn—especially when it comes to portion sizes since Sagittarius has a bigger-than-usual appetite—and you may have to lighten up a bit to save the family some drama.

VIRGO MOM + CAPRICORN CHILD

*

WHERE YOU CLICK

Aren't you just the proudest mama in town? The well-mannered, hardworking Capricorn child has inherited the halo hanging over your head. This good girl/boy thrives when there are benchmarks to reach, gold stars to earn, and clear-cut rules to follow. Sheer heaven! You'll crow with pride as high-achieving Capricorn scoops up trophies and blue ribbons, adding titles of distinction—class president, soccer team captain, German Club leader—to her ever-growing roster of honors. High standards? Check. Little Capricorn can be a status-conscious perfectionist who aims to keep up with the Joneses, just like you. At times you'll be outdone by your child's ambition. You may have to remind him to be a little *less* competitive—and less stern with himself to boot. In many ways, this child will hold up the mirror, reflecting back your proudest, and most intense, traits.

WHERE YOU CLASH

Did Debbie Downer just enter the building? Prone to pessimism, the Virgo mum and Capricorn child can get themselves in quite the funk. Damage control is a shared specialty: it's never hard for either of you to come up with a reason why something *can't* work or *shouldn't* be the way it is. You may inadvertently rain on your child's parade, and vice versa. The Virgo mom can be openly critical of both yourself and others. Little Capricorn is also naturally quite hard on herself. She may pick up this ball and run in a scary direction, becoming a snobbish elitist toward the other kids on the playground or holding herself to an impossible standard. Tip: say nice things about yourself and others in front of this child.

What goes around comes around. Virgo is the sign of service. You're always there in a pinch to help a neighbor, friend, or relative. Capricorn is the sign of ambition and you may find that your "I want to be the best" kid is a little too competitive or self-serving for your tastes. Teaching the importance of helping others would be a wise idea here.

VIRGO MOM + AQUARIUS CHILD

*

WHERE YOU CLICK

Caring, socially responsible Virgo is the sign of service; Aquarius is the zodiac's humanitarian. Your do-gooder mother-child pairing will lend itself toward family volunteer outings, charity races, and other hands-on community improvement projects. Little Aquarius is rational and scientific, which the logical Virgo mom will love. Here's a kid who loves to learn the why and how as much as you do.

By the same token, you both have a New Agey streak. This bohemian child will happily accompany you to your sitar lesson, raw-dessert-making class, and dream-catcher workshop. Virgo, you are an "activity mom," which is perfect for energetic Aquarius. This child also likes to geek out, so sharing nerdy trivia about obscure topics of interest will be like your own secret language. Both signs share a deep love for animals. It will be hard not to turn your home into a zoo!

WHERE YOU CLASH

The earthy Virgo mom has her feet planted on terra firma. The airy-fairy Aquarius child can drift off into the clouds. This kid's flights of fancy may be a bit too out there for you, especially when he starts talking about aliens, space travel, and visitations from unicorns. You operate on totally different timelines. Pragmatic Virgo is all about making the here-and-now better, but you also tend to dwell on the past. Future-oriented Aquarius lives for tomorrow and can be so distracted that she forgets to notice all the little things you do. Teaching this child to tune in to the moment and express gratitude will be important lessons to pass on.

The sensitive Virgo mom can get a little petty, your feathers ruffling at every slight. Fair-minded Aquarius likes to rise above and be cool. Your mellow kid may seem a bit too detached for your liking, and you should encourage him to get in touch with his feelings. There's wisdom coming from the mouth of this babe, too, who can teach you how to stop sweating the small stuff.

VIRGO MOM + PISCES CHILD

*

WHERE YOU CLICK

Pisces is your opposite sign, so this child will be a great complement and teacher for you (and vice versa). You're both bighearted: Virgo is all about selfless service, and Pisces is the sign of sacrifice. You'll beam watching your helpful little Fish in action on the playground and will secretly love it when your child gets a little bossy or starts finger wagging toward the other children.

Pisces will happily let you fuss over him. Your hands-on brand of nurturing is chicken soup to this child's soul. Pisces have sensitive systems and may deal with various allergies and infections as infants. The health-conscious Virgo mom is right on top of that, researching every natural remedy in town and getting your wee one in thriving shape. Pisces adores the arts and you're a bit of a culture vulture yourself, and both of your signs have an affinity for dance. Mother-child ballet routine, anyone?

WHERE YOU CLASH

The Virgo mom likes to make a plan and stick with it. Dreamy Pisces can drift in many directions and struggles with completing projects and sticking with schedules. Frustrating! Your pragmatic advice can wound this sensitive soul, who is prone to self-sabotage. Using positive reinforcement rather than punitive methods will be the best bet for building up your child's confidence—and getting your pokey Pisces to pick up the pace!

You are extremely selective about the people you allow into your world, and your little Fish's habit of befriending the underdog (and inviting her to sleep over . . . eek!) will challenge you to your very core. Elusive Pisces is prone to secrecy. You'll have a hard time figuring out what's going on in this kid's mind, which disrupts the need-to-know Virgo tendency. Both of you can be emotionally manipulative, too: you can send each other on epic guilt trips, so be mindful.

LIBRA

LIBRA MOM + ARIES CHILD

WHERE YOU CLICK

While *some* moms might get thrown off by spunky, self-expressed Aries, the easygoing Libra mom is totally up for the task of raising a Ram. You'll enjoy cultivating this kid's individualistic expression, in much the same way you enjoy supporting the arts. The forthright, single-minded Ram has no trouble making decisions, letting you know exactly what she does and doesn't like. This is great medicine for the wavering Libra mom who can get stuck in analysis paralysis. In turn, you'll smooth out your child's rough edges, teaching fiery Aries to play nice and use some diplomacy.

With your made-to-order tastes, you both have a touch of prima donna in you. Hey, you two simply like things done a certain way, even if that means making a few special requests. Lucky for you, people have trouble saying no to both of you!

WHERE YOU CLASH

Can't we all just get along? Harmonious Libra is the zodiac's peacekeeper. Mars-ruled Aries is the cosmic warrior. Your child's aggression and firepower can throw you off balance, big-time! You're not one to lose your cool, Libra, but this child could drive you over the edge. Spunky, independent Aries needs space to cultivate a separate identity—even the sweetest Ram will turn into a black sheep for a spell. This is especially true if you force a sense of togetherness or fixate on how similar you two are. Libra hates to rush, fast-and-furious Aries moves at a manic pace: exhausting! Forget about dressing this kid in the fussy outfits you adore. Your rough-and-tumble Ram will rip and stain them in no time.

LIBRA MOM + TAURUS CHILD

*

WHERE YOU CLICK

Like the Libra mom, little Taurus is ruled by creative, starry-eyed Venus. This child shares your fervor for life's finer—and beautiful—things. Drape your Bull in kiddie couture; puree the gourmet baby food; and fill your home with melodic sounds, gorgeous art, and delicate aromas. Taurus will be in heaven: you could groom an edified mini-me! A leisurely pace is how you both prefer to roll.

Forget the Sunday dinners. Instead, have an artful Saturday-morning ritual, lounging in pj's and making a special banana-hazelnut crepe recipe together in your chef's kitchen. Music soothes your twin souls. When your scales are off balance or Taurus starts seeing red, pump up the jams and have a dance break together. Harmonious Venus is at the helm! You'll have more moments of domestic bliss with little Taurus, who can be a homebody. In turn, the cultured Libra mom can get the stubborn Bull to open up and see more of what the world has to offer.

WHERE YOU CLASH

Libra is cultured and civilized; Taurus is brash and rough around the edges. This loud and opinionated child will ruffle your Miss Manners feathers from time to time, embarrassing you with matter-of-fact assessments of people (including you). Good luck trying to get Taurus to use his indoor voice!

Getting out of the house in time can be a doozy for you two. Little Taurus may take thirty-minute showers, fuss in front of the mirror, or do a few outfit changes before being ready to go. (Sound familiar?) Build in extra prep time in your mornings or you may be perpetually late.

Pushy Taurus can steamroll the patient Libra mom. It's a little too easy to spoil this child who doesn't back down easily when she has an agenda. Rule number one for raising this kid: remember that no is a complete sentence and set strict guidelines Taurus can remember and follow.

LIBRA MOM + GEMINI CHILD

*

WHERE YOU CLICK

Air sign soul mates, you both love to blow with the wind, breezing through the day with a sense of wide-eyed wonder. Little Gemini shares your curiosity about all things new. Life feels like a giant discovery mission when you're together. Break out the lightweight stroller! You're an on-the-go duo who prefer to be out and about rather than nesting at home for too long. Social butterflies, you both make friends wherever you go. Gemini will happily attend playdates, bonding with other kids while you gab endlessly with your adult friends. You'll connect with this child on an intellectual level, too, sharing books from your childhood and taking wee Gemini on interesting outings to places where they can learn new things. Gemini is the sign of the twins and Libra rules partnership: both of you love to have another person nearby at all times. You'll feel like BFFs with this child!

WHERE YOU CLASH

Between the Libra mom's constant wavering and Gemini's mercurial whims, you guys can have trouble making plans in advance. You can drive each other crazy trying to figure out where to go, what to eat, and who to have a playdate with that day. Gemini is cool and logical and some of your dreamy ideas can be a wee bit too out there for this kid. The sentimental Libra mom may get her feelings hurt when little Gem rebuffs your hugs or outright rejects your mushier gestures.

Don't expect Gemini to care about your rules of etiquette and social propriety beyond a point, either! This child likes to break the rules (or at least bend them), dancing near the edge of rebellion and hanging out with the troublemakers from time to time. Peacekeeping Libra moms are forever pushing for harmony, but Gemini gets a kick out of playing the devil's advocate. Your impish child may even start squabbles between family members just for the "fun" of it. Argh!

LIBRA MOM + CANCER CHILD

*

WHERE YOU CLICK

Sweet, sentimental souls, the Libra mom and Cancer child can bring out each other's best. You both love to create, then ruminate over, fond memories—all of which you'll photograph and organize in albums with helpful Cancer's input. (Can you say "scrapbooking party"?) Pampering is a big part of the Libra mom's world and the comfort-loving Crab will happily join you in these self-indulgent moments. It's basically domestic bliss when you two lounge lizards kick back at home.

Food holds a special place in both of your hearts, and you'll love teaching little Cancer all the family recipes, even if you add your own macrobiotic twist during one of your ever present health kicks. Cancers tend to revere their mothers, and you will love fawning over this well-behaved child. Little Cancer will fuss over you, too—you are the chicken soup for each other's souls.

WHERE YOU CLASH

The Libra mom is a party animal at heart and you can work a room like nobody's business. Close-knit Cancer kids embrace a chosen few, huddling with a tight circle of friends. Your clutchy kid may cramp your social style, becoming possessive and demanding of your time and attention. While you'll need to nudge the Crab off your apron strings, don't forget to focus on Cancer, too, giving special attention to your wee one even when you're surrounded by your 1,001 "friends."

Gushy, outspoken Libra moms like to let it all hang out while private Cancers hold their cards close to their vests. You're only bragging like a proud mother, but you could inadvertently blab this kid's business—grounds for slammed doors and silent treatments in Cancer's book. Your child's brooding moods can be a dark cloud over your sunny optimism. Though you prefer to look on the bright side, don't be dismissive of little Cancer's emotions. Minor situations really *do* feel that serious to this child, even if you never understand why.

LIBRA MOM + LEO CHILD

*

WHERE YOU CLICK

Diamonds are the Libra mom's best friend, and little Leo adores life's sparkly luxuries, too. You'll pass your elegant sensibilities on to this child, turning heads as you push your proud Lion around town in his stroller. A few of your favorite things to do together: dress up in stylish bright-colored clothes, eat rich and delicious food, dance to lively music, and give yourselves special treats on a daily basis. Musical and theatrical, you might even start a band together or star in a play with an all-ages cast.

You're both sunny optimists with huge hearts: when you adore people you'll do anything for them. Giving gifts is a way you both show love. Get ready to line your walls with tribute paintings and other little trinkets Leo bestows upon you. Warning: it's easy to spoil this child, so make sure your little one knows that some of those rewards must be earned.

WHERE YOU CLASH

Mirror, mirror on the wall. Vanity is a weakness for both the Libra mom and Leo child. Remember to teach your kid that it's what's inside that counts. Ruled by the radiant sun, Leos can forget that they are not the center of the universe. Give praise where praise is due or you can develop the worst trait of Leo: a huge ego. Fire sign Leo can be wild, loud, and domineering, which can overwhelm the mild-mannered Libra mom. Although you hate conflict, you'll have to push back and discipline your Leo lest she wrest control away from you. Alas, *no* is a word the Lion hates but needs to hear more often than most.

Leo needs long periods of undivided attention; Libra is a master crowd surfer, making light chitchat before moving on to the next conversation. Don't breeze over your child's need for one-on-one time. Young Leo may act out to get your attention, and it won't be pretty.

LIBRA MOM + VIRGO CHILD

*

WHERE YOU CLICK

Details, details! Both Libra mom and Virgo child are obsessed with the little things. So what if this slows everyone down a bit. You both know that the intricacies are what make the difference between good and great! Since Virgo is the sign of the critic and Libra the judge, you both have particular tastes. As your Virgo approaches the tween years, you might get a little snarky together, too. The fashion police have arrived—look out!

Modest Virgo can be prim and proper and loves to learn rules and etiquette. This child is your well-mannered mini-me and will make you one proud mama in the public eye. Earth sign Virgo loves to be helpful so clue your kid into your to-do list. Virgo will be great at remembering all the things that the airy Libra mom breezes right over. No need to set all those reminder alarms! You're both visual and love to pretty up your surroundings.

WHERE YOU CLASH

Fanciful Libra moms can get carried away with your creative expression, taking a hard left from anything sensible. The restrained Virgo child may blush or avoid you in moments like these. You're just too over the top for this pragmatic child at times. Your sunny optimism is a clash for little Virgo's glass-half-empty view of life. Your kid's neuroses will try your patience for sure—why can't he just let it go? When your Libra scales get off balance you can get swept up in a dramatic emotional spiral. Virgo will go into fixer mode, trying to help, which can stir up anxiety in your child. Try to keep your cool in front of Virgo, even if this old-soul child comforts you like a wise-beyond-her-years confidante. Otherwise, little Virgo's heart can get heavy with responsibility long before adulthood.

LIBRA MOM + LIBRA CHILD

*

WHERE YOU CLICK

What a lovefest! Venus-ruled Libra mother and child will share a great affection for each other. Call the kiddie stylist and set up the photo shoot, quick! You're the picture-perfect duo, and the camera loves you both. Don't be surprised if you're stopped on the street often with people fawning over you. Your mini-me adores beauty and harmony just as much as you do. Whether boy or girl, little Libra may be your young shopping mate, a kid who will happily tag along to outdoor music festivals, fashion shows, and artsy gatherings.

Party over here! This supersocial child loves people as much as you do. Drop little Libra anywhere and you'll both work the room with your respective peers. When your scales are both balanced, you'll coexist in blissful harmony, preferring peaceful, comfortable surroundings where you can relax and putter about without interruption or demands.

WHERE YOU CLASH

Libras are fussy with extremely particular tastes. So what happens when you and your child are both fixated but on different visions? Although your star sign hates conflict, there could be some serious standoffs here. Although you're generally sunny optimists, your scales can swing in opposite directions, making you both quite moody. This is especially true when Libra is hungry or tired. This child may hold up the mirror, revealing just how demanding you can be, Mom, when you want your way and you want it *now*!

The two of you can overemphasize appearances, too, perhaps because you look so good together as a pair. Don't forget to sharpen the intellectual connection you have with this kid, too. You're both deep thinkers, after all, and young Libra may enjoy all the books you read when you were a child, so share them with her. Spend more time at home together, too: just because you're both social butterflies, doesn't mean that young Libra doesn't need a sense of order and routine to feel secure.

LIBRA MOM + SCORPIO CHILD

*

WHERE YOU CLICK

The bond between Libra mom and Scorpio child can be rather intense. You feel a karmic connection with this child, who will stick close by your side, just the way you like it. You're both blessed with more than your average share of charm. Team up on school bake sales and charity fundraisers. Between your gracious personality and your Scorpio's irresistible charisma, you'll raise record funds. Who knows, maybe you'll launch a start-up together one day.

The laid-back Libra mom isn't thrown off so easily by Scorpio's powerful moods and reactions. This kid can get fixated on an emotion, fired up or stuck in a rut. Your fair-minded outlook comes in handy for helping Scorpio snap out of that obsessive groove and view the situation from another perspective. In turn, serious Scorpio helps you go beyond the superficial. You'll become an even deeper person, thanks to this kid's profound influence.

WHERE YOU CLASH

The Libra mom is a peacekeeper by nature: you'd rather extend the olive branch than stay mad at anyone. Not so for your Scorpio scion. This kid can hang on to a grudge for a lonnng time! Start early with the lessons in forgiveness, teaching young Scorpio the power of letting it go.

The social Libra mom is the queen of the scene: you're in demand the moment you step into a room, and you're the type who's never met a stranger. Alas, your extroverted nature can trigger Scorpio's jealousy issues. Your possessive child may lash out at you with a stinging remark or vicious tantrum if you make him feel like second fiddle to your myriad friends.

Both the Libra mom and Scorpio child can sink into an emo groove, but the difference lies in the magnitude of your moods. Your storm clouds pass a lot quicker than this child's. Scorpio's attraction to the darker side of life is tough for you to understand sometimes, causing you to wonder how you gave birth to such an intense child!

LIBRA MOM + SAGITTARIUS CHILD

*

WHERE YOU CLICK

Let the sunshine in! The optimistic Archer child shares your joie de vivre and sparkling outlook on life. Neither one of you likes to be down for long; your cheery child will shore you up with silly jokes and wise-beyond-his-years advice. You're a spontaneous, go-with-the-flow pair, so keep the lightweight stroller in the trunk at all times. A quick trip to the grocery store could turn into an all-day outing for you two explorers!

Sign up for the library card ASAP. You'll bond over books with young Sagittarius who shares your love of reading and eagerness to learn about the broader world. The two of you make great travel companions, too, whether you're going on a family road trip or flying overseas to explore your ancestral homeland. In many ways, the young Archer may feel like both your child *and* your BFF.

WHERE YOU CLASH

The rough-and-tumble Sagittarius can be a liability to the fussy Libra mom, and you might have to pack away a few of your pretty things (especially the white ones). Wild Sagittarius comes home covered in dirt and paint. Where you're graceful, the Archer is clumsy. Put those precious heirlooms on a high shelf! And forget about the kiddie couture with this one—there will be tears in the fabric before you have a chance to justify the ridiculous splurge.

The suave Libra mother is a natural diplomat. You always think before you speak. Not so for your child! Brash, outspoken Sagittarius is known for putting her tiny foot in her mouth. You'll be mortified on more than one occasion by this kid's tactless monologues. Unlike you, Sagittarius is not terribly sentimental. Save the Hallmark moments for another kid and show little Sag that you care with your sense of humor instead.

LIBRA MOM + CAPRICORN CHILD

*

WHERE YOU CLICK

The well-mannered, ambitious Capricorn is a bit of a mother's dream, particularly the etiquette-conscious Libra mum. You both like to shine in the public eye and this kid knows how to keep up appearances. Register for the country club membership ASAP; there's a touch of elitism in both of your signs. Little Capricorn will want to play with the "good kids" from "good families" and won't soil the precious tennis whites you outfit her in. You're definitely a picture-perfect pair!

Capricorn is loyal and traditional and, like you, loves to spend time with family. You'll coexist peacefully with this child especially since you both enjoy a calm and relaxing atmosphere. There's a perfectionist streak in both of you, too: Libra moms like things done just so, and little Caps hold themselves to a high standard and work ethic. You'll be inspired by your child's determination and may learn to stick to a goal by watching little Capricorn in action. In turn, you'll help your somber child lighten up and learn to roll with the punches without being too self-judgmental.

WHERE YOU CLASH

There's a bit of a role reversal in this mother-child pairing. The breezy Libra mom is often more playful than the earthbound Capricorn child. This solemn kid can be downright pessimistic, which can rain on your parade. When Capricorn starts something—a project, homework, a video game—he likes to see it through to the end. The socially active Libra mom may get stuck at home more often than you'd prefer, waiting for young Capricorn to complete a mission.

Capricorns thrive in a structured, traditional environment: this kid actually likes having rules! The spontaneous Libra mom is not always the best at creating routines, much less remembering your child's bedtime. Strive to be the traditional mom, not the cool mom—that's what this kid yearns for. Forward-focused Capricorns have a burning need to map out their futures. Live-for-the-moment Libra moms will need to become better planners for this kid's sake! Your constant "maybes" can trigger your kid's insecurities, too. Capricorn needs a yes or no answer from you; this is not a kid who likes spontaneity or surprises.

LIBRA MOM + AQUARIUS CHILD

*

WHERE YOU CLICK

Libra and Aquarius are both air signs, and you blow through life on a common cool breeze. This laid-back child shares your love of spontaneity and adventure. There will be no need to overplan your outings. Just pop Aquarius in the car seat and go! This sharp kid shares your intellectual curiosity and your jaunts could turn into all-day urban explorations through hands-on museums and specialty shops or on winding road trips through quaint little towns with rich histories. Not that you only go highbrow, of course. Should one (or both) of you leap out of bed with the urge to spend the day at an amusement park or the zoo, off you'll go without a second thought.

The humanitarian Aquarius child and "peace and love" Libra mom are both compassionate to the underdog, so volunteering together will be a great way to bond. Both signs are animal lovers as well. This kid may wind up going vegetarian with you at a young age, and for ethical reasons at that. Like you, little Aquarius has a talent for organizing people. Together, you'll keep family adventures lively, organizing fun and games while buoying the spirit of togetherness.

WHERE YOU CLASH

Although you're both incredibly social, Libra is more of a one-on-one person while your wee Water Bearer is the zodiac's team player. The bonding moments you long to share with your child will be regularly interrupted by visits from his entourage. "Can Brendan, Scott, and Jonah come along with us, too, Mom?" Aquarius will coo. Oh boy. You may have to put your foot down, lest you wind up feeling more like a shuttle bus driver than a dedicated mother.

Ruled by Venus, the Libra mom is a sentimental love bug. Aquarius is ruled by intellectual Uranus and may shrink from your sloppy kisses and frequent hugs. This kid is no one's dress-up doll or huggy bear, which might break your heart a little in moments. Don't take it personally! You'll connect beautifully to this child through the realm of books and ideas. You'll also be amazed by the mature quality of your conversations, too. From a young age, the sharp Water Bearer can grasp bigger, philosophical concepts. Sure, you may have to sacrifice a few warm embraces, but little Aquarius may one day count you as her BFF.

LIBRA MOM + PISCES CHILD

*

WHERE YOU CLICK

Creativity is the calling card for the Libra mom and Pisces child. Out come the finger paints, musical instruments, hand-illustrated books, and gorgeous ruffled canopy beds. The frills are what bring the thrills to your lives, and neither of you has limits when it comes to indulging. (Keep that cookie jar out of your Fish's reach—and yours, too!) The dreamy Pisces child shares your supersized imagination. Life feels like an enchanted journey when the two of you are together. Hey, you never *really* stopped believing in mermaids and fairies, did you, Libra? You'll get to relive the magic through your fantastical Pisces.

Bring on the hugs—and the beautiful mugs of delicious French hot cocoa. Not only are you both supersentimental, but you both love to pamper yourselves with comforting rituals. You'll share many blissful moments with this cuddly child who loves to be by your side.

WHERE YOU CLASH

You have a vivid imagination, but Pisces' oft-slippery grip on reality is another matter altogether. You may balk at your child's imaginary friends, eerie drawings, or irrepressible belief that there are ghosts in the room. Try not to judge, Libra. This gifted child does have superior sensory perceptions and, in some cases, prophetic dreams.

Little Pisces is a born caretaker, quick to comfort you when your Libra scales get off balance. But be careful here, Mom. This emotionally empathetic child is still a child! Don't put Pisces in the role of your nurturer too often or your little Fish may not gain a proper sense of safety in the world. You'll need to discipline yourself more when it comes to bedtimes, mealtimes, and other structures. Like you, little Pisces tends to lose track of time and may not announce hunger or sleepiness according to a normal schedule. Set reminder alarms for yourself. Keeping Pisces organized will help you get your own life into a more grounded groove. You're both emotionally sensitive, but water sign Pisces can be a big brooder. Shoring your child up from his darker moods could wear on your sunny groove. Although you crave constant company, the Fish needs solitude when he gets in these moods. Give him some space!

SCORPIO

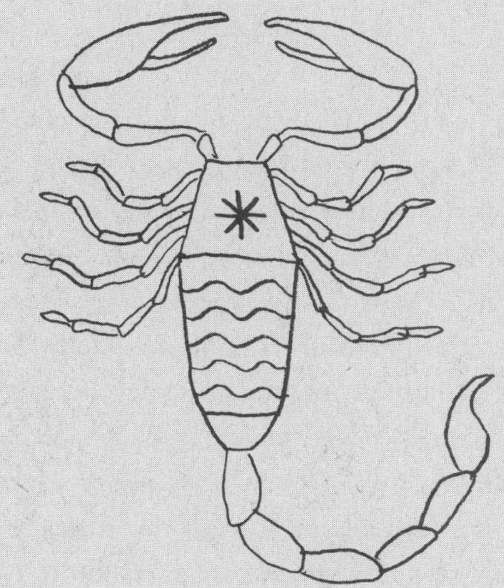

SCORPIO MOM + ARIES CHILD

*

WHERE YOU CLICK

Passionate and powerful, your Mars-ruled Aries is a chip off the old block. The Scorpio mom counts warrior planet Mars as her coruler, along with predominant Pluto. You will innately understand young Aries' competitive spirit and unstoppable drive. Whether captain of the soccer team, drum major, or child star, Aries kids often wind up leading the pack. The hands-on Scorpio is the perfect "mom-ager" for this wunderkind, directing your Ram's ascent and showing up for every game, audition, and performance.

The wild Aries child can be a hard one to tame, but the Scorpio "tiger mom" is up for the task. With your shrewd disciplinary style, you'll ensure that Aries remains humble, reminding your child that the world doesn't always revolve around her. While Aries kids exude confidence, they are also the zodiac's babies. Your intuitive brand of mothering comes in handy here, as you'll be able to sense just when to nudge Aries out of the nest and when to hold your little one close.

WHERE YOU CLASH

With aggressive Mars at the helm, there can be a combative connection between the Scorpio mother and Aries child. You are both brash and outspoken, sometimes blurting out hurtful comments that you later regret. For Aries, this is usually more of a thoughtless candor while the Scorpio mother will sting when feeling rejected or unappreciated. Tempers may flare quickly in this pairing, especially when the rebel Ram defies your rules at every turn—or simply forgets them completely. Your fiercely determined Aries child won't take kindly to the quiet control you exert, especially if you deny him the right to explore the world beyond your comfort zone.

The Ram is fundamentally independent, which can leave the Scorpio mom feeling uneasy. You're a bit needy and anxious, needing more reassurance of your lovable mommy status than the distracted Aries child knows how to give. Don't make the mistake of putting your self-worth in this charming child's hands or you could lose all parental controls.

SCORPIO MOM + TAURUS CHILD

*

WHERE YOU CLICK

Scorpio and Taurus are opposite signs. On a good day you are the perfect balance for one another. Your down-to-earth child is easy to read—there are no mysteries here, which is a relief for the somewhat suspicious Scorpio mom. It's not hard to cultivate an open communication style with this kid, who will consider you a confidant.

Much like you, Taurus is practical but also loves the good life. You'll have fun indulging together: bring on the ice-cream sundae parties! This dependable kid is a happy helper for the busy Scorpio mother. You're both creative and detail-oriented, so task wee Taurus with helping you pretty up the house for a party or make a playlist of background music. The luxury-loving Bull loves the finer things, but you're also both frugal. Little Taurus will sock away his pennies in that piggy bank and sniff out a great sale, just like his mama! Material comforts are a must for you both. Time at home will be sheer domestic bliss.

WHERE YOU CLASH

Stubborn much? Neither the bullheaded Taurus child nor strong-willed Scorpio mom back down easily when fixed on an idea. You're both prone to black-and-white thinking and may have trouble finding a compromise when the two of you clash. Sure, you could pull rank, Scorpio—and you'll probably have to on many occasions—but listen to little Taurus, too. This pragmatic child will often have a point worth considering, even if it takes him a while to verbalize it. Bear in mind that Taurus rules the throat, so encouraging your little Bull to voice her opinions is essential to building her confidence.

As fixed signs, neither one of you likes change, but when it's time to transform an area of life, you go into extreme makeover mode. Taurus rules the material world and gets attached to familiar objects. Tread lightly when tossing away those action figures or dollies. Just because your baby Bull hasn't played with them in months doesn't mean they no longer have security blanket status. Fights can get nasty between you two when the charging Bull meets the Scorpio's stinger. You might have to give yourself a time-out so you don't lose your cool!

SCORPIO MOM + GEMINI CHILD

✳

WHERE YOU CLICK

Sherlock Holmes meets Nancy Drew in this inquisitive mother-child pairing. Like you, little Gemini is endlessly fascinated by life's great mysteries—and you can both get obsessed with cracking the case. Solving puzzles is something you both love, too. Anything that's too straightforward just bores you both to tears; you'd rather figure out a perplexing code or unravel a series of clues to get your answers. Bring on the brainteasers and strategy games, a favorite way for you two to bond.

Like you, little Gemini is a rabid culture vulture, and you may share a special appreciation for films. Obsessing over the details is a common trait, too. While you may drive the other members of your household crazy, neither of you will be satisfied until things are done "just so."

WHERE YOU CLASH

The Scorpio mom is singular in focus. When you want to accomplish something, you won't veer off course until your goal has been conquered. Erratic Gemini has one of the shortest attention spans in the zodiac. This kid is notorious for leaving half-finished projects everywhere, driving you insane in the process.

Loyalty and trust are everything to the Scorpio mom, but good luck instilling those traits in *this* fickle child. Gemini has a reputation for being two-faced. If your child isn't outright gossiping, she will change best friends at least three times on the average day. You'll struggle to watch your child's mercurial social style, especially since BFF status is something you don't ever bestow lightly.

Silence is golden to the Scorpio mom. You need to retreat into your quiet cave to do your best thinking. Gemini's nonstop chatter will interrupt your meditative moments. You may have to leave the house in order to get a moment's peace!

SCORPIO MOM + CANCER CHILD

*

WHERE YOU CLICK

Sweet perfection! Little Cancer is your water sign soul mate, a child who is as intuitive and selective as you are. You'll form a cozy bubble world with this kid who will happily hang at your hip, mimicking your every move. Domestic bliss will not be in short order for you two family-oriented, traditional souls. Your comfortable home will serve as the enclave you private water signs so dearly crave. Thank your lucky stars: young Cancer understands the meaning of comfortable silence, giving you plenty of meditative moments to pause and recharge.

Your child's social style is similar to your own. Neither one of you trusts easily; you both prefer to have close connections to a chosen few. Like you, little Cancer is sensitive to perceived slights from friends. While you'll understand her high level of reactivity, be careful not to empower a victim mentality. You may both need to learn the power of not taking everything quite so personally!

WHERE YOU CLASH

This mother-child pairing may grow a little too close for comfort. You so adore each other's company that it's easy to tune out everyone else, including other family members who may grow jealous of your bond. When it comes to making friends, you're both prone to suspicion. Be careful not to form an "us against the world" mentality here. If you let life become too insular, your Cancer may never leave the nest! (You might think this is a good thing, but it's not—especially on the first day of kindergarten.)

Young Cancer is moody, but you have your dark spells, too. You can bring each other down with those storm clouds, raining on each other's parade. Little Cancer can be a goody-goody at times, both naive and preferring to be sheltered. The bawdy babe in you may feel confined by the little Crab's moralistic judgments. You want to be the cool mom, and this kid's desire for a June Cleaver replica can seriously cramp your style.

SCORPIO MOM + LEO CHILD

*

WHERE YOU CLICK

The child star and stage mother come together in this cosmic combination. While little Leo lights up the main stage, you'll be pulling strings behind the curtains, making sure your wunderkind gets top billing. There couldn't be a more supportive mom for this talented child's aspirations—even if you *do* veer into controlling terrain at times. While some children may feel smothered by so much attention, young Leo will revel in your constant care. You don't mind making your child the center of your universe, and the confident Lion believes such an esteemed position is her birthright. Leo's competitive nature and drive to be the best are traits you mirror in your own life. The mantel may grow crowded from the awards and trophies you two earn. You both have magnetic personalities and a striking style. You will attract a lot of attention when you're out together. A reality show about your lives would be fascinating, although *you* are probably far too private for that.

WHERE YOU CLASH

Who's the boss? There can be major power struggles in this parent-child pairing. Your mini-royalty may forget that it's *you* who reigns supreme, especially if you go overboard with the praise. Be careful not to inflate Leo's ego to outsized proportions by pointing out how much better he is than the other kids. This is a slippery slope you won't want to tumble down (even if you believe it to be true), or you could be fielding calls from the school about Leo's inability to share or play nicely.

The proud, brash Lion child is terrible at keeping secrets—and this may chill your deeply private heart. You'll have to monitor what information you share with Leo or you could find your dirty laundry aired on the loudspeaker. Fiery and independent, your little jungle cat needs lots of room to roam. Just try to keep this kid on that short, controlled leash, Scorpio. Young Leo could stage an epic rebellion or worse, make a huge public scene—the worst nightmare imaginable for your secretive sign.

SCORPIO MOM + VIRGO CHILD

*

WHERE YOU CLICK

The Virgo child is your kindred spirit, a comfortable sidekick for the Scorpio mother. Young Virgo takes life rather seriously; this kid can be almost as intense as you, especially when solving a perplexing puzzle or mystery. An anxious child, Virgo needs a lot of reassurance to feel secure. The intuitive Scorpio mother knows just how to soothe him, showing up as a steady, supportive presence in your Virgo's life. Rejoice! Here's a kid who appreciates your hands-on mommying style!

You're both a little neurotic, tuning in to every subtle nuance and shift in your surroundings. Virgo is just as fussy as you when it comes to her tastes: you'll make excellent shopping buddies one day whether you're cruising for couture or trying to find that needle-in-a-haystack antique on eBay.

Helpful Virgo can be a hardworking kid. Let him shadow you at work. Virgo will have great respect for your tireless drive, and you can teach your overly cautious kid how to take healthy, calculated risks in life.

WHERE YOU CLASH

Pick, pick, pick. Virgo is the sign of the critic and Scorpio can obsess over the details. You can get *way* too fussy together, needing everything custom ordered to your tastes. Be careful, Scorpio, or you could develop a demanding diva here. That won't go over well when Virgo heads off to school—the art teacher is not going to hand-blend paint colors for your kid's first watercolor painting.

You will see your own controlling tendencies mirrored in this child—an eye-opening reflection indeed. One day, young Virgo might even try bossing *you* around or weighing in on your adult decisions. This kid is definitely judgmental beyond her years! The sexy Scorpio mom is generally confident about her looks, but don't let those self-critical comments slip out as you gaze at your own reflection. Little Virgo is prone to perfectionism, especially body image issues, and will learn from your cues. Teaching this child self-love will be the best gift you can pass on. Gossiping is exacerbated when you two get together. Keep the snark in check, Mom, or you could bring out the mean girl in your Virgo!

SCORPIO MOM + LIBRA CHILD

*

WHERE YOU CLICK

Libra and Scorpio are both partnership-oriented signs. Like you, little Libra loves to engage in one-on-one interactions. Although your next-door-neighbor signs have little in common astrologically, you'll find yourselves chatting about every subject under the sun as soon as Libra's gift of gab kicks in.

Your differences are the charm in this parent-child pairing, in fact. Lighthearted Libra brings levity to your life. This kid knows how to look on the bright side and not get stuck sweating the small stuff. In turn, you help your flighty air sign child develop a bit of staying power. Little Libra hates to commit to a decision. Your surefootedness in this arena will set a great example for your child. With the purpose-driven Scorpio mom in his corner, choosing—and sticking with said selection—becomes less of an emotional ordeal for Libra. You both adore music and the arts. Little Libra may become your museum and symphony buddy while still in the stroller. Bring on the Picassos and twenty-piece jazz orchestras!

WHERE YOU CLASH

Could your child really be *that* naive? The wide-eyed wonder of young Libra makes the shrewd Scorpio mom break out in hives. This kid sees the world through rose-colored glasses while you hide behind spy goggles. You may veer into helicopter parenting, worrying constantly about your "overly trusting" offspring. Libra's mantra is "All you need is love," whereas the Scorpio mama feels the full, intense range of dark to light emotions. Your brooding spells could weigh heavily on cheery Libra's soul and may even cause your kid to pull away from the family structure. A word to the wise: close yourself in your room or go for a drive when you're having one of *those* moments.

Although you are both fussy about details—especially the way things look—flighty Libra is known for leaving loose ends and half-done projects. Teaching this child to finish what she starts may be one of your bigger challenges.

SCORPIO MOM + SCORPIO CHILD

✶

WHERE YOU CLICK

The Scorpio mom and child are as thick as thieves. Weaning this child, literally and figuratively, won't be a quick process—and you're perfectly fine with that. You both crave closeness and intensity; with your shared intuition it's as if you can read each other's minds. This soulful child may share your interest in mysticism and spirituality. Exploring the hidden side of life together will be important to you.

You both love elaborate schemes and will happily obsess over the details together, whether dressing up for a fancy celebration or devising an Easter Egg hunt for the neighborhood kids.

Little Scorpio can be a power-hungry child, but as long as you direct this tendency into a more humble groove you will groom a fine leader here. The two of you are charm personified; your magnetism will be striking while you're out in public together. Expect lots of stares but not much more since most people will be too intimidated to approach the cool cat and her kitten.

WHERE YOU CLASH

Obsess much? You're both attuned to unspoken vibes and hidden signals, but what about what's happening in front of your very eyes? There could be major pouting, huffing, and passive-aggressive moves between you two strategists. Honestly, your interactions don't have to be *so* complicated! Push yourself to communicate openly and make clear requests of young Scorpio. Just because this kid *can* read your mind doesn't mean she always will.

You recall your own attraction to danger and troublemakers from your own childhood and may see some of those traits mirrored in your pint-sized star mate. But does that give you the right to break into her diary or snoop through his room while he's at school? Um, no. Don't forget how much you need to have your own privacy respected, Mom. If you are suspicious that little Scorpio is heading down a wayward path, have a confidential conversation with him—and make sure you've created a safe space for your kid to divulge the details without reproach. This isn't too different from the way *you* would share with a loyal friend. While you may hear an earful from little Scorpio, have faith. You're the best possible guide since you can understand the lure of the dark side while simultaneously steering him in the opposite direction.

SCORPIO MOM + SAGITTARIUS CHILD

*

WHERE YOU CLICK

The soulful Scorpio mother and the philosophical Sagittarius child are both intrigued by the hidden realm of life. While you're more of a detective than your kid, the curious Archer child loves to discover new and hidden gems. Life may feel like an eternal treasure hunt for the two of you. You both like to achieve things on a grand scale—your broad-minded Sagittarius child is a visionary like you. With your knack for handling the details, you'll help make your enterprising Archer's dreams come true. Although as next-door-neighbor star signs you view the world in fundamentally different ways, you can help each other immensely.

The cautious Scorpio mom teaches harried Sagittarius that haste makes waste. In turn, your little optimist shores you out of your hopeless and obsessive spells, reminding you that there's often a rainbow after the rain.

WHERE YOU CLASH

The strategic Scorpio mom views life as a giant chess game. You rarely make a move without thinking it through from every angle. The impetuous Sagittarius child personifies "fools rushing in." Your control issues will rear up regularly watching the young Archer cross the lines of propriety and common sense. This kid's brash approach to life definitely gives you anxiety. The independent Archer seems to defy you at every turn, flagrantly ignoring your rules, especially the ones that limit her adventurous spirit or clip her wings in any way.

The Scorpio mother does not trust easily. People are put through Mafia-level loyalty tests before making it into *your* inner circle. The equal-opportunity Archer makes friends from every walk of life—yes, even *that* kid. Prepare to loosen up your standards a bit and perhaps become a bit more open-minded as a result of this child's influence.

SCORPIO MOM + CAPRICORN CHILD

*

WHERE YOU CLICK

The dynasty you've always dreamed of building is officially under way when little Capricorn comes out of the womb. As two of the most powerful, ambitious signs of the zodiac, your mini-mogul dreams of fame and fortune, just like Mom. You'll feel as if you're grooming a royal or a world leader, and indeed you may be. The Capricorn kid is born with an aristocratic air—you'll love watching him rise to the top in all that he does. Make a budget for luxury! This child has inherited your affection for fine goods, especially if those goods carry status. Like you, little Capricorn is highly selective of the company she keeps. Family means the world to both of your signs. Little Capricorn will be your second in command when it comes to rallying relatives together and keeping household affairs both orderly and lively.

WHERE YOU CLASH

Bossypants Capricorn can be a bit of a know-it-all. While you're happy to empower your child, you don't want her unseating you from your throne. Make sure it's abundantly clear who is in charge at *your* house. If you have other children, Capricorn can turn into a pint-sized dictator, especially if you put him in charge of siblings too often.

Both Scorpio and Capricorn can be drawn to the shadowy side of life—the land where jealousy, obsession, and power struggles live. Be extra mindful of what you expose this child to. Although you may not see a visible reaction, you don't want this child to become intrigued by darkness. The Scorpio mom can be secretive, and Capricorn can be closed off, too. Make sure that you talk about real deal subjects with this child so perfectionist Capricorn learns that it's safe to drop the mask and be vulnerable.

SCORPIO MOM + AQUARIUS CHILD

∗

WHERE YOU CLICK

Pass the sage and meditation pillow. There's a New Age bohemian living in both of your signs. Although Aquarius tends to be more logic-based than the intuitive Scorpio mom, your child will happily accompany you on those hippie-trippy pursuits that appeal to your inner mystic. All ages folk music festival, anyone?

You're both creative visionaries who love to think outside of the box. You can geek out over science, too! The curious Aquarius child is keen on studying people and gathering data to make a case. You're a natural detective yourself and will appreciate this wise kid's insights. You're both cool under pressure and may enjoy trying extreme or adventure-based sports together. Lighthearted Aquarius doesn't take things as personally as you do. Learn from this kid how not to sweat the small stuff.

WHERE YOU CLASH

Passionate Scorpio is the sign of attachment—you love your kids fiercely and want to keep them close. Cool-as-a-cucumber Aquarius is more detached; this kid wants to individuate from Mommy and roam without constraints. The Water Bearer may hurt your feelings by pushing away your affection. This can bring out the ice mom in you, and the cold front could be downright chilling if you start taking your Aquarian's need for space personally.

Your social styles are a major clash, too. Scorpio moms are suspicious of "strangers" (even the ones you've known for a decade), whereas the outgoing Water Bearer never met a stranger in his life. You'll have some nail-biting moments watching this child befriend every troublemaker in class or spark up a conversation with the sketchy-looking guy in the supermarket checkout line. Argh! You both have hidden tempers that can bubble up out of the blue. Fights can get nasty when the Scorpio mom's stinger comes out or the crackle of Aquarian lightning strikes. Try to avoid saying something to your rebellious Aquarius that you'll later regret.

SCORPIO MOM + PISCES CHILD

*

WHERE YOU CLICK

Dreamy Pisces is an easy child for the Scorpio mom to embrace. You're both highly intuitive and your bond runs deep. Indeed, it may feel as if you have a telepathic connection to this kid who you've surely known in at least three past lifetimes. This ethereal child can snap you out of your obsessive moods, reminding you to lighten up and find the beauty in the moment.

Pack a picnic and take your little mermaid to the beach! As fellow water signs, being near the sea soothes your souls—pure bliss. Swimming lessons should start as soon as the doctor okay's a dip in the pool for Pisces. You'll have a shared love of music and art. The mystical world beckons you both, too. Enchanted Pisces will happily accompany you on those "woo woo" pursuits like crystal healings, dream dances, and tarot-reading workshops. The prescient Pisces may inherit a few of your psychic powers, too. The little oracle in the stroller will amaze you with her insights!

WHERE YOU CLASH

When the Scorpio mom is on a mission you are well-nigh unstoppable—heck, some might even call you obsessed. The flowy Pisces child changes directions midstream, losing focus and often leaving projects unfinished. Forcing this child to be more directional is an exercise in futility, but you *can* make sure that your little Fish learns to clean up after herself. A toy- and art-supply-strewn home is not your idea of a dreamy decor scheme.

Scorpio and Pisces can both attract shady characters. You may see a few of your own less-than-perfect tendencies mirrored in this child. Teaching Pisces to be more socially selective would be a wise idea. Pisces are known for being passive, and while your child may readily follow your rules don't break your arm patting yourself on the back if there isn't any resistance from your kid. This child has sneaky tendencies. Better to cultivate a safe space for young Pisces to open up in than to find out your Fish has been rebelling behind your back.

SAGITTARIUS

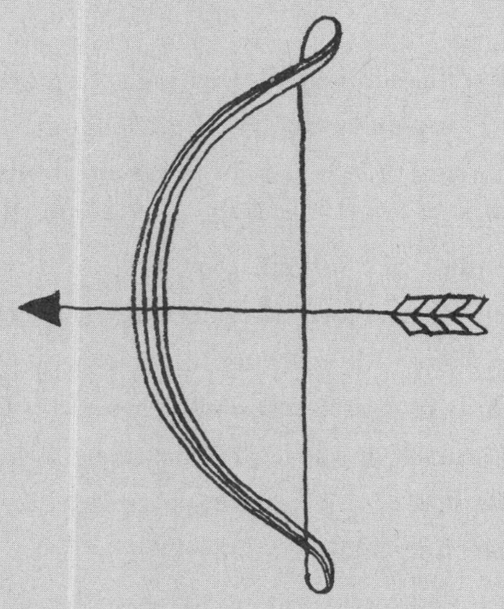

SAGITTARIUS MOM + ARIES CHILD

*

WHERE YOU CLICK

As fellow fire signs, you're kindred spirits at heart. Little Aries mirrors your confident "just do it" MO, and you'll appreciate the spark, drive, and hustle in each other. Bring on the field trips! Sitting still for more than ten minutes is not something either of you does well. Here's a kid who will be your coadventurer, although Aries is far fussier about the destination than suits your gypsy soul. Expect to return to a few favorite places over and over again until Aries is ready to explore elsewhere.

You'll also see your entrepreneurial spirit reflected in your Ram; in fact, your child may have more drive to achieve than you do! You'll glow with pride as your progeny takes on titles like team captain, class president, first chair clarinet, and leader of a peer-to-peer counseling group. The entrepreneurial gene is passed down here, too. You're both full of outrageous ideas that often turn into moneymakers. Aries' spin on the classic bake sale will leave you in awe. There couldn't be a more supportive parent for this ingenious child than the Sagittarius mama.

WHERE YOU CLASH

As the first sign of the zodiac, Aries are great at starting things but not always so keen on finishing them. It's irritating to see your house littered with half-done art projects, drying-out paints (little Aries got distracted and forgot to close the lids), partially constructed model airplanes, and so on. Encourage your Ram to finish what she starts, and teach her the rewards of completion.

Food could be a point of contention for you two. Gourmand Sagittarius has a zesty appetite and an experimental palette. Aries is picky, special-ordering everything and perhaps necessitating the preparation of a second meal to sate both of your tastes. Don't even bother trying to force this kid to try your braised short ribs or to wait for the timer on your slow cooker to ding. When Aries is hungry he Must. Eat. Now! Keep plenty of his favorite snacks on hand to avoid an appearance from a grumpy little troublemaker.

At times there may be a bit too much alpha energy in this parent-child pairing. You both love to be the best, but Aries is waaaay more competitive. Chasing after the restless Ram can be exhausting for you, especially if your kid wants to move in a different direction. This child can be bossy and demanding, throwing epic tantrums when you say no. Your people-pleasing nature could kick in causing you to lose the upper hand regularly.

SAGITTARIUS MOM +TAURUS CHILD

*

WHERE YOU CLICK

The indulgent Sagittarius mama has met her epicurean match in baby Taurus. Bring on the holiday cookie-baking marathons and meanderings through the outdoor food festivals. Your kitchen creations will be legendary, but set some limits before the two of you pile on the pounds or give yourselves cavities.

Earthy Taurus is a nature lover just like you and will accompany you on many of your outdoor jaunts—as long as they're not *too* taxing. Bring your little Bull along for gentle hikes, leisurely bike rides, and picnics in the park. Planting a garden is a great way to cultivate your mother-child connection, too. Little Taurus will love tending to the flowers and vegetable patch; in fact, your child will probably be better than you at remembering to water the plants.

You're both passionate when you believe in something (Taurus is the sign that rules ethics and values), and you'll see your kid get riled up with your same fiery spirit at times. Here's hoping you're aligned on a common cause! Candor and even outright tactlessness is a trait you both share. Your Bull babe calls it like she sees it, and you won't have to walk on eggshells when it comes to expressing your opinions, either.

WHERE YOU CLASH

Sagittarius is an experimental fire sign; Taurus is a traditional earth sign. Although both signs are concerned with faith and beliefs, little Taurus may develop completely different values and priorities than yours. While you're burning sage and meditating on the mountaintop, your Bull will crave more traditional forms of worship and celebration. Compared to your bawdy, offbeat style, Taurus can seem conservative and closed-minded. It's not hard for the outré Archer mum to embarrass this child! Do you really *have* to wear the gold lamé dress to your kid's band recital? Crisp white J.Crew shirts might just make their way into your closet as your child begs you to play the role of society mom when you're together in public.

Taurus is the zodiac's planner and thrives when she has a set schedule and routines. Repetition is not your forte, as Archers are guided by spontaneity, not some stuffy itinerary. You'll have to develop discipline in order to give your baby Bull the structure and stability she craves. Impatient Archer moms like to zip around at lightning speed. Taurus is slow and methodical. Waiting for this child to get ready for school can be as frustrating as watching paint dry, so be sure to have her set her clothes out the night before.

SAGITTARIUS MOM + GEMINI CHILD

*

WHERE YOU CLICK

Gemini and Sagittarius are opposite signs, and in many ways this kid is your perfect complement. You're both free spirits—curious, adventurous, and playful. Break out the BabyBjörn and lightweight stroller! Jet-setting Gemini will happily accompany you on your whimsical and impulsive jaunts around town. As she grows, you'll have the ideal companion for your unstructured adventures. Mother-child road trips will be legendary. You'll pull off the highway to pick strawberries, wander through a country fair, ride horses, or see 3D movie at an IMAX theater. Curious Gemini loves to sample all that life has to offer and will seldom resist your spunky ideas.

Your garrulous child can talk a blue streak and will be a lively conversational match for the Chatty Cathy in you. Both signs love to learn. Make room on the bookshelf! Erudite Gemini will be a reader just like Mama—but you'll both start more books than you ever finish. Hands-on workshops and DIY projects will amuse you both for hours. Break out the papier-mâché or the fabric paints. Of course, if either of you loses steam before finishing your latest masterpiece, you won't mind—you'll just move on to the next curiosity together.

WHERE YOU CLASH

You're both restless and impatient, but Gemini's attention span is far shorter than yours. Following this kid around can make you dizzy! You like to analyze a subject from every angle while Gemini changes topics midsentence. One minute you're planning Gemini's birthday dinner menu and the next you're hearing playground rumors, followed by a wish for a unicorn. Your chatty Gemini can drive you crazy at times and will need more interaction and validation than your independent sign can give. Bring in a peer to play sounding board, stat, instead of trying to fill the role of BFF Mom.

Gemini is impish and rebellious. Hold the lectures, Sag. Alas, this kid needs to learn things through the school of hard knocks. Sagittarius is the sign of the truth seeker; it's important that you imbue your children with honesty and integrity. Gemini can be a slick salesman, prone to concocting tales, telling fibs, and making promises she can't keep. Nip these habits in the bud. Just be careful about accusing your little one of being two-faced—Gemini genuinely needs to consider both sides of the coin before making a decision. You can't stop this kid from analyzing and verbalizing, even if you wish he'd keep those observations to himself.

SAGITTARIUS MOM + CANCER CHILD

∗

WHERE YOU CLICK

You're both intuitive and interested in what makes people tick—although little Cancer may be more of the shy observer, whereas you fearlessly interrogate folks with twenty-plus questions. Analyzing human behavior, and yes, gossiping a bit, too, will be a shared passion for you two.

Cancer rules the stomach while Sagittarius is governed by Jupiter, the god of the feast. Your bond is baked in—literally—so pull out the family recipes and whip up some comfort food together. Cancer's homey side brings out your own hidden domestic streak. You never thought you'd be the mom in the apron, but suddenly you're really getting into this neo-Betty Crocker thing. You'll have a partner in crime for your home decor projects, too, especially anything with a DIY twist. Better still, Cancers are patient and have plenty of staying power. You might actually *finish* sewing those curtains or refinishing the antique dresser with this mommy's little helper.

Erudite Cancer shares your intellectual curiosity. No skipping the bedtime stories with this child. You'll probably be listening to lots of audiobooks in the car, a great distraction for your Crab that's edifying, too.

WHERE YOU CLASH

What happens when the most insensitive sign (Sagittarius) winds up parenting the most notoriously sensitive one (Cancer)? The Archer mom's bluntness can wound the emotional Crab, though she was only trying to help! You may feel like you have to walk on eggshells with this kid.

Cancers can be clingy, needing lots of reassurance from Mom. Weaning this one could be a doozy and you might have to hang out in the classroom for hours during the early days of kindergarten. Cancer is also a nester, which can stifle your Sagittarian need to roam. You'll wind up staying home more often than you'd prefer to give your child a sense of security. Make sure you have plenty of toys and entertainment options around the house—both for your Cancer *and* for yourself. During the teen years, fights can get brutal when Cancer's pincers meet the slings of your arrows. Your child's nostalgia can grate on your nerves. While Cancer is humming the Beatles' "Yesterday," you'd rather cue Little Orphan Annie and sing "Tomorrow." To make matters worse, this child will not forgive or forget your mistakes. Hello, eternal guilt trip.

SAGITTARIUS MOM + LEO CHILD

WHERE YOU CLICK

Sagittarius and Leo are both fire signs, blazing with creative and adventurous energy. Little Leo shares your joie de vivre, and life is one big celebration for you two scene-stealers. Neither of you likes to be limited: you want to experience everything the world has to offer. No need to give up your social life, Mom. Your outgoing Lion easily gets chummy with your friend's kids (and a little bossy, too), leaving you free to gab away and have grown-up time while they play. Neither of you like to leave a party though. Set those "gotta go!" reminder alarms so you aren't the perpetually late parent-child duo.

Warmhearted Leo is a loyal child who enjoys learning from the scholarly Sagittarius mom. Finally: someone to whom you can impart your storehouse of wisdom! If you're an entrepreneur, you'll have a wunderkind by your side. Little Leo might just go into the family business or collaborate with you on a venture before he graduates from junior high. With Leo's flair for fashion, she'll play stylist for you, too. Hello, best-dressed mom in town!

WHERE YOU CLASH

With your bold, fiery personalities, this connection can get competitive. You both have strong ideas, and Leo can throw a world-class tantrum when he doesn't get his way. Being a mutable sign, you may buckle and back down in the face of these fits. Don't, Archer, or you could raise a tyrant! Praise-hungry Leo demands a *lot* of attention and loves to play long, complex games. The impatient Sagittarius mom loses interest in such follies after fifteen minutes. While you applaud your child's inventiveness and creativity, you'll also feel like an exhausted member of *The Leo Show*. Can we get an intermission? Please? You may find your kid's antics show-offy, and indeed they are. Don't forget, this sign is ruled by the sun—the center of the universe. Your feminist sensibilities may balk when your Leo daughter announces she wants to try out for head cheerleader or be entered into a pageant. An open mind is definitely required here. When Leo is inevitably cocky, you'll want to humble the kid, but be careful not to break his spirit with your blunt and unfiltered feedback.

SAGITTARIUS MOM + VIRGO CHILD

∗

WHERE YOU CLICK

In many ways, the philosophical Archer mum and analytical Virgo child are two peas in a pod. Both signs have an innate interest in what makes people tick—and you can both get a little preachy about your beliefs. Don't be surprised if your Virgo schools and scolds *you*, but you'll find this old soul's wisdom refreshing. In turn, this child enjoys your "truisms," and you can impart wisdom aplenty to Virgo's eager ears.

Both mom and child are bookworms. Virgo will love long bedtime stories, so read a few pages from an epic tale each night. Head to the planetarium, science center, and greenhouse: play-based learning will thrill this curious child. You both love animals, and there will be pets aplenty in your home. The Sagittarius mom is a nature lover and earthy Virgo adores the outdoors. Install the bike seat and take a scenic ride. Be sure to pack a picnic, since you both love good food. Planting an edible garden is another great way to cultivate this mother-child bond.

Virgo is loyal and supportive and far more detail-oriented than you. When it's chore time, your little helper will clean the baseboards, organize the spice rack, and handle all the methodical tasks you have no patience for.

WHERE YOU CLASH

Systematic Virgo thrives on routines and the Sagittarius mother loves spontaneity. This may be the child who forces you to organize your life . . . finally. Hey, it's probably good for you.

Virgo is sensitive to criticism; she is a hard-on-herself perfectionist. Your "helpful hints" could cut her to the core. Before you point out her mistakes, pause. There's a chance she is already beating herself up for these errors and needs encouragement and reassurance, not advice. Your live-out-loud approach to life can embarrass modest Virgo. Alas, you might have to tone down some of your bawdy behavior and off-color jokes. This kid is way more introverted than you and particular about whom he hangs out with. Indeed, Mom, you may feel judged by your critical offspring. While both signs can overanalyze, Virgos are more prone to worry. Your child may have neuroses and phobias that you'll never understand. Telling him to get over it will only make it worse. Help Virgo find coping mechanisms for her fears, even if you never understand what the fuss is all about.

SAGITTARIUS MOM + LIBRA CHILD

*

WHERE YOU CLICK

This lighthearted mother-child pairing is easy and breezy. You're both social butterflies who love to flutter from one thing to the next. Little Libra is a great activity buddy for the Sagittarius mama. With her agreeable, anything-goes attitude, this child will roll with your whimsical spontaneity just fine. Libras have a lifelong loyalty to their parents and are genuinely interested in hearing your stories (no matter how long they may be). The talkative Archer mom has plenty to share. It's flattering to have such an eager audience. Libras can be plenty chatty, too. As your child grows up, you'll enjoy great conversations, most with a sunny outlook and upbeat attitude. Although you move at different paces, this can be complementary.

Languid Libras often need a push, but you'll be able to get this child focused and in motion. In return, wee Libra gets you to stop and smell the roses. You can't help but enjoy life with this hedonistic soul in the stroller. More chocolate, please!

WHERE YOU CLASH

Libras can be vain: girlie girls and fussy little princes. They take their sweet old time washing up, picking outfits, and primping each morning and, oh, how they love to sleep. The on-the-go Sagittarius mom might pace a hole in the carpet (or finish up a half-day's work) waiting for Libra to get ready.

When you have an idea, you leap into production mode like Action Jackson. Libra deliberates endlessly, so get used to hearing a lot of pie-in-the-sky ideas that never become a reality. Also, don't force Libra to act upon every creative notion. This kid can be more of a dreamer than a doer, but that doesn't mean he won't find success. He might just teach you the meaning of "working smarter, not harder" one day.

The Sagittarius mom can easily embarrass posh Libra by not being refined enough, restrained, or decked out in the right labels. Libra is an etiquette sergeant, irritating the rugged Archer by correcting your table manners, steering you to the Career Separates department (when you'd rather shop in Juniors), or trying to instill a "no feet on the furniture" rule in *your* house!

SAGITTARIUS MOM + SCORPIO CHILD

*

WHERE YOU CLICK

Scorpio is innately curious, and you are the zodiac's scholar. Your wee one's interest in life's mysteries will send you on your own quest for bigger answers. Scorpio shares your zest for living, although she is far more serious and intense that you'll ever be.

The Sagittarius mom is a hunter and Scorpio loves to find hidden gems. Make games out of seeking rare treasures; start a collection together. From vintage bottle caps to rare baseball cards, you'll thrill over your shared discoveries and enjoy the process of unearthing these gems together. You're both resourceful and clever. Scorpio squirrels his goods away and can charm people into sharing their wealth. The lucky Sagittarius mom knows how to hone in on an opportunity and make a bold request. You'll give this normally reserved kid a necessary dose of chutzpah. In turn, your offspring can teach you to value your possessions (instead of accumulating more, more, more!) and invest in objects that stand the test of time.

WHERE YOU CLASH

The outspoken Archer mama's unfiltered style clashes with the secretive Scorpio who wants his private life kept under wraps. You think you're sharing a funny story, Scorpio feels exposed and betrayed. You can break trust by being too vocal about your child—even when you are gushing with pride!

Shrewd Scorpio will observe you in action, learning quickly how to push your buttons and get you to say yes to his outrageous requests. Don't get sucked in by this savvy child's games. "Because I said so" is an adequate reason for laying down the law and is probably your best bet if you want to keep the upper hand with this kid. As a fixed sign, Scorpio is not fond of change and needs repetition and routines to feel safe and grounded. It's curtains for the variety show that was your life, at least in the early years. You'll have to "lather, rinse, repeat" more than you care to for the sake of giving your child a sense of security.

Scorpio can be melancholy and brooding at times. Try as you might, your sunny optimism can't dissipate those storm clouds. Learn to let your Scorpio be when she is in one of those moods—and don't take it personally.

SAGITTARIUS MOM + SAGITTARIUS CHILD

*

WHERE YOU CLICK

Hello, mini-me. Your little carbon copy shares your adventurous, independent spirit. While you enjoy each other's company, this kid won't be overly clingy. You can comfortably coexist, working and playing independently in the same room—without demanding too much attention from each other. Sweet relief! Your curious, bookish kid will enjoy long bedtime stories and, when a little older, reading side by side. Get her a library card sooner rather than later! You can distract the Archer with an audiobook, too, but she won't sit still to listen for very long. Set up the LEGOs, craft supplies, or a puzzle. When it comes to being a multitasker extraordinaire, the apple doesn't fall far from the tree.

Active and outdoorsy, you'll enjoy nature walks, biking, hiking, and arranging flowers. Camping trips will be epic. Bring the wood and matches: you fire signs love to cook on the open flame. Traveling anywhere will be a blast since you both love to explore and learn. Little Sag probably shares your entrepreneurial spirit, and you'll be more than happy to encourage her along this path.

WHERE YOU CLASH

Temper, temper! You both get fired up easily and are known for having short fuses. This kid can truly push your buttons, especially when she inevitably starts yelling to get her point across. You'll forget to use your inside voice, too—and these fights can be stressful for the rest of the family. Your know-it-all kid is as preachy as you are and will start telling *you* what to do from a young age. Did you ask for this advice? Not at all! The trouble is there's more than a hint of truth in what your candid kid is pointing out. This child definitely holds up the mirror, forcing you to deal with your own shortcomings. Hey, you'll probably improve as a result, even if his blustery delivery makes you want to quarantine him to his room.

Neither one of you likes routines, but even Sagittarius children need a semblance of procedure from their parents. Try to do at least one thing at the same time every day—homework, dinner, bedtime—to help your Archer feel grounded and secure.

SAGITTARIUS MOM + CAPRICORN CHILD

*

WHERE YOU CLICK

This is not the easiest matchup, as your next-door-neighbor signs don't have much in common. Nevertheless, the enterprising Sagittarius mom has met her ambitious equal in little Capricorn. You're both goal-oriented achievers, though in different ways. The Sagittarius mom is experimental and willing to take risks. Little Capricorn colors within the lines, becoming the star pupil, team captain, and class president and earning other titles of distinction.

Sober Capricorn takes life more seriously than you, but this kid *does* have a wry sense of humor. You'll keep each other laughing with clever quips and witty observations, both seeing the divine comedy in life. Little Capricorn is a good little soldier. Since you're not so keen on being the disciplinarian, you'll be relieved to see how self-regulated your child is. This kid likes to follow the rules, so make sure you set them. Outdoor sports are a great way to bond—earthy Capricorn is a fellow nature lover who enjoys being active and physical as much as you. Hello, family softball games!

WHERE YOU CLASH

Wave the white flag and accept your role as the reluctant soccer mom. Capricorns crave structure and routine, challenging you to serve up some 1950s family values that are way out of your wheelhouse. You'll find young Capricorn's need to plan everything to the letter exhausting (and a wee bit boring, too). In turn, your child will wish you'd be more predictable. The headstrong Capricorn child has you beat in the stubbornness department. When she sets her sights on a goal, forget about swaying her. Patient, methodical Capricorn perseveres. You get impatient and change directions when results don't come fast enough. Be careful not to disrupt your child's process, though, just because *you're* getting restless.

Duty-bound Capricorn is a loyal friend who sticks to an exclusive, close-knit crew. Forget about dragging your child along on a million playdates just because *you* want to socialize with other moms. Cap likes consistency in friendships, so you'll be seeing a lot more of the same familiar faces as your child grows up.

SAGITTARIUS MOM + AQUARIUS CHILD

✳

WHERE YOU CLICK

Two independent idealists, Aquarius is your soul-mate child. The freethinking Water Bearer will dazzle you with wise-beyond-her-years assessments, offbeat clothing combinations (Tutu over snow pants? Well, why not?), and delightfully unpredictable moods. You're the perfect person to parent such a one-of-a-kind kid, since you're anything but a cookie-cutter mom yourself.

The Sagittarius mother is a global ambassador with friends from all walks of life. The humanitarian Aquarius child shares your love of the rainbow coalition and wants to help make the world a better place for everyone. Volunteering together is a great way to bond, especially if there is a travel component involved.

You both have wacky senses of humor—a mother-child comedy routine in action. Bon vivant Aquarius outdoes you in the friendship department. Since he gets along with most people, you won't have to tone down your socializing for a second.

WHERE YOU CLASH

Fire sign Sagittarius is warm and passionate. Air sign Aquarius can be cool and breezy. Your energy can be a bit too intense for your laid-back child, who may retreat from your overzealous hugs. In turn, your feelings may be hurt when your little Water Bearer withdraws or gives a less-than-effusive response to one of your playful ideas. Candid Sagittarians are quick to judge: they have an opinion on everyone and everything! Fair-minded Aquarius likes to give everyone the benefit of the doubt. This kid will definitely teach you to be more accepting of people's "flaws."

You're both gypsies at heart, but what about the structure kids need to feel safe? Although Aquarius might resist coming home for a set dinnertime or having a lights-out hour, you'll want to teach this mini-renegade to abide by a system, too. Aquarius is the sign of rebellion, so expect some pushback at the most unexpected moments. Here's where you'll have to remember that you're the mom, not her BFF—an easy thing to forget in this simpatico pairing.

SAGITTARIUS MOM + PISCES CHILD

*

WHERE YOU CLICK

Life is but a dream for the Sagittarius mom and Pisces child. Both signs are ruled by bountiful, expansive Jupiter (Pisces is also coruled by Neptune), eliciting a wide-eyed hopefulness and joie de vivre in you two. Magical Pisces awakens your sense of limitless possibilities, a baby muse if ever there was one. You'll stay up late together looking for shooting stars, paint a mural on the living room wall, and walk around town in feather boas and floppy hats, just for the fun of it.

Spiritual and metaphysical topics interest both signs. Let little Pisces tag along to your yoga class or Buddhist chanting circle. You might even get a deck of tarot or divination cards and learn to read them together—this child is a seer! Both Sagittarius and Pisces are mutable signs, adaptive chameleons who jive with people from all cultures and walks of life. Neither of you likes to be pinned down, so you'll have a rotating cast of people in your shared lives. Because Pisces has a soothing effect on Sagittarius, your Fish can help to calm you down. But while he'll happily rub your shoulders and bring you tea, don't forget who the parent is. Caretaking Pisces needs you to make the chicken soup sometimes, too.

WHERE YOU CLASH

The Sag mama is independent, optimistic, and proactive. Pisces can be clingy, pessimistic, and a bit of a victim. Your kid's "poor me" routine will try your nerves. Why can't she get over it already? Warning: you can be insensitive, too, lacking the compassion this child needs. Make sure to validate your child's feelings before delivering one of your (in)famous pep talks.

While little Pisces will grow to share your gypsy soul, his allergies, infections, and bouts of tummy sensitivities can interrupt your peripatetic parenting plans, at least in the first couple years. The Sagittarius mom is a people-pleaser, which can make you vulnerable to emotional manipulation by this shrewd kid. Pisces will know exactly how to push your buttons, sending you on guilt trips and, as a teen, firing off emotional barbs that hit a little too close to home. It's hard for you to weather those stormy moods and slammed doors when Pisces doesn't like the rules you make. Stay firm, even if your heart is aching. This is why you have to be careful about turning the compassionate Pisces into your confidant. Even though this old-soul child seems to understand your deepest emotions, becoming BFFs with your Pisces could be akin to handing over the reins. Boundaries!

CAPRICORN

CAPRICORN MOM + ARIES CHILD

*

WHERE YOU CLICK

Aries is the zodiac's baby and Capricorn the provider sign. You're the solid earth this fireball baby needs, giving your restless Ram a predictable pit stop between his many adventures and whims. The tantrums Aries is famous for throwing will be far less frequent in this parent-child pairing. The patient Capricorn mom gives little Aries lots of space to "just be."

You're both strong leaders who like to take charge. Hello, legacy child! Aries will scoop up the titles and awards that you once held, nabbing the gold in a few categories all his own. It's no secret that you both like to win and be the best. You'll glow with pride as little Aries gains public recognition for her feats. Both Capricorn and Aries are known for their athletic prowess. Grab your skis and hit the black diamond slopes!

WHERE YOU CLASH

The always-appropriate Capricorn mom abides by the rules. Rebellious Aries believes that rules were made to be broken . . . and then reinvented according to her desires. There will be plenty of power struggles in this parent-child pairing since you both feel as if you were born to reign. Rather than enforcing a strict code of conduct on the Ram, get her involved in creating the rules. She might just self-discipline if you do.

Conventional Capricorn mothers may feel embarrassed by young Aries' wild and dramatic style of expression. Good luck getting this kid into a pristine school uniform, and if you do, don't expect him to return home without rips and stains at the end of the day. Workaholic Capricorns can get so focused on achieving a grand goal that you forget to give little Aries the small "bytes" of attention the Ram needs to thrive. Praise Aries' process, not just the final product.

CAPRICORN MOM + TAURUS CHILD

*

WHERE YOU CLICK

This kid is your kindred spirit, a fellow earth sign who will happily plug into your well-ordered world. Routines and structure make both of you feel safe. Family traditions rank high in your books, and you're likely the matriarch of your extended family. The ancestral legacies you so cherish will live on through your baby Bull. Plus, crafty Taurus will be the happy helper for your elaborate table settings, decor schemes, and gift-wrapping sessions.

Your child is gifted with your common sense. You can both be no-nonsense worker bees when there's a job that needs to be done. But as dutiful and driven as you both can be, you adore the luxe life, too. Little Taurus loves the finer things and the Capricorn mom never met a status symbol she didn't like. Outfit your Bull in upscale brands and drive her to that elite private school in your Lexus if you'd like: you'll get zero objections from this kid when it comes to keeping up with the Joneses.

Goal-oriented Capricorn moms can help the languid Bull pick up the pace. Young Taurus teaches you to stop and smell the roses. How sweet it is.

WHERE YOU CLASH

Capricorn is ruled by stern, no-frills Saturn; Taurus counts decadent, romantic Venus as his cosmic ruler. Your hedonistic child will challenge your austere approach to life, tempting you to indulge rather than abstain from every little pleasure. Good luck keeping the sweets out of this kid's lunch box! You may have to lighten up some of your restrictions here.

Taurus is affectionate and not afraid to get a little sappy, writing a tribute song or long letter (read aloud at Mother's Day) in your honor. This may all be a bit much for the modest Capricorn mom to take. Your temperaments are different, too. Taurus has the "charging Bull" personality and can get riled up and *loud*! Making a scene is so not your bag. You're a fan of the indoor voice at all times and may struggle not to suppress your Taurus's wilder nature. Both signs are known for their stubbornness. When you lock horns with this kid, neither one of you wants to back down.

CAPRICORN MOM + GEMINI CHILD

*

WHERE YOU CLICK

You are both enterprising and full of big ideas. Little Gemini shares your drive to prosper—although he'll probably hit the jackpot out of the gate while you earn your chops from years of hard work and mastery. Nurture this kid's go-getter energy, Capricorn; your dedication to success is the best gift you can pass on. Besides ambition, your star signs don't have much in common, but you do have tons to learn from one another.

The persistent Capricorn mommy teaches changeable Gemini how to stay put and stick things out till the end. Playful, quirky Gemini gets you to loosen up, laugh, and experiment with more offbeat ideas. Since young Gems are all over the map, it's helpful for them to come home to the stable, grounded base that the Capricorn mom provides. You're definitely the rock for this little rolling stone.

WHERE YOU CLASH

The Capricorn mom likes to pick a lane and drive ahead without veering right or left; your Gemini kid merges all over the map. Your child's need for constant variety will exhaust you. Meanwhile, little Gemini will tear the hair out of her pigtails when made to go to *that* place again (read: your favorite haunts).

Since the Capricorn mom has sterling integrity, your word is as good as gold. The people-pleasing Gemini child makes and breaks promises left and right—her heart is usually in the right place, but she overcommits. Additionally, you'll cringe when your child's two-faced side shows up. Geminis can't help but gossip, and this is a trait that will earn a reprimand. Capricorn moms are straightforward: what you see, is what you get. Strategic Gemini can be a schemer. Stay on your toes, or this clever kid might play you like a violin.

CAPRICORN MOM + CANCER CHILD

*

WHERE YOU CLICK

Ahh, domestic bliss. The cozy, cuddly Cancer child loves the safe harbor of your home. This normally reserved child will blossom under your roof, thanks to the structure and security you provide. In turn, warm Cancer is like chicken soup for your soul. The caring Crab softens your harder edges, gets you to smile, relax, and give more hugs.

Cancer is the mother sign of the zodiac, and Capricorn is the father sign. Family is hugely important to both of you. This child will happily uphold traditions and help you tend to the rest of your flock, keeping a watchful eye on siblings. Tradition, tradition! From Sunday dinners to movie nights, to holiday decorating schemes, Cancer yearns for rituals as much as you. Socially, you're on the same page, preferring close-knit friendships with a chosen few.

WHERE YOU CLASH

Sensitive Cancers need lots of emotional validation and affection. While you're a solid force in your child's life, you only have so much patience for talking about feelings. Caution: just because *you* can't understand why something is such a big deal, don't make the mistake of minimizing the impact on your Crab. This kid's empathic angst may always be an enigma to you but a (long) reassuring hug will go a long way to center your child.

Cancers need security blankets in the form of treasured sentimental objects. Minimalist Capricorn moms may have to shelve plans of creating a Scandinavian modern showroom in your living quarters. Allow Cancer to hang up photos and birthday cards on the refrigerator, seat stuffed animals at the dinner table, and leave a few favorite blankets in the family room. At the very least, give your kid free rein to decorate *her* space.

Clutchy Cancers can get needy and dependent. You are eager to teach your little ones to stand on their own two feet. Getting this baby bird to fly out of the nest won't be easy.

CAPRICORN MOM + LEO CHILD

*

WHERE YOU CLICK

Bring on the trophies and blue ribbons! The ambitious little Lion wants to fill his mama's big footprints. Raise that bar as high as you'd like, Capricorn. Your achievement-oriented spawn loves the challenges you set before him, especially if you pile on the praise along the way. Nothing motivates Leo more than positive reinforcement. You're both strong leaders and you'll gush with pride as you watch Leo take charge of school groups and snag the awards you once earned. You definitely passed your competitive streak down to *this* kid! Leo and Capricorn want to be the best and have the best of everything. Dressing up and drawing public admiration is a big deal to both signs. You're the most enviable parent-child duo in town!

WHERE YOU CLASH

Cautious Capricorn moms see the glass as half empty (you never want to be caught unprepared, after all); the optimistic Leo child, bordering on overconfidence, often assuming the glass is overflowing with bottomless refills. You'll need to deliver some tough reality checks to this kid—and how painful it is to rain on his parade!

Theatrical Leo is showy, flashy, and sometimes outright egotistical. You, Capricorn, are all about modesty. You'd rather die than toot your own horn, preferring to have your work speak for itself. Teach your child humility, but don't dim her bright lights *too* much. Leo's confidence is also her greatest strength, even if it seems a bit over the top to you.

CAPRICORN MOM + VIRGO CHILD

*

WHERE YOU CLICK

Earth sign soul mates, you're both practical planners who like structure, stability, and routine. Your orderly lifestyle works well for Virgo, providing a foundation for your anxious child to relax and thrive. Helpful Virgo loves to be your right-hand man. Jump-start your kid's hardworking nature by assigning tasks and giving rewards for jobs well done. Virgo loves earning points and is motivated by praise.

Some may call you downers, but you're both masters of damage control. Little Virgo shares your eagle eye and can assess a brewing crisis long before it strikes. Together, you are guardians of your family's welfare, keeping a watchful eye over hot stoves, unlocked doors, and badly behaving siblings.

WHERE YOU CLASH

You are both extreme perfectionists who can be very hard on yourselves. While you hold the bar high, be careful not to set a standard that is too lofty for Virgo to reach. Warning: feeling like a failure can turn your little angel into a rebel! You may be a triathlete/CEO/PTA president, but it's not fair to expect your kid to keep pace. Make sure Virgo understands that everything in life doesn't have to be a competition and that it's okay to make mistakes. When you get into pessimistic moods, you can bring each other down with worrying or fussing. In such moments, turn on the music for a dance break or head to the playground with Virgo. You're probably both overthinking, well, everything.

The persistent Capricorn mom feels compelled to complete what she starts. Mutable Virgo may lose steam or change directions before tasks are done. Gentle encouragement from Mom can do wonders to get Virgo to the finish line.

CAPRICORN MOM + LIBRA CHILD

*

WHERE YOU CLICK

Melt! Upon arrival, the lovable Libra child softens the stern Capricorn mom. With an angelic gaze that exudes pure adoration, your Venus-ruled child knows exactly how to tug at your heartstrings. Rules . . . what rules? Your structured nature may fly out the window when you're under little Libra's spell. Surrender, Mom. This decadent child is here to remind you to have more fun. After all, your world won't come crashing down if you lift your dairy restriction and share a hot fudge sundae with your kid every now and again, will it? In turn, you'll teach Libra the rewards of discipline and delayed gratification, but be warned: it's gonna be tough not to spoil this child.

Libras love to dress up and wow the public with their enchanting personalities. Put your child in his Sunday best and let him tag along with you to your various prestigious functions. Wee Libra is the best icebreaker in your arsenal. Those stuffy types you roll with can't help but drop their guards when your scion walks up, politely extends a hand, and asks, "How do you do?" Too. Cute. For. Words.

WHERE YOU CLASH

Airy-fairy Libra is a huge daydreamer, spacing out and forgetting every rule and responsibility—including the ones you have posted on the neon chore chart. Disciplining this charmer won't be easy, but it's necessary. Alas, restricting privileges may be the only way to make an impact on Libra.

Sentimental Libra can get a little mushy for the cool Capricorn mother. Uh-oh. Not another sappy moment or five-minute hug! Yep. The goal-oriented Capricorn mom is forever focused on what lies ahead. Live-for-the-moment Libra likes to stop and smell every rose. You'll wish your kid would pick up the pace and stay focused. Don't waste your time trying to foist your work ethic on Libra, though. This child might just teach you the power of "working smarter, not harder."

CAPRICORN MOM + SCORPIO CHILD

*

WHERE YOU CLICK

Pint-sized Scorpio shares your ambition—you're a powerhouse parent-child duo indeed! Winning is a big deal to both of your signs, and you both love contests and competitive games. Motivate your child with big challenges, and be sure to reward Scorpio's inevitable victories. Snagging a prize (especially a coveted object of status) will keep this child aiming as high as you do.

Scorpios need lots of security; as a fixed sign, they dislike change. The reliable Capricorn mom knows just how to provide the orderly, predictable environment in which Scorpio can flourish. You're both highly selective about your friends, and your Scorpio scion doesn't trust anyone easily. (Sound familiar?) Just as you keep friends for years, so will your child. You'll love watching Scorpio and her loyal entourage grow up together, thick as thieves.

Scorpio kids need their fair share of privacy, and the cool Capricorn mom doesn't pry. There's a wonderful and easy affinity between you two.

WHERE YOU CLASH

While your eyes may be fixed on the prize, little Scorpio's competitive nature can get downright cutthroat. Encourage your kid's ambition, but make sure he knows that there's more to life than winning.

Neither Capricorn mom nor Scorpio child likes to feel vulnerable. You may both stuff down feelings or hide away when upset. Make sure your child has a healthy model of emotional expression. Those feelings have to go somewhere, after all, so when Scorpio shuts away in her room for too long, go and talk to her. You're both prone to brooding and can pull each other into gloomy spells. This empathic kid *will* pick up on your moods, Mom, so don't let your storm clouds go unchecked for too long. Scorpio needs focused, undivided attention, which the hardworking Capricorn mom may be "too busy" to give. Pause throughout your day to let Scorpio know he is special.

CAPRICORN MOM + SAGITTARIUS CHILD

WHERE YOU CLICK

The enterprising Archer shares your ambitious streak: this kid loves to strive for big goals as much as you do. Young Sagittarius may start his own business while still in grammar school, and he'd be hard-pressed to find a more supportive parent/CEO for this endeavor.

Clever Sagittarius is full of witty jokes and helps the serious Capricorn mom lighten up. You have a wry sense of humor yourself and the laughter this child brings is medicine for your soul. You're both active and outdoorsy. Spend time together in nature, riding bikes, hiking for a mountaintop picnic, riding horses. Join a community-supported agriculture farm in your area and make weekly jaunts to pick up fresh local produce a bonding experience. Experimental Sagittarius will come up with creative recipes, and dutiful Capricorn will chop, wash, and measure ingredients, making sure nothing burns on the stove.

WHERE YOU CLASH

Capricorn is the zodiac's stern pessimist. Sagittarius is the wide-eyed optimist. You and your child will have strikingly different outlooks on the world. Forget about proceeding with caution here. The risk-taking Archer will make your heart race with her daring bravado. While you don't want to take the wind out of your Sagittarian's sails, teaching your kid to look before she leaps is valuable.

Admit it, Capricorn: you like it when your children socialize with kids from "good" homes and families. The equal opportunity Archer is the antisnob, befriending kids from every socioeconomic category. Cancel the country club membership and let Sagittarius splash into the public pool. You're a creature of habit; Sagittarius needs constant variety. The traditions you adore will be turned on their ear, so make way for progress, Mom.

CAPRICORN MOM + CAPRICORN CHILD

*

WHERE YOU CLICK

Who wants to take over the family business? I do, I do! Loyal little Capricorns love legacies and will proudly play the role of chip off the old block. Just as you may have followed in your own mom or dad's well-heeled footsteps, your little Goat could show early signs of wanting to do the same. Even if mini-Cap seems destined for an entirely unique path, you'll recognize your own single-minded ambition in him. Give this kid a lofty goal, and like you, he'll strive to reach it. You two make an impressive team in all things.

Dutiful Capricorn shares your love of traditions. You can count on your pint-sized star mate to show up at the holiday table with bells on and organize games the whole family can enjoy. Just make sure it doesn't get *too* heated.

You're both competitive and love to be the best at all you do. Get little Capricorn involved in the sports you enjoyed as a child like soccer, skiing, and track. Like you, this responsible child is a born leader, and you'll encourage him to try out for team captain, class president, and other titles of distinction.

WHERE YOU CLASH

A pair of perfectionists, both Capricorn mom and child hold themselves to a high standard. This is the kid who tears up her drawings or hides the C+ paper from you. Uh-oh. Is the mirror being held up here, Mom? Cool down your quest for mastery a bit and let little Capricorn learn that it's okay to make mistakes. Banish your inner Debbie Downer, too, or you may see your somber, negative outlook reflected in your child.

According to astrological lore, Capricorn is born with an old soul but grows more youthful over time. There may be a strange role reversal in this pairing, with little Capricorn admonishing you for being too wild or having too much fun. You're both strong-willed and stubborn. If young Capricorn doesn't agree with your rules, you two Goats could lock horns in a major power struggle—and the silent treatments and cold wars won't blow over quickly!

CAPRICORN MOM + AQUARIUS CHILD

*

WHERE YOU CLICK

Capricorn and Aquarius are the "popular kids" of the zodiac. Like mom, the Water Bearer is charming, affable, and well liked. Here's a laid-back kid you can take pretty much anywhere and trust that he will play well with your friend's children or quietly entertain himself with a video game while you hold your third volunteer committee meeting of the day.

Aquarius likes an ambitious mission as much as you do. Your kid is more of an organizer while you're an alpha leader. As such, you make a great tag team for family projects with jovial Aquarius rallying other relatives and making work feel like play. You're both athletic with stamina for long-distance sports. Team up for long bike rides or sports competitions—especially if they have a charitable component as you both like to give back.

Class clown Aquarius will get you to lighten up with her antics; in turn, you'll ground your little space cadet before she rockets too far out of orbit.

WHERE YOU CLASH

Cap mamas are rule makers, whereas rebel Aquarius is the zodiac's rule breaker. Don't expect to foist your conventional standards on *this* kid. Aquarius will challenge your traditional views at every turn. Toss away the playbook and consider updating that third-generation recipe for holiday cookies. This child is here to help you evolve, not stay stuck ruminating about "the good old days."

Altruistic Aquarius loves to help out the underdog, making friends with kids from all walks of life. The edified Capricorn mom may come face-to-face with her inner snob.

Aquarius is always keen on starting projects, but gets distracted easily (or starts another scheme) and leaves them half finished. This frustrates the tenacious Capricorn mom who believes in pushing through to the finish line. You can both be cool and aloof. Don't forget to snuggle or share a sentimental moment every now and again.

CAPRICORN MOM + PISCES CHILD

*

WHERE YOU CLICK

In many ways, it feels like your Pisces dropped down from a different planet—and that is the beauty in this parent-child pairing. The dreamy Fish has a supersized imagination, a lovely complement to your matter-of-fact pragmatism. This kid will force you to look up from your computer so you don't miss that gorgeous sunset (or an entire spring).

The stable Capricorn mama creates the solid earth that little Pisces needs to find his "land legs." Yes, your child may space on the house rules at times, but the boundaries you set so naturally will help your unstructured child learn to do the same for herself one day. You both enjoy comfort and security. You'll share many moments of sweet domestic bliss with this child who will add a creative flourish to all your ideas.

WHERE YOU CLASH

Pisces is the sign of fantasy and escape. This kid lives in a magical kingdom, whereas the Capricorn mom keeps her feet planted solidly on earth. Your young Fish's ideas may run a little too "rainbows and unicorns" for your taste. Although you may think it helpful to bring a reality check, be careful not to crush this child's delicate dreams. Is there really any harm in her believing that mermaids are real? Nope, we think not.

Self-doubt plagues both of your signs, but you respond in opposite ways. The tenacious Capricorn mom pushes ahead, whereas escape-artist Pisces retreats and hides. Your tough-love style will fall flat with the Fish and might even discourage him. Meanwhile you'll wish Pisces would stop being so darn sensitive. Pisces colors outside the lines, but you'd prefer to paint by the numbers—it will be a struggle to mold this kid into anything that resembles conventionality, so stop trying.

AQUARIUS

AQUARIUS MOM + ARIES CHILD

*

WHERE YOU CLICK

The Aries child is a live wire, an energetic little prankster who will keep you in stitches. You'll love joining forces to play silly jokes on the other members of the household, who may or may not see the humor in it all the way you two do. Uh-oh.

Little Aries is a true original—a trait you hold dear. You'll encourage your kid's "mad scientist" ideas, and the two of you may even team up as coproducers. We can see the science-fair blue ribbons and mother-child TED talks already! In many ways, little Aries can be your BFF, as you're both fascinated by the future and innovative ideas. Since you're the zodiac's team player, you're also the perfect mom to teach sometimes-self-absorbed Aries how to share and play well with others. You both have an adventurous, daredevil streak. Little Aries will love riding in your sports car, joining you on the black diamond slopes, and trying out other extreme athletic adventures together.

WHERE YOU CLASH

Aries are sensitive to people's vibes and, for no tangible rhyme or reason, only like *certain* folks. The Aquarius mom is a social butterfly, willing to become friends with most anybody. Don't expect your little Ram to give hugs (or even a smile) to the latest so-and-so you bring around. Your dreams of setting up playdates with little Aries, and your pal's kids may be dashed by the Ram's fussy social energy. *Très* embarrassing for you!

Aquarius moms are generally laid-back and cool, and you won't know how to handle Aries' stormy moods, which can change at a moment's notice. You are both experts at giving the silent treatment, which could lead to a cold war. That said, the Ram's fiery tantrums will have you speed-dialing the Supernanny! Aries children love to win and can be intensely competitive. Since you usually wind up feeling sorry for the underdog, it can be hard for you to support your child's die-hard quest to be the best.

AQUARIUS MOM + TAURUS CHILD

*

WHERE YOU CLICK

In many ways, you're as different as night and day, but the open-minded Aquarius mom helps the myopic mini-Taurus learn to color outside the lines. You'll also nurture your young Taurus's creative expression—a good thing, since your child is ruled by Venus, planet of beauty. Aquarius is an idealistic humanitarian and Taurus is the sign that rules values and ethics. From a young age on, your baby Bull will be asking you big questions about life. You'll love engaging in these dialogues, but warning: your kid may wind up making a hard right from your values.

Fast-moving vehicles (usually sports cars) are a passion your signs share. If you have a son, he'll love seeing mom zip up to the school parking lot in her speedy two-seater. Little Taurus is more grounded than you, which can help you to slow down. You'll feel a bit more settled with this homebody child in your care, and you'll have to admit that the change of pace is probably good for you.

WHERE YOU CLASH

Your signs move at completely different paces! The mellow Bull seems downright lethargic compared to your quicksilver pace. The Aquarius mom adores oddities, bright and trendy clothes, gag gifts, and quirky objets d'art, but her Taurus child is more of a traditionalist. Even at an early age, Bulls' tastes run to high-quality goods that stand the test of time. While you're busy shopping in the trendiest boutiques, teen Taurus may be parsing through blazers in the career separates area or trying to steer you there so you'll fit the image of the "proper mommy" that this sign craves.

When angry, you both have lightning-bolt tempers. Taurus will fume (and even break toys) while you'll slam your door and tell her, "Talk to your father!" Relatives may duck for cover during one of your family feuds. Aquarius rules the future—you're the proud rebel mom who reinvents the wheel on family festivities. Traditional Taurus may grumble about the lack of customary fodder in your home, so you might have to tie on an apron and whip up a classic holiday meal on occasion to appease your child's desires to be like the other kids (something the unconventional Aquarius mama will never understand).

AQUARIUS MOM + GEMINI CHILD

*

WHERE YOU CLICK

The Aquarius mom and Gemini child are kindred spirits who move through life with playful curiosity, open minds, and wacky senses of humor. You're the quirky mom-kid combo that everyone adores. Gemini's constant "Why, Mommy?" inquisitiveness won't bother you one bit; in fact, you'll relish in discovering the answers together, especially if this means taking Gemini on educational field trips.

You're both technophiles: little Gemini's nimble fingers may soon be swiping your iPad or pulling up games on your mobile phone. Uh-oh! Better get some kid-friendly gadgets or your electronics will no longer be your own.

Variety is the spice of your lives, and it's never a dull moment when you're with this child. Both of you are social butterflies who make fast friends. You can drop little Gemini anywhere and she'll quickly be the life of the party—thank goodness since you often flutter from one get-together to the next on an hourly basis. The equally restless Gemini child is your perfect tagalong!

WHERE YOU CLASH

Chatty Gemini needs constant attention and validation, whereas the heady Aquarius mom needs moments of silence to space out. Here's hoping little Gemini has a sibling near in age or a playmate in close proximity, because keeping your restless Gemini entertained can be a full-time job. You won't have the patience for Gemini's exhausting bids for your focus, adorable as they may be.

Young Gemini can be fickle, even gossipy. If you have a girl, she may change best friends three times before the lunch bell rings—the egalitarian Aquarius mom likes everyone to get along. Teaching tolerance to quicksilver Gem will be an exercise in frustration.

A competitive dynamic can crop up between the Aquarius mom and Gemini child. While this kid will love that you're the cool mom, be careful not to steal the spotlight or upstage with your jokes, stories, and latest on-trend outfits. Gemini has a short attention span—even *you* can barely keep up. While you're listening to some street artist's sob story, Gemini will be tugging on your sleeve, insisting it's time to go. Argh!

AQUARIUS MOM + CANCER CHILD

*

WHERE YOU CLICK

Caring souls whose compassion flows toward the less fortunate, the Aquarius mom and Cancer child love to help people in need. Mother-child volunteer missions will begin early—a great way for your bighearted signs to bond—and lucky for the downtrodden and underrepresented in your community. Like you, the Cancer child treasures friendship and may turn amigos into extended family members. The main difference here is the guest list count. Little Cancer prefers a cozy, close-knit crew, whereas you have a minimum of ten BFFs at any given moment. There's a loner in both of you, too. The Cancer child will slip off to her room, cocooning with books, playing with dolls, drawing, listening to music. This gives you lots of space to zone out yourself, read your sci-fi novels, work on DIY projects, and chat on the phone with your friends.

You're both animal lovers and nary a stray can escape your adoring gazes. Your house may feel a bit like an animal shelter, but responsible, nurturing Cancer is a great caretaker who will always remember to feed the cats and close the door on the birdcage.

WHERE YOU CLASH

Cancer kids do not trust easily nor do they feel safe around strangers. You, Aquarius mom, never met a stranger. Your revolving cast of friends could traumatize your shy child, who craves familiarity. Forget about having an open-door policy (or relocating to a communal living situation) if you want your child to relax. Cancers are fussy and traditional. Think: crisp white shirts, flowered bedding, china tea sets. The über-modern Aquarius mom usually looks like a rainbow exploded on her life. Forget about picking out this child's clothes for too long. The Cancer kid's nesting instincts could cramp your on-the-go style *and* interfere with your decor scheme. Forget about painting the living room lime green on a whim and rearranging the furniture every weekend. This will upset the wee Crab, who wants to come home to a familiar space.

Cancers are bossy and maternal; Aquarius is the eternal rebel. Your wild larks will not go down well with this child; in fact, your mini-Crab may start mothering *you*! Let your kid be a kid and save the adult antics for times when he is not around.

AQUARIUS MOM + LEO CHILD

∗

WHERE YOU CLICK

As opposite signs, you two make quite the dynamic duo. Little Leo shares your spark of creativity and imagination. Bring on the art supplies. You're the mom who prizes individuality and this kid is definitely one of a kind.

Celebrations are what you both live for: no one adores a party quite like Leo and you are the queen of the epic shindig. Start a special fund just for Leo's birthday soirees (not to mention your own)! You're both leaders and organizers of your social groups and you'll beam with pride as your little Lion rallies friends together for scavenger hunts, softball tournaments, and talent shows. Born entertainers, you're like a mother-child vaudeville act. While you're humoring the crowds with your spot-on impressions and offbeat jokes, little Leo dances like a prima ballerina or rocks the house as a guitar-playing prodigy. Curtains up!

WHERE YOU CLASH

Little Leo can be *such* a drama queen, which disturbs the laid-back Aquarius mom. You cannot believe your child is making a fuss over something so minor. Your possessive little Lion wants *all* of your attention. You'll struggle to find the energy and focus for this child's needs, especially since you're also juggling the demands of your large group of friends. Your social circle may shrink markedly, in the interest of giving little Leo the quality time he craves. But be careful! Ruled by the sun, this kid is comfortable being the center of your universe to the expense of all else. You need to have a life, too, Mom.

Leos thrive on compliments and affirmation. Aloof Aquarius moms may fail to give Leo the gushing praise she craves. Don't slack on the high-fives and shiny gold stars! Leo may resort to slamming doors, huffing, and reprising *your* role as the rebel to get some attention.

AQUARIUS MOM + VIRGO CHILD

*

WHERE YOU CLICK

Intellectuals with quick minds, you're a gifted pair. Your inventive Virgo child shares your curiosity about the world. You'll geek out over instruction manuals, swap books, keenly and objectively analyze human behavior ("And *that's* why little Johnny keeps pulling my pigtails, Mommy!"), and perhaps attend a comic-book convention or Renaissance Fair on an annual basis.

Aquarius moms are innate humanitarians and Virgo is the sign of service. Teaming up on community service projects is a great way to bond and foster your child's giving spirit. (Fund-raiser bake sale, anyone?) Although you can both get lost in thought, you share a crunchy granola streak. Little Virgo will happily trot along to your drum circle, crystal meditation workshop, and yoga class. Animal lovers, you both have a soft spot for strays. Before you know it, the spare room could be devoted entirely to the kitties and puppies you adopt every couple of months.

WHERE YOU CLASH

Little Virgos are highly selective about people; strangers may give them anxiety. Your posse—as in the wacky tarot card reader friend who drops by for unannounced venting, the bassist from the reggae band who shows up at the family barbecue—may be a wee bit too sketchy for your straight-laced Virgo child to stomach. Simply put, little Virgo is pretty uptight compared to you. Alas, your trendy, "cool mom" clothes and *colors-that-don't-occur-in-nature* dye jobs may not be appreciated here.

The Aquarius mom's attempts to "teach tolerance" may be in vain. Virgos are critical perfectionists who zero in on "what's wrong" more often than "what's right." This child could even fall prey to gossiping about classmates. Do your best to correct this behavior, but know that you'll never be able to stop it altogether. Virgos are tuned in to every detail, which detached Aquamom may never understand. Don't accuse this child of overreacting—she really *is* that sensitive.

AQUARIUS MOM + LIBRA CHILD

*

WHERE YOU CLICK

Life is a nonstop party for you two social air signs. Your people-loving kid is generally easygoing and laid-back and will make fast friends with your pals' children. Bring on the playdates! You're both curious culture vultures. You'll love introducing your child to the arts with puppet shows, ballet and piano lessons, and Japanese brush-painting classes. Look for all-ages workshops so you can get your Picasso on, too.

Loving Libra brings out the softer side of the Aquarius mom. This kid will melt your heart, picking flowers from the grass for you and bringing home "I Love My Mommy" crayon drawings. Fair-minded Libra and humanitarian Aquarius both share a strong bent toward justice. You could be the adorable mother-child pair picketing for a social cause together. There's no shortage of creativity between you, either. Both Libra and Aquarius tend to live in a fantasy world, although yours is more sci-fi while Libra is a fairy-tale romantic. Your shared sense of wonder about the world makes every day feel magical!

WHERE YOU CLASH

Help . . . air! Affectionate Libras may need a little too much coddling for the independent Aquarius mom's preferences. Although you love your child, all that touchy-feely stuff is a little stifling for you. Weaning little Libra could take a while, much to your dismay. You're both such dreamers that structure may fly out the window. Libra may charm you into forgetting his bedtime or convince you that eating cookies before dinner really isn't such a bad idea. You'll have to discipline yourself a bit more in this pairing.

Easygoing Aquarius moms will hop in a power shower, throw their hair in a ponytail, and be ready to go with the wave of a mascara wand. Ruled by Venus, Libra is far more vain, taking lonnng baths, primping, and insisting on the latest fashions. While you'll love that your child is developing a personal style, you'll wish Libra would pick up the pace. You've got places to go and people to see, after all!

AQUARIUS MOM + SCORPIO CHILD

*

WHERE YOU CLICK

The Scorpio child shares your fascination with life's inexplicable oddities. You'll gaze at the heavens together, searching for shooting stars, UFOs, and rainbows. Little Scorpio is a dazzling charmer just like Mama: few can say no to the two of you. The school will boast record high numbers from the fund-raiser you teamed up on—and the cupcake recipes you creatively invent together will be legendary.

Both Scorpio and Aquarius are fixed signs. This child brings out the more traditional, disciplined side of you, which you'll both appreciate. Private time and personal space are a must for mom and child. Young Scorpio will retreat to his room and play independently, giving you the "me time" you so desperately crave. Although you're more of a team player than Scorpio, you share a competitive streak. You'll admire your diligent child's work ethic and desire for mastery.

WHERE YOU CLASH

The Aquarius mom treats everyone equally, which can be an issue if there are other siblings. Scorpio can be possessive, jealous even, and may vie to be *numero uno* with Mom. Scorpio requires undivided attention. Create special one-on-one time with this child, but set boundaries or Scorpio will dominate your time.

Scorpios are suspicious of strangers, which can totally cramp your social style. Forget about inviting new acquaintances to just drop by at a moment's notice. Your child will eye your pals up and down like a pint-sized CIA agent. You'll have to admit, though, this kid has sharp instincts. Perhaps you should listen when Scorpio warns you that someone is no good. Scorpio's fascination with the darker side of life may chill the rainbows-and-unicorns Aquarius mom. As well, this child's brooding temperament and stormy emotions will confound you. Can't this child just cheer up already? (Sigh.)

AQUARIUS MOM + SAGITTARIUS CHILD

*

WHERE YOU CLICK

Two free-spirited nomads, you'll roam the world together with wide-eyed wonder, making friends from all walks of life. You're both fascinated with eccentric people, and little Sag's social circle will be as multicultural and varied as your own. It's always "amateur night" when you two jokesters are together. Your child reprises your classic role as the class clown or wry cynic.

Both signs are future-oriented, always eager to discover what's next. The little Archer will engage your wild ideas—from changing your name to Starvox Moonray to camping at Burning Man's Kidsville section to starting an animal sanctuary in your own backyard. Be selective about what you expose your mini-mimic to at a young age or explain the importance of waiting for adulthood to, say, get a sleeve tattoo on your entire right arm. Living an edgy or bohemian lifestyle, however, is a lot easier to pull off with this child who loves to color outside the lines as much as you do.

WHERE YOU CLASH

Young Sagittarius is fiery and passionate while the Aquarius mama is cool and detached. Your Archer may overwhelm you with nonstop chatter and exhaust you with boundless zeal. Sometimes, you just wish this kid would pipe down and chill.

A competitive dynamic can crop up in this pairing, too, especially since you are both natural storytellers and entertainers. Be careful not to upstage your Archer around her friends. By the same token, don't let your kid turn into an attention hog or you could find yourself silenced and seething. It's okay to interrupt and teach the Archer to be a better listener. Sagittarius kids can be blunt and tactless, weighing in with advice when you didn't even ask for it. You may feel judged or scolded by your own child. Wait . . . who's the parent here? Since you're both über-social, your one-on-one time can fall by the wayside. Take a break from your many friends so you have special moments to bond.

AQUARIUS MOM + CAPRICORN CHILD

*

WHERE YOU CLICK

The ambitious Capricorn child is the perfect complement to the visionary Aquarius mother: there's nothing the two of you can't accomplish together! Little Capricorn's can-do spirit inspires you to bring your own wild ideas to life. In turn, you'll cheer for your go-getter child as he reaches for the gold.

Your signs are often quite athletic. You may train, family-style, for a mini-marathon together, take annual ski and snowboarding trips (both signs adore the mountains), and otherwise enjoy being active and outdoorsy.

Gushy sentimentality is not your thing, nor is it your cool-headed Capricorn's MO. Old-soul Capricorn is wise beyond his years. You'll talk to your child rationally, almost like a peer. Your earth sign offspring likes structure, order, and routine. This can help center the oft-flighty Aquarius mom, helping you plant your feet on solid ground. In turn, your wild, fun-filled ideas remind your solemn child not to take life *so seriously*.

WHERE YOU CLASH

The Capricorn child loves traditions and old-school family values—especially the ones handed down for generations. The offbeat Aquarius mom prefers to reinvent the wheel, which may greatly upset your little Cap. Tent camping in Kauai over Christmas sounds great to you; yet there you are, apron clad and cursing the cold as you and little Capricorn bake a German ancestor's Pfeffernüsse recipe and line the tree with perfectly wrapped presents instead.

Capricorn kids are competitive and like to surround themselves with the cream of the crop. Your open-armed friendship style is a total mismatch for your mini-social climber. Give up the Waldorf school fantasies and enroll your child in an elite private school or prestigious after-school activities. Capricorn likes to play by the rules and they feel safe when someone tells them what to do. Aquarius moms are the rule breakers. You'll scratch your head at this conventional kid, wondering at times how you gave birth to such a straight arrow.

AQUARIUS MOM + AQUARIUS CHILD

WHERE YOU CLICK

Two space cadets under one roof? What an adventure! Little Aquarius readily hops on board with your wild ideas—whether you're boarding a refrigerator box "spaceship" to Mars or touring the country for a year in an Airstream trailer. Your mini-Water Bearer will be as fascinated by life's oddities as you. Break out the lightweight stroller and head to the Star Trek convention or experimental music festival. Gypsy Aquarians will never have a dull moment together: it's anyone's guess where you will be on an hourly basis.

Young Aquarius was born sharing your humanitarian spirit, so get started early on the community service projects. You might even travel to another country together on a goodwill mission while your child is still in elementary school. Geek is chic for both Aquamom and child. Load up on gadgety toys for your little Water Bearer before he overtakes your iPad mini and DJ equipment—not that you'll mind sharing with your wunderkind, of course.

WHERE YOU CLASH

Two rebels under one roof? There could be some major blowups here. Aquarians are rumored to have lightning-bolt tempers that flash and strike out of nowhere. Those stormy electric crackles will show up often in this pairing, especially as you attempt to impose rules and limits on your insurgent offspring. You may have to tone down your own wild ways, just so you can parent without little Aquarius pointing out the hypocrisy of your demands.

Fill up a bin with colorful hair extensions, clip-on earrings, and temporary tattoos so your child can play dress-up and emulate your wild style. (Better that than a *real* tattoo or piercing at such a young age.) If little Aquarius adopts your bleeding-heart social MO, your home may wind up feeling like a youth hostel. If you weren't planning on adopting your kid's friends, you'll need to have stricter guidelines around when playtime ends.

AQUARIUS MOM + PISCES CHILD

*

WHERE YOU CLICK

With your bleeding hearts, both Aquarius mom and the sweet Pisces child love to take care of the underdog. You're a healing mother-child duo, always keen on helping a stranger. Nomadic souls, you'll love to wander and roam. Once she gets past her frail and fussy infant phase (Pisces can be fragile babies), little Pisces will be a wonderful travel companion for you.

Like you, little Pisces has a wacky streak. You'll adore your child's imagination and the outrageous things that come out of his mouth. There's a New Agey vibe between you, too. Here's your experimental who will gladly accompany you to guided meditation class and do fairy card readings together.

Dreamy Pisces can get lost in la-la land and her spacey Aquarian mother tends to zone out in her head. Comfortable silence is easy and natural here: you'll simply love being in each other's presence.

WHERE YOU CLASH

Your Fish is far more emotional than you! Your child is prone to brooding, and you won't have much tolerance for these spells. Pouty Pisces may rain on the free-spirited Aquarius mom's parade, forcing you to make unanticipated stops and detours when you were intent on getting to an event on time. In general, your child moves at a much slower pace than you: the Aquarius mom speeds along in a powerboat, whereas Pisces drifts on an oarless kayak. So. Frustrating.

Pisces need lots of cuddling and can even become clingy at times—tough for the "I need space" Aquarius mother. Weaning won't be easy nor will leaving this little one alone on the first day of kindergarten. Aquarius mom is a dreamer *and* a doer; Pisces, on the other hand, will talk about many ideas but never put them into action. Don't push this kid to match your ambitious pace. Relax, Aquarius: he'll find his way!

PISCES

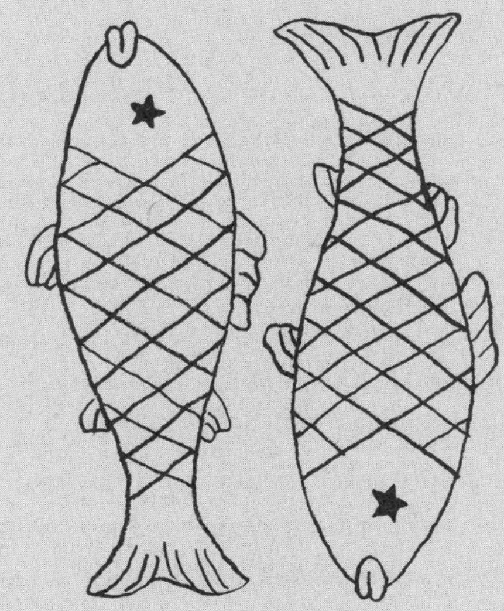

PISCES MOM + ARIES CHILD

✻

WHERE YOU CLICK

As next-door-neighbor signs, the Pisces mom and Aries child have little in common astrologically—and that may be the magic of this mother-child pairing. The Pisces mom is the gentle, rocking sea that helps cool down frenetic fire sign Aries. As the most compassionate sign of the zodiac, you have more patience than most for the Ram's mood swings, tantrums, and easily hurt feelings.

You prize creativity and your Ram has boatloads of it. Hello, superfan mom! You'll be the ultimate cheerleader for Aries' innovative ideas and star-powered endeavors. You're both a little bossy, too—you in a mother hen kind of way, Aries more like a military dictator. Nonetheless, you'll appreciate your child's budding leadership skills, and you can teach Aries to take charge with a gentler touch. In turn, your pint-sized pistol of a kid will help you strengthen your own backbone, setting an example of fearless confidence from which you'll want to borrow.

WHERE YOU CLASH

Ruled by warrior planet Mars, Aries is the most aggressive sign of the zodiac. Ruled by dreamy Neptune, the Pisces mom has a rep for being passive. At times, you'll feel overwhelmed by your child's firepower, which can disrupt your ethereal groove.

The Pisces mother is no stranger to sacrifice—setting limits can be a struggle for her. "Me first!" Aries was born with a sense of entitlement. This kid has no trouble asking for more, more, more—and throwing an epic fit when she doesn't get her way. Young Aries could easily steamroll you, leaving you exhausted from constantly trying to meet his demands. Consider yourself warned: no other sign has the ability to bring out the martyr mommy in you quite like Aries. You're going to have to learn to say no, Pisces, so you don't create a spoiled brat. Aries is independent whereas you can be codependent. Your hold-'em-close parenting style can suffocate the Ram. Don't take it personally when Aries inevitably wants to individuate!

PISCES MOM + TAURUS CHILD

*

WHERE YOU CLICK

Creatures of comfort, the Pisces mom and Taurus child will lounge together in style. Custom-order those overstuffed couches ASAP. Then kick back and cuddle together, drifting in and out of your respective daydreams. You might not have to interrupt your marathon sleep sessions for this child—little Taurus loves his shut-eye as much as you.

Taurus and Pisces are both a fascinating mix of tough and tender. Just as you can go from hypersensitive to thick-skinned in 0.2 seconds, young Taurus can flip from calm calf to raging Bull in no time. You'll admire this trait in your child as long as *you* aren't the reason she's seeing red.

Here's to the good life! Sensory Taurus loves luxury, fine food, and pampering just like mama. High-end field trips are in the cards for you two. (Think Eloise at the Plaza Hotel to "haute chocolate" at fancy pastry shops, even mommy-child spa days when your Taurus gets a little older.) For the most part, this pairing is a dream—meet your pint-sized BFF.

WHERE YOU CLASH

Strong-willed and stubborn, the Taurus kid wants what he wants *now*! This demanding, directional energy can cramp your go-with-the-flow style. Since you struggle with saying no, you may get bulldozed by the charging Taurus on many occasions, losing your grip on the parenting controls.

Tauruses thrive in a structured, repetitive routine. Doing the same thing day in and day out? Sounds like a tiny slice of hell to you, Pisces. Creating a predictable routine for Taurus leaves you feeling tethered at times—but on the upside, this could finally help you get your life into an orderly groove. (Admit it, Pisces, you could use a little discipline.) Little Taurus can be matter-of-fact, preferring to break things down to the simple black-and-white, but as a Pisces mom living in a fantasy world you're all about exploring the gray areas. This keep-it-real kid can stick a pin in your balloon, refusing to join you on your more "woo woo" quests. Hire a babysitter when it's time for your monthly tarot card reading or interpretive dance class.

PISCES MOM + GEMINI CHILD

*

WHERE YOU CLICK

Gypset (gypsy + jet-set) living, here you come! A pair of restless wanderers, you'll happily roam the world with this bundle of joy swaddled by your side. As the sign of the twins, Gemini is a happy and eager companion for the enchanting Pisces mom. Expose little Gemini to all the wonders you adore—art, music, literature, spirituality—and this child will quickly ripen into a culture vulture just like Mom. Movies and film are special loves for both signs, too. Bring on the buttered popcorn and 3D glasses!

Ruled by expressive Mercury, Gemini has the gift of gab, and poetic Pisces moms also have a way with words. Your conversations will be rich and colorful once little Gemini learns to talk. The patient Pisces mom won't mind this curious kid's games of Twenty *Thousand* Questions. You'll respond to these queries creatively—just try not to make anything up if you don't know the answer. Factual Gemini is more grounded in reality than you and won't take kindly to being misinformed.

WHERE YOU CLASH

Decisions, decisions: you've never been eager to make them, Pisces, and you won't get any help from *this* kid. Little Gemini wants to examine every option, whereas you simply hate to commit. Picking a playground to visit, selecting supplies for an art project (colored pencils or watercolor paints?), even leaving a radio station on for more than half a song—good luck with that! There's an exhaustive quality to this mother-child pairing, and in moments your mutually mutable ways will drive each other to Crazytown.

The Pisces mom is intuitive: you're not sure *why* you do what you do; you're just following your internal sensors. Little Gemini is a logic-based trivia hound. While you don't mind researching factoids for your child, you'll grow weary of your kid constantly questioning your motives. The live-for-the-moment Gemini child is happy to flow with your unstructured groove, but this is a slippery slope. Give this kid some semblance of consistency or Gemini may struggle when school (and all its rules) begins.

PISCES MOM + CANCER CHILD

*

WHERE YOU CLICK

As two emo water signs, you'll bask in the sweet security of each other's company. Both Pisces and Cancer crave closeness but can also be self-contained. As long as you're in the general proximity of each other, all is right in the world. Baking, decorating, making art—there's no shortage of creativity in this cosmic combination. Little Cancer understands the meaning of "comfortable silence," allowing you to quietly coexist when your dreamy nature kicks in. Fellow music lovers, your child will introduce you to new genres while you'll add the classic jams to your kid's repertoire. Likely scenario: you'll be the cool mom who takes little Cancer to her first live show, rocking out a few rows back yourself. Family time is ultra cozy. You can be a worrier, but this child is extra attentive to mother's moods. Likelihood of rebellion is low; in fact, you might sometimes feel as if *you* are the child and little Cancer the parent.

WHERE YOU CLASH

Too close for comfort? This combination can get a tad clutchy if your Cancer child isn't nudged toward independence. Then again, *you* may be the one clinging for dear life on that first day of kindergarten. Moody Cancers need to retreat into their shells on a regular basis, which the sensitive Pisces mom is prone to taking personally. Give your child space to lose herself in a book or glue together the intricate pieces of that model spacecraft without your constant bid for reassurance. There's a rebel rock star in every Pisces, but keep that side of your persona tucked away when in the presence of little Cancer. Your Crab can be "motherly," but let your kid be a kid instead of worrying him into a premature parental state of mind. Resist the urge to ask this old soul for advice too often! Both of you can be bossy. When it comes to taking things personally, this child gives you a run for your money. Cooldown breaks will be necessary, especially if emotions (tears and all) ramp up on a regular basis. And yes, you're probably both making mountains out of molehills.

PISCES MOM + LEO CHILD

*

WHERE YOU CLICK

Life imitates art with this mother-child pairing. There's no shortage of creativity and imagination between the dreamy Pisces mother and the fanciful Leo child. You'll live in a fairy-tale world together, teaming up on art projects, dancing till your feet ache, and perhaps even taking the stage together (the camera loves you both!). Little Leo is a superstar in his own right, earning accolades and awards while scooping up leadership roles right and left. The supportive Pisces mama is happy to cheer on your wunderkind; even hoist her up on the pedestal like the proudest stage mother in town.

You'll appreciate Leo's take-charge nature, too. Hey, at least *you* don't have to make all the decisions! The humble Pisces mom can also teach the proud Lion a little humility. In turn, your confident Leo models poise and self-reliance for you. To be certain, your signs can be as different as night and day, but you have a lot to learn from each other.

WHERE YOU CLASH

Dr-r-r-rama! Between Leo's theatrical nature and your extreme sensitivity, small situations get blown out of proportion very easily here. Little Leo won't be the only one slamming doors and bursting into tears. Can you say "mommy meltdown"? Your Lion's roar can be daunting at times, as can his egregiously large appetite. Since you have a tough time setting limits, disciplining this demanding royal may be one of your greatest challenges in life. You'll be guilt-ridden on many occasions when you're forced to say no to Leo. The alternative—creating a mini-megalomaniac—is far less appealing. Brace yourself to weather the fallout of disappointing Leo, which can be quite noisy and melodramatic.

Ruled by the sun (the center of our universe), Leo is self-focused. Pisces is the sign of sacrifice—you tend to put others before yourself. Little Leo may seem breathtakingly selfish to you at times, while your child may candidly advise you to start sticking up for yourself more often.

PISCES MOM + VIRGO CHILD

*

WHERE YOU CLICK

Be still thy bleeding hearts. The compassionate Pisces mom and charitable Virgo child make quite a caring pair. Like you, little Virgo can't walk by a less-fortunate soul without stopping to help. You'll swoon watching this young nurturer work the playground like a pint-sized Mother Teresa (also a Virgo). Volunteering together is a great way to bond. You'll fuss over one another, too, and happily so. This kid will sense your every mood, so much so that you might even decide to tone down the emotional outbursts around your child.

Virgo is your opposite sign, and you can be a great balance for each other. Where you rely on intuition, little Virgo is curious about the facts. Your child will remember the very rules that you forgot (even if you made them up in the first place!). Where Virgo can be uptight and judgmental, you're carefree and open-minded. You'll help your kid critic be more tolerant of other people's "imperfections" and to lighten up a little. In some cases, this pairing will feel like a bit of a role reversal with the Pisces mom feeling parented by stern little Virgo.

WHERE YOU CLASH

Mean-girl alert! Little Virgo's critical observations can wound the sensitive Pisces mom—but going cold fish on your kid can break Virgo's heart, too. The two of you are opposites on the astrological chart, and because of this your conflicts can be intense and painful. The Pisces mom is an emotional sponge. When you've soaked up too much, you can't stop the waterworks. Warning: your dramatic meltdowns can rock little Virgo to the core. This child is a worrier and a fixer (no surprise, many Virgos wind up becoming therapists for a living), but do you really want to burden your young one with that heavy load at such an early age? Excuse yourself and go cry in your room; call your sister or shrink instead of venting to your child. Virgo will comfort you and might actually seem to understand your plight, but it's not fair to lay that burden on her.

Virgo needs structure and rules in order to feel secure. You prefer to be spontaneous and go with the flow. You'll need to develop discipline to keep this child centered—you might even need to hire a coach to help with that.

PISCES MOM + LIBRA CHILD

*

WHERE YOU CLICK

Paging Hans Christian Andersen! There's a fairy-tale quality to the Libra-Pisces pairing. Your quixotic child views the world through the same starry-eyed lens as you do. Beauty moves you both and motivates your decisions. You'll stay up late to watch for shooting stars, take a horse-and-carriage ride for Libra's fifth birthday, paint with watercolors, write songs, and dance around the house with wild abandon.

There's a touch of vanity between you two, but when you look that good with your child, why *not* show it off? Decorating this child's room, selecting Libra's outfits (which might be miniature versions of your own style), arranging cups for a tea party—these are all detailed *processes* which you'll both greatly enjoy.

Like you, little Libra is a total love bug. You both melt for perfect strangers who you'll charm with your mutually adoring gazes. Libra has likely inherited your charitable nature, too. Engage Libra in your community service groups and volunteering missions—a fabulous way to bond with your bighearted offspring.

WHERE YOU CLASH

Both Pisces mom and Libra child are happiest when wearing rose-colored glasses, but when life delivers a reality check you may feel ill equipped to navigate Libra's sadness and disappointment. Avoid oversheltering Libra for this very reason—and perhaps seize the opportunity to develop some stronger crisis-coping skills yourself. You don't have to fall to pieces over these fairly minor ordeals, Pisces.

Indulgent Libra can turn into a material boy or girl if you put too much focus on the finer things in life. It's important to teach this child the value of money. Let Libra *earn* a few of those haute-kiddie benefits, okay? Indecisive Libra reserves the right to change his mind at a moment's notice; the commitment-shy Pisces mom always likes an escape hatch. You can drive each other—not to mention the people who are counting on you both—bonkers by altering plans in the last minute. Be careful not to pass on the flaky quality (a Pisces pitfall) to young Libra.

PISCES MOM + SCORPIO CHILD

✻

WHERE YOU CLICK

Is it a psychic hotline . . . or your home phone number? Keenly perceptive Scorpio is your intuitive partner. Like you, this child relies on gut instincts. You'll have an unspoken understanding between you, even if no one else is picking up on "vibes" or suddenly needing to leave a place because of a bad feeling. You're the perfect parent to help develop Scorpio's sixth sense. Like Pisces, Scorpio is an emotional water sign. The world of feelings is your mutual stomping ground—and this child is every bit as enchanting as you when he turns on the charm. You'll have people eating out of the palms of your hands—or turning over their palms to show you their love lines. Team up with your Scorpio to raise money for a holiday charity. Record highs will be the result!

WHERE YOU CLASH

Scorpio is the sign of power and control so you'll have to stay on your toes. Otherwise, this kid can easily run the show at Château Pisces, bringing out the subservient, sacrificing part of your nature. If you catch yourself racing to meet your child's intense and demanding whims, you'll know it's time to change course, stat!

Focused Scorpio kids require undivided attention. This child will remember everything that you say and will expect the same in return. Your natural inclination to drift off and tune out will not go down well with this child. A word to the wise: manage Scorpio's expectations of you early, and teach your kid that Mama needs to rest her brain sometimes! Scorpio kids can be possessive and jealous, which can cramp your free-spirited style. Young Scorpio is naturally suspicious of strangers and prefers to keep a close-knit crew of a few friends and relatives near. While you can be prone to paranoia yourself, you also attract some "interesting" characters. Put up a more discerning friendship filter, Pisces, so young Scorpio feels safe in the presence of your posse.

PISCES MOM + SAGITTARIUS CHILD

*

WHERE YOU CLICK

Two tickets for the Magical Mystery Tour! Little Sagittarius is ruled by jet-setting Jupiter (your sign's coruler), and oh, the places you'll go. Traveling together is a beautiful way to bond, so get that baby passport ASAP. The adventurous Archer is an ideal companion for the free-flowing Pisces mom.

You're both spontaneous and curious about life's bigger questions. Your spiritual outlook on life may dovetail perfectly with young, soulful Sagittarius. You're both quite philosophical, too, and will share many books as your child gets older. The active, outdoorsy Archer will inspire you to get out in nature more. Pack a picnic and head to the beach—Pisces' favorite place to have fun in the sun, and a wide-open wonderland for your mini-Centaur to romp. Sagittarius rules the hips, Pisces the feet: dancing will be another great way to bond, so crank up the music and turn your living room into an all-ages club!

WHERE YOU CLASH

Blunt, candid Sagittarians call it like they see it. The Pisces mom can be overly concerned about hurting people's feelings, censoring herself and avoiding conflict at all costs. Develop a thicker skin as soon as you can, Pisces. Little Sagittarius may wound you with the direct sling of her honesty arrows. In turn, you can frustrate your child by being vague and slippery when it comes to stating your feelings and opinions. Your kid just wants to know where you stand, which will force you to become more decisive (perhaps not such a bad thing, Pisces?).

Sagittarius is a fire sign; Pisces is a water sign. Your child's fierce temper and tantrums can send your sensitive feelings up in smoke. In turn, your fussing and fears can put out the Archer's fire. Sagittarius is fundamentally independent, whereas you err on the side of being codependent. Figuring out how to give young Sagittarius more personal space—and not take everything he says and does so personally—will be your biggest challenge in parenting this child.

PISCES MOM + CAPRICORN CHILD

*

WHERE YOU CLICK

There's a work hard-play hard matchup in this mother-child pairing. The industrious Capricorn child never met a project he didn't like . . . or finish! The quicksilver Pisces mama is easily distracted from pursuits by any opportunity to cut loose and have fun. Roles are reversed on many occasions, with the dutiful Cap kid reminding the Pisces mom to tend to the hearth and the spirited Pisces mom making sure her child plays hooky from all that responsibility every now and again.

You both adore the finer things in life—for you it's about beauty, whereas little Capricorn will be conscious of amassing status symbols from a young age. Although you're as different as night and day, there's an easy flow between your signs and you may feel more like friends at times rather than mother and child. With your compassionate nature, in fact, you may be the one person perfectionist Capricorn feels comfortable opening up to in life. Traditional Capricorn helps ground the flighty Pisces mother. You may stay put—at home, at your job, at family gatherings—longer than usual with this centered child's influence. In turn, you help pragmatic Capricorn embrace creative solutions and tap into her imaginative powers.

WHERE YOU CLASH

Is the glass half empty again? Both Capricorn and Pisces can be prone to pessimism and your gloomy spells may be contagious. Quarantine yourself when you're brooding so your kid doesn't catch your case of the blues.

Earth sign Capricorn needs lots of structure, especially in the financial department. This is problematic since money slips through Pisces' fingers. Your whimsical spending habits can find you scrapping to afford Capricorn's sports uniforms and competition entry fees. Economic uncertainty can bring out Cap's ultraresponsible nature but also spur your kid's worry and anxiety. Be careful, Pisces! Capricorn could miss out on her childhood if she feels burdened with rescuing the family in any way. Capricorn is conventional, preferring to keep up with Bobby and Susie Jones. Your habit of constantly reinventing the wheel could frustrate this kid to no end. Alas your bohemian, artsy side may be a bit much for this child to handle. You could get an earful for showing up at one of Capricorn's school events in a printed, off-the-shoulder caftan instead of a nice blazer and jeans. Tone it down sometimes, Mama.

PISCES MOM + AQUARIUS CHILD

*

WHERE YOU CLICK

Pixie-mermaid Pisces and space cadet Aquarius make a delightfully kooky mother-child combo. You'll adore your Water Bearer's unconventional outlook and support your child's mad scientist innovations. Aquarius may be more scientific in comparison to your beat poet vibes, but neither of you likes to color inside the lines.

Two superhero capes, please! Aquarius is the sign of the humanitarian and Pisces rules the charitable realm. Neither of you met an underdog you didn't want to rescue, revive, and empower. You'll watch proudly as your Water Bearer includes the frailest kid on the playground in his games. Making the world a better place for *everyone*—especially the disenfranchised—will be a shared mission. This logical kid is cool as a cucumber, but you can help young Aquarius tap into the realm of feelings and learn to express what's in her heart. In turn, your mellow Aquarius reminds you to let things roll off your back instead of getting up in arms over every slight. And with your child's wacky sense of humor, you'll get regular reminders that laughter is indeed the best medicine.

WHERE YOU CLASH

The sentimental Pisces mom is all heart, whereas logical Aquarius tends to get lost in his head. You may feel like your child is giving you the cold shoulder at times, especially when you go overboard with the love bombing. If you want to connect to this child, scooping him up in an embrace is not the way to go. Learn to talk to Aquarius, almost the way you would a friend. This wise kid responds to rational thinking above all else . . . *then* come the kisses and hugs.

Some Pisces moms veer into "cold fish" terrain and are less demonstrative than most. If you're of this cosmic ilk, work harder to bring the TLC. Aquarius is not likely to approach you for affection and your connection can grow distant and withdrawn if you don't make the effort. Hope springs eternal for the Aquarius child who prefers to stay in an upbeat, positive mood. The emotional Pisces mom can overwhelm this kid with gloomy sentiment, causing your child to pull away. Don't expect Aquarius to be your number-one confidant. Although you'll be wowed by this child's ahead-of-his-years insights, exposing Aquarius to too many of your meltdowns can cause your child to shut down emotionally and play out the more robotic tendencies of his sign.

PISCES MOM + PISCES CHILD

*

WHERE YOU CLICK

Life can be an enchanted wonderland for the Pisces mom and her little mermaid or merman. Sure, you might not always have the best grip on reality when together, but you'll bring forth the artiste in this child, whether his medium is dance, poetry, music, painting, or making breathtaking LEGO configurations. You won't judge Pisces' imaginary friends—hey, you had a few of your own when you were little. Sensitive and sometimes downright psychic, it's easy for you to intuit each other's feelings.

A cozy bubble of comfort envelops the Pisces mother and child. Nesting is sheer heaven with this cuddle bug. By the same token, you're a peripatetic pair, wandering the earth like a couple of nomads once your sensitive baby is old enough to be buckled into a stroller. Like you, your pint-sized star mate is a caretaker who shares your compassion for the underdog. There will be regular stops to help out people in need during your jaunts around town. You might even start a nonprofit together some day!

WHERE YOU CLASH

Too close for comfort? The Pisces mom and child can get carried away with the coddling, creating an "us against the world" vibe and losing a grip on reality. It's not unusual for you to fall into a codependent groove with little Pisces, enabling her bad habits in an effort to protect her from feeling pain. Little birds must one day be nudged from the nest if they are to survive, but it's especially hard for you to trust that this child will develop his wings. This hyperdependent vibe cuts both ways: if you emote too much around young Pisces she may take on the burden of shoring up your moods at her own expense. You both tend to hold in your feelings, then bubble over with resentment. At times, you may even feel controlled by the other's unspoken demands—you really are *that* tapped into each other. Make an effort to verbalize your wishes, encouraging your young Fish to do the same. You know what they say about assumptions, Mom, and they can be particularly toxic in this pairing. Gloomy spells can be especially weighty with you two under one roof, so repeat this saving mantra: "Feelings are not facts!"

ACKNOWLEDGMENTS

A thank-you vaster than the Milky Way goes out to the following people, who were integral to making *Momstrology* happen.

To our Taurus power agent, Yfat Reiss Gendell, and our savvy Scorpio publicist, Carol Leggett, thank you for being wise and wonderful sounding boards. Our Cancerian editor, Carrie Thornton, provided everything from a shared babysitter to friendship to championing this book.

To our patient and supportive husbands, Jeffrey Sleebos and Cory Verellen. We thank you (and your steadfast Taurus moons) for putting up with the best and the worst of us when we typed until the wee hours or got up before dawn, and you only got a few fleeting minutes of our cranky, distracted time. You were there to make coffee, cuddle the dachshunds, fill the fridge, and keep life humming along. We love you so much.

Team Astrostyle: Laura Bruzzese (Leo), Suzanne Guillette (Aquarius), and Melissa Gonzales (Taurus), our fellow "astro-geeks" who sat with us in cafes, parks, gardens, living rooms, libraries, and fancy restaurants to pontificate on the ways of Aries moms, Pisces kids, and everyone in between. Akima Briggs, aka Iscis Malone (Taurus), thank you for your generous copy editing. Saadi Chowdhury (Scorpio) our wise financial wizard and Yo-Dad—thank you for teaching us that time and numbers are sacred.

To the village that helped raise Ophira's child so these chapters could be written: Tina Guarasci, Nursery School of the Nyacks, Jennifer Marks and Imani Boswell, Leora Edut and Wendy Valentine—thank you for being mamas by proxy.

All good results require a little magic, too. Spirit-sister thanks to Dina Manzo, Michelle Seelinger, Terri Cole, Pam Colacino, Kat Tepelyan, Luke McKibben, and Kenny Arena for making new moon and full moon wishes with us—from fire pits in the East Village to chartered Escalades in the Nevada desert. To our "flower power" maven, Kerri Aab, of Seed to Blossom, your Bach flower essence potions and better-than-therapy talks kept us sane and productive. To the amazing Terye Trombley, thank you for your healing gifts and remedies.

All friends and followers who generously filled out our Momstrology survey, sharing your honest foibles and journeys so poignantly. You helped us round out the picture of each zodiac sign. We read each of your stories, and even if you don't see yourself quoted, know that your funny, honest, and poignant responses are all mixed into the final product of this book.